California Recreational Lakes & Rivers

California
Recreational
Lakes & Rivers

By Tom Stienstra

FOGHORN ☙ OUTDOORS

California Recreational Lakes & Rivers
Second Edition

Printing History
1st edition—1996
2nd edition—April 2000
5 4 3 2 1 0

Front cover photo: © International Stock Photography, Ltd.
Editors: Janet Connaughton, Ronit LeMon, Kyle Morgan, Carolyn Perkins
Design and Production: Janet Shade
Cartography: Mark Aver, Mike Morgenfeld, Chris Alvarez
ISBN: 1-57354-065-X
Library of Congress
Cataloging-in-Publication Data
has been applied for.

Published by
Avalon Travel Publishing
5855 Beaudry St.
Emeryville, CA 94608 USA
Printed in the United States of America

Please send all comments, corrections,
additions, amendments, and critiques to:
California Recreational Lakes & Rivers
Foghorn Outdoors
Avalon Travel Publishing, Inc.
5855 Beaudry St.
Emeryville, CA 94608 USA
e-mail: travel@moon.com
www.foghorn.com

Distributed in the United States and Canada
by Publishers Group West.

The Old Green Canoe

A stranger at the boat ramp laughed, then shook his head as I hoisted my old canoe from the top of my truck, then set it in the lake.

"That's a pretty old, worn-out looking boat," the stranger said. "Tippy looking, too. I'm surprised you don't have something better."

I looked at the old canoe and noticed that the outer green hull was chipped in about a dozen spots on each end, where the white inner layer was showing through from so many landings on rocky shores. The gunwale was bent from where a houseboat hit it. A seat was partially cracked—yeah, just old—the yoke was discolored from portages, and the inside was stained from fish, dirt, and 28 years of living, the past 18 with me.

After looking at the canoe for a minute, I turned back to the stranger. "You know, I don't like to brag, but this is quite a boat, and I really love this old green canoe." He moved closer to hear why, a mix of a little bit of logic and a lot of heart.

"Well, I bought it for $175 in 1981, a 17-foot Old Town Tripper, and it's been through four trucks, thousands of miles and hundreds of adventures. For paddling, it is stable enough to handle big lakes, slippery enough for Class II whitewater rivers. For camping, it will hold 1,100 pounds of people and gear. For fishing, I bolt a two-horsepower engine on a sidemount, which allows perfect approaches for a cast at a secret spot or precise control over trolling speed, and I've installed backrests for comfort. For the wilderness, it weighs 81 pounds, and I've carried that old green canoe on my shoulders for miles on portages between lakes.

"I've also learned that California has 190 lakes you can reach by vehicle where there are no boat ramps, lakes that are perfect for canoes and other car-top boats. In a state with 840,000 registered boats and 34 million residents, you can often count on having these places to yourself, even on a warm evening when the trout are jumping, right in the middle of summer. And at lakes with boat ramps, more than a hundred have speed limits that protect low-speed boats such as canoes. Sure, I love cruising out on a big lake in a power boat, and sometimes only that will fulfill your needs, particularly on big reservoirs, bays, or the open ocean.

"But while logic gives you what you need, logic has nothing to do with what really drives people. What drives people are the things they crave and must have, things that go to the heart of passions, memories, and the chance of fulfilling dreams in the days to come.

"Anybody who has almost lost their life knows this to be true, and so it was with me on a dark, icy day at a lake in the Cascades, when I misloaded that old green canoe—no weight in the front—and was paddling solo when it flipped because of the weight imbalance and dumped me into chilling waters.

"The canoe wouldn't turn upright and float, so I kept it upside down as a paddle board and tried to kick my way back to shore. After 15 minutes, my brother, Bob, judged from shore that I wasn't going to make it. He stripped, jumped in, grabbed the front of that capsized boat, and together we managed to struggle for another 15 minutes and make our way to land, ice-cold, too cold to shiver, our legs so numb that we couldn't stand up. But we were alive.

"Later when we turned the canoe over, everything was lost except lodged under a seat we found one paddle and a fishing rod, the one my grandfather gave me when I turned 12.

"'I think this is a message,' I remember my brother saying. 'You are supposed to paddle and fish a lot more in this boat.'

"And so I have been, adventuring across the West, seeing the best of America and western Canada, from diving ospreys and eagles to deer and moose swimming across lakes, to giant trout I have given names like Luther, Jargo, Horgon, and Herganon.

"Crazy stuff has happened. My old friend Ed Ow accidentally plowed right over the top of 'Old Green' in a houseboat, but it survived with a battle scar. Another time, amid a late-night poker game at a Redding hotel with other outdoors writers, I poked my head outside and saw that my beloved canoe was gone from the top of my truck, apparently stolen. I was distraught beyond imagination, but then I heard a happy shriek, looked down, a

"Two weeks later I made the trip, and yes, it was an Old Town Tripper, and after a short negotiation with the owner, John Morrill, I bought it for $175. Just as I was hoisting it on my truck, Morrill stopped me.

"'Before you take it away, you should know who really owned this canoe,' Morrill said. 'It actually belonged to my wife's dad, who was quite a guy. He was a great outdoorsman, canoed the Bowron Lakes, a real character, a great photographer. His name was Tom Bullock.'

"As I put the boat in the lake this week, I remembered that incident as if it had happened the previous day, about how the turns of fate had brought this canoe to my life, and the pleasure I have had from it. Sometimes at dusk, when the swallows are catching bugs and the eagle comes out for the rising trout, I swear that I can feel the angel of my old friend, Tom Bullock, watching over me."

Then I looked at the stranger at the boat ramp, who was inspecting the bent gunwale.

"You know, on second thought, I do like to brag," I told him, "because I'm pretty proud of this old green canoe."

Preface

This book was written with the intent that it will quickly become your bible for boating and water sports across California.

We have detailed every lake, river, bay, and coastal port—more than 400 listings—and the water sports popular at each, as well as precise directions to the state's 534 boat ramps. This includes 132 lakes for waterskiing, 282 lakes for swimming, 196 lakes and coastal areas for windsurfing, and 126 areas for Jet Skiing. There are also 190 lakes for cartop boating, many of which are perfect for a family with a canoe or raft. In addition, all of California's 45 premium rafting rivers are listed, including the rafting companies that run guided trips on 25 of these rivers.

California Recreational Lakes and Rivers is the most accurate, up-to-date resource guide of its kind. Each body of water is rated on a scale of 1 to 10, and activity icons show—at a glance—which activities can be enjoyed at every locale. Boating rules, speed limits, and safety zones are also described to make your trip as safe and fun as possible, and to help you select the best destination for your adventure. As an added bonus, we secured permission to reprint the "ABCs of the California Boating Law," a must-read for every boat owner in the state.

Beyond the scope of lakes, rivers, streams, bays, and coastal areas in California, I discovered a much more important lesson in writing this book: For anybody who desires adventure, excitement, fun, and a chance at true freedom, the fastest way to get it is with a boat. In a boat, there is nothing but open space, often for miles . . . no stoplights, no traffic jams . . . and in the outdoors, I have learned firsthand that heading out in a boat is the fastest and easiest way to put a giant smile on your face. See you out there!

—*Tom Stienstra*

Contents

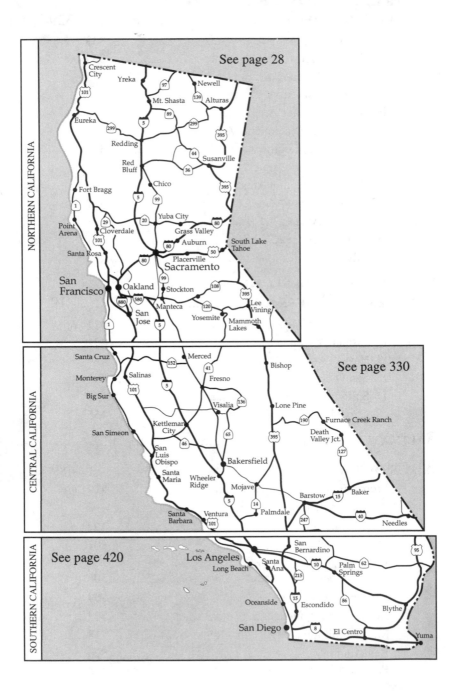

See page 28

See page 330

See page 420

NORTHERN CALIFORNIA

CENTRAL CALIFORNIA

SOUTHERN CALIFORNIA

How to Use This Book

You can search for your ideal boating or water sports spot in two ways:

    1) If you know the name of the area you'd like to visit, look for it in the index, beginning on page 525.

    2) To find a boating or water sports spot in a particular area of the state, refer to the map of California on the opposite page and on the last page of this book. Find the area you'd like to visit, then turn to the corresponding pages.

This book is conveniently divided into three regions: Northern, Central, and Southern California. Within these regions, the book is further divided into map sections for greater detail.

    Northern California (Chapters AØ-E5), pages 27-328
    Central California (Chapters F1-H9), pages 329-418
    Southern California (Chapters I6-J8), pages 419-458

What the Ratings Mean

Every boating spot in this book is rated on a scale of 1 to 10. The ratings are based on three factors: the quality of the boating, the diversity of the water sports, and scenic beauty.

Overall Rating

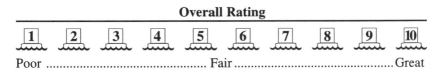

Poor .... Fair .... Great

What the Symbols Mean

Each listing features one or more activity icons. These symbols denote which recreational activities can be enjoyed at or near the boating area. Other symbols show whether a boat ramp or hot springs can be found at this location.

Key to the Symbols

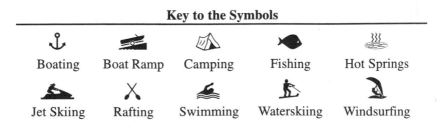

Boating   Boat Ramp   Camping   Fishing   Hot Springs

Jet Skiing   Rafting   Swimming   Waterskiing   Windsurfing

California Recreational Lakes and Rivers Reference Map

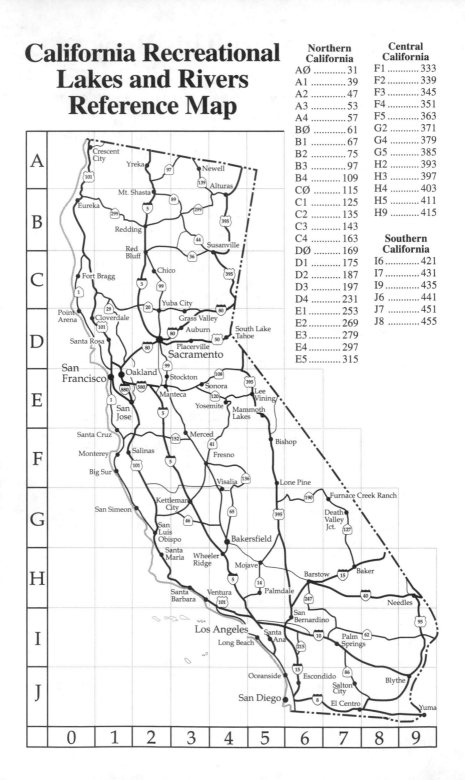

Author's Choice
Boating and Water Sports

Stienstra's Top Spots
for Boating and Water Sports

Want to know where to find California's best water-recreation areas? Here are the top picks from award-winning outdoors writer Tom Stienstra.

BEST HOUSEBOATING

1. Shasta Lake

This is the boating capital of the West. The giant Shasta Lake has 370 miles of shoreline, 400 houseboat rentals, 12 marinas, 14 boat ramps, 12 campgrounds, lakeshore lodging, and 22 species of sport fish. From a houseboat, it takes about five or six days to see the whole thing. With all the houseboaters on the water, it can seem like one big party of happy people. If you want peace and quiet, just head into one of the coves. See chapter B2, page 86.

2. Back Delta

What a great spot for houseboating, here on the threshold of 1,000 miles of waterways. Some of the houseboats on the delta are the scene of floating parties that kick off on a Friday evening and go nonstop through Sunday. If you want to experience complete insanity—the fun type—head out here for a three-day weekend. See chapter E2, page 274.

3. Lake Oroville

Lake Oroville has it all: houseboats, campgrounds, enough water for all kinds of boating, a fish for every angler, and accommodations tailor-made for boaters/campers, including floating campsites, floating toilets (no kidding), boat-in campgrounds, and two excellent marinas. This huge, man-made reservoir has extensive lake arms and a large central body of water, covering more than 15,000 acres, with 165 miles of shoreline. See chapter C2, page 140.

4. Don Pedro Reservoir

A giant lake with many extended arms, Don Pedro is one of the best boating and water sports destinations in California during high water years. Giant? When full, it covers nearly 13,000 surface acres and has 160 miles of shoreline. The lake arms provide zillions of hidden coves where you can park your boat, camp, swim, play, and fish. See chapter E3, page 291.

5. Trinity Lake

Many houseboaters consider Trinity Lake the ideal destination. The lake is set at an elevation of 2,300 feet at the eastern foot of the Trinity Alps. It covers 17,000 acres, ample room for all types of water sports, including waterskiing, personal watercraft, windsurfing, and fishing, yet is distant enough that it rarely attracts hordes of boaters. By August the lake feels like a huge bathtub, making it great for swimming; the best swimming is at the day-use areas and campgrounds operated by the Forest Service. See chapter B1, page 70.

BEST SCENIC DESTINATIONS

1. Emerald Bay, Lake Tahoe

Along with the Yosemite Valley and Oregon's Crater Lake, Lake Tahoe is one of those rare natural wonders that make you feel something special just by looking at it. One of the premier outdoor experiences in the world is boating in Emerald Bay, which brings you right into the heart of Tahoe's incomparable scenic beauty. No matter where you go in the bay, you'll be floating on clear, cobalt blue waters and surrounded by a mountain rim that is often topped with bright white snow. The sight is always remarkable, often breathtaking. See chapter D4, page 241.

2. Hell Hole Reservoir

Sapphire-blue water fills this lake, which is set at the bottom of a massive granite gorge. When viewed from an airplane, Hell Hole Reservoir resembles a mountain temple. Close up, it is just as sacred. The lake is set at an elevation of only 4,700 feet, but the surrounding walls and mountain country rise steep and high above the shore. The water is pure and is fed by the most remote stretches of the pristine Rubicon River. See chapter D3, page 217.

3. Upper Kings River

For the most part, this stretch of the river has been left untouched by humankind. It is extremely difficult and dangerous for rafters, and even experts rarely attempt to run it. Getting to the put-in requires a long, steep hike, and you must carry in your gear and your boat. Still with us? The first three miles are Class IV–V, with several possible portages. After that it's Class V+ all the way, with many portages, huge drops, and "brick-shitting rapids" (quote courtesy of a humbled river guide named Mike). The reward is unequaled wilderness scenery, including a spectacular view of the four-tiered, 640-foot Garlic Falls (on the right at mile five). See chapter F4, page 360.

4. Donner Lake

The first glimpse of Donner Lake is always a stirring one, and many vacationers cruising past on Interstate 80 stop to look at the sparkling blue waters. The remarkable beauty evokes a heartfelt response in all who witness it. Was it good for you, too? This is a big oblong lake, three miles long, three-quarters of a mile wide, with 7.5 miles of shoreline, and is set near the Sierra crest at an elevation of 5,900 feet. See chapter D4, page 236.

5. Sardine Lakes

Sometimes there just is no substitute for spectacular natural beauty. That is why no visit to the Plumas area is complete without a trip to the Sardine Lakes. Among the prettiest drive-to lakes in California, they are set in a rock bowl and are always full of fresh water thanks to the melting snow. The Sierra Buttes tower above. See chapter C3, page 158.

6. Smith River

Undammed and unbridled, the Smith River is the crown jewel of the nation's streams, a fountain of pure, emerald-green water that runs free through granite canyons. When you first see the Smith, you will probably exclaim: "Look how beautiful the water is!" Even after heavy winter rains, which can turn most rivers into brown muck, the Smith is usually pretty and clear. The river's hard granite base and the large volume of water drained from a huge mountain acreage give the river a unique ability to cleanse itself. See chapter AØ, page 34.

7. Channel Islands

Venturing out to any of the Channel Islands is one of the greatest boating odysseys in North America. This extraordinary habitat is surrounded by pristine, clear waters, with hardly anyone around for miles and miles—well, at least 20 miles. These islands are the perfect setting for hiking, swimming, snorkeling, and camping. And with the remarkable sea caves here, there is no better place to kayak, even for people who have never tried it. See the Saltwater Appendix, page 480.

8. Convict Lake

People who love untouched natural beauty can practice their religion at this mountain shrine. The lake is framed by a back wall of wilderness mountain peaks and is fronted by a shoreline dotted with giant rocks and a few scattered pines. Although it is set at 7,583 feet and bordered by the John Muir Wilderness to the west, it is easily accessed off US 395 to the east. See chapter E5, page 326.

9. Forks of the Kern River

This rafting run bears a Class V rating, one notch below a Class VI (which is certain death). It is known for many things: one heart-pumping rapid after another, a beautiful canyon setting, and extremely difficult access. The run is 17 miles long, most of it amid complete wilderness, and all of it on clear, icy water that is fed largely by Mount Whitney snowmelt from May through July. Right off the bat, you hit Class V water, a section of the river that is considered a world-class rafting run because of its series of sensational miniature falls. See chapter G5, page 387.

10. Monterey Bay

Monterey Bay is among the world's prettiest places. Even the water has a special look—more of a deeper blue-green than the murky green waters to the north and south. The water is often calmer and warmer than at points north, and it can lap at the sandy beaches. Big Sur to the south and its spectacular deep-cut canyons and rocky outcrops make this stretch of coast stand apart from all the others. See Saltwater Appendix, page 475.

BEST BOAT-IN CAMPING

1. Emerald Bay, Lake Tahoe

If you are looking for one of the best outdoor experiences on the planet, try boating in Emerald Bay followed by a stay at one of its boat-in campsites. With a boat you can do more than just stare in awe at the clear, cobalt blue waters and the nearby mountain rim; you can surround yourself with this incomparable beauty. And with a boat-in camp, you can wake up in the middle of it all, too. See chapter D4, page 241.

2. Santa Rosa Island

The "Painted Caves" of Santa Rosa Island make this a world-class destination for kayakers, as well as an ideal camping spot, from Friday through Sunday. Because the boat ride to Santa Rosa takes longer than the one to Santa Cruz Island, this place is often overlooked by visitors who are on a one-day round-trip adventure, making it extra special. See the Saltwater Appendix, page 481.

3. Englebright Lake

Boaters have access to a rare bonanza here: 17 boat-in campsites that provide both privacy and beautiful views. The reservoir, which covers just 815 acres yet offers 24 miles of shoreline, looks something like a water snake winding its way through the Yuba River Canyon. It is set in the Yuba County foothills at about a 500-foot elevation. See chapter D3, page 204.

4. Bullards Bar Reservoir

Bullards Bar Reservoir stands out like a silver dollar in a field of pennies when compared to the other reservoirs in the Central Valley foothills. Not only are there two boat-in campgrounds, but boaters are allowed to create their own primitive campsites anywhere along the lakeshore (a chemical toilet is required). See chapter C3, page 160.

5. Stone Lagoon

Stone Lagoon covers 521 acres and has a visitors center and a primitive boat ramp located at the parking area along the west side of US 101. From here you plunk into your canoe, wide-bodied kayak, or dinghy, then paddle or sail over to Ryan's Cove, which is straight across the lake and out of sight of the highway. There you will find a great, secluded boat-in campground with sites dispersed along 300 yards of shoreline. See chapter AØ, page 37.

6. Silverwood Lake

When full to the brim, Silverwood covers 1,000 acres and has 13 miles of shoreline. It is set at an elevation of 3,378 feet, and is bordered by San Bernardino National Forest to the south and the high desert to the north. The proximity to San Bernardino makes this place very popular with boaters, especially during hot summers. Hike-in and bike-in campsites are a unique bonus. See chapter I6, page 423.

7. Gaviota State Park

Even though Gaviota State Park is set on a beautiful and spectacular stretch of the California coast, it falls short of a perfect 10 rating due to the poor boating access. All that's provided is a hoist and a hook, nothing more. But those who come prepared will have the chance to experience outstanding camping and coastal boating. So there you have it, a lovely piece of Central California coastline and a state park that receives moderate use year-round. See chapter H2, page 395.

8. Lake Sonoma

Lake Sonoma is one of the best boater/camper destinations around. A 5 mph speed limit and no-wake zones have been established in many areas of the lake, a setup that guarantees peace and quiet, excellent swimming, and fishing while retaining a huge area of water for waterskiing. Add to that the 14 boat-in camps, and it's hard to top. See chapter DØ, page 171.

9. Trinity Lake

You can rent houseboats, stay in cabins (Cedar Stock Resort), or head out on the water and set up camp at a boat-in site (several good camps are available, including one at Captain's Point on the west shore of the Trinity River Arm). The lake is set at a 2,300-foot elevation at the eastern foot of the Trinity Alps and covers 17,000 acres, huge enough to accommodate all types of water sports, including waterskiing, personal watercraft, windsurfing, and fishing, yet distant enough that it rarely attracts large numbers of boaters. See chapter B1, page 70.

10. Klamath River
(Sarah Totten Campground to Happy Camp)

One spring week in March, I rafted the entire river at flood stage, from its headwaters in Oregon all the way to the Pacific Ocean. The 36-mile downstream stretch from Sarah Totten Campground is ideal for rafting, and there are private beaches where you are permitted to camp. The area is abundant with living creatures, not only fish but many species of birds and other wildlife. The river dishes out just enough excitement to set your heart racing, yet has plenty of flat water so you can catch your breath or beach the boat and go swimming. See chapter A1, page 43.

BEST RAFTING

1. Main Stem Tuolumne River

Many rafters are baptized by the cool, clear, pounding waters of the Tuolumne, commonly known as "The T." Here you'll find one of California's most thrilling rapids, Pinball, and one of the most terrorizing, Clavey Falls. The 18-mile run, from Meral Pool downstream to Ward's Ferry, is rated Class IV+. Anybody who runs it will have experienced the true essence of exhilaration. See chapter E4, page 308.

2. Salmon River

Most of the rapids on the Cal Salmon, as the Salmon River is affectionately known, alternate between Class IV and V, and only experienced paddlers who don't mind living on the edge need apply. Highlights include Bloomer Falls (Class IV), The Maze (Class IV), Whirling Dervish (Class IV+), and Last Chance (Class V). The latter is a mind-bender of a drop that will send your heart out of your body for what seems like an eternity. In fact, among rafters there is a clear-cut division between those who have run the Cal Salmon and those who have not. See chapter A1, page 41.

3. Forks of the Kern River

You have to be a little crazy to raft the Forks of the Kern, and that's exactly why we like it. This is expert-only territory, and attempting to run it can be a death-defying act even for the best. The run is rated Class V, just a bit saner than a suicidal Class VI. It is renowned for three things: heart-pumping rapids in quick succession, the stunning canyon setting, and its extremely difficult access. See chapter G5, page 387.

4. Upper Klamath River

Rafting Hell's Corner on the Upper Klamath is kind of like putting a saddle on the space shuttle and riding off into orbit. The worst stretch is Satan's Gate (Class IV), Hell's Corner (Class IV+), and Ambush (Class IV)—one right after the other. This is where boating turns into an act of faith. And it just keeps going. The last big rapids you'll encounter are Snag Islands Falls (Class III+) and Stateline Falls (Class III), providing two final chances to dump. See chapter A2, page 49.

5. South Fork American River

Here you have it: The most popular rafting river in America. For newcomers to the sport, the South Fork American is the best choice, offering easy access, enough of a white-water challenge to add some sizzle, and a huge array of guided trips to choose from. This is a Class III run, considered the perfect introduction to rafting, and there are plenty of takers. The white-water highlights include Meatgrinder (Class III), Troublemaker (Class III+), and Satan's Cesspool (Class III+), which can challenge even experienced paddlers and give most novices the opportunity to see if their heart can pound a hole through their chest. See chapter D3, page 223.

6. Upper Kings River

The Upper Kings is a scintillating stretch of water suitable only for daredevil experts. It features a Class V+ rating, incredible views, and near-death drops. The reward is unequaled wilderness scenery, including a breathtaking view of 640-foot Garlic Falls (on the right at mile 5). Note: There is no trail access to much of this stretch of river, except for the two-mile trail to the put-in. This means there is no chance of rescue. See chapter F4, page 360.

7. Merced River

The Merced features an extraordinarily long (29 miles) stretch of river that can be run from the put-in at Red Bud to the take-out at Bagby. It is rated Class IV+ for the first 9 miles and the last 13 miles, and is rated Class II for the 7 miles in between. The scenery is attractive and the run has a remote feel, even though much of it is paralleled by the highway. The first 2.5 miles contain some Class IV white water, most notably Chipped Tooth and Nightmare Island. See chapter E4, page 312.

8. Klamath River (Happy Camp to Green Riffle)

Nature's artwork can seem perfect here. The Klamath River tumbles around boulders and into gorges, then flattens into slicks, all the while framed by a high, tree-lined canyon rim and an azure blue sky. From Happy Camp to Green Riffle it's 37.5 miles, and highlights include Kanaka Falls (Class III) and Dragon's Tooth (Class III+). To sum it up, this is a very pretty run with lots of birdlife, pretty river bends, and a good number of easy runs interspersed by slicks, making it a kick for all comers. See chapter A1, page 43.

9. Middle Fork American River

The scenery is exquisite, remote, and lush. The water is cold and clear. Historical sites from the Gold Rush days abound. And the white-water rafting runs bear such names as Texas Chainsaw Mama and Murderer's Bar. Need more be said? Texas Chainsaw Mama? Hey, where do they get these names, anyway? Right, this is the Middle Fork American, the challenging alternative to the popular South Fork American. See chapter D3, page 216.

10. Lower Kern River

A challenging intermediate-advanced section is featured on this run. Most of the white water is rated Class III+, though there are a few Class IVs sprinkled along the route, including White Maiden's Walkway, Dead Man's Curve, Hari-Kari, Horseshoe Falls, and Pinball. Here's an insider's note: You'll find hot springs at the Miracle Hot Springs camping area. The area is not maintained, but you can still find hot pools if you search around a bit. See chapter G5, page 391.

BEST FISHING

1. San Diego Deep Sea

San Diego Bay is a world-class fishing destination, and boaters will find that the remarkable marine beauty, warm water, and benign seas put the bay and the nearby coast on a level rarely seen anywhere in the United States. There are trips that run to nearby Coronado and Catalina Islands for albacore, yellowtail, and white sea bass. Then there are trips lasting from a week and longer that head south of Cabo San Lucas to Clarion Island and other regional hot spots. When there are multiple hookups, it can be absolute bedlam, with anglers ducking under each other's rods and lines as they chase the fish along the railing, often in opposite directions. In other words, it's some of the most exciting fishing in the world. See Saltwater Appendix, page 487.

2. Lake San Antonio

Can you imagine catching 100 bass in a day? At San Antonio, that fantasy can become a reality. This lake is now one of the best in California for high catch rates of largemouth bass, which makes the whole San Antonio experience very special. Lake San Antonio is a long and narrow lake, covering 5,500 surface acres and offering 60 miles of shoreline. It is set at an elevation of 900 feet in the dry, hilly woodlands/grasslands of southern Monterey County. See chapter G2, page 373.

3. Golden Gate, San Francisco

A salmon-fishing trip here starts with a boat ride past such national treasures as Alcatraz and the Golden Gate Bridge. How can you beat that? Many people know they can't. Trips heading out beyond the Golden Gate venture to the richest marine region on the Pacific Coast, where anglers often get the highest catch rates for salmon anywhere. See Saltwater Appendix, page 468.

4. Santa Barbara Deep Sea

Beautiful beaches? An emerald-green sea that's warm to the touch? Waves that often lap at the shore? An excellent boat ramp and harbor that offers easy access to nearby fishing grounds? Perhaps the best climate anywhere on the California coast? Right on all counts, and that's what makes the Santa Barbara coastline extraordinary. Powerboaters who launch at the harbor can embark on an odyssey through dense kelp forests, oil platform drilling rigs, and the offshore Channel Islands, an abundant and varied saltwater habitat that will fulfill any angler's dream. See Saltwater Appendix, page 478.

5. Smith River

Smith River is unforgettable, thanks to its great natural beauty, redwoods, firs, pines, granite-lined gorges, and the free-flowing water. There's no place like it. There's also no place else in California with more big steelhead in the winter. The average catch here is a 10-pounder, and more 20-pounders are hooked, sometimes even caught, than anywhere in the state. See chapter AØ, page 34.

6. Lake Cachuma

Cachuma has become one of the hottest bass lakes in America, for both large-mouth and smallmouth bass. About 48,500 trout are stocked here yearly, and they are like growing pills for the bass. The lake is set at an elevation of 780 feet in the foothills east of Santa Ynez. When full, it is lovely and big, covering 3,200 acres. See chapter H3, page 399.

7. Lake Almanor

Lake Almanor is big and beautiful, featuring sapphire-blue waters and views of snowcapped Mount Lassen to the northwest. In the spring and fall, fishing for trout and salmon is often excellent, not so much for the number of fish, but rather for their size. Excellent, that is, providing you can handle them. Once you figure out this lake, trout and salmon in the four- and five-pound class might be your average catch. See chapter C3, page 147.

8. El Capitan Lake

The bassers call this place "El Cap," usually with a hint of reverence in their voices. While you might hear stories about the bass at other lakes, El Cap is the one that produces them. The water clarity is typically only fair here, which makes the bass far less spooky than at most lakes. Catch rates are high. See chapter J6, page 447.

9. Convict Lake

Although this lake features spectacular high mountain scenery, it is known primarily for fishing, particularly for the good catch rates of rainbow trout and the rare but huge brown trout. There's a dream brown here that I named Horgon; some say it's just a ghost memory, but one day I'm gonna hook and land that sucker. See chapter E5, page 326.

10. San Pablo Reservoir

Daybreak at San Pablo Reservoir is one of the prettiest boating scenes in the Bay Area, highlighted by blues and greens, placid water, and fishing boats trailing fresh, white wakes. Trout fishing serves as the main attraction here. The lake gets the highest trout stocks of any lake in California, with a large number of 12- to 15-inchers and a sprinkling of 8- to 15-pounders. See chapter E1, page 256.

BEST WATERSKIING

1. Lake Havasu

Giant Lake Havasu stands out like a lone sapphire in a pile of coal. Only the Colorado River breaks up a measureless expanse of desert, and when the Parker Dam was set across the river, Havasu was born. It is 45 miles long and covers 19,300 acres at the low elevation of 482 feet. This is one of the most popular boating destinations in the southwestern United States, and its size, weather, warm water, and proximity to Las Vegas make it one of the top vacation and waterskiing hot spots in the West. Most boaters do their own thing, heading off on this great stretch of water in search of wild fun and frolic. And most find it. Over the course of a year, enough suntan oil is used at Lake Havasu to flood the California Aqueduct. See chapter I9, page 437.

2. San Joaquin Delta

Yeah, it gets insane here, and that's exactly why so many people like the San Joaquin Delta. There are boats, boats, boats everywhere, not to mention boat owners who are on weekend vacations trying to completely escape the reality of their Monday-to-Friday lives. And the waterskiing? You've never seen so many boats ripping up and down, with happy (and somewhat insane) folks aboard and bright white wakes trailing behind. By early Saturday afternoon on the typical hot summer weekend, so much beer has been consumed that the scene deteriorates from crazed to maniacal. See chapter E2, page 272.

3. Colorado River

Hot weather and cool, calm water make this one of the water-ski capitals of America. Bring your suntan lotion and a beach towel. There are plenty of hot bodies and hot boats, and waterskiing is the dominant activity in the summer. The roar of the big V8s in the jet boats can be unbelievable, along with the bright wakes spewing from boats and skiers alike. It gets extremely crowded in the summer with happy boaters, skiers, swimmers, and general tourist traffic. Then there are the speedboat racers who show up every year for various competitions. See chapter H9, page 438.

4. Shasta Lake

Shasta has four lake arms—the Sacramento Arm, McCloud Arm, Pit Arm, and Squaw Creek Arm—and each arm is like a separate lake. That's in addition to the main lake near the dam. Add to that the thousands of little coves and secret inlets, and you've got a body of water that's so big no boater can ever fully explore it. In other words, this is one place that has plenty of room for everybody. With all the houseboaters and water-skiers, the scene resembles a giant party. Everybody's happy, and there's lots of sun, skin, oil, and liquid refreshments. See chapter B2, page 86.

5. San Vicente Lake

San Vicente is located in the arid San Diego foothills at an elevation of 659 feet, and when it's full it covers 1,070 acres and offers 14 miles of shoreline. An island completes the picture. To prevent conflicts, waterskiing is prohibited on fishing day (Friday), and fishing is prohibited on waterskiing days (Thursday, Saturday, and Sunday). Many people think this is an ideal setup. See chapter J6, page 445.

6. Lake Nacimiento

This big lake is set in the coastal foothill country of southern Monterey County. When full of water, it covers more than 5,000 acres with 165 miles of shoreline, plus there are a remarkable number of lake arms and coves. That combination—an enormous surface area and many private coves—provides the ideal conditions for high-speed boating, waterskiing, and personal watercraft, as well as for low-speed boating, canoeing, and fishing. In the main lake, there is even a slalom course for expert water-skiers. See chapter G2, page 373.

7. Lake Perris

In the summer and fall, the weather out here can make you feel like you're standing in a fire pit. That's why waterskiing and swimming are such big hits at Lake Perris. The lake is set in the Moreno Valley at an elevation of 1,500 feet, just southwest of The Badlands foothills. There are large ski beaches on the northeast and southeast shores, and this can be a great place to go waterskiing or ride personal watercraft. See chapter I6, page 427.

8. Lake Piru

Things can get crazy at Piru. Fortunately, it's usually a happy crazy, not an insane crazy. You see, this lake is pretty close to the Los Angeles Basin and it attracts quite a few people who come for the boating, waterskiing, fishing, sunbathing, and swimming. Temperatures are warm, and the water often seems to feel just right. And get this: No areas are off-limits to water-skiers. See chapter H4, page 409.

9. Lake Elsinore

Whoosh! Whoosh! What's faster than a speeding bullet? Whoosh! Whoosh! If you're at Lake Elsinore, then the answer is a water-skier being towed by a jet boat. The place is loaded with them. And why not? With day after day of barn-burner weather throughout summer and into fall, and few anglers to get in the way, it's the perfect place. Lake Elsinore is set at 1,239 feet in an area that gets hot enough to make the water here more valuable to water-skiers than gold. The lake is big enough to accommodate all kinds of boaters, too. It's a winner, and lots of people take advantage of it. See chapter I6, page 428.

10. Pyramid Lake

Although Pyramid Lake (elevation 2,600 feet) is surrounded by Angeles National Forest, Interstate 5 is routed right past several lake arms. This makes it one of the more easily accessed bodies of water in California. Because it's a showpiece, the water masters tend to keep it fuller than other lakes on line with the California Aqueduct. That makes it a favorite for powerboaters, especially water-skiers (a 35 mph speed limit is enforced). See chapter H4, page 406.

BEST FAMILY DESTINATIONS

1. Edison Lake

Here is one of the great family camping destinations in California. Edison Lake offers four lakeside camps, a resort, a boat launch, boat rentals, horseback riding rentals, a nearby trailhead to the Pacific Crest Trail, and yes, good fishing. A 15 mph speed limit keeps the water quiet, and there's twice-daily ferry service across the lake to the trailhead. Edison Lake, located at an elevation of 7,650 feet, is fed by Mono Creek, a cold, pure, and pristine trout stream. There are beach areas all along the shoreline for swimming. See chapter F5, page 365.

2. Big Bear Lake

Talk about a place that has it all: Big Bear is big and beautiful; it offers good trout fishing, quality boating opportunities, many campgrounds, a few resorts, and excellent swimming; and it is located near the highest regions of the San Bernardino National Forest, at 6,738 feet. Among all the bodies of water in the region, this lake has an unmatched beauty, particularly in the spring when the snow is melting. The deep-blue waters glisten in striking contrast with the surrounding white mountaintops. The lake covers more than 3,000 acres with 22 miles of shoreline, and has a faithful vacation following. See chapter I6, page 424.

3. June Lake

Awesome peaks that are often edged with snow tower above June Lake, a 160-acre mountain lake set at a 7,600-foot elevation. Amenities? If you need something, you can get it here. There are campsites near the shore, nearby cabins, a good boat ramp, and stores within a mile. June Lake is easily accessed off Highway 158. And for many reasons it gets the highest use by far of all the lakes in the June Lakes Loop. It is very beautiful, and it has the best fishing, best camping sites, best swimming, and best windsurfing. That's a lot of bests. Even when there are many people here, the 10 mph speed limit guarantees at least a semblance of serenity. See chapter E5, page 320.

4. Lake Siskiyou

Giant Mount Shasta rises 14,162 feet above Siskiyou, creating one of the prettier settings for a man-made lake anywhere in the country. The 10 mph speed limit ensures quiet waters, and the nearby campground makes the place ideal for family vacations, plus there's easy access off nearby Interstate 5. Children often play in the swimming area, which has a great swimming beach, or pedal around in paddleboats. The lake provides an excellent campground (clean and patrolled), decent trout fishing, and good leisure boating opportunities. See chapter B2, page 80.

5. Zaca Lake

Very few people know about Zaca, a small lake that makes the perfect family retreat, complete with cabin rentals. Covering just 25 acres, it is set at an elevation of 2,400 feet in Los Padres National Forest, about 40 miles north of Santa Barbara. Swimming is popular, and a buoy line designates a swimming area and rocky beach at the south end of the lake. Side trip options include hiking and horseback riding; good trails through national forest land start just north of here. See chapter H2, page 395.

6. Silver Lake

Beautiful and inviting, Silver Lake is set at an elevation of 7,200 feet in a classic granite cirque just below the Sierra ridgeline in Eldorado National Forest. Visitors have access to cabin rentals, a campground, boat rentals, decent trout fishing, great hiking trails, horseback riding campgrounds, and several other nearby lakes. Most people congregate on the north side of the lake, where the campgrounds, picnic areas, and marina are located. See chapter D4, page 246.

7. Klamath River

The rafting run from Sarah Totten Campground to Happy Camp is probably the best trip in California for families. Beautiful scenery and lots of birds and wildlife can be seen along the way. The run is lively enough to make the trip memorable, yet easy enough that it's doable for the whole family. White-water highlights are Upper Savage and Otter's Play Pen (both Class III-). There are plenty of thrills to get your blood pumping and lots of flat water so you can calm down or beach the boat and go swimming. See chapter A1, page 43.

8. Lake Alpine

In many people's minds, Lake Alpine fits the exact image of what a mountain lake is supposed to look like. For example, on a typical early summer evening, the surface of the lake is calm and emerald green, with little ripples made by hatching bugs and rising trout. The shoreline is well wooded (including some giant ponderosa pines), the smell of pine duff is in the air, and campsites are located within a short distance of the lake. Heaven on Earth? Almost. See chapter E4, page 299.

9. Goleta Beach County Park

The real attraction here is the huge beach—a sweeping, sandy oceanfront ideal for sunbathing, picnicking, swimming, and beachcombing. A buoy line designates a protected swimming area. There are summer days here when you'll see lots of people lolling around and you'll wonder, "Hey, doesn't any-body work anymore?" See chapter H3, page 400.

10. Rancho Seco Lake

For the ideal family picnic spot, give this place a try. The 160-acre lake is part of the 400-acre Rancho Seco Recreation Area, which has a boat ramp (no motors permitted) and several docks. There is a large, sandy swimming area, a pleasant picnic site, and a campground for tents or RVs. There are also trails for hiking, horseback riding, and bicycling, as well as several fishing docks along the shore. See chapter D2, page 194.

Northern California
Recreational Lakes
and Rivers

Overall Rating

| 1 | 2 | 3 | 4 | 5 | 6 | 7 | 8 | 9 | 10 |

Poor .... Fair .... Great

Key to the Symbols

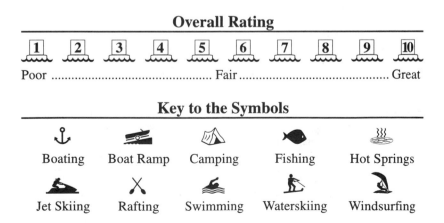

| Boating | Boat Ramp | Camping | Fishing | Hot Springs |

| Jet Skiing | Rafting | Swimming | Waterskiing | Windsurfing |

Northern California Overview

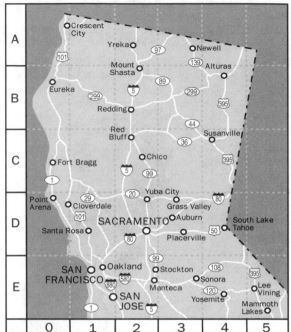

Chapter A0
Del Norte/ Smith River Coast

Overall Rating

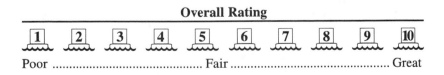

Poor .... Fair .... Great

A0–Del Norte/Smith River Map

One inch equals approximately 10.7 miles.
See page 12 for California state map.

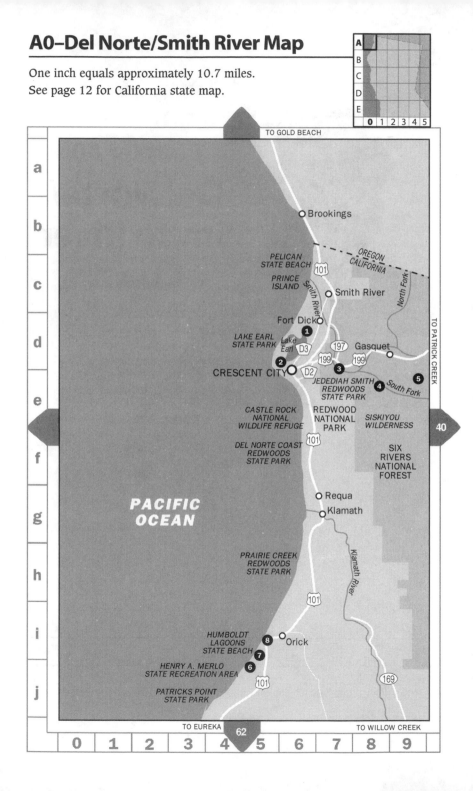

TO GOLD BEACH

Brookings

PELICAN
STATE BEACH

OREGON
CALIFORNIA

PRINCE
ISLAND

Smith River

North Fork

Smith River

Fort Dick

LAKE EARL
STATE PARK

Lake
Earl

Gasquet

CRESCENT CITY

JEDEDIAH SMITH
REDWOODS
STATE PARK

South Fork

TO PATRICK CREEK

CASTLE ROCK
NATIONAL
WILDLIFE REFUGE

REDWOOD
NATIONAL
PARK

SISKIYOU
WILDERNESS

40

DEL NORTE COAST
REDWOODS
STATE PARK

SIX
RIVERS
NATIONAL
FOREST

PACIFIC
OCEAN

Requa

Klamath

PRAIRIE CREEK
REDWOODS
STATE PARK

Klamath River

HUMBOLDT
LAGOONS
STATE BEACH

Orick

HENRY A. MERLO
STATE RECREATION AREA

PATRICKS POINT
STATE PARK

TO EUREKA   62

TO WILLOW CREEK

Chapter AØ features:

❶ Lake Earl

Location: Near Crescent City; map AØ, grid d6.

Directions: From Crescent City drive north on US 101. Turn northwest on Northcrest–Lake Earl Drive and then turn west on Morehead Road or north on Lower Lake Road or west on Kellogg Road.

Access: An unpaved boat ramp is provided. From Northcrest–Lake Earl Drive turn northwest on Lake View Road and continue to the ramp.

Facilities, fees: Boat rentals are not available. Five environmental walk-in campsites are provided. There is no piped water. Access is free.

Water sports, restrictions: There are no speed limits and no restrictions on water sports; however, the lake is generally considered too marshy to be used for anything except fishing.

Contact: California State Parks, North Coast Redwoods District, Redwood Coast Sector, (707) 464-6101.

About Lake Earl: Although Lake Earl is by far the largest lake in Del Norte County, it attracts very little attention. One reason is that motorists can't see it from US 101; another is that there are limited recreational opportunities here. Lake Earl is uniquely situated, near sea level less than a mile from the Pacific Ocean. Its neighbor to the west, Lake Talawa, is connected to Lake Earl by a short, narrow curve of water and borders coastal sand dunes, sometimes running into the ocean after heavy rainfall.

The lake is large, approximately 2,500 surface acres, but alas, it is both shallow and marshy. A boat ramp is available; however, boats rarely venture out on the water. If you just like to float around without a care, Lake Earl can provide peace and solitude. On the rare clear day, sunset watching from the eastern shore can be spectacular, with the light reflecting off the lake in a solitary beam. This is the perfect way to cap a day of camping in one of the little-known primitive campsites here, a world apart from the summer vacation traffic on US 101.

When you first arrive, Lake Earl looks like a great spot for fishing. Nope. Once in a while sea-run cutthroat trout and flounder are caught at the Narrows, the stretch of water that connects Earl and Talawa Lakes. Most anglers don't catch anything, which is why the locals tend to stay away.

❷ Dead Lake

Location: Near Crescent City; map AØ, grid e6.

Directions: From US 101 in Crescent City, take Washington Boulevard west and continue until you're almost at the airport. Turn north on Riverside Road and drive to the lake.

Access: There is no boat ramp.

Facilities, fees: No facilities are provided at the lake. However, full services and lodging are available two miles away in Crescent City. Access is free.

Water sports, restrictions: There are no speed limits and no restrictions on water sports; however, the lake is generally considered too marshy to be used for anything except fishing.

Contact: California State Parks, North Coast Redwoods District, Redwood Coast Sector, (707) 464-6101.

About Dead Lake: If you like secret fishing spots, file this one away in the back of your mind and then make sure you try it out when you are in the area. This little lake provides good bass fishing, is easy to reach, and is missed by virtually everyone who passes through the area. Unfortunately, it is small, narrow, and marshy, and has no boat ramp, making it extremely poor for other water sports. But that helps keep Dead Lake a secret for the few who know of it.

---

❸ Smith River

🎣🛶🏕🐟➤✕🚤　🛟 10

Location: East of Crescent City in Six Rivers National Forest; map AØ, grid e7.

Directions: At the junction of US 101 and US 199 in Crescent City, turn east on US 199. Direct access is available.

Access: A public boat ramp is located off US 199 near the confluence of the North and Middle Forks of the Smith River. Vault toilets are provided. A private ramp is available farther north at Salmon Harbor Resort on US 101, three miles north of the town of Smith River. There is no charge to use the private ramp, but you must be a guest at the resort.

There are two put-ins near the town of Gasquet. The upper put-in is located at the confluence of the North and Middle Forks off US 199. Turn north at the signed bridge just past Hiouchi, cross the river, and hike down on the left side to the bank. To reach the lower put-in, drive approximately two miles west on US 199 to a dirt turnout where the highway meets the river. Take out at a dirt turnout six miles west of Gasquet on US 199. Unless you're an expert, make sure you take out here, because the next section, Oregon Hole Gorge, offers only difficult Class V rapids.

Facilities, fees: Several campgrounds are available, including sites in Jedediah Smith Redwoods State Park and a few low-cost Forest Service camps. The camps are located along US 199 and provide streamside access. In addition the Wagon Wheel Motel near Gasquet and Patrick's Lodge on the upper river offer lodging along US 199. Smith River Outfitters and Hiouchi Market are the best sources for tackle and expert advice. No boat rentals are available. Access is free. Rafting permits are not required.

Water sports, restrictions: The Smith River is extremely popular for swimming. There are several good holes just off US 199; the best spots include Panther Flat Picnic Area, the Forks (the confluence of the South Fork and Middle Fork), and Mary Adams Peacock Bridge, all well signed and located just off US 199. A designated personal watercraft area is available near the mouth of the Smith River off US 101.

Contact: To obtain fishing information or to hire a fishing guide with a driftboat, contact Smith River Outfitters, (707) 487-0935. In the summer contact Ship Ashore, (707) 487-3141. For camping and general information, contact Six Rivers National Forest, Gasquet Ranger District, PO Box 228, Gasquet, CA 95543; (707) 457-3131; California State Parks, Jedediah Smith Redwoods State Park, c/o Redwoods National and State Parks, (707) 464-6101, extension 5112; North Coast Redwoods District, Redwood Coast Sector, (707) 464-6101. For guided rafting trips contact Aurora River Adventures, (530) 629-3843. For lessons or guided canoeing and kayaking trips, contact California Canoe & Kayak, (800) 366-9804.

About the Smith River: The crown jewel of the nation's streams, the Smith River is a fountain of pure water, undammed and unbridled, running free through sapphire-blue granite canyons.

When you first see the Smith, you will probably exclaim: "Look how beautiful the water is!" Even after heavy winter rains, which can turn most rivers into brown muck, the Smith is usually pretty blue and clear. The river's hard granite base, combined with the large volume of water drained from a huge mountain acreage, gives the river a unique ability to cleanse itself.

In the winter and spring, from November through May, this river is great for expert kayakers and fair for rafting and canoeing. In the summer it's decent for people heading far upstream looking for a swimming hole. The Smith is better known, however, as the number one producer of large steelhead from mid-December through mid-March.

The most tantalizing section of the river for kayakers and rafters is a six-mile stretch near Gasquet, rated as Class II+, with an additional one mile of Class V water directly below in the Oregon Hole Gorge. Only experts run the gorge, and doing so is a kind of rite of passage for kayakers ready to take the daredevil test. In the winter I have occasionally seen master kayakers giving lessons to small groups of people who want to conquer the gorge.

Canoeists should forget about the Gorge or any other stretch of upstream water. Instead put in at Ruby Van Deveneter County Park for a 10-mile Class I paddle down to the public boat ramp, a good easy day trip.

The best swimming holes in the Smith River drainage are well up the South Fork Smith River (see the following listing), accessible on South Fork Road, though a deep, calm spot is available in the summer at the Forks, the confluence of the Middle Fork and South Fork. Access is available just downstream from the bridge north of Hiouchi; from US 199 turn at the bridge, drive a quarter mile, and then turn right at the unsigned cutoff. By the way, this is also a good put-in spot for a canoe trip.

As with any river weather is the key variable, and the Smith gets more of the wet kind than any other place in the Lower 48. My pal Michael Furniss, one of the top hydrologists in America, set up a rain gauge at nearby Camp Six and documented 256 inches of rain in 1983, still a national record. Heavy rains mean the river can rise quickly and turn what would otherwise be a wild trip down The Gorge into an act of insanity.

But what you will remember best is the great natural beauty of the river; the redwoods, firs, and pines; granite-lined gorges; and the beautiful free-flowing water. There's no place like it.

❹ South Fork Smith River

Location: East of Crescent City in Six Rivers National Forest; map A∅, grid e7.

Directions: From Crescent City drive five miles north on US 101 and turn east on US 199. Continue for five miles to the small town of Hiouchi, drive for one mile, and turn right on South Fork Road. Drive over two bridges and then bear left on South Fork Road. Direct access is available.

Access: There is no boat ramp. To reach the put-in, follow the previous directions, driving south on South Fork Road for 13 miles. The put-in is at the fourth bridge over the river. You may also put in at the second and third bridges. Take out at a turnout on South Fork Road approximately one mile above the first South Fork bridge. Unless you're an expert, make sure you take out here, because the next section, South Fork Gorge, offers only difficult Class V rapids.

Facilities, fees: Big Flat Camp, a primitive Forest Service campground, is located adjacent to where Hurdy Gurdy Creek enters the South Fork Smith. There is no piped water. The nearest facilities are available in Hiouchi. Access is free. Rafting permits are not required.

Water sports, restrictions: There are several good swimming holes off South Fork Road; the best is located at the second bridge.

Contact: Six Rivers National Forest, Gasquet Ranger District, PO Box 228, Gasquet, CA 95543; (707) 457-3131. For lessons or guided canoeing and kayaking trips, contact California Canoe & Kayak, (800) 366-9804.

About the South Fork Smith River: The hallmarks of the South Fork Smith include beautiful scenery, good access, excellent white water for kayaking, pretty campsites, and decent swimming holes.

South Fork Road, a paved two laner, follows the river well up to its headwaters. On the way, you will pass one of the prettiest undammed streams you can see without having to hike, set deep in Six Rivers National Forest, with clear, emerald green water flowing free over a pristine granite base. There are frequent turnouts along the road, each with primitive, steep trails that anglers in search of steelhead use to reach prime river holes during the winter. These same routes provide access in the summer to the best swimming holes, especially far upstream.

The highlight of the South Fork Smith is an 11.5-mile stretch of Class III white water, all of it in virtual solitude, making this a great destination for skilled kayakers. The run features many short pool-and-drops feeding into rapids, with lots of breaks in moving flat water. That gives paddlers plenty of action, as well as a sufficient number of short breaks to let them catch their breath.

Newcomers should be warned about South Fork Gorge, which is located about a mile upstream from the confluence with the Middle Fork. The gorge starts with a set of falls, actually a fast-dropping rapid. If you dump here there's no way out and you'll have to float/swim the entire gorge. It is rated Class V and can be suicide for all but the best.

The prime kayaking season is fall, often mid-October through mid-June, when the river is pumped up from Del Norte County's legendary rains. The South Fork gets significantly less use than the Middle Fork because there are no commercial rafting trips available here.

⑤ Dry Lake

Location: Near Crescent City in Six Rivers National Forest; map AØ, grid e9.

Directions: From Crescent City drive five miles north on US 101 to US 199. Turn east and drive five miles, through Hiouchi, to South Fork Road. Turn east, cross two bridges, and then bear left after the second bridge. Drive 14 miles to Big Flat Ranger Station, turn left on County Road 405/ French Hill Road, and then drive five miles north to Dry Lake.

Access: There is no boat ramp.

Facilities, fees: The lake has one small, primitive campsite. No other facilities are provided. Access is free.

Water sports, restrictions: No motors are permitted on the lake. The lake is too small and muddy for swimming and other water/body contact sports.

Contact: Smith River National Recreation Area, PO Box 228, Gasquet, CA 95543; (707) 457-3131.

About Dry Lake: Dry Lake is a tiny, bowl-like lake situated in national forestland that even the locals don't venture into. The area is pretty, set at an elevation of 2,000 feet near the headwaters of Hurdy Gurdy Creek. This is a decent spot for paddling a raft or a canoe in complete seclusion. Because Dry Lake is small and shallow, it is not good for much else and receives very little use.

Note: If you continue north on the Forest Service road over Gordon Mountain (4,153 feet) and down the other side to Camp Six, about a 10-mile drive from the lake, you will reach the rainiest place in the

Lower 48. In 1983 it rained 256 inches, the highest amount ever recorded in the contiguous United States. Dry Lake? As the locals say, "Dry it ain't."

❻ Big Lagoon

Location: North of Trinidad in Humboldt Lagoons State Park; map AØ, grid j5.

Directions: From Eureka drive about 33 miles north on US 101 (eight miles past Trinidad). Turn west on Big Lagoon Road.

Access: A boat ramp is located on the east side of the lagoon off US 101.

Facilities, fees: A boat ramp and rest rooms are provided. Trinidad has two tackle shops: Salty's and Bob's Boat Basin. Campgrounds are available at Patrick's Point State Park in Trinidad and at Stone Lagoon to the immediate north. Access is free.

Water sports, restrictions: Waterskiing, windsurfing, and personal watercraft use permitted. Swimming is allowed, but it can be dangerous during spring runoff.

Contact: California State Parks, North Coast Redwoods District, Redwood Coast Sector, (707) 464-6101; Eureka Department of Fish and Game, (707) 445-6499.

About Big Lagoon: A series of three lagoons lies on California's northern coast, midway between Eureka and Crescent City along US 101. They look similar, but each has a distinct character and unique attractions.

Traveling north on US 101 from Eureka, you come to Big Lagoon, the first of the three lagoons, which covers 1,470 acres. The lagoon has brackish water, a mixture of fresh water and salt water, and is bordered on the west by a sand spit and the ocean, and on the east by second-growth forest.

This place is great for those who like to windsurf or sail small boats since it frequently gets winds out of the north, especially on spring and summer afternoons, and from the south during the winter. The water is cold, typically about 50 to 60 degrees, so most windsurfers will need to put on their wet suits.

On days when the wind is down, you can take advantage of an excellent beach walk out of Patrick's Point State Park. From the parking area for the Octopus Trees Trail, a staircase is routed down to a large beach. From here walk north all the way to the sand spit that borders the western edge of the lagoon, an extremely isolated setting.

❼ Stone Lagoon

Location: North of Trinidad in Humboldt Lagoons State Park; map AØ, grid j5.

Directions: From Eureka drive about 39 miles north on US 101 (14 miles past Trinidad).

Access: A boat ramp is located directly off US 101.

Facilities, fees: A boat dock and ramp are provided. Three campgrounds are available: Dry Lagoon, a walk-in camp; Big Lagoon; and the best, Stone Lagoon, a boat-in at Ryan's Cove, located on the western shoreline across the lagoon. Two good tackle shops are located in Trinidad: Salty's and Bob's Boat Basin. Access is free.

Water sports, restrictions: A 10 mph speed limit is strictly enforced. Swimming is permitted, but most swimmers prefer the clearer water of nearby Freshwater Lagoon.

Contact: California State Parks, North Coast Redwoods District, Redwood Coast Sector, (707) 464-6101; Eureka Department of Fish and Game, (707) 445-6499.

About Stone Lagoon: Of the three lagoons located along a 10-mile stretch of coastline in Del Norte County, this is my favorite. You get a boat-in shoreline campsite at Ryan's Camp, prime canoeing water, and decent trout fishing. Another plus: it is often overlooked by out-of-towners.

The lagoon covers 521 acres, with a visitor center and primitive boat ramp located at the parking area along the west side of the highway. From here you plunk in your canoe, wide-bodied kayak, or dinghy, and paddle or sail over to Ryan's Cove, straight across the water and out of sight of the highway, where you will find a great little boat-in campground. This is one of only seven lakes in California with boat-in camping.

Once your base camp is established, you can paddle and explore. Features include the pretty inlet stream, the open/shut sandbar "dam" along the ocean that bursts open during heavy rains, an occasional elk sighting, and a chance to fish for sea-run cutthroat trout. Like Big Lagoon to the south, this is also a good spot for windsurfing.

In addition you can land your craft on the far shore and gain access to a remote section of the Coastal Trail as well as the sand spit that separates this lagoon from the ocean. Most of those people zooming by on nearby US 101 don't have a clue that this pretty spot exists.

---

⑧ Freshwater Lagoon

Location: North of Trinidad in Humboldt Lagoons State Park; map AØ, grid j5.
Directions: From Eureka drive 41 miles north on US 101 (16 miles past Trinidad).
Access: A dirt launching area is located on the north end of the lagoon.
Facilities, fees: Rest rooms and an information center are provided. A large, flat area to the west of the highway is such a popular spot to park motor homes that they are sometimes lined up for a mile. Tent campers will find three campgrounds at Stone Lagoon. Two tackle shops are located in Trinidad: Salty's and Bob's Boat Basin. Access is free.
Water sports, restrictions: Personal watercraft and waterskiing are permitted.

A recreation area on the north end is popular with swimmers and windsurfers. There are several good swimming access points around the lagoon.

Contact: Humboldt Lagoons State Park, (707) 488-2041 or fax (707) 488-5555; Eureka Department of Fish and Game, (707) 445-6499. A visitor information center is located just north of Freshwater Lagoon, north of Lookout Point on the west side of the highway.

About Freshwater Lagoon: The lagoon's name gives it all away. From that alone all the vacationers cruising US 101 figure out that this is freshwater, not salt water. Of the three lagoons in the immediate area, this is the only one on the east side of the highway. Right, another tip-off.

That is why visitor traffic pours into this spot, while Stone Lagoon and Big Lagoon to the south get a relative trickle. And people galore are what you find here. The water is a lot warmer here than at the other two lagoons, so it attracts more of everything, more windsurfers, personal watercraft, water-skiers, swimmers, and yes, because it is stocked with rainbow trout, more anglers. Even scuba divers practice here.

At 241 acres this is the smallest of the three lagoons, yet it has the best boat ramp of the three, located at the north end.

In the summer when you first drive up, the number of motor homes and trailers parked in the extended shoulder along the highway can be unbelievable. Some days it looks like the Winnebago capital of the world, with vehicles lined up one after another, sometimes double-parked for miles.

All these people couldn't be wrong, could they? Nope. They've got it right. With the clear fresh water, easy access, and all those parking spaces for motor homes, this spot provides just what they want.

Chapter A1
Klamath Mountains Area

Overall Rating

| 1 | 2 | 3 | 4 | 5 | 6 | 7 | 8 | 9 | 10 |

Poor .... Fair .... Great

A1–Klamath Mountains Area Map

One inch equals approximately 10.7 miles.
See page 12 for California state map.

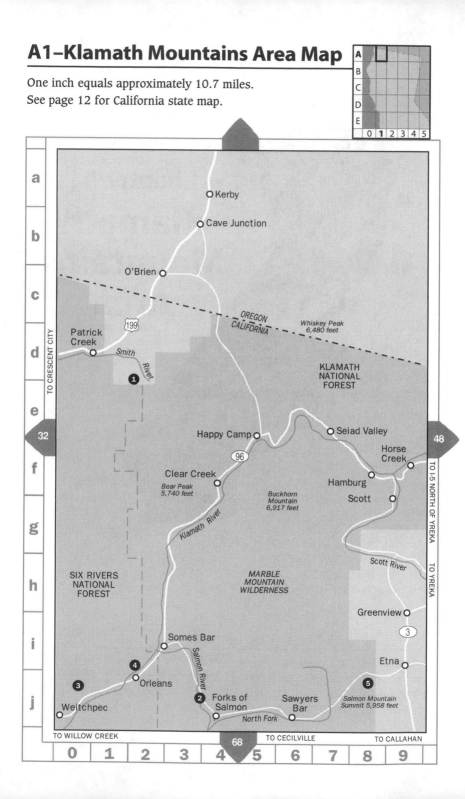

Chapter A1 features:

❶ Sanger Lake

Location: Near Gasquet in Six Rivers National Forest; map A1, grid d2.

Directions: From Crescent City drive five miles north on US 101 to US 199. Turn east and travel 14 miles to the small town of Gasquet. Continue 16 miles east on US 199. Turn east on Forest Service Road 18N02/Knopki Road, travel 13 miles, bear left, and travel a short distance to Sanger Lake.

Access: No boat ramp is available.

Facililties, fees: There are no on-site facilities. You can camp on a do-it-yourself basis. Access to the lake is free.

Water sports, restrictions: Swimming and canoeing are popular in the summer, although there is no beach. The lake is too small for other sports.

Contact: Six Rivers National Forest, Gasquet Ranger District, PO Box 228, Gasquet, CA 95543; (707) 457-3131 or fax (707) 457-3794.

About Sanger Lake: Little Sanger Lake is a small, out-of-the-way cold-water pond that provides peace, quiet, and a chance to catch tiny brook trout. Set just below Sanger Peak (5,862 feet) to the north, the lake is reached via a long drive on dirt roads, a trip that is daunting enough to keep most folks away—far away. Long? It seems to go on forever. From Eureka it takes two hours to reach the turnoff on US 199, and from there it's more than an hour to the lake.

When you finally arrive, you find six-acre Sanger Lake, set at an elevation of 5,100 feet on the edge of the Siskiyou Wilderness. The water is clear and cold, reaching a maximum depth of 25 feet. This is the kind of place where you can plop a raft or canoe in the water and just float around, enjoying the serenity. It is also good for swimming, especially in late summer after a hike. The trailhead for Young's Valley Trail, which is routed along Clear Creek, is located near here at the end of the access road that passes Sanger Lake.

For the most part the lake gets light use because it is small and it takes so long to get here. But that is exactly what some people are looking for.

❷ Salmon River

Location: Near Orleans in Klamath National Forest; map A1, grid i3.

Directions: From Eureka drive 12 miles north on US 101 to Arcata, turn east on Highway 299, and drive 42 miles. At the Highway 96 turnoff, turn north and drive 40 miles to the town of Orleans. Continue seven miles northeast to the town of Somes Bar and then turn east on Salmon River Road. Access is available along Salmon River Road.

Access: There is no boat ramp. To reach the put-in, drive approximately 17 miles east of Somes Bar on Salmon River Road to the town of Forks of Salmon. Look for a large gravel beach a little downstream of the schoolhouse in town. Beginners should take out at one of several points before mile five; the following 14 miles are Class IV–V. If you choose to continue through the rest of the run, take out at Oak Bottom Campground at mile 16.

Facililties, fees: A few campgrounds are located nearby, off Highway 96 on the Klamath River. Camps are also available upstream on the Salmon. Supplies can be obtained in Orleans or Somes Bar. Limited boat rentals and rafting gear are provided by Wilderness Adventures in Mount Shasta. Access is free. Rafting permits are not required.

Water sports, restrictions: There are several good swimming spots along the river; keep an eye out for the "River Access" signs as you drive on Salmon River Road. Two popular places are Blue Hole and Hogie's.

Contact: Klamath National Forest, Salmon River Ranger Station, (530) 467-5757 or fax (530) 467-5654. For supplies and fishing information, contact Somes Bar Store, (530) 469-3350; or Orleans Market, (530) 627-3326. For guided rafting trips contact American River Touring Association, (800) 323-2782; Aurora River Adventures, (800) 562-8475 or (530) 629-3843; Electric Rafting Company, (707) 826-2861; Turtle River Rafting, (800) 726-3223; or Wilderness Adventures, (800) 323-7238 or (530) 926-6282 or fax (530) 926-6283.

About the Salmon River: The Salmon River is one of California's greatest hidden treasures. It flows from the snowmelt in the nearby Trinity Alps, then runs through deep canyons en route to its confluence with the famous Klamath River. In the process it offers outstanding prospects for rafting, much of it suitable for advanced paddlers, as well as a wealth of great swimming holes.

Don't make the mistake of thinking that the Cal Salmon, as it is commonly called, is anything like its big brother, the Klamath. It isn't. The Salmon is clear, clean, and cold, set in a beautiful and remote deep canyon, and it gets far less use by the general public than the Klamath.

The main activity here is rafting. The best put-in spot is near the town of Forks of Salmon. From here the first five miles are Class II+, which makes a good run for beginners in inflatable kayaks. After that, however, the river really sizzles.

The rapids alternate between Class IV and V, and only experienced paddlers who don't mind living on the edge need apply. Highlights include Bloomer Falls (Class IV), the Maze (Class IV), Whirling Dervish (Class IV+), and Last Chance (Class V). The latter is a mind-bender of a drop that will have your heart leaving your body for what seems like an eternity. In fact, among rafters there is an unspoken division between those who have run the Cal Salmon and those who have not—once you have run this river, the pros figure you have captured one of the ultimate experiences in the outdoors.

The Otter Bar kayaking school, which is based in Forks of Salmon, offers week-long instructional packages that include food, lodging, and gear—a great way to learn the sport; phone the school at (530) 462-4772. Several commercial rafting companies lead trips on the Salmon, most lasting from one to four days.

Although the water is cold in early summer, this is the best stream in the Klamath river system for swimming. Trails that access pools begin from a number of pullouts on the gravel road along the river. One of the better spots is near the confluence of Wooley Creek, located at mile 14 on the access road. Smaller pools are located farther upstream.

❸ Fish Lake

Location: Southwest of Orleans in Six Rivers National Forest; map A1, grid j0.

Directions: From the junction of US 101 and Highway 299 near Arcata, turn east on Highway 299 and drive about 42 miles. Turn north on Highway 96 and drive to Weitchpec. From Weitchpec continue seven miles north on Highway 96. Turn left on Bluff Creek Road and drive about five miles. Turn right on Fish Lake Road/Forest Service Road 10N12 and drive three miles to the lake.

Note: The primary access road to this campground was closed by a landslide in

1996 but was reopened with a temporary dirt road graded over the landslide. The temporary road will be closed again if it becomes unstable. Call ahead for the status of road access.

An alternate route is available but requires an additional 2.5 hours of driving time: From Weitchpec drive north on Highway 96 for 15 miles (past Fish Lake Road) to Forest Service Road 12N12. Turn left at Forest Service Road 12N12 (very twisty, dirt logging road) and drive about 25 miles. Turn left on Forest Service Road 12N13 and drive about nine miles (extremely twisty, with a hairpin right turn at the junction with Road 12N10). Turn left at Forest Service Road 13N01, which is largely paved, and drive about 20 miles to Forest Service Road 10N12/Fish Lake Road. Turn left and drive three miles to the lake.

Access: A primitive area to launch cartop boats is located on the lake's east side.

Facililties, fees: A campground is provided at the lake. Access to the lake is free.

Water sports, restrictions: Motors are not permitted on the lake. Swimmers have a small beach to use.

Contact: Six Rivers National Forest, Orleans Ranger District, (530) 627-3291 or fax (530) 627-3401.

About Fish Lake: In many ways this lake provides the ideal summer camping/fishing destination. The key is in the out-of-the-way location: almost everybody misses it, yet it really isn't that difficult to reach.

Upon arrival you discover that Fish Lake is quite pretty, set in the woods with a Forest Service road going right around it. You get a lakeside camp that is practically within casting distance of the water. The lake covers 22 acres and is set at an elevation of 1,800 feet on the Six Rivers National Forest's eastern edge.

During peak summer months the lake and the adjoining campsites get what is best termed as "medium use," with most people coming for the scenery, tranquillity,

and good trout fishing. Because there is no boat ramp, some people bypass the place. But that makes it ideal for those with cartop boats, such as canoes or inflatable rafts. Fish Lake is pretty and intimate, and on warm summer days, this is a great place to just float around without a care in the world.

❹ Klamath River

Location: From Hamburg to Weitchpec in Six Rivers National Forest; map A1, grid j2.

Directions: From Eureka drive 12 miles north on US 101 to Arcata, turn east on Highway 299, and drive about 42 miles. Turn north on Highway 96 and drive 40 miles to the town of Orleans. Continue northeast on Highway 96, which runs parallel to the river. Direct access is available from turnouts along Highway 96 and from short spur roads that lead to the river.

Access: No boat ramps are available, but there are several primitive access spots, including Green Riffle just north of Somes Bar on Highway 96, and T-Bar, a popular access point a few miles upstream.

Rafters can put in at the following locations:

Sarah Totten Campground to Happy Camp: Put in at Sarah Totten Campground, located one-half mile east of Hamburg on Highway 96. Take out at the bridge in Happy Camp or at one of several access points just upstream.

Happy Camp to Green Riffle: Put in at the bridge in the town of Happy Camp. Take out at Green Riffle, 3.5 miles upstream of Ishi Pishi Falls, or at one of several access points upstream. Note: Unless you're an expert, be sure to take out above Ishi Pishi Falls, an extremely difficult Class VI run.

Salmon River to Weitchpec: Put in at a bridge where the Salmon River enters the Klamath, just south of Somes Bar on Highway 96. You can also put in farther upstream on the Salmon. Take out about one-half mile west of Weitchpec, just below the confluence of the Trinity and Klamath Rivers.

Facililties, fees: Several Forest Service and private campgrounds are located along Highway 96. Supplies can be obtained in the towns of Klamath River, Weitchpec, Somes Bar, Happy Camp, Seiad Valley, Horse Creek, and Orleans. Raft rentals and gear are available from Bigfoot Outdoor Company. Access is free. Rafting permits are not required.

Water sports, restrictions: Several swimming holes are located along Highway 96. One beauty is at Dillon Creek Campground, 15 miles north of Somes Bar on Highway 96.

Contact: Klamath National Forest, Orleans Ranger District, (530) 627-3291; Happy Camp Ranger District, (530) 493-2243. For fishing information contact Somes Bar Store, (530) 469-3350. For guided rafting trips contact Access to Adventure, (800) KLAMATH/552-6284 or (530) 662-7296; Aurora River Adventures, (800) 562-8475 or (530) 629-3843; Bigfoot Rafting Company, (530) 629-2263; Turtle River Rafting, (800) 726-3223; River Dancers, (800) 926-002 or Whitewater Voyages, (800) 488-7238.

About the Klamath River: This is one place where nature's artwork can seem flawless. The Klamath River tumbles around boulders, into gorges, and then flattens into slicks, all framed by a high, tree-lined canyon rim and an azure sky.

Rafters find prime territory here because the water runs at ideal flows throughout summer, courtesy of releases from Iron Gate Dam way up east of Hornbrook near the Oregon border.

One year when the river was near flood stage in March, I rafted the entire river in less than a week, from its headwaters in Oregon all the way to the Pacific Ocean. Dean Munroe of Wilderness Expeditions was the outfitter, and we completed the trip in five and a half days, the first documented descent of the entire river, covering more than 1,000 rapids. The story is detailed in my book *Epic Trips of the West.*

On that great adventure we discovered that the Klamath is abundant with not only fish, but with many species of birds and wildlife. They say this is the home of Bigfoot; there have been many sightings of the elusive creature in the Bluff Creek area, and that famous film of the Sasquatch strolling along the creek bank was shot along the Klamath in the 1960s.

The three most popular rafting runs on the Klamath are

Sarah Totten Campground to Happy Camp: 36 miles; Class III for the first 15 miles, then Class I+ until Happy Camp. Highlights: Upper Savage and Otter's Play Pen (both Class III-). Synopsis: Lively and doable in an inflatable kayak, this is also a good run for first-time rafters, with just enough excitement to get your heart pounding, yet plenty of flat water to catch your breath or beach the boat and go swimming.

Happy Camp to Green Riffle: 37.5 miles; Class III; take out above Ishi Pishi Falls. Highlights: Kanaka Falls (Class III), Dragon's Tooth (Class III+). Synopsis: A gorgeous run, with lots of birdlife, pretty river bends, and a good number of easy runs interspersed by slicks, making it a kick for all comers.

Warning: Green Riffle is the last take-out before Ishi Pishi Falls. Do not attempt to run Ishi Pishi, which has only been run once by a rafting crew without loss of life. Many people have perished here. In addition take special note of the sacred Native American ceremonial grounds along the banks of the Klamath eight miles past the put-in, where Clear Creek enters the river. For about a month in the summer, camping and stopping on the banks are banned.

Salmon River to Weitchpec (aka Ike's Run): 24 miles; Class III–IV. Highlights: The Ikes (Little Ike, Class III-; Big Ike, Class IV; and Super Ike, Class III+). Synopsis: The

Ikes are a fantastic series of big rollers, and the key for every rafter is to make sure you do not dump at the first one, which can have you swimming for your life as the current sweeps you through the other two sections. Once you pass the Ikes, the river rolls through one of its most beautiful sections—deep, emotive, and green, framed by granite walls.

The three featured runs offer stunning scenery, lots of wildlife, and solitude, despite the fact that Highway 96 runs alongside the river.

While the water is warm in the summer and fall, there are few clear, slow-moving deep pools for swimming. The nearby Salmon River is much better for swimming, as are Dillon and Elk Creeks.

There are several Forest Service campgrounds located along the Klamath River, and for those who are looking for a place to stay, a good spot is Young's Ranch Resort, which offers camping, lodging, and guided fishing and rafting trips.

If you prefer a do-it-yourself adventure and want to rent your own raft, Bigfoot Outdoor Company is the only game in town.

---

❺ Taylor Lake

Location: Southwest of Etna in the Russian Wilderness; map A1, grid j8.
Directions: Etna is located about a half-hour's drive west of Interstate 5 via Highway 3 from Yreka, or from the Gazelle turnoff just north of the town of Weed. From Etna head west on Sawyers's Bar Road, continue over Etna Summit, and then go just a mile down the other side. Make a left turn at the dirt road signed "Taylor Lake." A short, wheelchair-accessible path brings you to the lake.

Access: There is no boat ramp.
Facilities, fees: A primitive campground is provided, but there are no other facilities. There is a wheelchair-accessible path around the lake. Access is free.
Water sports, restrictions: There is no beach, but you can swim here.
Contact: Klamath National Forest, Headquarters, (530) 842-6131 or fax (530) 842-6327. For a detailed map of the area, send $4 to Map Sales, USDA-Forest Service, 1323 Club Drive, Vallejo, CA 94592.
About Taylor Lake: If you want the wilderness experience without having to endure a serious overnight hike, you've come to the right place.

Because Taylor Lake is located just inside a wilderness-area boundary, many people looking at a map mistakenly believe it is very difficult to reach. Not true. The walk in takes about 20 minutes.

Taylor Lake is at an elevation of 6,500 feet, covers 12 acres, and reaches a depth of 35 feet. None of the lakes in the Russian Wilderness are very sizable, but this is one of the biggest, shaped kind of like a kidney bean, with the outlet creek set along the access trail. It is a destination for hikers, campers, anglers, and swimmers.

For those people making their first overnight trek into a wild area, this lake provides what may be an ideal experience: a short hike to a remote area with good trout fishing.

Nothing is perfect, however, and that includes Taylor Lake. Because there is plenty of feed, horse traffic can be common, as packers prepare for trips on the nearby Pacific Crest Trail. In addition, even though this is wilderness, there are occasional bovine intrusions. Yep, cows, as hard as it may be to believe, are allowed to graze the immediate region.

Map of Northern California—Page 28

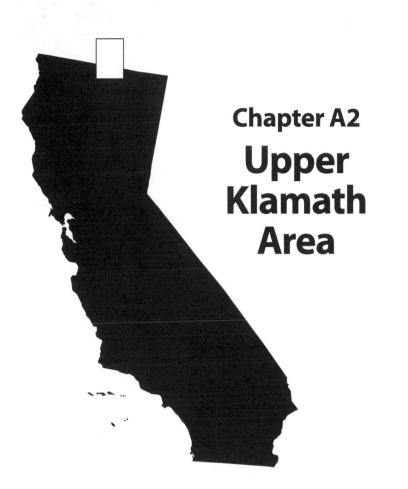

Chapter A2
Upper Klamath Area

Overall Rating

| 1 | 2 | 3 | 4 | 5 | 6 | 7 | 8 | 9 | 10 |

Poor .... Fair .... Great

A2–Upper Klamath Area Map

One inch equals approximately 10.7 miles.
See page 12 for California state map.

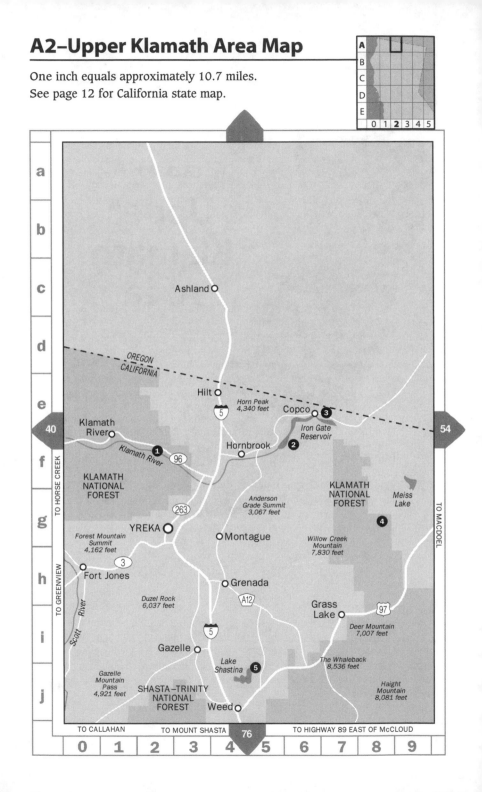

Chapter A2 features:

1 Klamath River

Location: From Ashland, Oregon, to the Klamath National Forest; map A2, grid f2.

Directions: From Redding drive 97 miles north on Interstate 5 to Yreka. Take the Yreka-Montague exit. Turn west toward Yreka and travel to the stop sign; then turn right on Highway 263. Drive six miles north (this is a narrow, twisty road) and then turn west on Highway 96 to access the river. To reach the Upper Klamath, see the directions to the rafting put-in below.

Access: A primitive boat ramp is available at the Tree of Heaven Campground, located on Highway 96 approximately five miles west of Interstate 5. Another boat launch is located just south of Iron Gate Reservoir. To reach it, drive north on Interstate 5 to the Henley-Hornbrook exit and then turn east on Copco Road and proceed about seven miles.

Drive north on Interstate 5 across the Oregon border to the town of Ashland. Take Exit 14 and turn east on Highway 66. Continue approximately 45 miles to John Boyle Reservoir. Just before you cross the reservoir, you will see a dirt road; turn right and drive about five miles to John Boyle Powerhouse. The signed put-in is just downstream of the powerhouse. Take out below Stateline Falls (just below the Oregon/California border) or farther downstream at Copco Lake.

Facilities, fees: Several private and Forest Service campgrounds are located along the river. Full services and facilities are available in Yreka. Boat rentals are not offered. Access is free. Rafting permits are not required.

Water sports, restrictions: There are several good swimming holes along Highway 96; look for the "River Access" signs. Swimming in the Upper Klamath is not recommended due to the algae-laden water and sharp volcanic rocks.

Contact: Klamath National Forest, Scott River Ranger Station, (530) 465-2241 or fax (530) 468-5654. For fishing information contact Quigley's General Store, (530) 465-2224. For guided rafting trips contact Access to Adventure, (800) KLAMATH/552-6284 or (530) 662-7296; American River Recreation, (800) 333-7238 or (530) 622-6802; Aurora River Adventures, (800) 562-8475 or (530) 629-3843; Turtle River Rafting, (800) 726-3223; or Whitewater Voyages, (800) 488-7238.

About the Klamath River: Rafting Hell's Corner is kind of like putting a saddle on the space shuttle and riding off into the stratosphere. This series of big water rapids is the highlight of the Upper Klamath and one of the most exciting runs in the western US. The put-in is in Oregon just below John Boyle Powerhouse (a good spot for trout fishing). From here the descent downstream is more like an assault, warming up with a series of Class III rapids for the first five miles.

Then things get exciting—and more difficult. The first big rapid is Caldera (Class IV+), a long siege of rollers. I dumped here my first time down and ended up swimming most of it. Here, though, "swimming" means being pulled under by the hydraulics of the river until the force of your life jacket pops you back up. You grab a quick breath, and a moment later the river pulls you right back down. Wild, wet, and crazy.

This is only the start. The worst stretch is Satan's Gate (Class IV), Hell's Corner (Class IV+), and Ambush (Class IV), one right after another. Boating here is an act of faith. Go only with an experienced guide in an oar boat, not a small paddleboat or inflatable kayak. The guy who taught me how to raft big water, guide Dean Munroe, lost an eye here when he tried to rescue a boatload of rafters who were pinned against a rock and the lead rope snapped, hurling a metal clasp into his face.

The challenges just keep coming. The final big rapids are Snag Islands Falls (Class III+) and Stateline Falls (Class III), providing two more chances to dump. But hey, a lot of people like dumping here. It feels like winning a merit badge, and survivors can say, "Yeah, I dumped at Ambush, but I made it anyway."

The run is 11 miles long, a hell of a day, though some rafting companies split the outing into two days over a weekend and make the 17-mile trip all the way to Copco Lake. This option requires a good deal of paddling in slow water at the head of the lake. Rafting season is April to October, and water released from John Boyle Dam keeps the run optimum even through warm, dry summers.

A few words of caution: Be aware of sharp volcanic rocks, and if you dump, keep your feet in front of you while you are floating downstream. In addition pack in your own drinking water. The Klamath is often warm and tinged with algae.

If you're looking for something easy, try the stretch of river from Iron Gate Dam past the Interstate 5 bridge to the Tree of Heaven Campground. This is Class I all the way, technically not even a run, but it is great for inner tubing and canoeing and for beginners in inflatable kayaks. While many commercial companies run Hell's Corner, none offers trips or rentals on this piece of river below Iron Gate Dam. But if you have your own craft and want a fun, stress-free day on the Klamath, this is the place.

❷ Iron Gate Reservoir

Location: North of Yreka near Klamath National Forest; map A2, grid f6.

Directions: From Redding drive north on Interstate 5 past Yreka to the Henley-Hornbrook exit. Turn east on Copco Road and drive eight miles to Iron Gate Reservoir.

Access: There are three boat ramps, all located on the west side of the reservoir off Copco Road.

Facilities, fees: Several primitive campsites, some with pit toilets, are located around the lake and are available on a first-come, first-served basis. Supplies can be obtained in Hornbrook. Access is free.

Water sports, restrictions: Waterskiing and windsurfing are permitted; however, there is a 10 mph speed limit in designated areas. Watch for signs. Swimming beaches are located around the reservoir.

Contact: Pacific Power, (530) 842-3521.

About Iron Gate Reservoir: This summertime vacation spot gets a fair amount of use, but most people overlook the place because of its remote location near the Oregon border.

Set at an elevation of 2,400 feet east of Interstate 5, the reservoir is nearly seven miles long and covers 825 surface acres. In early summer waterskiing and swimming are popular activities, but when the warm weather arrives, the water begins to develop an overabundance of algae. In fact, if you fall in while waterskiing, you will find yourself coated with green bits. Nobody appreciates this experience.

Iron Gate is more popular with those who enjoy catching bass and perch in good numbers.

❸ Copco Lake

Location: North of Yreka near Klamath National Forest; map A2, grid f6.

Directions: From Redding drive north on Interstate 5 past Yreka to the Henley-Hornbrook exit. To reach the north side of Copco Lake (via Iron Gate Reservoir), go east on Copco Road and drive 11 miles. (Midway between Iron Gate Reservoir and Copco Lake, the road becomes gravel, but it is not treacherous.) To reach the campground and boat ramp on the south side, drive six miles east to Montague and then 15 miles east on Ager Beswick Road. We advise the latter route.

Access: A paved boat ramp is located at Mallard Cove, which can be accessed on Ager Beswick Road.

Facilities, fees: A primitive campground is located at Mallard Cove. There are a store and some primitive toilets at the east end of the lake. Access is free.

Water sports, restrictions: Waterskiing and windsurfing are permitted; however, there is a 10 mph speed limit in designated areas. Watch for signs. You can swim at Mallard Cove.

Contact: Copco Lake Store, (530) 459-3655.

About Copco Lake: If you swim in Copco Lake in the summer, you'll emerge looking like you've got some kind of disease, or as if you have been exposed to radioactive material. You will practically glow with a fresh coating of green algae mire. Are we having fun yet?

No, we are not. But it can get very hot out here, and some people finally give in and take the plunge. Boat traffic is very light, and though waterskiing is permitted, nobody likes getting doused with all the "green stuff."

Copco Lake is set at an elevation of 2,613 feet, is five miles long, and covers 1,000 acres. In addition to the surplus algae, it offers something that no other lake can: fantastic opportunities in the summer to catch yellow perch. Imagine a scenario where families catch 40 or 50 (there's no limit) of the little buggers (seven to nine inches long) with little effort. I guess yel-

low perch don't mind all the algae.

Copco gets far less use than neighboring Iron Gate Reservoir, and in turn, the atmosphere is more remote. The boat ramp, by the way, is steep and somewhat primitive, and the adjacent parking area is small, but that's the price you pay for all the yellow perch you can catch.

❹ Juanita Lake

⚓ 🚤 🏕️ 🐟 ▶️   6

Location: Near Macdoel in Klamath National Forest; map A2, grid g8.

Directions: From Redding drive 65 miles north on Interstate 5 to Weed. Take the Weed–College of the Siskiyous exit. Drive north through town, take Highway 97 north, and drive approximately 40 miles to the town of Macdoel. Turn west on Meiss Lake–Sam's Neck Road and drive 8.5 miles to Butte Valley Road. Take Butte Valley Road south to the lake.

Access: A primitive boat ramp is located on the north end of the lake.

Facilities, fees: A campground is available. Supplies can be obtained in Macdoel. Access is free.

Water sports, restrictions: Motors are not permitted on the lake. The water is usually too cold for swimming and other contact sports.

Contact: Klamath National Forest, Goosenest Ranger District, (530) 398-4391 or fax (530) 398-4599.

About Juanita Lake: Juanita Lake is a perfect example of the kind of place that gets overlooked by so many Californians who hunger for exactly what it has to offer. It is small. It is out of the way, yet is accessible by car. It has lakeside camping and decent trout fishing. But you've probably never heard the name, right? Don't feel bad. Not many folks have, and the same goes for hundreds of similar lakes in the more remote areas of California.

Surrounded by high desert at an elevation of 5,100 feet in Klamath National Forest, Juanita is overlooked by Goosenest, a volcanic peak north of Mount Shasta.

The cold water, which is a little on the mucky side, and a rocky shore inhibit swimming, so Juanita Lake gets very light use. One of the highlights: the lake is ringed by a 1.5-mile paved, barrier-free hiking trail that is wheelchair accessible (the campground is also wheelchair accessible).

❺ Lake Shastina

Location: Near Weed and Klamath National Forest; map A2, grid j5.

Directions: From Redding drive 65 miles north on Interstate 5 to Weed. Take the Weed–College of the Siskiyous exit. Drive north through town and take the Highway 97 turnoff. Drive 2.5 miles northeast on Highway 97 and then turn west on Ordway Road. Travel one mile and turn north on Edgewood–Big Springs Road. Watch for the signed turnoff, travel northwest to Jackson Ranch Road, turn toward the lake, and continue to the public access area.

Access: A paved boat ramp is located off Jackson Ranch Road at the signed public fishing access.

Facilities, fees: There are a few primitive campsites. Supplies can be obtained in Weed. Access is free.

Water sports, restrictions: Waterskiing, windsurfing, and personal watercraft are permitted. There is a swimming beach near the public fishing area. No public facilities are provided. Boat rentals are not available.

Contact: For lodging and general information, call Lake Shastina Golf Course, (530) 938-3201.

About Lake Shastina: It seems as if it's always windy at Lake Shastina. The wind blows, blows, blows, and people just learn to put up with it.

Families have made this place a popular summer destination, one of the few lakes in the northern part of California where condo/house rentals are available. Shastina is located near Weed (named after a man, not a plant), set at 3,000 feet in elevation within close range of the north slopes of Mount Shasta. The country here is arid and desertlike, making Shastina sparkle and glow, especially when full in the spring and early summer.

In the spring, even though the water is cold, this is a good lake for windsurfing, but the sport has not caught on big time as it has in areas with warmer spring climates. Waterskiing and personal watercraft are more popular, especially when the warm weather sets in and the wind isn't blowing too much. For the most part, fishing for trout and crappie are the favored activities and lure the bulk of the visitors.

The surrounding land, including the Lake Shastina Golf Course, is privately owned. Condo rentals can be arranged by calling the golf course. Note that a once popular swimming area, complete with water slide, is now someone's personal playground and is closed to the public. Also be aware that although this is a good-size lake, by autumn it can be reduced to a large puddle due to irrigation demands by hay farmers located downstream. The water level can get so low that some locals dub the lake "River Shastina."

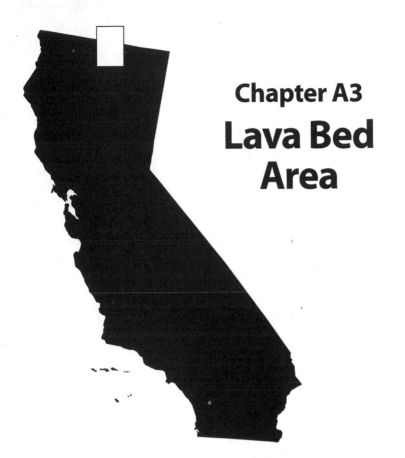

Chapter A3
Lava Bed
Area

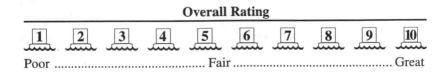

Overall Rating

| 1 | 2 | 3 | 4 | 5 | 6 | 7 | 8 | 9 | 10 |

Poor .... Fair .... Great

A3–Lava Bed Area Map

One inch equals approximately 10.7 miles.
See page 12 for California state map.

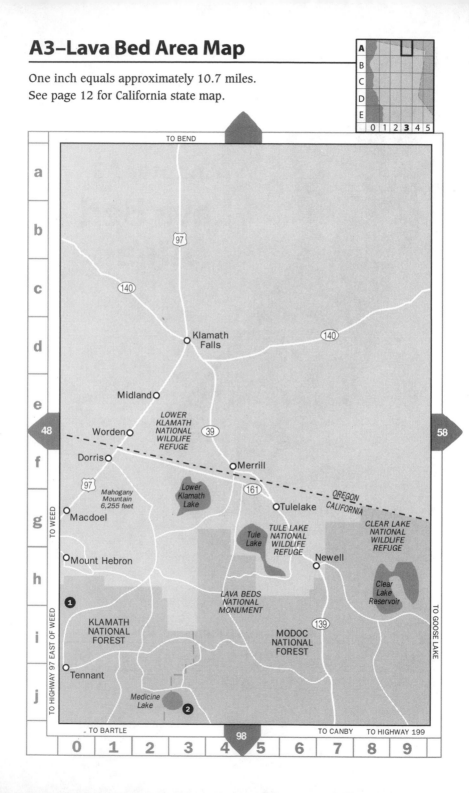

Chapter A3 features:

❶ Orr Lake

Location: Near Macdoel in Klamath National Forest; map A3, grid i0.

Directions: From Redding drive 65 miles north on Interstate 5 to Weed. Take the Weed–College of the Siskiyous exit. Drive north through town to the Highway 97 turnoff and then turn north and travel approximately 32 miles to the Bray–Tennant Road. Turn right on the Bray–Tennant Road and drive about six miles. After crossing the railroad tracks, turn left on the road to Bray. In Bray turn left on a dirt road (following along a creek) and drive about three miles to the lake.

Access: There is no boat ramp. Cartop boats may be hand launched.

Facilities, fees: Shafter Campground, run by the Forest Service, is located on the road that leads to the lake. Access to the lake is free.

Water sports, restrictions: The lake is too small for motorized boats and is usually too cold for swimming and other sports involving water contact.

Contact: Shasta Cascade Wonderland Association, (800) 474-2782 or (530) 365-7500 or fax (530) 365-1258.

About Orr Lake: Little Orr Lake is quite a place, both good and bad. Want the bad news first? Okay, here it is: The road in is in terrible shape, the larger fish can be very elusive, and in the hot summer months, visitors—especially those with kids—should be extremely careful about crossing paths with rattlesnakes. So drive a vehicle that can take the bumps, bring along your angling smarts, and keep your eyes on the ground. That accomplished, you're in for a treat.

The setting, in the high plateau country of northern Siskiyou County, affords a great view of Mount Shasta. Although the lake is quite small, unsuitable for boats with motors, it is ideal for floating around in a canoe, raft, or cartop boat and relaxing. No matter what you do, you will keep gazing northward to Shasta, a silver dollar in a field of pennies.

The land here is privately held, but the owners allow public access to the lake. Regardless, it gets light use. One reason is that the water tends to be cold and a bit murky, sometimes even mucky, making swimming and other contact water sports undesirable. Still, kids can have a good time splashing around, and they usually don't notice the difference.

❷ Medicine Lake

Location: Near McCloud in Modoc National Forest; map A3, grid j3.

Directions: From Redding drive 56 miles north on Interstate 5. Take the McCloud–Reno exit and travel 12 miles on Highway 89 to McCloud. Continue east for 17 miles to Bartle. Just beyond Bartle turn left at the signed and paved road (Forest Service Road 46) to Medicine Lake and drive for about 45 minutes. (When you reach the sign for the nearby ice caves, the lake is another 10 minutes away.)

Access: A paved boat ramp and a dock are available near the picnic area on the east side of the lake.

Facilities, fees: Four campgrounds are provided on the lake. Pit toilets are available. Supplies can be obtained in McCloud; Bartle Lodge has limited supplies. Access to the lake is free.

Water sports, restrictions: Waterskiing and personal watercraft are permitted. There are several sandy beaches for swimmers. The best ones are located near the campgrounds.

Contact: Modoc National Forest, Doublehead-Tulelake Ranger Districts, (530) 667-2246 or fax (530) 667-4808.

About Medicine Lake: A place of mystery, Medicine Lake has captivated many. The mystery is that the lake was originally a caldera, that is, the mouth of a volcano. It draws a natural comparison to Crater Lake in Oregon, although not as deep and not as blue. Nevertheless, the lake has a sense of history, unlike most lakes in California. It is beautiful here, with lakeside campsites and a paved road all the way in; the snow is cleared by June, sometimes earlier.

Undiscovered, however, Medicine Lake is not. The unique setting—at 6,700 feet in elevation in remote Modoc National Forest near the Lava Beds National Monument—attracts people from near and far.

The lake is oval, covers 640 acres, and reaches 150 feet at its deepest point. There is a good boat ramp, and all water sports are popular, including waterskiing, personal watercraft, windsurfing, and sailing. But most visitors come for the fishing and camping, and they usually leave surprised at the number of large brook trout they've caught. This area often gets buried in snow during the winter, and as a result, the water remains quite cold well into summer.

As this lake has become popular, rangers here have been very strict about enforcing rules. Their pet peeve is dogs. There is a leash law, and dogs are banned from the beach. You are hereby warned not to test them on how seriously they feel about this.

On a lighter note there are several exciting side-trip destinations in the area, including ice caves (created by glacial action), an abandoned Forest Service lookout on a mountaintop (great views), nearby Bullseye and Blanche Lakes (quite tiny but pretty), and Lava Beds National Monument (geologic phenomena). You can spend several days exploring the area, using Medicine Lake as your base camp.

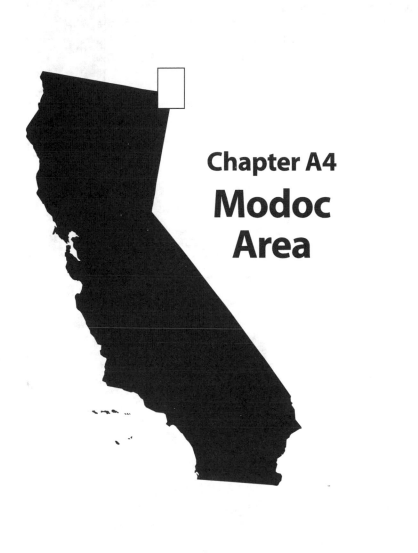

Chapter A4
Modoc
Area

Overall Rating

| 1 | 2 | 3 | 4 | 5 | 6 | 7 | 8 | 9 | 10 |

Poor .... Fair .... Great

A4–Modoc Area Map

One inch equals approximately 10.7 miles.
See page 12 for California state map.

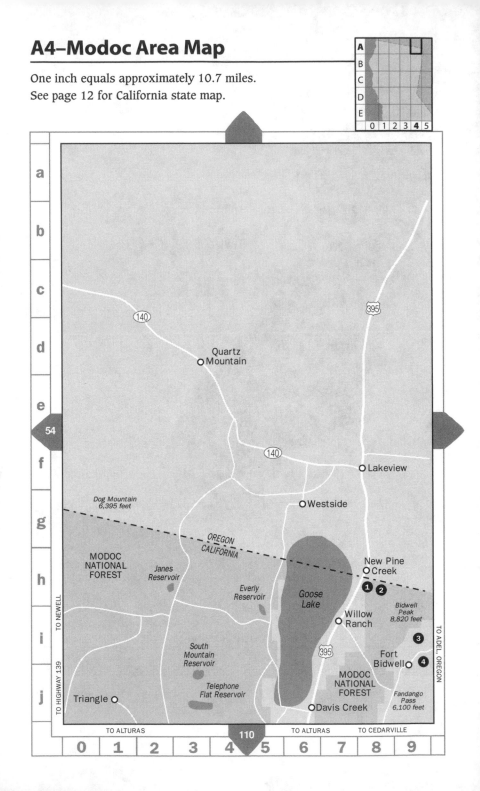

Chapter A4 features:

❶ Cave Lake

Location: In Modoc National Forest; map A4, grid h8.

Directions: From Redding drive 146 miles east on Highway 299 to Alturas. Turn north on US 395 and drive 40 miles to New Pine Creek (on the Oregon/California border). Drive six miles east on Highgrade Road/Forest Service Road 2. Trailers are not recommended.

Access: There is a primitive boat ramp suitable for small boats.

Facilities, access fees: A campground is provided, along with pit toilets. Supplies can be obtained in New Pine Creek and Fort Bidwell. Access is free.

Water sports, restrictions: Motors are not permitted on the lake. Swimming is allowed.

Contact: Modoc National Forest, Warner Mountain Ranger District, (530) 279-6116 or fax (530) 279-6107.

About Cave Lake: Two lakes are located here at the same destination, Cave Lake and Lily Lake. Together they make a nice set. Both are very quiet, get light user traffic, and offer decent fishing for trout in the foot-long class. Cave has very little surrounding vegetation, which makes Lily Lake the more attractive of the pair.

Tiny Cave Lake is set at 6,600 feet in elevation in remote Modoc County, far enough away from most people that it attracts little attention. It's the rare day when someone goes to the trouble of hauling a cartop boat, such as a canoe or johnboat, this far just to go trout fishing, even though you can camp overnight here. When people do venture this way, they usually go to neighboring Lily Lake, which is far prettier.

❷ Lily Lake

Location: In Modoc National Forest; map A4, grid h8.

Directions: From Redding drive 146 miles east on Highway 299 to Alturas. Turn north on US 395 and drive 40 miles to New Pine Creek (on the Oregon/California border). Drive 5.5 miles east on Highgrade Road/Forest Service Road 2. Trailers are not recommended.

Access: There is no boat ramp. Cartop boats may be hand launched.

Facilities, access fees: A campground and pit toilets are available at nearby Cave Lake. Supplies can be obtained in New Pine Creek and Fort Bidwell. Access is free.

Water sports, restrictions: Motors are not permitted on the lake. Swimming is allowed.

Contact: Modoc National Forest, Warner Mountain Ranger District, (530) 279-6116 or fax (530) 279-6107.

About Lily Lake: Little Lily is way out there in no-man's-land, but it is well worth the trip. People drive to this remote but premium destination for a day or two of camping (at neighboring Cave Lake), fishing, and solitude. Because there are some conifers sprinkled around the lake, Lily Lake is a lot prettier than Cave. Its remoteness makes it a treasured destination for the few people who venture here.

There is no boat ramp, but light cartop boats can be launched. Some people bring inner tubes so they can float around and fish. This is a remote, pretty spot that is ideal for a cool dip on a hot day. Due to the location, it gets light use even in peak summer months.

❸ Lake Annie

Location: Near Fort Bidwell; map A4, grid i9.

Directions: From Redding drive 146 miles east on Highway 299 to Alturas. Continue east on Highway 299 to Cedarville, then turn north on Surprise Valley Road, and head toward the town of Fort Bidwell. In Fort Bidwell turn north on Lake Annie Road and drive 2.5 miles.

Access: There is no boat ramp. Cartop boats may be hand launched.

Facilities, access fees: Lake Annie has no facilities. Supplies can be obtained in Fort Bidwell. Access is free.

Water sports, restrictions: Swimming is permitted, but there are no beaches.

Contact: Bureau of Land Management, Surprise Field Office, (530) 279-6101.

About Lake Annie: Lake Annie is the backyard fishing hole for the folks who live in Fort Bidwell, a unique community that time seems to have passed by. The small town is an anachronism and a beautiful little spot, with a grocery store, gas station, and hey, just west of town, a natural hot spring.

To the east of the lake is Annie Mountain, from which it gets its name. Bordering Lake Annie to the west are the Warner Mountains, a lonely, quiet place. The surrounding country is fairly sparse, and one thing is for sure: nobody arrives here by accident.

Lake Annie covers 30 acres and is situated at 4,700 feet in elevation, with a rocky shoreline surrounded by sagebrush and grassy hills. That's right: there are no trees. It's also right that the lake is too small for anything but cartop boats. The water can be on the cloudy side, but it is passable for swimming. Most of the few people who do visit this lake come primarily to fish for trout.

❹ Fee Reservoir

Location: Near Fort Bidwell; map A4, grid j9.

Directions: From Redding drive 146 miles east on Highway 299 to Alturas. At Alturas head north on US 395 to Fort Bidwell. From Fort Bidwell drive 7.5 miles east on Fee Reservoir Road, a good gravel road.

Access: There is a primitive, dirt launching area.

Facilities, access fees: A small campground is provided. Primitive toilets and well water are available. Supplies can be obtained in Fort Bidwell. Access is free.

Water sports, restrictions: Waterskiing, personal watercraft, and swimming are permitted.

Contact: Bureau of Land Management, Surprise Field Office, (530) 279-6101.

About Fee Reservoir: What's the price of a stunning high desert sunset? There's no fee at Fee Reservoir—just the time it takes to get here.

The setting is typical of Modoc County's high desert country. You get a chance to see that special orange glow at dawn and dusk, and in early summer the variety of wildflowers makes a normally stark landscape come alive with a multiplicity of colors.

It is set at 5,329 feet in elevation on the Modoc Plateau. When full, Fee Reservoir covers 337 acres, but because the water is used for irrigation, it is subject to major summer drawdowns and erratic level fluctuations based on water demand.

For this reason not many people come here for waterskiing, personal watercraft, or windsurfing, although these sports are permitted. In the future the Bureau of Land Management hopes to build a paved launch ramp. For now, boaters hoping to catch some trout just launch from the dirt road that heads down to the shore.

The water is often cloudy, and it's rare to see people on the lake.

Chapter B0
Humboldt Coast

Overall Rating

1	2	3	4	5	6	7	8	9	10

Poor .... Fair .... Great

B0–Humboldt Coast Map

One inch equals approximately 10.7 miles.
See page 12 for California state map.

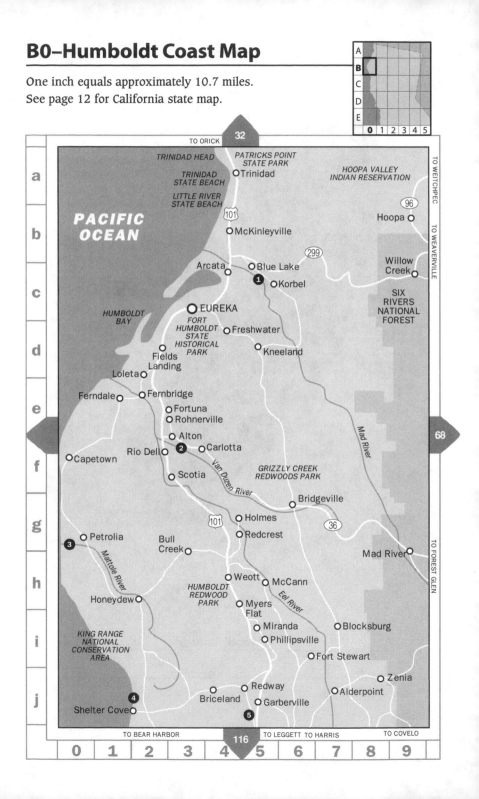

Chapter BØ features:

1 Mad River

Location: Near Arcata; map BØ, grid c5.

Directions: From Eureka drive about 12 miles north on US 101 to Highway 299. Turn east on Highway 299 and drive approximately six miles to the town of Blue Lake. From Blue Lake Boulevard turn right on Greenwood Road. At the four-way stop, bear right; Greenwood Road turns into Hatchery Road. Take Hatchery Road to the Mad River Fish Hatchery. Most fishing is done between the hatchery and the nearby bridge. To access swimming holes, hike up or downstream of the hatchery.

Access: There is no boat ramp.

Facilities, fees: A picnic area and public rest rooms are provided at the hatchery. RV camping is available at Mad River Rapid RV Park in Arcata. Access is free.

Water sports, restrictions: Several good swimming holes are located up and downstream of the hatchery.

Contact: Mad River Fish Hatchery, (707) 822-0592.

Special note: The Mad River is subject to emergency fishing closures if flows are below the prescribed levels needed to protect migrating salmon and steelhead. For a recorded message detailing the status of coastal streams, call the Department of Fish and Game at (707) 442-4502.

About the Mad River: This short coastal stream is viewed each year by thousands upon thousands who cross it on the bridge near McKinleyville. They give it a brief look, usually note the color and the flow, and then soon forget about it. Except for in the winter when anglers come in search of steelhead, the Mad River does not attract large numbers of recreational users. In ad-

dition, the water often runs brown in the winter and a shade of milky green the rest of the year.

Regardless, some locals have discovered a few good swimming holes upstream near the fish hatchery. To access them, you must park at the hatchery and walk up or downstream. The water isn't too cold during the summer, but that's not the reason swimmers stay away from here; it's the fact that there are so many cold, foggy days. If you don't want to get your feet wet, you might just come for a picnic, another popular pastime near the hatchery.

2 Van Duzen River

Location: Near Eureka; map BØ, grid f3.

Directions: From Eureka drive 16 miles south on US 101. At the junction of US 101 and Highway 36, drive east on Highway 36. River access points are located along the highway.

Access: There is no boat ramp. A put-in is located at Pepperwood Falls, four miles east of Grizzly Creek Redwoods State Park on Highway 36. Boaters can take out at Grizzly Creek Redwoods State Park; if you choose to continue, be aware of the difficult, unnamed Class IV–V run located just a few miles downstream. Be sure to scout the river from the road before proceeding.

Facilities, fees: You can camp at Grizzly Creek Redwoods State Park. Supplies can be obtained in Bridgeville or Carlotta. There is a day-use fee at Grizzly Creek Park.

Water sports, restrictions: A good swimming hole is located at Grizzly Creek Redwoods State Park.

Contact: Electric Rafting Company, (707) 826-2861; Grizzly Creek Redwoods State

Park, (707) 777-3683 or fax (707) 777-3683; Bucksport Sporting Goods, (707) 442-1832 or fax (707) 442-1837.

Special note: The Van Duzen River is subject to emergency fishing closures if flows are below the prescribed levels needed to protect migrating salmon and steelhead. For a recorded message detailing the status of coastal streams, call the Department of Fish and Game at (707) 442-4502.

About the Van Duzen River: The Van Duzen is known almost exclusively by two groups of people: the local expert kayakers who thrive on the short, difficult, and beautiful run available here, and the few anglers who come to fish for steelhead in the winter.

The most compelling feature is the four-mile run from Pepperwood Falls on down to Grizzly Creek Redwoods State Park, a decent stretch for kayaks and canoes. Although it is beautiful, bordered in part by lush forest, few rafters travel on this run. Unfortunately, the flow levels on the Van Duzen go up and down like crazy, ranging from extremely low in the summer, making it unrunnable by mid-May, to extremely high in the winter, when it's more like a flood. So you need to hit it when the flows are just right. That is why you typically see only locals on the water, since they have the luxury of being able to schedule their trips practically at a moment's notice. Because of the hit-and-miss nature of the river, commercial rafting trips are not offered.

The more ambitious rafters had better have their act together if they decide to continue beyond Grizzly Creek Redwoods State Park. There is a difficult stretch here that practically comes with a guarantee that river-runners will dump during late winter and early spring, which is when the river is most popular, though Grizzly Creek Redwoods State Park attracts many visitors in the summer months.

❸ Mattole River

Location: Near Eureka; map BØ, grid g0.

Directions: From Eureka take US 101 to the South Fork Road turnoff (just north of Weott), head west on the somewhat winding road (it turns to gravel) to Honeydew, and continue west on Mattole Road to Petrolia. The road parallels the river. The best public fishing access is located closest to the mouth of the river; fishing is permitted from the mouth of the river to the county road bridge at Petrolia. For rafting and swimming see directions below.

Access: There is no boat ramp. Canoeists and kayakers can put in at the Honeydew Store, located approximately 20 miles east of Petrolia on Mattole Road, and take out at the Fire Station, or farther downstream at AW Way County Park.

Facilities, fees: A campground is provided at AW Way County Park south of Petrolia. Supplies can be obtained in Petrolia and at the Honeydew Store. A day-use fee is charged at the county park (annual passes are also available).

Water sports, restrictions: There are two popular swimming holes on the Mattole. One area, called the Fire Station, is located just west of Honeydew on Mattole Road, off a dirt road across the street from the fire station. The other is located at AW Way County Park, 7.5 miles east of Petrolia on Mattole Road.

Contact: Honeydew Store, (707) 629-3310; AW Way County Park, (707) 629-3314. Special note: The Mattole River is subject to emergency fishing closures if flows are below the prescribed levels needed to protect migrating salmon and steelhead. For a recorded message detailing the status of coastal streams, call the Department of Fish and Game at (707) 442-4502.

About the Mattole River: The Honeydew Valley is one of Northern California's little paradises that most people know nothing about. It is set on the Lost Coast, bordered by mountains and oceans. Ah, but then there is the Mattole River, which cuts a charmed path down the center of the valley, a pretty, winding ribbon that is capable of handling a tremendous volume of water in the monsoonlike winter months.

Most people come either to explore the surrounding area in the summer or to go steelhead fishing during the late winter when the bite is on. But another option is to take a trip down a fairly benign stretch of water in a raft, canoe, or kayak. You put in at the Honeydew Store (say hi to my field scout Bob Fuel) and then float and paddle your way for 13 miles to AW Way County Park. Note that in the drier months, particularly late summer and fall, the river can be too low to run. It is usually runnable through June, sometimes well into July.

Visitors who make the trip here in the summer are treated to a demure stream and a county park that offers excellent picnicking, camping, and good swimming. Little do they know what a beast this river can be in the winter, when it can rain as much as anywhere in the Lower 48, sometimes getting pounded with up to an inch an hour. That is when the nice, sweet Mattole is transformed into a powerful torrent that inspires both trepidation and respect, and leaves an image in your mind that you will never forget.

❹ Shelter Cove

Location: South of Eureka; map BØ, grid j2.

Directions: From Eureka drive approximately 62 miles south on US 101 to the town of Garberville. Take the Shelter Cove–Redwood Road exit and drive 2.5 miles west on Redwood Road to Briceland–Shel-ter Cove Road. Turn west and drive 24 miles, following the truck/RV route signs. Turn south on Upper Pacific Drive and travel one-half mile.

Access: A multilane boat launch is located near the campground.

Facilities, fees: A campground is provided. Rest rooms, picnic areas, gas, tackle shop, restaurants, deli, and a grocery store are also available. Access is free.

Water sports, restrictions: The harbor has a designated swimming area. Windsurfing, waterskiing, and personal watercraft are permitted.

Contact: Shelter Cove Campground, (707) 986-7474.

About Shelter Cove: There's no mystery about why people come to Shelter Cove. It's pretty. It's remote. It's inexpensive. There's a great six-lane boat ramp. And in the summer months, the salmon are usually only a short boat ride away.

But hey, Shelter Cove is definitely off the beaten path, and the remote location discourages most people from making the trip.

The harbor is very attractive and is suitable for windsurfing and personal watercraft, but you must always wear a wet suit on the water. After all, the cove is quite chilly.

What really lures visitors is the salmon. The fish often school nearby, and because so few people attempt the long drive, boaters can't help but feel that somehow they have discovered a secret fishing spot. Well, even though it isn't exactly a secret, it certainly is special.

❺ Benbow Lake

Location: Near Garberville in Benbow Lake State Recreation Area; map BØ, grid j5.

Directions: From Eureka drive approximately 62 miles south on US 101 to the town of Garberville. Continue south for two miles and take the Benbow exit. The lake is located just inside Benbow Lake State Recreation Area.

Access: A gravel boat launch is located near the day-use area; it is available only in the summer.

Facilities, fees: A state campground is provided, and a private RV park and golf course are located across the highway. Supplies can be obtained in Garberville. Fees are charged for day use and camping. There is an additional fee to use the boat ramp. Paddleboats and other small craft can be rented at the concessionaire.

Water sports, restrictions: Motors are not permitted on the lake. A swimming beach is available near the picnic area.

Contact: Benbow Lake State Park, (707) 923-3238; Benbow Lake Campground, (707) 923-3238. For fishing information or tackle, contact Brown's Sporting Goods in Garberville, (707) 923-2533.

About Benbow Lake: "Benbow Lake? Where's Benbow Lake? I can't find it anywhere on the map!" That's a typical complaint of visitors to this area. You can look all you want and never find it on most maps. You see, Benbow Lake is a seasonal lake; that is, it is actually part of the Eel River. Sometime around Memorial Day weekend, a temporary dam is placed across the river in Benbow, at elevation 364 feet, creating this little lake. It makes a popular spot for sunbathing and nonmotorized boating.

The lake is long and narrow, of course, covering 230 acres. Only boats without motors are allowed on the lake. This is an ideal setting for canoeing, floating around on rafts, inner tubes and air cushions, and swimming. Temperatures are quite warm in the summer, and there is a beach that is perfect for people who want to take advantage of it by doing absolutely nothing. Picnickers will be happy to find a picnic area nearby.

There is rarely enough wind for windsurfing or sailing, but that's fine with the folks floating around in a lovely summer daze.

Chapter B1
Trinity
Area

Overall Rating

| 1 | 2 | 3 | 4 | 5 | 6 | 7 | 8 | 9 | 10 |

Poor .... Fair .... Great

B1–Trinity Area Map

One inch equals approximately 10.7 miles.
See page 12 for California state map.

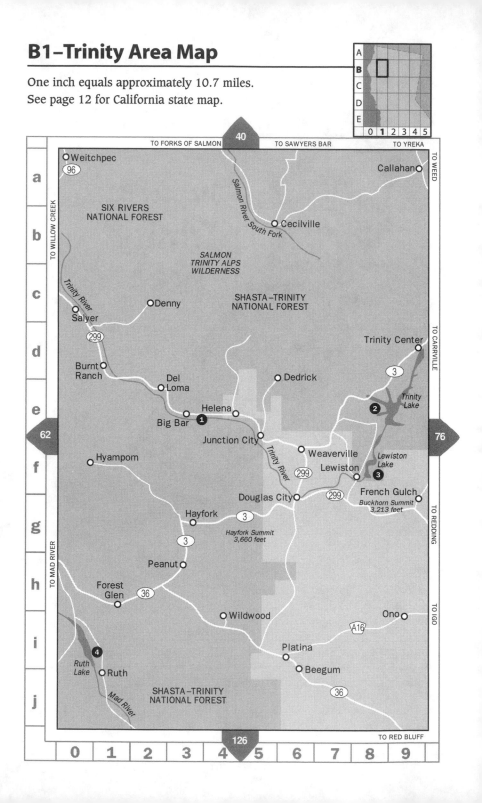

Chapter B1 features:

1 Trinity River

Location: In Shasta-Trinity National Forest; map B1, grid c0.

Directions: From Redding to the upper Trinity below Lewiston Dam, take Highway 299 west about 30 miles to the Lewiston turnoff. Drive four miles north on Trinity Dam Boulevard, turn left on Turnpike Road, and continue into the historic district of Lewiston. When you reach the bridge that crosses the river, turn left on Rush Creek Road. Direct access is available.

To reach the lower portion of the Trinity, drive west on Highway 299 from Redding to the town of Douglas City. Turn left (west) and follow Steiner Flat Road. Direct access is available off the road. Access is also available at several well-signed gravel roads and trails off Highway 299 west of Junction City.

Access: A primitive boat ramp (small, flat-bottomed boats and rafts only) is available at Trinity River Lodge RV Resort, located south of Lewiston off Trinity Dam Boulevard. Rafters can put in at the bridge in the town of Lewiston and take out at one of several points north of Douglas City.

There are no boat ramps on the lower stretch of the river. Rafters can put in at Pigeon Point Campground, 15 miles west of Weaverville on Highway 299. Take out five miles down at Big Flat Campground; those who want a longer run can take out 24 miles downstream at the highway bridge at Cedar Flat. Note: Unless you're an expert, take out at Cedar Flat or upstream. Downstream of Cedar Flat lies Burnt Ranch Gorge, a difficult eight-mile Class IV–V run.

Facilities, fees: Several campgrounds are located along Highway 299 and off Trinity Dam Boulevard. Limited boat rentals are available at Lewiston Lake; you can rent rafts and inflatable kayaks at Bigfoot Outdoor Company, located in Willow Creek and also at Big Flat on Highway 299. Supplies can be obtained in Lewiston. Access is free. Rafting permits are not required.

Water sports, restrictions: Both stretches of the river offer excellent swimming holes; two of the best are at Pigeon Point Campground on Highway 299 and at the bridge in the town of Helena.

Contact: Shasta–Trinity National Forest, Trinity River Management Unit, (530) 623-6106 or fax (530) 623-6123; Trinity River Lodge RV Resort in Lewiston, (530) 778-3791. For guided rafting trips contact Beyond Limits Adventures, (800) 234-7238; Bigfoot Rafting Company, (530) 629-2263; California Canoe & Kayak, (800) 366-9804; or Whitewater Voyages, (800) 488-7238.

About the Trinity River: The Trinity River runs clear and blue green, tumbling around boulders and into deep holes, all the while framed by a high, tree-lined canyon.

Located in Northern California west of Redding, the Trinity starts as a trickle in the Trinity Alps and then flows westward for 100 miles, eventually joining with the Klamath River in its journey to the sea. It is a fountain of beauty, rolling pure through granite gorges and abounding with birds and wildlife. Because flows are controlled by upstream dam releases, white-water rafting levels are guaranteed throughout summer.

This is a rafter's river and is especially suited to beginners for several reasons: Trips here are the lowest priced anywhere in California; the setting for rafters is a classic pool-and-drop, with most rapids in the Class II range; and the summer weather is often perfect. Renting an inflatable kayak for a day on the Trinity River runs as low as

$25 (at Big Flat), including all gear and a shuttle ride; guided oar-boat trips are also available at a higher price. A bonus at Big Flat are the Steelhead Cabins, which can be rented for a fairly low price.

The best trip for newcomers is near Big Flat, where the river has long, deep pools interspersed with sudden riffles and drops. Class II and III rapids such as Hell Hole, the Slot, Zig-Zag, Fishtail, Pinball, and others arrive every five minutes or so, providing bursts of pure thrill and then short rests that allow you to regain your composure. The commercial rafting company at Big Flat provides gear rentals and a shuttle service, and a survey we made revealed this was the lowest-cost rafting trip in California. The Trinity has two additional runs:

Lewiston Bridge to Douglas City: This is an easy paddle with Class I and II rapids, nothing difficult. The best put-in spots are at Lewiston Bridge and Trinity River Lodge RV Resort. Inner tubers looking for a great trip should plop in at Lewiston Bridge, float a few miles downstream, and take out at Trinity Lodge Resort. The entire 37 miles of river here is easy and manageable for longer trips. The surrounding vegetation is pretty, but the heavy traffic on adjacent Highway 299 is a common reminder that civilization is close at hand.

Pigeon Point to Cedar Flat: Pigeon Point, along with a Forest Service campground, is located just downstream of where the North Fork Trinity enters the main stem Trinity. This is the most popular put-in spot on the river, although there are a few other campgrounds upstream that also offer river access. The best bet here is to make the 12-mile run, taking out above Burnt Ranch Gorge, a mostly pristine river section that features deep pools and beautiful giant boulders. Burnt Ranch Gorge is rated Class V, clearly for experts in oar boats who like living on the edge and don't mind a little danger.

As for guided trips, only Beyond Limits

and Whitewater Voyages run Burnt Ranch Gorge. Meanwhile, Bigfoot and California Canoe & Kayak run other stretches of the river. Bigfoot offers a special evening dinner cruise on the lower Trinity, starting at Tish-Tang Gorge; it features a gourmet dinner, champagne, and tables set with candles, linen, and crystal. Just a few of these trips are offered each year, and reservations are required.

One of Northern California's greatest swimming areas is here at Tish-Tang Campground, located just upstream from the Hoopa Valley. In mid to late summer, it is the perfect place to laze around in an inner tube or to simply put on a life jacket and slowly float down the river in the warm, benign water.

❷ Trinity Lake

Location: Near Weaverville in Shasta–Trinity National Forest; map B1, grid e8.

Directions: From Interstate 5 at Redding, take the Highway 299 exit and drive 52 miles west to the town of Weaverville. Turn north on Highway 3/Weaverville–Scott Mountain Road and continue for 14 miles to the lake. The road will take you directly to a boat ramp. Boat ramps are also located farther north off Highway 3 and off Trinity Dam Boulevard.

Access: Eight boat ramps are located on Trinity Lake:

Bowerman: From Highway 299 at Weaverville, turn north on Highway 3 and drive approximately 20 miles to the sign for Alpine View Campground. A two-lane paved ramp is at the end of the road.

Cedar Stock Resort: From Highway 299 at Weaverville, turn north on Highway 3 and drive approximately 14 miles to the resort on the right, which has a paved ramp. A full-service marina is provided. Houseboat, fishing boat, canoe, paddleboat, powerboat, and personal watercraft rentals are offered. For information phone (530) 286-2225.

Clark Springs: From Highway 299 at Weaverville, turn north on Highway 3 and drive approximately 18 miles to the sign for the Clark Springs day-use area. The unpaved boat ramp is adjacent to the beach.

Estrellita Marina: From Highway 299 at Weaverville, turn north on Highway 3 and drive approximately 18 miles to the sign for Estrellita. Turn right and follow a dirt road for two miles to the two-lane, paved boat ramp. A full-service marina is available, along with houseboat, personal watercraft, fishing boat, and ski boat rentals.

Fairview: From Highway 299, take the Lewiston exit and turn north on Trinity Dam Boulevard. Continue straight to the two-lane, paved ramp, located northwest of the dam near Trinity Alps Marina.

Tannery Campground: From Highway 299 at Weaverville, turn north on Highway 3 and drive about nine miles. Look for the sign for Tannery Campground and turn right. A paved ramp is available for guests of the campground only.

Trinity Center Marina: From Highway 299 at Weaverville, turn north on Highway 3 and drive approximately 30 miles to the resort and the unpaved boat ramp on the right. A full-service marina is available. Houseboats and fishing boats can be rented through Cedar Stock Resort. For general information phone (530) 266-3432; to reserve a boat, phone Cedar Stock Resort at (800) 982-2279.

Facilities, fees: Several campgrounds are provided around the lake. Two good ones are Pinewood Cove Campground and Tannery Gulch. Free primitive boat-in campgrounds are also available. Full-service marinas can be found at several of the resorts listed above. Wyntoon Resort, (530) 266-3337, does not offer a launch ramp or gas but has a marina and rents fishing boats, ski boats, and patio boats. Lodging and groceries can be obtained in Trinity Center and at several of the resorts along Highway 3. Day-use access is free. There is generally no charge for boat launching, but some resorts require that you use only their boats.

Water sports, restrictions: A 5 mph speed limit is enforced near the marinas and at several of the coves where fishing is popular. Personal watercraft and water-skiing are permitted. Swimming, windsurfing, and sailing are also possible. There are several swimming spots here; the Clark Springs and Stoney Creek day-use areas have large beaches.

Contact: Shasta-Trinity National Forest, National Recreation Area Management Unit, (530) 623-2121 or fax (530) 623-6010; Trinity Chamber of Commerce, (530) 623-6101.

About Trinity Lake: If only Trinity Lake were a real lake and not a reservoir, it would be a virtual mountain paradise for fishing, boating, and camping. But it is a reservoir, and as such is subject to severe drawdowns because water is diverted and sent to the Sacramento River for farming. That means less water is around for Trinity Lake, particularly by late summer.

Trinity is a big lake with full-service marinas. You can rent a houseboat, stay in a cabin at Cedar Stock Resort, or head out and pitch a tent at a boat-in camp (there are several good camps, including one at Captain's Point on the west shore of the Trinity River Arm). There is a variety of fish for the catching, including smallmouth bass and rainbow trout. Even when the water level is down, there is still plenty of lake to explore and fish.

Nestled at the eastern foot of the Trinity Alps, the lake is set at an elevation of 2,300 feet and covers 17,000 acres. This is huge enough to provide plenty of room for all types of water sports, including waterskiing, personal watercraft, windsurfing, and fishing; yet it's sufficiently remote that large numbers of boaters rarely descend on the place. Most of the people who visit the area end up spending some time in Trinity Center, a big-time family resort destination.

The lake's surface temperature fluctuates greatly throughout the year, dipping to freezing cold in winter and only becoming tolerable for swimming by July. By August, however, the lake is practically a giant bathtub, great for swimming, with the best access at the day-use areas and campgrounds operated by the Forest Service.

---

❸ Lewiston Lake

Location: Near Lewiston in Shasta–Trinity National Forest; map B1, grid f9.

Directions: From Interstate 5 at Redding, take the Highway 299 exit and drive approximately 30 miles west. Turn north at the Lewiston exit and drive north on Trinity Dam Boulevard to access the lake.

Access: A paved ramp is located at Pine Cove Marina, 10.5 miles north of the Lewiston turnoff on Trinity Dam Boulevard. A primitive launch is provided at Lakeview Terrace Resort for resort guests only.

Facilities, fees: Several campgrounds are provided. The best is Mary Smith Camp. Fishing boats and houseboats can be rented at Lakeview Terrace. Pine Cove Marina offers full marina services and rents out fishing boats. Supplies can be obtained in Lewiston. Access is free.

Water sports, restrictions: A 10 mph speed limit is strictly enforced. Waterskiing and personal watercraft are not permitted. The water is generally too cold (40 to 50 degrees) for swimming and other water/body contact sports.

Contact: Shasta–Trinity National Forest, National Recreation Area Management Unit, (530) 623-2121 or fax (530) 623-6010; Trinity Chamber of Commerce, (530) 623-6101; Lakeview Terrace Resort, HC 01, Box 250, Lewiston, CA 96052; (530) 778-3803.

About Lewiston Lake: This is one of the prettiest reservoirs in California, always full to the brim and ringed by conifers, with the Trinity Alps to the northwest providing a beautiful backdrop. Features include a campground in a gorgeous lakeside setting (Mary Smith); a small, friendly resort with cabin rentals (Lakeview Terrace); and good trout fishing.

Long and narrow, Lewiston is set at 1,900 feet in elevation, spanning a length of nine miles and 750 acres, with 15 miles of shoreline. People often overlook this lake in favor of its big brother, nearby Trinity Lake, which covers 17,000 acres. When viewed from the air, it is easy to see how Lewiston Lake is actually the afterbay for Trinity, with the flows from Trinity Dam forming the headwaters of Lewiston. When those flows are running through the powerhouse, the trout fishing is outstanding anywhere from Lakeview Terrace on upstream, but it is usually best just below Trinity Dam.

For owners of small boats, the best thing about Lewiston Lake is the strictly enforced speed limit, 10 miles per hour, which keeps the lake quiet and calm. These are ideal conditions for canoes and small aluminum boats because all the powerboaters go to Trinity Lake. Also, the water here is quite cold, great for trout fishing but poor for swimming.

So despite Lewiston's beauty, it gets relatively light use. Water-skiers, personal watercraft, and powerboaters avoid the place, but it is treasured by people looking for a quiet day on a pretty lake.

---

❹ Ruth Lake

Location: Near Mad River in Six Rivers National Forest; map B1, grid i0.

Directions: From Eureka drive south on US 101 to Fortuna, turn east on Highway 36, and continue on the long, winding two-laner to the town of Mad River. Turn on Lower Mad River Road and drive southeast to the lake.

Boat ramp: There are three boat ramps:

Old Ruth Day-Use Area: From the turnoff at Highway 36, drive 15 miles south on Lower Mad River Road to the day-use area, which has a paved ramp.

Ruth Lake Marina: From the turnoff at Highway 36, drive nine miles south on Lower Mad River Road until you reach the marina and the two-lane paved ramp.

Ruth Recreation Area: From the turnoff at Highway 36, drive 14 miles south on Lower Mad River Road to the two-lane paved boat ramp at the recreation area.

Facilities, fees: Several campgrounds are located off Lower Mad River Road. Littlefield Ranch has cabins for rent. Ruth Lake Marina has full marina services and rents out fishing boats, ski boats, and pontoon boats. Picnic areas and a disposal station are also provided. Supplies can be obtained in Mad River. Access is free.

Water sports, restrictions: Waterskiing and personal watercraft are permitted. Swimming beaches are available at Sheriff's Cove Day-Use Area, Ruth Recreation Area, Old Ruth Day-Use Area, and at a small gravel bar adjacent to Ruth Lake Marina. Windsurfing and sailing are also popular.

Contact: Six Rivers National Forest, Mad River Ranger District, (707) 574-6233 or fax (707) 574-6273; Ruth Lake Marina, (707) 574-6524; Littlefield Ranch, (707) 574-6689 or (760) 732-3026 in winter.

About Ruth Lake: California's northwest corner is known for its great rivers—the Smith, Klamath, Trinity, Mad, Mattole, Eel, and Van Duzen to name just a few—but the entire region has scarcely any lakes. Ruth Lake, in fact, is the only major lake that offers significant recreational opportunities within a decent driving distance of Eureka. Even then it requires a long drive on twisty Highway 36. But in the summer, when the Humboldt coastline is fogged in, the hot climate here makes Ruth an attractive destination. The lake, really a reservoir that covers 1,200 acres, is located at an elevation of 2,600 feet on the western edge of Trinity County, remote by almost anyone's standards.

In the summer the warm water makes this an ideal place for families to spend some time swimming. Most water sports are permitted on the lake, including waterskiing and personal watercraft, but houseboats are not allowed (pontoon boats are okay). Fishing is fair for rainbow trout in the spring and for bass in the summer.

Horseback riding outfitters are available nearby at Flying AA Ranch in Ruth. Littlefield Ranch has cabins that you can rent.

Map of Northern California—Page 28

Chapter B2
Shasta Area

Overall Rating

| 1 | 2 | 3 | 4 | 5 | 6 | 7 | 8 | 9 | 10 |

Poor .... Fair .... Great

B2–Shasta Area Map

One inch equals approximately 10.7 miles.
See page 12 for California state map.

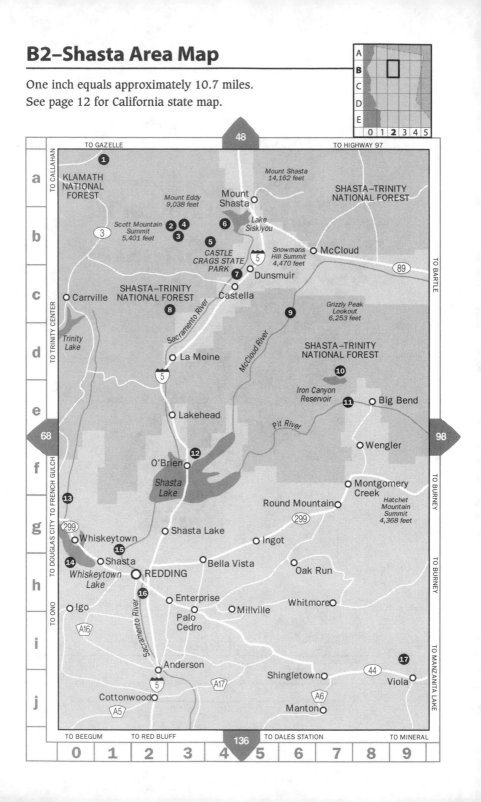

Chapter B2 features:

❶ Kangaroo Lake

Location: Near Callahan in Klamath National Forest; map B2, grid a1.

Directions: From Redding drive north on Interstate 5 past Weed to the Edgewood exit. Take the Edgewood exit, turn left at the stop sign, and then drive a short distance to another stop sign at Old Stage Road. Turn right on Old Stage Road and drive to Gazelle. In Gazelle turn west on Gazelle-Callahan Road and drive over the mountain to Rail Creek Road. Turn left on Rail Creek Road and drive to the lake.

Access: There is no boat ramp.

Facilities, fees: A campground and a fishing pier are provided. Supplies can be obtained in Callahan. The facilities are wheelchair accessible. A fee is charged for camping; day use is free.

Water sports, restrictions: Motors are not allowed on the lake. A sandy beach is available, but the water is very, very cold and hypothermia a danger to swimmers. Windsurfing is not permitted.

Contact: Klamath National Forest, Scott River Ranger District, (530) 468-5351 or fax (530) 468-5654.

About Kangaroo Lake: Little Kangaroo Lake is nestled in the Scott Mountains, a perfect hideaway for campers and anglers who want to get away from it all. The road in is quite pretty, especially below Scott Mountain, where there are scenic valleys filled with greenery and edged by forestland and mountains.

This small (25 acres) but deep (100 feet) alpine water is situated in a mountain bowl at an elevation of 6,500 feet. The campsites are reached via a short walk from the parking area, and the lake is just a few minutes from the campground. There's good shoreline fishing for large brook trout and decent-sized rainbow trout. And here's a rare plus: a wheelchair-accessible ramp. The water is cold, so only members of the Polar Bear Club try swimming here.

At the camp hikers will find a trailhead for the Pacific Crest Trail, which provides a route for an invigorating day hike up to a peak that has great views of the lake.

❷ Picayune Lake

Location: Near Mount Shasta in Shasta-Trinity National Forest; map B2, grid b3.

Directions: From Redding drive 58 miles north on Interstate 5 to Mount Shasta. Take the Central Mount Shasta exit and drive three miles southwest on W.A. Barr Road (off Interstate 5) past Lake Siskiyou to South Fork Road. Continue up the mountain past the Gumboot Lake turnoff (which is on the left). Continue up to the ridge, turn right (the lake will be below you to the left), and continue for another mile. Then turn left and drive to the gate. Park and hike the last half mile to the lake.

Access: There is no boat ramp.

Facilities, fees: A small dock and cabin have been built, but they are off-limits to the public. No other facilities are available on-site. There is a campground at nearby Gumboot Lake. Supplies can be obtained in Mount Shasta. Access is free.

Water sports, restrictions: Swimming is permitted.

Contact: Shasta-Trinity National Forest, Mount Shasta Ranger Station, (530) 926-4511 or fax (530) 926-5120.

About Picayune Lake: This is one of the prettiest alpine lakes in the Trinity-Divide country—almost always full, lined by firs, pines, and cedars, and bordered on the western side by a steep facing. It gets very little traffic because a gate blocks the access road's last half mile, and most people just don't want to hike in, and also because camping is prohibited. The lake is bordered by land owned by the Roseburg Lumber Company, not the US Forest Service, and while public access is permitted, the gate is there to discourage it.

Picayune is set at an elevation of 6,100 feet, covers 11.5 acres, and is 27 feet deep. Despite its beauty, it receives very light use, primarily by day hikers having picnics. It is too cold for swimming until midsummer, and the trout fishing is just fair. A few ambitious souls will carry in inner tubes or rubber rafts and float around in the center of Picayune Lake to take in all this great beauty.

Roseburg Lumber has built a nice cabin and dock at the lake, but they are strictly off-limits to visitors.

❸ Gumboot Lake

Location: Near Mount Shasta in Shasta-Trinity National Forest; map B2, grid b3.

Directions: From the town of Mount Shasta on Interstate 5, take the Central Mount Shasta exit and drive to the stop sign. Turn left, cross the highway, and continue to another stop sign at W.A. Barr Road. Turn left, drive past Lake Siskiyou, and continue up the mountain (the road becomes Forest Service Road 26). Near the summit look for the signed turnoff to Gumboot Lake on the left side of the road.

Access: No boat ramp is available. Cartop boats may be hand launched.

Facilities, fees: A small campground is provided, but there is no piped water, so bring your own. A few picnic tables and vault toilets are also available. Access is free.

Water sports, restrictions: Motors are not permitted on the lake. You can swim near the campground.

Contact: Shasta-Trinity National Forest, Mount Shasta Ranger Station, (530) 926-4511 or fax (530) 926-5120.

About Gumboot Lake: Gumboot is quite pretty, bordered on its far side by a meadow and a steep mountain face, and well forested on the other. A pool of emerald green water that's only 15 feet deep, the lake is set at an elevation of 6,050 feet and covers just seven acres.

Easy access makes this a popular stop for shoreline anglers and cartop boaters who haul in canoes, prams, and inflatable rafts. The water is chilly, too cold to swim in for very long and too cold to enjoy floating around in an inner tube.

If you're in the mood for a picnic and a hike, this is an excellent destination. There are some great hikes in the area. My favorite is to scramble up the mountain behind the lake to the ridgeline, hit the Pacific Crest Trail, then turn left, and claim the peak that is set just above the lake. This is a great vantage point, with a stellar view of Gumboot and Mount Shasta, and makes for a perfect rest stop on your afternoon adventure.

❹ Toad Lake

Location: Near Mount Shasta in Shasta-Trinity National Forest; map B2, grid b3.

Directions: From the town of Mount Shasta on Interstate 5, take the Central Mount Shasta exit and drive to the stop sign. Turn left, cross the highway, and continue to another stop sign at W.A. Barr Road. Turn left and drive past Lake Siskiyou and continue up the mountain (the road becomes Forest Service Road 26). Just past a concrete bridge, turn right, and drive a short distance. Turn left on Morgan Meadow Road and continue for 10 miles to the parking area. The road is bumpy and twisty. The final quarter mile to the trailhead is rough, and high-clearance four-wheel-drive vehicles are recommended. A 15-minute walk gets you to the lake. You are advised to carry a Forest Service map.

Access: There is no boat ramp.

Facilities, fees: A small campground is provided, but there is no piped water. Picnic tables and vault toilets are also available. Supplies can be obtained in Mount Shasta. Access is free.

Water sports, restrictions: Swimming is permitted. People who don't mind carrying in their boards can windsurf here.

Contact: Shasta-Trinity National Forest, Mount Shasta Ranger Station, (530) 926-4511 or fax (530) 926-5120. For a detailed map send $4 to Map Sales, USDA-Forest Service, 1323 Club Drive, Vallejo, CA 94592.

About Toad Lake: This is a pretty hike-in lake that sits on the edge of wilderness, providing good camping, swimming, hiking, and fair fishing—and you can be here after an easy 15-minute walk.

A lot of people stay clear of the lake because the road in is long and rough, particularly a terribly bumpy spot about a half mile from the parking area. At least you'll be rewarded for your efforts with a little solitude—solitude and a 23.5-acre, 40-foot-deep lake in an attractive setting at an elevation of 6,950 feet.

Swimming? Although the lake freezes over in winter, by midsummer it is refreshing and not too cold, and by summer it is excellent for swimming. Camping? Outstanding, with all the elements of a wilderness trip without a long tromp, allowing you to make repeat trips to carry in lots of bonus items. Hiking? A half-hour hike, starting by looping around the lake in a counterclockwise direction, will take you to a trail that is routed above the rock bowl and on to the Pacific Crest Trail. Another 15 minutes on foot will get you to Porcupine Lake, an absolutely pristine setting. Mountain climbing? An all-day, leg-straining grunt will help you reach the top of Mount Eddy, which peaks at 9,025 feet, making it the highest mountain in the local range.

Add it all up and put it in your mental cash register: Right, Toad Lake is quite a place to visit.

❺ Castle Lake

Location: Near Mount Shasta in Shasta-Trinity National Forest; map B2, grid b4.

Directions: From Redding drive 58 miles north on Interstate 5 to Mount Shasta. Take the Central Mount Shasta exit and drive 2.5 miles southwest on W.A. Barr Road (off Interstate 5), past Lake Siskiyou. Turn left on Castle Lake Road and continue to the lake.

Access: There is no boat ramp.

Facilities, fees: A small campground is provided nearby, but there is no piped water. A small picnic area with vault toilets and a fireplace is available. Supplies can be obtained in the town of Mount Shasta. Access to the lake is free.

Water sports, restrictions: Swimming is permitted. Windsurfing is also allowed, but no one windsurfs here.

Contact: Shasta-Trinity National Forest, Mount Shasta Ranger Station, (530) 926-4511 or fax (530) 926-5120.

About Castle Lake: Bring your camera. No, not to take pictures of big fish, because there are very few of those, but rather to take pictures from some of California's most scenic lookouts.

The view of Mount Shasta from the road in, just a half mile below the lake, is absolutely spectacular. More magazine pictures of the magic mountain are taken here than from any other lookout. But for an even better photo opportunity, hike in from Castle Lake to Heart Lake and then take a snapshot of Shasta with that little lake in the foreground. Unless you are careful, you might win an award for that one, it's just so beautiful! To get to Heart Lake, take the trail that starts on the left side of Castle Lake and when you reach the saddle, continue to the right and up; in all about a 25-minute hike.

Set at an elevation of 5,400 feet, the lake covers 47 acres and is 120 feet deep. Extremely pure water that is low in nitrogen (similar to Lake Tahoe) has resulted in a color that is deeper blue than any lake in the Trinity-Divide country and has been the focus of a study by UC Davis scientists for years. The depth of the lake keeps the water cold, even in summer, but some brave souls claim that if you take the plunge, you will be rejuvenated by the lake's magical properties.

Hand-launch boats, including canoes and rafts, are well suited for Castle Lake, especially for exploring the unusual rock face on the lake's back wall.

Castle Lake is easy to reach, with a paved road all the way in. Although in winter it provides one of the few good spots for ice fishing in Northern California, the views are what visitors find unforgettable.

---

❻ Lake Siskiyou

Location: Near Mount Shasta in Shasta-Trinity National Forest; map B2, grid b5.
Directions: From Redding drive 58 miles north on Interstate 5 to Mount Shasta. Take the Central Mount Shasta exit, turn left at the stop sign, head west over the freeway, and drive one mile to another stop sign at W.A. Barr Road. Turn left and drive for a mile, bear right where the road forms a Y, and continue over the dam to the far side of the lake, turning right at the sign for Lake Siskiyou Marina and Campground.

Access: A two-lane boat ramp with a dock is provided. To get there, drive past the entrance kiosk and continue straight for a half mile.

Facilities, fees: A campground, bathrooms with showers, small coin laundry, and a restaurant are provided. A small marina, snack bar, and tackle shop are located at the boat dock. Motorized fishing boats, pontoon boats, paddleboats, canoes, and kayaks can be rented. North shore access is limited to day use only; vault toilets are provided. A small access fee is charged to enter the beach and marina area; north shore access is free.

Water sports, restrictions: A 10 mph speed limit is strictly enforced. A sandy beach is located on the western shore of the lake, a five-minute walk south of the marina. The adjacent swimming area, protected from boats by a line of buoys, is popular in July and August. Windsurfing is permitted; note the speed limit.

Contact: Lake Siskiyou Campground, (530) 926-2610; Lake Siskiyou Marina, (530) 926-2617.

About Lake Siskiyou: This lake sits at the base of giant Mount Shasta, which towers above at 14,162 feet, giving it one of the loveliest settings for a man-made lake in America. Recreation—not water storage for farming—was the sole reason Siskiyou was built. Thus, while reservoirs in the foothills of California are drained when water is needed, Siskiyou remains full, often having a jewel-like quality. That is why people come here—to visit the most beautiful lake along the entire Interstate 5 corridor.

Lake Siskiyou covers 435 acres and is set

at an elevation of 3,181 feet. In the summer months the lake gets a lot of traffic from RV campers, sunbathers, and anglers. In the winter the shore is snowbound, but the lake does not freeze over. Favorite activities include fishing in the spring, and swimming and leisure boating in the summer, a time when many families take weeklong camping trips here. The campground is huge, with 125 RV spaces and 225 additional tent sites, yet it can fill up on summer weekends and reservations are advised. Camping season at the lake kicks off on Memorial Day weekend, and this spot is popular well into mid-September.

The 10 mph speed limit ensures quiet waters, and the nearby campground with easy access off Interstate 5 makes it ideal for family vacationers. Children often play in the swimming area and tool around in paddleboats. On hot summer weekends when the campground is full, Lake Siskiyou's beach can get pretty crowded. Windsurfing, which is usually fair on windy afternoons in May and early June, is practiced primarily near the less congested north shore.

This place is so wonderful that you can just stretch out on a beach blanket, gaze across the water at Mount Shasta, and be thankful to witness such a beautiful scene.

❼ Upper Sacramento River

🏕️ 🎣 ✕ 🏊   7️⃣

Location: Near Mount Shasta upstream of Shasta Lake; map B2, grid b5.

Directions: Direct access is available off Interstate 5 via nearly every exit between the towns of Lakehead and Mount Shasta.

Access: There is no boat ramp. To reach the uppermost put-in, take the Central Mount Shasta exit off Interstate 5, turn left at the stop sign, head west over the freeway, and drive one mile to the stop sign at W.A. Barr Road. Turn left, drive for a mile, bear right

where the road forms a Y, and continue over to Box Canyon Dam. Access to the put-in is just below the dam; there is no trail, and the descent is steep and difficult. Only lightweight craft are recommended, as equipment must be lowered part of the way down. Take out at one of several excellent access points about six miles downstream, just north of the town of Dunsmuir, or continue through Dunsmuir to Sims Flat. For those who wish to bypass the dangerous descent into Box Canyon, there's an alternate put-in that shortens the run by two miles: Follow the directions above, but bear left where the road forms a Y. Drive south on Old Stage Road to Cantara Road. Turn right and continue down to the river. The put-in is slightly above the Cantara Loop railroad bridge.

To reach a lower put-in, take the Sims Road exit off Interstate 5 about 12 miles south of Dunsmuir. Follow Sims Road to Sims Flat Campground. Put in here and boat 14 miles to the take-out above Dog Creek. **Facilities, fees:** Several full-facility campgrounds and RV parks are located along the river and near adjacent towns. Sims Flat is a popular put-in site. Railroad Park and Castle Crags State Park are also good options. Supplies can be obtained in Mount Shasta, Dunsmuir, Castella, Lakehead, and Redding. Access is free. Rafting permits are not required.

Water sports, restrictions: Several good swimming holes are situated along this entire stretch of river. The best, providing the easiest access, are at Sims Flat Campground at the end of Prospect Street in Dunsmuir, and at the Sweetbrier Bridge south of Dunsmuir.

Contact: Shasta-Trinity National Forest District Offices: Mount Shasta area, (530) 926-4511 or fax (530) 926-5120; Shasta Lake Ranger Station, (530) 275-1587. For guided rafting trips contact Turtle River Rafting, (800) 726-3223; or Wilderness Adventures, (530) 926-6282 or fax (800) 323-7238.

About the Upper Sacramento River: After going bankrupt several years ago, this stretch of river has experienced a resurgence, rebounding from the worst inland toxic spill in California history to become a flourishing ecosystem.

In 1991 I was on the scene when a Southern Pacific freighter derailed and dumped a tanker wheels-up into the river, spilling 19,000 gallons of an all-purpose herbicide. That seems so long ago, now that the entire aquatic food chain is again healthy and full, with trout filling the river from Box Canyon to Shasta Lake.

After Southern Pacific killed the river, few people would dare dream of such a recovery. All anybody could do was pray for a fresh start. Those prayers have been answered, and today this place offers the chance to experience nature in her prime.

The best way to see mother nature at work is for skilled kayakers, either in a hard shell or an inflatable, to run the river. Rafting in oar boats is usually limited to spring and early summer; after that the reduced stream flows can cause bottom scraping on too much of the route.

Skilled kayakers have two popular runs to choose from:

From Cantara Loop through Dunsmuir: This very demanding run is filled with Class IV rapids and requires a lot of technical paddling through pocket water sprinkled with boulders and quick turns. Although very pretty, with riparian vegetation again flourishing on the riverbanks, it is not secluded, especially right through Dunsmuir. In addition, the Southern Pacific railroad parallels the river all the way through Dunsmuir, and it is common to hear the cacophonous roar of passing trains. I have not run below Dunsmuir, but my research assistant, Robyn Schlueter, formerly of Mount Shasta, says the technical highlight of this run is Mears Creek Falls, which is rated Class V and is located below Dunsmuir at mile 21. "It's the largest rapid on the river, and during high flows it should be portaged," she states.

Sims Flat to Dog Creek: This is a more popular run than the previously detailed stretch of water, but its Class IV rapids and abundance of technical, quick turns around boulders and eddies render it challenging just the same. More so than most rivers, this section of stream varies wildly in character from spring through summer according to river flows. Even though you will be heading south as you venture downstream, be sure to pull over at clearings and look to the north for spectacular views of Mount Shasta.

❽ Tamarack Lake

Location: Near Castella in Shasta-Trinity National Forest; map B2, grid c3.

Directions: From Redding drive 44 miles north on Interstate 5 to the town of Castella. From Castella drive 11 miles west on Road 25/Castle Creek Road to Twin Lakes Road. Turn south and travel three miles; when the road forks, bear left and continue one mile to the lake. Note: The last four miles of road are very rough, suitable only for four-wheel-drive vehicles. You are advised to carry a map of Shasta-Trinity National Forest.

Access: There is no boat ramp.

Facilities, fees: No facilities are provided on site. Primitive, do-it-yourself campsites are available. Supplies can be obtained in Castella. Access is free.

Water sports, restrictions: Swimming is permitted. The lake is too small for other water sports.

Contact: Shasta-Trinity National Forest, Headquarters, (530) 964-2184 or fax (530) 964-2938. You can get a detailed map of the area for $4 from Map Sales, USDA-Forest Service, 1323 Club Drive, Vallejo, CA 94592.

About Tamarack Lake: Tamarack Lake is so pleasing to the eye. Set deep in the

Trinity-Divide country, this attractive alpine lake provides a refuge of peace and beauty. There are actually three lakes in the immediate area: Tamarack and, to the west, Upper and Lower Twin Lakes. Of the trio Tamarack is the biggest and has the most appeal for recreationists.

Tamarack makes a good base camp for people who have a taste for exploring. Of course if you just want to sit back and gaze at it, that's okay, too. This is one of the prettiest lakes in the Trinity-Divide country.

The lake is set at an elevation of 5,900 feet, covers 21 acres, and is 16 feet deep. To drive all the way in, you need a four-wheel-drive vehicle. Many people stop short where the access road gets rough and hike out the last half mile. Some four-wheelers bring canoes or rafts and enjoy the spectacular beauty from the water. Fishing for small trout is only fair here, and the water is often too cold for swimming until midsummer.

Side trips include a hike to the foot of Gray Butte, that craggy mountaintop to the northeast, and visits to nearby Twin Lakes and Lily Pad Lake. This is a great place for four-wheel-drive adventure.

---

❾ McCloud River

Location: Near McCloud in Shasta-Trinity National Forest; map B2, grid c7.
Directions: From Redding drive 56 miles north on Interstate 5. Take the McCloud-Reno exit and travel 12 miles east on Highway 89 to McCloud. To reach the lower portion of the McCloud River, turn south on Squaw Valley Road. Drive 7.5 miles on the paved road; then turn south on an unpaved road near the southwestern shore of McCloud Reservoir, and drive to a signed Forest Service turnoff to Ah-Di-Na Campground. Turn right and drive to the end of the gravel road, which terminates at the access point for the Nature Conservancy's McCloud River Preserve.

To reach the upper portion of the river, drive five miles east on Highway 89 from McCloud. Turn right at the sign for Fowler's Camp. Access is available along a trail out of the camp.
Access: There is no boat ramp. The put-in for the upper portion of the river is just below Lower Falls, near Fowler's Camp (see directions). During lower flows, put in about a mile below Fowler's Camp. You can reach this put-in via a steep path that leads down to the river. The section from here to Big Springs often has meager flows, and only kayaks and other small craft are recommended. Take out at the boat ramp at Tarantula Gulch in McCloud Reservoir; farther upstream is private property where taking out is prohibited.

The put-in for the Lower McCloud is just below McCloud Dam at Ash Camp, with the take-out at Gilman Road north of Shasta Lake. This Class IV–V run is for experts only.
Facilities, fees: The Forest Service provides a camp at Ah-Di-Na on the Lower McCloud. On the Upper McCloud, camping is available at Fowler's Camp, Cattle Camp, and Algoma Camp. A picnic area is located at Lower Falls. Supplies can be obtained in McCloud. Access is free. Rafting permits are not required.
Water sports, restrictions: Although the water is very cold, you can swim near Cattle Camp and at Lower Falls.
Contact: Shasta-Trinity National Forest, Headquarters, (530) 964-2184 or fax (530) 964-2938. For rafting information contact Turtle River Rafting, (800) 726-3223; or Wilderness Adventures, (530) 926-6282 or (800) 323-7238.
About the McCloud River: A visit to the McCloud River is about as close as you can get to an adventure in a time machine. Here, just walking, hiking, kayaking, or fishing can make you feel as if you have turned back the clock two centuries.

On the Upper McCloud out of Fowler's

Camp, a great 20-minute walk will take you to Lower Falls and to one of the prettiest waterfalls in Northern California: spectacular Middle Falls, a wide and tall silvery cascade that pounds into a deep pool. On the Lower McCloud starting at the Nature Conservancy, another wonderful hike is routed along the river, where you need to boulder-hop some of the way. Everything is pristine and untouched; the Nature Conservancy keeps it that way and I hope they always will.

The river is too cold for swimming in the Lower McCloud, painful even for a quick dunk. However, there is a nice hole in the Upper McCloud near Cattle Camp, and there are always lots of folks jumping off Lower Falls and playing in the deep hole below. A ladder runs up from this swimming hole to a flat, rocky area where people like to sunbathe and picnic. Please do not litter there (or anywhere)!

The Lower McCloud is too shallow and technical most of the year for kayakers or rafters and always presents a challenge for fly fishers. Regardless, the river gets the top rating for its dramatic scenery and challenging terrain for paddlers and anglers.

There are two primary runs for rafts and kayaks:

Upper McCloud, from Lower Falls to McCloud Reservoir, Class III: This 10-mile stretch includes three miles on the lake, a real drag. But the river passes the Hearst's Wyntoon Estate, complete with castles (look, but don't stop or touch). The first two miles of the run is typically shallow with a lot of bottom scraping, and then the flows pick up and make for a good yet technical run. By July it's all over. Commercial rafting companies tend to run this only on extremely rare occasions.

Rafting guide Diane Strachan told me that when she made the run, she stopped at a rock to look at the Hearst castles, then spotted this mean-looking gardener, who appeared to be glaring at her.

"Is it okay if I get out and look at the paintings on the walls of the castles?" she asked.

"Okay," the gardener answered, "but only for a moment."

Well, Diane looked closer and noticed the "gardener" was familiar. Could it be? It was. Turned out to be Clint Eastwood.

Lower McCloud, from Ash Camp to Gilman Road at Shasta Lake: With many of the rapids rated at Class IV and V, this is for expert kayakers only. Extremely technical work is required around shallow riffles sprinkled with boulders and pocket water. The season is extremely short, usually over by mid-May, and few try it. This is a long, exhausting, and grueling stretch of river for even the most skilled paddlers.

---

⑩ Iron Canyon Reservoir

Location: Near Big Bend in Shasta-Trinity National Forest; map B2, grid d7.

Directions: From Redding drive approximately 37 miles east on Highway 299. Turn north on Big Bend Road and drive 17 miles to the town of Big Bend. Continue north for two miles, turn left on Road 38N11, and drive 5.5 miles to Hawkins Landing.

Access: A paved launch ramp is available at Hawkins Landing. Small boats are recommended.

Facilities, fees: Two campgrounds are provided: Hawkins Landing (fee) and Deadlun Creek (free). Neither has piped water, so bring your own. Supplies can be obtained in Big Bend or Burney. Access is free.

Water sports, restrictions: You can swim near the campgrounds.

Contact: Shasta-Trinity National Forest, Shasta Lake Ranger Station, (530) 275-1587 or fax (530) 275-1512.; Shasta Lake Visitor Information Center, (530) 275-1589.

About Iron Canyon Reservoir: They screwed up when they built Iron Canyon Reservoir. Apparently the intake and dam are set up so the lake never fills. The result is this perpetual moonscape on the upper end of the lake, dotted with what's left of the trees that were once here, a kind of stump graveyard. It also means Deadlun Camp is too far away from the water.

Iron Canyon is located at 2,700 feet in elevation and covers 500 acres with 15 miles of shoreline. When the lake is at its fullest in the spring, this is a very pretty place, set in national forest land just above the elevation line where nature grows conifers instead of deciduous trees.

In winter the water masters drop the water levels down to almost nothing, rendering an unbelievable sight. Spring rains then make the shoreline extremely muddy, and since the water never fills the reservoir, all water sports are out of the question except for fishing and swimming. It is just too stumpy for waterskiing, personal watercraft, or windsurfing. Because the place doesn't have a beach, only exposed lake bottom, the swimming is just so-so.

Most people come here to camp, fish, and enjoy the remote, quiet setting and beautiful landscape. The water is a striking emerald green, and during a windless sunset, it appears to glow.

⑪ Pit River

Location: Northeast of Redding in Shasta-Trinity National Forest; map B2, grid e8.
Directions: From Interstate 5 at Redding, take the Highway 299 East exit and drive about 30 miles. Turn left on Fender's Ferry Road and travel four miles. Access is available on the left side of the river, below the dam. The river can also be accessed off several roads that intersect Big Bend Road, about 35 miles east of Redding. These roads are unimproved, so four-wheel-drive vehicles are recommended.
Access: There is no boat ramp.
Facilities, fees: A few campgrounds are available off Highway 299. Supplies can be obtained in Redding. Access is free.

Water sports, restrictions: You can swim at Fender's Flat (at the end of Fender's Ferry Road) and near the town of Big Bend. A natural hot spring is located just west of Big Bend. Note: Much of the shoreline is rugged and treacherous, with steep dropoffs into the river and deep pools below. Use care when walking.

Contact: Shasta-Trinity National Forest, Shasta Lake Ranger Station, (530) 275-1587 or fax (530) 275-1512.

About the Pit River: What makes the Pit great for most visitors is the natural hot spring pool that's bubbling away just a short distance from the river. That provides the rare opportunity to get heated up in the hot spring, then cooled down in the river, alternating between the two. The spring is located just downstream from the Pit River Bridge in the town of Big Bend, with access at Big Bend Hot Springs. The latter also has a series of concrete tubs perched on a bluff above the river, and the hot spring water pours in a series of miniature waterfalls from one tub to the next. This experience is not so much swimming as it is taking a dunk.

The river is strikingly pretty, a freestone stream, that is, where the water tumbles over boulders and into pools. Trout fishing is excellent. Flocks of bandtail pigeons course up and down the waterway, and the occasional bald eagle soars overhead. The best fishing spots are below Lake Britton Dam (near McArthur–Burney Falls State Park) and at the Big Bend Bridge. Other spots have difficult access and are extremely challenging for anglers to wade in. Many people take a tumble here, with slippery boulders and no obvious routes.

Big Bend Hot Springs has become well known to hippies heading over to Mount Shasta during the annual weeklong summer pilgrimage when they harmonically converge, or whatever it is they say they are doing.

⑫ Shasta Lake

⚓ 🚤 ⛺ 🪝   🔟 ≋

🤽 🚣 🎿 🐟 🦆

Location: Near Redding in Shasta-Trinity National Forest; map B2, grid f3.

Directions: Fishing access points are located all around the lakeshore and can be reached by taking one of several exits off Interstate 5 north of Redding. See directions to individual boat ramps.

Access: There are 14 boat ramps:

Antlers Boat Launch: From Interstate 5 take the Lakeshore Drive–Antlers Road exit and drive one mile south on Antlers Road to the four-lane paved boat ramp. A campground and picnic area are provided. For information phone the Shasta Lake Visitor Information Center at (530) 275-1589.

Antlers Resort: Take the Lakeshore Drive–Antlers Road exit off Interstate 5 and drive 1.5 miles south on Antlers Road. A paved ramp is available, along with a full-service marina, campground, grocery store, and picnic area. Houseboats, patio boats, aluminum fishing boats, personal watercraft, ski boats, and canoes can be rented. For information phone (530) 238-2553 or fax (530) 238-2340.

Bailey Cove: From Interstate 5 take the O'Brien–Shasta Caverns exit and follow the signs. There is a two-lane paved ramp. A campground and picnic area are provided. For information phone the Shasta Lake Visitor Information Center at (530) 275-1589.

Bridge Bay Resort & Marina: From Interstate 5 take the Bridge Bay exit and follow Bridge Bay Road to the resort, which has a paved ramp. A full-service marina, boat store, motel, grocery store, restaurant, and picnic area are provided. Houseboats, ski boats, patio boats, and aluminum fishing boats are available for rent. For boat rentals call (800) 752-9669. For general information phone (530) 275-3021.

Centimudi Boat Launch: From Inter-state 5 take the Shasta Dam exit and drive west on Shasta Dam Boulevard for about five miles. When you reach the four-way stop, turn right on Lake Boulevard. At the top of the hill, look for a sign on the right indicating Centimudi Boat Ramp. Turn right and continue to the four-lane paved ramp. Primitive toilets are provided. For information phone the Shasta Lake Visitor Information Center at (530) 275-1589.

Digger Bay Marina: From Interstate 5 take the Shasta Dam exit and drive five miles east on Shasta Dam Boulevard. Turn right on Shasta Park Drive (which becomes Digger Bay Road) and drive to the marina, which has a paved ramp. A full-service marina, gas, store, and picnic tables are provided. Houseboats, ski boats, personal watercraft, and aluminum fishing boats can be rented. For boat rentals call (800) 752-9669. For general information phone (530)275-3072.

Hirz Bay Launch Ramp: From Interstate 5 take the Gilman Road exit and drive approximately 10 miles northeast to the sign for the boat ramp. The road is narrow and winding. A two-lane paved ramp and a campground are provided. For information phone the Shasta Lake Visitor Information Center at (530) 275-1589.

Holiday Harbor: From Interstate 5 take the O'Brien–Shasta Caverns exit and drive three-quarters of a mile to the resort, which has a two-lane paved ramp. A full-service marina, RV park, grocery store, gas, picnic area, and playground are also provided. Houseboats, ski boats, patio boats, personal watercraft, aluminum fishing boats, and canoes can be rented. For information phone (530) 238-2383 or fax (530) 238-2132.

Jones Valley Launch Ramp: From Interstate 5 take the Highway 299 East exit and drive approximately 10 miles to the town of Bella Vista. Turn left on Dry Creek Road and follow it to the fork. Bear right and drive a quarter mile. To reach the private marina, turn left on Jones Valley Marina Drive; to reach the public boat ramp (two lanes, paved), continue straight. A full-service marina, campground, and grocery store are located at Jones Valley Resort. Houseboats, ski boats, patio boats, personal watercraft, canoes, and kayaks are available for rent. For marina information phone (530) 275-7950; for boat ramp information phone the Shasta Lake Visitor Information Center at (530) 275-1589.

Lakeview Marina Resort: From Interstate 5 take the O'Brien–Shasta Caverns exit and head east. Take a left at the mailboxes and continue to the marina. Only marina customers can use the paved boat ramp. A full-service marina, snack bar, and grocery store are provided. Houseboats are available for rent. For information phone (530) 223-3003.

Packer's Bay Access: This ramp is only accessible from Interstate 5 southbound. If you are driving on Interstate 5 northbound, take the O'Brien–Shasta Caverns exit and get back on the freeway heading south. Take the Packer's Bay exit and follow Packer's Bay Road to the four-lane paved ramp. A private marina is adjacent to the ramp, offering a dock, fuel, and a small store. Houseboats are available for rent. For marina and houseboat information, call (530) 275-5570; for boat ramp information phone the Shasta Lake Visitor Information Center at (530) 275-1589.

Shasta Marina: From Interstate 5 take the O'Brien–Shasta Caverns exit. Head east on O'Brien Inlet Road for one mile to a red building, which is adjacent to the marina. A paved ramp is available. A full-service marina, campground, showers, coin laundry, gas, and store are provided. Houseboats, patio boats, aluminum fishing boats, and ski boats can be rented. For information phone (530) 238-2284.

Silverthorn Resort: From Interstate 5 take the Oasis exit and drive east on Oasis Road (it turns into the Old Oregon Trail).

Continue approximately 10 miles to Bear Mountain Road; then turn right and continue to a stop sign at the T intersection. Turn left on Dry Creek Road and follow it to a fork. Bear left and follow the signs to Silverthorn Resort. A three-lane paved ramp, full-service marina, cabins, and a store are provided. Houseboats, patio boats, ski boats, aluminum fishing boats and personal watercraft are available for rent. For information phone (530) 275-1571 or fax (530) 275-1573.

Sugarloaf Marina: From Interstate 5 take the Lakeshore Drive–Antlers Road exit and turn left on Lakeshore Drive. Continue three miles to the building with the "Loaf on Inn" sign and turn left. At the sign for Sugarloaf, turn left again and continue to the marina. A two-lane paved ramp, full-service marina, campground, and store are provided. Houseboats, ski boats, patio boats, aluminum fishing boats, and kayaks are available for rent. For information phone (530) 238-8332.

Facilities, fees: Full services, campgrounds, and recreation areas are located around the lake; see boat ramp listings above for specifics. Four boat-in campsites are available as well. There is a charge for Forest Service boat ramps; charges for private ramps vary.

Water sports, restrictions: A 5 mph speed limit is enforced around the coves and marinas. Personal watercraft are permitted. Windsurfing is most popular on the McCloud Arm of the lake, where there is more wind. Two good jump-off points are Bailey Cove and Hirz Bay. There are no sandy beaches surrounding Shasta Lake, but swimming is possible all around the lakeshore. Two of the better spots to jump in for a dip are Gregory Creek and Jones Valley.

Contact: Shasta Lake Visitor Information Center, (530) 275-1589; Shasta Cascade Wonderland Association, (800) 474-2782 or (530) 365-7500.

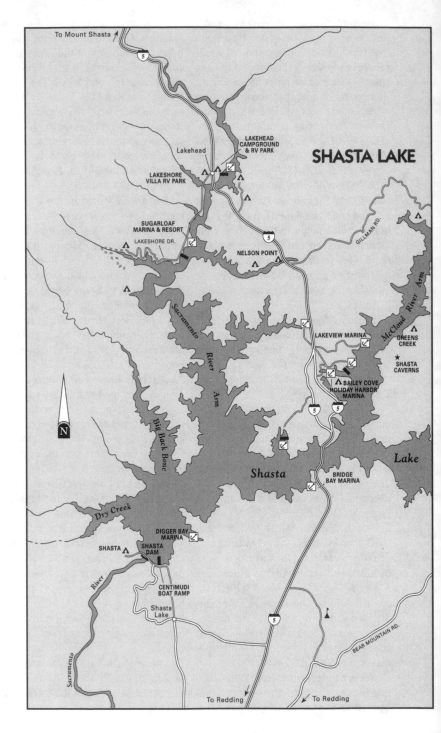

To Mount Shasta

5

Lakehead

LAKEHEAD
CAMPGROUND
& RV PARK

SHASTA LAKE

LAKESHORE
VILLA RV PARK

SUGARLOAF
MARINA & RESORT

LAKESHORE DR.

GILLMAN RD.

5

NELSON POINT

McCloud River Arm

LAKEVIEW MARINA

GREENS
CREEK

Sacramento River Arm

SHASTA
CAVERNS

BAILEY COVE

HOLIDAY HARBOR
MARINA

5

5

Big Back Bone

N

Shasta

Lake

BRIDGE
BAY MARINA

Dry Creek

DIGGER BAY
MARINA

SHASTA

SHASTA
DAM

CENTIMUDI
BOAT RAMP

River

Shasta
Lake

5

To Redding

To Redding

BEAR MOUNTAIN RD.

Sacramento

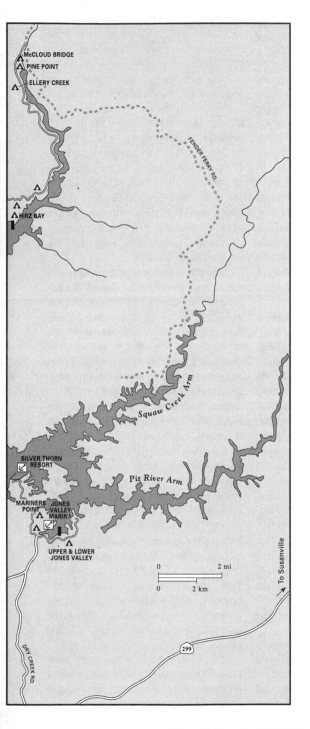

Map of Chapter B2—Page 76

About Shasta Lake: This is the boating capital of the west. This giant lake has 370 miles of shoreline, 400 houseboat rentals, 12 marinas, 14 boat ramps, 12 campgrounds, lakeshore lodging, and 22 species of sport fish. No matter what the season, Shasta is so big that there is plenty of room for everybody—water-skiers, personal watercraft, houseboaters, anglers, swimmers, windsurfers. You name it, Shasta can accommodate them all.

Shasta is really four bodies of water in one, with each lake arm forming a separate lake: Sacramento Arm, McCloud Arm, Pit Arm, and Squaw Creek Arm. That's in addition to the main lake near the dam. Add in the thousands of little coves and secret inlets, and you have the equivalent of a mansion that is so big you could never fully explore it.

Although it's not true of other lakes, it is easy to get accustomed to the large number of boaters at Shasta Lake. In the summer there are hundreds of houseboats here, plus quite a few water-skiers. But this is one place where there is plenty of room for all comers. With all the houseboaters on the water, it can seem like a giant party, with everybody happy, and you can bet on lots of sun, skin, lotion, and potent liquids. If you want to escape the festivities, just head into one of the quiet coves.

Shasta Lake is located just north of Redding, in the foothill country at an elevation of 1,000 feet. Covering 29,500 surface acres, this is the biggest reservoir in California, with 370 miles of shoreline. In a houseboat it takes about five or six days to tour the whole thing. Most people, however, develop an affinity for one section of the lake and return to it year after year, just like going to a second home.

Houseboating has become so popular that virtually every houseboat available for rent on the lake is booked the entire summer, Memorial Day through Labor Day. That makes planning and reserving far in advance a necessity. After a short instructional and safety lesson on how to operate the boat, you are set free to roam and play on your own.

Because surface water temperatures at Shasta range from the 70s to the low 80s in the summer, the lake can feel like a giant bathtub, ideal for waterskiing and personal watercraft. Swimming is only fair, primarily because most of the shoreline areas have steep drop-offs, as do most reservoirs. Two of the better spots to jump in for a swim are at Jones Valley and Gregory Creek, where the lake bottom contours are more gradually sloped. No matter where you take the plunge, children should always be supervised in the water.

Campgrounds never completely fill up, and boaters can take advantage of the additional boat-in sites, the best of which is at Ski Island. One problem at the drive-in campgrounds is the distance between the campsites and the water. Because the big reservoir is drawn down in late summer as water is shipped to points south, campgrounds located on the upper arms of the lake can end up being a steep hike from the water, with a wheezer of a climb up on the way back.

A few side notes: Windsurfing is best on the Pit River Arm. In the spring, bass fishers can have 30-fish days using plastic worms along the shoreline of the Squaw Creek Arm, Sacramento Arm, and McCloud Arm. Trolling for trout and salmon is often excellent at the Dry Creek Arm, and fishing for crappie is great at the submerged trees on the Pit Arm. The best hiking is on the Centimudi Trail near Jones Valley, and the Shasta Caverns offers a great tour of the limestone caves on the McCloud Arm. The lake has several full-time sheriff's patrol boats—whew.

When you put it all together, no place provides more boating recreation opportunities, diversity, and quality than Shasta Lake.

⑬ Clear Creek

Location: West of Redding; map B2, grid g0.

Directions: From Interstate 5 at Redding, take the Highway 299 West exit and drive 17 miles, past Whiskeytown Lake, to the French Gulch turnoff. Turn north on Trinity Mountain Road. Access is available off short roads that junction with Trinity Mountain Road, which parallels the creek.

Access: There is no boat ramp.

Facilities, fees: A small primitive campground is provided north of French Gulch; it has no piped water. More developed campsites are located at Whiskeytown Lake. Supplies can be obtained in Redding. Access is free.

Water sports, restrictions: Several good swimming holes are located off Trinity Mountain Road; look for the access roads.

Contact: Shasta-Trinity National Forest, National Recreation Area Management Unit, (530) 623-2121 or fax (530) 623-6010; Bureau of Land Management, Redding Office, (530) 224-2100.

About Clear Creek: "Pssssst. Want to hear a secret? Just don't tell anybody about it."

That is how people talk about Clear Creek. You see, everybody in this area goes to nearby Whiskeytown Lake. They don't know Clear Creek, along with the little campground here, exists. But it does.

Clear Creek is pretty, with beautiful riparian habitat bordering the water, yet it's far enough off the beaten path that it gets light use. So if you visit Whiskeytown Lake during the peak early summer season and are seeking a quiet alternative, little Clear Creek just might suit your needs.

Several excellent swimming holes, along with a couple of nice sandy bars, are available right off the access road. They are favorite retreats for a few locals. Fishing for small trout here is fair.

Whiskeytown Lake (see the next listing) is a National Recreation Area that offers full facilities, all water sports, hiking, biking, and camping. Despite all these attractions, Clear Creek has a special charm that is just as compelling.

⑭ Whiskeytown Lake

Location: Near Redding in Shasta-Trinity National Forest; map B2, grid g0.

Directions: From Interstate 5 at Redding, take the Highway 299 West exit and drive 10 miles. Turn left on Kennedy Memorial Drive (look for the visitor center, visible from the highway) or continue west on Highway 299 for four miles to the Oak Bottom access road on the left.

Access: There are three boat ramps:

Brandy Creek Marina: From Highway 299 turn left on Kennedy Memorial Drive, past headquarters, and follow the signs to Brandy Creek. The six-lane paved launch ramp is located one mile past the beach. A full-service marina, snack bar, and grocery store are available. Paddleboats and canoes can be rented.

Oak Bottom Marina: From Highway 299 continue past the Brandy Creek turnoff and drive for approximately four miles to the sign for Oak Bottom. Turn left toward the campground. To reach the four-lane paved launch ramp, continue straight down to the water. A full-service marina, store, and a snack bar are available; to reach the marina, turn left past the campground store. Patio boats, ski boats, sailboats, fishing boats, canoes, and paddleboats can be rented.

Whiskey Creek: From Highway 299 continue a short distance past the Brandy Creek turnoff. Just after you cross the bridge, turn right at the Whiskeytown Store and continue to the four-lane paved ramp.

Facilities, fees: There are three campgrounds: Brandy Creek, Oak Bottom, and

Dry Creek Group Camp. Tents are not permitted at Brandy Creek. Picnic areas are provided. Groceries and snacks are sold at Brandy Creek and Oak Bottom; full supplies can be obtained in Redding. Access and boat launching are free.

Water sports, restrictions: Waterskiing, personal watercraft, windsurfing, and sailing are allowed. Several sandy swimming beaches are located around the lake; the most popular are at the day-use areas at Brandy Creek and Oak Bottom.

Contact: Whiskeytown National Recreation Area, (530) 241-6584 or fax (530) 246-5154; Brandy Creek Marina, (530) 243-2733; Oak Bottom Marina, (530) 359-2269.

About Whiskeytown Lake: Whiskeytown is incredibly easy to reach, is sizable enough that you can spend a lot of time exploring, and has decent camping accommodations. Year-round this is a good place for boating, but the highlights here are excellent sailing in the spring, great hiking and biking, and typically high water levels. Is there any downside? Well, the wind can really kick up during the spring, but, hey, that is why this is the hands-down favorite in the area for windsurfers and sailboaters.

The good-sized lake covers 3,220 acres with 36 miles of shoreline and is just a short drive west of Redding at an elevation of 1,200 feet. In the summer the water is clear and warm, and with a few large sandy beaches, it is ideal for youngsters to kick around in. The popular picnic areas at Oak Bottom and Brandy Creek are exceptional, and the operators of both marinas are extremely helpful and friendly. Fishing is good for kokanee salmon and rainbow trout, although to be successful you'll need to be skilled in trolling techniques. But Whiskeytown really shines in the spring when west winds typically reach 10 to 15 knots, making it perfect for sailing and windsurfing.

One of the most romantic places on planet Earth is just beyond the western end of the lake at Mill Creek, where a hiking trail is routed along the stream for several miles. Covered by a canopy of oak/bay woodlands, Mill Creek runs gin-clear in the summer and strong in the spring, with lots of miniature waterfalls, pools, and drops. The trail parallels this pretty ribbon of water, crossing and recrossing the creek many times. The only sounds to accompany your thoughts are the twittering of birds, rushing water, and perhaps a light breeze rustling the leaves. Overall, Mill Creek is a great side trip.

Upon arrival, your first stop should be the visitor center, an outstanding facility located just off the highway. Free brochures and flyers are available, as is a staff of professionals who can answer any recreation questions.

⑮ Keswick Lake

Location: Near Redding in Shasta-Trinity National Forest; map B2, grid h1.

Directions: From Interstate 5 at Redding, take the Highway 299 West exit. Drive four miles, turn north on Iron Mountain Road, and travel another four miles to the lake.

Access: A paved boat ramp is located off Iron Mountain Road on the east side of the lake.

Facilities, fees: A day-use picnic area with rest rooms is provided. Campgrounds are available nearby at Whiskeytown Lake. Access is free.

Water sports, restrictions: Waterskiing and personal watercraft are permitted, but rarely seen. Swimming is allowed, but there are no beaches and the water is quite cold even in summer.

Contact: Bureau of Reclamation, 16349 Shasta Dam Boulevard, Shasta Lake, CA 96019 or phone (530) 275-1554 or fax (530) 275-2441.

About Keswick Lake: This long, narrow reservoir is situated directly below giant Shasta Lake, and with Shasta getting such heavy use, you might think Keswick would make a great, less-crowded alternative.

Well, there are indeed fewer people here. In fact, the lake is used by practically no one except for a few anglers. But great? Sorry.

The water entering 630-acre Keswick comes from the bottom of Shasta Dam, making this lake extremely cold, even in summer. The result is shabby opportunities for water sports, including waterskiing and swimming. It is doubly poor for swimming, because not only is the water painfully chilly, but the shoreline is rough and blocky with not a beach in sight.

Almost everybody in search of a good lake in the Redding area heads northbound on Interstate 5 to Shasta or west on Highway 299 to Whiskeytown, giving nary a thought to Keswick Lake. Everybody, that is, except a handful of anglers who have learned that there is a chance that giant rainbow trout will bite when the powerhouse is running at the head of the lake. Alas, when the powerhouse is down, fishing opportunities go kaput as well. When that happens you can head up here and never encounter another soul, even in summer.

⑯ Lower Sacramento River

⚓ 🚤 🏕️ 🐟 ✕   7️⃣

Location: Near Redding; map B2, grid h2.
Directions: From Redding drive south on Interstate 5. Access is available via the Riverside, Balls Ferry, and Jellys Ferry exits. Access is also available in the city of Redding, at Caldwell Park and near the Redding Civic Auditorium.
Access: There are four public boat ramps:

Balls Ferry Public Ramp: From Interstate 5 at Cottonwood, take the Balls Ferry Road exit. Drive east for about 200 yards, following the signs to the Coleman Fish Hatchery. Continue straight at a four-way stop; when you come to a T intersection, turn left on County Road A17 and continue

three miles. Turn right on Ash Creek Road and continue one mile. A public paved ramp is across the street from Balls Ferry Fishing Resort, which has a private, paved two-lane ramp.

Bonnyview: From Interstate 5 near Redding, take the Bonnyview–Bechelli Lane/Churn Creek exit. Turn west on Bonnyview and cross the river. Take the first left after the bridge and enter the paved parking area. A paved ramp and rest rooms are provided.

Lake Redding Park: From Interstate 5 in Redding, take the Lake Boulevard exit and head west. Turn south on North Market Street and continue down the hill about one-half mile. Turn west on Quartz Hill Road. Take the second entrance on the left into the park and look for signs indicating the boat ramp. A two-lane paved ramp and rest rooms are available.

Riverfront Park: From Interstate 5 south of Redding, take the Highway 44 west exit and continue to the Auditorium Drive exit. Stay to the right and follow the road behind the Civic Auditorium. The paved boat ramp is to the left of the concrete stage on the right side of the road. Rest rooms are provided.

Facilities, fees: Several full-facility campgrounds and RV parks are located along the river and near adjacent towns. A few good ones are Marina Motor Home Park, Sacramento River Motor Home Park, and Reading Island. A small marina is available at Balls Ferry Fishing Resort. Access to the river and the public ramps is free.

Water sports, restrictions: The river is too cold for swimming and other water/body contact sports.

Contact: Redding Parks and Recreation, (530) 225-4095; Balls Ferry Fishing Resort, (530) 365-8708.

About the Lower Sacramento River: For beginning canoeists the run from Redding downstream to Balls Ferry provides a great introduction to the sport. It's a pretty

Class I stretch, nothing tricky, just good flows for a pleasant paddle. On the 20-mile run, which is an easy half-day shot, you might see plenty of herons, mergansers, and turtles, and sometimes even deer, wild turkeys, and other critters along the riverbank.

To get the most out of this run, put in at Caldwell Park in Redding and take out at Balls Ferry Fishing Resort near Anderson (on the east side of the river). In the summer, river flows are typically 12,500 to 14,000 cubic feet per second, plenty of force to make you feel like your paddle strokes are really moving you along.

After that easy run you may yearn for something with a little sizzle. If so just paddle on. Some 10 miles past Balls Ferry you hit the Nunes Rapids (also known as Iron Canyon Rapids and China Rapids). In this short but swift chute, paddlers need to keep the canoe pointed straight ahead; if the bow starts to drift, you're in big trouble, and boom, over you go. As you blast through the chute, expect water to splash in the boat and on you, and be ready for the canoe to rock like a teeter-totter; dumping frequently occurs.

If you want to bypass the mellow stretch from Redding to Balls Ferry, put in at Balls Ferry and run downstream to Red Bluff. Except for that one rapid, the rest of the run is easy. The water is cold, the temperatures warm from spring through fall, and wildlife is abundant along the river.

This stretch of the Sacramento is also very popular for fishing, with plenty of trout from spring through early summer, and salmon from mid-August through October. Powerboaters should be aware of fluctuating water levels and shallow spots, which is why most boaters remove their propellers and switch to jet drives, despite the reduction in speed. Potentially dangerous obstacles include downed trees, floating debris, and, rarely, rebar from concrete blocks from failed riprap projects.

Some people try inner tubing on the river, but conditions are extremely poor, primarily because the water is so cold that it numbs the feet and because there are few places to stop along the bank. If these things don't bother you, be aware that, according to the law, inner tubers must wear life jackets. County sheriffs patrol the river and will yank violators right out of the water and deposit them on shore, citations in hand.

The river's water level fluctuates a great deal throughout the year. To find out when water is released from Shasta Dam, phone the Shasta Cascade Wonderland Association, (800) 474-2782 or (530) 365-1258.

---

⑰ McCumber Reservoir

Location: East of Redding; map B2, grid i9.

Directions: From Redding drive east on Highway 44 toward Viola, then turn north on Lake McCumber Road and drive two miles to the reservoir. Follow the signs to the boat ramp.

Access: There is a primitive boat launch for cartop boats.

Facilities, fees: A small campground is provided. Day-use access to the lake is free.

Water sports, restrictions: No specific speed limit is enforced here, but speedboating is prohibited. Gas motors are not permitted on the water. Swimming is allowed.

Contact: PG&E Building and Land Services, (916) 386-5164.

About McCumber Reservoir: Lots of folks bypass this little lake that is easy to get to from Redding. They just whiz by in their cars and never take notice. Whoa there. If you put your foot to the brake you'll discover little McCumber Reservoir, elevation 3,500 feet.

McCumber was created when a dam was placed across the North Fork of Battle Creek. Today it is a PG&E-run facility that is open to the public. This is a prime spot for small electric-powered boats, prams, and canoes; gas-powered motors are not permitted.

Swimming is allowed, but there are no beaches. Although the shoreline is pretty muddy, once you get out in the lake the water is clear. All these factors make it ideal for floating around in a raft and enjoying a warm summer day.

Chapter B3
Lassen Area

Overall Rating

1	2	3	4	5	6	7	8	9	10

Poor .... Fair .... Great

B3–Lassen Area Map

One inch equals approximately 10.7 miles.
See page 12 for California state map.

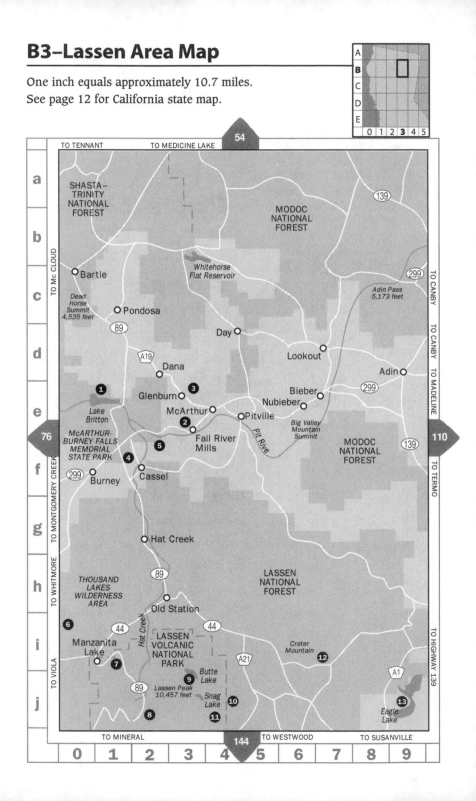

Chapter B3 features:

❶ Lake Britton

Location: Near Fall River Mills in Shasta–Trinity National Forest; map B3, grid e1.

Directions: From Redding drive 56 miles east on Highway 299 to the Highway 89 turnoff. Turn north and drive 10 miles. Turn left on Old Highway Road and drive one mile to the lake, or follow the signs to the campground entrances off Highway 89.

Access: There are boat ramps at the following locations:

Lake Britton: From Highway 89 about four miles north of the state park entrance, look for the "Fishing Access" sign. Turn west and continue to the picnic area and the paved launch ramp.

McArthur–Burney Falls Memorial State Park: Turn into the entrance on Highway 89 and follow the signs to the two-lane paved boat ramp.

North Shore: From Highway 89 about six miles north of the state park entrance, turn west on Clark Creek Road and drive one mile to the North Shore Campground and launch ramp.

Facilities, fees: Campgrounds, picnic areas, and limited supplies are available within McArthur–Burney Falls Memorial State Park. Also within the park is a small marina where you can rent canoes, kayaks, and motorized fishing boats. There is an entrance fee for the state park, and there are additional charges for boat launching at all three ramps.

Water sports, restrictions: Waterskiing and personal watercraft are permitted. A sandy swimming beach is available at McArthur–Burney Falls Memorial State Park; this is also a popular starting point for windsurfers.

Contact: PG&E Building & Land Services, (530) 386-5164 or fax (530) 386-5388; McArthur–Burney Falls Memorial State Park, (530) 335-2777.

About Lake Britton: Do you want the ideal camping/fishing/boating vacation? Lake Britton may be the answer to your prayers. Campgrounds are available on the north shore of the lake, as well as at nearby McArthur–Burney Falls Memorial State Park. Boat ramps provide easy access, and the lake is host to a wide variety of fish species.

Unlike so many lakes, this reservoir is easily accessible. Highway 89 runs right across it, and many people first learn of Lake Britton as they drive over the bridge on their way to or from McArthur–Burney Falls State Park. Burney Falls—a virtual freshwater fountain, 129 feet high—makes an excellent side trip. The peak offers outstanding viewing areas and hiking trails near the falls.

Lake Britton is set at an elevation of 2,700 feet, covering 1,600 acres with 18 miles of shoreline. Its close proximity to McArthur–Burney Falls State Park guarantees heavy use during the summer. Adjacent to the park's boat launch is a top-notch rental service where visitors can rent canoes, kayaks, small fishing boats with motors, and paddleboats.

The water is warm and surrounded by lush forestland, making this a prime spot for waterskiing and swimming. Because getting here requires a long drive, water-skier use is not high, yet it provides a great alternative for boaters who want something more forested and intimate than the giant lakes in the Central Valley foothills. All water sports are permitted; in the spring, when runoff is high, be on the lookout for floating debris.

With emerald green water set in a high-walled granite gorge, the lake headwaters are very pretty. The surrounding landscape is well forested with many giant ponderosa pines, which are best known for their impressive mosaic-like bark.

The hiking trails in this area are excellent. The Pacific Crest Trail runs along Burney Creek, through the park, and then past the dam on its 2,700-mile course to Canada. If you enjoy fishing, take note: the lake has fair prospects for trout and is sometimes excellent for crappie.

❷ Fall River Lake

Location: Near Fall River Mills; map B3, grid e3.
Directions: From Redding drive 69 miles east on Highway 299 to the town of Fall River Mills. Once in town turn left on Long Street and continue to the lake.
Access: A paved launch ramp is located on the southwest side of the lake, adjacent to the picnic area.
Facilities, fees: A picnic area is provided. Supplies can be obtained in Fall River Mills. Access is free.
Water sports, restrictions: Waterskiing and personal watercraft are permitted. A sandy beach for swimming is provided by the day-use area.
Contact: Fall River Valley Chamber of Commerce, (530) 336-5840.
About Fall River Lake: Most out-of-

towners overlook this little reservoir set behind the town of Fall River Mills. It's relatively small, but locals come here to water-ski. They know that the water is warm and conditions are excellent for waterskiing and swimming.

A lakeside picnic area with a few tables and grills is provided adjacent to a beach that makes a good spot for sunbathing and swimming. Again, these are popular hangouts with locals, their secret from the outside world. Fishing here is typically poor; instead, you should just plunk in a canoe and paddle around without a care. The nearest campgrounds are at Crystal Lake and Lake Britton.

❸ Big Lake

Location: Near McArthur; map B3, grid e3.
Directions: From Redding drive 73 miles east on Highway 299 to McArthur. Turn left on Rat Ranch Road and travel about 3.5 miles north to the lake. Note: the dirt road makes for a bumpy ride.
Access: From Rat Ranch Road turn right across a canal to reach the unpaved boat ramp.
Facilities, fees: A picnic area is provided. A boat-in campground is available across the lake at Ahjumawa Lava Springs State Park. Supplies can be obtained in Fall River Mills and McArthur. Access is free.
Water sports, restrictions: There is a 10 mph speed limit on the lake. You can swim near the picnic area.
Contact: Fall River Valley Chamber of Commerce, (530) 336-5840.
About Big Lake: How big is Big Lake? About 150 acres. This is intimate enough for a canoe, yet large enough for a powerboat, though a 10 mph speed limit keeps things relaxing and calm. That's right, no fast boats, no waterskiing, no personal watercraft, just a small, quiet lake with warm water, decent fishing, and lakeside camping. Oh yeah, this

just happens to be the site of one of Northern California's great boat-in campsites.

Although it is a mountain lake, the water is warm most of the year, a surprise for many newcomers who expect a chilly reception. That makes it good for swimming, floating around in a raft, or playing along the shore. Trout fishing is decent in the spring, but by summer anglers switch over to catfish and bass.

④ Baum & Crystal Lakes

⚓ 🚣 🏕️ 🐟   6️⃣

Location: Near Burney; map B3, grid f2.
Directions: From Redding drive 56 miles east on Highway 299. At the junction of Highways 89 and 299, drive two miles northeast on Highway 299 to Cassel Road. Turn right, drive two miles south, then turn left on Hat Creek–Powerhouse Road, and continue to Baum Lake and to adjoining Crystal Lake.
Access: A primitive boat ramp is located off Cassel Road.
Facilities, fees: A picnic area is provided. Cassel Campground is located nearby. Supplies can be obtained in Burney. Access is free.
Water sports, restrictions: Motors are not permitted on either lake. Swimming is not allowed.
Contact: For campground information or a free brochure, contact PG&E Building & Land Services, (916) 386-5164 or fax (916) 386-5388. For fishing information contact Vaughn's Sporting Goods in Burney, (530) 335-2381.
About Baum & Crystal Lakes: Baum (90 acres) and Crystal Lakes (60 acres) are adjoining bodies on Hat Creek that offer extremely limited boating opportunities. In fact this water is used almost entirely for trout fishing.

Motorboats are prohibited here, which limits watercraft to cartop, hand-powered boats, such as canoes and rowboats. Still, there are few of either on the water. Instead what you will see are a number of people fishing from the shore (never swimming, an illegal activity here). For a good side trip, visit the adjacent Crystal Fish Hatchery, which is operated by the Department of Fish and Game.
Special note: Some readers will wonder why this book does not contain a listing for Hat Creek. That is because swimming was banned following several drownings in the river section along Highway 89, where there are several campgrounds. If caught swimming you can be cited and evicted from your campsite. For information about trout fishing at Hat Creek, see the companion Foghorn Press book *California Fishing*.

⑤ Pit River

🏕️ 🐟 ♨️ ✗   7️⃣

Location: Near Fall River Mills; map B3, grid f2.
Directions: From Redding drive 34 miles east on Highway 299. Turn north on Big Bend Road. At the intersection of Big Bend Road and Hagen Flat Road in the town of Big Bend, drive east on Hagen Flat Road. Access is available directly off Hagen Flat Road, near Powerhouses Number 3 and 5 and at several spots in between. Access is also available below the Lake Britton Dam, which is just east of Lake Britton: At the junction of Highways 299 and 89, drive about seven miles north on Highway 299 to Powerhouse Number 1.
Access: There is no boat ramp. The rafting put-in is located just below PG&E Powerhouse Number 1. To get there look for the sign on Highway 299 for Powerhouse Number 1 and for the Bureau of Land Management Campground. Turn into the driveway and continue to the campground (to the right of the tennis courts). Put in below the spillway. Take out a couple of miles downstream on the right just below the Highway 299 bridge or, if you wish to go a little far-

ther, near the dam at Hat Creek. This take-out is logistically a bit more difficult, as it requires hiking with your boat up a small gully.

Facilities, fees: Campgrounds are located at Powerhouse Number 1, Lake Britton, and McArthur–Burney Falls State Park. A few small, primitive Forest Service campgrounds are also available along the river, but they offer no piped water. Supplies can be obtained in Fall River Mills and McArthur. Access is free. Rafting permits are not required.

Water sports, restrictions: The river is generally not suitable for swimming and other water sports. The one exception is adjacent to the hot springs at Big Bend.

Contact: Bureau of Land Management, Redding Field Office, (530) 224-2100; McArthur–Burney Falls Memorial State Park, (530) 335-2777 or fax (530) 335-5483.

About the Pit River: The Pit River is a phenomenon: a series of rivers interspersed by small hydroelectric dams called PG&E powerhouses.

For general recreation the best stretch of river is in the town of Big Bend, where you can relax in hot springs, swim, and fish for trout. The road crosses right over the Pit River here; looking upstream from the bridge, you get a glimpse of prime trout fishing water, while downstream you can view the hot springs and a good swimming hole. Trout fishing is also good below Powerhouse Number 3.

Big Bend Hot Springs provides a series of tiered concrete tubs that overlook the river, perfect for taking a dunk in the steaming mineral water. They also offer access, via a short hike, to a few natural hot spring pools right along the river. Adjacent to the hot springs there's a good swimming hole in the Pit River. The contrast between the 100-degree hot spring water and the 50-degree river water is enough to make you shout uncle.

The Pit River offers rafters a do-it-your-self special, a quality run that is short and obscure. Note that the directions given are for fishing access only; directions for rafting access are detailed under "Access."

The Class II+ run is extremely short, lasting just two to three miles, but is fairly easy and quite pretty. Because the ride is over so fast, few people make the effort, and commercial outfitters never run trips here.

It is best run in a canoe or a kayak, but small rafts and inflatable kayaks can be floated down, too. A key factor, of course, is the flow level, which can be obtained by phoning the Bureau of Land Management, Redding Field Office, (530) 224-2100. Water levels fluctuate depending on powerhouse activity.

❻ North Battle Creek Reservoir

Location: Near Viola; map B3, grid i0.
Directions: From Redding drive east on Highway 44 to Viola and then continue for 3.5 miles. Turn north on Road 32N17, drive five miles, turn left on Road 32N31, and drive four miles. Turn right on Road 32N18 and drive one-half mile to the reservoir.
Access: A primitive boat ramp is available for cartop boats only.
Facilities, fees: A campground is provided. Access to the lake is free.
Water sports, restrictions: Electric motors are permitted on the reservoir, but gas engines are prohibited. Swimming is allowed, but there is no beach.
Contact: PG&E Building & Land Services, (916) 386-5164 or fax (916) 386-5388.
About North Battle Creek Reservoir: A lot of folks bypass this lake. They're too busy and excited en route to Lassen Park on Highway 44. If they just slowed down, they might notice the turnoff for North Battle Creek Reservoir and discover a much less used spot than the nearby national park.

If the campgrounds are crowded at Lassen, what the heck, just roll on over to North Battle Creek Reservoir. The place appeals to vacationing families who are looking for a quiet spot to set up camp near the water.

Swimming is permitted, but there is no formal beach, and the water stays pretty cold through early summer. It's a good choice for cartop boaters, folks who haul in a canoe or rowboat. Most of them bring along a fishing rod and a few dreams of landing a couple of trout while they are here.

7 Manzanita Lake

Location: In Lassen Volcanic National Park; map B3, grid j1.

Directions: From Redding drive east on Highway 44. Manzanita Lake is located just beyond the visitor center on Highway 44 at the western boundary of Lassen Volcanic National Park.

Access: A primitive boat ramp that's suitable only for cartop boats is provided near the campground.

Facilities, fees: A campground and picnic area are provided. Groceries and propane gas can be purchased nearby. There is an entrance fee.

Water sports, restrictions: Motors are not permitted on the lake. Swimming is allowed here.

Contact: Lassen Volcanic National Park, (530) 595-4444; Manzanita Lake Camper Store, (530) 335-7557.

About Manzanita Lake: The centerpiece of Lassen Park is, of course, the old Mount Lassen volcano, and the climb up that beauty is one of the best two-hour (one-way) hikes in California. But Manzanita Lake and its idyllic surroundings also rate high among the park's attractions. In many ways the lake makes an ideal vacation destination.

Because it offers great natural beauty, a location close to Highway 89, and a large, easily accessible campground, Manzanita is the most popular lake in the park. On weekdays, when campground use is low, this place really shines. On busy weekends, though, when it is overrun with campers, it takes on quite a different character. Ah, but with a small boat, you can flee to the safety and sanity of the water and soak in the surroundings until you don't have a care in the world.

Manzanita is small but quite beautiful. Powerboats are not permitted on the lake, making it perfect for a canoe, raft, or pram. The pristine body of water is set at an elevation of 5,890 feet and covers 53 acres.

With 179 sites, the campground adjacent to the lake is Lassen's largest, and you will almost always find a spot there. It is also the easiest to reach, being so near a major entrance to the park.

The lake's prime attraction is trout fishing. There are restrictions mandating catch-and-release and the use of artificials with single barbless hooks. Show up with salmon eggs and Power Bait and you'll get strung up on the yardarm.

Swimming is permitted, but the lake lacks a swimming beach area, and the water is typically very cold until August. While there are no restrictions on windsurfing, you'll rarely see anyone doing this here; there is heavy fishing traffic and most windsurfers don't want to deal with user conflicts. Park rangers, too, want to keep this place serene and pristine.

8 Summit Lake

Location: Near Manzanita Lake in Lassen Volcanic National Park; map B3, grid j2.

Directions: From Redding drive east on Highway 44 to Lassen Volcanic National Park. Continue into the western entrance past the visitor center. From Manzanita Lake drive 12 miles south on Lassen Park Road.

Access: There is no boat ramp. Cartop boats may be hand launched.

Facilities, fees: A campground is provided. Groceries and propane gas can be purchased nearby. There is an entrance fee.

Water sports, restrictions: Motors are not permitted on the lake. Swimming and windsurfing are allowed.

Contact: Lassen Volcanic National Park, (530) 595-4444.

About Summit Lake: One of the best things about this lake is the large campground that's near the water and offers campers their pick of pretty sites. Campers often get a special treat when deer arrive at sunset to explore the meadow near the southeastern shore.

The 15-acre lake is set high in Lassen Volcanic National Park, at 6,695 feet in elevation. There is no boat launch, and if you hand-launch a canoe or other cartop boat, you must carry the craft some distance to reach the water.

Few people swim here, primarily because the water is cold throughout most of the year; every winter it freezes over solid. But because the lake is so small, the water temperature rises more quickly, and despite the high elevation, taking a dip here can be tolerable by midsummer. If your goal is to catch your dinner, forget it; ever since trout plants were suspended in the park, this lake has been largely fished out.

For an easy evening hike, just amble around the lake, making sure to keep an eye out for deer. There's a good chance you'll spot one of these beautiful creatures emerging from the trees to browse.

❾ Butte Lake

Location: South of Burney in Lassen Volcanic National Park; map B3, grid j3.

Directions: From Redding drive east on Highway 44 for 51 miles to the junction with Highway 89. Continue north on Highway 44/ 89 for more than 20 miles to the Susanville/ Reno turnoff. Turn east (still on Highway 44) and drive 11 miles. Turn southwest on Road 18 and drive 10.5 miles to the lake.

Access: A primitive boat ramp near the picnic area is available for cartop boats only.

Facilities, fees: A campground is provided, but is subject to closure. Phone the park in advance to find out the camp's status before you go. There is an entrance fee.

Water sports, restrictions: Motors are not permitted on the lake. Swimming and windsurfing are allowed.

Contact: Lassen Volcanic National Park, (530) 595-4444.

About Butte Lake: Butte Lake has a lot to offer: It is large (212 acres), has a high-mountain setting (6,049 feet elevation), and is beautiful. But because you must access it via an extremely obscure entrance to Lassen Volcanic National Park, most people overlook the place.

It is one of the most remote drive-to lakes in the park and also one of the largest. Butte is very appealing to cartop boaters, especially canoeists, who enjoy paddling around amid the unusual, spectacular scenery.

Hikers are not excluded from the fun. The lake borders some fantastic lava beds to the southwest, and there are trails leading to Snag Lake to the south and Prospect Peak to the west. Another good side trip is the day hike to Bathtub Lake, a fetching little spot.

Butte's size, along with the spring winds that come out of the northwest, makes it a wild card for windsurfing. This can be quite a place to practice the sport, providing you don't mind the long drive in.

The one mind-boggling problem is the campground's ambiguous status: sometimes open, most often closed. That can be a real doozy, so be sure to call ahead.

The area's remote location and lack of reliable camping facilities keep many people away. That in turn makes it a great day-use spot, pretty and private, for visitors who are camping elsewhere.

⑩ Silver Lake

⚓🛶⛺🐟🏊‍♂️ |6|

Location: Near Westwood in Lassen National Forest; map B3, grid j4.

Directions: From Redding drive 29 miles south on Interstate 5 to Red Bluff. Take the Highway 36 exit and drive 83 miles east to the town of Westwood (located east of Lake Almanor). Turn north on County Road A21 and drive 12.5 miles. Turn left on Silver Lake Road and continue to the lake.

Access: An unimproved boat ramp is located near the picnic area. Only cartop boats are permitted.

Facilities, fees: Two campgrounds are provided: Silver Bowl and Rocky Knoll. Supplies can be obtained in Westwood. Access is free.

Water sports, restrictions: Motors are not allowed on the lake. Swimming is permitted.

Contact: Lassen National Forest, Almanor Ranger District, (530) 258-2141 or fax (530) 258-5194.

About Silver Lake: Although Silver Lake is the largest of the little alpine lakes in the region, it is completely dwarfed by Lake Almanor, Mountain Meadows Reservoir, and Butt Valley Reservoir to the south. For that reason many vacationers pass it by.

Silver Lake makes a good first-night camp for an expedition into the adjoining Caribou Wilderness. From here hikers can access routes that will take them to Emerald Lake to the northwest and to Betty, Trail, and Shotoverin Lakes nearby to the southeast. That's right, this lake is primarily used as a jump-off point for a backpacking trip into the wilderness, though it's lovely enough in its own right to warrant a visit.

It is a small and pretty lake, set at 6,500 feet in elevation. That translates to cold water, freezing over in winter, with ice-out usually occurring by June. By then warm summer temperatures make the trout hungry, and the surface water is at least less frigid. With no boat ramp and motors banned from the lake, this is the kind of place where you can haul in a canoe on your rig and have the time of your life, paddling around, fishing for trout, enjoying the scenery, and maybe going for a midday swim. While the lake has no swimming beach, much of the shore slopes gradually. By August the water is warm enough for a dip.

The campgrounds are excellent, and so are the nearby hiking trails. In addition, Caribou Lake (see the next listing) provides a close alternative if you want to hit two lakes in one trip.

⑪ Caribou Lake

⚓🐟🏊‍♂️ |6|

Location: Near Westwood in Lassen National Forest; map B3, grid j4.

Directions: From Redding drive 29 miles south on Interstate 5 to Red Bluff. Take the Highway 36 exit and drive 83 miles east to the town of Westwood (located east of Lake Almanor). Turn north on County Road A21, drive 12.5 miles, then turn left on Silver Lake Road, and continue past Silver Lake to Caribou Lake.

Access: There is no boat ramp. Cartop boats may be hand launched.

Facilities, fees: Campgrounds are available nearby at Silver Lake. Access to the lake is free.

Water sports, restrictions: Motors are not allowed on the lake. Swimming is permitted.

Contact: Lassen National Forest, Almanor Ranger District, (530) 258-2141 or fax (530) 258-5194.

About Caribou Lake: Everyone should fly in an airplane over this area at least once to appreciate it. There are literally dozens of lakes here, most of them pristine little spots that are so quiet you can practically hear the flowers bloom.

Caribou is one you can reach by car rather than by parachute. Because it is set on the edge of the wilderness, it provides a jump-off point for hikes to several other small lakes. These include Jewel, Eleanor, Black, Turnaround, Twin, and Triangle Lakes, which you hit in that order as you venture into the wilderness interior.

Small and intimate Caribou is set at 6,500 feet in elevation, and is similar to nearby Silver Lake (see the previous listing) except without campgrounds, a real shame. Like Silver Lake, this is a good spot for cartop boaters because there is no boat ramp and motors aren't allowed, meaning you can typically have the place all to yourself. The water is cold year-round except for a few weeks from late July through mid-August, the only time when swimming is not just tolerable but exceptional.

⑫ Crater Lake

Location: Near Susanville in Lassen National Forest; map B3, grid j7.

Directions: From Redding drive 60 miles east on Highway 44. At Old Station continue southeast on Highway 44 for 30 miles to the Bogard rest stop, turn north on a Forest Service road, and follow the signs for seven miles to the lake. The road to Crater Lake is unimproved and rough; trailers are not recommended.

Access: A paved boat ramp is located on the lake's east side.

Facilities, fees: A campground and well water are provided. Supplies can be obtained in Susanville. Access is free.

Water sports, restrictions: Motors are not allowed on the lake. Swimming is permitted.

Contact: Lassen National Forest, Almanor Ranger District, (530) 257-2151 or fax (530) 258-5194.

About Crater Lake: Crater Lake Mountain rises just above little Crater Lake, an obscure spot that is set at an elevation of 6,000 feet within Lassen National Forest.

This really is a little lake, just 27 acres. When you consider that there are both a boat ramp and a campground, you would expect it to be quite popular. Nope. Not only is Crater Lake remote, but the access road is quite rough. A lot of people don't want to tangle with the drive just for the opportunity to fish for some small rainbow trout planted by the Department of Fish and Game.

The lake freezes over when winter sets in, and the water stays cold almost year-round. Very few people swim here, even in late summer after days of hot temperatures have made the surface layer at least tolerable.

Those brave souls who don't mind the bumpy access road to the lake are rewarded with a good side-trip option: take the Forest Service road that leads to the top of Crater Lake Mountain and loops around near the summit. From this vantage point you will have a great lookout to the east across a huge expanse of wildlands.

⑬ Eagle Lake

Location: Near Susanville in Lassen National Forest; map B3, grid j9.

Directions: From Red Bluff on Interstate 5, take the Highway 36 exit and head east for 105 miles. Turn north on County Road A1—Eagle Lake Road (three miles west of Susanville) and drive 15.5 miles.

Access: There are three boat ramps:

Eagle Lake Marina: Head north on Eagle Lake Road and follow the signs to the marina, which has a three-lane paved boat ramp.

Spaulding Tract: Head north on Eagle

Lake Road, past the signs for the marina turnoff, to Spaulding Tract on the west side of the lake. The paved ramp is near Eagle Lake RV Park.

Stones Landing: Head north on Eagle Lake Road, past the signs for the marina, to Stones Landing on the north end of the lake. There is a paved ramp.

Facilities, fees: Several campgrounds are provided. Two good ones are Aspen Grove and Merrill. Full marina services, fishing boat rentals, grocery store, coin laundry, and showers are available at Eagle Lake Marina. Access is free.

Water sports, restrictions: Waterskiing and personal watercraft are permitted. Swimming and windsurfing are allowed all around the lake. Gallatin Beach, a developed area near the marina, offers a large, sandy swimming area roped off with buoys for protection.

Contact: Lassen National Forest, Eagle Lake Ranger District, (530) 257-4188 or fax (530) 257-4150; Eagle Lake Marina, (530) 825-3454; Spaulding Tract General Store, (916) 825-2191.

About Eagle Lake: How does a huge lake with massive trout, hot summer temperatures, and lakeside campsites sound to you? Perfect? Hardly.

You see, the wind can really howl at Eagle Lake in the spring and early summer, which quickly results in waves and whitecaps that make boating unpleasant at the least, very dangerous at the worst. If you hit the lake when it is calm, you might want to move here, it is that pretty. But don't pack your bags quite yet.

Every Memorial Day weekend the lake opens to a lot of hoopla, and then windy and often foul weather usually sets in. If you're here in the early summer, the solution is to get out on the lake early before the wind kicks up. Either that or schedule your visit for late summer or early fall when conditions are much calmer.

Eagle Lake is set at 5,100 feet in elevation on the edge of high desert country in northeastern California (hence all the wind, which comes roaring across the plateau). The lake is huge, 27,000 acres and 100 miles of shoreline, yet relatively shallow; it's depth of just 10 to 15 feet in many areas helps the wind quickly whip the water to a froth.

Excellent campgrounds, large trout, and the proximity to Susanville guarantee heavy use all summer. Most visitors tend to congregate around the marina, where there are a beach, Forest Service campgrounds, and picnic areas. As a recreational facility it makes an ideal vacation destination.

Sooner or later, the trout become the most compelling attraction. The strain of Eagle Lake trout averages 18 to 22 inches; that's right, and they'll take a night crawler under a bobber. Fishing is best late in the year just outside the tules at the north end of the lake.

Because of the wind, this is an excellent place for windsurfing and sailing. Just be wary. When the whitecaps are too big to deal with, get off the water. If you hit it during moderate winds, however, you will think you've finally found nirvana.

The lake is so big that there is plenty of room for powerboaters and skiers. Cold water means that only the hardy can stay out for long, however. When the chips are down, you will usually only find a good number of hard-core fishermen in pursuit of their dream trout.

Map of Chapter B3—Page 98   107

Map of Northern California—Page 28

Chapter B4
South Warner Area

Overall Rating

| 1 | 2 | 3 | 4 | 5 | 6 | 7 | 8 | 9 | 10 |

Poor .... Fair .... Great

B4–South Warner Area Map

One inch equals approximately 10.7 miles.
See page 12 for California state map.

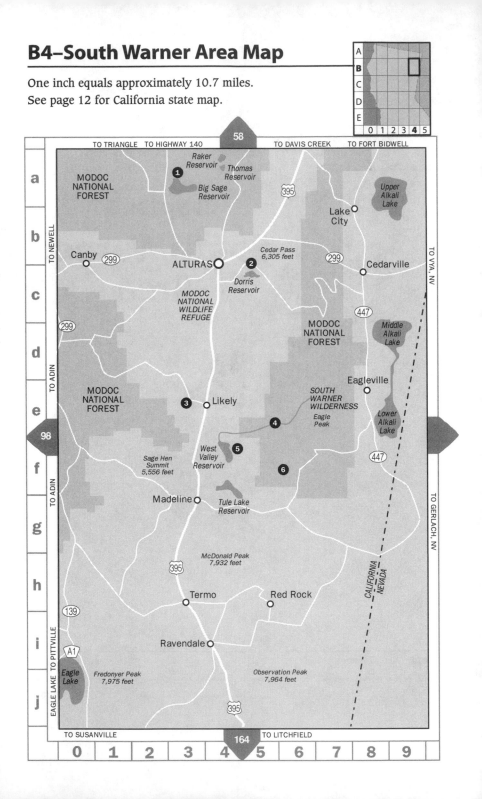

Chapter B4 features:

❶ Big Sage Reservoir

Location: Near Alturas in Modoc National Forest; map B4, grid a3.

Directions: From Alturas drive four miles west on Highway 299. Turn north on Crowder Flat Road and drive six miles; then turn right on the dirt access road (Big Sage Road) and continue to the reservoir.

Access: A paved boat ramp is located near the picnic area.

Facilities, fees: A campground and primitive toilets are provided, but piped water is not available. Access to the lake is free.

Water sports, restrictions: No water sports are available.

Contact: Modoc National Forest, Devil's Garden Ranger District, (530) 233-5811 or fax (530) 233-8709.

About Big Sage Reservoir: Don't be scared off by the dirt road that provides access to this lake. It's smooth enough to trailer a boat over, and it leads to a decent boat ramp and a campground.

The highlight of this reservoir is that there are no restrictions on powerboating and no opportunities for water sports, so if you have a fast boat, you can really let it rip. Despite Big Sage's considerable size, there are typically very few people here. On many days, you might have the place all to yourself. The water gets nice and warm by late summer, and a few islands dotting the waterscape provide habitat for largemouth bass.

Upon arriving in the sparse sagebrush country at elevation 4,900 feet, you will find that Big Sage makes a pretty sight. When you consider that this is the biggest recreational lake in Modoc County, covering 5,400 surface acres, you might think you've really found something special. Well, that's what you get for thinking.

The shoreline is made of clay and mud, and the water is often very murky. Algae growth is usually a problem in midsummer, and by late summer, anybody who tries waterskiing or swimming here will most likely emerge coated in green muck. See ya'.

❷ Dorris Reservoir

Location: Near Alturas in Modoc National Wildlife Refuge; map B4, grid c5.

Directions: From the south end of Alturas, drive about three miles east on Parker Creek Road/County Road 56 until the road forks. Bear right and travel a short distance to the boat ramp, or bear left and continue to the north end of the reservoir.

Access: A primitive boat launch is located on the northwest side of the lake. Note: Due to fluctuating water levels, boating is permitted only from April through September.

Facilities, fees: Campsites are located several miles east of the reservoir, near Cedar Pass. Supplies can be obtained in Alturas. Access is free.

Water sports, restrictions: Waterskiing is permitted from June through September. Swimming is allowed.

Contact: Modoc National Wildlife Refuge, (530) 233-3572 or fax (530) 233-4143.

About Dorris Reservoir: Drive a short way out of Alturas and you will find Dorris Reservoir in the Modoc National Wildlife Refuge, which provides a safe habitat for ducks, geese, and other waterfowl.

The lake is big enough to water-ski on, but boaters should be wary of submerged stumps, which pose serious hazards especially when the lake is not full to the brim. As with many lakes in Modoc County, this one has some problems with water clarity, although you won't encounter anything like the slimy green mess you will elsewhere. Waterskiing, swimming, and other sports involving water contact are legal, but they're not very popular due to the fairly turbid water.

The lake's shoreline is composed more of gravel and sand than mud, which makes the place somewhat appealing for sunbathers and swimmers. Dorris Reservoir is open for day use only—that is, no camping is allowed here—and closes at 8 PM during the summer.

❸ Bayley Reservoir

Location: South of Alturas; map B4, grid e3.

Directions: From the south end of Alturas, drive about two miles south on Centerville Road to Westside Road. Turn left and drive south for 6.5 miles. Turn right on Bayley Reservoir Road and travel 10 miles southwest to the reservoir.

Access: A primitive boat launch is available for cartop boats only.

Facilities, fees: A few primitive campsites are provided, but there is no piped water. Supplies can be obtained in Alturas. Access is free.

Water sports, restrictions: Motors are not allowed on the water. No water sports are permitted here.

Contact: Bureau of Land Management, Eagle Lake Field Office, (530) 257-0456 or fax (530) 257-4831.

About Bayley Reservoir: This lake is way out in the middle of nowhere. What makes it worth seeing? Mainly that it is far away from anything. In fact, the first time I stopped in nearby Likely, which consists of a gas station/store and a cemetery, I asked this old fella at the gas pump why, of all

things, they named the town Likely.

"Because you are likely not to get there," he answered. That's the way they are in Modoc. You're in cow country now, and if you want to have a lake all to yourself, this is the one. The trees are small, there is plenty of chaparral, and there are more trout than people.

But be forewarned that the only thing this lake is good for is paddling around in a boat (no motors allowed) and fishing for trout. Speaking of trout, this lake is stocked with more of 'em than any other in the region.

When you arrive, it's likely that you will not find what you were looking for, just like the man said, because this lake is very small and is often yucky and smelly. A ranger we spoke to told us about the time when while doing some research work, he waded into the lake for a short time, then later on the trip home discovered a terrible rash had broken out all over his legs. No thanks!

❹ Mill Creek

Location: Near Likely in Modoc National Forest; map B4, grid e6.

Directions: From Alturas drive 18.5 miles south on US 395 to the town of Likely. Turn east (left) on Jess Valley Road/County Road 64 and drive east until the road forks. Bear left and follow the road to Mill Creek Falls. Access is available off Forest Service roads near Mill Creek Falls Campground, and also along the numerous trails that lead into the South Warner Wilderness.

Access: There is no boat ramp.

Facilities, fees: A campground is located at Mill Creek Falls. Supplies can be obtained in Likely. Access is free.

Water sports, restrictions: You can swim just downstream of Mill Creek Falls.

Contact: Modoc National Forest, Warner Mountain Ranger District, (530) 279-6116 or fax (530) 279-6107.

About Mill Creek: Mill Creek emerges right out of the South Warner Wilderness, those lonely mountains of the northeast. The best strategy for a good trip is to go sight-seeing at Mill Creek Falls, then head onward, park at Soup Springs Camp, and hike into the South Warner Wilderness along the creek's pretty headwaters.

The waterfall is beautiful, and it has far more power than most people realize. Do not try to swim there or explore too closely on the adjacent rocks, which are slippery. Enjoy the view, move on, and get ready for more fun.

And you will have fun when you follow the trail over the hill and into the valley floor, where Mill Creek awaits. The product of snowmelt, the creek water is cold, making swimming (actually more like a taking a dunk) impossible until late in the summer, when the water flows slower and warms up a bit. Early in the summer, it is so cold that all you can do is have contests with your hiking friends to see who can keep their feet in the stream the longest.

Pretty, pristine, and calm, Mill Creek is primarily a wilderness fishing stream, a great place to take a relaxing hike. When you're ready to rest a spell, dunk your feet in the water and enjoy the quiet paradise.

⑤ West Valley Reservoir

Location: Near Likely; map B4, grid f4.
Directions: From Alturas drive 18.5 miles south on US 395 to the town of Likely. Turn east (left) on Jess Valley Road/County Road 64 and drive two miles. To reach the west side of the lake where the boat ramp and campgrounds are, turn right at the sign for West Valley Reservoir and drive four miles south. The north end of the lake can be accessed via a short road off Jess Valley Road.
Access: To reach the paved boat ramp,

turn right at the sign for West Valley Reservoir and drive four miles south.
Facilities, fees: A few unimproved campsites are provided, along with water and toilets. Supplies can be obtained in Likely. Access is free.
Water sports, restrictions: Waterskiing and personal watercraft are permitted. Windsurfing and swimming are also allowed.
Contact: Bureau of Land Management, Alturas Field Office, (530) 233-4666 or fax (530) 233-5696.

About West Valley Reservoir: Nothing is perfect, but in Modoc County, West Valley Reservoir will have to do.

If you come on a calm, warm day, this is one of the better choices in the entire region. West Valley Reservoir provides good access, has a quality boat ramp, and usually fills up during the winter with runoff from the South Fork Pit River.

In the hot summer months, the place is ideal for swimming, with warm water and a gravelly shore. Summers are also great for windsurfing, good for waterskiing and personal watercraft, and fair for trout fishing.

The lake is set at 4,770 feet, covers 970 surface acres, and has seven miles of shoreline. A great bonus is that boat-in camping is permitted anywhere along the shore, a do-it-yourself affair with no resorts, marinas, or facilities of any kind.

This lack of facilities, as well as the long drive most people have to undertake to get here, keeps most boaters away. Those who do come find that West Valley makes a good alternative destination with plenty of room, few boats, and warm water.

Windsurfers will be thrilled to find that the lake is exceptionally suited to their sport. Perched on the edge of the great basin and the high desert, the location is perfect for catching prevailing winds in the spring and early summer.

Unfortunately, sometimes it is too perfect. In the spring whipping winds can churn the lake into a froth, making conditions extremely hazardous for boaters; there have been several accidents. Some boaters claim that ghosts of past accident victims hover overhead.

Other problems to be aware of: By late summer it is advised that you call ahead and check the water level at the reservoir. During that time of year, the reservoir is often drained to very low levels to supply local ranchers with water. Finally, it gets really cold in the winter. Up here on the Modoc Plateau, temperatures often dip to around zero degrees Fahrenheit for several weeks starting in mid-December, and this lake freezes hard.

❻ Blue Lake

Location: Near Likely in Modoc National Forest; map B4, grid f6.

Directions: From Alturas drive 18.5 miles south on US 395 to the town of Likely. Turn east (left) on Jess Valley Road/County Road 64 and drive nine miles, until the road forks. Bear right, travel seven miles on Blue Lake Road; then turn right at the signed turnoff and continue to the lake.

Access: A paved boat ramp is located next to the picnic area on the north end of the lake.

Facilities, fees: A campground and a picnic area are provided. Supplies can be obtained in Likely. Access is free.

Water sports, restrictions: Waterskiing, personal watercraft, swimming, and windsurfing are permitted.

Contact: Modoc National Forest, Big Valley Ranger District, (530) 299-3215 or fax (530) 299-3210.

About Blue Lake: Shaped like an egg and rimmed by trees, this is one pretty lake. Bordering on pristine, it is one of the most attractive lakes you can reach on a paved road in northeastern California, and makes an ideal vacation site for campers, boaters, hikers, and anglers.

Despite being located so near to the South Warner Wilderness, Blue Lake's access is quite good, with a paved road that leads all the way to the northeast shore. The campground has an attractive setting, will accommodate RVs, and is close to a good boat ramp.

With the surrounding landscape and clear water, the lake has great appeal for all water sports enthusiasts, although it is typically on the cold side until mid-July. Of the lakes in Modoc County that are decent for waterskiing, this one edges out West Valley as the best. The shoreline is a gravel/sand mix, not mud, which makes it good for wading or just horsing around.

A good hiking trail that is routed around the lake and a wheelchair-accessible fishing platform are two good touches. Trout fishing is only fair, but the fish here are often larger than at other lakes in the region. In addition, you have the chance to make a great side trip to nearby Mill Creek Falls, which most local campers consider a must-see destination.

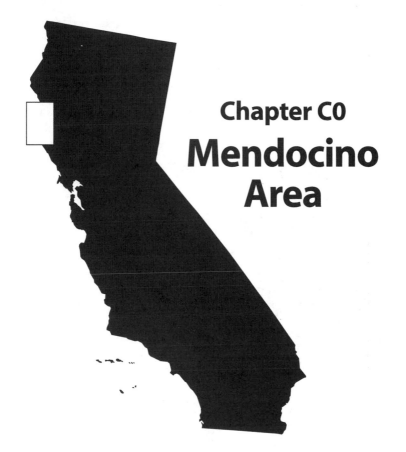

Chapter C0
Mendocino Area

Overall Rating

1	2	3	4	5	6	7	8	9	10

Poor .... Fair .... Great

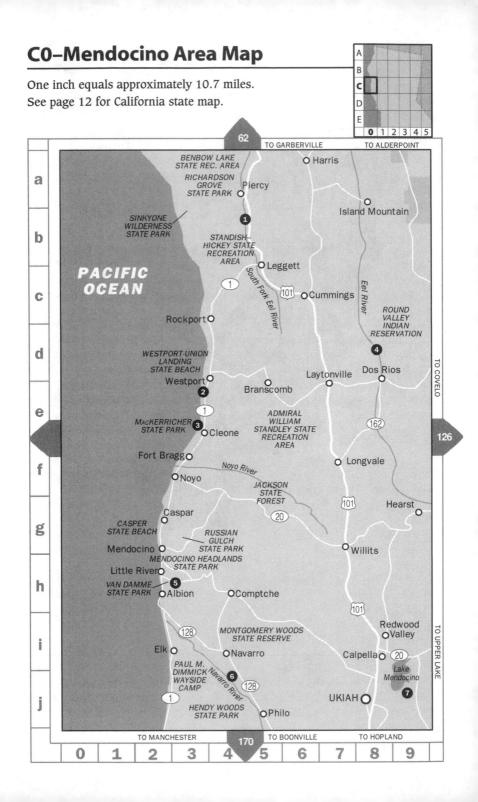

C0–Mendocino Area Map

One inch equals approximately 10.7 miles.
See page 12 for California state map.

PACIFIC OCEAN

TO GARBERVILLE
TO ALDERPOINT

62

BENBOW LAKE STATE REC. AREA

Harris

RICHARDSON GROVE STATE PARK

Piercy

Island Mountain

SINKYONE WILDERNESS STATE PARK

STANDISH–HICKEY STATE RECREATION AREA

Leggett

Cummings

Eel River

ROUND VALLEY INDIAN RESERVATION

Rockport

WESTPORT-UNION LANDING STATE BEACH

Westport

Branscomb

Laytonville

Dos Rios

MACKERRICHER STATE PARK

Cleone

ADMIRAL WILLIAM STANDLEY STATE RECREATION AREA

126

Fort Bragg

Noyo

Noyo River

JACKSON STATE FOREST

Longvale

Hearst

Caspar

CASPER STATE BEACH

RUSSIAN GULCH STATE PARK

Willits

Mendocino

MENDOCINO HEADLANDS STATE PARK

Little River

VAN DAMME STATE PARK

Albion

Comptche

Redwood Valley

MONTGOMERY WOODS STATE RESERVE

Calpella

Elk

Navarro

PAUL M. DIMMICK WAYSIDE CAMP

Navarro River

Lake Mendocino

UKIAH

HENDY WOODS STATE PARK

Philo

TO MANCHESTER
TO BOONVILLE
TO HOPLAND

170

TO COVELO

TO UPPER LAKE

South Fork Eel River

❶ South Fork Eel River

Location: North of Leggett; map CØ, grid c6.

Directions: From the San Francisco Bay Area, drive north on US 101 to Leggett. Continue north on US 101. Fishing access is excellent near the Smithe Redwoods State Reserve at Bridges Creek and Dora Creek, and near Standish-Hickey State Recreation Area, off the South Leggett exit. Access is also available off the Highway 271 exit (four-wheel drive is advisable here).

Access: No boat ramp is available. There are two standard put-ins:

Wilderness Lodge: From US 101 at Laytonville, turn west on Branscomb Road and drive approximately 17 miles, through Branscomb, to Wilderness Lodge Road. Turn north and continue to the lodge at the end of the road. The put-in is adjacent to the lodge. Note: The first 10 miles of this run are Class II, but at the confluence with Tenmile Creek, boaters will run into South Fork Gorge, a Class V, experts-only run. There is no feasible take-out upstream of the gorge.

Black Oak Ranch: This put-in is actually on Tenmile Creek, on which you can descend to meet the South Fork Eel. To get there, look for the sign indicating Black Oak Ranch on the west side of US 101 north of Laytonville. The creek is directly off the highway, and access is limited to a wide spot in the road. Parking here is risky, and shuttling is highly recommended (see "Contact" below). Note: This run, from the put-in through South Fork Gorge is Class V and for experts only.

Facilities, fees: Several campgrounds are located along the river on US 101, including Rock Creek, Standish-Hickey, and Redwood River Retreat. Supplies can be obtained in Leggett, Laytonville, and Piercy. Access is free except at the state parks, where an entrance fee is charged. Rafting permits are not required.

Water sports, restrictions: Excellent swimming holes and riverside beaches can be found at Richardson Grove State Park and Standish-Hickey State Recreation Area.

Contact: Richardson Grove State Park, (707) 247-3318 or fax (707) 247-3300; Standish-Hickey State Recreation Area, (707) 925-6482; Big Bend Lodge, (707) 984-6321. For guided river trips contact Aurora River Adventures, (800) 562-8475 or (530) 629-3843, or ask at Big Bend Lodge about local guides. Note: For a small fee the folks at Big Bend Lodge will sometimes provide shuttles to the Tenmile Creek put-in.

About the South Fork Eel River: Like a chameleon the South Fork Eel is always changing, both in color and character. In its appeal to the public, the shifts tend to be even more dramatic.

Most visitors see the South Fork Eel in the summer while vacationing in the Redwood Empire. They cruise on US 101 right alongside the river as it runs north from Leggett, through Cooks Valley, past Benbow, and into Richardson Grove State Park. At this time of year, the river slows to a warm trickle, interrupted with the occasional deep pool that's ideal for swimming. A bottom scraper all the way, this river is really out of the question for canoeing, kayaking, and rafting. Instead, a favorite activity here is a picnic along the rock-strewn banks, possibly followed by a dip in one of the swimming holes. The best and most easily accessible holes are found near

Richardson Grove State Park and Standish-Hickey State Recreation Area.

As you motor down US 101 in this area, you will eventually spot one of the "High Water Mark" signs along the roadside. Trying to imagine the river running that high, way over the highway, is inconceivable to most people. But it did indeed swell that high in the winter of 1962, which should tell you everything you need to know about how much the character of this river can change. Remember the chameleon.

To understand how such changes can be wrought, you must know that in the winter it doesn't just rain here, it pours and can just keep on pouring. Hey, why do you think the trees grow so tall? Well, before long the ground becomes saturated and the storm runoff streams right into the South Fork Eel. After a day or two of nonstop rain, the river becomes very muddy, then starts to rise. As the deluge continues, the river keeps on climbing, swelling bank to bank with cold, brown water that is running high, fast, and powerful on its northward course to the Pacific Ocean.

Even expert kayakers shudder to think what would happen if their little plastic boats were to get wrapped around a boulder in such conditions. Right, this is no river to tangle with.

The best time to run this river is when the high water is receding and the green color is beginning to return. This occurs primarily in late winter and early spring, when there are significant breaks in the storm pattern and rain. Even then beginners need not apply.

To get the most out of the run, use the put-in at Wilderness Lodge (see "Access"), and meander down the 10-mile Class II run to the South Fork Gorge. This, however, is only a warm-up. Once you head downstream, there are no take-outs above the gorge, which means you are committed to going all the way. In high water this would be suicide. Even in moderate water flows,

kayakers are right out there on the edge of life and death. That's what Class V is all about. There are so many tricks and turns, suckholes and boulders, chutes and swallows, and its makeup changes so often according to river height, that few attempt the run.

The skilled and ambitious souls who do take the risk will find themselves guided downstream surrounded by forest and vegetation, and with it a sense of lush isolation. The stretch from Wilderness Lodge at Branscomb is particularly beautiful. Once you hit the gorge, though, you will no longer notice your surroundings. You won't have time. Also, enjoying the Class II portion is difficult, knowing that the overbearing shadow of the Class V gorge looms ahead. **Special note:** The South Fork Eel may be subject to emergency fishing closures if flows are below prescribed levels needed to protect migrating salmon and steelhead. For a recorded message detailing the status of coastal streams, phone the Department of Fish and Game, (707) 442-4502.

---

❷ Ten Mile River

Location: North of MacKerricher State Park; map C0, grid e3.

Directions: From Fort Bragg drive three miles north on Highway 1 to MacKerricher State Park. Ten Mile River is located at the park's north end, and is accessible by driving east on Camp 1 Ten Mile Road or south on Camp 2 Ten Mile Road.

Access: No boat ramp is available. There is no standard put-in, but boaters with small craft (canoes or kayaks) may park at the bridge and put in at the beach at the river's mouth.

Facilities, fees: Campgrounds are provided at MacKerricher State Park. Supplies can be obtained in Fort Bragg. Access is free. Rafting permits are not required.

Water sports, restrictions: You can swim near the beach at the river's mouth.

Contact: MacKerricher State Park, (707) 937-5804 or fax (707) 937-2953.

About the Ten Mile River: Little Ten Mile River starts in the mountains just north of Bucha Ridge and tumbles some 20 miles on its short journey to the Pacific Ocean. In the winter when fierce coastal squalls pound the ridge, water rushes down the canyon, forming this stream.

Only a tiny stretch of the river, from the mouth on upstream for a few miles, is appropriate for canoeing or kayaking and swimming. The river narrows here and runs slowly most of the year, creating conditions that are suitable only for canoes and kayaks. Easy access is the big plus. Farther upstream the Ten Mile cuts through private property, and the riverbanks are smothered by thick brush.

Most people playing in the lower river are doing so as a side trip from another destination, usually MacKerricher State Park. MacKerricher is a great park, boasting a beautiful beach, outstanding walks, lookout for viewing harbor seals, small freshwater lake (see the next listing) with trout fishing, and excellent campgrounds, including great walk-in campsites. Day-use access is free at MacKerricher, which is an extreme rarity for a state park.

---

❸ Cleone Lake

⌈6⌉

Location: North of Fort Bragg in MacKerricher State Park; map CØ, grid e3.

Directions: From Fort Bragg drive three miles north on Highway 1 to MacKerricher State Park. The lake is located in the park.

Access: There is no boat ramp, but cartop boats may be hand launched.

Facilities, fees: MacKerricher State Park provides a campground. Supplies can be obtained in Fort Bragg. Day use is free.

Water sports, restrictions: Motors are

not permitted on the lake. Swimming is allowed.

Contact: MacKerricher State Park, (707) 937-5804 or fax (707) 937-2953.

About Cleone Lake: Cleone Lake is one of the few lakes in the state that is actually located west of Highway 1, nestled in a little pocket between the highway and Laguna Point. Along with the surrounding MacKerricher State Park, the lake makes an ideal destination for a weekend vacation.

Although small, the lake is gorgeous, bordered by tules on one side, forest on another, and opening to the coast on the west (the ocean is about 100 yards away). A parking area and rest room are available right next to the lake. This is where visitors can hand launch their cartop boats; canoes, rafts, prams, and the like are recommended. From the shoreline, anglers fish for trout, which are stocked by the Department of Fish and Game.

The grassy shoreline on the northwest side makes getting in and out of the water a snap, but few people swim here. The water is too cold most of the year because summers are foggy and the lake never gets a chance to heat up.

Rather, Cleone Lake holds more appeal for hikers, offering a great short trail around its circumference, much of it on a raised wooden walkway that passes in some spots like a tunnel through the lush greenery. Other great hikes at MacKerricher include one that leads to a harbor seal viewing area and tide pools. Camping is also excellent here, especially at the walk-in campsites.

---

❹ Eel River

⌈8⌉

Location: Longvale to Alderpoint; map CØ, grid e8.

Directions: From US 101 at Longvale, turn east on Highway 162 and drive northeast. The highway parallels the river, and direct access is available.

Access: There is no boat ramp. The put-in is at the small town of Dos Rios. If you're approaching from US 101 southbound, turn east at Laytonville onto Laytonville–Dos Rios Road and drive approximately 15 miles to Dos Rios. The road is narrow and winding. If you're coming northbound on US 101, turn east on Highway 162 at Longvale and continue northeast to Dos Rios. Put in below the Eel River Bridge. Take out 45 miles downstream at Alderpoint.

Facilities, fees: Campgrounds are located along US 101, and there are a few primitive spots along the river north of Dos Rios. Access is free. Rafting permits are not required.

Water sports, restrictions: A few swimming holes are located off Highway 162, but they may be difficult to access. Several sandbars north of Dos Rios provide opportunities for sunbathing and swimming; however, they are accessible only by raft or boat.

Contact: Bureau of Land Management, Arcata Field Office, (707) 825-2300. For guided rafting trips contact Aurora River Adventures, (800) 562-8475 or (530) 629-3843, or Big Bend Lodge, (707) 984-6321.

About the Eel River: A handful of rafters and campers are going to cringe when they read this. They are going to be filled with worry that a once secret and stellar run will become known to all. But fear not, because this place is too remote. It requires skills in wilderness camping and intermediate boating, and most people just don't have the time, equipment, and talent to make the trip.

Those that do, get what they deserve—a 45-mile run from Dos Rios to Alderpoint. The run has everything going for it: seclusion (there are practically no access roads along the route), beauty (set in a gorgeous canyon that's forested on both sides), great camping (at several good beaches on the banks), and a stretch of water just challenging enough to keep things interesting.

With a Class II–III rating, the run is doable in an inflatable kayak as well as rafts and hard-shell kayaks. Canoeists must be skilled and experienced, as there are many trick eddies that can turn and flip a canoe. In any case, make sure that all your gear is waterproof and strapped in tight as you'll most likely need your warm clothes.

Unpredictable water flows and weather are the biggest problems on the Middle Fork Eel. For the most part the best time to run is in March, although cold temperatures (for the Humboldt coast) can sap the energy from some boaters, particularly if you get wet weather on your trip. By April this run is largely a goner, and by May and June the flows become more like a dribble, rendering the river unrunnable. If you try to make the trip before March, downpours can be a problem; it can rain, rain, and keep on raining to the point that you might consider boarding an ark instead of an inflatable.

Special note: The Eel River is subject to emergency fishing closures if flows are below the prescribed levels needed to protect migrating salmon and steelhead. For a recorded message detailing the status of coastal streams, phone the Department of Fish and Game, (707) 442-4502. Also note that the main stem Eel is subject to special regulations, which may be changed on a yearly basis.

---

❺ Albion River

Location: South of Mendocino; map C∅, grid h2.

Directions: From Mendocino drive 5.5 miles south on Highway 1 to the town of Albion. At the north side of the bridge, turn left (south). Go about one-quarter mile to the bottom of the hill, take another left at the "Campground" sign, and drive to the harbor.

Access: A paved boat ramp is located at Schooner's Landing.

Facilities, fees: A campground and a dock are available at Schooner's Landing. More campsites, gas, and groceries are available nearby. Access is free. There is a charge for boat launching.

Water sports, restrictions: The water is too cold for swimming and other water sports. Canoeists may put in at the boat ramp and paddle upstream.

Contact: Schooner's Landing, (707) 937-5707; Noyo Harbor District, (707) 964-4719 or fax (707) 964-4710.

About the Albion River: A lot of people with trailered boats bypass this area because they do not realize that there is a boat ramp. Well, there is. If you are touring along the coast, a stop here can add the missing piece to your vacation puzzle.

The area in the vicinity of Schooner's Landing is well protected, making it a good launch site for trailered boats. With campgrounds on grassy sites and full hookups available for RVs, this is an ideal base camp for a multiday trip.

A great plus is the short cruise to the fishing grounds. Most boaters head around Albion Head to the north, then make a left turn, and cruise around Salmon Point to the south. There are good chances you'll catch rockfish here, and salmon often school in this area in midsummer.

If you do not wish to venture to the ocean, another option is to canoe in the lower river. It is more like a lagoon, with the tidal forces extending about three miles upstream, providing a great little day paddle.

Because this is a coastal environment, temperatures stay in the 50s throughout the year. It is too cold for water sports unless you don a wet suit. However, this stretch of the Mendocino coast is exceptional for snorkeling and abalone diving. There are dozens of secluded spots along the coast that have giant rocks set in sheltered tidal lagoons, perfect grounds for snorkeling.

The ocean is within walking distance of Schooner's Landing, which has a good beach for beachcombing. Wear heavy or layered clothing because the weather is typically foggy or windy.

---

❻ Navarro River

Location: South of Mendocino; map CØ, grid j5.

Directions: From Mendocino drive 10 miles south on Highway 1. Turn left on Highway 128 and drive east. The highway parallels the lower river. Fishing is permitted from the river mouth to Greenwood Road Bridge. Access the upper river through Hendy Woods State Park, located off Highway 128.

Access: There is no boat ramp. Canoeists and kayakers can put in at the junction of Highway 128 and Mountain View Road in Boonville, which is about eight miles east of Hendy Woods State Park on Highway 128. You can boat all the way to the mouth of the river, but standard take-outs are located at Hendy Woods State Park and Paul Dimmick State Park.

Facilities, fees: You'll find campgrounds at both Hendy Woods State Park and Paul Dimmick State Park. Supplies can be obtained in Mendocino. Access is free. Rafting permits are not required.

Water sports, restrictions: Several good swimming spots are located along Highway 128; one of the best, at Iron Bridge (mile marker 3.66), offers a sandy beach and deep swimming hole.

Contact: Hendy Woods State Park, (707) 895-3141 or fax (707) 895-2012; Fort Bragg–Mendocino Coast Chamber of Commerce, (707) 961-6300 or fax (707) 964-2056.

About the Navarro River: Highway 128 follows the river all the way to the ocean, providing visitors easy access and a good look at conditions.

In the spring and summer months, this river gets very heavy use. It is excellent for swimming in the summer, when the water heats up a little and the rafters have departed for the season. Many pullouts along Highway 128 offer access to short trails routed to the river, with dozens of great picnic spots along the way.

While the river is too narrow and brushy for large rafts, it is great for beginners in canoes, inflatable kayaks, and hard-shell kayaks. Class I+ all the way, you'll have a relatively easy paddle no matter what stretch of water you choose.

One favorite starts at Hendy Woods State Park, from where it takes four hours to get downstream to Paul Dimmick State Park and another two to reach the mouth of the river. Time it so you hit an outgoing tide on the lower river and you'll have an easy ride all the way. The route is very pretty, graced with a variety of riparian vegetation throughout; some stretches feature redwood forest.

---

❼ Lake Mendocino

Location: Near Ukiah; map CØ, grid j9.
Directions: From the San Francisco Bay Area, drive north on US 101 to the junction with Highway 20, about 4.5 miles north of Ukiah. Turn east on Highway 20 and travel three miles to the lake entrance road. Turn right and continue to the lake.
Access: There are two boat ramps:

Che-Ka-Ka Picnic Area: From US 101 take the Lake Mendocino Drive exit and head east to the paved ramp, which is located near the Che-Ka-Ka picnic area.

Ky-en Campground: From Highway 20 take the Marina Drive exit and follow the signs to the marina, which has a multilane paved ramp.
Facilities, fees: A full-service marina, campgrounds, groceries, snack bar, boat

fuel, and picnic areas are available. Three boat-in campgrounds are located on the east side of the lake. Powerboats, pontoon boats, ski boats, canoes, and fishing boats can be rented at the Lake Mendocino Marina. Full services and supplies can be obtained in Ukiah. Access is free. There is a fee for boat launching.
Water sports, restrictions: Waterskiing, personal watercraft, and windsurfing are permitted. A sandy swimming area roped off with buoys for protection is available in the Pomo Day-use Area.
Contact: US Army Corps of Engineers, Lake Mendocino, (707) 462-7581 or fax (707) 462-3372; Lake Mendocino Marina, (707) 485-8644 or fax (707) 485-7081.
About Lake Mendocino: Quite a transformation has occurred at Lake Mendocino. At one time this was a quiet place, with little boating traffic and few campers, lost in the shadow of Clear Lake to the east. Apparently more and more boaters are becoming enamored with it each year, and now the campgrounds sometimes fill up, the lake is abuzz with ski boats, and the swimming beach is sprinkled with lots of happy folks.

The lake is set at 750 feet in elevation in the foothill country east of Ukiah, covers 1,750 acres, and has 15 miles of shoreline. It is a major destination point for boater and campers, especially families who appreciate the warm, clear water, and the easy access (compared to Clear Lake).

One treat is that there are excellent opportunities to windsurf, especially in May and June, when the weather is warm, yet the wind is coming out of the northwest—the perfect combination. Once school is out in June, waterskiing activity picks up, especially on weekends, and windsurfers have to be on a constant lookout.

Another bonus is an excellent swimming beach, which is adjacent to such amenities as a snack bar and rest room. Swimmers and waders should not stray too far from the primary beach area because Lake Mendocino is the home of the man-biting catfish. One summer several swimmers were actually chomped quite severely on their legs, leaving large red welts. You see, Fish and Game placed several "catfish condominiums" in the lake. Catfish hole up in these little homes, and when a wader steps too close—wham! They get nailed. Strange, but true.

Map of Northern California—Page 28

Chapter C1
Yolla-Bolly
Area

Overall Rating

| 1 | 2 | 3 | 4 | 5 | 6 | 7 | 8 | 9 | 10 |

Poor .... Fair .... Great

C1–Yolla-Bolly Area Map

One inch equals approximately 10.7 miles.
See page 12 for California state map.

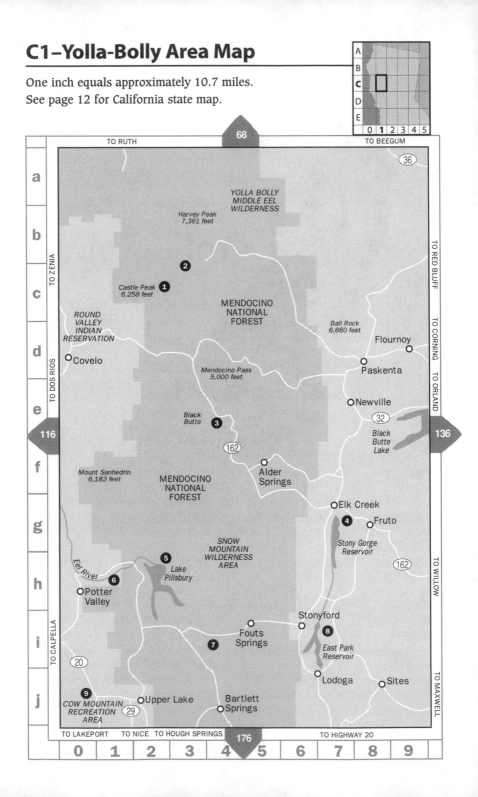

Chapter C1 features:

1 Howard Lake

Location: Near Covelo in Mendocino National Forest; map C1, grid c3.

Directions: From the San Francisco Bay Area, drive north on US 101 about 12 miles past Willets. From the junction of US 101 and Highway 162, drive northeast on Highway 162 about 34 miles (one mile past Covelo). Turn right onto Highway 162 East and drive 13 miles to the Eel River Bridge. Turn left at the bridge and continue 11 miles northeast on Forest Service Road M1/Indian Dick Road to Little Doe Campground. Turn left and drive six miles to the lake.

Access: A primitive boat ramp for cartop boats only is located on the northwest side of the lake.

Facilities, fees: The Little Doe Campground is available just north of the lake. Piped water is not provided, so bring your own. Supplies can be obtained in Covelo. Access is free.

Water sports, restrictions: Motors are not permitted on the lake. Swimming is allowed.

Contact: Mendocino National Forest, Covelo Ranger District, (707) 983-6118 or fax (707) 983-8004.

About Howard Lake: Little Howard Lake is tucked deep in the interior of Mendocino National Forest between Espee Ridge to the south and Little Doe Ridge to the north. For a drive-to lake, it is surprisingly remote and provides good fishing and primitive camping.

Set at an elevation of 3,500 feet, it covers about 15 or 20 acres. As you might have guessed, this is not a big water-recreation destination. Instead, this is a pretty, remote spot that you can paddle your canoe around in, perhaps trying to catch a trout now and then. By early June the water is usually warm enough for swimming, but the shoreline is a little muddy and it is rare to see people taking a dip. While there is no campground at the lake, there are a few camps nearby in the surrounding Mendocino National Forest.

2 Hammerhorn Lake

Location: Near Covelo in Mendocino National Forest; map C1, grid c3.

Directions: From the San Francisco Bay Area, drive north on US 101 about 12 miles past Willets. Turn northeast on Highway 162 and drive about 13 miles (one mile past Covelo). Turn right on Highway 162 East and continue 13 miles to the Eel River Bridge. Turn left at the bridge and drive about 17 miles northeast on Forest Service Road M1/Indian Dick Road to Hammerhorn Lake.

Access: There is no boat ramp. Cartop boats may be hand launched.

Facilities, fees: A small, primitive campground is provided. Supplies can be obtained in Covelo. The lake has two wheelchair-accessible piers. Access is free.

Water sports, restrictions: Motors are not allowed on the lake. Swimming is permitted.

Contact: Mendocino National Forest, Covelo Ranger District, (707) 983-6118 or fax (707) 983-8004.

About Hammerhorn Lake: A veritable

dot of a lake at just five acres, Hammerhorn is more like a mountain pond set at an elevation of 3,500 feet in remote Mendocino National Forest. Despite the small size there are a few factors that make the place special: the lake is quite pretty, there is a campground, and the location is near the border of the Yolla-Bolly Wilderness.

There is no boat ramp, of course (after all, it's only five acres), but small cartop boats and inflatables can be launched by hand. That is exactly what some campers do, possibly tossing out a line for trout, though the lake's population of hardhead shiners has cut into fishing success. The lake is warm enough for swimming by mid-June, but few people make it out here just to take a dip.

The place typically attracts the hiking crowd. Backpackers will make the drive into the Mendocino wildlands and camp here before heading off the next day for a trip into the Yolla-Bolly Wilderness; a trailhead is located nearby to the northeast.

❸ Plaskett Lakes

Location: Northwest of Willows in Mendocino National Forest; map C1, grid e4.

Directions: From Sacramento drive 90 miles north on Interstate 5 to Willows. Turn west on Highway 162 and drive toward the town of Elk Creek. Just after you cross the Stony Creek Bridge, turn north on Road 306 and drive four miles. Turn left on Alder Springs Road, drive 31 miles, and then turn left over the final piece of rough road to reach the lakes. Trailers over 16 feet long are not recommended.

Access: There is no boat ramp. Cartop boats may be hand launched.

Facilities, fees: Two campgrounds and a picnic area are provided. Supplies can be obtained in Elk Creek. Access is free.

Water sports, restrictions: Motors are not permitted on the lake. Swimming is allowed.

Contact: Mendocino National Forest, Grindstone Ranger District, (530) 934-3316 or fax (530) 934-1212.

About Plaskett Lakes: Plaskett Lakes are a pair of connected dot-size mountain lakes that form the headwaters of little Plaskett Creek. They are difficult to reach, located at the end of a rough road out in the middle of nowhere.

The lakes are set at an elevation of 6,000 feet. They cover just three and four acres and get very light use. You'll typically find just a few people out here floating around in rafts and fishing for trout. Swimming is not recommended because the lake bottoms are mucky and your feet will sink into the ooze when you enter and leave the water.

But the area is pretty, gets little traffic, and is remote—the nearest town is 35 miles away. There are good opportunities for hiking (one trail is routed along Plaskett Creek) and a number of Forest Service roads (the best in the area is routed up Chimney Rock).

❹ Stony Gorge Reservoir

Location: Near Elk Creek; map C1, grid g7.

Directions: From Sacramento drive 90 miles north on Interstate 5 to Willows. Turn west on Highway 162, drive about 15 miles, turn left at the signed entrance, and continue one mile to the reservoir.

Access: A paved boat ramp is located on the northeast side of the lake at Skipper's Point.

Facilities, fees: Three campgrounds and two picnic areas are provided, but there is no piped water, so bring your own. Limited supplies can be obtained in Elk Creek. Access is free.

Water sports, restrictions: Waterskiing, personal watercraft, windsurfing, and swimming are permitted. A beach is available at Skipper's Point.

Contact: Bureau of Reclamation, Mid-Pacific Construction Office, (530) 934-7066 or fax (530) 934-1302.

About Stony Gorge Reservoir: If only the Bureau of Reclamation made recreation a top priority at Stony Gorge Reservoir, this place would have a chance of being something special.

This is a long, narrow lake set in a canyon, with an elevation of 800 feet, 1,300 surface acres, and 25 miles of shoreline. A classic foothill reservoir, it gets hot weather and experiences summer water drawdowns. The setting is fairly pretty, and all boating and water sports are permitted. In the spring when the lake is full, the water is starting to warm up, and the surrounding hills are green, you might think you've really found something.

Other than the boat ramp and vault toilets, there are no developed facilities of any kind, not even potable water. A marina? Gas? A bait shop? You've got to be kidding.

In the late spring, conditions are excellent for waterskiing and swimming, with swimmers congregating at a beach near the boat ramp. Then summer arrives and puts an end to all the festivities.

The Bureau of Reclamation virtually gives the water away at subsidized prices to farmers, and by June, the lake level starts dropping rapidly. Most years the launch ramp is unusable by summer, and even if you do manage to get a boat in the water, you will have to negotiate lots of underwater hazards and deal with the day-to-day fluctuations in the water level.

❺ Lake Pillsbury

Location: Near Ukiah in Mendocino National Forest; map C1, grid h2.

Directions: From the San Francisco Bay Area, drive north on US 101 to the junction with Highway 20, about 4.5 miles north of Ukiah. Turn east on Highway 20 and drive five miles. Turn northwest on County Road 240/Potter Valley–Lake Pillsbury Road and drive 26 miles to the lake.

Access: There are three paved boat ramps: one at Fuller Grove Campground on the lake's northwest end, one just past Sunset Campground on the northeast end, and one at Lake Pillsbury Resort on the west end.

Facilities, fees: Several campgrounds are provided, including primitive boat-in campsites. Lodging, a full-service marina, a restaurant, gas, and groceries are available at Lake Pillsbury Resort. You can rent fishing boats, canoes, kayaks, and paddleboats at the resort. Access is free. There is a charge for boat launching.

Water sports, restrictions: Waterskiing and personal watercraft are permitted. Windsurfing and swimming are best on the lake's north end, which has large, sandy beaches.

Contact: Mendocino National Forest, Upper Lake Ranger District, (707) 275-2361 or fax (707) 275-0676; Lake Pillsbury Resort, (707) 743-1581 or fax (707) 743-2666.

About Lake Pillsbury: Bit by bit, Lake Pillsbury is growing more popular every year. At one time not so long ago, this was just a mountain lake that had good weather, plenty of water, few people, and lots of trout. Well, with all those attractions, it isn't surprising that more vacationers than ever before are heading here.

Covering some 2,000 acres, Pillsbury is by far the largest lake in the Mendocino National Forest. Besides the surrounding forestland, highlights include lakeside camping and good boat ramps. Groceries and gas are also available, and hey, just north of the lake there's even a primitive soil-cement airstrip whose runway is a long cast from the water's edge.

Set at an elevation of 1,800 feet, Pillsbury is big and pretty when full, with 65 miles of shoreline. It is becoming a popular vacation destination with Bay Area folks, who tend to congregate at the north end of the lake, where beaches, Forest Service camps, and a boat ramp are located.

Most visitors will fish a little and water-ski a little, enjoy the sun, and maybe take a dunk in the cool green waters. Though conditions are decent for windsurfing in the early summer, few windsurfers are willing to make the circuitous drive for less than great prospects. Ironically, you are more apt to see hang gliders here.

The lake remains just difficult enough to reach that it probably will never get inundated with people, as occasionally occurs at Clear Lake. If you're staying at Pillsbury, one great side trip is a rafting run down the nearby Eel River (see the Eel River listing).

➏ Eel River

Location: Scott Dam to Van Arsdale Reservoir; map C1, grid h1.

Directions: From the San Francisco Bay Area, drive north on US 101 to the junction with Highway 20, about 4.5 miles north of Ukiah. Turn east on Highway 20 and drive five miles. Turn northwest on County Road 240/Potter Valley–Lake Pillsbury Road and follow the signs to Lake Pillsbury and Scott Dam. Limited access is available along Potter Valley Road and below the Scott Dam.

Access: There is no boat ramp. The put-in is just below Scott Dam, southwest of Lake Pillsbury off Potter Valley Road. Take out at one of several points above Van Arsdale Reservoir, located approximately 15 miles north of Highway 20 off Potter Valley Road.

Facilities, fees: Campgrounds and full facilities are available at Lake Pillsbury. Access is free. Rafting permits are not required.

Water sports, restrictions: Swimming is possible, but the river may be difficult to access. When driving on Potter Valley Road, look for spots where you can turn off and park.

Contact: Mendocino National Forest, Upper Lake Ranger District, (707) 275-2361 or fax (707) 275-0676; Bureau of Land Management, Ukiah Field Office, (707) 468-4000. For guided rafting trips contact Aurora River Adventures, (800) 526-8475 or (530) 629-3843.

About the Eel River: Of all the rafting runs on the main stem Eel River, the Pillsbury Run is the most popular. One reason might be that the area is so close to the campgrounds at Lake Pillsbury, a great bonus.

The nine-mile run to the final take-out above Van Arsdale Reservoir makes a doable day trip. You can shorten the trip by using one of several other take-outs available upstream.

With a Class III+ rating, the run has a few technical rapids and is an excellent choice for those whose skills are at the intermediate level. Along the way, rafters are treated to beautiful scenery. The river is bordered for the most part by dense forest, and the setting makes you feel far removed from civilization.

When it comes to rafting, the Eel River (see chapter C0) is hardly a star attraction. But of all the available runs, this stretch is the best.

➐ Letts Lake

Location: West of Maxwell in Mendocino National Forest; map C1, grid i4.

Directions: From Interstate 5 at Maxwell (67 miles north of Sacramento), turn west on Maxwell-Sites Road and drive to Sites. In Sites turn left on Sites-Lodoga Road and continue to the town of Lodoga. Turn right on Lodoga-Stonyford Road and loop around East Park Reservoir to reach Stonyford. From Stonyford drive 16 miles west on Road M10/Fouts Springs Road. Continue three miles southeast on Forest Service Road 17N02 to the lake. Trailers longer than 16 feet are not recommended.

Access: A primitive boat ramp that's suitable for cartop boats is located on the east side of the lake.

Facilities, fees: Several campgrounds are provided. A wheelchair-accessible fishing pier is available. Supplies can be obtained in Stonyford. Access is free.

Water sports, restrictions: Motors are not permitted on the lake. Swimming is allowed.

Contact: Mendocino National Forest, Stonyford Ranger District, (530) 963-3128. For a detailed map of the area, send $4 to Maps, Office of Information, US Forest Service, 1323 Club Drive, Vallejo, CA 94592.

About Letts Lake: Okay, c'mon now, admit it: you've never seen directions like the ones provided here for Letts Lake, right? If you think they are confusing, imagine how difficult it would be to find the lake without this book. Result? Advantage, you.

When you eventually get here, you find a small lake (35 acres) set at 4,500 feet in elevation within the edge of Mendocino National Forest, along with a few campgrounds on the north shore.

Because boats with motors are not allowed and the access road is quite circuitous, people with cartop rowboats, canoes, and rafts will fare well at Letts Lake. Swimming prospects are good; although there is no sandy beach area, there is a rocky shoreline.

The surrounding area is pretty, with excellent views and good hiking. You can turn a hike into a fortune hunt by trying to discover one of several natural springs in the area: Fir Rock Springs, Summit Springs, Cold Springs, Freezeout Springs, Board Camp Springs, Young's Corral Springs, and Sylar Springs.

❽ East Park Reservoir

Location: Near Stonyford in Mendocino National Forest; map C1, grid i7.

Directions: From Interstate 5 at Maxwell (67 miles north of Sacramento), turn west on Maxwell-Sites Road and drive to Sites. In Sites turn left on Sites-Lodoga Road and continue to the town of Lodoga. Turn right on Lodoga-Stonyford Road and loop around East Park Reservoir to reach Stonyford. From Stonyford turn east on East Park Road and drive to the reservoir.

Access: A primitive boat ramp is located on the lake's northwest side at the end of the access road.

Facilities, fees: Primitive campsites and a picnic area are provided. Supplies can be obtained in Stonyford and Lodoga. Access is free.

Water sports, restrictions: A five 5 mph speed limit is enforced around the swimming areas. Waterskiing, personal watercraft, and windsurfing are permitted. Swimming beaches are located near the campgrounds.

Contact: East Park Reservoir, (530) 968-5267; Bureau of Reclamation, (530) 275-1554 or fax (530) 275-2441.

About East Park Reservoir: It can get hot here, absolutely sizzling. In midsummer, temperatures in the 90s and 100s are common, and some summers the area is hit with a string of 100-degree days that seems to go on forever. The water levels drop a bit almost daily, and by August, East Park Reservoir has been transformed into a bathtub, complete with the ring.

But until that happens, this is a great lake for powerboating, waterskiing, and swimming. Although the place is primitive, the foothill setting is pretty, launching and access are free, and all water sports are permitted. The best swimming areas are near the campgrounds.

In low rain years and after late July, powerboaters should check water levels before heading out. The dropping levels result in navigational hazards, and tree stumps are often just beneath the surface.

⑨ Blue Lakes

Location: Near Upper Lake; map C1, grid j0.

Directions: From the San Francisco Bay Area, drive north on US 101 to Ukiah. Continue 4.5 miles north to Highway 20. Turn east and continue for 12 miles to Blue Lakes. The lake is accessed off Highway 20 or Blue Lakes Road.

Access: There are four private boat ramps:

Blue Lakes Lodge: The lodge, which is located on the east side of the lake off Highway 20, provides a paved launch ramp and a dock. Aluminum fishing boats are available for rent. For information phone (707) 275-2181.

Le Trianon Resort: A paved launch ramp and a dock are provided at this resort, which is located on the north end of the lake, off Highway 20. Rowboats are available for rent. For information phone (707) 275-2262.

Narrows Lodge: The lodge is located on the west side of the lake, off Blue Lakes Road. There's a paved launch ramp and a dock. Motorized boats, kayaks, rowboats, paddleboats, and canoes can be rented. For information phone (707) 275-2718 or fax (707) 275-0739.

Pine Acres Resort: This resort, located on the west side of the lake off Blue Lakes Road, has a paved launch ramp and a pier. You can rent motorized boats, rowboats, and paddleboats. For information phone the resort, (707) 275-2811.

Facilities, fees: Most of the private resorts offer campsites. Picnic areas, limited marina facilities, lodging, restaurants, groceries, and gas are available at the lake. Access is free. There is a charge for boat launching.

Water sports, restrictions: A 5 mph speed limit is strictly enforced. Protected, sandy swimming beaches are located near the lakeside resorts. Windsurfing is allowed (note the speed limit); the best windsurfing spot is near Pine Acres Resort.

Contact: For general information contact the Lake County Visitor Information Center, (800) 525-3743 or fax (707) 263-9564, or any of the private resorts listed above.

About Blue Lakes: Lake County is home to these Blue Lakes, which are not to be confused with several other Blue Lakes elsewhere in the state. There are Blue Lakes in Toiyabe-National Forest, Modoc National Forest, Inyo National Forest, Tahoe National Forest, and Hoover Wilderness. There's even a town called Blue Lake near Arcata, where there are no lakes at all, and then there is Big Blue Lake in the Russian Wilderness.

Located along Highway 20 north of Clear Lake, these two lakes feature quiet water, low-speed boating, trout fishing, and a lakeside resort with rental units. The lakes are long and narrow, created from the flows of Cold Creek, which eventually meets up with the East Fork Russian River and empties into Lake Mendocino. The upper lake is by far the better of the pair.

The calm, cool, and clean water, combined with the opportunity to catch trout, is very compelling in this region, and Blue Lakes gets heavy use. As for that 5 mph speed limit, don't ignore it or your vacation will end abruptly; they're very strict about enforcing it.

The setting at elevation 1,400 feet is very pretty, with a forested shoreline and a fair number of sandy beaches. You can swim just about anywhere here. Of course most windsurfers don't give Blue Lakes the time of day because the speed limit is more like a stop sign. But beginners will find a good spot on the west shore near Pine

Acres Resort, which gets a fair wind out of the north in the spring.

If you end up loving this place and worry that other people will make the same discovery, hey, just tell 'em you're going to Blue Lakes. They won't have a clue.

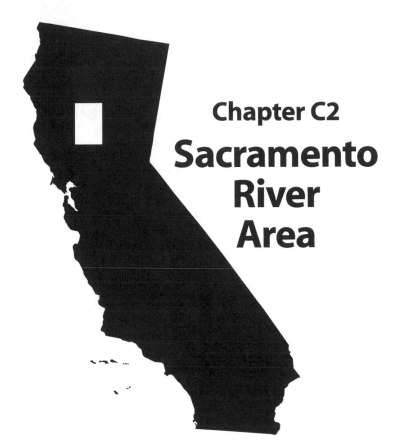

Chapter C2
Sacramento River Area

Overall Rating

| 1 | 2 | 3 | 4 | 5 | 6 | 7 | 8 | 9 | 10 |

Poor .... Fair .... Great

C2–Sacramento River Area Map

One inch equals approximately 10.7 miles.
See page 12 for California state map.

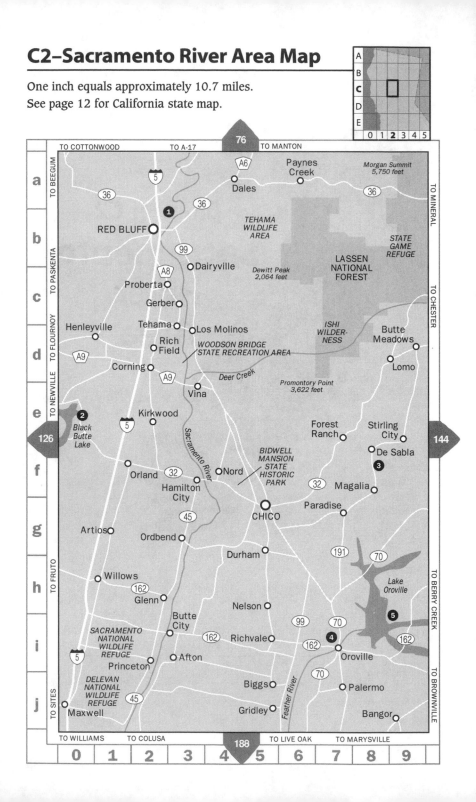

Chapter C2 features:

❶ Sacramento River

Location: From Red Bluff to Colusa; map C2, grid b3.

Directions: The river is accessible off roads that join with Interstate 5 near Red Bluff, Corning, and Orland. Highway 45 parallels the river southeast of Orland, and direct access is available.

Access: There are four boat ramps. Rafters should put in at the Red Bluff Diversion Dam (see directions below) and float down to Woodson Bridge State Recreation Area.

Bend Bridge Public Ramp: From Interstate 5 north of Red Bluff, take the Jellys Ferry Road exit and head east. Follow the signs to Bend RV Park; a two-lane paved ramp is located just behind the park.

Red Bluff Diversion Dam: From Interstate 5 at Red Bluff, take the Susanville–Highway 36 exit. Drive east to Sale Lane and turn right. Follow the road to the end; a paved ramp is available nearby. Another paved ramp, which gives access to the other side of the dam, is located a little farther down by the campgrounds.

Red Bluff River Park: From Interstate 5 at Red Bluff, take the Red Bluff exit and head west. At the second stoplight turn left on Main Street and continue four blocks to the Red Bluff River Park entrance. Turn left into the park and continue through the parking area to the paved ramp. Rest rooms are provided.

Woodson Bridge State Recreation Area: From Interstate 5 at Corning, take the South Avenue exit and drive nine miles to the park. Follow the signs to the paved boat ramp.

Facilities, fees: Several campgrounds and RV parks are located along the river. A few good ones are Bend RV Park and Fishing Resort (near Red Bluff), Hidden Harbor RV Park (near Los Molinos), and Woodson Bridge State Recreation Area (near Corning). Lodging and supplies can be obtained in Red Bluff and Corning. Access is free. Rafting permits are not required.

Water sports, restrictions: Rafting, canoeing, and kayaking are allowed; boaters must wear life preservers. You can waterski, use personal watercraft, windsurf, and swim at Lake Red Bluff.

Contact: US Forest Service, Lake Red Bluff Recreation Area, (530) 527-2813; Bend RV Park, (530) 527-6289; Woodson Bridge State Recreation Area, (530) 839-2112. For general information about the area, contact the Shasta Cascade Wonderland Association, (800) 474-2782 or (530) 365-7500 or fax (530) 365-1258.

About the Sacramento River: The old river is an emerald green fountain, the lifeblood of Northern California, and a living, pulsing vein in the heart of the state. Heh, heh. To phrase it a little more directly, this section of the river from Red Bluff downstream to Colusa is the prettiest part of California's Central Valley, a place filled with beauty and power.

What a shame that most people never see this. The river's most visible aspect is the variety of recreation offered at Lake Red Bluff, created by a fish-killing atrocity called the Red Bluff Diversion Dam. Lake Red Bluff has calm water for ski boats and personal watercraft, and some areas for swimming. Conditions are often perfect in the spring and early summer for windsurfing, with a strong wind, calm water surface, and warm temperatures, yet it is extremely rare to see anyone practicing the sport. While there are no beaches at Lake Red Bluff, there is a large grassy area on the west bank where people sunbathe and swim. This is the only practical spot for wading and swimming because water temperatures are much colder out on the main lake body.

Below the Red Bluff Diversion Dam, there is a great stretch of easy canoeing water, Class I all the way. Woodson Bridge State Recreation Area is the most popular take-out. The river is wide, cool, and bordered by riparian habitat, and this is an outstanding opportunity to cool off on a typical hot summer day in the north valley.

Commercial outfitters do not offer rafting trips here. Instead, this is a do-it-yourself special, as you plop in and enjoy the scenery and the wildlife. When giant blue herons lift off before your eyes, they look almost prehistoric. Other common sights are turtles sunning on rocks, hawks soaring overhead, and deer venturing out to the riverbanks. If you're lucky, you might see an eagle or even a wild turkey.

Water flows often run at 14,500 cubic feet per second in the summer months, a good, strong rate that makes your paddle strokes seem quite powerful. Most people take their time, with more floating than paddling, but those aboard eventually end up paddling a bit anyway. Either way you go, you gain a personal glimpse of one of the Central Valley's least-visited paradises.

❷ Black Butte Lake

Location: Near Orland; map C2, grid e0.
Directions: From Interstate 5 at Orland (100 miles north of Sacramento), take the Black Butte Lake exit. Drive 10 miles west on Highway 32/Newville Road to the lake.
Access: There are three boat ramps:
Black Butte Marina: Heading west on

Highway 32, go past the dam and watch for signs indicating the marina and Buckhorn Campground. Turn left and continue to the paved ramp and dock.

Eagle Pass: Heading west on Highway 32, watch for signs for the dam and Eagle Pass Picnic Area. Turn left and continue to the paved boat ramp.

Orland Buttes: Heading west on Highway 36, watch for the Orland Buttes turnoff on your left. The paved ramp is located past the campground.

Facilities, fees: Two developed campgrounds are provided: Orland Buttes and Buckhorn. Black Butte Marina offers full boating services and rents out fishing boats, canoes, and paddleboats. A sanitary disposal station, groceries, and propane gas are also available. Access is free. There is a fee for boat launching.

Water sports, restrictions: Waterskiing, personal watercraft, and windsurfing are permitted. Swimming areas are available near Buckhorn Picnic Area and at Eagle Pass Day-Use Area, near the dam.

Contact: US Army Corps of Engineers, Black Butte Lake, (530) 865-4781 or fax (530) 865-5283; Black Butte Marina, (530) 865-2665.

About Black Butte Lake: Hit this lake at the wrong time and you'll get the vacation from hell. Hit it right and you'll wonder why more people aren't taking advantage of paradise on earth. The reality here is that there is rarely an in-between.

If you come in late March, April, or May, you will find a pretty lake amid freshly greened foothills, with some 40 miles of shoreline and lakeside camps.

But arrive in late July or August and you will find a low water level, brown and mostly barren hillsides, and camps like sweat pits. Let there be no doubt as to when you should plan your trip.

Black Butte is set at 500 feet in elevation in the west valley foothills and covers 4,500 surface acres. Just a short jog off Interstate 5, the lake is easily accessible, making it very attractive to people with trailered boats. It gets heavy use during the prime season, when warm temperatures set in and spring gives way to summer.

This is the best time for waterskiing and powerboating as well as for fishing for crappie, a prize that attracts many anglers.

The best launch points for windsurfing as well as for wading or swimming are near the Orland Buttes Campground and at the Buckhorn Day-Use Area.

Black Butte's marina offers full boating services, including boat storage. However, gasoline is not always available, so boaters should either call before they arrive or fill up their tanks ahead of time.

The water is warm at Black Butte and as mentioned previously, the lake is best visited in spring and early summer. By fall not only do the surroundings turn brown, hot, and dusty, but the water levels drop, creating a number of boating hazards just under the surface.

❸ Paradise Lake

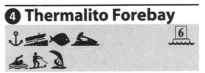

Location: Near Paradise; map C2, grid f8.
Directions: From Interstate 5 at Orland (100 miles north of Sacramento), take the Highway 32/Chico exit. Drive about 18 miles east to Chico, turn on Highway 99 south, turn east on Skyway Road, and drive 10 miles to Paradise. In Paradise turn north on Coutolenc Road and drive 3.5 miles.
Access: A primitive boat ramp is located near the picnic area.
Facilities, fees: A day-use picnic area is provided. There is a campground north of Paradise Lake at Philbrook Reservoir. Supplies can be obtained in Paradise. There is a day-use fee.
Water sports, restrictions: Gas motors are not allowed on the lake; swimming, windsurfing, and water/body contact sports are prohibited.

Contact: Paradise Lake Irrigation District, (530) 873-1040; Lassen National Forest, Almanor Ranger District, (530) 258-2141 or fax (530) 258-5194.

About Paradise Lake: There are a lot of things you can't do at Paradise Lake. You can't have a motor on your boat. You can't swim. You can't windsurf. There's no campground, yet they charge a day-use fee. Cartop boats are strictly regulated by lake officials; only "approved" craft (that is, approved by them) are permitted. Kayaks cannot be completely self-enclosed, inflatables must have two outside air chambers, and all boaters must wear life jackets at all times.

Despite all the can'ts, Paradise Lake has earned a fair rating. Set at 3,000 feet in the Mount Lassen foothills, the pretty lake is in the transition zone where the valley woodlands give way to alpine country. With all the boating restrictions, the lake is primarily visited by trout fishermen. There is also a pretty picnic area, and you can plunk in a cartop boat.

Because motors are not allowed on the lake, you don't have to worry about getting plowed under by water-skiers, a real concern at Lake Oroville. Instead you get quiet water that is ideal for small paddle-powered boats. In early summer this can be the perfect place to bring your canoe and spend a few calm, relaxing hours.

❹ Thermalito Forebay

Location: Near Oroville in Lake Oroville State Recreation Area; map C2, grid i7.
Directions: The forebay is divided into two areas: the North Forebay and the South Forebay. To reach the North Forebay from Oroville, drive about two miles north on Highway 70. Turn west on Garden Drive and drive one mile to the picnic area. To reach the South Forebay, drive three miles west on Grand Avenue to the parking area.

Access: The North Forebay has a two-lane paved ramp, and the South Forebay has a four-lane paved ramp; see Directions.

Facilities, fees: A day-use picnic area is provided at the North Forebay. Nearby Lake Oroville has several campgrounds. Supplies can be obtained in Oroville. There is a day-use fee.

Water sports, restrictions: Motors are not permitted on the North Forebay. A sandy beach is available for swimming, and windsurfing and sailing are allowed. The South Forebay is open to all boating; however, there is a 5 mph speed limit within 100 yards of the shoreline. You can swim all along the shore.

Contact: North Thermalito Forebay, (530) 538-2221; Lake Oroville State Recreation Area, (530) 538-2200.

About Thermalito Forebay: With so many boaters, campers, and anglers heading to nearby Lake Oroville, Thermalito Forebay is becoming a surprisingly attractive option to those who prefer quiet water and freedom from motorized boats. Although small compared to the giant Lake Oroville, the Forebay is not exactly pint-sized, covering 300 acres in the Oroville foothills at an elevation of 900 feet.

The North Forebay is the prettiest area here and makes the best spot for swimming and windsurfing. Only nonmotorized boats are allowed, so you get quiet water and don't have to keep looking over your shoulder. There is also a swimming beach and a picnic area with drinking water, shaded shelters, and lots of trees. What a concept.

The South Forebay, on the other hand, is visited almost entirely by people hoping to land a few fish. It is much more primitive, offering only vault toilets and not a tree (or a fire hydrant) in sight. Dogs have it tough.

At less than 1,000 feet in elevation, this area gets hit with blowtorch heat day after day once midsummer arrives. Visit then and you might as well camp in the caldera of a volcano.

⑤ Lake Oroville

Location: Near Oroville; map C2, grid i9.

Directions: From Highway 70 in Oroville, take the Oro Dam Boulevard exit, turn right, and drive 1.5 miles to Highway 162/Olive Highway. Turn right and follow the highway east; access is available off several signed turnoffs. The west arm of the lake is accessible off Highway 70 north of Oroville; follow the signs.

Access: A few primitive boat ramps are located in remote areas of the lake. They are difficult to reach and are sometimes closed, depending on water levels. Phone ahead to check conditions and obtain specific directions. Four paved boat ramps are available:

Bidwell Canyon Marina: From Highway 70 in Oroville, take the Oro Dam Boulevard exit, turn right, and drive 1.5 miles to Highway 162/Olive Highway. Turn right and drive approximately seven miles to Kelly Ridge Road. Turn left and continue to Arroyo Road. Turn right and continue to the marina and the paved boat ramp. Houseboats, ski boats, fishing boats, and patio boats are available for rent.

Lime Saddle Marina: From Oroville drive approximately nine miles north on Highway 70. Turn left on Pentz Road and drive about three miles; look for signs indicating the marina. A multilane paved boat ramp and a dock are provided. Houseboats, ski boats, fishing boats, patio boats, and canoes are available for rent.

Loafer Creek: From Highway 70 in Oroville, take the Oro Dam Boulevard exit, turn right, and drive 1.5 miles to Highway 162/Olive Highway. Turn right and drive approximately eight miles to the turnoff for Loafer Creek Campground. A paved launch ramp is adjacent to the campground.

Spillway: From Highway 70 in Oroville, take the Oro Dam Boulevard exit and follow the signs heading to the dam and the adjacent multilane paved boat ramp.

Facilities, fees: Several campgrounds are provided, including Bidwell Canyon and Loafer Creek. Boat-in camping is an option. Groceries, gas, snacks, and boat supplies can be obtained at the marinas. Day-use and boat launching fees are charged.

Water sports, restrictions: Waterskiing, personal watercraft, and windsurfing are permitted. Swimming beaches are located near Loafer Creek and Bidwell Canyon Campgrounds. Diving into the water is not permitted.

Contact: Lake Oroville State Recreation Area, (530) 538-2200; Bidwell Canyon Marina, (530) 589-3165; Lime Saddle Marina, (530) 877-2414.

About Lake Oroville: A huge, man-made reservoir with extensive lake arms and a large central body of water, Lake Oroville covers more than 15,000 acres and offers 165 miles of shoreline. Throughout much of the year, Oroville has it all: campgrounds, enough water for all kinds of boating, a fish for every angler, and accommodations that are tailor-made for the boater/camper, including floating campsites, floating toilets (no kidding), boat-in campgrounds, and two excellent marinas.

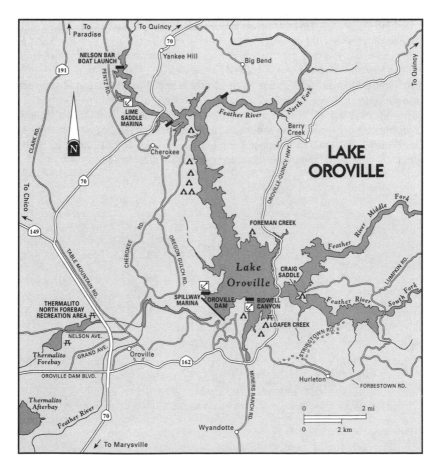

You will find this beauty in the foothills east of Chico at an elevation of 900 feet. The fully developed recreation sites make it a favorite family destination. Most newcomers head to the Bidwell Canyon area, where the primary marina, boat ramp, and most of the campgrounds are located. But there are many alternatives. Lime Saddle Marina, on the less-crowded northwest arm of the lake, is preferred by many boaters because there are fewer people, a high-quality marina, and access to the upper arm of the lake. In addition to renting every kind of boat, Lime Saddle Marina has docks, overnight moorings, boat slips, a boat shop, marine supplies, water-ski sales and rentals, and fuel. The campgrounds closest to Lime Saddle are boat-in sites, not drive-to sites.

Fishing has improved in recent years at Oroville. Anglers seek out the quiet water in the lake coves, and they get irate when invaded by water-skiers or personal watercraft "hitting the coves." So don't do it. With so much water to choose from, why invade somebody else's space?

In the summer the water in the main lake warms up, making it ideal for waterskiing. Water temperatures in June can be 5 to 10 degrees colder up in the lake arms. Most skiers prefer the warm water, and anglers tend to prefer the cold water. By mid-July, though, even the water up in the lake arms begins to warm significantly. When the water levels are high, it creates a dramatic setting, especially for waterskiing in the old Feather River Canyon.

Several problems at Lake Oroville prevent its being awarded a perfect 10 rating. First, in years with light rains, so much water is drained out of the lake for farmers that the place can look like the Grand Canyon of Oroville by September, with acres and acres of exposed lake bottom. That makes the hike up to the boat-in campsites long and steep. After heavy winters, however, the problem isn't nearly as severe. Another dilemma is the weather. At an elevation of 900 feet in foothill country, the lake gets some very hot temperatures in the summer. Anybody who isn't prepared for it will shrivel like a prune. Using sunscreen—while on your boat and at your camp—is critical.

Improvements at Lake Oroville, including upgraded boat-in campsites, make this big lake an ideal destination for an overnight boating/camping trip.

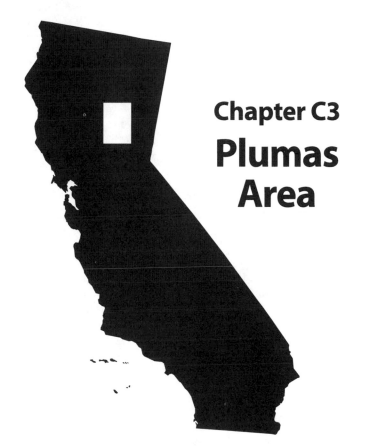

Chapter C3
Plumas
Area

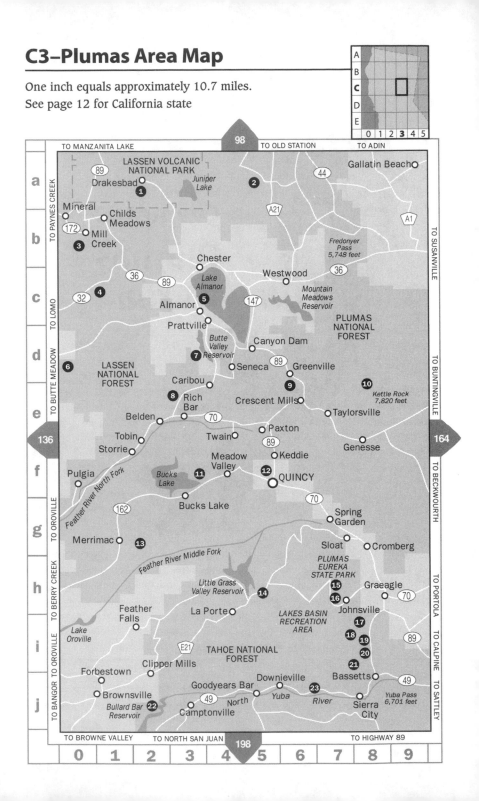

C3–Plumas Area Map

One inch equals approximately 10.7 miles.
See page 12 for California state

Chapter C3 features:

---

① Willow Lake

Location: Near Chester in Lassen National Forest; map C3, grid a2.

Directions: From Redding drive 29 miles south on Interstate 5 to Red Bluff. Take the Highway 36 exit and drive 70 miles east to the town of Chester. Turn north on Warner Valley Road and drive about five miles north. When the road forks, bear left, drive one mile; then bear right and continue on a dirt road to Willow Lake.

Access: There is no boat ramp. Cartop boats may be hand launched.

Facilities, fees: A primitive campground is provided, but no piped water is available. Supplies can be obtained in Chester. Access is free.

Water sports, restrictions: Swimming is permitted; a small stretch of shoreline near the campground is available for sunbathing.

Contact: Lassen National Forest, Almanor Ranger District, (530) 258-2141 or fax (530) 258-5194.

About Willow Lake: This little egg-shaped lake always comes as a surprise. Although located near some of California's top vacation destinations, it is so far off the ol' beaten path that it gets missed by out-of-towners every time.

Willow Lake is located in national forestland just west of Kelly Mountain, only three miles from the southeastern border of Lassen Volcanic National Park at Drakesbad and 10 miles northwest of giant Lake Almanor. Still, it manages to provide an intimate, quiet atmosphere.

Set at an elevation of approximately 6,500 feet, the lake is tiny, and marshy in some places. It is too small for any boating other than cartop or inflatable craft, and gets very light use. The water is too cold for swimming until midsummer; swimmers who do come when things warm up are treated to a small shoreline clearing (more dirt than sand) where they can sunbathe.

Nearby Drakesbad at Lassen Park provides a great side trip for hikers, with destinations such as Devil's Kitchen and several alpine lakes within an hour's walk.

② Echo Lake

Location: Near Chester in Lassen National Forest; map C3, grid a5.

Directions: From Redding drive 29 miles south on Interstate 5 to Red Bluff. Take the Highway 36 exit and drive 78 miles east to Chester Dump Road (about eight miles east of the town of Chester). Turn left on Chester Dump Road, drive west a short distance on a connector road, and then continue north for 9.5 miles to Echo Lake.

Access: There is no boat ramp. Cartop boats may be hand launched.

Facilities, fees: A primitive campground is provided, but no piped water is available. Supplies can be obtained in Chester. Access is free.

Water sports, restrictions: Swimming is permitted.

Contact: Lassen National Forest, Almanor Ranger District, (530) 258-2141 or fax (530) 258-5194. For a detailed map of the area, send $4 to Maps, Office of Information, US Forest Service, 1323 Club Drive, Vallejo, CA 94592.

About Echo Lake: Obscure? Hard to reach? Primitive camping? Trout fishing? Not many people around? That is what most people want on a vacation, and that is exactly what Echo Lake provides. The one drawback is its small size, but that's only a problem on extended trips.

The miniature and marshy lake is set at an elevation of about 6,500 feet. A highlight is the small, primitive campground that provides seclusion and a very pretty setting. Almost too small for hand launching boats, the lake is better suited for rafts. Swimming conditions are fair once the water warms up by midsummer, but you can expect the bottom to be mushy.

The Caribou Wilderness is located less than a mile to the northwest. With a national forest map to help you find your way, it can be easy to make a short trek into the nearby wilderness and hit a lake loop. Hidden Lakes, Long Lake, Posey Lake, and Beauty Lake are all on the same loop trail.

❸ Mill Creek

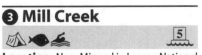

Location: Near Mineral in Lassen National Forest; map C3, grid b0.

Directions: From Redding drive 29 miles south on Interstate 5 to Red Bluff. Take the Highway 36 exit and drive about 45 miles northeast to the town of Mineral. Turn south on County Road 172 and drive five miles to the town of Mill Creek. Turn right at a signed Forest Service road and continue for three miles to a parking area and trailhead. A hiking trail follows Mill Creek for several miles.

Access: There is no boat ramp.

Facilities, fees: Two campgrounds, Hole in the Ground and Mill Creek Resort, are available off the Forest Service road mentioned above. Supplies can be obtained in Mineral. Access is free.

Water sports, restrictions: Several excellent swimming holes are located along the Mill Creek Trail.

Contact: Lassen National Forest, Almanor Ranger District, (530) 258-2141 or fax (530) 258-5194; Mill Creek Resort, (530) 595-4449. For a detailed map of the area, send $4 to Maps, Office of Information, US Forest Service, 1323 Club Drive, Vallejo, CA 94592.

About Mill Creek: Here is an attractive little trout stream running through national forestland, complete with streamside trail. It is the kind of place where you go for a walk in the summer, maybe stopping at a swimming hole on a hot day or casting for trout on a cool evening.

With Lassen National Forest surrounding the lake, which is set at 4,500 feet in elevation, this is a heavily forested, picturesque area. Mill Creek is a popular destination for vacationers staying at Mill Creek Resort. The prime time here is from mid-July on through summer; with the snow-melt over, the stream drops and the water warms up.

Highlights here include good hiking and two developed campgrounds. Mill Creek is too small for any rafting or boating. Instead, after parking you hit the trail for access to several swimming holes. Do not think of wandering from the trail; some of the land bordering this stream is privately owned.

❹ Deer Creek

Location: Near Mineral in Lassen National Forest; map C3, grid c1.

Directions: From Chico drive about 10 miles northeast on Highway 32. Or from Redding drive 29 miles south on Interstate 5 to Red Bluff. Take the Highway 36 exit and drive about 45 miles northeast to the town of Mineral. Continue for about 12 miles southeast on Highway 36. Turn right on Highway 32 and travel south. Access the creek directly off Highway 32.

Access: There is no boat ramp.

Facilities, fees: Campgrounds are provided on the creek on Highway 32. Supplies can be obtained in Mineral. Access is free.

Water sports, restrictions: Several good swimming holes are located along Highway 32, with the best at Potato Patch, Elam Creek, and Alder Creek Campgrounds.

Contact: Lassen National Forest, Almanor Ranger District, (530) 258-2141 or fax (530) 258-5194. For a detailed map of the area, send $4 to Maps, Office of Information, US Forest Service, 1323 Club Drive, Vallejo, CA 94592.

About Deer Creek: From its headwaters on downstream, Highway 32 parallels Deer Creek, providing easy streamside access at three campgrounds, a series of roadside pullouts, and a hiking trail.

Don't think the proximity to Highway 32 means that the drive here is painless. Just the opposite. Highway 32 is not even close to being an actual highway and is very twisty, extremely narrow in spots, and far away for most visitors. That is why we advised accessing the road from the junction with Highway 36 and then driving downhill, the easiest route by far.

Deer Creek, at an elevation of 4,000 feet, is primarily a trout stream, with large numbers of trout stocked here each summer mainly near the three campgrounds. A trail that is routed right along the stream provides good hiking and takes you to a hidden waterfall. People rarely take a dunk in the pools because the water, which is fed from snowmelt, is cold until late in the summer.

The traffic ranges from very light early and late in the season, to medium in early summer, then heavy in midsummer when the trout plants are high, the weather is warm and clear, and the stream flows are perfect. Regardless, Deer Creek makes a good alternative to the oft-crowded scene at nearby Lake Almanor (see the following listing).

❺ Lake Almanor

Location: East of Red Bluff in Lassen National Forest; map C3, grid c4.

Directions: From Red Bluff drive east on Highway 36 about 70 miles to the junction with Highway 89 (about three miles before Chester). Turn right on Highway 89 and drive south for about six miles. Turn left (east) on County Road 310 and drive to the lake.

From Susanville drive approximately 28 miles west on Highway 36, past the town of Chester, to Highway 89.

Access: Eleven boat ramps are available at resorts and campgrounds around the lake:

Big Cove Resort: A paved ramp, docks, and a full-service marina are available. Pontoon boats and fishing boats can be rented. For information phone (530) 596-3349.

Camp Prattville: A dirt ramp, docks, and limited marina services are provided. For information phone (530) 259-2464 or fax (530) 259-3434.

Knotty Pine Resort: A paved ramp, docks, and a full-service marina are available. Pontoon boats, fishing boats, kayaks,

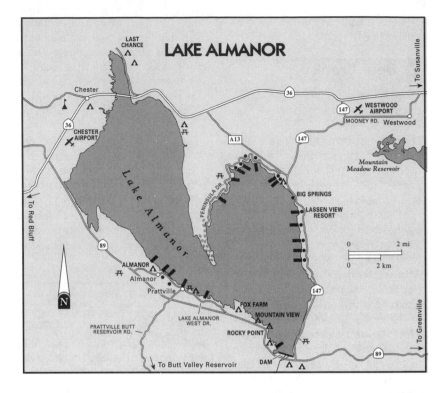

and paddleboats can be rented. For information phone (530) 596-3348.

Lake Almanor Resort: There is a paved ramp and docks. For information phone (530) 596-3337.

Lake Cove Resort and Marina: A paved ramp and dock are provided. They rent fishing boats, too. For information phone (530) 284-7697.

Lake Haven Resort: A paved ramp, docks, and limited marina services are available. For information phone (530) 596-3249.

Lassen View Resort: A three-lane paved ramp and docks are provided. Cabins, fishing boats, pontoon boats, and personal watercraft are available for rent. For information phone (530) 596-3437 or fax (530) 596-4437.

Little Norway Resort: There is a paved ramp and a full-service marina where you can rent fishing boats, ski boats, pontoon boats, and personal watercraft. For information phone (530) 596-3225.

Northshore Campground: A paved ramp and dock are available. You can rent small fishing boats here, too. For information phone (530) 258-3376.

Facilities, fees: Several campgrounds are provided. Lodging, cabins, restaurants, laundry facilities, hot showers, groceries, and gas are available. For boat rentals see the resorts listed under "Access." Access is free. There is a fee for boat launching.

Water sports, restrictions: Waterskiing and personal watercraft are permitted. Swimming beaches are located at Canyon Dam Picnic Area, Eastshore Picnic Area, and Camp Conery Group Camp, all situated on the lake's southeast end. Windsurfing is best at these areas, too.

Contact: For a free travel packet, contact

the Plumas County Visitors Bureau, Box 4120, Quincy, CA 95971; (800) 326-2247 or (530) 283-6345. For Forest Service campgrounds contact the Lassen National Forest, Almanor Ranger District, (916) 386-5164. For group camping information contact PG&E Building & Land Services, (916) 894-4687 or fax (916) 386-5388. For camping details, see the Foghorn Press book *California Camping*. For information on boating and other water sports, phone one of the resorts listed above.

About Lake Almanor: Northern California's answer to Lake Tahoe, Lake Almanor is a jewel ringed by conifers. It's a big lake, about 13 miles long with 28,000 surface acres, set at an elevation of 4,500 feet. Although Almanor is a reservoir built by PG&E, it looks more like a natural lake because it is kept full most of the year and much of the shoreline is wooded. Big and beautiful, Almanor has sapphire blue water and views of snow-capped Mount Lassen to the northwest.

Almanor's popularity has been undergoing a boom in the 1990s, with the price of lakeside homes doubling in some cases, and lakeview homes on the peninsula are now exorbitantly priced. People have figured out that there are precious few lakes in California where it is possible to build a vacation home, and that not only is Almanor one of the few, but with all things considered, it just might be the best. There are also opportunities to stay in a lakeside vacation home or rent a cabin here.

The water is clear, ideal for all kinds of boating and water sports, and a large number of vacationers take advantage of it every summer. Waterskiing is excellent in July and August. The best spots for swimming and windsurfing are located almost exclusively along the east shore, but like most reservoirs, the beaches here are few and far between.

In the spring and fall, fishing for trout and salmon is often excellent, not so much for the number of fish you can land, but rather for their size. The lake is so big that many newcomers are unsure where to try their luck. To get the lowdown, always call Lassen View Resort at (530) 596-3437; fishing guides are also available there.

Spring winds and a long winter will always prevent this place from turning into a year-round vacation paradise. Wind? Yow, it can really howl. For instance, in May it can be as calm as a small pond at daybreak; then it starts to blow by 9 AM, and by 10 AM, the whitecaps start churning and continue for the rest of the day. This occurs in the spring, from April through early June, and while not a daily event, it happens plenty enough to keep owners of small boats especially wary. Winter is long and cold here, often with tremendous amounts of snow. Sometimes the lake even freezes over, an amazing sight for such a large body of water.

Regardless, Almanor is a jewel. It's one of the best recreation lakes in California, and an excellent destination for boaters, campers, and anglers.

6 Philbrook Reservoir

Location: Near Paradise in Lassen National Forest; map C3, grid d0.

Directions: From Interstate 5 at Orland (100 miles north of Sacramento), take the Highway 32–Chico exit. Drive about 18 miles east to Chico and then south on Highway 99. Turn east on Skyway Road and drive 37 miles (about 27 miles past Paradise). Bear right at Humbug Summit Road and drive two miles. Turn right on Philbrook Road and drive three miles to the next intersection. Turn right, continue a half mile to the boat ramp, and another half mile past that to the campground.

Access: A cartop boat ramp is provided.

Facilities, fees: A campground and a picnic area are available. Access to the lake is free.

Water sports, restrictions: Cartop boats are permitted. Swimming and windsurfing are allowed; the best spots are at the campground or the picnic area.

Contact: Lassen National Forest, Almanor Ranger District, (530) 258-2141 or fax (530) 258-5194.

About Philbrook Reservoir: Maybe they got the name wrong. Paradise Lake is located very near to the southwest. After getting a glimpse of this lake, you might think Philbrook Reservoir deserves to have the name Paradise more than the original does.

That is because after traversing a very rough access road, you discover a pretty alpine lake at elevation 5,000 feet, with forest campsites, swimming beaches, and a picnic area. All in all, it's the ideal spot for cartop boats and inflatables, especially canoes and rafts.

Getting here is just difficult enough to keep most folks away. The road is jarring at times, very rough on vehicles not built to handle unpaved roads.

Once here the hardy few tend to set up camp and then fish for trout or plunk their canoe or raft in and paddle around, submersing themselves in the rapture of this pretty alpine setting.

---

❼ Butt Valley Reservoir

Location: Near Chester; map C3, grid d3.

Directions: From Red Bluff drive east on Highway 36 about 70 miles to the Highway 89 junction (about three miles before Chester). Turn right on Highway 89 and drive about seven miles to Butt Valley Road. Turn right on Butt Valley Road and drive 3.2 miles to the north end of the reservoir.

Access: A paved boat ramp is located near Cool Springs Campground on the east shore of the lake.

Facilities, fees: Two campgrounds and a picnic area are provided on the eastern shoreline. Supplies can be obtained in Chester. Access is free.

Water sports, restrictions: Ski boats and personal watercraft are not allowed. Swimming areas are available near the campgrounds and picnic area. Windsurfing is permitted.

Contact: For general information or to order a free brochure, contact PG&E Building & Land Services, (916) 386-5164 or fax (916) 386-5388.

About Butt Valley Reservoir: While the official name of this place is Butt Valley Reservoir, nobody calls it that. The reservoir goes by Butt Lake, and it is a peculiar place, despite having lakeside campgrounds and the occasional giant rainbow trout. What is so peculiar is that it has the potential for greatness but usually falls just a bit short.

A PG&E-run lake that receives its water via a tunnel coming from nearby Lake Almanor, Butt Valley is set at an elevation of 4,100 feet and is five miles long. In water plumbing terminology, this is the afterbay for Almanor. When full, Butt Lake is very pretty, with campsites set within view of the water and a boat ramp for launching small trailered boats, mainly used by people fishing for trout. When the powerhouse runs at the head of the lake, pond smelt from Lake Almanor get poured right into the water, inspiring every big resident trout to go on a feeding frenzy.

In the spring and early summer, a predictable wind plows right down the Feather River Canyon, making conditions good for expert windsurfers. The water, which can be cold, warms up enough for a short swim by summer.

As a collective vision this seems just right, eh? Unfortunately, it rarely lives up to the expectations.

The biggest problem is that the lake is often quite low, with lots of stumps on the bare lake bed. Even though there is no speed limit, waterskiing is not permitted because of the underwater hazards, and drivers of fast boats who stray from the channel run the risk of hitting one of those stumps. Another minus is that the trout have grown so fat from feeding on the pond smelt pumped in from Almanor that they usually bite only when the power-house is running, an unpredictable event. Also, other than the boat ramp and the campgrounds, the place lacks facilities and a marina.

Hence, what you have here is a lake that's got tons of potential. Curiosity about Butt Lake causes many vacationers from nearby Almanor to at least swing by to take a look-see at the possibilities.

❽ North Fork Feather River

 6

Location: South of Belden Forebay in Plumas National Forest; map C3, grid e3.

Directions: From Oroville drive northeast on Highway 70. Just 1.5 miles after passing Belden, turn left (north) on Caribou Road. The North Fork Feather borders this small road all the way to Belden Forebay.

Access: There is no boat ramp.

Facilities, fees: Four campgrounds are set right along the river, with access off Caribou Road. Others are provided off Highway 70. Gansner Bar is a good one to check out. Supplies can be obtained along Highway 70. Access is free.

Water sports, restrictions: The best swimming spots are at Queen Lily, North Fork, and Gansner Bar Campgrounds, all located on Caribou Road. Rafting is not permitted.

Contact: Plumas National Forest, Headquarters, (530) 283-2050 or fax (530)2 83-4150.

About the North Fork Feather River: The highlight at the North Fork Feather is a series of campgrounds and an access road that is routed up to Belden

Forebay. The campgrounds have become very popular for their pretty settings along the stream, and the road that parallels the river provides easy access to swimming holes and trout fishing spots.

Early in the year, the water is swift and cold from snowmelt and only an otter would dare swim here. By summer the flows are greatly reduced, temperatures have warmed considerably, and a few swimming holes near the campgrounds are usually passable for taking a dunk.

Most of the people you see around here are fishing for trout. Stocks are made at each of the campgrounds, as well as upstream at Belden.

❾ Round Valley Reservoir

4

Location: Near Greenville in Plumas National Forest; map C3, grid e6.

Directions: From Red Bluff drive east on Highway 36 about 70 miles to the Highway 89 junction (about three miles before Chester). Turn right on Highway 89 and drive south about 25 miles to the town of Greenville. Turn south on Greenville Road, drive three miles, turn left, and follow the signs leading to Round Valley Lake Resort. From Susanville drive approximately 28 miles west on Highway 36, past the town of Chester, to Highway 89.

Access: A gravel boat ramp is located on the east side of the lake near Round Valley Lake Resort.

Facilities, fees: A private campground and fishing boat rentals are available at Round Valley Lake Resort. A picnic area is provided for day use. Supplies can be obtained in Greenville. Access is free.

Water sports, restrictions: Boat motors are restricted to a maximum of 7.5 horsepower. Swimming and other water/body contact sports are prohibited.

Contact: Round Valley Lake Resort, (530) 258-7751 or (714) 637-3181 for a brochure and general information; Plumas National Forest, Greenville Service Center, Mount Hough Ranger District, (530) 284-7126.

About Round Valley Reservoir: Considering that Round Valley Reservoir is set at an elevation of 4,500 feet, you might wonder why it's got all those weeds and lily pads. Well, the answer is that this is one of the few warm-water lakes in California's mountain country. If you've never visited here before, it's bound to pleasantly surprise you.

The area surrounding the lake is quite pretty, with trails for hiking and horseback riding nearby, and the campground provides a relatively secluded option to nearby Lake Almanor.

But there are rules restricting most boating and water sport opportunities. No body contact with the water and no motors over 7.5 horsepower are allowed. What you end up with is a rare mountain lake where anglers can try for bass and catfish, not trout, without having to worry about fast boats or swimmers.

⑩ Taylor Lake

Location: Near Taylorsville in Plumas National Forest; map C3, grid e8.

Directions: From Sacramento drive approximately 100 miles east on Interstate 80. Turn north on Highway 89 and drive 70 miles to Quincy. From Quincy continue about 18 miles north on Highway 89 to the turnoff for Highway 22. Turn right and drive five miles east to Taylorsville. Turn north on County Road 214 and drive about two miles. Turn right on Forest Service Road 27N10 and drive about 10 miles east (stay to the left). Turn left on Forest Service Road 27N57 and drive one mile to the lake.

Access: There is no boat ramp. Small cartop boats may be hand launched.

Facilities, fees: A few primitive Forest Service campsites are available, but there is no piped water, so bring your own. Supplies can be obtained in Taylorsville. Access is free.

Contact: Plumas National Forest, Greenville Service Center, Mount Hough Ranger District, (530) 284-7126. For a detailed map of the area, send $4 to Maps, Office of Information, US Forest Service, 1323 Club Drive, Vallejo, CA 94592.

Water sports, restrictions: Swimming is permitted. The lake is too small for windsurfing and other water sports.

About Taylor Lake: Very few campers pay attention to this small and obscure mountain lake located at an elevation of 5,000 feet. It is too small for most boats, but large enough for a float tube or a raft; visitors occasionally use one of those little float boats to fish for brook trout.

The water is clear, very cold in early summer but quite tolerable by midsummer. Although there are no beaches, there are swimming access spots all around the lakeshore. The surrounding region of Plumas National Forest is well forested, with a network of jeep roads in the area just waiting to be explored.

⑪ Bucks Lake

Location: Near Quincy in Plumas National Forest; map C3, grid f3.

Directions: From Sacramento drive approximately 100 miles east on Interstate 80. Turn north on Highway 89 and drive 70 miles to Quincy. In Quincy turn west on Bucks Lake Road and drive 16.5 miles to the lake.

Access: There are three paved boat ramps, all on the east side of the lake. When you're driving in on Bucks Lake Road, look for the signs for Lakeshore Resort, Bucks Lake Lodge, and Haskins Resort.

Facilities, fees: Several campgrounds and a picnic area are provided on the lake. Lakeshore Resort has a full-service marina and offers fishing boat and paddleboat rentals. Cabins, a restaurant, and groceries are also available. Access is free. There is a fee for boat launching.

Water sports, restrictions: Waterskiing and personal watercraft are permitted. You can swim everywhere, but the best beach is at the Sandy Point Day-Use Area on the northwest end of the lake. Windsurfing is also best in that area.

Contact: Plumas National Forest, Mount Hough Ranger District, (530) 283-0555 or fax (530) 283-1821; Lakeshore Resort, (530) 283-6900; Bucks Lake Lodge, (530) 283-2262.

About Bucks Lake: Here's one of the perfect boating/camping/fishing spots if only—if only it attracted fewer people. Bucks Lake is set at an elevation of 5,150 feet in Plumas National Forest, about a 25-minute drive out of Quincy. That's remote enough to make you feel like you're on the edge of wilderness and high enough to give you a full dose of the four seasons. It's an ideal destination for a family on a camping trip with a boat.

At 1,800 acres the lake is big enough for all water sports. Campers tend to congregate on the lake's northwest side, where the cheaper Forest Service campgrounds are located; the marina, cabins, and developed facilities are all on the east side. The campsites are pretty and wooded, some with views of the lake, and provide excellent shoreline access. Trout fishing is outstanding here, and not only does the lake yield high catch rates of rainbow trout, but some huge Mackinaw and brown trout as well.

When the water levels are high, the lake has a gemlike beauty, its deep blue-green surface contrasted with a forested backdrop and an azure summer sky. But even when the water is low, there are benefits, as several beaches become accessible. In high water, only the beach at the Sandy Point Day-Use Area is available.

The lake freezes over every winter, and snow typically buries the access road. The road is usually plowed by the end of April or very early in May, and even with snow still on the ground at the campgrounds, fishing is usually outstanding. By late June the surface waters start to warm and powerboaters and skiers come out to take advantage of the warm midday temperatures. The combination of clear water and frequent afternoon winds makes Bucks Lake by far the best in the region for windsurfing, a fact that is not well known.

What is well known, however, is that this lake is just about the perfect destination for families who are hauling their boats along in search of some camping fun. That fact keeps the place full of happy folks.

⑫ Spanish Creek

🐟 🏊 ⛵   3 ≋

Location: Near Quincy in Plumas National Forest; map C3, grid f5.

Directions: From Sacramento drive approximately 100 miles east on Interstate 80. Turn north on Highway 89 and drive 70 miles to Quincy. In Quincy continue west on Bucks Lake Road and drive 16.5 miles to the lake. Excellent access is available from the road.

Access: There is no boat ramp.

Facilities, fees: Campgrounds and lodging are provided nearby. Supplies can be obtained in Quincy. Access is free.

Water sports, restrictions: Swimming access points are found at several spots along the roads mentioned above.

Contact: Plumas National Forest, Mount Hough Ranger District, (530) 283-0555 or fax (530) 283-1821.

About Spanish Creek: Little Spanish Creek is known primarily by the local residents who fish for trout here, but a handful of people are aware that this is also a good spot for swimming on hot summer days.

Although there are no designated swimming areas, there is excellent access right off the road. Visitors can simply look for a wide spot in the road, pull over, and jump into a good swimming hole. The place gets light use, mostly by local folks.

---

⑬ Middle Fork Feather River

🏕️ 🎣 ✕ 🚣   [4]

Location: Northeast of Oroville in Plumas National Forest; map C3, grid g2.

Directions: From the junction of Highways 70 and 162 in Oroville, drive 26 miles north on Highway 162/Olive Highway. At the town of Brush Creek, turn right (south) on Bald Rock Road and drive one-half mile to Forest Service Road 22N62/Milsap Bar Road. Turn left and continue northeast. The road is steep and rough. Access is available directly off the road. From Blairsden drive north on Highway 70/89. Access is available off the highway between the towns of Blairsden and Sloat, and off trails that junction with it.

Access: There is no boat ramp. To reach the put-in, start at Quincy on Highway 70/89 and drive east for three miles to La Porte Road. Turn south and continue about seven miles. The put-in is on the left bank, just past the bridge. To reach the take out, start at Oroville and drive northeast on Highway 162/Olive Highway to Brush Creek. Turn south on Galen Ridge Road, continue to Milsap Bar Road, turn left, and continue to the Middle Fork Bridge. Note: This Class V+ run is considered one of the most difficult in the state. Only highly skilled and experienced boaters should attempt it, and then only in kayaks or self-bailing rafts.

Facilities, fees: Campgrounds are available along the river. Supplies can be obtained in Oroville and Blairsden. Access is free. Rafting permits are not required.

Water sports, restrictions: Various swimming holes are available off the access roads mentioned above. Getting to some spots requires extensive hiking; consult a map of Plumas National Forest for specifics.

Contact: Plumas National Forest, Mount Hough Ranger District, (530) 283-0555 or fax (530) 283-1821. For a detail map of the area, send $4 to Maps, Office of Information, US Forest Service, 1323 Club Drive, Vallejo, CA 94592.

About the Middle Fork Feather River: The Middle Fork Feather River is one of the wildest streams in Northern California. Cutting through the bottom of a deep canyon, it is beautiful and free-flowing, remote and untamed. Most people who venture here are hikers and backpackers taking steep butt-kicking trails in and out of the canyon, some crossing the river on the Pacific Crest Trail. There are a number of pools for fishing and swimming, though the water is cold.

Only a handful of expert rafters will try conquering the Middle Fork Gorge, a wild and woolly run that can be terrifying. A series of Class IV and V rapids, as well as some unrunnable suicide portions must be portaged. These include several waterfalls, even the dramatic Granite Dome Falls. Newcomers should have at least one person in their party who knows the river well, and they should attempt running the river only during low water.

That said and done, you have a 32-mile run at the bottom of a canyon in beautiful, extremely remote country. It is a virtual wilderness, where rafters are commonly treated to wildlife sightings and lush vegetation borders much of the river. Once you embark on this run, there is no way out of the canyon, so you are committed to heading downstream all the way to the take-out. Rescues are nearly impossible.

⑭ Little Grass Valley Reservoir

Location: Near La Porte in Plumas National Forest; map C3, grid h5.

Directions: From Oroville drive about 15 miles east on Highway 162 to La Porte Road. Bear right on Forbestown Road and drive east, two miles past the town of La Porte. Turn left on County Road 514/Little Grass Valley Road, drive one mile to a Y, bear left, and drive one more mile to the Wyandotte Campground entrance at the reservoir.

Access: Three paved boat ramps are available. One is on the west side of the lake, adjacent to Black Rock Campground, and the other two are on the east side, near Little Beaver and Peninsula Campgrounds.

Facilities, fees: Several campgrounds are provided. Two good ones are Wyandotte and Running Deer. Supplies can be obtained in La Porte. Access is free.

Water sports, restrictions: Waterskiing, personal watercraft, and windsurfing are permitted. Swimming beaches are available at Running Deer and Little Beaver Campgrounds.

Contact: Plumas National Forest, Feather River Ranger District, (530) 534-6500 or fax (530) 532-1210.

About Little Grass Valley Reservoir: This lake has become quite popular, and why not? It has a little bit of everything, and most of it is high quality. The lake is set at an elevation of 5,000 feet in Plumas National Forest and covers 1,600 acres, so you get alpine beauty plus plenty of room for people to enjoy all water sports.

Boat launching is free, a nice perk. The water is clear and, by midsummer, has warmed up. Lake levels are usually quite good. A recent plan to establish kokanee salmon has given the fishery a boost, too.

The best places for windsurfing and swimming are near the campgrounds on the east side of the lake. This is a great spot for recreation, with hiking trails (the Pacific Crest Trail runs nearby) and a number of Forest Service roads in the area.

But it is the camper/boater who benefits most. You name it, you can probably get it here. Except for solitude, that is. A growing number of summer visitors are becoming quite enamored with the place, so expect company.

⑮ Eureka Lake

Location: Near Graeagle in Plumas-Eureka State Park; map C3, grid h7.

Directions: From Truckee drive about 48 miles north on Highway 89 (about one mile past Graeagle), turn left (west) on County Road A14/Graeagle-Johnsville Road, and drive about five miles to the Plumas-Eureka State Park Entrance.

Access: There is no boat ramp at the lake. You may launch cartop boats by hand.

Facilities, fees: A campground and picnic area are provided in Plumas-Eureka State Park. Supplies can be obtained in Graeagle. A day-use fee is charged at the park.

Water sports, restrictions: Motorized boats are not permitted on the lake. Windsurfing is not allowed. There is a swimming beach on the north side of the lake.

Contact: Plumas-Eureka State Park, (530) 836-2380 or fax (530) 836-0498.

About Eureka Lake: The centerpiece of Plumas-Eureka State Park is Eureka Lake. Set at an elevation of 6,300 feet, the small lake is nestled below Eureka Peak (7,447 feet) and is surrounded by a mix of forest and meadow, with a good wildflower bloom in early summer.

The lake is used mostly for fishing and picnicking and as a jump-off point for the great hike to Eureka Peak. There is no boat ramp, but cartop boats are well suited for the lake because they can be hand launched. Although the surrounding parkland gets heavy use, the lake itself does not, and boaters can enjoy a day free from competition with motorized boats.

A beach is available on the northern shore, and some visitors will swim or bob around a bit late in the summer when the water warms up a bit. However, after big snow years result in heavy runoff, the beach is often submerged.

Rangers are experimenting with closing the access road on busy summer weekends from Friday through Sunday. Even when the road is open, however, it is rough enough to compel most people to hike to the lake, and deters a lot of RV campers from making the trip.

⑯ Jamison Creek

Location: Near Graeagle in Plumas-Eureka State Park; map C3, grid h7.
Directions: From Truckee drive about 48 miles north on Highway 89 (about one mile past Graeagle), turn left (west) on County Road A14/Graeagle-Johnsville Road, and drive about five miles to the Plumas-Eureka State Park Entrance. Creek access is available off the road near the campground.
Access: No boat ramp is available.
Facilities, fees: A campground and picnic area are provided at Jamison Creek. Supplies can be obtained in the town of Graeagle. A day-use fee is charged at the park.
Water sports, restrictions: Several swimming holes are available along the creek, which runs directly through the park's campground. Start at the campground and follow the stream to access the various spots.
Contact: Plumas-Eureka State Park, (530) 836-2380 or fax (530) 836-0498.
About Jamison Creek: Little Jamison

Creek is a prime spot for families with youngsters who want to cool off on a hot summer day. Several excellent swimming holes can be found along the creek and are easily accessible. The best time to swim here is from mid- to late summer, when the water is not only warmer but the flows are low and calm.

Though out-of-towners have no idea that this little creek exists, it is a favorite with the locals. The elevation is approximately 5,000 feet.

⑰ Gold Lake

Location: Near Sierraville in Plumas National Forest; map C3, grid i8.
Directions: From Truckee drive about 30 miles north on Highway 89. Just past the town of Sattley, turn left (west) on Highway 49 and drive over Yuba Pass to Bassetts (about 20 miles). In Bassetts turn right (north) on Gold Lake Road and drive about six miles, following the signs to the lake.
Access: A paved ramp is located on the north side of the lake.
Facilities, fees: Cabins, campground, fishing boat rentals, and limited supplies are available at Gold Lake Beach Resort. Other supplies can be obtained in Graeagle and Bassetts. Access is free.
Water sports, restrictions: Waterskiing, personal watercraft, and windsurfing are permitted. A swimming beach is available at Gold Lake Beach Resort.
Contact: Plumas National Forest, Beckwourth Ranger District, (530) 836-2575 or fax (530) 836-0493; Gold Lake Beach Resort, (530) 836-2491. For a detailed map of the area, send $4 to Maps, Office of Information, U.S Forest Service, 1323 Club Drive, Vallejo, CA 94592.
About Gold Lake: Imagine a beautiful, sky blue lake set in a rock basin in the

northern Sierra, the kind of place where you might want to hide out in a cabin and plan on never leaving.

That is how a visit to Gold Lake can make you feel. It is set near theSierra crest at an elevation of 6,400 feet, and because it is a natural lake, not a reservoir, it is always full of water, a beautiful sight. On the whole this place makes a great vacation destination, with one disclaimer.

The lone drawback, alas, is the wind, which can really blow here, particularly during the afternoon throughout the summer. But that is why windsurfers love the place. Gold Lake is rated as one of the top 10 spots to windsurf in California, and it lures windsurfers from great distances. Every summer day around 2 PM it's a giant Hobiefest around here.

The water is very cold until late in summer, and sometimes the snow and ice aren't gone until late June, but lots of people swim anyway during the vacation season. There's a swimming beach at the resort. The heart of the lake is Gold Lake Lodge, where cabins are typically booked solid in July and August.

⑱ Haven Lake

Location: Near Sierraville in Plumas National Forest; map C3, grid i8.

Directions: From Truckee drive about 30 miles north on Highway 89. Just past the town of Sattley, turn left (west) on Highway 49 and drive over Yuba Pass to Bassetts (about 20 miles). In Bassetts turn right (north) on Gold Lake Road and drive about five miles. There is no formal access road to the lake; look for dirt roads that lead off the main road toward the lake.

Access: There is no boat ramp. Cartop boats may be hand launched.

Facilities, fees: A few primitive campsites are provided, but there is no piped water. Other campgrounds and lodging are available nearby. Supplies can be obtained in Sierra City and Bassetts. Access is free.

Water sports, restrictions: The lake is too small for windsurfing and most boating. Swimming is permitted.

Contact: Plumas National Forest, Beckwourth Ranger District, (530) 836-2575 or fax (530) 836-0493.

About Haven Lake: This small lake with a forested shoreline is very pretty and is always full of water. It is set at an elevation of 5,500 feet in the Lakes Basin Recreation Area.

Most of the folks you'll see around here have come to fish for brook trout, but there are a handful of people who like to swim in Haven Lake. Fewer yet will plunk in a cartop boat and paddle around a bit. Use is very light, due to the fact that there are so many great destinations nearby.

⑲ Snag Lake

Location: Near Sierraville in Plumas National Forest; map C3, grid i8.

Directions: From Truckee drive about 30 miles north on Highway 89. Just past the town of Sattley, turn left (west) on Highway 49 and drive over Yuba Pass to Bassetts (about 20 miles). In Bassetts turn right (north) on Gold Lake Road and drive about six miles, following the signs to the lake. There is no formal access road to the lake; look for dirt roads that lead off the main road toward the lake.

Access: There is no boat ramp. Cartop boats may be hand launched.

Facilities, fees: A primitive campground is provided, but there is no piped water. Supplies can be obtained in Sierra City and Bassetts. Access is free.

Water sports, restrictions: The lake is too small for windsurfing or large boats. Swimming is permitted.

Contact: Tahoe National Forest, North Yuba Ranger Station, (530) 288-3231 or fax (530) 288-0727.

About Snag Lake: There are better lakes in this area, and then there are worse. So as far as the competition goes, Snag Lake rates in the so-so range. But when you consider how beautiful this section of Plumas National Forest is, on a larger scale you could do a lot worse.

This lake is very small and is used by hardly anyone except a few trout anglers. The shoreline is forested; there's not much beach area, but it is possible to get in the water. The water stays quite cold throughout the summer, but some brave souls do manage to swim around, though their immersion is typically brief.

When you do see a boat in use here, it's almost always a raft or a canoe, with the occupants floating about and enjoying themselves, usually casting a line for rainbow trout.

⑳ Salmon Lake

Location: Near Sierraville in Tahoe National Forest; map C3, grid i8.
Directions: From Truckee drive about 30 miles north on Highway 89. Just past the town of Sattley, turn left (west) on Highway 49 and drive over Yuba Pass to Bassetts (about 20 miles). In Bassetts turn right (north) on Gold Lake Road and drive about three miles; turn left at the sign for Salmon Lake and drive one mile to the lake.
Access: There is no boat ramp. Small fishing boats and cartop boats may be hand launched at the shore near the dock.
Facilities, fees: Lodging and limited boat rentals are available at Salmon Lake Lodge. A dock and a pier are also provided. Campgrounds are available nearby. Supplies can be obtained in Sierra City and Bassetts. Access is free.
Water sports, restrictions: The lake is too small for windsurfing or large boats. Swimming is permitted.
Contact: Tahoe National Forest, North

Yuba Ranger Station, (530) 288-3231 or fax (530) 288-0727; Salmon Lake Lodge, (415) 771-0150.
About Salmon Lake: This is a gorgeous setting, absolutely pristine and beautiful with crystal-clear water and wilderness-like surroundings. The Salmon Lake Lodge is unpretentious (they don't have a telephone there), but the cabins are among the most difficult to get reservations for anywhere in California.

Set at an elevation of 6,000 feet, the lake is sheltered from the wind, but the water is typically cold. That doesn't stop kids from jumping off the pier at the lodge, and while they might complain about the cold water, if you listen close you will actually learn that they are bragging.

The lake is excellent for canoeing and kayaking, with rentals available at Salmon Lake Lodge. An extremely primitive dirt launch is provided, but it is intended primarily for hand launching cartop boats. If you use a motor, note that a few underwater boating hazards are marked with buoys.

Several other hike-to lakes, including Lower Salmon Lake, Horse Lake, and Deer Lake, are located nearby. Deer Lake is the prettiest of the lot.

㉑ Sardine Lakes

Location: Near Sierraville in Tahoe National Forest; map C3, grid i8.
Directions: From Truckee drive about 30 miles north on Highway 89. Just past the town of Sattley, turn left (west) on Highway 49 and drive over Yuba Pass to Bassetts (about 20 miles). In Bassetts turn right (north) on Gold Lake Road and drive about one mile. Turn left at Sardine Lake Road, drive a short distance, veer to the left at the Y, and drive one-half mile to Lower Sardine Lake.
Access: A hand-launching area is available on the lower lake.

Facilities, fees: Lodging, restaurant, and rowboat and fishing boat rentals are available at Sardine Lake Lodge. A campground is provided at Lower Sardine Lake. Supplies can be obtained in Sierra City and Bassetts. Access is free.

Water sports, restrictions: A 5 mph speed limit is strictly enforced. Swimming is permitted at Upper Sardine Lake, just a short walk from the parking area at Lower Sardine Lake, or at little Sand Pond down the road. Swimming is not allowed at Lower Sardine.

Contact: Tahoe National Forest, North Yuba Ranger Station, (530) 288-3231 or fax (530) 288-0727; Sardine Lake Resort, (916) 645-8882.

About Sardine Lakes: Sometimes there is just no substitute for spectacular natural beauty, which is what you'll find when you visit the Sardine Lakes. The Sardine Lakes are among the prettiest drive-to lakes in California. They are set in a rock bowl beneath the impressive Sierra Buttes and are always full of water, thanks to the melting snow. That right there is reason enough to justify a visit. The lakes need no extra selling point, but they get it.

Small and intimate, the lakes are perfect for low-speed boats, and on the water you are surrounded by this dramatic beauty. Sometimes it feels as if you are literally soaking it up. A primitive boat ramp—accessible to cartop boats and small trailered boats—is provided next to the lodge. There is also a small marina with boat docks where visitors can rent aluminum boats with motors.

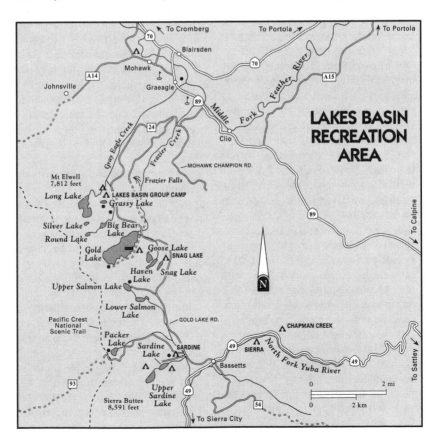

Map of Chapter C3—Page 144

Trout fishing is good here, and most boaters bring along a rod. Some visitors rent a boat and venture to the head of the lake, where they can beach and make the short walk to the inlet stream's hidden waterfall.

The water at Lower Sardine is too cold for swimming, but nearby Upper Sardine (which you have to hike to) and Sand Pond offer decent swimming opportunities and excellent hiking.

The cabins at Sardine Lake Lodge are small, well kept, and utterly adorable. Getting a reservation to stay in one can require literally years on a waiting list.

㉒ Bullards Bar Reservoir

Location: Near Camptonville in Tahoe National Forest; map C3, grid j2.

Directions: From Sacramento drive 40 miles north on Highway 70/89 to Marysville. Turn east on Highway 20 and drive 12 miles. Look for the sign for Bullards Bar Reservoir and turn left on Marysville Road. Turn north and drive about 10 miles. Turn right on Old Marysville Road and drive 14 miles to Bullards Bar Reservoir. Turn just before the dam to access the Emerald Cove Marina.

Access: Two paved ramps are available, one at Dark Day Day-Use Area on the west side of the lake, and one at Emerald Cove Marina on the south end of the lake.

Facilities, fees: Two developed boat-in campgrounds are provided, along with many primitive boat-in sites, but they offer no piped water and require reservations. Campgrounds, rest rooms, and a day-use area are available. A full-service marina is provided at Emerald Cove, along with fishing boat, ski boat, patio boat, and houseboat rentals. A snack bar and limited groceries are also available. Full supplies can be obtained in Marysville, Camptonville, and Dobbins. Access is free.

Water sports, restrictions: Ski boats and personal watercraft are permitted. Swimming access points are available all along the shore; the best areas are in the various coves around the lake, which are accessible only by boat.

Contact: Emerald Cove Resort and Marina, (530) 692-3200 or fax (530) 692-3202; Yuba County Water Agency, (916) 741-6278; Tahoe National Forest, North Yuba Ranger Station, (530) 288-3231 or fax (530) 288-0727.

About Bullards Bar Reservoir: Bullards Bar Reservoir shines like a silver dollar in a field of pennies when compared to the other reservoirs in the Central Valley foothills.

The lake is set at an elevation of 2,300 feet, and with 4,700 surface acres and 55 miles of shoreline, it covers a lot of territory. Not only are there two boat-in campgrounds, but boaters are allowed to create their own primitive campsites anywhere along the lakeshore (a chemical toilet is required). This is a great breakthrough for boater/campers, and the combination of boat-in campgrounds and do-it-yourself sites make this one of the best bets in California.

There's more, too. The average surface temperature in the summer is 78 degrees, ideal for all water sports. The steep shoreline makes this a poor place for children to go wading, but most people here have boats, and the warm water makes it great for boats towing just about anything—skiers, kids on Boogie boards, and even inner tubes.

The fishing runs hot and cold here. Prospects are best when trolling for kokanee salmon, a growing fishery. Rainbow trout also live in the lake.

Many of the 155 major reservoirs in California are just water-storage facilities, drawn down at the whims of the water brokers regardless of the effects on recreation and fisheries. But the folks who control the plumbing at Bullards Bar somehow manage to keep this lake nearly full through July, even in low-water years when other reservoirs have been turned into dust bowls. So right off, you get good lakeside camping, boating, and general beauty along with a lot of water.

㉓ North Yuba River

Location: Near Sierra City in Tahoe National Forest; map C3, grid j7.

Directions: From Sacramento drive northeast on Interstate 80 to Auburn and then turn north on Highway 49. Direct access is available east or west of Sierra City.

Access: No boat ramp is available. There are two popular runs on the North Yuba:

Downieville Run: To reach the put-in, drive six miles east of Downieville on Highway 49 to Union Flat Campground. Take out 10 miles downstream at the Goodyears Bar Bridge or continue through the Goodyears Bar Run. Note: This run is Class IV–V with some very difficult sections and should be run by experts only.

Goodyears Bar Run: From Downieville drive approximately five miles west on Highway 49 to Goodyears Bar. Take out downstream at Fiddle Creek Campground or continue an additional eight miles to Bullards Bar Reservoir.

Facilities, fees: Numerous campgrounds are available off Highway 49. Two good ones are Union Flat and Chapman Creek. Supplies can be obtained in Bassetts, Sierra City, Downieville, and Camptonville. Access is free. Rafting permits are not required.

Water sports, restrictions: There are several excellent swimming holes along Highway 49, with the best at the Forest Service campgrounds.

Contact: Tahoe National Forest, Headquarters, (530) 265-4531 or fax (530) 478-6109. For guided rafting trips contact Whitewater Voyages, (800) 488-7238.

About the North Fork Yuba River: The North Fork Yuba is one of the prettiest streams to flow westward out of the Sierra Nevada. The stretch of river near Downieville is especially gorgeous; it is fed by the melting snow from the Sierra crest, has deep pools and miniature waterfalls, and is in places edged by slabs of granite and punctuated with boulders.

In the spring this can be a wild and cold force of water, running blue-white during peak snowmelt. In the summer and fall, it greens up, warms considerably, and takes on a more benign demeanor in its routed canyon course.

Highway 49, which is shaped more like a pretzel than a highway, parallels much of the river, providing access not only to the stream but to a series of campgrounds operated by the Forest Service. Right alongside the road are many good swimming holes that are accessible from the camps, such as the one six miles east of Downieville near Quartz Point at Union Flat Campground.

Rafting season generally lasts from April through June here, and the river offers several great runs. The two best are the Downieville Run and the Goodyears Bar Run (for directions see "Access"):

Downieville Run: Spanning 19 miles, the run features white water rated Class IV–V. The Class V highlights include Moss Canyon and Rossasco Ravine. This is a tight canyon with lush vegetation and cold water. Wet suits or dry suits are necessary; they are available for rent from Whitewater Voyages.

Goodyears Bar Run: This is one of the prime one-day rafting trip runs in California. It covers eight miles with a series of Class III–IV rapids and one monster Class V called Maytag, which rafters who are unfamiliar with the river may choose to portage. The trip can be extended farther downstream to Bullards Bar Reservoir, and the reward for doing so is a six-mile stretch with Class IV–IV+ white water. You pay for this encounter, however, by having to paddle 12 slow miles across flat water at the reservoir to the nearest take-out, Dark Day Boat Ramp. It would be wise to make advance arrangements for a tow.

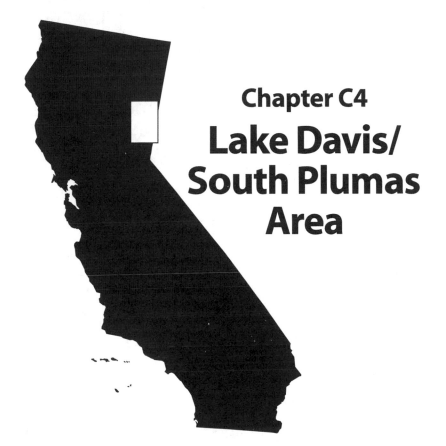

Chapter C4
Lake Davis/
South Plumas
Area

Overall Rating

| 1 | 2 | 3 | 4 | 5 | 6 | 7 | 8 | 9 | 10 |

Poor .... Fair .... Great

C4–Lake Davis/South Plumas Map

One inch equals approximately 10.7 miles.
See page 12 for California state map.

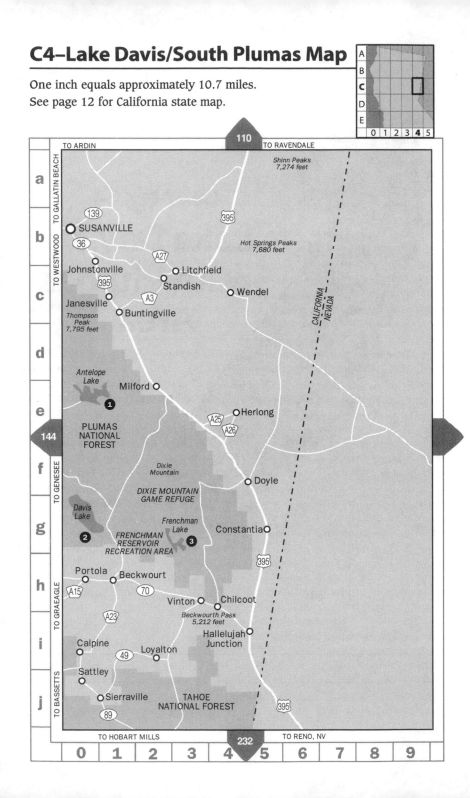

❶ Antelope Lake

Location: Near Taylorsville in Plumas National Forest; map C4, grid e1.

Directions: From Red Bluff drive east on Highway 36 to Susanville and US 395. Turn south on US 395 and drive about 10 miles (one mile past Janesville) to County Road 208. Turn right on County Road 208 (signed for Antelope Lake) and drive about 15 miles to a Y, one mile before Antelope Lake. Turn left at the Y and drive four miles to the northwest end of the lake.

Access: To reach the two-lane paved ramp, continue on Indian Creek Road toward Boulder Creek and Lone Rock Campgrounds and proceed around the lake's north side to the ramp.

Facilities, fees: Campgrounds are provided at the lake. A small store with limited supplies is available. Extensive supplies can be obtained in Taylorsville. Access is free.

Water sports, restrictions: Waterskiing, personal watercraft, and windsurfing are permitted. Swimming access is available near the campgrounds.

Contact: Plumas National Forest, Headquarters, (530) 283-2050 or fax (530) 283-4156.

About Antelope Lake: Wanted: Mountain lake circled by conifers with campsites, good boating, and trout fishing.

Some people might want to put an advertisement in the newspaper to find such a place, but that isn't necessary for in-the-know visitors to northern Plumas County. They'll direct you to Antelope Lake, which is ringed by forestland, provides campgrounds at each end of the lake, and has a boat ramp conveniently located just a few miles from each camp.

Antelope Lake is just about perfect for a boating/camping vacation. Seclusion is practically guaranteed—the lake is located approximately 100 miles from Oroville by our estimate—and the road in is accessible to trailered boats. Although not huge, Antelope Lake is big enough, with 15 miles of shoreline and plenty of little islands, coves, and peninsulas to create an intimate atmosphere.

The lake is set at 5,000 feet elevation and covers 930 surface acres. Even though the shoreline is heavily forested, there are good swimming areas adjacent to the campgrounds. Windsurfers will find the prime spots for their sport on the west side near the boat ramp and at Long Point Campground (both offer more wide-open access).

What makes Antelope Lake special is that the drive here is too daunting for most visitors. If it were any closer to civilization, the place would be loaded with vacationers everyday throughout summer. Still, it is by no means unknown. On summer weekends it can even get crowded. Hey, it makes sense. After all, a description of this lake reads like an advertisement for a good time.

❷ Lake Davis

Location: Near Portola in Plumas National Forest; map C4, grid g0.

Directions: From Sacramento drive approximately 100 miles east on Interstate 80 to Truckee. Turn north on Highway 89 and drive to Sattley. Turn right on County Road A23 and drive 13 miles to Highway 70. Turn left on Highway 70 and drive one mile; then turn right on Grizzly Road and drive six miles to the lake.

Access: There are three boat ramps:

Honker Cove: Continue north on Grizzly Road to Grasshopper Flat Campground. A paved ramp is located just north of the campground at Honker Cove.

Lightning Tree: Continue north on Grizzly Road to Lightning Tree Campground, the northernmost site on the lake. There is a paved ramp.

Old Camp Five: At the south end of the lake, turn left on Davis Lake Road and drive west past the dam to the primitive boat ramp.

Facilities, fees: Campgrounds and cabin rentals are available. The Grizzly Store rents out fishing boats and sells limited supplies. Access is free. There is no charge for boat launching.

Water sports, restrictions: Waterskiing and personal watercraft are not permitted. Windsurfing is allowed. Swimming is possible all around the lakeshore; a good spot is the cove at Grasshopper Flat Campground.

Contact: Plumas National Forest, Headquarters, (530) 283-2050 or fax (530) 283-4156; Davis Lake Cabins; (530) 832-1060.

About Lake Davis: If you want to cap off your boating/camping trip with a little gambling binge, come to Lake Davis, located in the southern reaches of Plumas National Forest just 50 miles from Reno. Set high in the northern Sierra at 5,775 feet in elevation, this is a good-size lake that covers 4,000 acres and has 32 miles of shoreline.

The character of the lake undergoes great changes according to the season. In the spring, after ice-out, winds are often ideal for sailing and windsurfing (a thick wet suit is essential). At times the winds can even be dangerous for small boats, and only extremely experienced boaters in appropriate craft should be on the water.

Then summer suddenly arrives, along with hot weather and plenty of campers. Many campers bring small boats, which they use to go fishing for trout and bass, netting fair results. Waterskiing and personal watercraft are prohibited, a rule that ensures that the water remains calm. That is a bonus for anglers as well as for swimmers. While there are no beaches, several good coves provide good swimming areas. As summer progresses camper use increases greatly.

A summer's worth of hot weather spurs a rich aquatic food chain into existence, and much of the lake can become quite weedy by the end of August. Fouled propellers are a real problem here at this time. Then, after the first cold nights of October, the trout go on a feeding binge. This results in outstanding trolling for large rainbow trout, which often reach lengths of 16 to 22 inches, and sometimes even bigger.

Because of the elevation the area gets a lot of snow dumped on it in the winter. This lake can freeze over, despite the fact that it is large. By winter just about everything is shut down, except for the cabins that are rented by people who want to play in the snow or go cross-country skiing. Say, how far away is Reno?

---

❸ Frenchman Lake

Location: Near Portola in Plumas National Forest; map C4, grid g3.

Directions: From Sacramento drive approximately 100 miles east on Interstate 80 to Truckee. Turn north on Highway 89, drive about 50 miles, then turn east on Highway 70, and drive 28 miles to Chilcoot. Turn north on Frenchman Lake Road and drive about eight miles to the lake. The lake is also easily accessed from Reno.

Access: A paved boat ramp is located at Frenchman Campground, east of the dam.

Facilities, fees: Several campgrounds are provided on the south and west shores. There are five boat-in campgrounds on the north side. Groceries can be purchased near the campgrounds. Access is free.

Water sports, restrictions: Waterskiing, personal watercraft, and windsurfing are permitted. Swimming access is available all around the lake, with the best spots in the small coves near the boat-in camps.

Contact: Plumas National Forest, Headquarters, (530) 283-2050 or fax (530) 283-4156.

About Frenchman Lake: High desert borders the east side of Frenchman Lake. A game refuge and Plumas National Forest lie to the west. So visitors to this lake get a piece of two different worlds, as well as the opportunity for good boating, fishing, and camping throughout much of the summer.

Frenchman is set in fairly high country, at an elevation of 5,500 feet, which means things get cold and windy in the spring and fall as wind sails over the Sierra crest and plunges eastward toward the Nevada desert. In addition, due to water demands, the lake level often drops substantially in late summer and fall. During this time of the year, you are advised to phone the Forest Service before planning a boating trip to make sure the water level isn't below the ramp.

That leaves a relatively short period, mid-June through early August, when the temperatures are warm, the wind is down, and the lake level is up. At that time boating and camping are good, the trout bite, and the swimming is decent. A number of people have figured this out, so the place can be bustling in midsummer and then seem as deserted as a ghost lake a month later.

The lake—which is surrounded by a mix of sage and pines—has 21 miles of shoreline, including a few deep secluded coves on the west side that are protected from the early summer winds. The best windsurfing spots are near the ramp at Frenchman Campground and at Big Cove Campground.

Frenchman Lake can be used as a base camp for two good excursions. Dixie Mountain State Game Refuge is just to the northwest; and another favorite, Reno, is only 35 miles away. Odds are you'll wind up at the latter anyway.

Chapter D0

Sonoma Coast

Overall Rating

1	2	3	4	5	6	7	8	9	10

Poor .... Fair .... Great

D0–Sonoma Coast Area Map

One inch equals approximately 10.7 miles.
See page 12 for California state map.

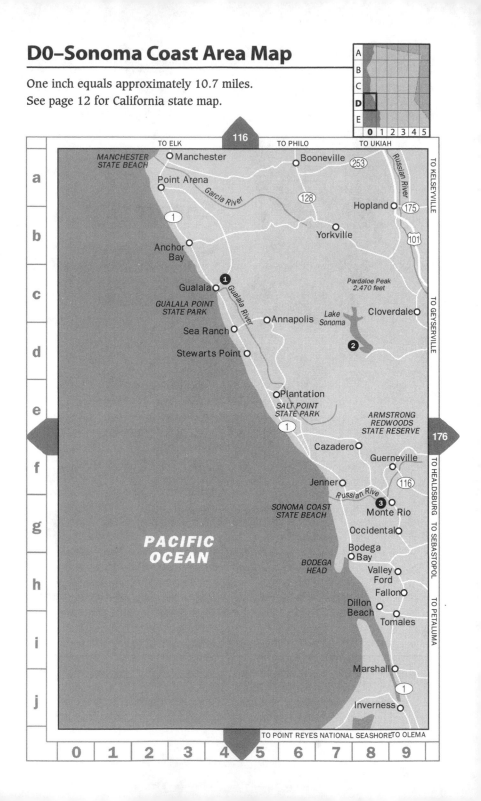

Chapter DØ features:

❶ Gualala River

Location: South of Point Arena; map DØ, grid c4.

Directions: To reach the upper fishing limit of the river, drive south on Highway 1 from Point Arena for 20 miles to Annapolis Road. Turn left (east) and drive to the twin bridges. To access the lower river from the town of Gualala, turn east on Old Stage Road (Road 501), then right on Old State Highway (Road 502). Direct access is available.

Access: There is no boat ramp. To reach the standard put-in, called Switchvale, follow the directions above for access to the lower river. Once on Old State Highway, drive three miles to a parking area. Park and carry your gear a short distance down to the beach. An alternate put-in is located about six miles upstream at an access known as Hot Spot, but it is generally only boatable very early in the season.

Facilities, fees: Campgrounds are available near Gualala. Kayak rentals, shuttle service, and boating supplies can be obtained at Adventure Rents. Full facilities are available in Gualala. Access is free. Rafting permits are not required.

Water sports, restrictions: Several swimming holes are located off the roads mentioned above.

Contact: Adventure Rents, (707) 884-4386 or fax (707) 884-1231.

About the Gualala River: Remote and pretty, the Gualala River is the best of the smaller rivers flowing along the Sonoma and Mendocino coastline. Families and novice rafters find that it makes a great place to enjoy an easy float in a canoe or a kayak. The water is clean and warm in the summer, and the lower river is good for swimming.

Because the river's upper stretches are often too shallow in the summer, the lower section gets pretty heavy recreational use. The run down in a kayak or canoe is an easy Class I affair that gets a lot of traffic in the summer months. About 50 kayaks are available for rent, and customers are provided with all of the necessary accessories and shuttle service. Bikes and canoes are also available.

The river is very scenic, and boaters should be able to see lots of wildlife and a variety of bird species. Swimming is good all along the lower river, which has deep swimming holes and even rope swings in a couple of places. One word of warning: Don't try to find swimming spots upstream because that river section is bordered by private property.

❷ Lake Sonoma

Location: North of Santa Rosa; map DØ, grid d7.

Directions: From Santa Rosa drive 12 miles north on US 101 to the town of Healdsburg. Turn left at the Dry Creek Road exit and drive 11 miles to the lake.

Access: A five-lane paved boat ramp is located on the lake's west side. To reach it, take Dry Creek Road past the dam and cross the bridge. The ramp is on the north side of the road. A primitive, hand-launch area is available at Yorty Creek (see directions for the swimming beach under "Water sports, restrictions").

Facilities, fees: Primitive, developed, and boat-in campsites are provided at the lake. A full-service marina, rest rooms, snack bar, and a small store are available at Lake Sonoma Resort. Ski boats, fishing boats, personal watercraft, canoes, and paddle-boats can be rented at the marina. Supplies can be obtained in Healdsburg. A day-use fee is charged, and there is an additional fee for boat launching.

Water sports, restrictions: Waterskiing and personal watercraft are allowed only in designated areas. The rest of the lake has a strictly enforced 5 mph speed limit. There is one swimming beach; to reach it take the South Cloverdale Boulevard exit off US 101 and turn right. Continue to Hot Springs Road, turn left, and continue to the beach at Yorty Creek. This is also the best spot for windsurfing.

Contact: US Army Corps of Engineers, Lake Sonoma, (707) 433-9483; Lake Sonoma Marina, (707) 433-2200. For a map write to US Army Corps of Engineers, Lake Sonoma, 3333 Skaggs Springs Road, Geyserville, CA 95441.

About Lake Sonoma: Nestled in the rich foothill country of Sonoma County, Lake Sonoma offers one of the best boater/camper experiences around. A 5 mph speed limit and no-wake zones have been established in many areas of the lake, along with 14 boat-in campsites. This guarantees peace, quiet, and excellent swimming and fishing opportunities; yet there's still a huge section of water available for waterskiing.

There's plenty of room for everybody. The lake is set at an elevation of 450 feet and covers 2,500 surface acres, with 53 miles of shoreline and hundreds of hidden coves. In addition, the lake is adjacent to an 8,000-acre wildlife area that has 40 miles of hiking trails. From the dam the lake extends nine miles north on the Dry Creek Arm and four miles west on Warm Springs Creek. Each of the lake arms has several fingers and miles of quiet and secluded shore. One of the great things about this lake is that boat rentals are available at the marina.

Any potential conflict between speed demons and anglers has been resolved by setting aside a large area in the main lake for water-skiers and personal watercraft.

Water-skiers usually stick to the Warm Springs Arm, which gets less wind than the Dry Creek Arm. Swimmers and beginning windsurfers will find the best conditions near Yorty Creek, although speed-loving windsurfers can venture into the waterskiing area on the Dry Creek Arm. How is the water? Well, after the winter storm runoff turns it a bit off-color, the lake quickly turns green in the spring, and by summer surface temperatures are in the high 70s.

The lake attracts heavy use, with most visitors staying at the Liberty Glen Campground. The only fully developed camp on the lake, it encompasses 118 campsites. Boaters have the advantage of being able to access the boat-in camps, which are great if you're looking for a personal, secluded site. These are primitive sites without piped water, but they provide chemical toilets, garbage cans, tent sites, picnic tables, fire rings, and lantern poles (you can hang your food on them)—and the sites are free. Be sure to bring some kind of sunscreen, even if it's just a light tarp rigged with poles and ropes. Sites are taken on a first-come, first-served basis.

To get the most out of a stay here, stop at the visitor center below the dam to pick up maps, brochures, and other information, and ask about boat-in campsite availability.

All in all, Lake Sonoma provides the perfect example of how to do something right.

---

❸ Russian River

Location: Northwest of Santa Rosa; map DØ, grid g8.

Directions: From San Francisco drive north on US 101 and then west on Highway 116 past Sebastopol and Guerneville. Four miles past Guerneville at an intersection with a stop sign, continue straight into Monte Rio where Highway 116 veers to the right. Turn left on the Bohemian Highway and drive a short distance to the river. Direct access is available from the road.

Access: Access points to numerous hand-launch areas for canoes and other small craft are located along Highway 116. In addition, paved boat ramps are provided at these locations:

Casini Ranch Family Campground: From Highway 116 at Duncans Mills, turn southeast on Moscow Road and drive one-half mile to the campground.

Monte Rio Fishing Access: In the town of Monte Rio, turn south on Church Street and continue down to the ramp.

Canoeists and kayakers may put in at one of the areas mentioned above or farther upstream at Burke's Canoes, located about 10 miles east of Guerneville at 8600 River Road. Note: Private boats are permitted to launch only on weekdays. On weekends private boats are not permitted to launch from here; rentals are available.

Facilities, fees: Several campgrounds are located on and near the river. A good one is Casini Ranch Family Campground, which also provides canoe rentals. Canoes can also be rented at Burke's Canoes. Public beaches with rest rooms, picnic facilities, and snack bars are available as well. Access is free. There is a fee for boat launching at Casini Ranch and Burke's.

Water sports, restrictions: Several excellent swimming beaches are available along Highway 116. Good spots include Johnson's Beach in Guerneville, the public beach at Monte Rio, and the beach at Casini Ranch Campground.

Contact: Casini Ranch Family Campground, (707) 865-2255 or (800) 451-8400; Burke's Canoes, (707) 887-1222.

About the Russian River: Want to find out just how well you get along with somebody? Try paddling a canoe with them down the Russian River. By the end of the day, you either will have bonded with your companion or will want to jam a paddle down their throat.

Rest assured that this is a great place for such an experiment because the results are likely to be positive. Most of the year the river is fresh and rolling green, with a prime 10-mile stretch between Forestville and Guerneville that is routed through redwoods. All this makes for a great first-time paddle.

The most popular launching spot for canoeists is Burke's Canoes. From there you take your time floating lazily down to their private beach in Guerneville, where you can catch a shuttle ride back (it's included in the price). Without guides, you set the pace of your trip. It's an easy paddle along one of the prettiest sections of the entire river, winding through the heart of the redwoods. The area is green and lush, yet also has many sunny beaches where you can picnic. And whereas other river sections have temporary dams to retain water, here there are no dams to cross.

There are several other places to put in downstream, however, and it's an easy float nearly all the way to the ocean. Casini's is another popular put-in, the beginning of a six-mile paddle trip.

In the summer the river gets heavy use, with lots of boaters and swimmers at every imaginable access point. There are large, sandy beaches all along the highway. The best are at Johnson's Beach and Monte Rio, which offer full-facility beaches with lifeguards.

Way upstream on the Russian River, between Cloverdale and Hopland, is a challenging bend and rapid at Squaw Rock where kayakers like to practice. You'll sometimes see people taking kayaking lessons here.

From Cloverdale down past Geyserville, it's an easy paddle. The river is more sedate, and there are far fewer people than the stretch downstream of Forestville. With only a handful of short, unrated rapids, this is the kind of place where you can enjoy being close to the water as it helps to propel you downstream, and you gain a sense of exhilaration from the freedom of riding a river. Regardless of which section you pick, the Russian River is an ideal first-time destination for canoeing or kayaking.

Chapter D1
Clear Lake/ Berryessa Area

Overall Rating

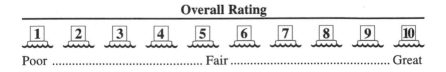

| 1 | 2 | 3 | 4 | 5 | 6 | 7 | 8 | 9 | 10 |

Poor .... Fair .... Great

D1–Clear Lake/Berryessa Area Map

One inch equals approximately 10.7 miles.
See page 12 for California state map.

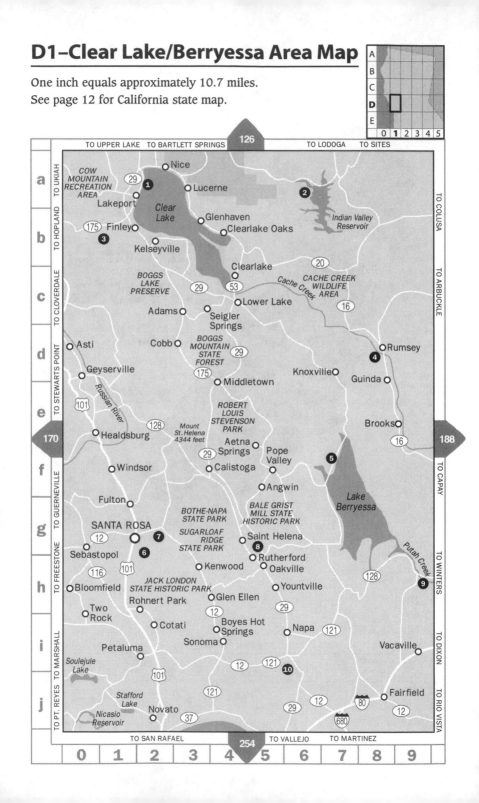

TO UPPER LAKE   TO BARTLETT SPRINGS   **126**   TO LODOGA   TO SITES

TO UKIAH

a
COW MOUNTAIN RECREATION AREA
Nice ①
Lucerne
Lakeport
Clear Lake
②
Indian Valley Reservoir

TO HOPLAND
TO COLUSA

b
⑳ 175 Finley
③
Kelseyville
Glenhaven
Clearlake Oaks

TO CLOVERDALE
TO ARBUCKLE

c
BOGGS LAKE PRESERVE
29
Clearlake
53
Cache Creek
20
CACHE CREEK WILDLIFE AREA
16
Adams
Seigler Springs
Lower Lake

d
Asti
Cobb
BOGGS MOUNTAIN STATE FOREST
29
Knoxville
Rumsey ④
Guinda

TO STEWARTS POINT
Geyserville
175
Middletown

TO CLOVERDALE

Russian River

e
101
128
Mount St. Helena 4344 feet
ROBERT LOUIS STEVENSON PARK
Brooks
16
170   Healdsburg   **188**

TO GUERNEVILLE
TO CAPAY

f
Windsor
29 Aetna Springs
Calistoga
Pope Valley
⑤
Lake Berryessa

g
Fulton
SANTA ROSA
12 ⑦
⑥
BOTHE-NAPA STATE PARK
SUGARLOAF RIDGE STATE PARK
BALE GRIST MILL STATE HISTORIC PARK
Angwin
Saint Helena ⑧

TO FREESTONE
Sebastopol
116

h
101
Bloomfield
JACK LONDON STATE HISTORIC PARK
Rohnert Park
Kenwood
Rutherford
Oakville
Yountville
128
⑨

TO WINTERS

i
Two Rock
Cotati
Glen Ellen
12
Boyes Hot Springs
Sonoma
29
Napa
121
Vacaville

TO MARSHALL
Petaluma
Souleujule Lake

TO DIXON

j
101
121
Stafford Lake
Nicasio Reservoir
Novato
37
12
121
⑩
29
12
80
680
Fairfield
12

TO PT. REYES
TO RIO VISTA

TO SAN RAFAEL   **254**   TO VALLEJO   TO MARTINEZ

0   1   2   3   4   5   6   7   8   9

Chapter D1 features:

❶ Clear Lake

Location: North of San Francisco; map D1, grid a2.

Directions: From San Francisco drive north on US 101 past San Rafael to Highway 37. Drive east on Highway 37 about 23 miles to Vallejo. Turn north on Highway 29 and drive about 69 miles to the town of Lower Lake.

From Sacramento/Interstate 5, take Interstate 5 north to Williams, turn west on Highway 20, and continue to the town of Clearlake.

From the North Coast take US 101 south to Calpella (17 miles south of Willits); then turn east on Highway 20 and continue to the town of Nice.

Access: Clear Lake has 10 free boat launches, along with dozens and dozens of others at private resorts. For a complete list contact the Lake County Visitor Information Center at the phone number given below. The following is a list of free public ramps:

Lakeside County Park: From Highway 29 south of Kelseyville, turn north on Soda Bay Road/Highway 281 and drive to Park Drive. Take Park Drive north and continue to the paved ramp at 1985 Park Drive.

Redbud City Park: In the town of Clearlake, look for the park entrance at 14655 Lakeshore Drive. A four-lane paved ramp is available.

First Street Ramp: From Main Street in the town of Lakeport, turn east on First Street and continue to the two-lane paved ramp.

Third Street Ramp: From Main Street in the town of Lakeport, take Third Street east to the two-lane paved ramp.

Fifth Street Ramp: From Main Street in the town of Lakeport, turn east on Fifth Street and drive to the two-lane paved ramp.

Clear Lake Avenue: From Main Street in the town of Lakeport, take Clear Lake Avenue east and head to the paved ramp located at the lake's edge.

Lakeshore Drive and Crystal Lake Way: From Main Street in the town of Lakeport, turn west on Clear Lake Avenue and continue to High Street. Turn north, drive to Lakeshore Drive, turn north, and continue to the paved ramp at the junction with Crystal Lake Way.

Lucerne Harbor County Park: A paved ramp is available at this park, located in the town of Lucerne at 6225 East Highway 20.

H. V. Keeling County Park: This park is located in the town of Nice at 3000 Lakeshore Boulevard and has a paved ramp.

Hudson Avenue: From Highway 20 in Nice, turn south on Hudson Boulevard and continue to the two-lane paved ramp at the lake's edge.

Facilities, fees: You can camp at Clear Lake State Park near Kelseyville as well as at several private campgrounds and resorts around the lake. Boat rentals, bait and tackle, and supplies are available. Full marina services and boat rentals are available at Ferndale Marina in Kelseyville, (707) 279-4866; Tally's Family Resort in Nice, (707) 274-1177; Glenhaven Marina in Glenhaven,

(707) 998-3406; and Will-O-Point Resort in Lakeport, (707) 263-5407. Access is free. There are fees for boat launching at the private marinas.

Water sports, restrictions: Waterskiing, personal watercraft, windsurfing, and swimming are permitted. There are good beaches at Clear Lake State Park in Kelseyville, Redbud City Park in Clearlake, Star Beach in Lucerne, H.V. Keeling Park in Nice, and at 16th Street in Lakeport.

Contact: For general information and a free travel packet, contact the Greater Lakeport Chamber of Commerce, (707) 263-5092 or fax (707) 263-5104; or the Lake County Visitor Information Center, (800) 525-3743 (in California only) or fax (707) 263-9564.

About Clear Lake: What a vision Clear Lake is the first time you drive over the hills and lay your eyes on it: So big, so full, perhaps a few cumulus clouds sprinkled in the sky over nearby Mount Konocti. It is one of the prettiest sights in California, particularly in the spring when the surrounding hills are green and everything is so fresh and clean.

This is one of those rare places where reality can equal the vision. There is just something about Clear Lake that makes a visit here a special experience. Maybe it's the knowledge that this is a true lake fashioned entirely by the forces of nature rather than a reservoir created by humans to serve humans.

For one thing the body of water is vast, covering more than 40,000 surface acres amid the foothills of Lake County, the largest natural freshwater lake within California's borders. It often seems full right to the brim, and with Highway 20 running aside the eastern shore, there is a sense of intimacy that large reservoirs just can't claim, where the water levels can be low and roads far distant from the water. With doz-

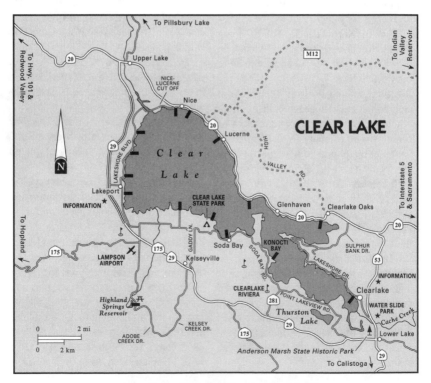

ens of resorts and private campgrounds sprinkled along the 100 miles of shoreline, the lake can accommodate huge numbers of visitors without making one feel crowded. In addition there are almost 100 boat ramps (including 10 free ramps). That makes Clear Lake ideal for boater/camper weekends.

Every imaginable water sport—even parasailing—can be enjoyed here, and just about every kind of watercraft is available for rent. Add to that staying at a resort, camping, fishing, hiking, horseback riding, bicycling, rockhounding, golfing, touring wineries, taking glider flights, exploring Indian village archaeological sites, and well, you've got it all.

The lake is shaped somewhat like an hourglass, with the northern section much larger and rounder than its southern counterpart, which is divided by an extended peninsula. Waterskiing is best on calm summer days on the lake's northern part. Note that the shoreline along the north and west shores, and along the southern half of the lake is very popular for bass fishing, so water-skiers should avoid the shoreline, particularly in the coves. To ensure that water-skiers stay where they're supposed to, a sheriff's boat patrols the lake full time.

The water is very warm in summer, with surface temperatures often approaching 80 degrees, ideal for all water sports. But nothing is perfect, and such is the case at Clear Lake. Warm water combined with high nutrients and a productive aquatic food chain can result in large amounts of algae. By late summer there can even be mats of the gunk. For the most part by the time the hot weather arrives, it is more like a lot of green bits in pea soup. During this time, anybody emerging from the water can be covered with the stuff; people wearing white bathing suits covered with green bits make an especially bizarre sight.

The lake's marinas are complete and well staffed, and the marinas that have lodging and docking facilities are extremely popular all summer long. Reservations are always advised. The same is true at Clear Lake State Park, which provides campgrounds as well as boater access to an adjacent section of tule-edged shoreline that is especially good for fishing for bluegill and bass.

Dozens of mom-and-pop operations are located around the lake. They vary greatly in quality, but virtually all have their own boat ramps or are situated very close to a public ramp. The most developed operation is at Konocti Harbor Inn, which has condo-style units, a restaurant, full marina, and a small concert hall.

Windsurfing is possible just about anywhere there's a beach. The best time for the sport is in the spring when the wind is up and the algae problem is minimal.

There are several beaches around the lake. The Lake County Visitor Information Center provides a free map that details all the public boat ramps and beach access points.

❷ Indian Valley Reservoir

Location: Near Clear Lake; map D1, grid a6.

Directions: From the north end of Clear Lake at the town of Nice, drive one mile south on Highway 20 and turn left on Bartlett Springs Road. The twisty road is routed to the north end of the lake, where a boat launch is located. From Interstate 5 at Williams, turn west on Highway 20 and drive about eight miles. Turn left on Highway 53 and drive three miles. Turn right on Lakeshore Drive in Clearlake. Access to the lake is off Lakeshore Drive.

Access: To access the boat ramp at the north end of the lake, take Leesville-Walnut Road from Leesville and jog left on Bear Valley Road. Drive two miles, turn right on Brim/Bartlett Springs Road, and drive to the north end of the lake. To access the southern boat ramp, from Interstate 5 at Williams, turn west on Highway 20 and drive 24 miles to Walker Ridge Road. Take Walker Ridge Road for five miles, turn left on the access road, and continue about two more miles to the boat ramp, located near the Indian Valley Store.

Facilities, fees: Campgrounds are located near the Indian Valley Store, which has limited supplies. There is a day-use fee.

Water sports, restrictions: A 10 mph speed limit is strictly enforced. Waterskiing and personal watercraft are prohibited. Although there are no designated beaches, you can swim all along the shoreline; the most popular swimming spots are near the campgrounds. Windsurfing is permitted, but note the speed limit.

Contact: Bureau of Land Management, Folsom Field Office, (916) 985-4474; Indian Valley Store, (530) 662-0607.

About Indian Valley Reservoir: Imagine a lake so ugly that it is beautiful. Such is the case at Indian Valley Reservoir.

Ugly? To some people it is one downright ugly dog. The water level is often very low, turning the lake into a long, narrow strip with miles of exposed shore. For most of the year, the surrounding hills are brown and barren. The road in from either side is a twisted nightmare.

But after a while Indian Valley Reservoir becomes more like a homely dog that you love more than anything in the world, because inside beats a heart that will never betray you.

When full, the lake covers about 4,000 acres and has 41 miles of shoreline. The water harbors many submerged trees, which provide an excellent habitat for bass and catfish. This is some of the best bass fishing territory in Northern California.

A 10 mph speed limit, clear water, and hot days create a quiet setting for fishing and make for good swimming all summer long.

Indian Valley is a long, narrow reservoir

set at 1,500 feet elevation. There are no sandy beaches, but the clear, warm water is good for swimming, and those who want to take the plunge can jump in wherever and whenever they desire. After all, it is fairly remote and primitive out here. There are two campgrounds in the area, both operated by the Bureau of Land Management. They are nondeveloped, hard to find (see the companion book *California Camping*), and best suited for Cro-Magnon types. Rental boats are not available.

The saving graces are the little Indian Valley Store at the lake's south end and the boat ramps located at the north and south ends. Boater traffic is low, consisting primarily of people who come to fish for bass. Few know about this place, and of those who do, the long twisty drive, ugly surroundings, and enforced speed limit keep most of them away.

But for anglers that makes it just beautiful.

❸ Highland Springs Reservoir

Location: West of Clear Lake; map D1, grid b1.

Directions: From the San Francisco drive 15 miles north on US 101 to Highway 37. Turn east and drive about 23 miles to Vallejo. Turn north on Highway 29 and drive to the town of Lower Lake. Veer left on Highway 29 and drive about four miles past Kelseyville. Turn left on Highland Springs Road and drive four miles to the reservoir.

Access: A primitive boat ramp is located on the lake's east side adjacent to the picnic area.

Facilities, fees: A large grassy picnic area, horseshoe pits, basketball court, and rest rooms are provided. Access is free.

Water sports, restrictions: Gas-powered motors are not permitted on the lake.

Swimming is available at the picnic area. Windsurfing is permitted.

Contact: Lake County Flood Control, (707) 263-2343.

About Highland Springs Reservoir: People can drive to giant Clear Lake many times over a lifetime and never learn about nearby Highland Springs Reservoir or the adjacent Adobe Creek Reservoir. Yet these two lakes are so close, only about 10 miles west of Clear Lake, and between them they fulfill many needs.

Highland Springs Reservoir is located in the foothills just southwest of Big Valley, about a mile west of Adobe Creek Reservoir. Created when a dam was built on Highland Creek, a tributary of Adobe Creek, it covers about 150 acres.

Because no gas-powered motors are allowed on the lake, Highland Springs offers a perfect alternative for people with small, hand-powered boats, such as canoes, rafts, or prams. Boaters are guaranteed calm water, even on three-day weekends when nearby Clear Lake just about gets plowed under by all the hot jet boats.

This is a nice, quiet, day-use-only lake that's ideal for a few hours of picnicking and splashing or wading around. With warm, fairly clear water and no motorized boats to disturb the peace, the swimming here is decent and windsurfing is excellent. The lake gets moderate use, and most of the visitors are anglers. A golf course is available next to the lake.

---

❹ Cache Creek

⚓ 🚐 🏕 🐟 🍴 ✕ 🏊 ⛰   7️⃣

Location: Southeast of Clear Lake; map D1, grid d8.

Directions: From Sacramento drive 19 miles north on Interstate 5 to the Woodland/Main Street exit (Main Street becomes Highway 16). Turn left and drive 43 miles to Cache Creek Regional Park. Direct access is available from Rumsey to four miles upstream at the confluence of Bear Creek. South of Rumsey the creek runs on private property; be aware of the boundaries.

Access: There is a boat ramp at Shaw's Shady Acres Campground, located near Lower Lake on Highway 53. Rafters may put in along Highway 16 just before the point where the highway and the creek split off into different directions (this is roughly 10 miles north of the town of Rumsey, near the county line). Take out about six miles downstream at Camp Haswell.

Facilities, fees: Several campgrounds are located along Highway 16 and farther north, near Lower Lake. One good camp is at Cache Creek Canyon Regional Park on Highway 16 north of Rumsey. Supplies can be obtained in the Clear Lake area. Shaw's Shady Acres rents out fishing boats. Access is free.

Water sports, restrictions: Swimming access is available at most of the campgrounds and picnic areas along Highway 16.

Contact: Cache Creek Canyon Regional Park, (530) 666-8115; Shaw's Shady Acres, (707) 994-2236. For information and guided rafting trips, contact Whitewater Voyages, (800) 488-7238.

About Cache Creek: Cache Creek is best known as the closest place to go whitewater rafting by people who live in the San Francisco Bay Area.

From San Francisco it is 110 miles away, and for residents of Napa in the northern Bay Area, it is only 65 miles away. The most accessible area is right along Highway 16, the little two-laner that links tiny towns such as Guinda and Rumsey and eventually connects with Highway 20 near the Cache Creek Wildlife Area.

This is an ideal river for inflatable kayaks, a first-time white-water experience, or an easy overnight trip.

For one-day trips the best put-in spot is about 10 miles north of Rumsey. You can cover about eight miles of river, including shooting three Class II rapids, and use adjacent Highway 16 as your shuttle road. The best take-out is at Camp Haswell, which has a good picnic area that closes at dusk.

The warm water is ideal for swimming, and many rafters fall in on purpose. Although not spectacular, the rural foothill country setting is quiet. There is a good deal of traffic here in the summer, mostly Bay Area people taking a quick trip. But if you leave enough room between boats when you get on the river, you can go a full day and not see anyone anyway.

An insider's note: The upper reach of Cache Creek, just south of Clear Lake, is largely inaccessible. However, few people know that a two-mile stretch of water can be reached on the obscure road that runs out of Anderson Flat.

---

⑤ Lake Berryessa

Location: North of Vallejo; map D1, grid f7.

Directions: From Vallejo drive north on Interstate 80 to the Suisun Valley Road exit. Take Suisun Valley Road to Highway 121, then turn north and drive five miles. Turn left (west) on Highway 128, drive five miles to Turtle Rock (look for the gas station and bar), then turn right (north) onto Knoxville Road, and travel north.

Access: There are six boat ramps on Lake Berryessa:

Lake Berryessa Marina Resort: From Highway 128 turn north on Knoxville Road and drive nine miles to the resort. A two-lane paved ramp, docks, and a full-service marina are available. Patio boats, ski boats, fishing boats, and canoes can be rented. For general information phone the resort, (707) 966-2161.

Markley Cove Resort: From the junction of Highways 121 and 128, turn right (east) on Highway 128 and drive approximately 12 miles to the resort. A multilane paved ramp and fishing boat rentals are available. For information phone (707) 966-2134.

Putah Creek Resort: From Highway 128 turn north on Knoxville Road and drive approximately 16 miles to the resort, which has a multilane paved ramp and a full-service marina. For information phone (707) 966-2116.

Rancho Monticello Resort: From Highway 128 turn north on Knoxville Road and drive about 9.5 miles to the resort and the multilane paved ramp. For information phone (707) 966-2188.

Spanish Flat Resort: From Highway 128 turn north on Knoxville Road and drive five miles to the resort, which has a multilane paved ramp and a full-service marina. Patio boats, ski boats, personal watercraft, and fishing boats are available for rent. For information phone (707) 966-7700.

Steele Park Resort: From the junction of Highways 121 and 128, turn west on Highway 128, drive a short distance, then turn right (north) on Steele Canyon Road, and continue to the resort. A multilane paved boat ramp and a full-service marina are available. For information phone (707) 966-2123.

Facilities, fees: Several private campgrounds are located around the lake. Oak Shores provides a picnic area with bathrooms. The resorts listed above have full-service marinas. Boats can be rented at Lake Berryessa Marina, Spanish Flat Resort, and Action Sports Rentals. Lodging, gas, and groceries are also available. There is a fee for boat launching, and most resorts charge day-use fees.

Water sports, restrictions: Waterskiing, personal watercraft, and windsurfing are permitted. A public swimming beach is available at Oak Shores, about three miles south of Lake Berryessa Marina on Knoxville Road. Beaches are also available at Lake Berryessa Marina, Spanish Flat Resort, and Steele Park Resort.

Contact: Bureau of Reclamation, Lake

Berryessa, (707) 966-2111 or fax (707) 966-0409. For boating information phone any of the marinas listed above or Action Sports Rentals, (707) 966-1303.

About Lake Berryessa: When full, this is a big lake, covering some 21,000 acres with 165 miles of shoreline, complete with secret coves, islands, and an expanse of untouched shore on the eastern side.

Berryessa is the Bay Area's backyard boating headquarters, often a wild scene on hot weekends with lots of fast boats, water-skiers, suntan oil, and flowing liquid refreshment of various origins. During the week the place is more peaceful and the natural beauty really shines; this is the best time for fishing and family recreation.

All water sports are permitted, but the focus is on powerboaters and water-skiers, who have a field day on summer weekends in the warm, clear water. It can get crowded, and by Sunday afternoon, after two days of sun and drink, problems of one kind or another typically erupt, usually regarding conflicts over lack of boating courtesy. The Berryessa Boat Patrol resolves such disputes by any means necessary and restores some semblance of sanity to Planet Berryessa.

Berryessa does not provide free public boat ramps. Instead, there are several resorts, all of which have ramps, marinas of varying size, small stores, and campgrounds. The largest is Steele Park Resort, which has waterside condo units, motel, marina, RV park, cabins, pool, tennis courts, and a water-skiing school. Most of the marinas offer boat rentals, but surprisingly, Steele Park does not.

The main body of Berryessa is upstream of the Narrows. To the north is a wide expanse of water that is so roomy that jet boats, water-skiers, and personal watercraft can go crazy without running into too many problems. To the south of the Narrows, where fishing is more popular, the lake is much smaller and more intimate. Owners of fast boats would be wise to stay to the north and leave the lake's southern end to those who are fishing.

Another unique element of Berryessa is at the far northern end of the lake, well up the Putah Creek Arm. There, a buoy line marks the point where powerboats aren't permitted upstream, making it ideal for canoeists to paddle into the rarely traveled lake section, bordered on the west by a dramatic granite wall and on the east by a meadow where deer often graze. The scene is so different from the one played out on the main lake that you will never forget it.

---

⑥ Lake Ralphine

Location: In Santa Rosa at Howarth Park; map D1, grid g2.

Directions: From US 101 in Santa Rosa, drive east on Highway 12 until it becomes Hoen Avenue. Continue east for about two miles to Summerfield Road. Turn left and drive to Howarth Park.

Access: A boat ramp is adjacent to the picnic area.

Facilities, fees: The park provides picnic facilities. Rowboat, canoe, and sailboat rentals are available. A campground is located nearby at Spring Lake. Access to the lake is free.

Water sports, restrictions: Motors are not permitted on the lake. Swimming and other water/body contact sports are not allowed. All boaters must wear life jackets.

Contact: Howarth Park Boathouse, (707) 543-3424; Santa Rosa Parks Department, (707) 543-3282 or fax (707) 543-3288.

About Lake Ralphine: Located within Santa Rosa's Howarth Park, little Lake Ralphine is available for day use only and is used primarily for fishing, paddling, and rowing small boats, or for enjoying a picnic on the shore.

People come here just to watch the water and feed the ducks. On the lake's edge are a snack bar and a boathouse where you can rent a small boat. In early spring Ralphine is stocked with trout twice a month.

The surrounding Howarth Park is strictly a destination for families with kiddies, who delight in the pony rides, petting barn, carousel, and miniature steam train.

❼ Spring Lake

Location: In Santa Rosa in Spring Lake County Park; map D1, grid g2.
Directions: From US 101 in Santa Rosa, drive east on Highway 12 until it turns left at a stoplight. Go straight, onto Hoen Avenue. Drive two miles on Hoen Avenue to Newanga Avenue, turn left, and drive to the end of the road. To reach the visitor center and swimming lagoon, turn right on Montgomery Drive off Highway 12 and follow the signs to the park entrance.
Access: A two-lane paved boat ramp is located on the lake's south end, just west of the dam (follow the directions to the Newanga Avenue entrance).
Facilities, fees: A campground and picnic areas are provided at the lake. The campground is only open on weekends and holidays from September through mid-May. Rowboats, canoes, kayaks, and paddleboats are available for rent. A day-use fee is charged.
Water sports, restrictions: Gas-powered motors are not permitted, but electric motors are okay. All boaters must wear life jackets. Swimming is allowed only at the swimming lagoon on the lake's east side, near the visitor center. Windsurfing is permitted (sailboarders must wear life jackets), with the best sailing on the south end near the boat ramp.
Contact: Spring Lake County Park, (707) 539-8092.
About Spring Lake: A precious handful of parks in the San Francisco Bay Area have both campgrounds and lakes, and this

is one of them. The others are Del Valle Reservoir, Lake Chabot, Uvas Reservoir, Coyote Reservoir, and Pinto Lake.

Spring Lake covers 75 acres and is set within 320 acres of parkland. It is pretty, with tules on one side of the water, an exceptional sight in the spring when the surrounding hills have greened up.

This is the kind of place where you hand launch a cartop boat, then float around and enjoy the sun, watch the resident ducks, and maybe have a picnic. Some people come here to fish for trout, which are stocked in spring and early summer.

Windsurfing is a wild card at Spring Lake, best from April through early June when there are good winds in the afternoon. Wind Toys in Santa Rosa occasionally gives windsurfing demos at the lake; remember that windsurfers are required to wear life jackets. Swimming conditions are good in the early summer months, but people are only permitted to swim in the lagoon area.

Spring Lake County Park offers many recreational opportunities, with hiking, biking, and horseback riding trails, and picnic areas available.

❽ Lake Hennessey

Location: North of Napa in Lake Hennessey City Recreation Area; map D1, grid g5.
Directions: From Napa drive east on Trancas Street to the Silverado Trail. Turn north, drive about 15 miles; then take the Highway 128 east turnoff, and continue for three miles to the boat launch facility.
Access: An unpaved boat ramp is located on the lake's south side, just off the highway.
Facilities, fees: A picnic area is provided near the dam. Supplies can be obtained in Napa. Access is free. There is a fee for boat launching.
Water sports, restrictions: No engines over 10 horsepower are permitted on the

lake. Swimming, kayaking, and water/body contact sports are not allowed.

Contact: City of Napa, Public Works & Water, (707) 257-9520.

About Lake Hennessey: The City of Napa owns Lake Hennessey, and it does a good job of keeping quiet about it. Most people from elsewhere in the Bay Area have never heard of the place.

The lake is quite small and is used almost exclusively for fishing. The fish population is supplemented with light doses of trout plants from winter through spring.

Even in the summer Hennessey receives very little recreational traffic other than anglers. The main reason is that body contact with the water is not allowed, and that rules out swimming and windsurfing.

In addition, only boats with small engines are permitted, which at least makes for a nice, quiet visit. The shoreline is rough and covered with oak trees. A picnic area is available off the highway.

⑨ Lake Solano

Location: Near Lake Berryessa in Lake Solano County Park; map D1, grid h9.

Directions: From the town of Winters on Interstate 505, turn west on Highway 128. Drive about five miles and turn left (south) on Pleasant Valley Road. Continue to Lake Solano County Park.

Access: There is a boat ramp near the campground.

Facilities, fees: A campground and picnic areas are provided. Paddleboats and canoes are available for rent. Supplies can be obtained nearby. A day-use fee is charged. There is no additional fee for boat launching.

Water sports, restrictions: Motorized boats are not permitted on the lake. There are no restrictions on swimming, but the water is generally too cold.

Contact: Lake Solano County Park, (530)

795-2990 or write Yolo County Parks, 8685 Pleasant Valley Road, Winters, CA 95614.

About Lake Solano: Sometimes a lake is not a lake at all. That is the case with Lake Solano, which is actually Putah Creek with a small dam on it.

Whatever you call it, it does provide a quiet alternative to nearby Lake Berryessa, located immediately upstream. The water entering Lake Solano comes from Lake Berryessa's Monticello Dam.

Because motorized boats are prohibited from the water, this lake is a good bet for folks with canoes, rowboats, or other small people-powered craft. When Berryessa is teeming with too many people and too many fast boats, you can escape to Lake Solano to enjoy a much quieter day.

Fed by water that comes straight down from the dam, Solano is usually too cold (around 50 degrees) for swimming. As for windsurfing and sailing, the winds aren't strong enough for those sports. Instead, the place appeals to those who are looking for some quiet trout fishing and overflow camping when Berryessa is crowded.

⑩ Napa River

Location: Near Napa; map D1, grid i6.

Directions: From Napa drive southwest on Highway 121/Highway 12. Turn left on Cuttings Wharf Road and travel to the end of the road and on to the boat ramps.

Access: There are two boat ramps:

Moore's Landing: Once on Cuttings Wharf Road, continue to where the road forks. Bear right, continue to a yield sign, then bear left and head down to the water. A paved ramp and marina are available.

Napa Valley Marina: Once on Cuttings Wharf Road, travel to where the road forks. Continue straight, and at the next intersection turn left. Proceed to Milton and follow the signs to the full-service marina, which has a paved ramp.

Kayakers and canoeists may put in at Moore's Landing and float for several miles to one of numerous take-out spots downstream.

Facilities, fees: Marina services are available at the boat ramps. There are no campgrounds nearby, but lodging is available in Napa. Access is free. There may be a fee for boat launching.

Water sports, restrictions: There are no swimming access points.

Contact: Napa Visitor's Bureau, (707) 226-7459. For fishing information contact the Napa Valley Marina, (707) 252-8011, or Moore's Landing Restaurant, (707) 253-2439 or fax (707) 253-7038.

About the Napa River: When people embark on a river trip, they usually refer to it as a "float trip." On the Napa River it is just that: a float, along with a good deal of paddling, on water that is dead flat and placid.

This is not the kind of raging river that will tip you over. And you'll be thankful because the water is typically muddy and cold, with the downstream portions of the river within the tidal reach of the bay and the ocean.

The lower river is wide and quiet, and appeals to people fishing for striped bass and sturgeon, both long shots. Occasionally, a kayaker or canoeist drifts by.

As mentioned this is literally a float. After putting in, you drift downstream, paddling to keep moving at a decent pace. You can extend your trip all the way to San Pablo Bay at Mare Island. The surrounding wetlands attract a large number of birds, including herons, egrets, ducks, and the inevitable mud hen.

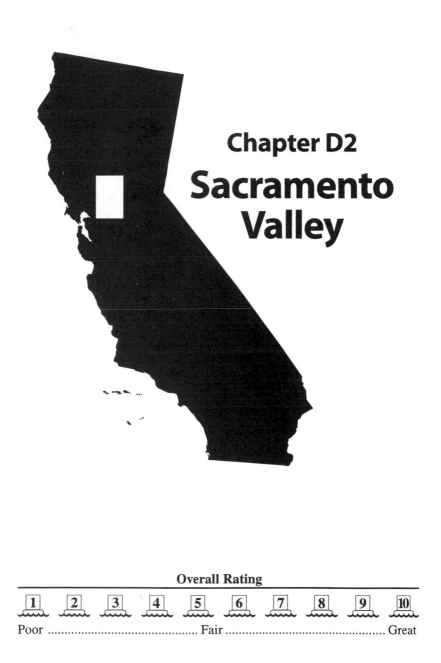

Chapter D2
Sacramento
Valley

Overall Rating

| 1 | 2 | 3 | 4 | 5 | 6 | 7 | 8 | 9 | 10 |

Poor .... Fair .... Great

D2–Sacramento Valley Map

One inch equals approximately 10.7 miles.
See page 12 for California state map.

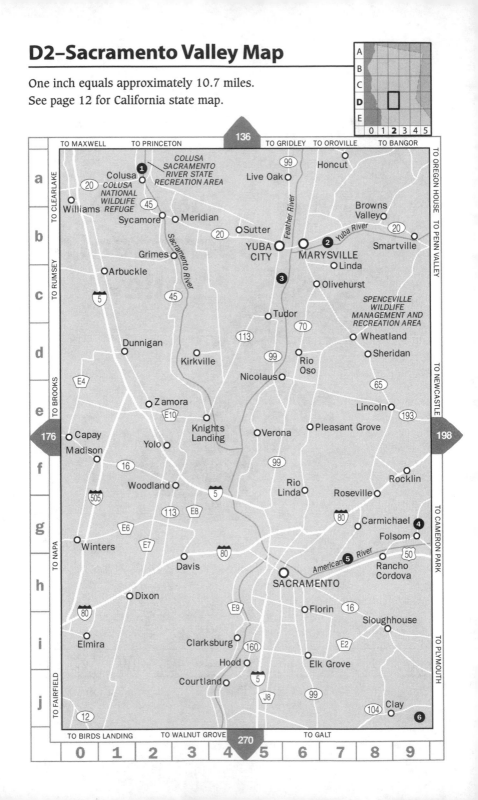

Chapter D2 features:

❶ Sacramento River

Location: From Colusa to Sacramento; map D2, grid a2.

Directions: Access is available off roads that junction with Interstate 5.

Access: Boat ramps are available at several locations. Canoeists and kayakers can also put in at the boat ramps described below:

Colusa–Sacramento River State Recreation Area: From Interstate 5 in Williams, turn east on Highway 20 and drive to Colusa. Turn north on 10th Street and continue to the park entrance. There is a paved ramp. For information phone (530) 458-4927.

Ward's Boat Landing: From Interstate 5 at Williams, turn east on Highway 20 and drive to Colusa. Turn right on Market Street and continue all the way to the road's end. Turn left (you're still on Market), go over the bridge, and then turn right on Butte Slough Road. Continue five miles to the marina. There is a paved ramp. For information phone (916) 696-2673.

Verona Marina: From Interstate 5 north of Sacramento, take the Garden Highway north and drive approximately nine miles to Verona. Or at the junction of Interstate 5 and Highway 99 north of Sacramento, drive eight miles north on Highway 99 to Sankey Road. Turn left and travel two miles west to Verona Marina, which has full services and a paved ramp. For information phone (916) 927-8387.

Alamar Marina: From Interstate 5 north of Sacramento, take the Garden Highway north and continue to Alamar Marina, where there is a paved ramp. For information phone (916) 922-0200. Patio boats, ski boats, and fishing boats are available for rent next door at Metro Marina, (916) 920-8088.

Discovery Park: From Interstate 5 at Sacramento, take the Garden Highway exit and turn left. Drive to Natomas Park Drive, turn right, continue to the traffic signal, and follow the signs into Discovery Park. For information phone County Parks, (916) 875-6672 or fax (916) 875-6632.

Miller Park: From Interstate 5 at Sacramento, turn east on Interstate 80. Take the Sixth Street exit and drive south to Broadway. Turn right and continue to Miller Park. A paved ramp and a marina are provided. For information phone City of Sacramento Marina, (916) 264-8163.

Clarksburg Flat: From Interstate 5 south of Sacramento, take the Pocket Road exit and turn left on Pocket Road. Continue to Freeport Boulevard and turn right. Drive about one mile until you come to a bridge. Turn right, cross the bridge, make an immediate left, and follow the road through Clarksburg. The paved ramp is located about 2.5 miles south of Clarksburg on the left side.

Facilities, fees: Picnic facilities are provided at Discovery Park. Campgrounds, lodging, and supplies are available in the Sacramento area. A day-use fee is charged at the state park. All private marinas charge boat launching fees.

Water sports, restrictions: Due to the river's murky water and steep drop-offs, swimming is generally not recommended along this section's northern reaches. However, sandy beaches are available at the Colusa–Sacramento River State Recreation Area, and people may swim at their own risk. Swimming beaches are available along the Garden Highway north of Sacramento, at Discovery Park, and south of Sacramento near Clarksburg. Waterskiing, personal watercraft, and windsurfing are allowed.

Contact: Sacramento Chamber of Commerce, (916) 552-6800 or fax (916) 443-2672. For boating information contact any of the marinas listed above, or any of the following: Freeport Bait in Sacramento, (916) 665-1935; Sherwood Harbor Marina, (916) 371-3471; Broadway Bait in Sacramento, (916) 448-6338; or Freeport Marina, (916) 665-1555.

About the Sacramento River: When I canoed the entire Sacramento River, this particular section left the most lasting memories, both good and bad.

Near Colusa the river is quite beautiful as it winds its way southward. The banks are lined with trees, and there are some deep holes, gravel bars, and good fishing for salmon in the fall and for striped bass in the spring. Most of the boaters are there to go fishing. You will occasionally see a waterskier or personal watercraft, as well as a few power cruisers out for a scenic river drive.

The bulk of the recreational traffic is near the Feather River mouth at Verona and the American River mouth in Sacramento near Discovery Park. In fact, the latter is sometimes inundated with people on warm summer weekend afternoons.

After all, nearby Sacramento is just another large city in the valley, and this beautiful river represents to a lot of people the best chance to enjoy freedom and fun.

The scenery is dramatic in Sacramento. In addition to the riparian zone along the river, you see some old bridges, the occasional ship, and a wide variety of boats, from runabouts to yachts. Both waterskiing and personal watercraft have become quite popular, along with power cruising and patio boating. Fishing is generally fair at the mouths of the American and Feather Rivers, with the best prospects for salmon in the fall and for striped bass in the winter and spring.

The river is quite benign in the summer months when it has a decent flow, green water, and a predictable nature. Such is not the case, however, the rest of the year. Runoff causes the water to turn murky and run swiftly, and is highest in the spring and early summer. After big storms all manner of debris is sent floating down the river, even trees, creating dangerous boating hazards. In addition, dead fog is common from mid-December through early February.

For the most part the Sacramento River is a great recreational resource, made even more important by the number of people living nearby. Unfortunately, the river section between Colusa and Verona is largely a nightmare. Many long segments have been converted into a virtual canal by the Army Corps of Engineers; they have turned the riverbanks into riprapped levees, complete with beveled edges and 90-degree turns. These parts of the river are treeless, virtually birdless, and the fish simply use it as a highway, migrating straight upriver without pausing. There are a few river holes near Grimes, but that's about it.

The best reason to venture to this section is the outstanding fishing for crawdads. Commercial crawdad traps are found all along the rocky, riprapped banks.

---

❷ Yuba River

Location: From Browns Valley to Marysville; map D2, grid b7.

Directions: At the junction of Interstate 5 and Highway 20 just north of Williams, drive about 30 miles east on Highway 20 to Marysville. Access is available at the Simpson Lane Bridge in Marysville and at the E Street Bridge on Highway 20.

Access: There is no boat ramp. Canoeists and kayakers can put in at Parks Bar, located at the bridge where Highway 20 crosses the river, approximately 20 miles east of Marysville. Note: Boaters must take out above Daguerra Dam (there are warning signs for boats); another put-in is available just below the dam, and from there boaters can continue all the way to Marysville.

Facilities, fees: Lodging and supplies can be obtained in Marysville or Yuba City. Access is free.

Water sports, restrictions: Due to the Yuba's swift current, swimming is generally not recommended; however, people do swim at various sandbars along the river.

Contact: Marysville Parks and Recreation, Yuba County, (530) 741-6666; Johnson's Tackle in Yuba City, (530) 674-1912.

About the Yuba River: The Yuba is one of California's great rivers for inner tubing. Unfortunately, that means that it is not so great for other water sports.

Throughout the Central Valley the condition of many rivers depends on water releases from the reservoirs located upstream. In this case the fact that Bullards Bar Reservoir is always so full of water means that the Yuba is often quite low.

That makes it perfect for inner tubing. Tubers should be aware that they are advised to wear life jackets, that access here is difficult, and that if you hit the river on a rare day when water releases are up out of Bullards Bar, the flows of the Yuba can be swift. Several sandbars along the river make the best spots for swimming, but they are inaccessible by car. Some tubers will float to these spots, set up a day camp and picnic site, then enjoy themselves and jump in the river now and then. Camping is not permitted on the river.

The Yuba is usually too shallow for boats larger than canoes or kayaks, and even kayakers must occasionally get out and portage their boats to deeper water. Another pain is that it is necessary to take out above Daguerra Dam, where you portage, and then put in below the dam and continue downstream to Marysville.

The Yuba is used mostly by locals. Many people just bypass this place in favor of the nearby Sacramento River, which has river flows more suited to recreation.

❸ Feather River

Location: From Marysville to Sacramento; map D2, grid c6.

Directions: Drive-to river access is limited. There are two good access points:

Riverfront Park: From Yuba City drive east on Highway 20 toward Marysville. Cross the bridge to Marysville; at the second stoplight, turn left and continue to a stop sign. Go straight to a second stop sign and then turn left. Continue over a levee and follow the signs to Riverfront Park.

Verona Marina: From Interstate 5 north of Sacramento, take the Garden Highway north and drive approximately nine miles to Verona. Or at the junction of Interstate 5 and Highway 99 north of Sacramento, drive eight miles north on Highway 99 to Sankey Road. Turn left and travel two miles west to Verona Marina.

Access: Paved boat ramps are available at Riverfront Park and Verona Marina.

Facilities, fees: Picnic facilities are provided at Riverfront Park. Boating services are available at Verona Marina. Campgrounds and lodging are available in the Sacramento area. Supplies can be obtained in Yuba City. Access is free.

Water sports, restrictions: Waterskiing, personal watercraft, and windsurfing are permitted. Due to the river's swift current, swimming is not generally recommended; however, people do swim at Riverfront Park. Life jackets are advised for participants of all water sports.

Contact: Yuba City Parks and Recreation, (530) 741-4650; Verona Marina, (916) 927-8387.

About the Feather River: The placid appearance of the Feather River often belies its true nature. Actually, the river has quite a strong current, and anyone thinking of getting into the water should be prepared to wear a life jacket. This goes for swimmers, windsurfers, water-skiers, and personal watercraft.

Many of the people on the river, however, are in powerboats whose engines have been converted to jet drives. As you might guess, most of them are here to bring in a few fish. The river attracts striped bass in the spring, shad in the early summer (best at Shanghai Bend), and salmon in late summer and fall (best at Verona).

The most popular general recreation area, complete with boat ramp, is at Riverfront Park near Marysville. Another boat ramp is at Verona Marina, located near where the Feather feeds into the Sacramento River; this is primarily a boat-access point used by anglers.

❹ Lake Natoma

Location: East of Sacramento at Nimbus Dam; map D2, grid g9.

Directions: From Sacramento on Interstate 80, drive east on Madison Avenue or Greenback Lane as far as you can go. Turn left and continue to Negro Bar. Or take US 50 east of Sacramento to Hazel Avenue and drive to the boat ramp at the west end of the lake.

Access: Boat ramps for launching small boats are located at the California State University System (CSUS) Aquatic Center on the lake's south end, and at Negro Bar on the west end (see Directions).

Facilities, fees: A campground is provided at Negro Bar. Rowboats, sailboats, and sailboards are available for rent at CSUS Aquatic Center, which also offers sailing and windsurfing classes. A day-use fee is charged at the lake. There is a fee for boat launching.

Water sports, restrictions: Motors are not allowed on the lake, and a 5 mph speed limit is strictly enforced. Windsurfing is permitted; note the speed limit. A sandy swimming beach is available at Negro Bar. You can also swim at Nimbus Flat, but there is no beach.

Contact: Folsom Lake State Recreation Area, (916) 988-0205; CSUS Aquatic Center, (916) 985-7239.

About Lake Natoma: Below every major reservoir is usually a small lake called an afterbay, and Lake Natoma is just that for big Folsom Lake to the east. Natoma provides water-sports enthusiasts in the area with a decent alternate destination for windsurfing, sailing, fishing, and low-speed boating.

This narrow lake covers 500 acres with 13 miles of shoreline. Because it gets its water from the bottom of Folsom Dam, Natoma tends to be colder than big brother Folsom.

The real plus here is quiet and calm water. Waterskiing is prohibited and a 5 mph speed limit is enforced, so visitors never have to compete with personal watercraft and speedboats.

The CSUS Aquatic Center draws a college-age crowd who come to learn about windsurfing and sailing. Sailing and rowing are the two most popular activities on the lake. Recreation is concentrated at two points: the Aquatic Center for boaters, and Negro Bar for campers, swimmers, and picnickers. Use is fairly heavy in the summer.

❺ Lower American River

Location: From Nimbus Dam to Sacramento; map D2, grid h7.

Directions: Easy access is available off the roads in Rancho Cordova and Fair Oaks that cut off from US 50. A free map can be obtained from Fran & Eddy's Sports Den. By boat the best and most easily accessible spot is at the confluence of the Sacramento and American Rivers in Sacramento's Discovery Park.

Access: Several boat ramps and rafting put-ins and take-outs are available on the Lower American:

Ancil Hoffman Park: From Interstate 80 at Sacramento, take the Arden Way exit and turn east. Drive 4.5 miles, turn left on Fair Oaks Boulevard, and continue about 1.5 miles to Oak Avenue. Turn right, proceed to California Avenue, turn left, and drive one-half mile to Tarshes Drive. Turn right and drive west into Ancil Hoffman Park. Follow the signs to the cartop boat ramp or launching area.

Discovery Park: From Interstate 5 at Sacramento, take the Garden Highway exit and turn left. Drive to Natomas Park Drive, turn right, continue to the traffic signal, and follow the signs into Discovery Park. This is the only paved ramp on the Lower American. It is also a rafting site.

Goethe Park: From Interstate 50 east of Sacramento, take the Bradshaw Road exit and turn north. Turn right on Folsom Boulevard and drive about one mile, then turn left on Rod Beaudry Drive and continue to the ramp at Goethe Park.

Harrington Way: From Interstate 80 in Sacramento, take the Arden Way exit. Turn west on Arden Way, drive approximately 4.5 miles, and then turn right on Kingsford Drive, which turns into Harrington Way. Proceed down to the cartop boat ramp or launching area.

Howe Avenue: From Interstate 50 east of Sacramento, take the 65th Street exit and turn north. Proceed a short distance to Folsom Boulevard, turn right, and drive about a mile west to Howe Avenue. Turn left, drive one-half mile, turn right on La Riviera Drive, and continue to the sign for the cartop boat ramp or launching area.

Mira Del Rio: From Interstate 50 east of Sacramento, take the Bradshaw Road exit and turn north. Proceed to Folsom Boulevard, turn left, and drive a short distance west to Butterfield Way. Turn right, continue to Stoughton Way, turn right, and proceed to Mira Del Rio Drive. Turn left and then immediately right to access the cartop boat ramp.

Rossmoor Drive: From Interstate 50 east of Sacramento, take the Sunrise Boulevard exit and turn north. Drive about one-half mile, take a left turn on Coloma Road, and drive about 1.5 miles west. Turn right on Rossmoor Drive and continue into the park to the cartop boat ramp at the end of the road.

Sailor Bar: From Interstate 50 east of Sacramento, take the Hazel Avenue exit and turn north. Drive about 1.5 miles to Winding Way, turn left, and drive about one-half mile. Turn left on Illinois Avenue and continue to the end of the road.

Upper Sunrise: From Interstate 50 east of Sacramento, take the Sunrise Boulevard exit and turn north. Drive about 1.5 miles to South Bridge Street, turn right, and continue to the cartop boat ramp or launching area.

Watt Avenue South: From Interstate 50 east of Sacramento, take the Watt Avenue exit and drive about one-half mile to the sign for the launching area.

Rafting put-ins and take-outs are available at the following sites:

Lower Sunrise: From Interstate 50 east of Sacramento, take the Sunrise Boulevard exit and turn north. Drive about 1.5 miles, then turn right on South Bridge Street, and continue past the Upper Sunrise turnoff, looping around to Lower Sunrise located just past the bridge. No ramp is available.

Sacramento Bar: From Interstate 50 east of Sacramento, take the Sunrise Boulevard exit and turn north, continuing for two miles to Fair Oaks Boulevard. Turn left, drive a short distance, then turn left on Pennsylvania Avenue, and continue one-half mile to the river. No ramp is available.

Facilities, fees: Campgrounds, lodging, and supplies are available in the Sacramento area. Rest rooms, picnic areas, and barbecues are provided at many river access points. An entrance fee is charged at a lot of the county parks. Rafting permits are not required.

Water sports, restrictions: A 5 mph speed limit is strictly enforced. Boaters must carry life jackets. Boating, swimming, and rafting are prohibited from Nimbus Dam to 150 feet downstream. Swimming is allowed at most of the parks listed above and at several other access points along the river. Phone Sacramento County Parks for a free map (see below).

Contact: Sacramento Chamber of Commerce, (916) 552-6800 or fax (916) 443-2672. For information on boat ramps and river access (a free map is available), contact Sacramento County Parks, (916) 875-6672 or fax (916) 875-6632, or the California Department of Boating and Waterways, (916) 263-1331. For information on guided rafting trips, contact California Canoe & Kayak, (800) 366-9804. For raft or kayak rentals, contact American River Recreation, (916) 635-6400.

About the Lower American River: From Memorial Day weekend until several months later, the American River is the site of some of the biggest water parties in California. Just about anybody can get into a raft here and go for a float on a hot summer day, and that is exactly what a lot of folks do. It's great fun, even though there are many people on the river, some of them absolutely ripped from the combination of too much beer and too much sun. There are a few drownings every year, and the typical victim is someone who got drunk, didn't wear a life jacket, then fell overboard. Don't drink alcohol and do keep your life jacket on, and you'll surely enjoy the float.

This section of the American flows from the outlet at Nimbus Basin on downstream past Fair Oaks and Rancho Cordova before entering the Sacramento River at Discovery Park. The entire run is 23 miles. Within that span are several excellent access points.

Rated Class I, this is an easy rafting river. A couple of Class II rapids are thrown in: Suicide Bend, located about three miles downstream of the dam; San Juan Rapids, one mile farther; and Arden Rapids, another five miles past that. These rapids are not difficult, but newcomers may want to scout them from the shore. Portaging is easy at all the runs.

One great bonus is that American River Recreation rents out kayaks and rafts of all sizes. When renting, you always put in at their shop on Sunrise Boulevard, then enjoy the 2.5-hour float down to Goethe Park. For a small fee they will give you a shuttle ride back.

The only outfitter offering guided trips is California Canoe & Kayak. But this is an easy float, and novice boaters can do most of it alone.

Though temperatures around here get hot, the water is often cold, which can come as a big surprise. Rafters sometimes discard their life jackets to enjoy the sunny weather, then are stunned by the cold water when they fall in. After big winters the river can be quite high and cold on Memorial Day weekend, the traditional kickoff of the party/rafting season on the American River.

❻ Rancho Seco Lake

Location: Southeast of Sacramento in Rancho Seco Recreation Area; map D2, grid j9.

Directions: From Sacramento drive about 12 miles south on Highway 99. Take the Highway 104 exit and drive 12 miles east on Highway 104/Twin Cities Road. Turn right at the signed entrance for Rancho Seco Recreation Area and continue to the lake.

Access: A boat ramp is located near the picnic area.

Facilities, fees: A campground and a picnic area are provided. Lodging and supplies can be obtained in Sacramento. A day-use fee is charged.

Water sports, restrictions: Gas-powered motors and live bait are not allowed on the lake. Windsurfing is permitted. A large swimming beach is available near the picnic area.

Contact: Rancho Seco Recreation Area, (209) 748-2318.

About Rancho Seco Lake: Looking for the ideal spot for a family picnic? Here it is. Rancho Seco Lake (160 acres) is part of the 400-acre Rancho Seco Recreation Area and offers a boat ramp (no motors permitted), picnic area, and several docks. The park is open for day use only, closing each day at sunset. Because no motors are allowed, you get quiet water, fair fishing, and good access and picnic sites. Bring the family.

There is a large, sandy swimming area, pleasant picnic site, and a campground for tents or RVs. In addition there are trails for hiking, horseback riding, and bicycling, as well as several fishing docks along the shore.

This lake is also popular with windsurfers. Every afternoon from spring through summer, you will usually see about a dozen people on sailboards catching the afternoon breeze.

Map of Northern California—Page 28

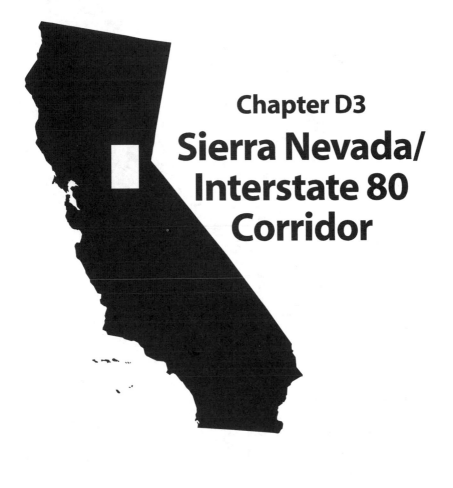

Chapter D3
Sierra Nevada/ Interstate 80 Corridor

Overall Rating

Poor .... Fair .... Great

D3–Sierra Nevada/I80 Corridor Map

One inch equals approximately 10.7 miles.
See page 12 for California state map.

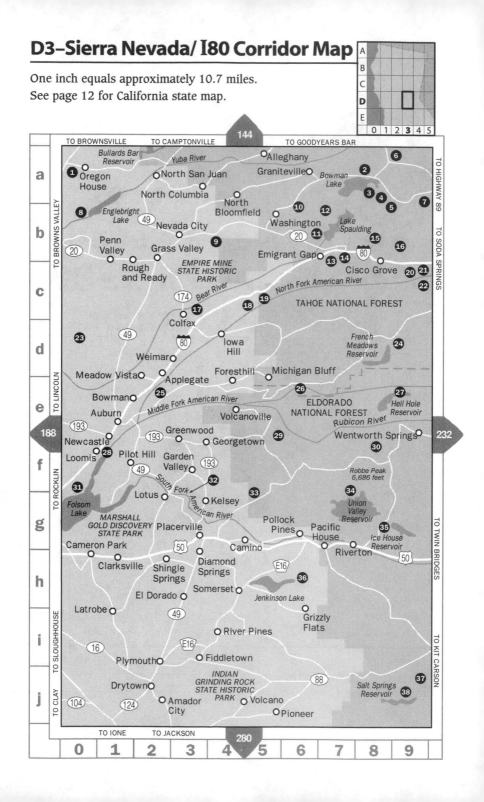

Chapter D3 features:

---

1 Collins Lake

Location: North of Marysville in Collins Lake Recreation Area; map D3, grid a0.

Directions: From Sacramento drive 40 miles north to Marysville on Highway 70. Take Highway 20 east and drive 12 miles. Turn north on Marysville Road and drive eight miles to the lake entrance on the right.

Access: A paved boat ramp is located between the picnic area and the southern-most campground.

Facilities, fees: One 40-acre, dispersed camping area, one designated campground, and a picnic area are provided. There's a full-service marina where you can rent fishing boats, rowboats, and paddleboats. A snack bar, gas station, and small grocery store are also available at the lake. A day-use fee is charged. There is an additional fee for boat launching.

Water sports, restrictions: Waterskiing is permitted from May 15 through September 15 only. Personal watercraft are not allowed. Certain lake areas are reserved solely for fishing, with a 5 mph speed limit; skiers should watch for signs. Windsurfing is allowed. A large, sandy swimming beach and diving raft are available near the picnic area.

Contact: Collins Lake Recreation Area, (530) 692-1600 or (800) 286-0576 or fax (530) 692-1607.

About Collins Lake: The boating rules have resolved most of the potential user conflicts at Collins Lake, setting an example for lakes across the rest of the state.

Conflicts between water-skiers and anglers are kept to a minimum because each group has a separate area to roam in the summer. In addition, skiing is not allowed after September 15, when the water-skier crowds tend to dwindle anyway and cool water attracts more people who want to fish at the lake.

Set at 1,200 feet in the foothill country of Yuba County, Collins Lake is a pretty spot that's ideal for the camper/boater. The lake covers 1,000 acres and has 12 miles of shoreline. Temperatures are warm from March through October, and in the summer visitors enjoy day after day of hot weather and cool water. In late spring, when the foothills are green and the lake sparkles, the area can almost appear to be glowing.

A recreation area has been developed to accommodate hordes of summer visitors. It includes a huge swimming beach with rest rooms, showers, and snack bar, and well-maintained picnic and camping facilities. Many folks use the swimming beach as a jump-off point for windsurfing; conditions for this sport are fair here.

Personal watercraft are prohibited at Collins Lake because far too many accidents occurred when they were permitted. If you see someone pulling into the campground towing a trailer with a personal watercraft, don't panic; personal watercraft users will often camp here, then drive 20 minutes up the road to Bullards Bar for the day.

Are you starting to think that this quality operation must attract a good number of people? Well, you got that right. On weekends from Memorial Day through Labor Day, the campgrounds are almost always filled to capacity.

❷ Weaver Lake

Location: North of Emigrant Gap in Tahoe National Forest; map D3, grid a7.
Directions: From Sacramento drive east on Interstate 80 past Emigrant Gap to High-

way 20. Drive west on Highway 20 to Bowman Road, turn right, and drive north for 19 miles to Meadow Lake Road. Turn left on Meadow Lake Road, drive one mile, turn north on McMurray Lake Road, and drive two miles to Weaver Lake. The road is rough, and although four-wheel-drive vehicles are not required, they are recommended.
Access: There is no boat ramp. Cartop boats may be hand launched.
Facilities, fees: No facilities are available on-site. A primitive campground is located at Jackson Creek just east of Bowman Lake; no piped water is provided. Access to the lake is free.
Water sports, restrictions: There is a 10 mph speed limit. Swimming is permitted. The lake is too small for windsurfing.
Contact: Tahoe National Forest, Nevada City Ranger District, (530) 265-4531 or fax (530) 478-6109. For a detailed map of the area, send $4 to Maps, Office of Information, US Forest Service, 1323 Club Drive, Vallejo, CA 94592.
About Weaver Lake: For the mom and dad who want to get away from it all but whose family is not ready for the wilderness experience, Weaver Lake provides a rare drive-to alternative.

One of dozens of lakes within a 10-mile radius tucked away in the granite slopes of Sierra Nevada country, Weaver is set at an elevation of 6,000 feet. On the way in you will pass several lakes, including both little McMurray Lake and large Bowman Lake within a mile to the south.

Most of the visitors to the lake are anglers, but the rough road in makes the place attractive to people who want a wilderness experience without having to hike.

The lake is small, and only cartop boats such as canoes, rowboats, and inflatables are appropriate. Despite the fact that the area can be hit with some hot summer days, the water is chilly, making it quite a feat to jump in and paddle around a bit, even for a short while.

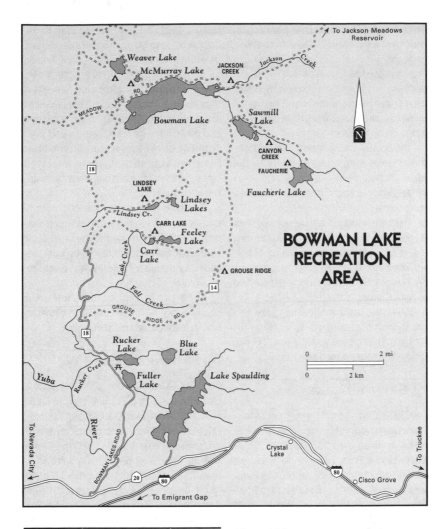

❸ Bowman Lake

🏕🎣🏊⛴ 　　　　　5⃞

Location: North of Emigrant Gap in Tahoe National Forest; map D3, grid a8.

Directions: From Sacramento drive east on Interstate 80 past Emigrant Gap to Highway 20. Drive west on Highway 20 to Bowman Road, turn right, and drive 19 miles north to Meadow Lake Road. Turn right (east) on Meadow Lake Road and drive one mile. The lake will be on your right. The last part of the drive is rough, and four-wheel-drive vehicles are recommended.

Access: There is no boat ramp. Cartop boats may be hand launched.

Facilities, fees: A primitive campground is provided at Jackson Creek, just east of the lake. Access to the lake is free.

Water sports, restrictions: A 10 mph speed limit is enforced. Swimming is permitted.

Contact: Tahoe National Forest, Nevada City Ranger District, (530) 265-4531 or fax (530) 478-6109.

About Bowman Lake: Many get their

first glimpse of Bowman Lake from the access road, fully intending to drive onward to nearby Weaver Lake to the north or to Jackson Meadow Reservoir six miles to the northeast. But Bowman is so pretty, a sapphire jewel set in granite at an elevation of 5,568 feet, that it is difficult to pass by without wanting to set up camp.

The access road is rough and not conducive to towing trailered boats. In the ideal situation you would have a four-wheel-drive vehicle with a canoe strapped to the top.

This lake is just a bit more popular than its northerly neighbor, Weaver. On the plus side it is larger than Weaver, but when water levels are down in drought years the shoreline can become quite steep and rocky, a minus.

Pine trees surround Bowman Lake, and the shoreline is sprinkled with large granite slabs. Though the water is usually cold, it's decent enough for a quick dunk.

❹ Sawmill Lake

Location: North of Emigrant Gap in Tahoe National Forest; map D3, grid a8.

Directions: From Sacramento drive east on Interstate 80 past Emigrant Gap to Highway 20. Drive west on Highway 20 to Bowman Road, turn right, drive 19 miles (past Bowman Lake) to Meadow Lake Road, and then east to Jackson Creek Campground. Turn right (south) on a Forest Service road and travel about two miles to Sawmill Lake.

Access: There is no boat ramp. Cartop boats may be hand launched.

Facilities, fees: No facilities are available on-site. A campground is provided at Jackson Creek. Access to the lake is free.

Water sports, restrictions: A 10 mph speed limit is enforced. Swimming is permitted.

Contact: Tahoe National Forest, Nevada City Ranger District, (530) 265-4531 or fax

(530) 478-6109. For a detailed map of the area, send $4 to Maps, Office of Information, US Forest Service, 1323 Club Drive, Vallejo, CA 94592.

About Sawmill Lake: Tiny Sawmill is the classic "nice little spot." It's very pretty, set at about 6,000 feet amid Sierra granite and pines, but without a campground, boat ramp, or direct access for swimming or launching a cartop boat. So why would you come here? For the beauty, which is sometimes enough.

The lake attracts the curious, mainly people fishing for trout. Cartop boats (canoes, kayaks) are okay, but you must carry your boat in from wherever you park because, as mentioned, there is no vehicle access to any of the shore.

The water is cold, and the shoreline is partly rocky, partly weedy, and provides only fair conditions for swimming.

❺ Faucherie Lake

Location: North of Emigrant Gap in Tahoe National Forest; map D3, grid a8.

Directions: From Sacramento drive east on Interstate 80 past Emigrant Gap to Highway 20. Drive west on Highway 20 to Bowman Road, turn right, and drive 16 miles (past Bowman Lake) to Jackson Creek Campground. Turn right (south) on a Forest Service road and travel about three miles past Sawmill Lake to Faucherie Lake.

Access: There is no boat ramp. Cartop boats may be hand launched.

Facilities, fees: A campground is provided at the lake; reservations are suggested. Access to the lake is free.

Water sports, restrictions: There is a 10 mph speed limit on the lake. Swimming is permitted.

Contact: Tahoe National Forest, Nevada City Ranger District, (530) 265-4531 or fax (530) 478-6179. For a detailed map of the area, send $4 to Maps, Office of Information,

US Forest Service, 1323 Club Drive, Vallejo, CA 94592.

About Faucherie Lake: It's hard to believe that you can simply drive to beautiful Faucherie Lake. But here it is, a classic alpine lake in the Sierra Nevada. The glacier-carved granite bowl is filled with clear, pure water from melting snow.

This is the kind of place that backpackers will hike many miles to reach. Quiet and pristine, it has a completely wilderness-like feel, a rare quality in a drive-to lake. Imagine arriving at Faucherie Lake on a summer afternoon, plopping in a canoe, then paddling around, and enjoying the natural beauty.

Not only is it an excellent venue for cartop boating, but there's decent fishing for trout and fair conditions for swimming.

This is the most popular lake in the area, mainly because it is the only one with a developed campground, which attracts so many campers that it is on the US Forest Service reservation system. The entire area to the west of the lake is closed to vehicles, and there is some good hiking out there.

⑥ Jackson Meadow Reservoir

Location: Northwest of Truckee in Tahoe National Forest; map D3, grid a8.

Directions: From Sacramento drive approximately 100 miles east on Interstate 80 to Truckee. Turn north on Highway 89 and drive 17.5 miles. Turn west on Forest Service Road 7 and drive 16 miles west to the reservoir.

Access: Two paved boat ramps are provided, one on the east side and one on the west side. Both are adjacent to the campgrounds.

Facilities, fees: Several campgrounds, including a boat-in campground, and two picnic areas are provided. Supplies can be obtained in Truckee and Sierraville. Access is free.

Water sports, restrictions: Waterskiing, personal watercraft, and windsurfing are permitted. Two developed swimming beaches are available.

Contact: Tahoe National Forest, Sierraville Ranger District, (530) 994-3401 or fax (530) 994-3143; Truckee-Donner Chamber of Commerce, (530) 587-2757. For a detailed map of the area, send $4 to Maps, Office of Information, US Forest Service, 1323 Club Drive, Vallejo, CA 94592.

About Jackson Meadow Reservoir: Water levels here are often kept higher than at the typical mountain reservoir, which makes the lake quite beautiful and provides for a much wider variety of top-quality boating and recreation than offered by the area's other lakes.

Jackson Meadow is set at an elevation of 6,200 feet, and the surrounding area is just as pretty, featuring forest, meadows, and the trademark granite look of the Sierra Nevada. This is a very popular recreation area, with developed campsites, well-maintained picnic areas, and two large, sandy swimming beaches. As it is the only lake in the immediate area where all boating is allowed, it gets heavy use in the summer. Access is fairly easy, just a few miles from Highway 89, and the beautiful forest setting attracts a lot of tourists.

Families on vacation and people who just want a quiet spot to bed down will find all they need here. Rangers strictly enforce noise level laws, a courtesy rarely found at Forest Service campgrounds.

Some campers use Jackson Meadow Reservoir as their headquarters for multiday trips into the surrounding mountain country. Many lakes in the vicinity make good destinations for side trips, and the trailhead for the Pacific Crest Trail is located just east of the lake along the access road.

❼ Meadow Lake

Location: Northwest of Truckee in Tahoe National Forest; map D3, grid a9.

Directions: From Sacramento drive approximately 100 miles east on Interstate 80 past Emigrant Gap to Highway 20. Drive west on Highway 20 to Bowman Road, turn right, and drive 19 miles (past Bowman Lake) to Meadow Lake Road. Turn right on Meadow Lake Road and drive about six miles to Meadow Lake.

Access: There is no boat ramp. Cartop boats may be hand launched.

Facilities, fees: No facilities are available on-site. Camping is not permitted. Access is free.

Water sports, restrictions: There is a 10 mph speed limit on the lake. Swimming is permitted.

Contact: Tahoe National Forest, Sierraville Ranger District, (530) 994-3401 or fax (530) 994-3143; Truckee-Donner Chamber of Commerce, (530) 587-2757. For a detailed map of the area, send $4 to Maps, Office of Information, US Forest Service, 1323 Club Drive, Vallejo, CA 94592.

About Meadow Lake: Few people know about this lake, and most of those few come here to picnic and fish. But what is even less known is that of all the primitive, hard-to-reach lakes in this area, Meadow Lake is among the better ones for swimming. That is because there are some small beachlike areas—stretches of sand/gravel mix along part of the shore—that provide good access and sunbathing territory.

Meadow Lake is set at an elevation of 6,000 feet. It is narrow but pretty good sized, about 1.5 miles long. The water is clear and cold.

Boating is limited to cartop boats, and because the place lacks a campground, most people exploring the region scratch it off their list of places to visit. Hikers will find a good side trip by heading just south,

where a trail is routed to the Meadow Lakes Mine, an old gold mine.

❽ Englebright Lake

Location: Northeast of Marysville; map D3, grid b0.

Directions: From Sacramento drive 40 miles north on Highway 70 to Marysville. From Marysville drive 20 miles east on Highway 20 to Mooney Flat Road (just past Smartville). Drive three miles north to the lake.

Access: Two paved ramps are available, one just east of the dam, adjacent to the picnic area, and one at the marina at Skipper's Cove. There are signs for each on the entrance road.

Facilities, fees: Camping is limited to boat-in sites only. A full-service marina and houseboat, patio boat, ski boat, fishing boat, canoe, and paddleboat rentals are available. Groceries and gas are available also. Access is free. There is a fee for boat launching.

Water sports, restrictions: Waterskiing and personal watercraft are permitted only below the lake's Upper Boston area. Sandy beach areas are located near several of the boat-in campgrounds.

Contact: US Army Corps of Engineers, Englebright Lake, (530) 639-2342; Skipper's Cove, (530) 639-2272.

About Englebright Lake: The reservoir has an unusual appearance, resembling something like a water snake winding its way through the Yuba River Canyon. Although it covers just 815 acres, it has 24 miles of shoreline.

Because it is set at about a 500-foot elevation in the Yuba County foothills, Englebright Lake gets hot in the summer, ideal for sun-loving water enthusiasts. Water-skiers really like this place because the nearby shoreline gives an illusion of greater speed—something you don't get on a wide-open lake.

But the real bonanza here is for boaters. There are 17 boat-in campsites, all offering privacy and beautiful views. These campsites rarely fill up, even in summer when the lake can get crowded on weekends with day-use water-skiers.

As with any narrow lake where high-speed water-skiers run the risk of rounding a point and plowing into a low-speed fishing boat, crowded conditions can present major conflicts. But rules have been enacted to resolve that problem; all boating is permitted up to Upper Boston, yet boating is restricted from Upper Boston upstream to the North Fork Yuba for the sake of anglers. So you find people happily waterskiing below Upper Boston, and people contentedly fishing above Upper Boston.

Because Englebright Lake is set in a river canyon, the shoreline drops abruptly and is quite rocky. Hence most of the lake provides poor swimming access, but there are still a few sandy stretches adjacent to the campgrounds.

The water level is fairly stable, but boaters should be aware of underwater hazards. With a boat at Englebright Lake, you can enjoy water sports to your heart's desire and still have the luxury of a secluded and pretty campsite.

❾ Scotts Flat Reservoir

Location: East of Nevada City in Scotts Flat Recreation Area; map D3, grid b4.

Directions: From Sacramento drive about 31 miles east on Interstate 80 to Auburn. Turn north on Highway 49 and drive about 25 miles to Nevada City. From Nevada City continue five miles east on Highway 20. Turn south on Scotts Flat Road and continue about four miles (three miles paved and one mile gravel) to the lake.

Access: There are two boat ramps:

Cascade Shores: From Nevada City turn south on Red Dog Road, drive three miles, then turn left on Quaker Hill Road, and continue east to the sign for the Cascade Shores Day-Use Area.

Scotts Flat Marina: After you turn south on Scotts Flat Road, head about four miles down to the marina.

Facilities, fees: Two campgrounds and a picnic area are located on the lake's northwest side. A day-use area is provided on the southeast side. Fishing boat and paddleboat rentals and a full-service marina are available. There's a restaurant and a place to purchase groceries. A day-use fee is charged.

Water sports, restrictions: Waterskiing and windsurfing are permitted. No personal watercraft are allowed. Roped-off, sandy swimming beaches are available at the day-use area at Scotts Flat Marina and on the lake's other side at Cascade Shores Day-Use Area. No horses or motorcycles are allowed in the recreation area.

Contact: Scotts Flat Recreation Area, (530) 265-5302 or fax (530) 265-3777; Scotts Flat Marina, (530) 265-0413.

About Scotts Flat Reservoir: When Scotts Flat Reservoir is full to the brim, it is one of the prettier lakes in the Sierra Nevada foothills. The reservoir is shaped like a teardrop, with 7.5 miles of shoreline circled by forestland at an elevation of 3,100 feet. With a campground located close to the water's edge and a nearby boat launch, it makes for an ideal family camping destination.

The lake covers 850 surface acres. While the primary activities are camping and fishing, be aware that there are also some surprisingly outstanding windsurfing conditions as there is nearly always an afternoon breeze. The best places to windsurf are at Scotts Flat Marina and on the other side at Cascade Shores. All boating (except for personal watercraft) is permitted.

Visitor use is high on summer weekends, when the campgrounds almost always fill up. Note that if you want to avoid the developed area (Gate 1, which has a store, boat ramp, and large campground) on the lake's north side, a more primitive campground called Gate 2 is available on the undeveloped, primitive southern shore.

The surrounding scenery is beautiful and heavily forested, and there are lots of hiking trails nearby.

⑩ South Fork Yuba River

Location: East of Nevada City in Tahoe National Forest; map D3, grid b6.

Directions: Limited access is available from Interstate 80 near Donner Summit, via the Eagle Lakes or Big Bend/Rainbow Road exits. Much of the land bordering the South Yuba is private; be on the lookout for signs.

Access: There is no boat ramp. Three of the best swimming holes are available north of Nevada City:

Edwards Crossing: From Highway 49 in Nevada City, turn north on North Bloomfield Road and drive up a hill until you come to a Y intersection. Bear right and continue about five miles to the parking area at Edwards Crossing.

Highway 49 Bridge: From Nevada City turn north on Highway 49 and continue approximately five miles to the Highway 49 bridge.

Purdon Crossing: From Highway 49 in Nevada City, turn north on North Bloomfield Road and drive up a hill until you come to a Y intersection. Bear left at the sign for Lake Vera–Purdon Crossing and continue about five miles on a dirt road to the river at Purdon Crossing.

Facilities, fees: Campgrounds are available off Interstate 80; there is also a campground just over the river from Purdon Crossing. Rest rooms are provided at Edwards Crossing. Supplies can be obtained in Nevada City and off Interstate 80. Access is free.

Water sports, restrictions: See directions for swimming areas above.

Contact: Tahoe National Forest, Nevada City Ranger District, (530) 265-4531 or fax (530) 478-6109; Bureau of Land Management, Folsom Field Office, (916) 985-4474.

About the South Fork Yuba River: With beautiful, clear blue water and forested banks flanked by granite boulders and walls, this is a particularly scenic river. Recreational options include swimming and sunbathing, as well as hiking, fishing, and panning for gold.

Although swimming in the river can be excellent, things sometimes turn dangerous. On hot days the pools look cool and inviting, but swimmers who are new to the river may not recognize how cold and swift the water can be or just how quickly they can get into trouble. The risk is heightened greatly when swimmers down a lot of beer and their judgment is impaired. Despite the river's fun nature, several people drown here each year, usually during a period of high snowmelt.

Explorers will discover a number of spots along the river that are ideal for picnicking and sunbathing. The prettiest one is at Purdon Crossing, which has become notorious for nude bathing; if that isn't what you have in mind, head in the other direction to Edwards Crossing.

This river is generally too shallow and rocky for rafting, but early in the season and at high water it is possible for expert kayakers to have a go at it. A 12-foot waterfall below Humbug Creek must be portaged. Again, this is done by experts only, usually in the company of at least one or two others who have experience on the river and can recognize the portage spot before everyone goes sailing over the waterfall.

⑪ Lake Spaulding

Location: Near Emigrant Gap in Tahoe National Forest; map D3, grid b7.

Directions: From Sacramento drive east

on Interstate 80 past Emigrant Gap to Highway 20. Drive west on Highway 20 to Lake Spaulding Road. Turn right and drive one-half mile to the lake.

Access: A paved boat ramp is available at the end of the access road.

Facilities, fees: PG&E provides a campground and a picnic area. Supplies can be obtained in Nevada City. Access is free. There is a fee for boat launching.

Water sports, restrictions: Waterskiing and windsurfing are permitted. Personal watercraft are not allowed. A swimming area is available near the picnic area.

Contact: Tahoe National Forest, Nevada City Ranger District, (530) 265-4531 or fax (530) 478-6109. For campground information or a free brochure, contact PG&E Building & Land Services, (916) 386-5164 or fax (916) 386-5388.

About Lake Spaulding: Here are the requirements: Spectacular beauty. Easy to reach. Good boat ramp. Campground. Splendid hiking trails in the area.

Lake Spaulding is one of the few lakes that can provide all of these perks. Covering 698 acres, the lake is set at an elevation of 5,000 feet in the Sierra Nevada. This is classic granite country, and the setting features huge boulders and a sprinkling of conifers around a gray, slablike shoreline. The entire area looks like it has been cut and chiseled.

The drive here is nearly a straight shot up Interstate 80. If there is one problem, it is the amount of company you'll have at the campground.

The boat ramp is paved, but it is not really intended for large boats. After launching you will enter a beautiful setting that's suitable for most water sports. The water is spectacularly clear and cold; waterskiing is quite popular amid such grandeur and beauty, and is really fun—until you fall in. By August however, even that problem has for the most part abated, with the surface waters becoming considerably warmer.

Some people even try swimming. Windsurfing is popular because winds can be good and this is one of the few large lakes in the area.

Because the lake has a campground and is conveniently located right off Interstate 80, access is extremely easy and the place gets a lot of attention and use.

There's just one word of caution: Water levels tend to drop in late summer, creating visible hazards for boaters. For waterskiing that can mean that two spotters are necessary, one to keep an eye on the skier and another to be on the lookout for the occasional obstacle.

⑫ Fuller Lake

Location: East of Nevada City in Tahoe National Forest; map D3, grid b7.

Directions: From Sacramento drive east on Interstate 80 past Emigrant Gap to Highway 20. Drive west on Highway 20 to Bowman Road. Turn right and drive four miles to Fuller Lake on the right.

Access: A primitive boat launching area is located on the lake's west side.

Facilities, fees: A primitive campground is provided; no piped water is available. Supplies can be obtained in Nevada City. Access is free.

Water sports, restrictions: The lake is too small for windsurfing or powerboating. Swimming is permitted.

Contact: Tahoe National Forest, Nevada City Ranger District, (530) 265-4531 or fax (530) 478-6179. For a detailed map of the area, send $4 to Maps, Office of Information, US Forest Service, 1323 Club Drive, Vallejo, CA 94592.

About Fuller Lake: As you drive north on Bowman Road, little Fuller Lake is the first lake you'll come to. There are dozens of other lakes set farther back in the mountains. But if you just can't wait any longer, or the lakes nestled deeper in the national forest are inaccessible, stopping here just might prove to be a good idea. The place is ideal for camping, cartop boating, and maybe even a bit of fishing or swimming.

Though there are many lakes in the immediate region, this little lake stands apart because it is relatively easy to reach, has a campground and something that at least resembles a boat ramp; most other lakes around here don't have either.

Fuller is a tiny lake, best suited for cartop boating, fishing, and swimming. The water can remain quite cold through midsummer, but is clear and pretty.

The setting is at an elevation of 5,600 feet, and the road is usually free of snow by mid-May. Late snowstorms are common in this area, so always phone the Forest Service in advance to get road conditions.

⑬ Lake Valley Reservoir

Location: Near Yuba Gap in Tahoe National Forest; map D3, grid b7.

Directions: From Interstate 80 west of Truckee, take the Yuba Gap exit and head south about one-quarter mile. Turn right on Lake Valley Road and drive for one mile until the road forks. Bear right and continue for 1.5 miles.

Access: A paved boat ramp is located next to the picnic area on the north side of the lake.

Facilities, fees: PG&E provides a campground and a picnic area. Supplies can be obtained off Interstate 80. Access is free.

Water sports, restrictions: Waterskiing and personal watercraft are not permitted. Windsurfing is allowed. Swimming is available at the picnic area.

Contact: For campground information or a free brochure, contact PG&E Building & Land Services, (916) 386-5164 or fax (916) 386-5388.

About Lake Valley Reservoir: When full, Lake Valley Reservoir is gorgeous, its shoreline sprinkled with conifers and boulders. It is set at an elevation of 5,786 feet, has a surface area of 300 acres, and offers a decent campground and nearby boat ramp.

Upon arrival you get your first bonus: the very pretty campground, located near the lake but set right in the forest. It is one of the best camps run by PG&E.

Though no powerboating is permitted, the lake earns a pretty high rating anyway because of easy access, scenic beauty, great camping, and outstanding cartop boating conditions. Canoes are perfect for this lake, and paddling about while you fish for trout can be great fun.

Excellent windsurfing is another wonderful aspect of this lake, with a strong west wind on most afternoons. The shoreline is steep and rocky, but there is a suitable swimming area by the picnic area. This is also the best put-in spot for sailboarders.

When you add it all up, Lake Valley Reservoir is a winner. Quite a few vacationers have done the math, too, and they flock here in the summer.

⑭ Kelly Lake

Location: East of Nevada City in Tahoe National Forest; map D3, grid b7.

Directions: From Interstate 80 west of Truckee, take the Yuba Gap exit and head south about one-quarter mile. Turn right on Lake Valley Road and drive for one mile until the road forks. Bear left and continue for 1.5 miles to the lake.

Access: There is no boat ramp. Cartop boats may be hand launched.

Facilities, fees: A picnic area is provided. A campground is available nearby at Lake Valley Reservoir. Access to the lake is free.

Water sports, restrictions: Motors are not permitted on the lake. Swimming is possible near the picnic area. The lake is too small for windsurfing.

Contact: For campground information or

a free brochure, contact PG&E Building & Land Services, (916) 386-5164 or fax (916) 386-5388.

About Kelly Lake: Kelly is the little brother of nearby Lake Valley Reservoir. It has a similar look, set at an elevation of 5,900 feet and surrounded by granite boulders and conifers, but is just 15 percent of Lake Valley's size.

Many travelers on nearby Interstate 80 take a break here, either for a picnic lunch or to enjoy the pretty scenery. There's usually a handful of people who've hopped over from crowded Lake Valley Reservoir in search of a smaller, more intimate setting.

Before a picnic, some people take a dip in the water. Although there is no designated beach, there is a nice shoreline for swimming.

As no motors are permitted, boating opportunities are only available for cartop boaters. Also, there is no campground or any overnight use facility.

⑮ Fordyce Lake

Location: East of Nevada City in Tahoe National Forest; map D3, grid b8.

Directions: From Sacramento drive east on Interstate 80, take the Cisco Grove exit northbound. Immediately turn left on the frontage road (just prior to reaching Thousand Trails) and then right on Rattlesnake Road. Drive three miles north. When the road forks, bear left (this road is recommended for four-wheel-drive vehicles only) and travel three miles to the lake.

Access: There is no boat ramp. Cartop boats may be hand launched.

Facilities, fees: No facilities are provided on-site. A primitive campground is available at nearby Lake Sterling. Supplies can be obtained off Interstate 80. Access is free.

Water sports, restrictions: Motors are not permitted on the lake. Swimming is allowed.

Contact: Tahoe National Forest, Nevada City Ranger District, (916) 265-4531 or fax (530) 478-6109. For a detailed map of the area, send $4 to Maps, Office of Information, US Forest Service, 1323 Club Drive, Vallejo, CA 94592.

About Fordyce Lake: Some strangely shaped lakes were created when dams were built in Sierra gorges, and Fordyce is one of them. This long, curving lake has a very deep southern end near the dam, several coves, and six feeder streams. It is set at an elevation of about 7,000 feet.

It is ideal for four-wheel-drive cowboys with cartop boats who can make their way to the lake's narrow west side and then hand launch their craft. Other visitors with less ambition had best pass.

The shoreline is steep and rocky, making it difficult to launch boats or to find access for swimming or windsurfing. It is, however, large, and if you can get your boat or board into it, you can enjoy a private paddle in a wilderness-like setting. You are duly warned that the water does stay quite cold through most of the summer.

Some good hiking trails are available in the area and are detailed on a Forest Service map. If your car can't handle the access road, you can camp at nearby Lake Sterling to the south and make the short hike to Fordyce on a well-marked trail.

⑯ Lake Sterling

Location: East of Nevada City in Tahoe National Forest; map D3, grid b9.

Directions: From Sacramento drive east on Interstate 80 and take the Cisco Grove exit northbound. Turn left at the frontage road (just prior to reaching Thousand Trails) and then right on Rattlesnake Road. Drive four miles to Sterling Lake Road. Turn left and drive 2.5 steep, curvy miles to the lake. Four-wheel-drive vehicles are recommended.

Access: A primitive boat ramp is next to the campground.

Facilities, fees: A small primitive campground is provided; no piped water is available. Access to the lake is free.

Water sports, restrictions: Gas-powered motors are not permitted on the lake. Swimming access is available all along the shore.

Contact: Tahoe National Forest, Nevada City Ranger District, (530) 265-4531 or fax (530) 478-6109.

About Lake Sterling: Small and extremely pretty Lake Sterling is perched in a granite pocket at an elevation of 7,000 feet. Before you decide to make this your destination, though, be sure to call ahead and ask the key question: "How high's the water?" Because throughout its history, Lake Sterling has been subject to severe fluctuations.

This is a small, secluded lake with a primitive but pretty campground and a tree-lined shore. The access road is very rough, which sharply limits the number of visitors and often guarantees that a stay at Lake Sterling will be a private affair, even on summer weekends.

The boat ramp is suitable for small boats, and for the most part only anglers use it. No motors are permitted on the water. What you get here is the chance to go camping and cartop boating, with some good swimming by day and trout fishing during the early evening.

The water is clear and cold. The surface waters don't start to warm up considerably until late July, when swimming prospects can really shine.

---

⑰ Rollins Lake

Location: Southeast of Grass Valley; map D3, grid c3.

Directions: From Sacramento on Inter-

state 80, drive east about 60 miles to Highway 174 at Colfax. Drive east on Highway 174 to the lake.

Access: There are four paved boat ramps:

Greenhorn: From the Highway 174 turnoff, drive about eight miles north to Greenhorn Road. Turn right and continue to the ramp, located next to Greenhorn Campground.

Long Ravine: From the Highway 174 turnoff, drive a short distance north, then turn right on Rollins Lake Road, and drive 1.5 miles east. Turn left at the sign for Rollins Lake Resort and Long Ravine Campground and continue to the boat ramp and marina, located adjacent to the campground.

Orchard Springs: From the Highway 174 turnoff, drive about four miles north to Orchard Springs Road. Turn right and continue to the ramp, located next to Orchard Springs Campground.

Peninsula: From the Highway 174 turnoff, drive approximately 14 miles north, and then turn right on You Bet Road. After three miles the road becomes gravel. Continue to the sign for Peninsula Campground, turn right, and continue south to the boat ramp, located adjacent to the campground.

Facilities, fees: Four campgrounds, convenience stores, a restaurant, and rest rooms with showers are provided. A full-service marina and fishing boat, paddleboat, and canoe rentals are available. Supplies can be obtained in Grass Valley and Colfax. A day-use fee is charged. There is an additional fee to bring a boat in.

Water sports, restrictions: Waterskiing, personal watercraft, and windsurfing are allowed. Roped-off swimming beaches are available at each of the four on-site campgrounds.

Contact: Rollins Lake Resort/Long Ravine Campground, (530) 346-6166; Orchard Springs Campground, (530) 346-2212; Greenhorn Campground, (530) 272-6100;

Peninsula Campground, (530) 477-9413.

About Rollins Lake: Just a short drive north from Colfax brings you to Rollins Lake, set at an elevation of 2,100 feet at the point where the foothill country becomes forest. In late winter the snow line is somewhere around here as well. The result is a lake that crosses the spectrum as a trout lake and bass lake, water-ski lake, and a swimming lake.

Rollins extends far up two lake arms, covering 825 acres with 26 miles of shoreline. It can get quite hot in summer, which makes this place attractive for swimming and waterskiing. The latter is very popular, with boaters drawn to the warm summer weather and lukewarm water. Sunny weather, good campgrounds, cabin rentals, and the opportunity for all water sports make Rollins Lake a winner in the summer.

Another plus is that boat ramps and large, sandy swimming beaches are available near all four campgrounds. With all this to offer, it's no surprise that the lake draws fairly large crowds throughout the summer. Your best bet for snagging a remote campsite is at Peninsula Campground (reached via Highway 174 and You Bet Road); although it's developed and has full facilities, it gets less traffic than Orchard Springs or Long Ravine. Long Ravine is by far the most popular area because it is located next to the marina and restaurant. This is also the best put-in spot for windsurfing, a sport that's just starting to catch on at Rollins Lake.

⑱ Sugar Pine Reservoir

⤓〰️🏕🐟🏄🛶 7

Location: Northeast of Auburn in Tahoe National Forest; map D3, grid c4.

Directions: From Sacramento drive 31 miles east on Interstate 80 to Auburn. Take the Foresthill Road exit at the north end of town and drive 20 miles northeast to Foresthill. Continue east on Foresthill Road

(it becomes Baker Ranch–Soda Springs Road) for eight miles and then turn north on Sugar Pine Road. Drive about five miles, turn left on Finning Mill Road, and continue to the lake.

Access: From Finning Mill Road, continue past the sign for Forbes Creek Campground to the sign for the unpaved boat ramp. Turn right and drive down to the lake.

Facilities, fees: Campgrounds and a picnic area are provided. Supplies can be obtained in Foresthill. Access is free.

Water sports, restrictions: A 10 mph speed limit is strictly enforced. Windsurfing is allowed; note the speed limit. Swimming is available near the campgrounds and picnic areas on the north side of the lake.

Contact: Tahoe National Forest, Foresthill Ranger District, (530) 367-2224 or fax (530) 367-2992.

About Sugar Pine Reservoir: Lakeside campgrounds make Sugar Pine Reservoir a popular summer vacation spot. Covering 160 acres, the lake is set at 3,600 feet in the lower alpine region of the Sierra Nevada. The surrounding area is heavily forested, the lake is quite scenic, and for the most part, access is not difficult.

The 10 mph speed limit ensures that activities are subdued and the water remains calm. Fishing, canoeing, swimming, and windsurfing appeal to most visitors. The recreation area is fully developed, and the campgrounds can fill up. There are nice areas for swimming, windsurfing, and with the water always calm and quiet, canoeing.

A bonus is that the facilities are wheelchair accessible.

⑲ Big Reservoir

⤓〰️🏕🐟🏄🛶 6

Location: Northeast of Auburn in Tahoe National Forest; map D3, grid c5.

Directions: From Sacramento drive 31 miles east on Interstate 80 to Auburn. Take the Foresthill Road exit at the north end of town and drive 20 miles northeast to the town of Foresthill. Continue east on Foresthill Road (it becomes Baker Ranch–Soda Springs Road) for eight miles; then turn north on Sugar Pine Road and drive about three miles to Forest Service Road 24 (signed for Big Reservoir). Bear right on the signed access road and drive one mile to the lake.

Access: A primitive boat ramp is available next to the picnic area.

Facilities, fees: A campground and picnic area are provided. Rest rooms with showers, a small store, and paddleboat rentals are available at Morning Star Lake Resort. Supplies can be obtained in Foresthill. A day-use parking fee is charged.

Water sports, restrictions: Gas-powered motors are not permitted on the lake. Windsurfing is allowed. Swimming beaches are provided, but you can swim anywhere along the shoreline.

Contact: Tahoe National Forest, Foresthill Ranger District, (530) 367-2224 or fax (530) 367-2992; Morning Star Lake Resort, (530) 367-2129.

About Big Reservoir: Beautiful Big Reservoir is a 70-acre freshwater pocket surrounded by forest and set at an elevation of 4,100 feet. In addition to being quite pretty, it is also quiet because no gas-powered motors are permitted.

A picnic area is provided at the lake's edge, and a campground is available nearby. With all these features this little lake is becoming a favorite for families. Many families find that the lake is easily accessible, located a relatively short distance from Sacramento.

Another wonderful aspect of Big Reservoir is that conditions are about perfect for windsurfing. A breeze kicks in around 9 AM and continues into the late afternoon, only to pick up again around 7 PM. In addition you can swim anywhere on the lake because the entire shoreline is sandy and gently sloped.

Morning Star Resort offers a developed campground with showers. It receives only moderate use in the summer months, even lighter in late spring.

⑳ Kidd Lake

Location: West of Truckee in Tahoe National Forest; map D3, grid c9.

Directions: From Sacramento drive approximately 90 miles east on Interstate 80 toward Truckee. Take the Norden exit (12 miles west of Truckee). Turn south on Soda Springs Road and travel one mile to Pahatsi Road. Turn west and drive one mile (the pavement ends one-third mile past the turnoff). When the road forks, bear south, drive one mile to the next fork, bear west, and continue three-quarters of a mile to the lake entrance.

Access: A primitive boat ramp is available on the lake's west side.

Facilities, fees: PG&E provides group campsites; reservations are required. Supplies can be obtained in Truckee. Access to the lake is free.

Water sports, restrictions: There is a 10 mph speed limit. Windsurfing is allowed. Swimming is available around the lake's edge.

Contact: Tahoe National Forest, Truckee Ranger District, (530) 587-3558 or fax (530) 587-6914. For campground reservations phone PG&E Building & Land Services, (916) 386-5164 or fax (916) 386-5388.

About Kidd Lake: Kidd Lake is the first of three lakes bunched in a series along the access road, and one of seven in a six-mile radius. A campground and primitive boat ramp make it one of the better choices.

The lake is set in the northern Sierra's high country at an elevation of 6,750 feet. Of course it gets loaded with snow every winter. In late spring and early summer, be sure to call ahead to ask about conditions on the access road.

Forestland surrounds the small, round

lake. The shoreline is somewhat rocky, but there are a couple of good spots that are suitable for swimming. Windsurfing is decent in the afternoon, when the wind picks up. And if you want a break from the water, you'll find some good hiking trails in the area.

Kidd Lake gets a lot of traffic in the summer from Interstate 80 travelers, mainly anglers who bring small boats and camp overnight. There are usually enough visitors to make campsite reservations necessary.

㉑ Cascade Lakes

Location: West of Truckee in Tahoe National Forest; map D3, grid c9.
Directions: From Sacramento drive approximately 90 miles east on Interstate 80 toward Truckee. Take the Norden exit (12 miles west of Truckee). Turn south on Soda Springs Road and travel one mile to Pahatsi Road. Turn west and drive one mile (the pavement ends one-third mile past the turnoff). When the road forks, bear south, drive one mile to the next fork, and bear west. Drive about three miles past Kidd Lake to Cascade Lakes.
Access: There is no boat ramp.
Facilities, fees: No facilities are provided on-site. A group campground is available nearby at Kidd Lake (reservations required). Supplies can be obtained in Truckee. Access to the lake is free.
Water sports, restrictions: There is a 10 mph speed limit. Swimming is allowed.
Contact: Tahoe National Forest, Truckee Ranger District, (916) 587-3558 or fax (530) 587-6914; Mountain Hardware, (530) 587-4844.
About Cascade Lakes: A channel connects these two tiny lakes, which are set at an elevation of about 4,000 feet. Both are too small for much boating, but a few diehard fishermen do haul in their small cartop boats to fish for trout now and then.

There's no boat ramp, and the shorelines are not conducive to hand-launching. Much of the shore is rocky and steep, which also discourages many swimmers. By midsummer, however, the water is warm and clear, a good place to take a quick dunk on a hot day after driving on Interstate 80, providing you don't mind searching around a bit to find the best access points.

Cascade Lakes are better known among hikers as a good trailhead site and jump-off point for a backpacking trip. A trailhead that is located at the lake's northwest side is routed south into Tahoe National Forest, up into the drainage to the headwaters of the North Fork American River.

㉒ Serene Lakes

Location: West of Truckee; map D3, grid c9.
Directions: From Sacramento drive approximately 90 miles east on Interstate 80 toward Truckee. Take the Norden exit (12 miles west of Truckee). Turn south on Soda Springs Road and travel approximately two miles to the lake.
Access: A boat ramp is located on the lake's east side at Serene Lakes Lodge.
Facilities, fees: A campground and picnic area are provided. Rooms, restaurant, and paddleboat and canoe rentals are available at Serene Lakes Lodge. Access is free.
Water sports, restrictions: Motors are not permitted on the lake. Windsurfing is allowed but is not that popular. A swimming beach is available in front of the lodge.
Contact: Serene Lakes Lodge, (530) 426-9001.
About Serene Lakes: Not only is the scenery around Serene Lakes gorgeous, but this is one of the few lakes in California that has adjoining private property where vacation homes have been built.

The lake (two connected lakes, actually)

is too small and shallow for motorized boating, which isn't permitted anyway, but it is perfect for canoes, rowboats, and paddleboats.

An excellent sandy beach is available at the lodge. Another beach nearby is technically reserved for the lake's home owners, but lodge guests and day-use visitors go there frequently.

Visitor use at Serene Lakes is moderate—pretty much just guests of the lodge and campground. Some good hiking trails are routed through the area.

㉓ Camp Far West Reservoir

Location: East of Marysville; map D3, grid d0.

Directions: From Sacramento drive east on Interstate 80 to Roseville. Turn north on Highway 65 and drive to the town of Wheatland. Turn east at the sign for Camp Far West/Main Street and follow the signs for about six miles to the reservoir. A road circles the lake's west side, providing access to camps and boat launches at both the north and south entrances to the lake.

Access: There are two paved boat ramps, one on the north side and one on the south side. Clearly marked signs for both boat ramps are posted on the entrance road.

Facilities, fees: Campgrounds and picnic areas are provided. A marina with boat docks and limited facilities is available on the south side. Groceries, snack bar, and personal watercraft, paddleboat, and kayak rentals are available on the north side. A day-use fee is charged; boat launching is included.

Water sports, restrictions: Waterskiing, personal watercraft, and windsurfing are permitted. A large day-use and swimming area is provided on the north side near the campground; a smaller swimming area is available on the lake's south side.

Contact: Camp Far West, (530) 633-0803; Water Toys, (916) 955-6880.

About Camp Far West Reservoir: Camp Far West is set at an elevation of 320 feet in the foothill country, which means it gets an early spring followed by a hot summer. Covering 2,000 surface acres with 29 miles of shoreline, the reservoir is an outstanding destination for boating and water sports, with warm water, hot weather, and plenty of room for everybody.

For the most part, users split the lake into two areas. Most powerboaters and water-skiers head to the lake's southern side. It can get outrageous on the weekends when a few impromptu water-skier parties get under way with lots of liquids and suntan lotion flowing almost as fast as the jet boats.

The northern side of the lake, on the other hand, tends to be quieter, a setting for more family-oriented activities. This is also where the lake's best day-use area is located. Water-skiers should note that there is a large rocky area on the northwest side of the lake that should be avoided.

Because the lake is used to store water for agricultural use, by late summer the levels can fall quite a bit. In fact, in low rain years the change can be quite drastic. By late August it is recommended that visitors call ahead for conditions.

Use is moderate on summer weekends, high on three-day holidays, and light during the week.

㉔ French Meadows Reservoir

Location: Northeast of Auburn in Tahoe National Forest; map D3, grid d9.

Directions: From Sacramento drive 31 miles east on Interstate 80 to Auburn. Take the Foresthill Road exit at the north end of town and drive 20 miles northeast. Just before the town of Foresthill, turn right on Mosquito Ridge Road and travel 36 miles east to the French Meadows Reservoir dam. Cross the dam, turn east, and drive along the lake.

Access: There are two paved boat ramps, one at the picnic area two miles east of the dam, and one on the opposite side of the lake next to Maguire picnic area. Both are directly off the lake's access road and are well signed.

Facilities, fees: Several campgrounds and two lakeside picnic areas are provided. Supplies can be obtained in Foresthill. Access to the lake is free.

Water sports, restrictions: Waterskiing, personal watercraft, and windsurfing are permitted. Be aware that low water levels in summer can pose hazards for powerboaters; call ahead to check conditions. A swimming beach is available at Maguire picnic area on the north shore.

Contact: Tahoe National Forest, Foresthill Ranger District, (530) 367-2224 or fax (530) 367-2992.

About French Meadows Reservoir: If you don't mind a do-it-yourself camping/boating trip, French Meadows just might be the vacation destination you're looking for. Do it yourself? Right. Facilities are limited to campgrounds, picnic areas, and two boat ramps. There is no marina, and there are no boats for rent. All the necessary supplies (as well as gas for your boat) must be obtained before you arrive.

What you do get are several sandy areas around the lake that are suitable for sunbathing and swimming; the largest is the designated day-use area at Maguire picnic area on the lake's north side. There's also the chance for some good trout fishing from spring through early summer.

French Meadows Reservoir is set at an elevation of 5,300 feet on a dammed-up section of the Middle Fork American River. When full in the spring, it is big, nearly 2,000 acres.

In years with good snowpacks, there is enough melt-off to keep the lake high and beautiful. That is often not the case, however, in years following winters with even slightly below normal precipitation.

The water masters who control the dam have a way of turning it into a little lake by fall. That's right, they drain this sucker down until acres and acres of lake bottom are exposed and all kinds of stumps and boulders start poking through the surface. It creates a multitude of navigational hazards and leaves the campgrounds stranded far from the shoreline.

㉕ Clementine Lake

Location: Northeast of Auburn on the American River; map D3, grid e2.

Directions: From Sacramento drive 31 miles east on Interstate 80 to Auburn. Take the Foresthill Road exit and drive five miles east. Turn north on Clementine Road and drive four miles to the boat ramp.

Access: There's a paved ramp at the end of the access road.

Facilities, fees: Boat-in campgrounds and picnic areas are provided. A concessionaire sells gas. Supplies can be obtained in Auburn. Access to the lake is free. There is a fee for boat launching.

Water sports, restrictions: Waterskiing and personal watercraft are permitted. Swimming areas are available in front of the campgrounds; access is limited to boats only.

Contact: Auburn State Recreation Area, (530) 367-2224 or fax (530) 367-2992; Auburn Chamber of Commerce, (530) 885-5616.

About Clementine Lake: Sometimes you just plain need a boat. When you visit Clementine Lake, you will discover that this is one of those situations.

A dammed-up gorge on the North Fork American River, Clementine Lake is 3.5 miles long and quite narrow. It is ideal for the boater, with boat-in campsites, great boat-in swimming beaches, and a 25-boat limit that practically guarantees tranquillity.

Highlights include very pretty scenery, easy access from Auburn, and the boat-in campgrounds, which provide visitors with a wilderness-like atmosphere.

It is critical to understand the ramifications of the 25-boat quota implemented by the Auburn State Recreation Area. What it all boils down to is that boaters who are camping at the lake get priority, and if you're coming on a weekend to spend the day, you run the risk of being shut out. Arriving during the week is a better bet for day use; if you're scheduling a trip for a summer weekend, you should reserve a campsite.

No services are offered at the lake, except for gasoline, which is a great plus.

Shoreline access is virtually impossible without a boat. But with a boat? Heh, heh, what a payoff!

㉖ Middle Fork American River

Location: Near Foresthill; map D3, grid e6.
Directions: Access is limited to the rafting put-in downstream of the Oxbow Powerhouse (see Boat ramp, put in) and a few rough dirt roads out of Foresthill. See a USGS map for details.
Access: There is no boat ramp. To reach the rafting put-in, drive east of Auburn on Interstate 80 and take the Foresthill exit. Turn east on Auburn-Foresthill Road and drive approximately 20 miles to Foresthill. Once in town turn right on Mosquito Ridge Road and follow the road down to the North Fork of the Middle Fork American crossing. Continue for about two miles, turn right, and drive toward the Oxbow Powerhouse. The put-in is

just downstream of the powerhouse.

The closest take-out is 16 miles downstream at Greenwood Bridge, accessible by taking Auburn-Foresthill Road to Drivers Flat Road and then turning down toward the river. An alternate take-out is another seven miles downstream at Mammoth Bar, which is reached by taking Old Foresthill Road north from Highway 49 (east of Auburn) to Mammoth Bar Road and then down to the river. Note: You must take out here if you want to avoid the Class V–VI rapid above Murderer's Bar (experts only). Those who wish to continue may take out two miles downstream at the Highway 49 bridge, located at the confluence of the Middle and North Forks of the American. This is the last possible take-out before Folsom Lake.

Facilities, fees: A few remote Forest Service campgrounds are available on Mosquito Ridge Road, past French Meadows Reservoir. Boats can be rented at California Canoe & Kayak and Wilderness Sports in the Sacramento area. Supplies can be obtained in Auburn and Foresthill. Access is free. Rafting permits are not required.

Water sports, restrictions: There are a few excellent swimming holes; the best are reached by boat. You can also swim at Greenwood Bridge and at Ahart Campground on Mosquito Ridge Road.

Contact: Eldorado National Forest, Visitor Center, (530) 644-6048, or fax (530) 295-5624; Eldorado National Forest, Georgetown Ranger District, (530) 333-4312 or fax (530) 333-5522. For guided rafting trips contact All-Outdoors Whitewater Rafting, (800) 247-2387; American River Recreation, (800) 333-7238 or (530) 622-6802; American Whitewater Expeditions, (818) 352-3205; American River Touring Association (ARTA), (800) 323-2782 or (209) 962-7873; Beyond Limits Adventures, (800) 234-7238; Koolriver Adventure Tours, Inc, (800) 931-8999; Mariah Wilderness Expeditions, (800) 462-

7424; Mother Lode River Trips, (530) 626-4187; Outdoor Adventure River Specialists (OARS, Inc), (800) 346-6277; RAM River Adventures, (800) 466-7238; River Runners, (818) 222-4260; Whitewater Voyages, (800) 488-7238; or Zephyr River Expeditions, (209) 532-6249.

About the Middle Fork American River: The scenery is exquisite, remote, and lush. The water is cold and clear. Historical sites from the Gold Rush days dot the landscape. And the white-water rafting runs have names such as Texas Chainsaw Mama and Murderer's Bar. Need more be said? Texas Chainsaw Mama? Hey, where do they get these names?

Right, this is the Middle Fork American, the challenging alternative to the popular South Fork American. Because river access is difficult and there are several challenging expert sections of water, including some portages, many people opt for the South Fork instead. For those willing to take the challenge, however, rafting here means rewards of considerable solitude and excitement. One word of caution. Do not plan to stop and venture onto the adjoining lands; they are privately owned and the landowners do not take kindly to trespassers, no matter how honorable the intention.

The run stretches for 25 miles and has a very long season, typically from May through September, courtesy of upstream dam releases. The first 14 miles are rated Class IV, with one Class V–VI section (Tunnel Chute). That is a definite portage for most, unless you have a yearning to make an early visit to the big hydraulic suckhole in the sky. Many rafters take out at Greenwood Bridge.

Continuing downstream from Greenwood Bridge to Mammoth Bar, the run is Class II–III, pleasant and inspiring most of the way. But this piece is difficult to enjoy to the fullest because awaiting in the last two miles is a wild run, rated Class V–VI. It

is heaven for some, hell for others. This stretch includes Murderer's Bar, Ruck-a-Chucky Falls (beautiful but unrunnable, and always portaged), Parallel Parking (Class IV), and finally, the one you have been waiting for, Texas Chainsaw Mama (Class IV).

Special note: The proposed Auburn Dam project would eliminate the possibility of rafting on both the Chamberlain Falls and Big Bend Runs of the North Fork, as well as the entire stretch of the Middle Fork. An alternate proposal seeks to turn these areas into a protected National Recreation Area, an idea that's much more appealing to rafters for obvious reasons. Many of the rafting companies listed above have information on how individuals can support this effort.

㉗ Hell Hole Reservoir

Location: Northeast of Auburn in Eldorado National Forest; map D3, grid e9.

Directions: From Sacramento drive 31 miles east on Interstate 80 to Auburn. Take the Elm Avenue exit in Auburn and drive to High Street. Drive straight through the third signal onto Highway 49 and into the canyon about 3.5 miles. Turn right over the bridge and drive back up the canyon about 2.5 miles into the town of Cool. Turn left on Georgetown Road/Highway 193 and drive on Wentworth SpringsRoad/Forest Service Road 1 to Eleven Pines Road/Forest Service Road 2. Turn left and drive to the reservoir.

Access: A paved ramp is located on the access road past Hell Hole Campground.

Facilities, fees: A primitive Forest Service campground is provided on the access road, and several boat-in sites are available on the far eastern end of the lake. A picnic area is also provided. Supplies can be obtained in Georgetown and Foresthill. Access is free.

Water sports, restrictions: Waterskiing and personal watercraft are permitted, although it can be difficult to haul boats on trailers up the twisty, narrow access road. Windsurfing is allowed; sailors should be aware of potentially hazardous winds in the afternoon. Swimming is permitted, but the shoreline is steep and rocky.

Contact: Eldorado National Forest, Visitor Center, (530) 644-6048 or fax (530) 295-5624; Eldorado National Forest, Georgetown Ranger District, (530) 333-4312 or fax (530) 333-5522.

About Hell Hole Reservoir: The first time I saw this lake was from an airplane, which afforded a spectacular view of one of the most awesome drive-to destinations in California. The lake is set at the bottom of a massive granite gorge, filled with water the color of sapphires. From the sky it has the appearance of a mountain temple.

Close up, Hell Hole Reservoir is just as sacred. The lake elevation is only 4,700 feet, but the surrounding walls and mountain country rise steep and high above the water. The water is crystal pure, fed by the most remote stretches of the pristine Rubicon River.

But understand something right off. This lake is extremely remote and access is very poor, requiring a terribly long, slow, twisty drive on mountain back roads to get here. Trailered boats can take a pounding, and so will your nerves. Also, there are no drive-to campsites on the lake, which means trailering a boat involves a pain-in-the-butt drive back and forth from the nearest campground. Campers are much better served here with a cartop boat equipped to handle a small engine.

The lake covers 1,300 acres and has 15 miles of shoreline, if you can call it that. It's really more like canyon walls plunging down into the water, so beautiful that it is dramatic, even breathtaking. Most of the people you'll see out on the lake are camper/anglers, fishing for brown trout, Mackinaw trout, and kokanee salmon.

Because the long, circuitous drive is so inconvenient, water-skiers are scarce. The handful that make the trip, however, will find that this is the most picturesque lake for waterskiing in California, and possibly anywhere in North America.

With no real shoreline to speak of, access for swimming is difficult, though some boaters with ladders on their boats will occasionally take a quick plunge. Quick? Right, this water is very cold, even through summer.

Windsurfing can be excellent. Afternoon winds are predictable, and on a good day, this is a spectacular setting for such a sport. But note that winds can really howl up here, and sometimes windsurfing as well as boating can become dangerous.

Despite the incredible grandeur, the long drive to get here keeps use down to moderate levels in summer. The typical visitor is a vacationer who has time to burn, time to enjoy a veritable paradise.

㉘ North Fork American River

Location: Near Auburn; map D3, grid f1.
Directions: From Sacramento drive 31 miles east on Interstate 80 to Auburn. From Auburn drive northeast on Highway 49. Access is available where the bridge crosses the river. Limited access is also available off roads that intersect with Interstate 80 near the town of Colfax (see directions to put-ins).
Access: A boat ramp is located off Highway 49 north of Folsom Lake, on Rattlesnake Bar Road. There are four well-known put-ins (see "About the North Fork American River.")
Facilities, fees: Campgrounds are available in Auburn and off Interstate 80 at the above locations. Supplies can be obtained in Auburn, Colfax, and in the Emigrant Gap

area. Boat rentals can be obtained at California Canoe & Kayak and Wilderness Sports in the Sacramento area. Access is free. Rafting permits are not required.

Water sports, restrictions: Swimming is available at the Highway 49 bridge and at or near the rafting put-ins for the Big Bend and Clementine Runs (see directions above).

Contact: Bureau of Land Management, Folsom Field Office, (916) 985-4474. For guided rafting trips, contact All-Outdoors Whitewater Rafting, (800) 247-2387; American River Recreation, (800) 333-7238 or (530) 622-6802; American Whitewater Expeditions, (818) 352-3205; ARTA, (800) 323-2782 or (209) 962-7873; Mariah Wilderness Expeditions, (800) 462-7424; Mother Lode River Trips, (530) 626-4187; O.A.R.S., Inc, (800) 346-6277; RAM River Adventures, (800) 466-7238; River Runners, (530) 622-5110; Sierra Mac River Trips, (800) 457-2580; or Whitewater Voyages, (800) 488-7238.

About the North Fork American River: The scenery is superb, with impressive canyons, lush vegetation, clear and cold water, and a wilderness-like feel to the entire canyon. Of the three forks of the American River, the North Fork is the most difficult to run. Anybody who makes it through Locomotive Falls, Dominator, and Nutcracker Chute is bound to feel lucky to be alive and may even want to kiss the nearest available rock rooted firmly in solid ground.

The rafting season generally runs from April to June; in high water years, it starts a bit later and lasts into the first few weeks of July. While access is limited, there are plenty of campsites along the river below the Giant Gap Run.

Although the water's clear and cold, you must always purify it before drinking. The water is cold enough that most rafting outfitters require all participants to wear wet suits or dry suits on guided trips.

Here are the breakdowns on the available runs:

Big Bend and Clementine Runs: From Interstate 80 east of Auburn, take the Colfax exit and turn south on Canyon Way. Continue to Yankee Jim's Road (watch for the sign for Foresthill), and turn left. Drive east to the put-in, located slightly upstream from the bridge on the left. Take out 4.5 miles downstream at Ponderosa Way or continue through the Clementine Run.

To access the Clementine Run, from Interstate 80 east of Auburn, take the Weimar Cross Road exit and turn left on Canyon Way. Proceed to Ponderosa Way and turn east, continuing down to a bridge that crosses the river. Put in on the right bank, just below the bridge. Take out 4.5 miles downstream at Clementine Lake, where Upper Clementine Road intersects on the left bank.

Ah, anybody who makes it this far deserves what lies ahead. This is a nine-mile stretch of all Class I and II water—a nice, scenic traverse where you can catch your breath and congratulate yourself on making it out alive.

Chamberlain Falls Run: From Interstate 80 east of Auburn, take the Colfax exit and turn south on Canyon Way. Continue to Colfax–Iowa Hill Road and turn east. Follow the road down to the bridge that crosses the river. Take out five miles downstream at the Shirttail Canyon access or continue through the Big Bend Run. Note: Chamberlain Falls Run is Class IV–V+; experienced paddlers only.

A very popular run, this is a particular favorite with commercial rafting companies. It is named after Chamberlain Falls, rated Class IV+, but includes a heart-thumping vertical drop of eight feet. You'll never forget it. Other highlights include Slaughter's Sluice (Class IV), Tongue & Groove (Class IV), Bogus Thunder (Class IV), and Staircase (Class IV+).

Giant Gap Run: From Interstate 80

east of Auburn, take the Alta exit. Turn south on Casa Loma Road and drive approximately three miles to the Eucre Bar Trailhead. A two-mile hike is required to reach the river. The put-in is just past a small bridge that crosses the river. Take out 14 miles downstream at the bridge at Colfax–Iowa Hill Road, or continue through the Chamberlain Falls Run. Note: Giant Gap run is Class IV+; experts only.

This is the most difficult run on the North Fork, and it is very popular. It's rated Class IV+, which means it's for experts only. Rafters who are new to the river should be in rafts guided by experts.

The run cuts through a very narrow, scenic gorge. Just to reach the put-in requires a steep, two-mile hike, which means boats and gear must be carried in. For this reason, most commercial trips start farther downstream at the Colfax–Iowa Hill Road bridge access.

For those willing to pay the price, encounters with some of the most daredevil white water imaginable await. You will meet Nutcracker Chute (Class V), then Locomotive Falls (Class V–V+ with a vertical drop), and Dominator (Class V). All three may be portaged. But in the usual scenario, a guide will make the run first, and after (hopefully) emerging alive, will provide scouting information for future trips run by other guides. Then everybody has a hell of a time. Heaven or hell? You decide.

Special note: The proposed Auburn Dam project would eliminate the possibility of rafting on both the Chamberlain Falls and Big Bend Runs of the North Fork, as well as the entire stretch of the Middle Fork. An alternate proposal seeks to turn these areas into a protected National Recreation Area, an idea that's much more appealing to rafters for obvious reasons. Many of the rafting companies listed above have information on how individuals can support this effort.

㉙ Stumpy Meadows Reservoir

Location: Northeast of Placerville in Eldorado National Forest; map D3, grid f6.
Directions: From Sacramento drive 31 miles east on Interstate 80 to Auburn. Take the Elm Avenue exit in Auburn and drive to High Street. Drive straight through the third signal onto Highway 49 and into the canyon about 3.5 miles. Turn right over the bridge and drive back up the canyon about 2.5 miles into the town of Cool. Turn left on Georgetown Road/Highway 193 and drive 18 miles on Wentworth Springs Road/Forest Service Road 1 to Stumpy Meadows Reservoir.
Access: A paved boat ramp is located just south of the dam, right off Wentworth Springs Dam near Vista picnic area.
Facilities, fees: Campgrounds and a picnic area are provided. Supplies can be obtained in Placerville and Georgetown. Access to the lake is free.
Water sports, restrictions: A 5 mph speed limit is strictly enforced. Motorized boats are limited to 10 horsepower. Windsurfing is allowed; note the speed limit. Swimming is available at Vista picnic area, near the boat ramp.
Contact: Eldorado National Forest, Visitor Center, (530) 644-6048 or fax (530) 295-5624; Eldorado National Forest, Georgetown Ranger District, (530) 333-4312 or fax (530) 333-5522.
About Stumpy Meadows Reservoir: Don't let the name fool you into thinking Stumpy Meadows is a stodgy old place full of algae. Quite the opposite. The water is cold and clear, the lake is surrounded by national forest, and it is an ideal place to camp, fish, and boat.

The only stodgy thing about the place is the 5 mph speed limit for boaters, which keeps the lake quiet.

Stumpy Meadows covers 320 acres and

is set at an elevation of 4,400 feet in Eldorado National Forest, up in the snow country. The water is quite cold, so swimming is only for the brave at heart. However, the lake is perfect for windsurfers, who don't have to contend with motorboats and water-skiers.

No facilities are available at the lake, save for the campgrounds. Use is moderate on weekdays in the summer, but the campgrounds usually fill up on weekends; you can book a spot through the Forest Service reservation system.

㉚ Gerle Creek Reservoir

Location: West of Lake Tahoe in Eldorado National Forest; map D3, grid f8.

Directions: From Sacramento drive 45 miles east on US 50 to Placerville. Continue for about 20 miles east on US 50 to Riverton and the bridge across the American River. Turn north on Ice House Road and drive about 32 miles (passing Union Valley Reservoir) and drive three miles to the Gerle Creek turnoff on the left.

Access: No boat ramp is available. Cartop boats may be hand launched.

Facilities, fees: A campground, a picnic area, and a fishing pier are provided. Supplies can be obtained in Placerville. Access to the lake is free.

Water sports, restrictions: Motors are not permitted on the lake. Swimming and windsurfing access is available near the picnic area.

Contact: Eldorado National Forest, Visitor Center, (530) 644-6048 or fax (530) 295-5624; Eldorado National Forest, Pacific Ranger District, (539) 644-2349 or fax (530) 647-5405.

About Gerle Creek Reservoir: This is a small, pretty lake, although boating options are somewhat limited. It is set at an elevation of 5,300 feet in Eldorado National Forest.

Small? No boat ramp is provided, mak-

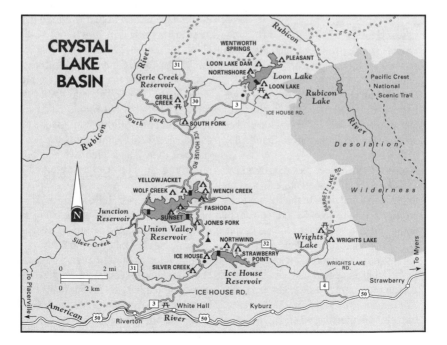

ing it perfect for people with cartop boats that are easily hand launched, such as canoes. Pretty? Definitely, nestled right in the Gerle Creek Canyon, which feeds into the South Fork Rubicon. Limited? Another affirmative, because here all motors are prohibited.

Among the things this small reservoir does have are clear water and a scenic campground set in old-growth conifer forest.

As mentioned, boating at Gerle Creek Reservoir is suited only for small, human-powered craft. Windsurfing can be excellent on summer afternoons. The shoreline is grassy and rocky, and some visitors go swimming adjacent to the picnic area, where there is a grassy/dirt area that is good for sunbathing.

Traffic is light here. Most folks head to nearby Loon Lake when they want full-facility boating opportunities.

㉛ Folsom Lake

Location: Northeast of Sacramento in Folsom Lake State Recreation Area; map D3, grid g0.

Directions: From Sacramento drive northeast on Interstate 80. Take the Douglas Boulevard exit and travel nine miles east on Douglas Boulevard to Granite Bay at the lake.

Access: There are five paved boat ramps:

Dike 8: From Sacramento, turn east on Interstate 50 and drive to the Folsom turnoff. Go into the town of Folsom on Folsom Boulevard and turn right on Blue Ravine Road. Drive approximately four miles to East Natoma Road, then turn right and continue to the multilane paved boat ramp, located adjacent to a picnic area.

Folsom Marina: From Sacramento, turn east on Interstate 50 and drive to the Folsom turnoff. Go into the town of Folsom

on Folsom Boulevard and turn right on Blue Ravine Road. Continue straight past the turnoff for Dike 8 to the sign for Folsom Marina, where there is a multilane paved boat ramp.

Granite Bay: From Interstate 80 east of Sacramento, take the Douglas Boulevard off-ramp and drive east on Douglas Boulevard to where it dead-ends at Granite Bay. A multilane paved ramp is available.

Peninsula: From Sacramento, take Interstate 80 east to Auburn and exit on Maple Street. Stay right on Maple Street and continue south as it turns into Auburn-Folsom Road. Drive four miles, then turn right on Rattlesnake Bar Road and continue 2.5 miles to the entrance. A paved ramp is available.

Rattlesnake Bar: From Sacramento, take Interstate 80 east to Auburn and take the Elm Street exit. Turn east and drive one-half mile; turn left on High Street, which turns into Highway 49; continue east for 10 miles to the town of Pilot Hill. Turn right on Rattlesnake Bar Road and continue nine miles to the entrance. A paved ramp is available.

Facilities, fees: Campgrounds, picnic areas, rest rooms, and a snack bar are provided at the lake. Folsom Marina has full services and rents out fishing boats and small sailboats. Windsurfing lessons are available at Beals Point. A day-use fee is charged. There is an additional fee for boat launching. Supplies can be obtained in Folsom.

Water sports, restrictions: Waterskiing, personal watercraft, and windsurfing are permitted. Designated swimming beaches are available at Granite Bay and Beals Point. Swimming is permitted anywhere along the shoreline except within the boat launching areas. Note: Private boats must be registered at either the marina or Granite Bay before launching.

Contact: Folsom Lake State Recreation

Area, (916) 988-0205; Folsom Marina, (916) 933-1300; Fran and Eddy's Sports Den in Rancho Cordova, (916) 363-6885.

About Folsom Lake: This is Sacramento's backyard playland, where thousands and thousands of people come to fish, water-ski, camp, and just lie around in the sun.

Because of the lake's shallow arms, water levels can fluctuate as dramatically from winter to spring as at any lake in California. This lake can look almost empty before any rains start in December, then seem to fill to the brim virtually overnight. When full, it covers some 12,000 acres with 75 miles of shoreline.

This is an extremely popular (and populated) spot in summer. Families, college students, and anyone in Sacramento with a yearning for some lake-oriented fun seem to flock here, sometimes at the same time. Some come for the waterskiing, some for the fishing, some for the camping, and some apparently for the beer.

Visitors have the use of attractive swimming beaches with lifeguards and buoys, several boat ramps, boat rentals, and nice campgrounds and day-use areas. The adjoining recreation area has a network of trails for jogging, hiking, and horseback riding.

Temperatures get extremely hot in the summer here. Hundred-degree days are common, and as early as May the mercury often hits the 90s. Given these conditions, what more could you ask for than a huge recreation lake just minutes from Sacramento? Well, you might desire a little more evidence of functioning brain matter, but at a huge urban lake that's asking for a bit much.

Plan on seeing a number of drunken young sailor/cowboy types at Folsom, roaring around at high speeds, often with the steering wheel in one hand and a beer in the other. If you stick around long enough, you'll witness just about every imaginable stunt that is born out of the combination of hot sun, cold suds, and lots of people.

㉜ South Fork American River

Location: Near Placerville in Eldorado National Forest; map D3, grid g3.
Directions: From US 50 at Placerville, drive north on Highway 49. Access is available via Highway 193 to the east or from short roads that intersect Highway 49 to the west.

Access: There is no boat ramp. To reach the rafting put-in, take Highway 49 north from Placerville to Highway 193. Turn right and drive three miles down to the bridge at Chili Bar. Take out 20 miles downstream just above the Salmon Falls bridge or farther upstream at one of several other access points, including the Highway 49 bridge in Coloma, Henningsen-Lotus County Park, or Camp Lotus (off Highway 49 on Lotus Road). Note: Access is available at Marshall Gold Discovery State Park, but only put-ins are allowed, no take-outs.

Facilities, fees: Private campgrounds are available on Highway 49. Ten miles downstream of the Chili Bar put-in, there are campsites provided for noncommercial rafters. Boat rentals can be obtained at California Canoe & Kayak and Wilderness Sports in the Sacramento area. Supplies are available in the town of Placerville. A private concession charges a fee to put in at Chili Bar. Access fees are charged at Marshall Gold Discovery State Park, Henningsen-Lotus County Park, and Camp Lotus. People with private boats and rafts must obtain use tags (free) at one of these main river access points.

Water sports, restrictions: Swimming is available at all the parks listed above.

Contact: Bureau of Land Management, (916) 985-4474; Eldorado National Forest, Visitor Center, (530) 644-6048 or fax (530) 295-5624. For guided rafting trips, contact

Action Whitewater Adventures, (800) 453-1482; All-Outdoors Whitewater Rafting, (800) 247-2387; American River Recreation, (800) 333-7238 or (530) 622-6802; American Whitewater Expeditions, (818) 352-3205; ARTA, (800) 323-2782; Beyond Limits Adventures, (800) 234-7238; California Adventures, (510) 642-4000; ECHO River Trips, (800) 652-3246; Environmental Travel Companions, (415) 474-7662; Gold Rush River Runners, (800) 344-1013; Koolriver Adventure Tours, Inc, (800) 931-8999; Mariah Wilderness Expeditions, (800) 462-7424; Mother Lode River Trips, (530) 626-4187; OARS, Inc, (800) 346-6277; RAM River Adventures, (800) 466-7238; River Runners, (818) 222-4260; South Bay River Rafters, (310) 545-8572; Whitewater Voyages, (800) 488-7238; or Zephyr River Expeditions, (209) 532-6249.

About the South Fork American River: Behold, the most popular rafting river in America. For newcomers to the sport, the South Fork American is *the* choice, with easy access, enough white-water challenge to add some sizzle, and a huge array of trips offered by rafting outfitters. No experience needed; just hop on for the ride.

This is a Class III run, considered a perfect introduction to rafting, and there are plenty of takers. River traffic is very heavy starting on Memorial Day weekend, especially on weekends, and anybody desiring any semblance of solitude should go elsewhere.

The river can usually be run from May through October, but there are no guarantees, as flows are determined from upstream hydro releases. The scenery is pleasant, not sensational, but there's an open, rugged feel and lots of Gold Rush–oriented historical sites along the way.

White-water highlights include Meatgrinder (Class III), Troublemaker (Class III+), and Satan's Cesspool (Class III+), which can challenge even experienced paddlers and give most any beginner the opportunity to

see if their heart can pound a hole through their chest.

Guides always point out to the occupants in the raft that there is a seven-mile stretch running past several private homes and campgrounds that boaters are asked to treat as a quiet zone. That means rafters have to try to not act like lunatics for about two hours, no mean feat for some people.

Many rafting companies offer an array of specialty trips on this river. These include family trips, youth trips, theme trips, service trips (where participants clean up trash on the river in exchange for a large discount), and express trips (inexpensive, no-frills, half-day trips). Environmental Travel Companions, a company located in the Bay Area, specializes in rafting trips for the disabled.

㉝ Finnon Lake

Location: North of Placerville; map D3, grid g5.

Directions: From Sacramento drive 45 miles east on US 50 to Placerville. In Placerville, turn left at the second stop onto Highway 49 and drive one mile. Turn right on Highway 193 and drive eight miles. Turn right on Rock Creek Road and drive eight miles to the lake.

Access: There is no boat ramp. Cartop boats may be hand launched.

Facilities, fees: A campground is provided. A store, snack bar, and rowboat rentals are available at Finnon Lake Resort. Supplies can be obtained in Placerville. A day-use fee is charged.

Water sports, restrictions: Gas-powered motors are not permitted. Windsurfing is allowed. Swimming access is available all along the shoreline.

Contact: Finnon Lake Resort, (530) 622-9314.

About Finnon Lake: Most folks just keep on driving when they see the Rock

Creek Road turnoff that leads to little Finnon Lake. Why? Well, this is a county recreation lake equipped for small boats that are hand launched and paddle powered, with a small campground and a few hiking trails.

In other words, this is not exactly the boating capital of the world. It's a small lake, set at 2,400 feet elevation in the Placerville foothills, and is best suited for a variety of low-impact use. It attracts a moderate number of visitors.

Recreational use includes riding in small boats powered with oars, paddles, or electric motors; swimming; windsurfing; sunbathing; picnicking; and camping. While there is no designated swimming area, the shoreline, a mix of grass and dirt, slopes gently into the water. That's fine for walking into the lake, and decent enough for throwing down a blanket or towel to have a picnic or sunbathe. The campground is clean and has some facilities, and there are hiking and horseback riding trails in the area.

Windsurfing is permitted, but conditions are unpredictable. Sometimes there's a lot of wind, and sometimes there's none, and you never know what's going to happen. Just another happy day at good ol' Finnon Lake.

③ Union Valley Reservoir

Location: West of Lake Tahoe in Eldorado National Forest; map D3, grid g8.

Directions: From Sacramento drive 45 miles east on US 50 to Placerville. Continue about 20 miles east on US 50 to Riverton and the bridge across the American River. Turn north on Ice House Road and drive about 20 miles (past the turnoff to Ice House Lake).

Access: Three boat ramps are available:

Fashoda: From Riverton, turn north on Ice House Road and drive approximately 17 miles to the turnoff for Fashoda and Sunset Campgrounds. Turn left and continue 1.5 miles to the unpaved boat ramp.

West Point: From Riverton, turn north on Ice House Road and drive approximately four miles to Peavine Ridge Road. Turn left and drive about three miles west to Bryants Spring Road. Turn right and continue five miles north to the paved ramp, located adjacent to the dam.

Yellow Jacket: From Riverton, turn north on Ice House Road and drive approximately 23 miles (winding around the east and north sides of the lake) to the sign for Yellow Jacket Campground. Turn left and continue to the paved ramp.

Facilities, fees: Campgrounds are provided. Supplies can be obtained in Placerville. Access to the lake is free.

Water sports, restrictions: Waterskiing, personal watercraft, and windsurfing are permitted. A swimming beach is available at Fashoda Campground, and it is possible to swim at various other spots along the shoreline.

Contact: Eldorado National Forest, Visitor Center, (530) 644-6048 or fax (530) 295-5624; Eldorado National Forest, Pacific Ranger District, (530) 644-2349 or fax (530) 647-5405.

About Union Valley Reservoir: The Crystal Basin Recreation Area is one of the most popular backcountry regions for campers from the Sacramento area. Union Valley Reservoir, a big lake covering nearly 3,000 acres, is one of the centerpieces.

The area gets its name from the prominent granite Sierra ridge, which looks like crystal when it is covered with frozen snow. The lake is set at 4,900 feet elevation, along with nearby Ice House Reservoir to the south and Loon Lake farther to the north.

Facilities at the lake are limited to the Forest Service campgrounds and three boat ramps. There is no marina, no store. After all, Union Valley sits right on the edge of wilderness. So boater/campers must be sure to purchase and pack all supplies before heading to the lake.

All boating and water sports are allowed, and for many this is the perfect destination for camping, boating, and fishing, as well as sailing in small boats and windsurfing. There are additional opportunities for swimming and hiking nearby.

The water is clear and cold, but not too cold for swimming by midsummer. Although there are no true beach-type areas, much of the shoreline is grassy. There is also a swimming area at Fashoda Campground, where the shore is primarily hard-packed soil.

Summer mornings here feature good trout fishing. By the afternoon, the wind usually comes up, the anglers leave the lake, and out come a few windsurfers with sailboards in hand and a sprinkling of little sailboats. As they sail across the lake, they often look around as if relishing the sensation of being in the midst of a great paradise.

㉟ Ice House Reservoir

Location: West of Lake Tahoe in Eldorado National Forest; map D3, grid g9.

Directions: From Sacramento drive 45 miles east on US 50 to Placerville. Continue about 20 miles east on US 50 to Riverton and the bridge across the American River. Turn north on Ice House Road and drive 10 miles; then turn right on the Ice House Lake access road and head two miles east.

Access: A paved boat ramp is located next to Ice House Campground.

Facilities, fees: Three campgrounds and a picnic area are provided. Supplies can be obtained in Placerville and at the Ice House Resort, located a few miles south of the reservoir on Ice House Road. Access to the lake is free.

Water sports, restrictions: Waterskiing, personal watercraft, and windsurfing are permitted. A swimming beach is available at Ice House Campground. Swimming is also available at the other two campgrounds and at the picnic area west of the dam.

Contact: Eldorado National Forest, Visitor Center, (530) 644-6048 or fax (530) 295-5624; Eldorado National Forest, Pacific Ranger District, (530) 644-2349 or fax (530) 647-5405; Ice House Resort, (530) 293-3321.

About Ice House Reservoir: Of the three major lakes in the beautiful Crystal Lakes Basin, Ice House is the first one you'll drive past. The others are Union Valley Reservoir and farther north, Loon Lake.

Ice House, which sits at an elevation of 5,500 feet, was created by a dam on South Fork Silver Creek. When full, it covers about 675 acres. There are many recreational opportunities here, but the lake is best known for having quality trout fishing and a number of primitive campsites.

All boating is allowed. The best prospects are for sailing and windsurfing on midsummer afternoons. Another good prospect is swimming. The water is quite cold, but there are nice swimming areas at the campgrounds and a gently sloping shoreline all around the lake.

There is one well-developed campground at the lake, Ice House, which has piped water, wheelchair-accessible sites, a swimming beach, and an adjacent boat ramp. That is the favorite of boater/campers. The other camps are more primitive and have no water, but they're free and less crowded.

Visitor use at the lake is moderate during the week, but quite heavy on summer weekends.

One note: The rumor you may have heard about the major flea invasion here does have a shred of truth to it. However, the Forest Service believes the problem has largely been eradicated and the risk is minimal after repeated sprayings. The most dangerous part of the trip by far is the drive here.

㊱ Jenkinson Lake

Location: East of Placerville in Sly Park Recreation Area; map D3, grid h6.

Directions: From Sacramento drive 45 miles east on US 50 to Placerville. Continue 11 miles east on US 50 to the town of Pollock Pines. Take the Sly Park Road exit and travel five miles south on Sly Park Road.

Access: Two paved boat ramps are available:

Stonebraker: Continue straight through on the entrance road, past Pine Cone and Arrow Head Campgrounds, to the Stonebraker Campground and launch ramp.

West Shore: Once inside the lake entrance, go 50 feet past the kiosk and turn right. Continue about one-quarter mile to the ramp.

Facilities, fees: A campground and picnic areas are provided. A small marina with docks is available. Limited supplies are sold at the Sly Park Store. Full supplies can be obtained in Placerville. A day-use fee is charged. There is an additional fee for boat launching.

Water sports, restrictions: Waterskiing and personal watercraft are allowed, but there is a 5 mph speed limit north of Sierra Point on the north side of the lake. Windsurfing is permitted. A roped-off swimming beach is available at the Pine Cone Day-Use Area.

Contact: Sly Park Recreation Area, (530) 644-2545 or fax (530) 644-1003.

About Jenkinson Lake: The only thing wrong with Jenkinson Lake is that it's hardly a secret. In fact, it may just be the ideal vacation destination.

The lake is set at 3,500 feet elevation, covering 640 acres with eight miles of shoreline. All water sports are permitted, and rules that separate high-speed users from low-speed users help to resolve potential conflicts and set the stage for first-class water recreation.

The 5 mph zone covers 80 acres of the lake north of Sierra Point; of course, water-skiers and personal watercraft should stay clear of there. The Stonebraker launch ramp lies within this zone and is used primarily by anglers. Visitors with ski boats and other fast craft should launch instead at the other ramp.

Swimming is available all along the shoreline, but swimmers are cautioned to stay within 50 feet of the shore to avoid any chance of getting in the way of fast boats towing water-skiers. Windsurfing is also good here, usually best from 11 AM to 3 PM, when a steady wind courses over the lake.

A bonus at Sly Park is the variety of campgrounds, with campsites available for individuals, youths, families, and equestrians.

㊲ Bear River Reservoir

Location: Southwest of Lake Tahoe in Eldorado National Forest; map D3, grid j9.

Directions: From Stockton on Highway 99, turn east on Highway 88 and continue for 75 miles, through the foothill country and into the mountains. Turn right on Bear River Road and drive two miles; then turn left and drive a half mile to Bear River Resort.

Access: A paved ramp is available at Bear River Resort.

Facilities, fees: Campgrounds are provided. Groceries are available nearby. Bear River Resort has a full-service marina and rents out fishing boats, paddleboats, and canoes. Access to the lake is free. There is a fee for boat launching.

Water sports, restrictions: Waterskiing, personal watercraft, and windsurfing are permitted. A developed swimming beach is provided at Bear River Resort; swimming is also good near the campgrounds.

Contact: Eldorado National Forest, Visitor Center, (530) 644-6048 or fax (530) 295-5624; Eldorado National Forest, Amador Ranger District (209) 295-4251 or fax (209) 295-5994; Bear River Resort, (209) 295-4868.

About Bear River Reservoir: As you venture into the mountains on Highway 88, this is the first of three quality mountain lakes you will come to. The others are Silver Lake and Caples Lake.

One advantage at Bear River Reservoir is its lower elevation—5,800 feet. That means the ice melts off far earlier in the year than at its two brothers farther up the line.

The lake is decent sized, 725 acres. Cold, you say? Well, I might add, it's deep, too.

Even though the location is some distance from Jacksonville on curvy Highway 88, the roads are paved all the way to the boat ramp, and on weekends many people are willing hitch up their boats and make the trip. So it gets a fair number of boaters, most out for fishing, some for waterskiing. In addition, windsurfing and sailing are excellent, with brisk afternoon winds daily.

On summer weekends, campground reservations are essential. Bear River Resort at the lake also has lodging, and adds trophy-size trout to supplement the little rainbow trout stocked by the Department of Fish and Game. A clean, developed campground and swimming beach are also available at the resort.

㊳ Salt Springs Reservoir

⚓ 🛶 ⛺ 🐟 🏊 🚤   9️⃣

Location: East of Jackson in Eldorado National Forest; map D3, grid j9.

Directions: From Sacramento drive 45 miles east on US 50 to Placerville. Turn south on Highway 49 and drive 32 miles to Jackson. At Jackson, drive 36 miles east on Highway 88. Turn right and drive south on Ellis Road for five miles south at Inspiration Lodge and drive five miles on Ellis Road. When the road forks, bear south and cross the bridge that goes across Bear River. Continue three miles to the dam.

Access: A primitive boat launch is located at the north end of the base of the dam.

Facilities, fees: A picnic area is provided. Three free, primitive campgrounds are available nearby on the Mokelumne River. No piped water is available. Supplies can be obtained in Ham's Station. Access is free.

Water sports, restrictions: Motors are not allowed on the reservoir. Windsurfing is allowed, but high winds can be hazardous. Swimming is permitted.

Contact: Eldorado National Forest, Visitor Center, (530) 644-6048 or fax (530) 295-5624; Eldorado National Forest, Amador Ranger District, (209) 295-4251 or fax (209) 295-5994. For a detailed map of the area, send $4 to Maps, Office of Information, US Forest Service, 1323 Club Drive, Vallejo, CA 94592.

About Salt Springs Reservoir: Everyone should visit this place at least once in his or her life. You'll find everything here.

Salt Springs Reservoir is a long, narrow lake set in the Mokelumne River Gorge, a dramatic canyon with spectacular surroundings for boaters. It's a good spot for hikers, too. A trail that is routed into the Mokelumne Wilderness starts just north of the dam. Want more? Got more. A series of small, primitive campgrounds—all very pretty spots—is situated west of the lake, below the dam along the Mokelumne River.

The lake is set at an elevation of 4,000 feet and covers 950 acres. Even though the location is fairly obscure, the scenic beauty attracts vacationers who return year after year.

Swimming access is difficult because the shoreline is steep and rocky. If you can find a good spot to wade in, though, the water is great—fresh, clean, and often just the right temperature.

The surrounding area is particularly scenic, and because no motors are allowed (hence no waterskiing), the lake stays pretty quiet.

The only bugaboo is the high winds that kick up in the late morning and afternoon and can rudely disrupt the idyllic setting. The safest times to boat are before 10 AM and after 4 PM. If you're planning on boating here, keep this in mind.

Map of Northern California—Page 28

Chapter D4
Tahoe Area

Overall Rating

| 1 | 2 | 3 | 4 | 5 | 6 | 7 | 8 | 9 | 10 |

Poor .... Fair .... Great

D4–Tahoe Area Map

One inch equals approximately 10.7 miles.
See page 12 for California state map.

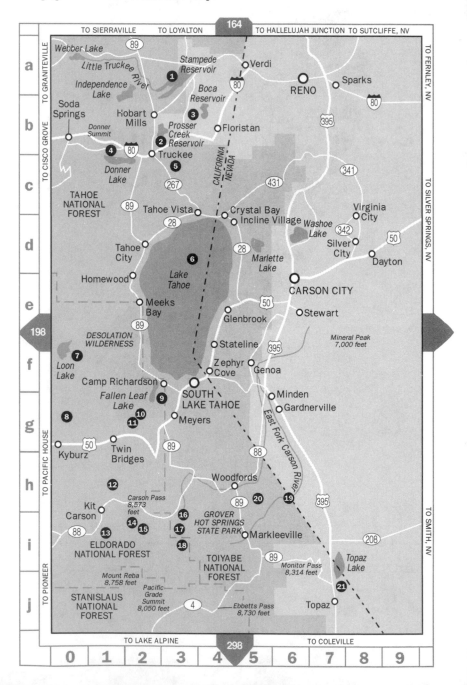

Chapter D4 features:

1 Stampede Reservoir

Location: North of Truckee in Tahoe National Forest; map D4, grid a3.

Directions: From Sacramento drive approximately 100 miles east on Interstate 80 to Truckee. Continue seven miles east on Interstate 80 and take the Boca-Hirschdale exit. Continue north (past Boca Reservoir) for eight miles on Stampede Meadows Road to the reservoir.

Access: From Stampede Road turn west on Forest Service Road 19N69 and travel toward the dam. Pass the dam and continue past Logger Campground to the paved, extended launch ramp on the lake's south side.

Facilities, fees: A developed campground is provided. A more primitive campground is located to the north of the reservoir, at Davies Creek. Supplies can be obtained in Truckee. Access to the lake is free.

Water sports, restrictions: Waterskiing, personal watercraft, and windsurfing are permitted. Swimming access is available near the campground.

Contact: Tahoe National Forest, Truckee Ranger District, (530) 587-3558 or fax (530) 587-6914; California Land Management, (530) 544-5994.

About Stampede Reservoir: Offering the classic Sierra Nevada experience, Stampede Reservoir is an easy-to-reach drive-to lake that is hard to beat.

The setting is gorgeous, complete with Sierra granite, sage, and pine trees. For dramatic effect there are the occasional classic summer thunderstorms in the late afternoon and stellar starry nights best viewed from a sleeping bag.

Covering 3,400 acres with 25 miles of shoreline, the lake is huge, the second largest in the area after Lake Tahoe. Stampede is set at an elevation of 6,000 feet in the Sierra granite country and usually becomes accessible by late May.

There's just one problem. Note the extended launch ramp. Why would a ramp need to be extended? Right, because the water level gets quite low in the late summer and fall, when water is poured out the dam via the Little Truckee River and Boca Reservoir to keep the fish going in the Truckee River along Interstate 80.

Use is high on summer weekends, and the developed campground is usually filled on Friday and Saturday nights. Most of the visitors are campers who are fishing for trout; a number of them bring along small trailered boats. On warm weekends you'll also typically see several fast boats towing water-skiers. During weekdays the scenario is pretty quiet, with relatively few folks out, trolling slowly and hoping to land a big brown trout.

Afternoons bring winds out of the west, shooting right up the Interstate 80 canyon corridor. Wind conditions regularly make sailing and windsurfing quite good. The water, fresh from snowmelt pouring into the lake, is very cold, of course, until midsummer. That prevents most people from swimming here until late July; although there is no designated beach area, you can swim at various spots along the shoreline.

❷ Prosser Creek Reservoir

Location: North of Truckee in Tahoe National Forest; map D4, grid b2.

Directions: From Sacramento drive approximately 100 miles east on Interstate 80 to Truckee. From Truckee drive about four miles north on Highway 89 to the Prosser Reservoir turnoff on the right. Turn east and travel about two miles on Prosser Dam Road to the dam. Or continue north on Highway 89 for three miles, then turn east at the signed turnoff, and travel to the reservoir's north shore.

Access: From Highway 89 turn east at the sign for Lakeside and Prosser Campgrounds. A paved ramp is available near the Prosser group camp.

Facilities, fees: Campgrounds and a picnic area are provided. Supplies can be obtained in Truckee. Access to the lake is free.

Water sports, restrictions: A 5 mph speed limit is strictly enforced. Windsurfing is permitted. Swimming access is available all along the shoreline.

Contact: Tahoe National Forest, Truckee Ranger District, (530) 587-3558 or fax (530) 587-6914; Mountain Hardware, (530) 587-4844.

About Prosser Creek Reservoir: This pretty and often serene spot is set at an elevation of 5,800 feet in Tahoe National Forest. One of the reasons it is so serene is the 5 mph speed limit that ensures all the fast boats are making waves at other lakes. Access is extremely easy, situated just a few miles off Interstate 80, so the place gets a lot of visitor traffic throughout the summer, especially on weekends.

Prosser Creek Reservoir covers 740 acres with 11 miles of shoreline. Highlights include good scenery and opportunities for fishing, camping, windsurfing, and swimming.

To snag the best campsites, check out Prosser Campground, which is perched on a wooded lake. As you drive in on the access road from west to east, it's the last camp you will come to.

There are no sandy beaches, but much of the shore is gently sloping, making it easily accessible to windsurfers and swimmers. When the lake is full, the prime jump-off spot for windsurfing is at Prosser Campground.

❸ Boca Reservoir

Location: Northeast of Truckee in Tahoe National Forest; map D4, grid b3.

Directions: From Sacramento drive approximately 100 miles east on Interstate 80 to Truckee. Continue for seven miles east on Interstate 80 and take the Boca-Hirschdale exit. Drive 1.5 miles north on Stampede Meadows Road to Boca Reservoir.

Access: From Stampede Meadows Road turn left on Boca Road and drive 14 miles west to the sign for the boat ramp. Turn right and continue three miles to the paved ramp.

Facilities, fees: Two free primitive campgrounds are provided. Supplies can be obtained in Truckee. Access to the lake is free.

Water sports, restrictions: Waterskiing, personal watercraft, and windsurfing are permitted. Swimming access is available all along the shoreline.

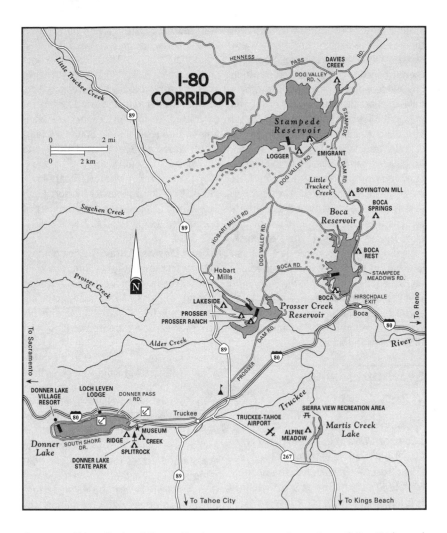

I-80 CORRIDOR

Contact: Tahoe National Forest, Truckee Ranger District, (530) 587-3558 or fax (530) 587-6914; Mountain Hardware, (530) 587-4844.

About Boca Reservoir: Accessing this lake is very simple, just a quick hop off Interstate 80. However, a lot of folks miss it because the dam faces the highway, unlike nearby Donner Lake, which is set right along the highway and presents a scenic view to thousands of travelers every day. Still, enough people have discovered this gem, and use is very high all summer. The campgrounds are always full on Friday and Saturday nights, and on hot weekend afternoons there can be a lot of boats zipping around in the water.

Occasionally there are conflicts between slow-trolling trout fishermen and warp-speed ski boats and personal watercraft. If the fast boats would just stay well clear of the shoreline, where most people are fishing, there would be no problem.

Swimming conditions are much like those at Prosser Creek Reservoir (see the previous listing), with access available around most of the shoreline, although there are some steep sections.

Like so many lakes in this region, Boca is extremely pretty. It is set at an elevation of 5,700 feet and covers 980 acres with 14 miles of shoreline. Once on the water, you may find it hard to believe that Interstate 80 is only two miles away. No foolin'.

In common with other lakes in the area, Boca has no sandy beaches for swimming and sunbathing and no picnic spots. After all, this is the Sierra! Shoreline access, however, is quite good; parts of the lakeshore are grassy and meadowy, with lots of pine trees. These are the prime spots, of course.

In drought years Boca can be drained so low that the boat ramp is rendered totally unusable. It's a long drive to the boat ramp, so if you are unsure about conditions, call ahead before starting out. In high snow years the lake is usually full by June, a beautiful and inviting sight.

❹ Donner Lake

Location: West of Truckee in Donner Memorial State Park; map D4, grid c1.

Directions: From Auburn drive east on Interstate 80 just past Donner Lake to Donner Pass Road. Take that exit and drive south for one mile to the park entrance and the southeast end of the lake.

Access: A paved public ramp is located on the lake's west end, about one-half mile from Donner Lake Resort on Old Highway 40.

Facilities, fees: Campgrounds are available at Donner Memorial State Park. Picnic areas are provided on the east, west, and south sides of the lake. A motel is also available. Powerboats, fishing boats, personal watercraft, and paddleboats can be rented at Donner Lake Resort, and paddleboat, canoe, and kayak rentals are available at the state park. Supplies can be obtained in Truckee. A day-use fee is charged at Donner Memorial State Park. There is a fee for boat launching.

Water sports, restrictions: Waterskiing, personal watercraft, and windsurfing are permitted. Swimming beaches are available at Donner Memorial State Park (east side), West End Beach (west side), and Shoreline Park (south side).

Contact: Donner Memorial State Park, (530) 582-7894; Donner Lake Resort, (530) 587-6081; Truckee-Donner Chamber of Commerce, (530) 587-2757 or fax (530) 587-2439.

About Donner Lake: The first glimpse of Donner Lake is always a stirring one, even though the lake has become a common stop for millions of vacationers cruising past on Interstate 80. Its remarkable beauty evokes a heartfelt response. Was it good for you, too?

Set near the Sierra crest at elevation 5,900 feet, this big, oblong lake—three miles long by three-quarters of a mile wide, with 7.5 miles of shoreline—is filled with gem blue water. It is easy to reach and provides a good option for family campers. The area is well developed, with cabins and maintained access roads. A public boat ramp is available at the lake's west end near Donner Village Resort. Those very factors, however, are often cited as the reasons why some people never stay at Donner. They want more seclusion.

If you go by boat, take fair warning that afternoon winds can run you off the lake during the spring and that afternoon thunderstorms can do the same late in the summer. Also note that the lake's spectacular beauty and prominence as a national landmark attract tons of people throughout the summer. All boating and water sports are available, in addition to good hiking, biking, and horseback riding.

West winds are common during the afternoon, providing outstanding conditions for sailing and windsurfing. The best put-in spots for windsurfing are at Shoreline Park and Donner State Park. Sailing is so popular that a sailing club has been established here.

Though the water is cold, it heats up by midday. Many people like to swim here. The designated swimming beaches are truly spectacular—large, developed stretches of sand.

Because the lake is such a favorite, reservations are an absolute must if you want to camp at the state park, the only campground at the lake. Also note that there is only one boat ramp, and that boats rented at the state park can be hand launched only.

❺ Martis Creek Reservoir

Location: Near Truckee; map D4, grid c3.
Directions: From Sacramento drive approximately 100 miles east on Interstate 80 to Truckee. From there drive five miles southeast on Highway 267 to the signed entrance to the lake. Turn left and travel two miles.
Access: No boat ramp is available. Cartop boats may be hand launched.
Facilities, fees: A developed campground is provided near the lake. A picnic and recreation area is also available. Supplies can be obtained in Truckee. Access to the lake is free.
Water sports, restrictions: Motors are not permitted on the lake. Fishing is limited to catch-and-release with single barbless hooks and artificials; no bait is permitted. Swimming and windsurfing are allowed at Sierra View Recreation Area.
Contact: US Army Corps of Engineers, Martis Creek Reservoir, (530) 639-2342; California Trout, Inc, (415) 392-8887.
About Martis Creek Reservoir: Little Martis, just 70 acres, is well known among a cult of fly fishers for its status as one of

the few wild trout lakes in the country. Because the lake is not stocked with trout, you are restricted to catch-and-release fishing using artificials.

The lake is set at the edge of a large valley near the Tahoe-Truckee Airport, and the wind can really howl in the afternoon. It was originally built to provide flood control and water storage for Truckee, and then was set aside as one of the first wild trout lakes in the state. Motors are prohibited, which keeps things quiet, and most of the visitors are fly fishers in float tubes, casting and retrieving, over and over again, prisoners of hope.

The place does lure a few non-anglers, too. It is an excellent destination for windsurfing, or on a calm morning, plunking a canoe in and paddling around a bit. There is a developed recreation area on the west side of the lake where you'll find a beach and picnic spot.

Despite all of the lake's strong points, most folks in the area flock to nearby Lake Tahoe, and Martis gets low to medium use.

❻ Lake Tahoe

Location: East of Sacramento in Lake Tahoe Basin; map D4, grid d3.
Directions: From Sacramento drive east on Interstate 50 to get to the south shore. An alternate route is to take Interstate 80 to Truckee, then head south on Highway 267 to Tahoe City (west shore) or Highway 89 to Kings Beach (north shore).
Access: Boat ramps are located at the following locations:

SOUTH LAKE TAHOE
Camp Richardson Marina: Located on Highway 89, 2.5 miles north of South Lake Tahoe. A paved ramp and a full-service marina are provided. Ski boats and fishing boats are available for rent. For boat rent-

als phone (530) 541-1801. For marina information phone (530) 542-6570.

Cave Rock Ramp: Located on Highway 50, three miles north of Zephyr Cove. A paved ramp is available. For information phone (702) 831-0494.

Lakeside Marina: At the junction of Lakeshore Boulevard and Park Avenue, off Highway 50 in South Lake Tahoe. A paved ramp and a full-service marina are provided. Ski boats, sport boats, pontoon boats, and inflatables can be rented. For information phone (530) 541-6626.

Sand Harbor Ramp: On Highway 28 four miles south of Incline Village. A paved ramp and limited marina facilities are available. For information phone (702) 831-0494.

South Lake Tahoe Recreation Area: On Lakeview Avenue off Highway 50 in South Lake Tahoe. A paved ramp is available (but it's closed to the public on Sundays). For information phone (530) 542-6055.

Tahoe Keys Marina: Located on Tahoe Keys Boulevard, off Highway 50. A paved ramp and full-service marina are available. You can rent ski boats. For boat rentals phone (530) 544-8888. For marina information call (530) 541-2155.

Timber Cove Marina: At 3411 Lake Tahoe Boulevard in South Lake Tahoe. An unimproved boat ramp and limited marina services are provided. Ski boats and personal watercraft are available for rent. For information call (530) 544-2942.

Zephyr Cove Marina: On Highway 50 in Zephyr Cove. A paved ramp and full-service marina are available. Ski boats, fishing boats, personal watercraft, canoes, and paddleboats are available for rent. For information phone (702) 588-3833.

NORTH LAKE TAHOE

High & Dry Marina: Located on Highway 89 in Homewood. A hoist and a full-service marina are provided. Ski boats, tours, and lessons are available. For waterskiing information phone (530) 525-1214. For marina information phone (530) 525-5966.

Kings Beach Recreation Area: Located off Highway 28 in Kings Beach. There is a paved ramp suitable for small boats. Ski boats, sailboats, and personal watercraft can be rented. For boat rentals phone (530) 546-4889. For park information phone (530) 546-7248.

Lake Forest Public Ramp: Located on North Lake Forest Road, off Highway 28 in Lake Forest. A paved ramp is available. For information phone (530) 583-5544.

Meeks Bay Resort and Marina: Located on Highway 89, 10 miles south of Tahoe City. A paved ramp and full-service marina are provided. Canoes, kayaks, and paddleboats, are available for rent. A high-speed shuttle to Emerald Bay is available. For information phone (530) 525-5588 or (530) 525-6946 or fax (530) 525-4028.

North Tahoe Marina: Located on Highway 28 in Tahoe Vista. There is a paved ramp for powerboats only and a full-service marina. Powerboats can be rented. For information phone (530) 546-8248.

Obexers Boat & Motor Sales: At 5355 West Lake Boulevard in Homewood. A paved ramp, travel lift, and limited marina services are available. You can rent ski boats, too. For information phone (530) 525-7962.

Sierra Boat Company: At 5146 North Lake Boulevard in Carnelian Bay. A hoist and a full-service marina are provided. For information phone (530) 546-2551.

Facilities, fees: Campgrounds, picnic areas, lodgings, groceries, gas, restaurants, and full facilities are available at several locations around the lake. Boats can be rented at several of the marinas listed above and at the following locations: Action Water Sports, (530) 541-4386; Lighthouse Water Sports Center, (530) 583-6000; Tahoe Water Adventures, (530) 583-3225; Ski Run Marina, (530) 544-0200; and Lakeview Sports, (530) 544-0183. Parasailing can be arranged through Ski Run Boat Company, (530) 544-0200. Boat cruises are available through

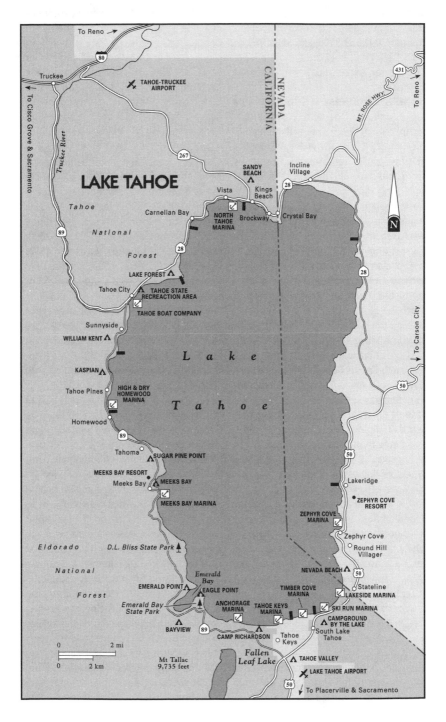

To Reno

80

Truckee

To Cisco Grove & Sacramento

89

Truckee River

✈ TAHOE-TRUCKEE AIRPORT

NEVADA
CALIFORNIA

431

To Reno

MT ROSE HWY.

267

LAKE TAHOE

SANDY BEACH ⚲

Incline Village

Tahoe

Vista

Kings Beach

Carnelian Bay

NORTH TAHOE MARINA

28

Brockway

Crystal Bay

National

28

N

Forest

28

LAKE FOREST ⚲

Tahoe City ⚲

TAHOE STATE RECREACTION AREA ⚲

To Carson City

TAHOE BOAT COMPANY ⚲

Sunnyside

L a k e

WILLIAM KENT ⚲

50

KASPIAN ⚲

T a h o e

Tahoe Pines

HIGH & DRY HOMEWOOD MARINA ⚲

Homewood

50

89

Tahoma

SUGAR PINE POINT ⚲

MEEKS BAY RESORT

Lakeridge

Meeks Bay ● ⚲ MEEKS BAY

ZEPHYR COVE RESORT

MEEKS BAY MARINA ⚲

ZEPHYR COVE MARINA ⚲

Eldorado

D.L. BLISS STATE PARK ⚲

Zephyr Cove

Round Hill Villager

National

NEVADA BEACH ⚲

Emerald Bay

50

Forest

EMERALD POINT ⚲

Stateline

EAGLE POINT

TIMBER COVE MARINA ⚲

LAKESIDE MARINA ⚲

Emerald Bay State Park

ANCHORAGE MARINA ⚲

TAHOE KEYS MARINA ⚲

SKI RUN MARINA ⚲

BAYVIEW ⚲

89

CAMP RICHARDSON

Tahoe Keys

CAMPGROUND BY THE LAKE ⚲

South Lake Tahoe

0   2 mi

0   2 km

Mt Tallac 9,735 feet

Fallen Leaf Lake

TAHOE VALLEY ⚲

✈ LAKE TAHOE AIRPORT

50

To Placerville & Sacramento

Tahoe Queen, (530) 541-3364; North Tahoe Cruises, (530) 583-0141; Woodwind Sailing Cruises, (702) 588-3000; and M.S. Dixie II, (702) 588-3508. Fees are almost always charged for parking, day use, and boat launching.

Water sports, restrictions: All four-stroke engines are permitted. Also permitted are two-stroke engines with direct fuel injection (DFI) and any watercraft engine that meets the California Air Resources Board 2001 or the US Environmental Protection Agency (EPA) 2001 emissions standards. Prohibited are 1) non-direct fuel injection engines (electronic or Rotax fuel injection) purchased after January 27, 1999, (auxiliary sailboat engines excepted) and 2) carbureted two-stroke engines with more than 10 horsepower. Windsurfing and swimming are permitted. There are two undeveloped beaches, Chimney Beach and Secret Cove, both on the east shore (in Nevada), south of Incline Village. Developed beaches are available at the following locations:

South Shore: Baldwin Beach, on Highway 89 four miles north of the junction with Highway 50; Emerald Bay Beach at the base of Emerald Bay; Camp Richardson Beach, on Highway 89 2.5 miles north of the junction with Highway 50; Connolly Beach on Highway 50 at Timber Cove Lodge; Kiva Beach, on Highway 89 2.5 miles north of the junction with Highway 50; Nevada Beach, on Elk Point Road off Highway 50 near Roundhill; Pope Beach, on Highway 89 two miles north of the junction with Highway 50; Regan Beach west of Highway 50 on Lakeview and Sacramento in South Lake Tahoe; Zephyr Cove Beach on Highway 50 at Zephyr Cove.

North Shore: Agatam Beach on Highway 28 in Tahoe Vista; D.L. Bliss State Park on Highway 89 south of Meeks Bay; Kaspian Recreation Area on Highway 89 south of Sunnyside; Kings Beach Recreation Area in Kings Beach; Lake Forest Beach one mile east of Tahoe City; Meeks Bay Campground

10 miles south of Tahoe City; Moondunes Beach in Tahoe Vista; North Tahoe Beach Center in Kings Beach; Patton Beach on Highway 28 in Carnelian Bay; Sand Harbor State Park (Nevada) south of Incline Village on Highway 28; Secline Beach on Secline Street in Kings Beach; Tahoe City Commons Beach in Tahoe City; Tahoe State Recreation Area in Tahoe City; William Kent Campground on Highway 89 in Sunnyside.

Contact: For boating information phone any of the marinas listed above or the California Department of Boating and Waterways, (916) 263-1331 or fax (916) 327-7250; For general information call Lake Tahoe Basin Management Unit, (530) 573-2600; North Lake Chamber of Commerce, (800) 824-6348 or (530) 581-6900; or South Lake Chamber of Commerce, (530) 541-5255 or fax (530) 541-7121.

About Lake Tahoe: So few places evoke an emotional response at first glance. Lake Tahoe, along with Crater Lake in Oregon and Yosemite Valley, is one of the rare natural wonders that makes you feel something special just by looking at it.

Of course it is huge, but there is also an unmatched purity. Huge? Try 22 miles long, 12 miles wide, 72 miles of shoreline, and 1,645 feet at its deepest point. It is filled with 39 trillion gallons of water, enough to cover California to a depth of 13.8 feet and (as long as we're speaking hypothetically) enough so that it would require 300 years of severe drought for it to drain significantly.

Pure? Only 99.9 percent pure, similar to the purity of distilled water. It is so clear that on a calm day in late summer, you can see a dinner plate 75 feet below the surface.

To capture this essence of purity after you've had your fill of the nearby casinos, you can sit on the ridge above Emerald Bay or take the chairlift to the top of Heavenly Valley and just admire the lake. It conjures one of the greatest feelings ever.

Yet you can take it a giant step further by hopping in a boat. One of the premier outdoor experiences in the world is boating in Emerald Bay, topped off by an overnight stay at one of the boat-in campsites there. The beauty is incomparable. Regardless of where you go by boat, you are out in the middle of clear, cobalt blue waters, surrounded by a mountain rim that's often topped with bright white snow. It is always a remarkable sight, often breathtaking.

This is a place for everyone—and at times it seems that everyone is showing up at once. All boating and water sports are permitted, but it is the roads around the lake that get crowded, not the water. There is always plenty of room on the lake for everybody. Conflicts among users are extremely rare, and hey, just cruise around for five minutes and you'll notice a remarkable phenomenon: suddenly, all the stressed-out people become relaxed and nice.

Other recreational opportunities include bicycling, bungee jumping, airplane and hot-air balloon rides, parasailing, gambling, horseback riding, kayak tours, golfing, hiking, tram rides, musical entertainment, railroad tours, sportfishing charters, and four-wheel-drive buggy rides on the Rubicon Trail.

To make your visit the best one possible, it is imperative that you make extensive plans for lodging and recreation; reservations are mandatory on weekends. That's true whether you'll be staying in a cabin, campground, or casino. The Lake Tahoe Basin gets approximately three million visitors per year. The highest use occurs on winter weekends during the ski season, followed by the summer, from the Fourth of July through early October. There are two periods of relatively light use: after the ski season has ended, in April and early May, and then again in the fall after summer is over, in October and early November.

Despite the teeming masses, Lake Tahoe is always a stellar vacation spot. Traffic and parking difficulties are the main problems. Many vacationers rent condos or cabins and spend their days playing or lounging at the expansive beaches. Only the brave try swimming. Because Tahoe is fed by snowmelt from 63 streams, the water is often cold. The warmest it gets is 68 degrees on the surface, and that only happens after days of hot summer temperatures.

Tahoe was created when the center of three earthquake faults collapsed, forming this giant mountain lacuna, which was then filled with snowmelt. Glaciers carved out Emerald Bay.

The water is so blue because it lacks nutrients. More specifically, there is no algae; as algal growth increases in a lake, the water becomes greener. Some people fear that Lake Tahoe may one day turn green because it has been introduced to nitrogen from car exhaust and phosphorus from storm runoff in the form of silt from topwater soil damage caused by logging. When nitrogen and phosphorus meet, they increase algae growth, reduce water clarity, and can, in time, cause a lake to change from blue to green. A consortium of government agencies is working to reverse this trend, funded by grants, taxes, and the newly implemented Tahoe License Plate Fund.

There is no place on Earth like Lake Tahoe. The South Lake Tahoe's Visitor Authority provided the following facts about the lake:

- It is North America's largest alpine lake.
- The elevation is 6,226 feet, making it the highest lake of its size in the United States.
- With a depth of 1,645 feet (near Crystal Bay), it is the third deepest lake in North America and the 10th deepest in the world (Lake Baikal in Russia is the deepest, at over 4,600 feet). The average depth is 989 feet.
- About 95 percent of the lake's fish live in only 5 percent of the water available.
- If drained, the lake would take 700 years to refill.
- Sixty-three streams flow into Lake Tahoe,

but only one, the Truckee River, flows out, running past Reno and into Pyramid Lake.
- The sun shines at Lake Tahoe an average of 274 days per year, but snowfall has been recorded every month and averages 420 inches per year.
- The water is so deep, cold (39 degrees below 700 feet), and devoid of light and oxygen on the bottom, that, according to legend, 1930s mobsters wearing "cement shoes" have been perfectly preserved on the lake bottom, complete with vintage clothing.

❼ Loon Lake

Location: South of Lake Tahoe in Eldorado National Forest; map D4, grid f0.

Directions: From Sacramento drive east on US 50 to the town of Riverton and the bridge across the American River. Turn north on Ice House Road and drive 32 miles to the lake.

Access: To reach the paved boat ramp, take the cutoff from Ice House Road to Loon Lake Campground and the picnic area.

Facilities, fees: A picnic area and campgrounds are provided. A primitive campground on the lake's north end can be accessed by boat or trail. Supplies are available at Ice House Resort. Access to the lake is free.

Water sports, restrictions: Waterskiing, personal watercraft, and windsurfing are permitted, but wet suits are advised due to the extremely cold water. Swimming is not recommended.

Contact: Eldorado National Forest, Visitor Center, (530) 644-6048 or fax (530) 295-5624 or Pacific Ranger District, (530) 644-2349; Ice House Resort, (530) 293-3321.

About Loon Lake: Loon Lake is a good destination for a weekend camping trip, especially if you have a small boat. It also can make for a jump-off point for a weeklong backpacking trip.

Set near the Sierra crest at 6,400 feet, this is a good-size lake, covering 600 acres and reaching depths of up to 130 feet. It is bordered by Eldorado National Forest and Desolation Wilderness, and a trail from this area is routed out to Winifred Lake, Spider Lake, and Buck Island Lake, all located to the east. If you don't like roughing it, you can opt to stay at Ice House Resort, which you'll pass on the access road about three miles from the lake.

Boating is very popular at Loon Lake, where there are no boating restrictions. However, water-contact sports can be dangerous due to heavy use on weekends, very cold water, and the typical high winds in the afternoon. In the early summer these afternoon winds can drive anglers off the lake. But their loss is a boon to sailboarders, who can only cheer.

Water-skiers and windsurfers should always wear wet suits; one dunk in the lake will convince anyone of that. Swimming is not a good idea, and not all that fun, anyway, unless you're a member of the Polar Bear Club (you know—the group of psychos who pride themselves on being the first every year to go swimming in freezing cold lakes). Windsurfers must take into consideration both the cold water and the potentially hazardous winds that can kick up in the afternoon. That is why windsurfers are generally better off heading to Union Valley Reservoir, located to the nearby south.

❽ Wrights Lake

Location: Southwest of Lake Tahoe in Eldorado National Forest; map D4, grid g0.

Directions: From Sacramento drive east on US 50 about 20 miles past Placerville. Turn left on Ice House Road and drive 10 miles. Turn right on Ice House Campground

Road and drive one mile. Watch for signs to Wright Lake on the left.

Access: No boat ramp is available. Cartop boats may be hand launched.

Facilities, fees: A campground and picnic area are provided. Supplies can be obtained in South Lake Tahoe. Access to the lake is free.

Water sports, restrictions: Motors are not permitted on the lake. The lake is not large enough or windy enough for windsurfing. Swimming is permitted.

Contact: Eldorado National Forest, Visitor Center, (530) 644-6048 or fax (530) 295-5624 or Pacific Ranger District, (530) 644-2349.

About Wrights Lake: This is your classic alpine lake, small (just 65 acres) and set high in the Sierra Nevada at a 7,000-foot elevation. Wrights Lake is an ideal jump-off point for a backpacker, day hiker, or a great destination for folks with cartop boats. Note that no motors are allowed on boats.

The beauty of the little lake is the number of side trip options available. You can drive less than a mile to little Dark Lake, and from there hike farther north to the Beauty Lakes or Pearl Lake. For multiday trips another option is routing a backpack trip to the east in the Crystal Range and the Desolation Wilderness (permit required).

On the lake itself the main activity is canoeing. Most folks head up just to paddle around, and maybe fish a little. Swimming is permitted, but the water is pretty cold and the shoreline is mostly rocks and grass, not really suitable for sunbathing.

The campground and nearby trailhead make this a very popular spot, and it gets lots of visitor traffic in the summer.

---

⑨ Fallen Leaf Lake

Location: Near South Lake Tahoe in Lake Tahoe Basin; map D4, grid g2.

Directions: From South Lake Tahoe drive three miles north on Highway 89 to Fallen Leaf Lake Road. Turn south and travel another two miles to the lake.

Access: Take Fallen Leaf Lake Road south to its end and then take the turnoff toward the marina. Note: RVs are not allowed on this road, and there is no turnaround for trailers.

Facilities, fees: A campground is located on the lake's north side. A small marina with fishing boat, pontoon boat, and sailboat rentals is available near the lodge. Within the marina is a sailing center that offers sailing and windsurfing rentals and lessons. Limited supplies can be obtained at the lake. Access to the lake is free. There is a fee for boat launching.

Water sports, restrictions: All four-stroke engines are permitted. Also permitted are two-stroke engines with direct fuel injection (DFI) and any watercraft engine that meets the California Air Resources Board 2001 or the US Environmental Protection Agency (EPA) 2001 emissions standards. Prohibited are 1) non-direct fuel injection engines (electronic or Rotax fuel injection) purchased after January 27, 1999, (auxiliary sailboat engines excepted) and 2) carbureted two-stroke engines with more than 10 horsepower. Waterskiing, Windsurfing and swimming are permitted. A large, roped-off swimming beach is available next to the marina; there are several smaller beaches around the shoreline.

Contact: Fallen Leaf Lake Marina, (530) 544-0787; Fallen Leaf Lake Lodge, (530) 541-6330; Lake Tahoe Basin Management Unit, (530) 573-2600 or fax (530) 573-2693.

About Fallen Leaf Lake: Millions of people drive within a mile of this large, beautiful lake and don't even know it's there. It is located just one mile from Highway 89 along Lake Tahoe, only three miles from the town of South Lake Tahoe.

Fallen Leaf Lake, which is set at a 6,300-foot elevation, has water that's almost as deep a shade of blue as nearby Lake Tahoe.

It's a big lake, three miles long and three-quarters of a mile wide, and is 430 feet at its deepest point. Because the lake is circled by forest, some of it on private property, shoreline access to the public is poor, and you need a boat to be able to enjoy the lake to its full potential.

This place presents a nice alternative to huge, crowded Lake Tahoe. It gets its share of traffic, too, but has a slightly more wilderness-like feel. Though the water is very cold, the setting is absolutely spectacular for waterskiing.

Several pretty swimming beaches are provided around the shore's south and north sides, with the most developed beach located next to the marina. Also at the marina is a sailing center that offers rentals and windsurfing lessons. Winds are common in the afternoon, often ideal for sailing and windsurfing, and with the surrounding beauty, either activity can prove to be an extraordinary experience.

⑩ Echo Lake

Location: South of Lake Tahoe in Lake Tahoe Basin; map D4, grid g2.
Directions: From Sacramento drive east on Interstate 80. About two miles past the Sierra-at-Tahoe Ski Area, turn left on Johnson Pass Road and drive less than one mile. Turn left on Echo Lake Road and drive to its end.
Access: A paved boat ramp is located next to Echo Chalet.
Facilities, fees: Echo Chalet offers lodging, picnic areas, groceries, and a snack bar. A marina with docks and canoe and fishing boat rentals is available. Camping is allowed in the adjacent Desolation Wilderness with a permit. Developed drive-to campgrounds are available nearby at Lake Tahoe. Access to the lake is free. There is a fee for boat launching.

Water sports, restrictions: All four-stroke engines are permitted. Also permitted are two-stroke engines with direct fuel injection (DFI) and any watercraft engine that meets the California Air Resources Board 2001 or the US Environmental Protection Agency (EPA) 2001 emissions standards. Prohibited are 1) non-direct fuel injection engines (electronic or Rotax fuel injection) purchased after January 27, 1999, (auxiliary sailboat engines excepted) and 2) carbureted two-stroke engines with more than 10 horsepower. Windsurfing is permitted. Swimming is available anywhere along the shore except in the main harbor area; the best spot is on the far end of Upper Echo Lake, where there used to be an old Boy Scout camp.

Contact: Echo Chalet, (530) 659-7207; Lake Tahoe Basin Management Unit, (530) 573-2600 or fax (530) 573-2693.

About Echo Lake: Afternoon sunlight and a light breeze will cover the surface of Echo Lake with slivers of silver. By evening the lake, now calm, takes on a completely different appearance, deep and beautiful, almost foreboding. Watching the transformation is like watching the changing expressions of the person you care for.

Echo Lake is carved out of granite near the Sierra ridge. Set at 7,500 feet, it's the gateway to the southern portion of the Desolation Wilderness. The lake is big and blue, covering 300 acres and reaching depths of 200 feet. At one time this was actually two lakes, but a small dam on Lower Echo Lake raised the water level, and now there is a narrow connecting link to Upper Echo Lake.

Lower Echo gets most of the traffic, both from water-skiers and anglers. On the main lake there can be tons of water-skiers during the hot summer months. The setting is spectacularly beautiful for all boating, and though the water is cold, it gives water-skiers an added incentive not to fall in.

Upper Echo Lake, on the other hand, provides guaranteed quiet water. Waterskiing is not permitted. Use is far less than at Lower Echo, and here you will even see people paddling about in little rowboats and canoes, swimming, and piloting low-speed boats. Swimming is permitted anywhere you can find access, and there are lots of rocks and grassy areas, but no beach. The old Boy Scout camp on the Upper Lake provides the best stretch of shoreline, with a large, fairly flat grassy area and gentle slope.

The Pacific Crest Trail runs right alongside the lake, and this is a main trailhead for the Desolation Wilderness, so the lake gets a lot of traffic, sometimes hordes of hikers. Echo Chalet offers a self-registration box for day-use wilderness permits, and also a taxi service for backpackers to the upper end of the lake, which shaves 3.25 miles off the hike.

Many outstanding destinations are accessible along the Pacific Crest Trail, including Tamarack Lake and many other nearby lakes.

⑪ Angora Lakes

⚓🐟🏊   6

Location: South of Lake Tahoe in Lake Tahoe Basin; map D4, grid g2.
Directions: From Sacramento drive east on US 50 to Highway 89 in South Lake Tahoe. Drive north on Highway 89 to Fallen Leaf Lake Road. Turn left and drive up the hill about three miles. When the road forks bear left and drive one-quarter mile. Bear right on Forest Service Road 12N14 (a dirt road) and drive about six miles, past the Angora Fire Lookout. Park in the lot provided and hike one-half mile to Angora Lakes.
Access: There is no boat ramp.
Facilities, fees: Piped water and rest rooms are provided. Cabin rentals, small store, and rowboat rentals are available at Angora Lake Resort. A campground is located nearby at Fallen Leaf Lake. Supplies can be obtained in South Lake Tahoe. Access is free.

Water sports, restrictions: Motors are not permitted on the lake. Swimming access is available all along the shoreline.
Contact: Angora Lake Resort, (530) 541-2092; Lake Tahoe Basin Management Unit, (530) 573-2600 or fax (530) 573-2693.
About Angora Lakes: For many visitors to Lake Tahoe, Angora Lakes provides the perfect side trip.

Just a short drive from South Lake Tahoe, followed by a brief walk, lands you at these two small lakes that are set in a bowl below Echo and Angora Peaks.

The quick, uphill hike deters some people, but certainly not all. For many, particularly families with young children, it is the perfect distance to walk, especially at this high elevation. The trek to Angora Lakes is a small price to pay for such a beautiful destination, ideal for swimming, renting a rowboat, staying in a cabin (a real long shot getting in), and visiting the legendary lemonade stand.

This is a very popular lake for swimming, with stretches of beach interrupted by large boulders that are excellent for jumping into the drink. After taking this leap of faith, you may have second thoughts in midair about touchdown in the cold water. Many youngsters express their reservations with a howl before landing with a splash.

Boating is pretty much restricted to the rowboats that are rented at Angora Lake Resort, unless you want to carry in your own canoe or inflatable on the half mile hike. Few people are willing.

Cabin rentals are available at the resort, but reservations can be booked years in advance. The only way to get in is to sign up on a cancellation list, then wait for years, hoping somebody eventually dies and leaves their spot open. Heh, heh.

The resort has a little store where you can buy sandwiches and lemonade. The woman who provides the latter is somewhat famous here and is known as the "lemonade lady."

If you want to camp, you'll have to head on over to Fallen Leaf Lake, but no matter, this is still a great day-use spot.

⑫ Kirkwood Lake

Location: South of Lake Tahoe in Eldorado National Forest; map D4, grid h1.

Directions: From Jackson drive east on Highway 88 for approximately 60 miles (four miles past Silver Lake) to the access road entrance (if you reach the sign for Kirkwood Ski Resort, you have gone a half mile too far). Turn left and drive a quarter mile to the campground (the road is not suitable for trailers or RVs).

Access: There is no boat ramp. Cartop boats may be hand launched.

Facilities, fees: A campground and picnic areas are provided. Access to the lake is free.

Water sports, restrictions: Motors are not permitted on the lake. Swimming is allowed, but the water is quite cold.

Contact: Eldorado National Forest, Amador Ranger District, (209) 295-4251 or fax (209) 295-5994; Kirkwood Ski Resort, (209) 258-6000.

About Kirkwood Lake: The Carson Pass area has become a great alternative to crowded Lake Tahoe nearby to the north (it's an hour's drive to the casinos). At the center of it all is Kirkwood Ski Resort, which now offers year-round accommodations, as well as a deluxe base of operations for a hiking trip.

Here, in this beautiful Sierra setting at an elevation of 7,600 feet, you will find little Kirkwood Lake. At this very small, very pretty lake, no motorized boating is allowed, which helps keep things pretty quiet.

Most of the land bordering the lake is private, with summer homes sprinkled about. Public recreation is limited to the west side, where there's a campground that is almost always full during the summer.

Even though the trout fishing here is only fair, most lake users are anglers out in small boats. Some campers do try swimming on hot days, but most of the shoreline is rocky and the water is quite cold. No matter how hot the sun is shining, swimming at Kirkwood usually means taking an in-and-out dunk.

The nearby Kirkwood Ski Area has been transformed into a year-round facility, offering lodging, restaurant, and good hiking opportunities.

⑬ Silver Lake

Location: In Eldorado National Forest; map D4, grid i1.

Directions: From Jackson drive east on Highway 88 for 52 miles to the lake entrance road.

Access: A paved ramp is available at Kay's Silver Lake Resort, located on the northwest side of the lake on Highway 88.

Facilities, fees: Two campgrounds, picnic areas, groceries, restaurants, gas, and a coin laundry are provided at the lake. Cabins and motels are available. Kay's Silver Lake Resort has a marina where you can rent fishing boats, and Kit Carson Lodge rents fishing boats, rowboats, canoes, and kayaks. Access to the lake is free. There is a fee for boat launching at Kay's Silver Lake Resort.

Water sports, restrictions: Waterskiing, personal watercraft, and windsurfing are permitted. Wet suits are recommended due to the cold water. Although the water is quite cold for swimming, there are several sandy beach areas for sunbathing; the best are at Sandy Cove and Kit Carson Lodge.

Contact: Eldorado National Forest, Amador Ranger District, (209) 295-4251 or fax (209) 295-5994; Kay's Silver Lake Resort, (209) 258-8598; Kit Carson Lodge, (209) 258-8500.

About Silver Lake: The Highway 88 corridor provides access to several excellent lakes, including three right in a row from west to east: Lower Bear River, Silver, and Caples. Of the three, Silver Lake is most often overlooked.

Silver Lake is set at an elevation of 7,200 feet in a classic granite cirque just below the Sierra ridgeline. The surrounding area is extremely scenic.

The water is quite cold, and unfortunately it stays that way throughout the summer. That doesn't stop people from waterskiing and windsurfing and using personal watercraft, but only the truly brave and/or crazy try it without a wet suit. Windsurfing can be particularly good because winds are often brisk on summer afternoons. Sometimes they're a little too brisk, though, and boaters should take extra care. Swimming is usually a jump-in, jump-out situation, but there are good sunbathing beaches.

Silver Lake also provides decent trout fishing, great nearby hiking trails, horse rentals, campgrounds, and cabins. Full facilities are offered at the three resorts that operate here.

Usually the lake is free of ice by late May or early June, and by summer it's getting quite a lot of use. Most visitors congregate on the lake's north side, where the campgrounds, picnic areas, and marina are located.

One great activity to try when you're here is horseback riding. Visitors can rent horses at Plasse's Resort on the lake's south side (no phone).

⑭ Caples Lake

Location: South of Lake Tahoe; map D4, grid i2.

Directions: From Jackson drive east on Highway 88 for 63 miles (one mile past the entrance to Kirkwood Ski Area) to the lake entrance road on the right.

Access: A boat ramp is available at Caples Lake Resort on Highway 88.

Facilities, fees: A campground is provided across the highway from the resort. A lodge, cabins, and groceries are available also. Fishing boats, canoes, and kayaks can be rented at Caples Lake Resort. Access is free. There is a fee for boat launching.

Water sports, restrictions: A 5 mph speed limit is strictly enforced. Windsurfing and swimming are allowed, although the water is quite cold. Wet suits are recommended for windsurfers.

Contact: Eldorado National Forest, Amador Ranger District, (209) 295-4251 or fax (209) 295-5994; Caples Lake Resort, (209) 258-8888.

About Caples Lake: A high mountain lake set at an elevation of 7,950 feet, Caples is surrounded by dramatic scenery and is easily accessed off Highway 88. It provides good trout fishing, low-speed boating (5 mph speed limit), nearby hiking trails, and fair swimming.

In the spring just pray that the cold wind out of the west doesn't howl. It can go right through you and make you feel like petrified wood.

The 600-acre lake is filled by snowmelt, and though the water is cold, people do swim here. Much of the shoreline is rocky and steep in places, but there is a beach area near the resort that is suitable for sunbathing. It is extremely rare to see anyone windsurfing, even though conditions are often ideal—the lake is sizable and wide open, and typically gets good afternoon winds—providing sailboarders wear wet suits.

Use of the lake is moderate on most summer days, primarily attracting anglers who come looking for trout. On weekends use is heavy, with campers showing up in force. Many visitors go hiking. The best opportunity is at the trail that starts just off the highway near the dam at the lake's westernmost portion, and is routed into the Mokelumne Wilderness.

⓯ Woods Lake

Location: In Eldorado National Forest; map D4, grid i2.

Directions: From Jackson drive east on Highway 88 for 64 miles (one mile past Caples Lake) to the signed turnoff for Woods Lake. Turn south and drive two miles on Woods Lake Road to the lake (trailers and RVs are not recommended).

Access: An unimproved launch ramp is adjacent to the campground.

Facilities, fees: A campground and picnic area are provided. Supplies can be obtained nearby. Access to the lake is free.

Water sports, restrictions: Motors are not permitted on the lake. The lake is too small for windsurfing. Although the water is quite cold, swimming is permitted. The best spots are near the campground and picnic area.

Contact: Eldorado National Forest, Amador Ranger District, (209) 295-4251 or fax (209) 295-5994.

About Woods Lake: Woods Lake may be located only two miles off Highway 88, yet when you're here, you get the feeling that you are visiting some far-off land.

Set in the high Sierra, elevation 8,200 feet, this small lake comes complete with a campground and an area where you can launch cartop boats. The lake always seems to be full, making a very pretty picture against the granite Sierra backdrop.

Cartop boating in Woods Lake is excellent, as you enjoy beautiful, wilderness-like scenery, quiet water, and decent trout fishing. Because the water is so cold, swimming is for the brave only.

Despite the backcountry atmosphere, the place is easy to access. Use can be quite high in summer, when the campground is almost always full. Many visitors take advantage of the hiking opportunities in the area, including an outstanding short tromp to nearby Winnemucca Lake.

⓰ Red Lake

Location: South of Lake Tahoe in Humboldt-Toiyabe National Forest; map D4, grid i3.

Directions: From the junction of US 50 and Highway 89 at the town of Meyers (two miles south of South Lake Tahoe), drive 20 miles southeast on Highway 89 to Highway 88. Turn right and drive about six miles southwest on Highway 88 to the turnoff for Red Lake. Turn left and continue to the lake.

An optional route from the Central Valley: From Jackson drive east on Highway 88 all the way over Carson Pass to the turnoff for Red Lake. Turn right and drive to the lake.

Access: An unimproved boat ramp is located on the lake's northeast corner.

Facilities, fees: A few primitive campsites are available on the lake's east side. Supplies can be obtained along Highway 88. Access is free.

Water sports, restrictions: Motors are not permitted on the lake. Although the water is quite cold, windsurfing and swimming are permitted.

Contact: Humboldt-Toiyabe National Forest, Carson Ranger District, (775) 882-2766 or fax (775) 884-8199.

About Red Lake: If you have a canoe or any other type of cartop boat or inflatable, Red Lake is an ideal place to come and do your own thing. No motors are permitted, and most boaters just paddle or float around a bit, often with a fishing rod so they can be on the ready for trout.

Red Lake is a high mountain lake set at 8,200 feet elevation just southeast of Carson Pass. It is a fair-sized body of water, about four times bigger than nearby Woods Lake, and is shaped like a lima bean.

Camping is allowed only on the far east end of the lake. Use is light compared to the other lakes in the area, even in midsummer; for the most part only people who want to fish for trout bother to make the trip out.

Vigorous afternoon winds can make this a great lake for windsurfing. Be aware that the water is very cold and wearing a wet suit is highly recommended.

The lake once was the subject of intense disputes over public access on the part of some nearby landowners. That was resolved in 1993, when the Department of Fish and Game purchased most of the land adjoining the lake as well as the water rights. It was a great move: end of problem.

⑰ Upper Blue Lake

⚓ 🛶 🏕 🐟 🏊 🚤   ⬛ 6

Location: South of Lake Tahoe in Humboldt-Toiyabe National Forest; map D4, grid i3.

Directions: From the junction of US 50 and Highway 89 at the town of Meyers (two miles south of South Lake Tahoe), drive 20 miles southeast on Highway 89 to Highway 88. Turn right (west) and travel 2.5 miles southwest to Blue Lakes Road. Turn left and drive approximately 14 miles, passing Lower Blue Lake, to Upper Blue Lake.

Access: Primitive boat launching areas are available on the southern and northern ends of the lake, just off the access road.

Facilities, fees: Several PG&E campgrounds are located in the vicinity. Access to the lake is free.

Water sports, restrictions: Only small motorized or cartop boats are suitable for the lake. Although the water is quite cold, swimming is permitted.

Contact: PG&E Building & Land Services, (916) 386-5164 or fax (916) 386-5388; Humboldt-Toiyabe National Forest, Carson Ranger District, (775) 882-2766 or fax (775) 884-8199.

About Upper Blue Lake: Upper Blue Lake is one of two lakes that are linked by Middle Blue Creek.

This is the high country, set at 8,200 feet. The landscape is fairly sparse but pristine, featuring sandy soil sprinkled with pines,

and bare granite mountains looming above nearby. But it's the good trout fishing and decent campgrounds that provide the true appeal.

The water is cold, with ice-out usually occurring by Memorial Day weekend, later in big snow years. Of the two Blue Lakes here, Upper Blue gets most of the boater traffic. Even then it is primarily anglers out trolling for trout in small boats.

Other than fishing and low-speed boating, it is extremely rare to see water sports being performed here. Some people swim, but the water is pretty cold and the shoreline fairly rugged.

Of the campgrounds in the area, Upper Blue Lake, operated by PG&E, is the most remote and private. Hiking is fair here; the best trek is the climb out on the Pacific Crest Trail, which rises on the barren slopes above the lake and awards hikers with scenic views.

⑱ Lower Blue Lake

⚓ 🛶 🏕 🐟 🏊   ⬛ 5

Location: South of Lake Tahoe in Humboldt-Toiyabe National Forest; map D4, grid i3.

Directions: From the junction of US 50 and Highway 89 at the town of Meyers (two miles south of South Lake Tahoe), drive 20 miles southeast on Highway 89 to Highway 88. Turn right (west) and travel 2.5 miles southwest to Blue Lakes Road. Turn left and drive about 12 miles to Lower Blue Lake.

Access: A primitive boat launching area is available on the lake's far southern end.

Facilities, fees: Several PG&E campgrounds are located in the vicinity. Access to the lake is free.

Water sports, restrictions: The lake is suitable only for cartop boats. Although the water is quite cold, swimming is permitted.

Contact: PG&E Building & Land Services, (916) 386-5164 or fax (916) 386-5388; Humboldt-Toiyabe National Forest, Carson

Ranger District, (775) 882-2766 or fax (775) 884-8199.

About Lower Blue Lake: This is the smaller of the two Blue Lakes, suitable only for leisurely paddles in a canoe or inflatable. For many that makes for a perfect day.

As the little brother of the pair, Lower Blue receives less traffic, and that means fewer boaters, campers, anglers, and hikers. Since trout fishing is the main appeal at the Blue Lakes and the fishing is far better at Upper Blue than at Lower Blue, it's no wonder this one is often overlooked.

Few people swim here, but it is still an option on a hot summer day. The shoreline is rocky and fairly sparse, and you'll need to have footwear to reach the water's edge.

⑲ East Fork Carson River

Location: Near Markleeville in Humboldt-Toiyabe National Forest; map D4, grid i5.

Directions: From the small town of Markleeville on Highway 89 (southeast of Lake Tahoe), drive south on Highways 89 and 4 for six miles. Direct access along the highway is available in this area. Access is also available off Wolf Creek Road (see directions).

Access: A boat ramp is not available. There are two standard rafting runs on the East Fork:

Upper East Fork: From Markleeville drive south on Highways 89 and 4 to where they divide. Continue south on Highway 4 for three miles, turn left on Wolf Creek Road, and drive 1.5 miles. Put in anywhere you can find good access. Take out seven miles downstream at Hangman's Bridge, or continue through to Ruhenstroth Dam.

Wilderness Run: From Markleeville drive two miles south on Highways 89 and 4 to Hangman's Bridge. Take out 20 miles downstream just above the dam. To reach the take-out, start at Markleeville and drive seven miles north on Highway 89 to High-

way 88. Turn right and drive northeast for 14 miles, crossing into Nevada. At US 395 turn south and drive to Gardnerville, Nevada. Continue five miles south and look for a dirt road on your right. Turn there and drive to a parking area.

Note: It is essential that you take out here because just downstream is a 30-foot vertical drop over a dam.

Facilities, fees: A campground is provided near Markleeville. Supplies can be obtained in Markleeville. Access to the river is free. Rafters running the Wilderness Run must register at the put-in.

Water sports, restrictions: Although the East Fork Carson River is quite cold through the summer, several swimming holes are available along Highways 89 and 4 and on Wolf Creek Road. Look for turnouts and trails leading to the river.

Contact: Humboldt-Toiyabe National Forest, Carson Ranger District, (775) 882-2766 or fax (775) 884-8199; Monty Wolf's Trading Post, (530) 694-2201. For guided rafting trips contact Ahwahnee Whitewater Expeditions, (800) 359-9790; California Adventures, (in Berkeley), (510) 642-4000; or RAM River Adventures, (800) 466-7238.

About the East Fork Carson River: This rafting run is just enough. That is, there's just enough excitement to make it fun, just enough scenic beauty to provide a sense of the natural grace of the great outdoors, and just enough surprises along the way to keep you guessing about what awaits around the next bend.

The best surprise of all on the river is a hot spring, located nine miles downstream of the Hangman's Bridge put-in spot. Almost nobody passes that by, and anybody who does should be committed to an institution! Heh, heh. The rafting season here tends to be in May and June, when both the weather and the water are cold. Jumping into that hot spring and warming up, then taking a quick dunk in the cold river, then bobbing back into the hot spring—in pretty surroundings with no-body around—well, that can be one of the most exhilarating of life's little experiences.

Pines and high desert chaparral make up the streamside scenery. While it may not be the gorgeous backdrop of granite canyons that you'll find in the western Sierra, the setting does feel remote.

The length of the entire run is 27 miles. The season is usually over in June, though in years with big snowpacks it can extend into July. Because the water is so cold (as well as being very clear), it is essential that rafters wear wet or dry suits.

Upper East Fork Run is rated Class III, and the Wilderness Run is Class II. The highlight is Sidewinder, a Class II+ rapid and the most difficult piece of white water on the run. It is located just upstream of the hot spring. Got it? Right, that means you whip through Sidewinder, then jump in the hot spring. If you fall in at Sidewinder, the pain of being in such cold water, even while wearing a wet suit, is largely mitigated by the knowledge that you will soon be soaking in the hot spring. **Special Note:** Note the warning about taking out above the dam; missing the take-out would result in what rafting guides call "disastrous consequences," otherwise known as being dead very quick.

⑳ Indian Creek Reservoir

⬇🚣⛺🐟🏊🧍   [6]

Location: Near Markleeville in Indian Creek Reservoir Recreation Area; map D4, grid i5.
Directions: At the intersection of Highways 88 and 89 at the small town of Woodfords, drive three miles south on Highway 89 to Airport Boulevard. Turn left and travel five miles to the reservoir.
Access: A paved launch ramp is available on the west side of the lake, adjacent to the picnic areas. Another, more primitive

launching area is located on the east side, at the end of Airport Road.
Facilities, fees: Several campgrounds and two picnic areas are provided. Supplies can be obtained nearby. Access to the lake is free.
Water sports, restrictions: Only small motorized or cartop boats are permitted on the lake. Windsurfing and swimming are allowed.
Contact: Bureau of Land Management, Carson City Field Office, (775) 885-6100 or fax (775) 885-6147.
About Indian Creek Reservoir: In the space of just a few miles, the terrain completely changes in this country. When you cross from the western Sierra over the ridge to the eastern Sierra, the land becomes sparsely forested on the high desert edge, with none of the classic granite-based features of the high Sierra.

That is why Indian Creek Reservoir gets overlooked by so many people. It's on the Sierra's eastern side, at 5,600 feet in elevation, and most vacationers are off yonder. Access, however, is quite easy (there's even a small county airport within a mile of the lake).

People don't know what they're missing. This is an excellent lake for small boats. In addition, fishing can be good, it's fairly scenic, and the Bureau of Land Management campsites are free or low-cost.

Like so many lakes set just east of the Sierra, wind is common, particularly in the afternoon. This is due to a katabatic phenomenon, that is, when wind crosses the Sierra ridge then dives down the other side to the east, picking up speed as it goes. That can make conditions for windsurfing excellent at Indian Creek Reservoir, and it makes sailing pretty popular here, too.

Because there are no beaches and the water is cold, swimming is not popular, although it is permitted. Most campers are here in small boats to fish for trout, while others come to hike in the area.

One possible side trip is the one-mile hike to little Summit Lake, located just west of Indian Creek Reservoir. The trailhead is southwest of the campground area. Another popular side trip is to nearby Grover Hot Springs, located right outside of Markleeville.

㉑ Topaz Lake

Location: On the California/Nevada border in Humboldt-Toiyabe National Forest; map D4, grid j7.

Directions: From Carson City, Nevada, drive south on US 395 for 33 miles to Topaz Lake and the campground/marina on the left side of the road. From Bridgeport, California, drive north on US 395 for 45 miles to the campground/marina on the right side of the road.

Access: There are three boat ramps on Topaz Lake:

Douglas County Recreation Area: From US 395 at the California/Nevada border, drive north into Nevada and look for the park entrance on your right. The paved boat ramp is at the end of the access road.

Topaz Lake RV Park: A paved ramp is available at the park, located just a short distance south of Topaz Marina on US 395. There is no public access; use is limited to guests of the RV park.

Topaz Marina: A paved boat ramp is available at the marina, located on US 395 just south of the California/Nevada border.

Facilities, fees: RV camping is available at Topaz RV Park. Tent camping and picnic facilities are available at Douglas County Recreation Area on the lake's northeast side. Full services and fishing boat rentals are provided at Topaz Marina. A day-use fee is charged at the county park. There is a fee for boat launching.

Water sports, restrictions: Waterskiing, personal watercraft, and windsurfing are permitted. Swimming access is available at various areas within the county park and along the west shore.

Contact: Topaz Landing, (775) 266-3550; Douglas County Recreation Area, (775) 266-3343; Topaz Lake RV Park, (530) 495-2357.

About Topaz Lake: Topaz is set at 5,000 feet in the eastern Sierra and is surrounded by high desert country. The Nevada border runs right through the lake. Some people say the place is cute, as in "cute like an iguana." When the wind kicks up, it can get downright ugly.

In addition to the wind, Topaz is best known for providing premium fishing for rainbow trout, with lots of large rainbow trout for trollers. If you fish out of a small aluminum boat, always remember: Safety first. And if the wind starts to come up, then get off the lake, because once it starts it rarely dies, and instead crescendos until the lake is whipped to a froth.

The lake covers 1,800 acres of pretty much wide-open water. All boating and water sports are allowed. In July and August it can be a premium destination for all kinds of water sports enthusiasts, and it does get a lot of stopovers from travelers on adjacent US 395. The RV park, in particular, receives a lot of traffic.

On the typical day anglers are out on the lake early, before the wind comes up, trolling for trout. By 11 AM the powerboaters and water-skiers start to appear, but rarely in great numbers. By mid-afternoon there is enough wind for windsurfing, and on most days it can be exceptional.

While swimming is permitted anywhere along the shoreline, there are no designated swimming areas and it is not common to see people in the water. There are several gravel-type beach areas that are suitable for sunbathing; on the rare occasions when someone decides to take a dunk, that's where they go.

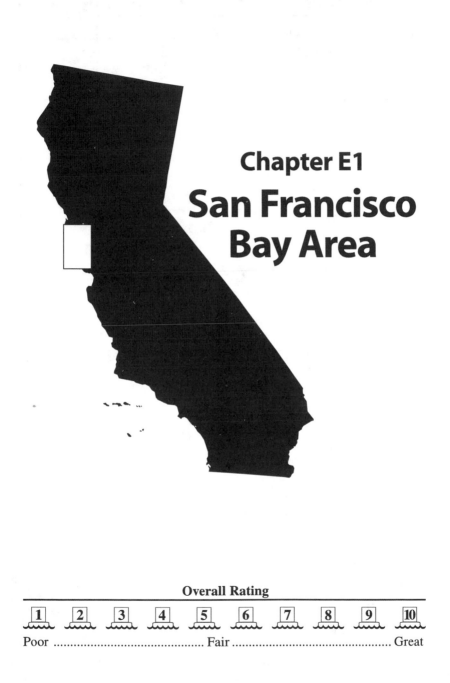

Chapter E1
San Francisco Bay Area

Overall Rating

1	2	3	4	5	6	7	8	9	10

Poor .... Fair .... Great

E1–San Francisco Bay Area Map

One inch equals approximately 10.7 miles.
See page 12 for California state map.

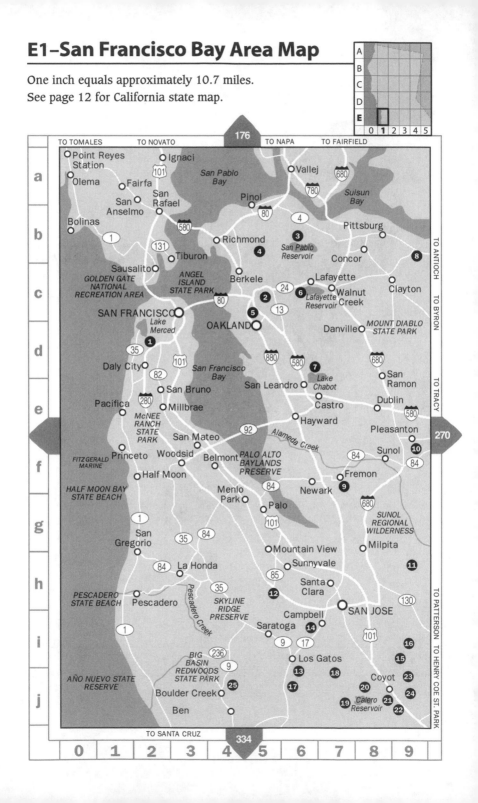

Chapter E1 features:

❶ Lake Merced

Location: In San Francisco; map E1, grid d2.

Directions: From Interstate 280 in Daly City, take John Daly Boulevard west, turn right at Skyline Boulevard, and continue to the lake.

Access: There is a paved ramp at the North Lake; an unimproved ramp is provided at the South Lake.

Facilities, fees: A picnic area is provided. A bar and restaurant are available at the boathouse. Rowboats, canoes, paddleboats, and boats with electric motors can be rented. Windsurfing lessons and rentals are available. Access is free. Fees are charged for day use and boat launching.

Note: Lake Merced has rented boats with electric motors for the past 30 years. At press time a new concessionaire has been contracted, and at least for the forseeable future, only rowboats will be available. For an update call the San Francisco Recreation & Parks Department, Property Management Unit, (415) 831-2773 or fax (415) 831-2099.

Water sports, restrictions: Gas-powered motors are not permitted on the lake.

Swimming and water/body contact are prohibited. Windsurfing is allowed, but you must wear a wet suit.

Contact: San Francisco Recreation & Parks Department, Property Management Unit, (415) 831-2773 or fax (415) 831-2099; Lake Merced Boathouse, (415) 753-1101. For windsurfing lessons and rentals, phone (415) 753-3235.

About Lake Merced: If you try sitting in a boat along Lake Merced's tule-lined shore, San Francisco and her 700,000 residents will seem like a whole different world. That is because they are. This is a place of peace.

There is actually a total of three lakes here: Lake Merced North (105 acres), Lake Merced South (203 acres), and the Merced Impoundment (17 acres, but typically too low on water for public use).

Lake Merced North is where the largest trout recorded in Bay Area history was caught. The rainbow trout weighed 17 pounds, eight ounces and was landed by Jesse Rappenecker of San Bruno. This is a pretty spot, surrounded by tules for the most part, with a beach area for shore fishing on the west shore, and the Harding Park Golf Course along the south shore.

The South Lake, the largest of the trio, is

more of a recreation lake for rowers and sailboaters. Larger than most newcomers expect, the lake is quite pretty, with a shore almost completely enclosed by tules. A small hoist is provided for boats, ideally small sailboats.

Getting afternoon winds off the nearby coast, the South Lake is excellent not only for small sailboats but for novice windsurfers. Beginning classes for windsurfing are even taught here. It is rarely crowded (most of the people fishing are at the North Lake) and is a good place to practice before you head out to a more challenging environment.

Because the lake is right on the coast, fog is sometimes a problem and temperatures are often cool, even in summer. When the Central Valley is baking in the 100s day after day, Merced can be shrouded in mist from a heavy fog.

❷ Lake Temescal

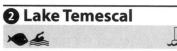

Location: In the Oakland hills; map E1, grid c5.
Directions: From Oakland on Highway 24, take the Broadway exit. Bear left through the intersection, continuing on Broadway (toward Highway 13 southbound). Within one-half mile look for the signed entrance to the Temescal Regional Recreation Area on the right.
Access: Boating is not permitted on the lake.
Facilities, fees: Picnic areas, rest rooms, and a snack bar are provided. Most facilities are wheelchair accessible. Fees are charged for parking and swimming.
Water sports, restrictions: There is a sandy swimming beach.
Contact: East Bay Regional Park District, (510) 635-0135, extension 2200.
About Lake Temescal: Little Lake Temescal, encompassing only 10 surface acres, is set in the Oakland hills and pro-

vides a good retreat for shore fishing and swimming. There is a nice sandy beach and a picnic area for day use.

The lake is used primarily for trout fishing from winter through spring, when the water is cool enough for trout stocks. From May through the summer, it becomes the site of picnics and swimming parties.

The hills surrounding Temescal were burned in the terrible Oakland firestorm that devastated the area in the fall of 1991. Even though the hills are revegetating quite well and the lake is once again green, nobody forgets.

❸ San Pablo Reservoir

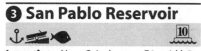

Location: Near Orinda; map E1, grid b5.
Directions: From the north take Interstate 80 and exit on San Pablo Dam Road. Go right, toward Orinda, and drive six miles to the main lake entrance. If you have a boat to launch, continue to the second entrance. From the south (from San Jose), take Interstate 680 and then take the Highway 24 exit toward Orinda. Take the Orinda exit and turn left on Camino Pablo Road (Camino Pablo Road becomes San Pablo Dam Road). The first entrance leads to the boat ramp; the second is the main entrance.
Access: A multilane paved launch ramp is located on the east side of the reservoir.
Facilities, fees: Picnic areas, playground, small marina, docks, and a snack bar are provided. Fishing boats and rowboats can be rented. Fees are charged for parking and boat launching.
Water sports, restrictions: There is a 5 mph speed limit along the shoreline and in the coves, and a 25 mph limit on the main lake body. Personal watercraft, windsurfing, and swimming are not allowed. All boaters must wear Coast Guard–approved life jackets.
Contact: San Pablo Reservoir, (510) 223-1661 or fax (510) 223-0832.

About San Pablo Reservoir: Daybreak at San Pablo Reservoir highlights one of the prettiest boating scenes in the Bay Area, distinguished by blues and greens, placid water, and boats leaving fresh, white trails. San Pablo is the Bay Area's number one lake, providing a unique combination of beauty, good boating, and good fishing.

The lake is big for one so close to so many people—860 acres. Two major lake arms are featured. The main arm extends south into a waterfowl management area with a 5 mph speed limit, while the Scow Canyon Arm, located across the reservoir from the San Pablo Recreation Area, extends east into the remote foothills of Contra Costa County.

All in all, this is a great destination for boating, big enough to accommodate sizable fiberglass boats, yet small enough to provide intimate settings for tiny aluminum boats and even canoes. The lake supplies drinking water to the Bay Area, so body contact with the water is forbidden; hence, swimming, wading, waterskiing, personal watercraft, and inner tubing are strictly prohibited.

The excellent marina supplies a variety of boat rentals, as well as good over-the-phone reports on wind and fishing conditions. One drawback is that the boat ramp is located some distance from the marina and the recreation area—an odd setup.

Fishing is the main attraction at San Pablo Reservoir, which gets the highest trout stocks of any lake in California. But good conditions for all styles of boating make this lake tops in the Bay Area.

➍ Lake Anza

Location: In Berkeley in Tilden Regional Park; map E1, grid b5.
Directions: From Orinda take Highway 24 to Fish Ranch Road. Turn right on Grizzly Peak Boulevard and continue to South Park Drive. Then turn right again, travel one mile, and turn left on Wildcat Canyon Road. Turn right on Central Park Drive, then right again on the Lake Anza entrance road, just before the merry-go-round.

Access: Boating is not permitted on the lake.

Facilities, fees: Picnic areas and rest rooms are provided. The facilities are wheelchair accessible. Fees are charged for swimming and parking.

Water sports, restrictions: There is a sandy swimming beach.

Contact: East Bay Regional Park District, (510) 635-0135, extension 2200.

About Lake Anza: Don't expect this lake to set your heart a-pumping. It is small, just 11 acres, and the main attraction is the surrounding parkland.

While Lake Anza does provide an opportunity to take a dunk and swim around a bit, the warm water can turn a bit soupy in mid- to late summer. The fishing isn't all that great either. The surrounding Tilden Regional Park gets quite a lot of use, but few parkgoers make a point of visiting Lake Anza. Picnics and other group events are often held here, but rarely do people come just to see the lake itself.

➎ Lake Merritt

Location: In Oakland; map E1, grid c5.
Directions: From Interstate 580 in Oakland, take the Grand Avenue exit and drive west to the lake entrance.

Access: A launch ramp is located on the northeast side of the lake.

Facilities, fees: Rest rooms and grassy areas for picnicking are provided. Rowboats, paddleboats, canoes, and sailboats can be rented at the boat center. Sailing and windsurfing lessons are also available there. Boat tours are conducted on weekends. There is a fee for boat launching, and an entrance fee is charged on weekends.

Water sports, restrictions: Motors are not permitted on the lake. Windsurfing is allowed, but you are advised to wear a wet suit. Swimming is prohibited.

Contact: Lake Merritt Boat Center, (510) 444-3807.

About Lake Merritt: Believe it or not, such a place does exist right in the heart of downtown Oakland. It is one of the city's prettiest settings and has become a very popular spot for jogging and picnicking.

This is one of the few lakes in the area where boat rentals are available. Lake Merritt has a boat center where you can pick up a canoe, paddleboat, or little sailboat, all ideal for spending a few hours on these waters. In fact, this is an excellent place for beginners to learn how to sail, with winds predictable and steady on spring and summer afternoons, not wild and erratic.

Or you can learn how to windsurf here. This is the perfect lake for novices; lessons are available, the water is calm, and the wind is just strong enough most of the time to give you a thrill.

A small barred gateway separates Lake Merritt from San Francisco Bay, and though heavy rains turn the lake to fresh water in the winter, it becomes brackish and then salty by summer and fall. That means no fish, because the changing salinity levels make the water uninhabitable for freshwater species.

❻ Lafayette Reservoir

Location: Near Walnut Creek; map E1, grid c6.

Directions: From Walnut Creek drive east on Highway 24. Take the Acalanes exit, which feeds you onto Mount Diablo Boulevard, and drive about a mile to the signed entrance to the park on the right.

Access: A primitive launching area (hand launching only) is provided.

Facilities, fees: Picnic areas, rest rooms, and hiking and bicycling trails are provided. A sailing dock and paddleboat and rowboat rentals are available. There is a fee for parking.

Water sports, restrictions: Gasoline motors are not permitted on the lake. Swimming, windsurfing, and water/body contact are prohibited.

Contact: Lafayette Reservoir, (925) 284-9669.

About Lafayette Reservoir: This 115-acre lake is very pretty, truly a little paradise in the East Bay hills. The surrounding oak-covered hills create a pleasant, quiet setting.

The reservoir is used only for fishing, canoeing, and sailing, and with access restricted to boats that can be hand launched, you are assured peace and lots of space on the water. Gas motors are not permitted, but electric motors are okay, which keeps things quiet. Talk about the ideal spot for canoeing.

Peak use is in late winter and spring, when the weather begins to warm yet the water temperature is still cool, making for good trout fishing. A small boathouse and a dock are provided.

❼ Lake Chabot

Location: Near Castro Valley; map E1, grid d6.

Directions: In Oakland on Interstate 580, take the 35th Avenue exit. Turn east on 35th Avenue and drive up the hill and across Skyline Boulevard, where 35th Avenue becomes Redwood Road. Drive six miles on Redwood Road to the park entrance on the right.

Access: There is no boat ramp. Private boats (except canoes and kayaks) are not permitted on the lake.

Facilities, fees: A campground is provided on the lake's north side. Rest rooms, picnic areas, snack bar, boathouse, hiking and biking trails, and drinking water are available. Electric motorboats, rowboats, paddleboats, and canoes can be rented. Fees are charged for parking and day use.

Water sports, restrictions: Motorized boats are restricted to the electric boat rentals. Swimming, windsurfing, and all other water/body-contact activities are strictly prohibited.

Contact: East Bay Regional Park District, (510) 635-0135, extension 2200; Lake Chabot Marina, (510) 582-2198.

About Lake Chabot: The lake is the centerpiece of a 5,000-acre regional park that includes 31 miles of hiking trails, horseback riding rentals, and a campground.

Covering 315 acres, Lake Chabot has a small island, secluded coves, a marina where you can rent boats, and decent fishing. Considering all these factors, it could be just about perfect, except for one thing: privately owned boats are not permitted on the lake. That right there rules out its value to many people. Oh yeah, and the fact that swimming and windsurfing aren't allowed either.

If you don't mind renting a boat, head to the small dock, where you have your pick of rowboats, electric motorboats, canoes, kayaks, and paddleboats. Lake Chabot's cool waters provide a respite from the intense summer heat as you paddle around in a canoe or try to master the art of kayaking.

---

❽ Contra Loma Reservoir

Location: Near Antioch; map E1, grid b9.
Directions: In Antioch take Contra Loma Boulevard south to the park entrance.
Access: There is a paved boat launch.
Facilities, fees: A fishing pier, picnic areas, and a snack bar are provided. Kayak rentals and windsurfing lessons are available in the summer months. The facilities are wheel-

chair accessible. A fee is charged for parking.

Water sports, restrictions: Boats with electric motors are permitted on the reservoir (limit 17 feet), but gasoline motors are not allowed. There's a sandy beach suitable for swimming and windsurfing.

Contact: Contra Loma Reservoir, (925) 757-0404. For kayak rentals or windsurfing lessons, phone (925) 778-6350.

About Contra Loma Reservoir: Contra Loma Reservoir is the first stop for water being shipped out of the Delta and bound for points south. It covers 70 acres, is easily accessible to residents of Antioch and nearby towns, and provides a good place for fishing, swimming, and boating. The surrounding parkland is crisscrossed with hiking and horseback riding trails.

One thing to remember is that it gets hot here in the summer and afternoon winds are common. This makes it ideal for windsurfing and sailing. Both sports are popular here, and the conditions are particularly attractive to beginning windsurfers.

Swimming prospects are also good, with a large beach and play area available for youngsters. Boating rules (no gas-powered motors and no boat more than 17 feet long) ensure that the reservoir remains quiet and peaceful.

---

❾ Lake Elizabeth

Location: In Fremont; map E1, grid f7.
Directions: From Fremont on Interstate 880, turn east on Stevenson Boulevard and drive about two miles. Turn right on Paseo Padre Parkway and drive about one block. Turn left on Sailway Drive and continue a short distance to Central Park.
Access: A paved launch ramp is located on the lake's west side.
Facilities, fees: Picnic areas, snack bars, rest rooms, and athletic facilities are provided. Canoes, paddleboats, kayaks, and sail-

boats can be rented on weekends. Access is free. There is a fee for boat launching.

Water sports, restrictions: Motors are not permitted on the lake. Swimming, windsurfing, and water/body contact are prohibited, but in the summer months an adjacent swimming lagoon is available.

Contact: Lake Elizabeth Boathouse, (510) 791-4340.

About Lake Elizabeth: During the hot summer in the East Bay flats, Lake Elizabeth and the surrounding parkland provide a relatively cool retreat. The lake is located in Fremont's Central Park and covers 80 acres.

Strong afternoon winds create excellent sailing conditions. Sailboats are available for rent on the weekend, but you must have your sailing license with you to rent one.

Although your body is not allowed to come into contact with the water at the lake, an adjacent lagoon provides a cool place to take a dip in the summer and is really one of the best swimming spots in the Bay Area. The park offers full facilities, including a jogging/biking trail, baseball fields, tennis courts, grassy lawns, and picnic areas. Use is heavy in summer; during the remainder of the year you'll encounter only a few picnickers and anglers.

⑩ Shadow Cliffs Lake

Location: In Pleasanton; map E1, grid f9.

Directions: From Interstate 680 take the Pleasanton exit. Turn northeast on Sunol Boulevard and continue to the lake.

Access: There is a paved launch ramp.

Facilities, fees: Picnic areas, fishing docks, and a snack bar are provided. Rowboat, canoe, and paddleboat rentals are available. Some facilities are wheelchair accessible. There are fees for parking and boat launching.

Water sports, restrictions: Boats with electric motors are permitted on the lake (limit 17 feet), but gas-powered engines are

not. There is a sandy beach for swimming and windsurfing.

Contact: Shadow Cliffs Lake, (925) 846-3000; or East Bay Regional Park District, (510) 635-0135, extension 2200.

About Shadow Cliffs Lake: Shadow Cliffs is proof that good ideas do work. Once a good-sized water hole for a former rock quarry, it has since been converted into a lake that offers fishing and boating opportunities.

Warm summer temperatures and clear water make for good swimming. While much of the 75-acre lake is bordered by a steep sloping bank, the beach area offers a gentle grade and warm water. Afternoon winds are fair for windsurfing, making Shadow Cliffs an ideal place for beginners to practice the sport.

The lake is stocked with trout when the water is cool, from fall through spring, then with catfish in the summer. Most of the boaters you'll see are in hot pursuit of those species.

⑪ Sandy Wool Lake

Location: Near Milpitas in Ed Levin County Park; map E1, grid h9.

Directions: From San Jose take Interstate 680 north to Milpitas. Take the Calaveras Road East exit and follow it to the park.

Access: There is no boat ramp. Cartop boats may be hand launched.

Facilities, fees: Rest rooms, golf course, horseback riding trails, and picnic areas are available. A day-use fee is charged.

Water sports, restrictions: Motors are not permitted on the lake. Swimming is not allowed. Windsurfing is permitted, but not recommended.

Contact: Ed Levin County Park, (408) 262-6980; Santa Clara County Parks and Recreation, (408) 358-3741 or fax (408) 358-3245.

About Sandy Wool Lake: At just 14 acres this is a small lake, but it is surrounded by parkland with 16 miles of hiking trails. Nonpowered boats are allowed on the water, which makes it a nice spot to paddle around in a raft, canoe, or rowboat.

Sandy Wool is very popular with families. It is set along a migratory path for waterfowl, so there are always ducks here, including Canada geese in early fall. The youngsters seem to enjoy feeding them. Some kids bring their little remote-controlled model boats and float them around.

Swimming is not allowed, but you probably wouldn't want to swim anyway, because the water is algae-laden and quite shallow. This is also why windsurfing is not recommended; only a small area of the lake is deep enough to windsurf in, and the water is mucky enough to keep windsurfers away. There is plenty of wind, and the park attracts hang gliders.

Use of the park is moderate, mostly by families in the summer. A sprinkling of people come out to fish during the winter months when the lake is stocked with trout.

⑫ Stevens Creek Reservoir

Location: Near Cupertino; map E1, grid h5.

Directions: In San Jose on Interstate 280, take the Foothill Boulevard exit. Drive south on Foothill Boulevard, which becomes Stevens Canyon Road, to the reservoir. The approximate distance from the Foothill Boulevard exit to the reservoir is four miles.

Access: A paved boat ramp is located on the lake's west side.

Facilities, fees: Rest rooms, picnic areas, and hiking and riding trails are available. Fees are charged for lake use and boat launching.

Water sports, restrictions: Electric motors are permitted on the lake, but gas-powered motors are not. Windsurfing is permitted. Swimming is not allowed.

Contact: Stevens Creek County Park, (408) 867-3654; Santa Clara County Parks and Recreation, (408) 358-3741 or fax (408) 358-3245.

About Stevens Creek Reservoir: When full, Stevens Creek is quite pretty, covering 90 acres. It can fill quickly during a series of heavy rains. In other years, though, the place just about dries up in the summer.

This is primarily a small water-storage facility that happens to have pretty surroundings. That means it has marginal boating and recreational appeal. The saving grace is the boat ramp, which at least provides access for small rowboats and canoes. But there's no swimming, no gas motors, and lousy fishing.

While windsurfing is permitted, conditions are marginal at best. Only rarely are there sufficient winds to power a sailboard. Most visitors come here to picnic and look at the lake, not to boat on it.

⑬ Vasona Lake

Location: In Los Gatos; map E1, grid i6.

Directions: Take Highway 17 to the Los Gatos exit and follow the signs to the lake entrance.

Access: A paved launch ramp is located on the lake's west side.

Facilities, fees: Picnic areas, rest rooms, playground, and fishing pier are provided. Rowboats and paddleboats are available for rent. Fees are charged for parking, lake use, and boat launching.

Water sports, restrictions: Motors are not permitted on the lake. Windsurfing is permitted. Swimming is not allowed.

Contact: Stevens Creek County Park, (408) 867-3654; Santa Clara County Parks and Recreation, (408) 358-3741 or fax (408) 358-3245.

About Vasona Lake: This is the kind of place you would visit for a Sunday picnic, maybe getting in a good game of softball or volleyball, and perhaps sailing around in a dinghy or paddling a canoe. The 55-acre lake is bordered by a large grassy area and is a popular destination for families, especially in the summer.

The best thing going here are the boat rentals. This is the only lake in the Santa Clara County Parks and Recreation District where you can rent a boat. Water levels are usually kept high, and the easy accessibility and pretty setting (especially for being so close to so many people) make it quite attractive.

⑭ Campbell Percolation Pond

Location: In Campbell; map E1, grid i7.
Directions: In Campbell on Highway 17, take the Camden Avenue/San Tomas exit. Follow west on San Tomas Avenue to Winchester. Go south on Winchester to Dell Avenue. Turn left and follow the signs to the lake entrance.
Access: Boating is not permitted on the ponds.
Facilities, fees: Rest rooms, water, and a grassy picnic area are available. Fees are charged for parking and day use.
Water sports, restrictions: Swimming is not allowed. Windsurfing is permitted.
Contact: Santa Clara County Parks and Recreation, (408) 358-3741 or fax (408) 358-3245
About Campbell Percolation Pond: A veritable dot of water, this little pond covers a total of just five acres. In the cooler months the water is stocked with trout, while in the summer it provides opportunities for visitors to go windsurfing or model boating.

In fact, one section of the tiny lake is reserved solely for model boats, a real rar-

ity. Throughout the rest of the lake, shoreline fishing (for trout) and windsurfing are allowed.

Windsurfing is quite popular here because on most days the lake gets steady afternoon winds, and conditions are ideal practically every summer afternoon. On weekends, however, it can get crowded.

In the surrounding area you'll also find paths for hiking, biking, and horseback riding.

⑮ Lake Cunningham

Location: In San Jose; map E1, grid i9.
Directions: In San Jose on US 101, drive south to the Tully Road East exit. Follow the signs to the lake.
Access: A boat launch is available.
Facilities, fees: Rest rooms, water, picnic areas, and a small marina are provided. Rowboats, canoes, paddleboats, and sailboats can be rented. A parking fee is charged in the summer months (weekends only in the off-season). There is also a fee for boat launching.
Water sports, restrictions: Motors are not permitted on the lake. Windsurfing is allowed. Swimming in the lake is prohibited, but a swimming lagoon is available at the adjacent Raging Waters park.
Contact: Lake Cunningham Marina, (408) 277-4792; Lake Cunningham Regional Park Headquarters, (408) 277-4319; City of San Jose Parks Department, (408) 277-4573.
About Lake Cunningham: Fifty-acre Lake Cunningham is located adjacent to the Raging Waters water slide, which is the best insurance policy for vacation success a family could possibly ask for. If you have a passel of youngsters who are disappointed because the fish just aren't biting, you can always turn them loose at the water slide.

Although best known for offering fair trout fishing, the lake is a popular spot for sailing and windsurfing as well. The water warms up considerably through April, May, and June, and afternoon winds provide rather good prospects for sailing.

The rules are par for the course for a small lake: no motors and no swimming allowed. Use is moderate in summer, and light the rest of the year.

⑯ Cottonwood Lake

Location: In San Jose at Hellyer County Park; map E1, grid i9.

Directions: In San Jose drive south on US 101 to the Hellyer exit. Follow this exit to Hellyer County Park.

Access: A paved launch ramp is available on the lake's south side.

Facilities, fees: This lake is located in a county park and has full facilities, including rest rooms, water, parking, and picnic areas. Fees are charged for parking and lake use.

Water sports, restrictions: Motors are not permitted on the lake. Windsurfing is allowed. Swimming is prohibited.

Contact: Coyote-Hellyer County Park, (408) 225-0225; Santa Clara County Parks and Recreation, (408) 358-3741 or fax (408) 358-3245.

About Cottonwood Lake: Calling this place a lake is stretching the truth just a bit. It's more like a pond, eight acres in all, but still it's a pretty spot in the center of Hellyer Park. Access is quite easy, a short hop off US 101. It is a favorite local destination for windsurfers and sailboaters, and for others there are good picnic sites and six miles of bike trails.

Like most lakes in Santa Clara County, no motors or swimming are permitted. Those rules make the lake perfect for windsurfing, sailing, and fishing. Fair winds and uncrowded waters are ideal for neophyte windsurfers and sailors in small dinghies. More than anything, Cottonwood is a great picnic spot.

⑰ Lexington Reservoir

Location: Near Los Gatos in the Santa Cruz foothills; map E1, grid j6.

Directions: From Los Gatos drive south on Highway 17. Take the Bear Creek Road exit, turn right, cross over the freeway, and then drive left back on the freeway heading north. Turn right on Alma Bridge Road and drive to the reservoir.

Access: A paved launch ramp is available on the lake's north side.

Facilities, fees: Picnic areas are provided. There is a fee for lake use.

Water sports, restrictions: Motors are not permitted on the lake. Windsurfing is allowed. Swimming is prohibited.

Contact: Lexington Reservoir, (408) 356-2729; Santa Clara County Parks and Recreation, (408) 358-3741 or fax (408) 358-3245.

About Lexington Reservoir: If you ask questions about Lexington Reservoir, you'll get a few yes's and a lot of no's.

Yes, you can windsurf, and it's the best activity possible here. The reservoir is big, 450 acres when full, and gets a predictable 10 to 20 mph wind out of the northwest, so there is plenty of room, calm water, and enough kick to let it rip with a sailboard. In the summer when conditions are ideal, windsurfing traffic can even get heavy. Conditions are also good for piloting small sailboats.

Yes also for fishing, with an improving fishery for largemouth bass. Yes for hand-powered boating and the chance to canoe or row in calm water along the quiet western shore and inlet.

Sound good? Unfortunately there are a few no's. No swimming. No motors on boats. And worst of all, sometimes there is no water.

Even when Lexington fills up, creating this big, beautiful lake, the local water agency just drains it anyway some years. They say it is necessary in order to clear silt from the outlet hole, but in the eyes of the public, they're just taking a pretty spot and turning it into a dust bowl.

⑱ Guadalupe Reservoir

Location: Near Los Gatos; map E1, grid j7.
Directions: From San Jose drive south on the Almaden Expressway. Turn right at Coleman Road and continue for three miles to Camden Avenue. Turn right on Camden Avenue, then immediately left onto Hicks Road. Continue to the reservoir (about four miles from Camden Avenue).
Access: There is no boat ramp. Cartop boats may be hand launched.
Facilities, fees: A picnic area is provided. Fees are charged for parking and lake use.
Water sports, restrictions: Motors are not permitted on the reservoir. Swimming and windsurfing are prohibited.
Contact: Santa Clara County Parks and Recreation, (408) 358-3741 or fax (408) 358-3245.
About Guadalupe Reservoir: If only looking good beat doing good. Guadalupe Reservoir covers 75 acres in the foothills of the Sierra Azul Range just southeast of Los Gatos. It looks so appealing that in the spring newcomers to the area can practically have heart palpitations upon first glance.

But when you actually get out here and maybe fish a little, you discover all kinds of problems. The bass and other fish are contaminated with mercury, courtesy of runoff from a nearby mine, which has since been closed down. In fact, that is why the surrounding parkland was named Quicksilver.

Then you learn about the many things that aren't allowed: no motors, water contact sports, windsurfing, swimming, or wading. There seem to be few fish here, too. Only then do you realize that doing good beats looking good, every time.

So what you end up with is a small lake for nonpowered boating and poor fishing, with nearby picnic spots and some hiking trails, and that's about it.

⑲ Almaden Lake

Location: Near San Jose; map E1, grid j7.
Directions: From San Jose drive south on the Almaden Expressway for about five miles to the lake, located just past the junction with Blossom Hill Road.
Access: A primitive launch ramp is available on the lake's south side.
Facilities, fees: Picnic areas are provided. In the summer months you can rent paddleboats, inflatable canoes, and windsurfing boards. Parking and day-use fees are charged.
Water sports, restrictions: Motors are not permitted on the lake. Windsurfing is allowed. From Memorial Day to Labor Day, you can swim in an adjacent swimming lagoon.
Contact: Almaden Lake, (408) 277-5130.
About Almaden Lake: Don't confuse Almaden Lake with nearby Almaden Reservoir, which doesn't allow boating or water sports. At the reservoir you can do nothing else but fish from the shore.

Almaden Lake, on the other hand, is a perfect destination for families with kids and for beginning windsurfers. Winds are fairly calm but are consistent enough to power some good sailing. The lake is quite small, so it can get crowded with boards on summer weekends.

Motors are not allowed on the lake, which keeps things quiet.

Another bonus is the adjacent swimming lagoon, an excellent perk in the summer for families.

Almaden Reservoir? No. Almaden Lake? Yes.

⑳ Calero Reservoir

Location: Near Coyote; map E1, grid j8.
Directions: From San Jose drive south on US 101 and take the Bernal Road exit. Travel west to the Monterey Highway exit. Take this

exit, head south to Bailey Avenue, and make a right. Follow Bailey Avenue to McKean Road. Turn right and continue about one-half mile to the reservoir entrance.

Access: A paved launch ramp is available on the lake's east side. Launching reservations are required on weekends and holidays.

Facilities, fees: Portable rest rooms and a picnic area are provided. Fees are charged for parking, day use, and boat launching.

Water sports, restrictions: A 35 mph speed limit is strictly enforced. A maximum of 20 personal watercraft per day is set for this reservoir. Windsurfing is permitted. Swimming is not allowed.

Contact: Calero Reservoir, (408) 268-3883; Santa Clara County Parks and Recreation, (408) 358-3741. For boat launching reservations phone (408) 927-9144 or fax (408) 358-3245.

About Calero Reservoir: Calero is the one lake in the Santa Clara County foothills that is often full to the brim, even when other lakes are nearly dry from extended droughts. That makes it very popular for boating, fishing, and all forms of lakeside recreation.

Covering 333 acres, this big lake looks quite pretty in the foothills just west of the south valley, its green water contrasted against the golden hills. Calero is also one of the few lakes in the region that allows powerboating.

To solve the problem of too many boaters showing up at the same time on weekend mornings, the County Parks and Recreation Department has established a special system wherein boaters make reservations for launching priority. Thus they avoid what would otherwise be a real jam.

The powers that be have also resolved the personal watercraft vs. everybody else conflict by setting aside a special water section just for personal watercraft, leaving the rest of the reservoir safe for all other boaters.

Fishing for crappie and bass can be quite good at Calero. However, note the health warnings about eating any fish you catch. The fish are contaminated with mercury from metals leeching in from a nearby mine. Almost everybody follows the catch-and-release rule.

Windsurfing conditions are decent on weekdays, but the reservoir gets so crowded on weekends that boarders are generally better off heading to one of the smaller lakes in the area.

㉑ Chesbro Reservoir

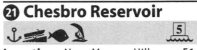

Location: Near Morgan Hill; map E1, grid j9.

Directions: From San Jose drive south on US 101 to the Bernal Avenue exit. Travel west to the Monterey Highway exit. Head south to Bailey Avenue and turn right. Continue on Bailey Avenue to McKean Road and turn left. Follow this road, which becomes Uvas Road, for about five miles to Oak Glen Avenue and then turn left. This road will lead you right to the reservoir.

Access: A paved launch ramp is available on the lake's southeast side.

Facilities, fees: Picnic areas are provided. There is a fee for parking. If the boat ramp is in use, there is a launch fee.

Water sports, restrictions: Electric motors are permitted on the reservoir, but gasoline motors aren't allowed. Windsurfing is permitted. Swimming is prohibited.

Contact: Santa Clara County Parks and Recreation, (408) 358-3741 or fax (408) 358-3245; Coyote Discount Bait & Tackle, (408) 463-0711.

About Chesbro Reservoir: A series of lakes is set in the foothills on each side of the south Santa Clara Valley, including Chesbro, Calero, and Uvas on the west, and Coyote and Anderson on the east. Chesbro, which is most often referred to as Chesbro Dam, is known primarily as a bass fishing lake.

Other prospects for boating and water recreation are poor. Gas-powered motors are not permitted, which sharply limits your boating possibilities. Also, you can't swim here, a shame since this would be a great place for swimming.

Windsurfing is permitted, but winds are typically light, making conditions fair at best, even for beginners who aren't seeking the challenge that comes with a gale. That pretty much leaves the reservoir free for anglers, some of whom take to the water in float tubes, casting into the lake's quiet coves.

㉒ Uvas Reservoir

Location: Near Morgan Hill; map E1, grid j9.

Directions: From San Jose drive south on US 101 to the Bernal Avenue exit. Travel west to the Monterey Highway exit. Take this exit and head south to Bailey Avenue. Turn right. Continue on Bailey Avenue to McKean Road and turn left. Follow this road, which becomes Uvas Road, for about eight miles to the reservoir.

Access: A paved launch ramp is located on the lake's southeast side.

Facilities, fees: A picnic area is provided. A campground is available at Uvas Canyon County Park. A parking fee is charged. If the boat ramp is in use, there is a launch fee.

Water sports, restrictions: Electric motors are permitted on the reservoir, but gasoline motors aren't allowed. Windsurfing is permitted. Swimming is not allowed.

Contact: Santa Clara County Parks and Recreation, (408) 358-3741 or fax (408) 358-3245.

About Uvas Reservoir: South of Chesbro Reservoir (see the preceding listing) is Uvas Reservoir, and conditions at the two are nearly identical.

Uvas gets slightly more use because there's a campground nearby, trout is stocked in late winter, and there are rare periods when bass fishing is excellent. For the most part, it is used primarily by anglers, with boating and water sports just an afterthought.

㉓ Lake Anderson

Location: Near Morgan Hill; map E1, grid j9.

Directions: From San Jose drive south on US 101 toward Morgan Hill. As you come into Morgan Hill, take the Cochran Road East exit and continue to the base of the dam, about 1.5 miles.

Access: A paved ramp is located on the lake's west side, off Cochran Road. Launching reservations are required on weekends and holidays.

Facilities, fees: Picnic areas and rest rooms are provided. There are fees for day use and boat launching.

Water sports, restrictions: A 35 mph speed limit is strictly enforced. Personal watercraft are prohibited. Swimming is not allowed. Waterskiing and windsurfing are permitted.

Contact: Santa Clara County Parks and Recreation, (408) 358-3741 or fax (408) 358-3245. For boat launching reservations phone (408) 927-9144.

About Lake Anderson: Anderson is the boating capital of Santa Clara County. A big lake, it covers nearly 1,000 acres and is set among the oak woodlands and foothills of Mount Hamilton's western slope.

It takes a lot of water to fill the lake, and boating and fishing are only good here when water levels are high. When that occurs, typically after most winters, the place turns into a madhouse on warm weekends.

The lake is long and wide enough for powerboaters to let it rip, and waterskiing is extremely popular on the main lake body. The 35 mph speed limit sets up a kind of game between the jet boaters and the boat patrol, with the speed boaters often gauging just how far they can push it without getting kicked off the lake.

In early summer a midday wind kicks up, making conditions ideal for windsurfing and sailing. Be aware that the wind can really howl here; after all, the lake is set in a canyon. First it gets choppy and uncomfortable, then whitecaps pop up, and then things can get potentially dangerous. When the wind starts to blow, stay alert and don't get caught too far offshore.

On hot weekends and holidays, expect to encounter a lot of people and a lot of boats, including many ski boats. That is the nature of Anderson. If you want quiet water, head over to the section at the lake's south end at the Dunne Avenue Bridge, a popular fishing area where a 5 mph speed limit keeps things sane.

㉔ Coyote Reservoir

Location: Near Gilroy; map E1, grid j9.
Directions: From San Jose drive south on US 101 toward Gilroy. Take the Leavsley Road exit east and drive for about three miles. Turn left on New Avenue and drive to Roop Road. Turn right on Roop Road (it will become Gilroy Hot Springs Road). Drive up over the hill and drop down onto Coyote Lake Road. Continue to the reservoir.
Access: A paved ramp is located on the reservoir's west side.
Facilities, fees: A campground, picnic areas, and rest rooms are provided. Fees are charged for parking, day use, and boat launching.
Water sports, restrictions: A 35 mph speed limit is strictly enforced. A maximum of 40 personal watercraft per day is set for this reservoir. Only one powerboat per five surface acres is permitted. Windsurfing is permitted. Swimming is not allowed. Boats must follow a counterclockwise traffic pat-

tern. Certain sections of the reservoir are designated environmental areas and are subject to a 5 mph speed limit.
Contact: Coyote Lake County Park, (408) 842-7800; Santa Clara County Parks and Recreation, (408) 358-3741 or fax (408) 358-3245.
About Coyote Reservoir: At one time Coyote Reservoir was considered simply an alternative to Lake Anderson, its big brother just to the north. Those days are over. The appeal of this lake has made it equally popular, and a visit here will quickly demonstrate why.

The long, narrow lake is set at an elevation of 770 feet in a valley in the foothills southeast of San Jose. One of only a handful of lakes in the greater Bay Area with a nearby campground, the place is usually packed most summer weekends. All boating is permitted, bass fishing is good during the summer, trout fishing is good in the spring, hiking trails are available along the shoreline, and the entire setting provides a pretty respite from the chaos of crowded San Jose to the north.

Its location is ideal for picking up strong, steady breezes as they sail down the canyon on afternoons in the spring and early summer, making this lake excellent for windsurfing and sailing. The clear, warm waters would also be ideal for swimming, or at least bobbing around in a life jacket, but swimming is not permitted, a real shame.

Regardless, this lake is still a popular spot, one of the best in the Bay Area for campers/boaters.

㉕ Loch Lomond Reservoir

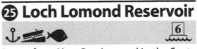

Location: Near Ben Lomond in the Santa Cruz Mountains; map E1, grid j4.
Directions: From the peninsula or Santa Cruz take Highway 9 west into Ben Lomond, turn east at the intersection

with the sign for Loch Lomond Reservoir, and drive to the lake.

From San Jose take Highway 17 south. Take the Mount Hermon Road exit west for about three miles to Graham Hill Road. Turn left and head south on Graham Hill Road for about 0.8 mile. At Zayante Road turn left and travel about 2.5 miles until you reach Lompico Road. Turn left on Lompico and continue for about 1.5 miles until you hit West Drive. Turn left on West Drive and drive until you reach Sequoia Drive. Turn right and continue into the lake area. Sequoia Drive dead-ends there. Most of this route is well-marked.

Access: A paved boat ramp is located on the reservoir's west side.

Facilities, fees: Rest rooms, picnic areas, and a snack bar are provided. Rowboats and fishing boats with electric motors are available for rent. The lake is closed from fall through spring. Fees are charged for day use and boat launching.

Water sports, restrictions: Only boats with electric motors are allowed. Powerboats, sailboats, and windsurfers are not permitted. Swimming is not allowed.

Contact: Loch Lomond Reservoir, (831) 335-7424.

About Loch Lomond Reservoir: Just add water and this is one of the prettiest places in the greater Bay Area.

The lake, which was created when Newell Creek was dammed, is nestled in a long, narrow canyon in the Santa Cruz Mountains. It is a beautiful spot, complete with an island and well forested, with redwoods and firs growing right down the shoreline.

Although the boat ramp is small, it is big enough to handle similarly small aluminum boats with electric motors, rowboats, and canoes. Boat rentals are available at the adjacent dock. Unfortunately, swimming, wading, windsurfing, and other water contact sports are not allowed. Also note that the lake is closed to the public every year from fall through spring.

While most visitors are here for the trout fishing, others do come to row a boat or paddle a canoe for fun. A boat-in picnic site, complete with barbecue, is provided on the island. Imagine that, a boat-in picnic site on an island to call your own.

The surrounding parkland features an excellent hike that parallels the south shore of the lake, then climbs to the small mountain overlooking the water for an incredible view. You gaze down, watch the boats purring around, and realize this is one of the greatest day-trip destinations in the Bay Area.

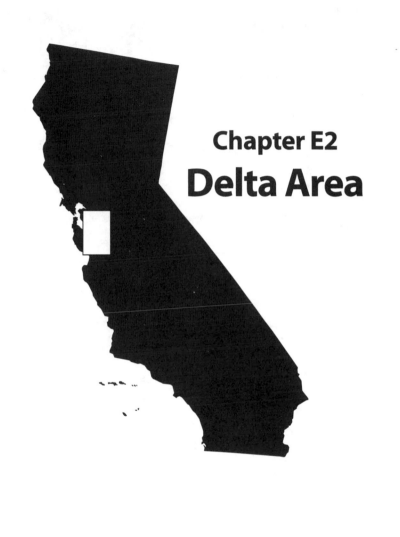

Chapter E2
Delta Area

Overall Rating

| 1 | 2 | 3 | 4 | 5 | 6 | 7 | 8 | 9 | 10 |

Poor .... Fair .... Great

E2–Delta Area Map

One inch equals approximately 10.7 miles.
See page 12 for California state map.

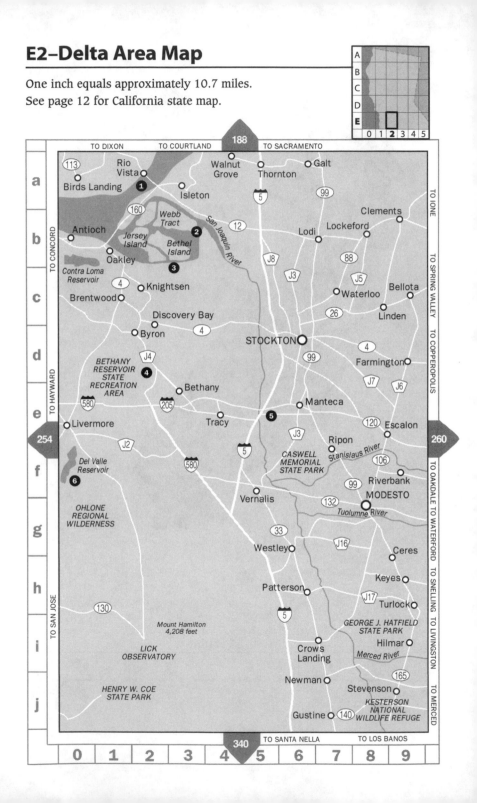

Chapter E2 features:

---

❶ Sacramento River Delta

Location: Near Rio Vista; map E2, grid a2.

Directions: From Sacramento take Interstate 5 south from Sacramento for about 35 miles, turn west on Highway 12, and drive to Rio Vista. See directions to specific access points below.

From the San Francisco Bay Area, take Interstate 80 east to Fairfield, turn east on Highway 12, and drive to Rio Vista. See directions to specific access points below.

Access: Paved boat ramps are available at the following locations:

B&W Resort, Isleton: From Interstate 5 south of Sacramento, turn west on Highway 12 and drive 11 miles. After the second bridge, turn right; the resort is on your immediate left. For information phone (916) 777-6161 or fax (916) 777-5199.

Brannan Island State Recreation Area, Rio Vista: From Interstate 5 south of Sacramento, turn west on Highway 12 and proceed to the sign indicating Brannan Island State Park. Turn and follow the signs into the park. For information phone (916) 777-7701 or fax (916) 777-7703.

Ko-Ket Resort, Isleton: From Interstate 5 south of Sacramento, take the Thornton–Walnut Grove exit and turn left. Drive six miles to the town of Walnut Grove. Continue until you reach a bridge, take a left, and cross it. Turn immediately right onto Highway 160 and continue two miles to the resort on your right. For information phone (916) 776-1488.

Korth's Pirate's Lair Marina, Isleton: From Interstate 5 south of Sacramento, turn west on Highway 12 and drive 11 miles. After the second bridge, turn right onto Brannan Island Road and continue to the marina. For information phone (916) 777-6464.

Vieira's Resort, Isleton: From Interstate 5 south of Sacramento, turn west on Highway 12. Drive all the way to a four-way stop just before the Rio Vista Bridge. Turn right on Highway 160 and travel three miles north to the sign for Vieira's. Turn left and continue into the resort. For information phone (916) 777-6661.

Facilities, fees: Campgrounds are provided at Brannan Island State Recreation Area. Lodging, full-service marinas, and supplies are available at or near many of the boat ramps listed above. Ski boat, personal watercraft, patio boat, and fishing boat rentals are available in Stockton at Herman & Helen's Marina, (209) 951-4634. Korth's Pirate's Lair rents out fishing boats. Most river access is free. There is a day-use fee at Brannan Island State Recreation Area, as well as at some private resorts. Boat launching fees are also charged.

Water sports, restrictions: Waterskiing and personal watercraft are permitted. A sandy swimming beach is available at Brannan Island State Park, which also has a designated windsurfing area called Windy Cove. Another swimming beach is available at Vieira's Resort in Isleton. Numerous beach access points for swimming and windsurfing are available along Highway 160 near Rio Vista.

Contact: Brannan Island State Recreation Area, (916) 777-6671; Bob's Bait in Isleton, (916) 777-6806. For general information phone any of the marinas listed above.

About the Sacramento River Delta:

Some people curse the wind. Some people love it. When the wind is down on a warm summer day, the Sacramento River Delta is a great place to go waterskiing, power-boating, houseboating, and fishing.

Waterskiing is permitted throughout the delta, and the most popular spot along this stretch of the Sacramento River is in the Rio Vista area. The river is wide here, with plenty of room for all water sports, and the water is warmer than farther upstream. There is a good access ramp right at Rio Vista. You'll also find beach access in Rio Vista for swimming and windsurfing.

Boating traffic in the Sacramento River Delta is extremely heavy in the summer. Most boat rentals are booked up on week-ends. One of the reasons it is so popular is that in a boat you gain access to a network of adjoining waterways, many with excellent sheltered areas suitable for water-skiing.

One of the best of these areas is known as the Meadows, and is located on Snodgrass Slough near Walnut Grove. It is fed from the Mokelumne River, not the Sacramento River. A boat launch at Walnut Grove Marina provides nearby access.

There's just one problem on the Sacramento River Delta in the summer: the wind. When temperatures reach the 100 degree range in the Central Valley yet it is foggy on the coast, the wind whistles west, using the river as a passageway. That means rough going for most boating and water sports. These winds tend to come and go in three-day cycles, that is, three days of wind, then three days of calm. Not always, of course, but that is the general pattern.

Some people, however, love the wind, and when it comes to water sports, those people are windsurfers.

When the wind rips across the delta, it turns these waterways into some of the best windsurfing territory in California. The most developed facility in the area for windsurfing (and swimming) is Brannan

Island State Recreation Area. The best place at Brannan Island is Windy Cove, which is rated as one of the top 10 windsurfing spots in the nation.

If you want to avoid the wind, the San Joaquin Delta (see the next listing) provides a number of sloughs and adjoining river waterways with more shelter.

➋ San Joaquin Delta

Location: Near Antioch; map E2, grid b1.
Directions: From Interstate 5 south of Sacramento, take the Highway 12 exit, travel west to Highway 160, turn south, and continue, driving over the Antioch Bridge to Antioch.

From the San Francisco Bay Area, take Interstate 80 east to the Hercules/Rodeo area and turn east onto Highway 4. Drive east on Highway 4 to Antioch.
Access: Launching facilities are available at the following locations:

Ann & Chuck's Boat Harbor, Bethel Island: From Antioch take Highway 4 south to Oakley. Turn left on Cypress Road and continue north to Bethel Island. Once on the island turn right on Stone Road and continue 1.5 miles to the sign for the marina. A paved ramp is available. For information phone (925) 684-2388.

Bethel Harbor, Bethel Island: From Antioch take Highway 4 south to Oakley. Turn left on Cypress Road and continue north to Bethel Island. Continue to the island's northern side and look for Harbor Road. Turn right and proceed to the end of the road. An elevator launch is available. For information phone (925) 684-2141 or fax (925) 684-0450.

Carol's Harbor & Marina, Oakley: From Antioch take Highway 4 south to Oakley. Turn left on Cypress Road and continue north to Bethel Island. Once on the island turn right on Sand Mound Road and continue 200 feet to the marina. A lift is available. For information phone (925) 684-2803.

Eddo's Harbor & RV Park, Rio Vista: From Antioch turn north on Highway 160, drive a short distance; then turn left on Sherman Island–East Levee Road, and continue to Eddo's, located at 19530 East Levee Road. A paved ramp is available. For information phone (925) 757-5314.

Lauritzen Yacht Harbor, Antioch: From Highway 4 in Antioch, take the Wilbur Avenue exit and turn right. Continue to the stop sign and then turn left on Bridgehead Road. Drive one-quarter mile to the sign for the yacht club, turn right, and continue a short distance. A paved ramp is available. For information phone (925) 757-1916.

Russo's Marina & Trailer Park, Bethel Island: From Antioch take Highway 4 south to Oakley. Turn left on Cypress Road and continue north to Bethel Island. Once over the bridge look for Gateway Road and turn right. Proceed to Piper Street, turn left, and follow it to the marina at the end of the road. A paved ramp is available. For information phone (925) 684-2024.

Facilities, fees: Campgrounds are provided in the Bethel Island area, at Eddo's Boat Harbor, and at several places near Stockton. Ski boat, personal watercraft, patio boat, and fishing boat rentals are available in Stockton at Aqua Sports, (209) 334-3272, and Herman & Helen's Marina, (209) 951-4634. Aluminum fishing boat rentals are available at Carol's Harbor & Marina, (925) 684-2803. Lodging and supplies can be obtained in adjacent towns. Fees are charged for parking and boat launching.

Water sports, restrictions: Waterskiing and personal watercraft are permitted all along the delta. Windsurfing and swimming are also allowed, although access is somewhat limited. Two popular spots are Ski Beach and Swing Beach, both located near Frank's Tract. The best beach access is available in the sloughs, which are reachable by boat only.

Contact: For general information phone any of the marinas listed above.

About the San Joaquin Delta: You could go boating every weekend of the year and not see the entire delta in your lifetime. There is just so much of it. Thus it can be inundated with people and boats in the summer, particularly water-skiers, who descend in unbelievable numbers. The place gets wild, with partiers drinking heavily, bikini contests staged at the marinas, and so many boaters having trouble launching and loading their craft that some marinas set up football stands at the ramps so people can sit and watch. For newcomers the sheer number of boats on the water can seem incredible—all kinds, all sizes.

The prime waterskiing areas are in the sloughs, and there are dozens and dozens of them. False River and Old River are two of the best. The sloughs are better protected from winds than the wide-open areas, such as Frank's Tract and Sherman Lake (where the San Joaquin and Sacramento Rivers join), which means smooth, warm water for waterskiing. Don't underestimate the value of these sheltered areas. At times the wind can be howling 15 miles away on the Sacramento River while False River is being stroked by a gentle breeze.

The problem is that these waterways can be narrow in places, meaning there is sometimes limited forward visibility, yet there are a lot of boats out on weekends. That is one of the reasons the law says you must have a spotter on board to watch the trailing water-skier; thus the driver can stay alert to what is going on ahead without watching the action behind the boat and plowing into somebody. To further prevent accidents, sheriff's patrol boats are constantly out to bust boaters in this area who are driving drunk.

Because water-ski traffic is so heavy on weekends, most windsurfers will head instead to Windy Cove near Brannan Island

Map of Chapter E2—Page 270   273

State Recreation Area (see the previous listing). There's no sense battling so many fast boats on the San Joaquin. In addition, most beach areas in the San Joaquin Delta are accessible by boat only.

Anglers, too, have largely been driven from the delta in the summer months by all of the water-ski boats. Some stay and fight, fishing primarily for catfish and small striped bass. The best fishing is from fall through spring, when the main thrust of striped bass migrate through the area, and also when cold water and fog keep the water-skiers at home.

❸ Back Delta

Location: Near Stockton; map E2, grid c3.
Directions: Access is available near Antioch, off Highway 4 near Bethel Island and Frank's Tract; off Interstate 5 at Stockton; and at various sloughs in between. See "Access" for specific directions.
Access: Boat launching facilities are available at the following locations:

Discovery Bay Yacht Harbor, Byron: From Interstate 5 at Stockton, take the Charter Way exit and turn west on Highway 4, driving toward Discovery Bay. Turn north on Discovery Bay Boulevard and follow the signs to the harbor and the paved ramp. Note: Launching costs $30 for nonresidents. For information phone (925) 634-5928.

Herman & Helen's Marina, Stockton: From Interstate 5 north of Stockton, take the Eight Mile Road exit, turn west, and drive to the marina at the end of the road. A paved ramp is available. For information phone (209) 951-4634.

Holland Riverside Marina, Brentwood: From Interstate 5 at Stockton, take the Charter Way exit and turn west on Highway 4. Drive past Discovery Bay to the sign for Knightsen (Byron Highway). Turn right, drive to Delta Road; then turn on

Delta, and proceed to the marina at the road's end. A paved ramp is available. For information phone (925) 684-3667 or fax (925) 684-3902.

King Island Resort, Stockton: From Interstate 5 north of Stockton, take the Eight Mile Road exit and head west. Follow the signs for King Island Resort, which has an elevator launch. For information phone (209) 951-2188.

Ladd's Stockton Marina, Stockton: From Interstate 5 at Stockton, take the March Lane exit and drive 1.5 miles west. A paved boat ramp is located next door to Ladd's Marina. For information phone (209) 477-9521 or fax (209) 477-8595.

Lazy M Marina, Byron: From Interstate 5 south of Stockton, turn west on Interstate 205 and drive west toward Tracy. Turn west on Grant Line Road and follow it until you come to a stop sign at a fire station. Turn right on Byron Highway and continue to Clifton Court Road. Follow the signs to the marina, which has a paved ramp. For information phone (925) 634-4555.

Mossdale Crossing, Lathrop: From Interstate 5 south of Stockton, take the Louise Avenue exit and drive west to a stop sign. Turn right, proceed to the next stop sign, turn left, and continue to the paved ramp at Mossdale Crossing. For information phone Mossdale Marina at (209) 982-0358.

Orwood Resort, Brentwood: From Interstate 5 at Stockton, take the Charter Way exit and drive west on Highway 4 to Discovery Bay. Just past Discovery Bay turn right on Bixler Road. Proceed to the stop sign at the road's end and turn right on Orwood Road. The resort is two blocks down on the right. A paved ramp is available. For information phone (925) 634-2550.

Paradise Point Marina, Stockton: From Interstate 5 north of Stockton, take the Eight Mile Road exit and head west. Drive about 2.5 miles; then turn left on Rio Blanco Road, and continue to the launching area with a paved ramp. For information phone (209) 952-1000 or fax (209) 941-4575.

Tiki Lagun Resort Marina, Stockton: From Interstate 5 at Stockton, take the Charter Way exit and turn west on Highway 4. Drive 5.5 miles to Inland Drive and turn right. Inland Drive turns into McDonald Road; follow the road to the resort. A paved launch is available. For information phone (209) 941-8975.

Turner Cut Resort, Stockton: From Interstate 5 at Stockton, take the Charter Way exit and turn west on Highway 4. Drive 5.5 miles to Inland Drive and turn right. Inland Drive turns into McDonald Road; follow the road to the resort, located just past Tiki Lagun Resort. For information phone (209) 465-4129.

Village West Marina, Stockton: From Interstate 5 at Stockton, take the Benjamin Holt exit and turn west. Benjamin Holt turns into Embarcadero; follow the road until you see a sign for Village West Marina. A paved ramp is available. For information phone (209) 951-1551 or fax (209) 951-9352.

Whiskey Slough Harbor, Holt: From Interstate 5 at Stockton, take the Charter Way exit and turn west on Highway 4. Drive approximately six miles to Whiskey Slough Road. Turn right and continue through a stop sign to Whiskey Slough Harbor, where there is a paved ramp. For information phone (209) 464-3931.

Windmill Cove Marina, Stockton: From Interstate 5 at Stockton, take the Charter Way exit and turn west on Highway 4. Drive 5.5 miles to Inland Drive and turn right. Inland Drive turns into McDonald Road; follow the road to Holt Road (one mile after the road becomes McDonald). Turn right and follow the road to a T intersection at its end; then turn right on Windmill Cove Road and continue to the marina. A paved ramp is available. For information phone (209) 948-6995.

Facilities, fees: Campgrounds, lodgings,

and supplies are available in the Stockton area. Ski boats, personal watercraft, patio boats, and fishing boats can be rented in Stockton at Herman & Helen's Marina, (209) 951-4634. Ski boat and personal watercraft rentals are also available at Five Star Boat Rentals in Stockton. Access is free. Fees are charged for boat launching and parking.

Water sports, restrictions: Waterskiing and personal watercraft are permitted. Swimming and windsurfing access is available in many of the sloughs. Some popular sandy beaches: Orwood Tract, north of Discovery Bay; the Mandeville (south) side of Venice Island, east of Frank's Tract; and Lost Isle, north of Holt.

Contact: For general information contact any of the marinas listed above.

About the Back Delta: Yeah, things get pretty insane here, and that's exactly why so many people like it. There are boats, boats, boats everywhere, and their owners are on mini weekend vacations in which they completely escape the reality of their Monday-to-Friday lives.

And the waterskiing? You've never seen so many boats ripping up and down, with happy folks aboard and bright white wakes trailing behind. By early afternoon on a typical hot summer weekend, enough beer has been consumed that the atmosphere goes from crazed to maniacal in a few hours. That is when the bikini contests get rocking in the marinas, the sheriff shows up and starts arresting people for all manner of violations, a few engines inevitably break down, and people are begging for tows to a marina.

Since the Back Delta is so close to Stockton and Interstate 5, access is easy, and developed marinas get more traffic than any other delta areas. Campgrounds, lodgings, and boat rentals are booked solid, and at times some resorts refuse to allow boat owners to launch unless they have booked a room.

Houseboating is also popular on the

Back Delta, which is on the threshold of a thousand miles of waterways. Houseboats are sometimes the scene of floating parties that start on a Friday evening and continue—often without a break—through Sunday.

If you want to experience sheer insanity, then just try spending a three-day weekend out here. Like I said, that is part of the attraction.

Special note: During low tides a number of sandy beaches are unveiled at numerous small, unnamed islands. You can tie up your boat and spend a couple of hours swimming and sunbathing while water-skiers and personal watercraft buzz by as if you and your friends or family members were slalom gates in a racecourse.

4 Bethany Reservoir

Location: Near Livermore in Bethany Reservoir State Recreation Area; map E2, grid e2.

Directions: From Interstate 580 at Livermore, travel east and take the Altamont Pass exit. Turn right on Altamont Pass Road and travel to Kelso-Christianson Road. Turn right and continue to the park entrance.

Access: A two-lane paved launch ramp is available not far from the first picnic area.

Facilities, fees: Picnic areas and portable toilets are provided. There are fees for day use and boat launching.

Water sports, restrictions: A 5 mph speed limit is strictly enforced. Personal watercraft are not permitted. Windsurfing is allowed; note the speed limit. Swimming is allowed.

Contact: California State Parks, Four Rivers District, (209) 826-1196 or fax (209) 826-0284.

About Bethany Reservoir: Best known as the northern hub for the California Aqueduct Bike Path, on which you can ride for hundreds of miles to points south, this reservoir is part of a day-use recreation area, complete with picnic areas, a good boat ramp, and great windsurfing conditions.

Winds can really kick up here in the afternoon, and while the water is a bit choppy, expert windsurfers are able to catch some great rides. Along with fishing, windsurfing is the most popular activity here.

Bethany Reservoir covers 162 acres and like its cousin to the north, Contra Loma Reservoir, it receives its water via the California Aqueduct. Though there are no restrictions on the size of boats allowed on the lake, a 5 mph speed limit helps keep things quiet.

5 Oakwood Lake

Location: Near Manteca; map E2, grid e6.

Directions: From Interstate 5 south of Stockton, take the Highway 120 exit east and drive to Airport Way. Turn right on Woodward Avenue and drive two miles to the lake on your right.

Access: There is no boat ramp.

Facilities, fees: A campground, store, snack bar, and numerous activities are available. Children's kayaks are available for rent. There is an entrance fee.

Water sports, restrictions: Motors are not permitted on the lake. Windsurfing is allowed, but you must wear a life jacket. Life jackets are also required for all other boaters. Swimming is not permitted.

Contact: Oakwood Lake Resort, (209) 239-2500.

About Oakwood Lake: Oakwood Lake Resort is basically a big funpark for the kiddies. The attractions include the famous high-tech Manteca Water Slides, "river rapid" rides, video arcades, roller skating rink, playgrounds, bungee jumping, movie theater, bingo, and a softball field. And for those who want to spend more than one day here, there's a 400-site campground.

No motors are allowed on the lake, but all human-powered craft, including sailboards, are welcome. Life jackets are required. There are bass and catfish in the lake, but only resort guests are permitted to fish. Get the picture? Right, this is the kind of place where you bring the youngsters on a hot summer day so they can have the time of their lives.

---

❻ Del Valle Reservoir

⚓🚤🏕️🐟🏊🛶   7️⃣

Location: Southeast of Livermore in Lake Del Valle State Recreation Area; map E2, grid f0.

Directions: In Livermore on Interstate 580, take the North Livermore Avenue exit. Turn south and travel on North/South Livermore Road (this will turn into Tesla Road) to Mines Road. Turn right and drive about three miles south on Mines Road to Del Valle Road. Turn right and continue for four miles to the lake entrance.

Access: A multilane paved boat ramp is available at the end of the entrance road.

Facilities, fees: A campground and several picnic areas are provided. There are paved walking and bicycling trails. A full-service marina offers fishing boat, rowboat, patio boat, paddleboat, and canoe rentals. The facilities are wheelchair accessible. Fees are charged for parking and boat launching.

Water sports, restrictions: A 10 mph speed limit is strictly enforced. Windsurfing is permitted; note the speed limit. A large, sandy beach is available at the day-use area, and you can swim all along the shoreline.

Contact: East Bay Regional Park District, (510) 635-0135, ext. 2200; Del Valle Regional Park, (925) 373-0332; Del Valle Marina, (925) 449-5201.

About Del Valle Reservoir: Here is one of the Bay Area's top adventurelands for fishing, camping, boating, and hiking.

Del Valle Reservoir sits in a long, narrow canyon in Alameda County's foothill country south of Livermore, covering 750 acres with 16 miles of shoreline. This is one of the few lakes in the Bay Area that provides camping, rental boats, and a good ramp for powerboats. On top of all that, the trailhead for the Ohlone Wilderness Trail is located nearby.

In the summer the weather gets very hot around here and hordes of sunbathers, swimmers, and boaters cram into the park. Only the 10 mph speed limit keeps the scene from turning into something like the weekend nuthouse over at the nearby delta. Despite the speed restriction, almost everybody is having fun; after all, it beats working, and the big lake and adjoining park provide a great place for a respite from the rat race.

Swimming and water sports are permitted year-round, but the water gets cold in the winter and spring. The prime time for swimming is from May to September, when lifeguards are posted at the beaches.

The wind is strong on spring and summer afternoons, making windsurfing here very popular. However, experts may find the speed limit confining.

One great thing about Del Valle is that the trout fishing has improved. Not only are the catch rates good, but there's a sprinkling of huge rainbow trout in the eight- to 12-pound class. In addition, there are also some large striped bass swimming around, providing a wild card challenge for the ambitious few.

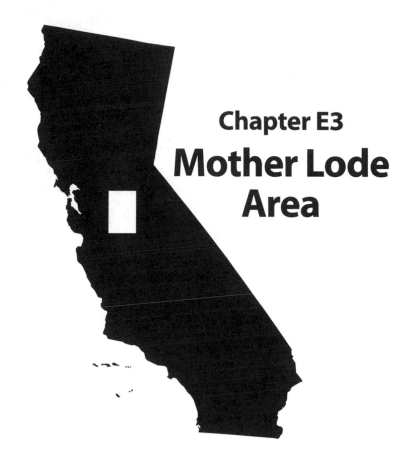

Chapter E3
Mother Lode
Area

Overall Rating

1	2	3	4	5	6	7	8	9	10

Poor .... Fair .... Great

E3–Mother Lode Area Map

One inch equals approximately 10.7 miles.
See page 12 for California state map.

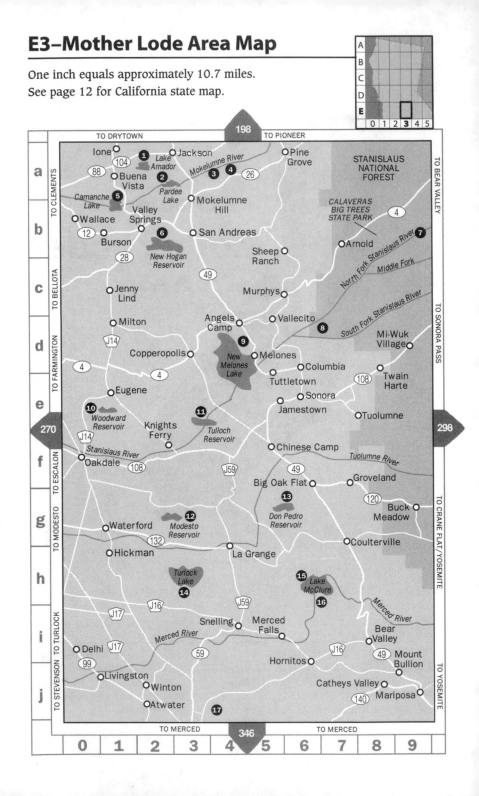

Chapter E3 features:

❶ Lake Amador

⌁⚓≋🏕🐟⛵   5

Location: Northeast of Stockton; map E3, grid a1.

Directions: From Stockton drive 24 miles east on Highway 88/12. Just east of Clements continue straight on Highway 12 and drive about 11 miles. Turn right on Jackson Valley and drive four miles to Lake Amador Drive. Continue to the lake.

Access: A paved boat ramp is available at Lake Amador Marina, located just off Lake Amador Drive.

Facilities, fees: Campgrounds, picnic area, groceries, gas, showers, and a snack bar are available at the lake. There is a small marina where you can rent fishing boats. Fees are charged for day use, fishing permits, and boat launching.

Water sports, restrictions: A 5 mph speed limit is enforced within the coves and around the marina. Waterskiing, personal watercraft, and windsurfing are not allowed. A sandy swimming pond is available near the campgrounds.

Contact: Lake Amador Marina, (209) 274-4739 or fax (209) 274-6755.

About Lake Amador: Yeah, this lake seems like it was planted on Earth for one reason: fishing.

Although there is a campground and swimming pond nearby, Amador is better known for providing excellent fishing for trout and bass, with good catch rates for rainbow trout and a fair number of giant Florida bass. The lake is set at an elevation of 485 feet in the foothill country east of Stockton, covering 425 acres with 13.5 miles of shoreline. Of the four lakes in the immediate area—Camanche, Pardee, New Hogan, and Amador—it is Amador and Pardee that have enacted the most restrictive boating rules to guarantee that anglers have quiet water and the best chances for success.

That means no waterskiing, personal watercraft, or windsurfing. And while swimming is not prohibited, much of the shoreline is rocky, swimming access is poor, and hey, with a one-acre pond specifically designated for swimming near the campground, you never see people taking a dunk in the lake. The pond is family oriented, with a playground, water slide, and gently sloping sandy beaches. Use is high year-round, the campground is often full in early summer, and reservations are suggested. There are also hiking and mountain biking trails in the area.

❷ Pardee Lake

⌁⚓≋🏕🐟   5

Location: Northeast of Stockton; map E3, grid a2.

Directions: From Stockton drive 24 miles east on Highway 88/12. Just east of Clements continue straight on Highway 12 and drive 11 miles to Jackson Valley Road.

Turn right and drive to the four-way stop at Buena Vista. Turn right and drive about three miles to Stony Creek Road on the the left. Turn left and drive about one mile to the lake.

Access: A paved ramp is available at Pardee Recreation Area, located on the northeastern arm of the lake.

Facilities, fees: A campground, picnic area, restaurant, gas, coin laundry, and groceries are available. A full-service marina offers fishing boat rentals. Fees are charged for day use and fishing permits.

Water sports, restrictions: No body contact with the water is permitted, which rules out waterskiing, personal watercraft, and swimming. A large swimming pool is available at the campground.

Contact: Pardee Recreation Area, (209) 772-1472.

About Pardee Lake: Of all the lakes in the Mother Lode country, Pardee is the prettiest, covering more than 2,000 acres with 43 miles of shoreline. It is most beautiful in early spring, when the lake is full, the hills are green, and the wildflowers are blooming. And one other thing: the trout are biting then, too.

Like Amador, this lake was designed exclusively for fishing. Waterskiing, swimming, and windsurfing are prohibited. While there is no designated speed limit for boats, most boaters heed a "common courtesy" rule, making the lake safe and comfortable, even those with small, low-speed craft, such as canoes or small fishing boats. Pardee has full facilities for boating, even a marina, and in spring this is the ideal destination for the camper/boater/angler.

The lake opens each year in mid-February, often kicking right off with good trolling for trout and kokanee salmon. With good fishing and good weather, it doesn't take long before the campground can get quite crowded.

Many families take advantage of the swimming pool near the campground, which tends to be deluged with throngs of youngsters and their parents.

---

❸ Mokelumne River

Location: Northeast of Stockton; map E3, grid a4.

Directions: From Stockton drive 24 miles east on Highway 88/12 to the town of Clements. Continue on Highway 88 past Camanche Lake and Pardee Lake. At Martell turn south on Highway 49/88, drive through Jackson, and continue to Electra Road. Turn east on Electra Road and drive east. The river is accessible off this road for four miles upstream to the Electra powerhouse.

Access: There is no boat ramp. Kayakers, canoeists, and inner tubers can put in just below Electra Powerhouse (see directions). Take out three miles downstream at the Highway 49 bridge.

Facilities, fees: A PG&E picnic area is provided on Electra Road. Access to the river is free.

Water sports, restrictions: Swimming access is available at Electra Picnic Area.

Contact: Bureau of Land Management, Folsom Field Office, (916) 985-4474. PG&E Building & Land Services, (916) 386-5164 or fax (916) 386-5388. For guided kayak or canoe trips or lessons, contact California Canoe & Kayak, (800) 366-9804.

About the Mokelumne River: Much of the Mokelumne River has been devastated by low flows, toxic runoff, and channelization by the East Bay Municipal Utility District, but this short three-mile stretch provides a window to the way the entire river once was. It's a great spot for inner tubing and easy kayaking and is decent for swimming.

The rafting season is a long one, from March to September, when the river features warm water and good scenery. It's an easy river to kayak, mostly Class I with a couple of Class II rapids, ideal for beginning and practicing kayakers (especially in inflatable kayaks), as well as for inner tubers.

The three-mile-long run cuts through the Gold Rush towns of Jackson and Mokelumne Hill, and there are many historic sites in the area. By far the best spot for swimming is at Electra Picnic Area. While use is moderate, and no guided trips are available, there can be lots of inner tubers here on hot summer weekends, and kayaking is extremely popular in the spring and early summer.

But there is a major problem. The river is a prisoner of water releases, which means that flows can fluctuate wildly according to the whims of the water master, not rainfall and snowmelt. You should always call the Bureau of Land Management to check flow levels before scheduling a trip on the Mokelumne.

❹ Lake Tabeaud

Location: Near Jackson; map E3, grid a4.
Directions: From Stockton drive approximately 45 miles east on Highway 88/12 to the town of Jackson. Turn south on Highway 49 and drive one-half mile; then turn left on Clinton Road. Drive five miles east, then turn right on Pine Grove–Tabeaud Road, and continue two miles to the lake.
Access: No boat ramp is available. Cartop boats may be hand launched.
Facilities, fees: A picnic area is provided by PG&E. Supplies can be obtained in Jackson. Access to the lake is free.
Water sports, restrictions: Motors are not allowed on the lake. Swimming is not allowed. The lake is too small for windsurfing.
Contact: PG&E Building & Land Services, (916) 386-5164 or fax (916) 386-5388
About Lake Tabeaud: It is always funny to hear people try to pronounce the name of this lake on their first visit. My pal Foonsky, who commonly mangles names, called it

Lake "Tay-Be-A-Ud," then smiled like he screwed it up on purpose. Yeah, surrrre.

It's pronounced "Tah-Bow." Got it, Foonsky?

An hour's drive east of Stockton, the lake is set at an elevation of 2,000 feet, just high enough to keep the water cool into early summer. The lake gets light use, primarily by anglers.

The surrounding area is pretty and attracts a small amount of vacation traffic. No motors are permitted, which limits boating to rowboats, canoes, and inflatables. Swimming and windsurfing are also not allowed, just paddling, fishing, and picnicking. That's about it. And sometimes that's just plenty.

❺ Camanche Lake

Location: Northeast of Stockton; map E3, grid b1.
Directions: From Stockton drive 24 miles east on Highway 88/12. Just east of Clements bear left on Highway 88 and drive six miles to Comanche Parkway. To access the south shore, turn left and drive six miles to the entrance gate. To reach the north shore, turn right and drive seven miles to the Comanche Northshore entrance.
Access: Multilane paved boat ramps are available at both recreation areas (see the directions).
Facilities, fees: Campgrounds, picnic areas, lodging, and groceries are available at the lake. Both resorts offer full-service marinas and rent out fishing boats and patio boats. Fees are charged for day use and boat launching.
Water sports, restrictions: Waterskiing and personal watercraft are permitted only on the lake's lower portion. Windsurfing is permitted anywhere, as is swimming. There are no designated beach areas, but almost all of the shoreline is rocky or sandy and gradually sloped.

Contact: North Shore Marina, (209) 763-5166; South Shore Marina, (209) 763-5915.

About Camanche Lake: Camanche is a large, multifaceted facility that covers 7,700 acres and has 53 miles of shoreline. It is set in the foothills east of Lodi at an elevation of 325 feet. Here you will find the best of everything—boating, camping, fishing, waterskiing, swimming, and windsurfing—with enough space for everyone and rules to keep user conflicts to a minimum.

The water is clear and warm, resorts and campgrounds are available at both the north and south ends of the lake, and as you might expect, visitor turnout is high, especially during the peak months in late spring and early summer.

All boating is allowed on the lake, but fast boats are prohibited in the northern end. In the typical scenario anglers work the lake's northern end and water-skiers and personal watercraft take over the southern portion. On busy summer weekends this works out just fine.

Windsurfing conditions at Camanche Lake are excellent because the afternoons are breezy just about every day. Most windsurfers will plunk their sailboards in the water near the campgrounds, then venture out from there. When the wind comes up on summer afternoons, it is ideal for windsurfing, with hot weather, warm surface temperatures, and enough wind to get you sailing along at a good clip. By late in the afternoon, most of the anglers and many of the water-skiers have quit for the day, leaving the lake to the windsurfers.

The swimming is also good here. Most people sunbathe for a spell, then jump into the lake to cool off and have a little fun. While there are no designated swimming beaches, much of the shoreline has suitable access; the two most popular spots are at Campers Cove on the north shore and the area near the snack bar on the south shore.

One constant concern at Camanche is the water level. This lake can get extremely low when the snowpack is light in the Sierra Nevada and the resulting melt-off is minimal, particularly during the late summer and fall. In a year that has seen a low mountain snowpack, you are advised to call ahead before finalizing your plans.

❻ New Hogan Reservoir

Location: Northeast of Stockton; map E3, grid b2.

Directions: From Stockton drive about 35 miles east on Highway 26 to Valley Springs. Turn southeast on Hogan Dam Road and drive four miles to the reservoir.

Access: Three paved ramps are available at the marina, and one adjacent to the campgrounds. All ramps can be accessed from the entrance road; watch for signs.

Facilities, fees: Two drive-in campgrounds and one boat-in campground are provided. A picnic area, showers, gas, golf course, and groceries are available. There's a full-service marina that offers fishing boat rentals. A day-use fee is charged.

Water sports, restrictions: A 5 mph speed limit is enforced around the coves. Waterskiing, personal watercraft, and windsurfing are permitted on the lake's main body. After sundown boating is restricted to 15 mph. Swimming access is available all along the shoreline; a popular spot is at Wrinkle Cove, located off the entrance road into the lake.

Contact: New Hogan Reservoir, (209) 772-1462.

About New Hogan Reservoir: New Hogan is a big lake, covering 4,000 acres with 50 miles of shoreline. There are many good spots along the eastern shore near Deer Flat that are suitable for boat-in camping. It's that last factor that makes this a tremendous vacation spot for anglers who have boats and want to camp overnight.

All water sports are popular here. The

large marina provides three boat ramps, docks, moorings, dry storage, and boating supplies. Since the water is quite warm in the summer, swimming, waterskiing, and windsurfing are extremely popular. The place is consistently packed from Memorial Day to Labor Day.

In addition, numerous sandy areas are available all along the shoreline for swimming, although none is designated specifically for that activity. Some boaters will pull up at one of these spots for a picnic, and the youngsters aboard will jump out and cavort in the shallows. In a few of these areas, the underwater drop-off is steep, so kids should always wear life jackets.

A fair lake for fishing, New Hogan Reservoir offers the unique opportunity to try to fish for striped bass. Of the four lakes in the immediate area, Amador attracts anglers who are looking for bass and trout, Camanche gets those who want bass and crappie, Pardee lures anglers seeking trout and kokanee salmon, while New Hogan gets those who are in search of stripers and largemouth bass.

A 5 mph speed limit in the coves keeps the atmosphere decent enough for fishing. That leaves the rest of this big lake wide open for fast boats, and on hot summer days, they really let it rip out here.

❼ North Fork Stanislaus River

Location: Near Arnold in Stanislaus National Forest; map E3, grid b9.

Directions: From the junction of Highways 4 and 49 at the town of Angels Camp, turn east on Highway 4 and drive approximately 28 miles, through Arnold, to Dorrington. Turn south on Boards Crossing Road and continue down to the river. Access is also available at Calaveras Big Trees State Park on Highway 4.

Access: There is no boat ramp. To reach the rafting put-in, follow the directions above to Boards Crossing Road, and then drive four miles to Sourgrass Campground. Put in on the left bank above the bridge. Note: A difficult Class V drop is located immediately downstream of the put-in; boaters who wish to avoid it can put in below the rapid (on the right bank). Take out just downstream of the bridge when you reach Calaveras Big Trees State Park.

Facilities, fees: Campgrounds are available on Boards Crossing Road and at Calaveras Big Trees State Park. Picnic areas are provided. Supplies can be obtained in Dorrington and Arnold. Access is free except at Calaveras Big Trees State Park, where an entrance fee is charged. Rafting permits are not required.

Water sports, restrictions: Excellent swimming areas are available near Sourgrass Campground, Boards Crossing Campground, and at Calaveras Big Trees State Park. Farther downstream is a popular area called Candy Rock, which is accessed by taking Hunter Dam Road south off Highway 4 (just east of Hathaway Pines) for five miles to the river. Several large pools and rock slides are available.

Contact: Stanislaus National Forest, Calaveras Ranger District, (209) 795-1381 or fax (209) 795-6849; Calaveras Big Trees State Park, (209) 795-2334. For guided rafting trips contact All-Outdoors Whitewater Rafting, (800) 247-7238; Beyond Limits Adventures, (800) 234-7238; Whitewater Voyages, (800) 488-7238; or Zephyr River Expeditions, (209) 532-6249.

About the North Fork Stanislaus River: Beautiful, wild, and exciting—this stretch of river has everything going for it but length. Only the rafting run's relatively short length, a mere five miles, keeps the North Fork Stanislaus from snagging the highest rating.

Rated as Class IV–V, the run is ideal for most rafters, difficult enough for plenty of excitement, yet with only one truly mind-bending piece of white water. That stretch, Sourgrass Ravine, will launch you to the edge and beyond, then release you back to your senses, as well as to the seat of your raft. The scenery is beautiful, with big granite boulders peppered about the river, and pines and sequoias lining much of the adjacent shore, plus a sprinkling of fragrant azaleas.

Not only is the run short, but right out of the starting gate you encounter the big one, Sourgrass Ravine, a Class V monster. After conquering that (or not), you face a number of challenging Class IV rapids and drops, including Beginner's Luck, Sierra Gate, The Claw, Convulsion, Wallet Slot, and Emerald Falls. You couldn't demand more from a five-miler.

The water is clear, cold, and beautiful. How cold? In the spring dry suits or wet suits are mandatory, but they become optional by summer, when temperatures are considerably warmer. In most years the season runs from April through August, though it can be shortened due to a low snowpack and the resultant minimal melt-off.

Only a few commercial companies are permitted to raft here, so the water is significantly less crowded than the main stem Stanislaus. Regardless, it is becoming increasingly popular, especially among non-guided experts who want a trip that can be completed in a day.

The North Fork Stanislaus is a real favorite for swimming and sunbathing, with the most popular spot being at Candy Rock. Note that this is an infamous spot for nudists, not a typical hangout for families from Stockton. There are natural and man-made rock slides here, as well as several large, deep pools, and the water is warmer than at places farther upstream.

Families are better off heading to the series of pools located about a mile upstream past Sourgrass Campground; there's a parking area there and a short hiking trail down to the swimming hole.

8 Stanislaus River

Location: Above New Melones Reservoir to below Knights Ferry; map E3, grid c7.

Directions: To access the river section above New Melones Reservoir, start at the junction of Highways 4 and 49 at Angels Camp and head east on Highway 4. Access is available off Parrott's Ferry Road. Below New Melones access is available near Knights Ferry on Highway 108/120.

Access: No boat ramp is available. There are three standard runs on the main Stanislaus:

Camp Nine Run: To reach the put-in, drive east of Angels Camp on Highway 49 for approximately five miles to Parrott's Ferry Road. Turn right, drive about 1.5 miles south, turn left on Camp Nine Road, and continue nine miles to the put-in. Take out nine miles downstream at the old Parrott's Ferry Bridge. Note: This river section can be run only when drought conditions allow New Melones Reservoir to recede. Always call ahead for conditions.

Goodwin Canyon Run: To reach the put-in, start at Oakdale on Highway 108/120 and continue east on Highway 108/120 for approximately 17 miles to Tulloch Road. Turn left and drive north to the river. Put in one-half mile downstream from the dam. Take out four miles downstream at Knights Ferry, just down from the bridge. Note: This river section is rated Class V and is for experts only. It can be run only when water is released from the dam upstream, usually in spring and fall. Call ahead to check conditions.

Knights Ferry Run: From Oakdale drive east on Highway 108/120 to the town of Knights Ferry. Put in at the new bridge. The standard take-out is eight miles downstream at Orange Blossom Park, although there are several other access points.

Facilities, fees: Campgrounds are available around New Melones Reservoir and at

Knights Ferry. Canoes and kayaks can be rented at River Journey or Sunshine River Adventures. Supplies are available along Highway 4. Access is free. Rafting permits are not required.

Water sports, restrictions: The river is generally too dangerous for swimming upstream of Knights Ferry, although there are some good swimming areas that can be accessed by boat. Downstream, swimming is available at several parks along Highway 108/120. A good one is Knights Ferry Resort in Knights Ferry.

Contact: For guided trips or information about the Camp Nine Run or the Goodwin Canyon Run, contact Ahwahnee Whitewater Expeditions, (800) 359-9790; All-Outdoors Whitewater Rafting, (800) 247-2387; ARTA, (800) 323-2782; American Whitewater Expeditions, (818) 352-3205; Beyond Limits Adventures, (800) 234-7238; Mother Lode River Trips, (530) 626-4187; OARS, Inc, (800) 346-6277; RAM River Adventures, (800) 466-7238; Sierra Mac River Trips, (800) 457-2580; Sunshine River Adventures, (800) 829-7238; or Zephyr River Expeditions, (209) 532-6249. For guided trips, information, or raft and canoe rentals for the Knights Ferry Run, contact River Journey, (209) 847-4671, or Sunshine River Adventures, (800) 829-7238.

About the Stanislaus River: You get everything from heaven to hell on the Stanislaus River, sometimes on the same day.

At one time this was one of the premier rafting runs in America, and in drought years it still is. I'm referring, of course, to the Camp Nine Run, the sensational and beautiful stretch of white water that is drowned in high water years when the water backs up the river canyon from the enlarged New Melones Dam. During a drought the water level at New Melones Reservoir drops to the point that the Camp Nine Run reemerges to be treasured more than ever.

In high water years, however, two other runs are available: the Goodwin Canyon Run, which is exciting and challenging, and the Knights Ferry Run, an easy float. Here are the details of both, followed by a synopsis of the Camp Nine Run:

Goodwin Canyon Run: As it pours through an untouched granite canyon in a wilderness setting, this stretch of water can only be called beautiful. The Class V white water is exciting and difficult, winding through a narrow canyon with steep rapids and drops, and is a favorite among the commercial rafting companies. The highlights are Mr. Toad's (Class V), Off-Ramp (Class V–VI), Pinball (Class III–V), and Haunted House (Class V). Off-Ramp was not named haphazardly; it is treated like an off-ramp by many rafters who choose to portage this scary piece of white water.

Note that this river section can be run only when the water masters see fit to release enough water downstream to get it going. This usually happens twice a year, once in spring and again in fall.

Knights Ferry Run: Not to worry, this is an easy float, all Class I water with one Class II rapid, Russian Rapid. Rafts and canoes can be rented at Sunshine River Adventures and River Journey, which also provide shuttle services. The Knights Ferry Run is a great opportunity for newcomers, and most people adopt the do-it-yourself approach, alternating between paddling and floating, and stopping occasionally to jump in and swim. Half-day to multiday trips can be arranged, depending on one's schedule. Most people take out within 10 miles of Knights Ferry, but it is possible to float about 45 miles downstream, all the way to the San Joaquin River confluence.

Camp Nine Run: Talk about a heartbreaker. This is one of the saddest stories in rafting history: For many years the Stanislaus was considered one of the prime stretches of water in the state and was run more often than any other river. But that all changed in 1982, when the New Melones Dam was built, creating New Melones Reservoir and backing up the lake so far that it covered the entire Camp Nine Run. Now it can only be run in drought conditions, when lake levels are lowered enough for the river to emerge. Boaters were delighted when this occurred from about 1987 to 1994. Although droughts are typically devastating for boating, this place is the exception.

When it can be run, it's fantastic. The river cuts through the deepest limestone canyon in the country, flowing past tree-lined banks and beautiful wildflower displays. Most companies do not require their customers to have previous experience in order to raft it, even though there is one Class IV drop, called Big Dog, located just below the put-in. The remaining rapids are rated Class III and include Rock Garden, Death Rock, Devil's Staircase, Bailey Falls, and Widowmaker. A bonus on the Stanislaus is that there's good swimming in eddies and pools at the bottoms of deep canyons.

So you see, this river has everything: dramatic canyon beauty, plenty of excitement, one mind-bending rapid, seclusion, and great swimming. Alas, in most years it is flooded out, now typically the headwaters of New Melones Reservoir.

❾ New Melones Reservoir

Location: Near Sonora; map E3, grid d4.
Directions: From the San Francisco Bay Area, drive east on Interstate 580 past Livermore; continue east on Interstate 205 until it bisects Interstate 5. Drive north on Interstate 5 for two miles. Turn east on Highway 120 and continue through Manteca and Oakdale (where it becomes Highway 108/120) to Sonora (some small roads west connect to the lake). At Sonora turn north on Highway 49 and drive north to the lake. Turnoffs are available for Tuttletown Recreation Area and farther north, Glory Hole Recreation Area.

Access: There are three paved boat ramps, two at Glory Hole Recreation Area and one at Tuttletown Recreation Area. Watch for signs indicating access off Highway 49.
Facilities, fees: Campgrounds and picnic areas are provided. A full-service marina and fishing boat, patio boat, ski boat, and houseboat rentals are available at New Melones Lake Marina. Supplies can be obtained in Sonora. Access is free. There is no fee for boat launching.
Water sports, restrictions: Waterskiing, personal watercraft, and windsurfing are permitted. A sandy swimming beach is available at Glory Hole Recreation Area, on the Angel Arm of the lake.
Contact: US Bureau of Reclamation, New Melones Lake, (209) 536-9094; New Melones Lake Marina, (209) 785-3300 or fax (209) 785-3303.
About New Melones Reservoir: Rafters may hate this lake (to find out why, see the preceding listing, Stanislaus River), but boaters love it.

When full, it is huge, covering 12,500 acres with more than 100 miles of shoreline, so there's plenty of room for all boating and water sports. It is set in the valley foothills near Angels Camp at an elevation of 1,085 feet.

New Melones is still getting established as a recreational facility, with relatively new campgrounds, and still more on the drawing board. The response to this lake has been phenomenal, and if the Bureau of Reclamation doesn't make good on its promises made in the 1980s to add more campgrounds, the whole lot of bureau officials should be strung up to the yardarm.

The place gets very crowded on summer weekends. On holiday weekends it resembles something like an aquatic zoo on parade. Weekdays are much more quiet.

Temperatures are warm, the surface waters are perfect for waterskiing, personal watercraft, and swimming, and there is so much water that low-speed anglers and high-speed boaters have room to stay out of each other's way. For the most part, fishermen stick to the lake's upper arms, while the high-speed boaters head to the more open, main lake body.

All water sports are permitted. Waterskiing and houseboating are particularly popular. When there are afternoon winds, common in the spring and early summer, it is possible to windsurf. Swimming is limited to the swimming beach; elsewhere the shoreline is fairly rocky or tree-lined.

⑩ Woodward Reservoir

Location: Near Oakdale in Woodward Reservoir County Park; map E3, grid e1.
Directions: From Stockton drive south on Highway 99 to Manteca. Turn east on Highway 120 and travel about 20 miles to County Road J14/Twenty-Six Mile Road. Turn left (north) and drive five miles to the reservoir.
Access: Three boat ramps are available: a paved, multilane ramp at the marina (go left at the stop sign at the entrance), a paved ramp at Area 24 (turn right at the stop sign), and another paved ramp at Heron Point (turn right at the stop sign).
Facilities, fees: Developed and primitive campsites and picnic areas are provided. There is a full-service marina where you can rent rowboats, paddleboats, canoes, and personal watercraft. Groceries and a snack bar are also available. Fees are charged for day use; boat launching is included.
Water sports, restrictions: Waterskiing, personal watercraft, and windsurfing are permitted. Swimming is available at Office Point, near the marina; that is also the best spot for windsurfing.
Contact: Woodward Reservoir County Park, Stanislaus County, (209) 847-3304.
About Woodward Reservoir: The only solution to the waterskiing vs. fishing con-

flict is to separate the two groups. At Woodward Reservoir that is exactly what has happened. May each go thine own separate way and live in peace and happiness.

The two large coves on the lake's south and east ends, as well as the area behind Whale Island, are for low-speed boats only; no waterskiing or personal watercraft. Meanwhile, the jet boats have full run of the main lake, where they can make all the fun they want. This is an example of the correct way to organize a recreational lake.

Woodward covers 2,900 acres with 23 miles of shoreline, set in the rolling foothills just north of Oakdale at an elevation of 210 feet.

All boating is allowed, but note the aforementioned restrictions designed to prevent user conflicts. In addition to powerboating sports, windsurfing and swimming are excellent at Woodward Reservoir. The best area for windsurfing is at Office Point, located on the west side of the lake, near the marina. This is also the best place for swimming.

Because this is one of the largest reservoirs in the area near Modesto and Stockton, it gets lots of local traffic, especially on summer weekends. It can be extremely hot here in July and August, and by the end of summer, jumping in the lake may feel like stepping into a large hot tub.

⑪ Tulloch Reservoir

Location: Near Jamestown; map E3, grid e3.
Directions: From Stockton drive south on Highway 99 to Manteca. Turn east on Highway 120 and travel 35 miles, just east of Knights Ferry. Turn north on Tulloch Road to get to the south shore, or continue for 10 more miles on Highway 108/120 to Byrnes Ferry Road and turn left to reach the north shore.

Access: There are three boat ramps:

Copper Cove: From Highway 108/120 turn north on Byrnes Ferry Road and drive approximately seven miles to Copper Cove, where there is a paved ramp. Note: The ramp is extremely steep, and getting boats out is often difficult.

Poker Flat: From Highway 108/120 turn north on Byrnes Ferry Road and drive approximately five miles to Lake Tulloch Resort. A paved ramp is available.

South Shore: From Highway 108/120 east of Knights Ferry, turn north on Tulloch Road and drive four miles to Lake Tulloch Marina, where there is a multilane paved ramp.

Facilities, fees: A campground is available at South Shore. Day-use areas are provided on both sides of the lake. Shower facilities, coin laundry, groceries, lodging, restaurant, and a bar are available at the lake. At South Shore there's a full-service marina and a place to rent fishing boats, pontoon boats, and personal watercraft. Another marina, as well as rentals of ski boats, patio boats, and fishing boats, is located at Poker Flat. Fees are charged for day use and boat launching.

Water sports, restrictions: Waterskiing, personal watercraft, and windsurfing are permitted. Large, sandy swimming beaches are available at South Shore and Poker Flat.

Contact: South Shore Marina, (209) 881-0107; or Lake Tulloch Resort, (209) 785-2286.

About Tulloch Reservoir: The first time I flew an airplane over Tulloch Reservoir, I couldn't believe how different it looked by air than from a boat. It resembled a giant X rather than a lake. After landing at the runway in Columbia and making the trip to the lake, I understood why.

The reservoir is set in two canyons that crisscross each other, and by boat you never see the other canyon. The lake is actually the afterbay for New Melones Reservoir, and the water that fills Tulloch Reservoir comes from the New Melones Dam on the northeastern end of the X. These extended lake arms give the reservoir a total of 55 miles of shoreline.

This has a profound effect on boating. Because the water is basically set in filled canyons, the waterway is relatively narrow. So despite the lake's size, there are a lot of blind points. When the weather is hot and the water-ski traffic is high, there can be some close calls between fast boats running in opposite directions. All boaters should be wary of this danger, stay out in the main channel, keep an alert spotter on duty, and forbid drinking and driving. That done, the waterskiing can be sensational, with the shore so close it creates the illusion of great speed.

If you pick your spots well, windsurfing and swimming can also be excellent. The best area for windsurfing is along the north shore, where the most predictable wind can be found. But because this lake lies in a deep canyon, winds can be erratic. In addition windsurfing is not advised on summer weekends, when the narrow lake is swarming with speedboats and the danger factor is raised a few notches.

Both of the lake's resorts offer great swimming opportunities. Each has large, sandy beaches complete with developed facilities.

The only campground here is at South Shore, and the thought of bedding down there sends off alarm bells for some campers. Why? Although it rarely occurs, tarantulas have been known to invade the campground. In turn they send loads of campers running to stay at the lodge at Poker Flat. Like I said, rare but true.

⑫ Modesto Reservoir

Location: Near Modesto; map E3, grid g3.
Directions: From Modesto drive 16 miles

east on Highway 132, past Waterford. Turn left (north) on Reservoir Road and then continue to the reservoir.

Access: Two paved boat ramps are available: one at the marina, located on the south shore just west of the campgrounds, and one on the reservoir's west side, off Rio Linda Drive.

Facilities, fees: Campgrounds, picnic areas, groceries, gas, and a snack bar are available. A full-service marina and rowboat, canoe, and paddleboat rentals are also available. Fees are charged for day use and boat launching.

Water sports, restrictions: A 5 mph speed limit is enforced on the lake's southern arm and around the day-use areas. Windsurfing is permitted. Waterskiing and personal watercraft are permitted in designated areas. Sandy swimming beaches are available at various spots around the shoreline; there's a designated swimming area next to the marina.

Contact: Modesto Reservoir, (209) 874-9540; or Modesto Marina, (209) 874-1340.

About Modesto Reservoir: You'll find Modesto Reservoir set in the hot foothill country, just east of guess where.

This is a big lake, covering 2,700 acres with 31 miles of shoreline. One of the great things about the place is the boat-in camping. Many coves at the lake's southern end provide an opportunity to set up primitive self-made boat-in campsites. It's a good idea to bring a shovel in order to dig out a flat spot for sleeping, something that is often necessary when boat-in camping at a reservoir.

The reservoir is set at 200 feet on the edge of the Central Valley, where it gets very hot for days upon days in the summer. The proximity to, uh, (what's the name of that town?) and the diverse recreation opportunities make it very popular, and it often gets extremely crowded in the summer months. On weekends the scene can be wild, with fast boats and lots of liquid refreshments adding to the insanity.

Regardless, in addition to good waterskiing and jet boating, the swimming in Modesto Reservoir is great. The best spots for swimming and playing in the water are near the day-use areas, where a 5 mph speed limit is in effect and boaters stay well clear of the near shore. That ensures calm water for non-boaters.

Windsurfing is also good because steady, strong winds are common almost every afternoon from spring through ummer.

⓭ Don Pedro Reservoir

Location: Northeast of Modesto; map E3, grid g6.

Directions: From the San Francisco Bay Area, drive east on Interstate 580 past Livermore. Continue east on Interstate 205 until it bisects Interstate 5; then drive north on Interstate 5 for two miles. Turn east on Highway 120 and continue through Manteca and Oakdale (where it becomes Highway 108/120). Turn east on Highway 120 and drive to the town of Chinese Camp. To reach the lake's upper end, continue east on Highway 49/120 for five miles and then turn left toward Moccasin Point. To reach the lake's southern end, turn south from Chinese Camp, take Redhill Sims Road–La Grange Road, veer east on Bond Flat Road, and drive to the dam.

From Modesto drive approximately 32 miles east on Highway 132 to the town of La Grange. Turn north on County Road J59/La Grange Road and travel to the dam.

From Sonora drive east on Highway 108/49, then turn east at Highway 49, and drive to the town of Chinese Camp. To reach the lake's upper end, continue east on Highway 49/120 for five miles, and then turn left toward Moccasin Point. To reach the southern end, turn south from Chinese Camp, take Redhili Sims Road–La Grange Road, veer east on Bond Flat Road, and drive to the dam.

Access: There are three boat ramps: two on the southern end of the lake, near the dam, and one at Moccasin Point (see directions for both).

Facilities, fees: Campgrounds, picnic areas, snack bars, restaurant, grocery store, coin laundry, showers, and gas are provided at the reservoir. Full-service marinas and fishing boat, houseboat, and patio boat rentals are available at Don Pedro Marina (south shore) and Moccasin Point Marina (north shore). Some facilities are wheelchair accessible. Fees are charged for day use and boat launching.

Water sports, restrictions: Waterskiing, personal watercraft, and windsurfing are permitted. A sandy swimming beach is available on the south shore at Fleming Meadows Picnic Area.

Contact: Don Pedro Recreation Agency, (209) 852-2396; Don Pedro Marina, (209) 852-2369.

About Don Pedro Reservoir: In high water years Don Pedro—a giant lake with many extended lake arms—is one of the best boating and recreation lakes in California.

Did I say giant? When full, it covers nearly 13,000 surface acres with 160 miles of shoreline. Not only do the lake arms extend far, but they harbor zillions of hidden coves and secret spots where you can park your boat, camp, swim, play in the water, and fish.

Temperatures soar here in the summer because the lake is set low, at an 800-foot elevation. To protect yourself from the sun, it is critical that you have a canvas canopy on your boat and bring along a light tarp with poles and rope. That done, prepare to have the time of your life on Don Pedro Reservoir. The water is often lukewarm on top

and cool a few feet down, perfect for water sports.

The best areas for waterskiing are offshore near the Don Pedro Marina and Don Pedro Recreation Area. Because anglers tend to head well up the narrow lake arms and into coves, conflicts with water-skiers are less common than at many lakes. Personal watercraft can cause problems, however, if their riders zip into the coves and disrupt low-speed boaters.

Don Pedro has one designated swimming area at Fleming Meadows, located on the south shore. There is a fairly sandy beach here and a nearby concession stand. On the lake's northern end there are no beach areas, but people swim anyway, either from the shoreline or by jumping off their boats. Some shoreline areas have quick drop-offs, so children should always wear life jackets and be supervised.

Hey, newcomers, here's a great insider's note: The lake's northern, upper end sits in a deep, narrow canyon. Because of this, water-skiers and jet boaters stay away. That makes it ideal for fishing and other low-speed use, such as paddling a canoe or kayak, or floating about in a raft.

The lake gets sufficient wind in the afternoon to make sailing and windsurfing fairly popular. The best areas for these activities are at the lake's southern end, which is largely open and receives more predictable winds.

The big problem at Don Pedro occurs in low rain years. In the summer much of the water is delivered to farmers in the Central Valley, and not only do the levels drop, but the day-to-day changes can be amazing. You can park your boat on the shore, only to discover later in the day that the water has receded to the point that you risk having your boat stuck on the bank. Low water also creates considerable boating hazards, and water-skiers should pay special attention at all times.

⓮ Turlock Lake

Location: East of Modesto in Turlock Lake State Recreation Area; map E3, grid h3.

Directions: From Modesto drive about 20 miles east on Highway 132, past Waterford, to Crabtree Road on the right. Turn south, drive one mile, then turn left on Lake Road, and travel three miles east to the lake entrance.

Access: A paved boat ramp and dock are located on the northwest shore, about one mile east of the Lake Road turnoff.

Facilities, fees: A campground is available nearby on the Tuolumne River. Picnic areas are provided. There is a day-use fee.

Water sports, restrictions: Waterskiing, personal watercraft, and windsurfing are permitted. You'll find large, sandy swimming beaches at the day-use area.

Contact: Turlock Lake State Recreation Area, (209) 874-2008 or fax (209) 874-2611.

About Turlock Lake: When full, Turlock Lake covers 3,500 acres and has 26 miles of shoreline. The Tuolumne River feeds the lake with cold, fresh water in the spring. In the summer the water heats up like a big bathtub and the place is converted into a great spot for waterskiing and swimming. Excellent swimming beaches, big and sandy, are a special highlight.

But get this: the developed facilities—marina, grocery store, and gas station—are gone. That's right, the owner folded his tent and said *adios*. Lacking these facilities, this is now one of the more primitive major recreation sites in the valley.

It does still get a lot of traffic, but Turlock Lake has become far more family oriented than the old days when fast jet boats absolutely dominated the scene. One major factor in the personality change is that alcohol is no longer allowed on the lake or beaches, which keeps away the rowdiest water-skiers.

The way things work here is that families and go-slow users head to one area of the lake, while water-skiers go to another. When you arrive on the entrance road, note that the first beach you come to is the "family" beach, where people take their kids. Drive farther down the road and you will arrive at another beach known as Ski Beach; this is where the young adult crowd hangs out.

In addition to waterskiing, personal watercraft and windsurfing are pretty popular at Turlock.

⓯ Lake McClure

Location: East of Modesto; map E3, grid h6.

Directions: From Modesto drive 32 miles east on Highway 132 to the town of La Grange. Continue for 11 miles east to Merced Falls Road. To reach the lake's northernmost arm, continue 5.5 miles east on Highway 132 to Horseshoe Bend; to access the west shore, turn right on Merced Falls Road and drive three miles to the entrance at Barrett Cove. To reach the southernmost access point, continue south to Lake McClure Road and head east to McClure Point. If approaching from Highway 49, access is available south of Coulterville at Bagby Recreation Area.

Access: Paved ramps are located at Barrett Cove, McClure Point, Horseshoe Bend, and Bagby (see directions to each).

Facilities, fees: Campgrounds and picnic areas are provided around the lake. Full-service marinas are available at McClure Point, Barrett Cove, and Bagby. You can rent houseboats, patio boats, ski boats, and fishing boats at Barrett Cove Marina. Groceries, snack bars, and gas are available at all major access points. Fees are charged for day use and boat launching.

Water sports, restrictions: Waterskiing and personal watercraft are permitted. The lake is usually not windy enough for windsurfing. The shoreline has no beaches, but there are swimming lagoons at each recreation area.

Contact: Barrett Cove Marina, (209) 378-2441; McClure Point, (209) 378-2521.

About Lake McClure: Some people think that Lake McClure and adjoining Lake McSwain (see the next listing) appear to be the same lake. That will teach them to think. Even though McClure and McSwain are connected by the Merced River, they are two separate lakes, each with its own unique identity.

Of the pair McClure is the giant, a huge H-shaped lake that covers 7,000 surface acres with 82 miles of shoreline. The water is warmer and there is more water sports activity here, including skiing and houseboating.

This is a full-facility recreation area that offers developed campgrounds, picnic areas, and boating services. Waterskiing, personal watercraft, and houseboating are all very popular. In the summer the place gets extremely crowded, but for the most part everybody seems to be having the time of their lives. In the off-season it gets low to moderate use.

Swimming is pretty much limited to the lagoons in the campgrounds, which have sandy sunbathing areas. While swimming is not prohibited in the lake, you'll rarely see people swimming or playing along the shore, mainly because of the typically steep drop-off. A more common sight is that of folks using their boats as swimming platforms, jumping in, treading water, floating around, and then scrambling back into the boat for a repeat performance.

⑯ Lake McSwain

Location: East of Modesto; map E3, grid i6.

Directions: From Modesto drive 32 miles east on Highway 132 to the town of La Grange. Continue for 11 miles east to Merced Falls Road. Turn right (south) and drive 13 miles to Lake McClure Road. Turn left and continue for one mile to the lake entrance.

Access: A paved boat ramp is available next to Lake McSwain Marina, located on Lake McClure Road.

Facilities, fees: A campground is provided. There's a full-service marina where you can rent fishing boats and paddleboats. A snack bar, grocery store, coin laundry, and showers are available. Fees are charged for day use and boat launching.

Water sports, restrictions: A 10 mph speed limit is strictly enforced. No houseboats are permitted. The lake is too small and not windy enough for windsurfing. A sandy swimming beach is available adjacent to the marina.

Contact: Lake McSwain Marina, (209) 378-2521 or (209) 378-2534.

About Lake McSwain: If you find that Lake McClure is simply too large and filled with too many big boats, then little Lake McSwain provides a perfect nearby alternative. You won't have to contend with the crowds that descend on McClure to the east because this lake is small, waterskiing is prohibited, and the water is much colder.

McSwain may be like a puddle compared to McClure, but the water level is usually near full capacity here. That makes it the more attractive option, especially in low water years when McClure can look almost barren in comparison by late fall.

Although McSwain is developed, recreation is far more low-key than at big brother McClure. It is evolving into an excellent destination for families who want to avoid the rowdy water-skiers and houseboaters. It is quite small, and the campground fills up fast on summer weekends, so reservations should be made in advance.

One of the bright spots is that unlike at McClure, much the shoreline is favorable for swimming, and there's even a good, sandy beach. However, the lake is colder because the water that fills McSwain comes from the bottom of McClure Dam. But that cold water is what makes the trout fishing better at here than at McClure.

⑰ Yosemite Lake

Location: North of Merced in Lake Yosemite Park; map E3, grid j4.

Directions: From Merced on Highway 99, turn north on Highway 59 and travel four miles to Bellevue Road. Turn right, drive five miles east to Lake Road, turn left, and continue to the lake.

Access: A paved boat ramp is available just past the park entrance.

Facilities, fees: Picnic areas and rest rooms are provided. A concessionaire with fishing boat rentals may be in business; phone ahead for status. Lodging and supplies can be obtained in Merced. Fees are charged for day use and boat launching.

Water sports, restrictions: Waterskiing, personal watercraft, and windsurfing are permitted in designated areas. Two large, sandy swimming beaches are available along the southern shore, off Lake Road.

Contact: Yosemite Lake Caretaker, (209) 722-2568; Merced County Parks and Recreation, (209) 385-7426.

About Yosemite Lake: Now don't get confused. Yosemite Lake is not in Yosemite National Park. In fact it has nothing to do with Yosemite National Park, which is covered in chapter E4.

Yosemite Lake, on the outskirts of eastern Merced County, is a 390-acre lake where all water sports are permitted. Unlike the national park with which is shares a name, it doesn't quite make the major leagues. Although not stellar in any way, this is still a nice spot, particularly for cooling off on a hot summer evening.

The best things going here are opportunities for swimming and windsurfing. Large swimming beaches are available, and lifeguards are posted on weekends. That's a winner. Another winner is windsurfing, with steady winds nearly every afternoon.

It is also popular with powerboaters and water-skiers, especially with the weather being so hot almost all summer long. Rate prospects good, but not great.

One problem is that the marina operations are in a state of flux. In 1995 no boat rentals or services were available. At press time they were slated to reopen soon, but the status of these operations is still unclear.

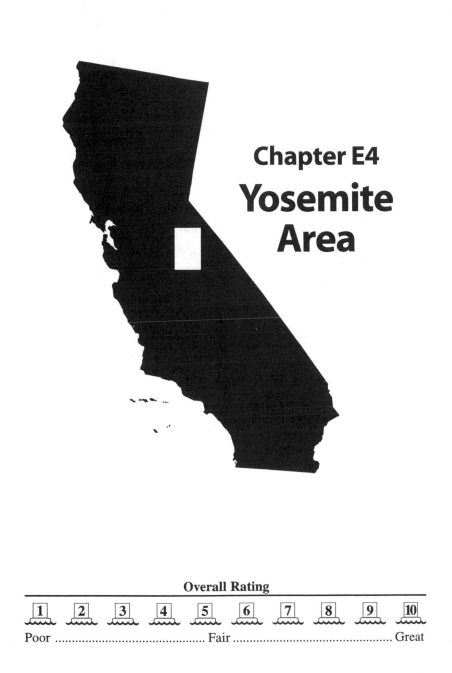

Chapter E4
Yosemite Area

Overall Rating

| 1 | 2 | 3 | 4 | 5 | 6 | 7 | 8 | 9 | 10 |

Poor .... Fair .... Great

E4–Yosemite Area Map

One inch equals approximately 10.7 miles.
See page 12 for California state map.

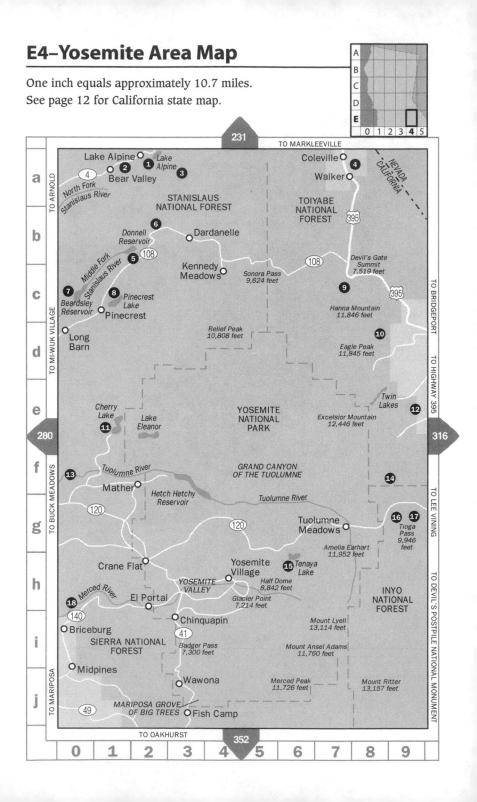

Chapter E4 features:

❶ Lake Alpine

Location: Northeast of Arnold in Stanislaus National Forest; map E4, grid a2.

Directions: From Highway 99 at Stockton, turn east on Highway 4 and drive to Angels Camp at the junction of Highways 4 and 49. Continue east on Highway 4 for approximately 51 miles to the lake.

Access: To reach the paved boat ramp, turn right at the entrance road across from Alpine Resort.

Facilities, fees: Several campgrounds and picnic areas are provided. Cabins, restaurant, store, and a snack bar are available at Lake Alpine Lodge. You can rent fishing boats, rowboats, canoes, and kayaks at the lodge. Access to the lake is free.

Water sports, restrictions: A 10 mph speed limit is strictly enforced. Windsurfing is allowed. Swimming is permitted anywhere along the lake's shoreline.

Contact: Stanislaus National Forest, Calaveras Ranger District, (209) 795-1381 or fax (209) 795-6849; Lake Alpine Lodge, (209) 753-6358; Ebbetts Pass Sporting Goods, (209) 795-1686.

About Lake Alpine: In a lot of people's minds, Lake Alpine fits their vision of what a mountain lake is supposed to look like. By early evening during the summer, the surface is calm and emerald green, with little pools created by hatching bugs and rising trout. The shoreline is well wooded (includ-ing some giant ponderosa pines), the smell of pine duff is in the air, and campsites are within a short distance of the lake. Heaven? Almost.

The only problem with this slice of heaven is that a lot of people want to get in. At Alpine that means filled campgrounds, lots of anglers, and on popular weekends, even difficulty renting a boat at the dock.

Lake Alpine covers 180 surface acres and is set at 7,320 feet in the Sierra Nevada, just above the snowplow stopping point. Highway 4 is gated just below the lake; in mid-April, CalTrans opens that gate and plows the highway all the way to the lake.

Most vacationers here are campers who like to hike and fish. Some bring along small boats, either cartop boats, such as canoes or inflatables, or trailered boats. Many others rent a fishing boat, canoe, or kayak at the lake's small marina, and paddle around and bask in the great mountain beauty.

The water is clear and cold, especially early in the season. By July, however, on hot summer days there are always plenty of people jumping in anyway. Most are just taking a dunk, but a few swim around a bit. While there is no designated swimming beach, there are lots of spots along the entire shoreline suitable for taking the plunge.

Windsurfing can be excellent, with steady winds out of the west kicking up on most afternoons. It is quite a sensation to clip along in the midst of all this supreme mountain lake charm.

But as mentioned, this area gets very crowded, especially on weekends between Memorial Day and Labor Day. The 10 mph speed limit and the long, twisty drive in keep out the fast boats and personal watercraft, but they don't guarantee much silence. Occasionally there are loud campers who disturb the peace. Sometimes there are also off-road motorcycles in the area, and you can hear their engines wailing, which is extremely upsetting if you are trying to enjoy a quiet paddle with a friend in a small canoe.

The best times to visit and avoid the masses are from late April through May and again in October, even though the nights are cold and the weather can be unpredictable.

❷ Union Reservoir

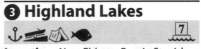

Location: Northeast of Arnold in Stanislaus National Forest; map E4, grid a2.
Directions: From Highway 99 at Stockton, turn east on Highway 4 and drive to Angels Camp at the junction of Highways 4 and 49. Continue for approximately 32 miles east on Highway 4 to Forest Service Road 7N01/Spicer Reservoir Road. Turn right, travel about 8.5 miles east; then turn left on Forest Service Road 7N75 and travel two miles to the reservoir.
Access: There is no boat ramp. Cartop boats may be hand launched.
Facilities, fees: Walk-in campsites are available off Forest Service Road 7N75 at the reservoir. Supplies can be obtained in Tamarack off Highway 4. There is no piped water here, so bring your own. Access to the lake is free.
Water sports, restrictions: The lake is only suitable for small, cartop boats. Swimming is permitted.

Contact: Stanislaus National Forest, Calaveras Ranger District, (209) 795-1381 or fax (209) 795-6849. For a detailed map of the area, send $4 to Maps, Office of Information, US Forest Service, 1323 Club Drive, Vallejo, CA 94592.

About Union Reservoir: For some just getting here is far enough "out there." But you can get a lot farther "out there" if you want.

Along with the adjoining Utica Reservoir, Union Reservoir is set in Sierra granite at an elevation of 6,850 feet. The surrounding area is very scenic, and this is an excellent spot for kayakers and canoeists. You got it: if you can't cartop your boat and then launch it by hand, you won't find any boating access. But with a canoe you can paddle yourself into the center of this exceptionally beautiful mountain setting.

The water is very cold up here, but Union, because it is small and quite shallow, probably offers the warmest water for swimmers. It's still darn cold, though. Use is light to medium, even in summer. Only dispersed camping is allowed, and campers are asked to practice minimum-impact techniques to protect the fragile shoreline.

❸ Highland Lakes

Location: Near Ebbetts Pass in Stanislaus National Forest; map E4, grid a3.
Directions: From Highway 99 at Stockton, turn east on Highway 4 and drive to Angels Camp at the junction of Highways 4 and 49. Continue for approximately 64 miles east on Highway 4, past Lake Alpine, to Forest Service Road 8N01/Highland Lakes Road. Turn right and travel five miles to the lakes. From US 395, proceed to the junction of US 395 and Highway 89 (just south of Topaz Lake on the Nevada/California border). Turn west on Highway 89 and drive about 15 miles to the Highway 4 junction. Turn south and travel 15 miles to Ebbetts Pass. Con-

tinue west for one mile and turn left at Forest Service Road 8N01/Highland Lakes Road. Proceed to the lakes.

Access: A primitive boat ramp is available on Upper Highland.

Facilities, fees: A campground is provided at Lower Highland. Supplies can be obtained at Lake Alpine Resort on Highway 4. Access is free.

Water sports, restrictions: A 15 mph speed limit is strictly enforced. Swimming and windsurfing are not recommended due to the extremely cold water.

Contact: Stanislaus National Forest, Calaveras Ranger District, (209) 795-1381 or fax (209) 795-6849. For a detailed map of the area, send $4 to Maps, Office of Information, US Forest Service, 1323 Club Drive, Vallejo, CA 94592.

About Highland Lakes: This scenic lake pair is set high near the Sierra crest at an elevation of 8,600 feet, just below Ebbetts Pass. They are popular with anglers, canoeists, and kayakers, but swimming is for the insane only. You can figure out why: the water is frigid, all of it fresh snowmelt, and at this elevation it rarely warms up.

A developed campground and boat launch, along with easy access off the highway, attract a lot of travelers from nearby Highway 4. On summer weekends the campground is often full, usually with camper/anglers who have small trailered boats. They like the intimacy that you can only find at tiny lakes that have a small, primitive campground.

Because the water is so cold, nobody swims. A ranger told us he's only seen one person swim here in his entire career, and that person was of questionable mental stability. For the same reason (the chilly water, not your state of mind), windsurfing is almost as rare.

What makes this place a winner to so many people is that it is the perfect jump-off spot for hikes, including backpacking trips into the nearby Carson-Iceberg Wilderness. Because you're just below Ebbetts Pass, you don't have to start your trip by hiking up, up, and up. Instead, you're already about as far up as you can get in this area.

❹ West Walker River

Location: Northwest of Bridgeport in Humboldt-Toiyabe National Forest; map E4, grid a8.

Directions: From US 395 at the town of Bridgeport, continue northwest. Excellent roadside access is available on US 395 north of Sonora Junction, as well as off of Highway 108 going west.

Access: No boat ramp is available. To reach the put-in start at the junction of US 395 and Highway 108, and drive three miles west on Highway 108 to the Sonora Bridge picnic area. The standard take-out is eight miles downstream at China Garden. Note: This take-out is difficult; there are no eddies or pools available, which means you must turn hard into the bank. At high flows the river's rapids are rated Class IV–V; only experienced paddlers should attempt this run.

Facilities, fees: Several campgrounds are available off US 395 and Highway 108. Supplies can be obtained in Bridgeport. Access is free. Rafting permits are not required.

Water sports, restrictions: Swimming is not permitted.

Contact: Humboldt-Toiyabe National Forest, Bridgeport Ranger District, (760) 932-7070 or fax (760) 932-1299. For guided rafting trips contact Beyond Limits Adventures, (800) 234-7238, or American Whitewater Expeditions, (818) 352-3205.

About the West Walker River: The West Walker is best known as a pretty trout stream on the eastern side of the Sierra where there are a sprinkling of Forest Service campgrounds.

What is less known, however, is that for a short period in the early summer, the West

Walker provides a very challenging rafting run. While the Forest Service does not recommend rafting on this river, we included it in this book anyway because commercial trips are available, and it does have a cultlike following among rafters.

First, note that the season is very short, typically from mid-June through mid-July. In the spring the flows are over 2,000 cubic feet per second, far too high, cold, and dangerous for anybody. Yet by the end of July, the river is usually too low to try anything but a butt bumper.

Second, even when the flows are safe, it's considered a very difficult run. From put-in to take-out, you encounter eight miles of steady, challenging rapids. At high flows that means eight miles of Class IV–V water.

Third, taking out can be a very frustrating experience, to put it nicely. To put it unnicely, it's a downright pain in the butt. The Forest Service requires commercial companies to take out at China Garden, and there are no quiet eddies for boats to slip into. That means rafters must crank abruptly into the bank immediately after a rapid, so you must be very alert as well as skilled at paddling.

In years with a low snowpack, the river is unrunnable at all times because of low flows. That has been the case several times in the recent 10-year period that California experienced a drought.

Needless to say, the Walker is not exactly a hot spot. And that is exactly why some expert rafters and kayakers love this place, because they often have the river to themselves.

It's an attractive river, set mostly in high desert country. One drawback is that after the first few miles, the river directly parallels US 395, not exactly a wilderness atmosphere. But hey, you're going to be navigating Class IV–V rapids, so you probably won't even notice. No foolin' you won't notice.

❺ Donnell Reservoir

Location: Near Strawberry in Stanislaus National Forest; map E4, grid b1.

Directions: From Stockton drive south on Highway 99 to Manteca. Turn east on Highway 120 and drive 56 miles. At the junction of Highways 120 and 108, take Highway 108 northeast and continue to Sonora. From Sonora continue 29 miles east on Highway 108 (a winding two-laner) to the town of Strawberry. Continue northwest for four more miles to Beardsley Road. Turn left and proceed for a short way and then turn right on Forest Service Road 5N06/Hells Half Acre Road. Drive four miles, then turn right again on the access road to Donnell Reservoir.

Note: A heavy-duty four-wheel-drive vehicle is required to get near the lake, followed by a difficult hike over boulders. Light-duty four-wheel-drive vehicles can be damaged on the access road.

Access: There is no boat ramp.

Facilities, fees: No facilities are provided. Access is free.

Water sports, restrictions: There are no boating restrictions, but boating is not advised due to the difficult access. Swimming is permitted.

Contact: Stanislaus National Forest, Summit Ranger District, (209) 965-3434 or fax (209) 965-3372; Rich & Sal's Sporting Goods in Pinecrest, (209) 965-3637.

About Donnell Reservoir: Only the deranged need apply. But sometimes being a little crazy can keep you from going insane.

Donnell Reservoir, set in the Stanislaus River canyon at 4,921 feet, is one of the toughest lakes to reach in California.

So the first question is how do you get a boat in? Answer: only by dragging it for a considerable distance over boulders down to the dam at the lake's western end. And once you do that, it is "Good-bye, boat." You might somehow get a boat in, but getting it back out is damn near impossible, since you have to climb out of the canyon over boulders.

Believe it or not, there are a couple of boats here. Permanently. There is no way to get them out of the lake. They are beat up and chained up, but they are boats. People bring along bolt cutters, cut them free, use them to catch fish, then chain them back up. Yeah, it's crazy.

Since the lake's shoreline is steep and covered with giant rocks, there is no beach or good swimming access. The water is clear, cold, and deep; if you decide to swim, pick your access point carefully to make sure you have a safe place to get out of the water. Because of the difficult access, use here is very light. Most of the summer traffic comes from hikers.

Now don't go jumping off on this trip without taking a good look in the mirror and having a long talk with yourself. If you go anyway, I have one thing to say: Don't blame me. I warned you.

❻ Spicer Meadow Reservoir

Location: Northeast of Arnold in Stanislaus National Forest; map E4, grid b2.
Directions: From Highway 99 at Stockton, turn east on Highway 4 and continue to Angels Camp at the junction of Highways 4 and 49. Continue for approximately 32 miles east on Highway 4 to Forest Service Road 7N01/Spicer Reservoir Road. Turn right, travel about 8.5 miles, turn right (south) on Forest Service Road 7N75, and continue to the lake.
Access: A paved boat ramp is located on the lake's west end, near the campground.
Facilities, fees: A campground is provided. Access to the lake is free.
Water sports, restrictions: Motors are not permitted on the lake's eastern end. A

10 mph speed limit is enforced on the western arm. Swimming is not recommended due to the extremely cold water. Windsurfing is permitted; wet suits are recommended.

Contact: Stanislaus National Forest, Calaveras Ranger District, (209) 795-1381 or fax (209) 795-6849. For a detailed map of the area, send $4 to Maps, Office of Information, US Forest Service, 1323 Club Drive, Vallejo, CA 94592.

About Spicer Meadow Reservoir: This is one of the older reservoirs in the high central Sierra Nevada. Spicer Meadow Reservoir was established in 1929 when a dam was built in the canyon on Highland Creek, creating a short, narrow lake.

By reservoir standards this lake isn't big, covering 227 acres. But it is quite pretty from a boat, surrounded by canyon walls and set at 6,418 feet.

The water is very cold, way too cold for swimming—unless, that is, you have a dream of become a human Popsicle. And while winds are typically steady from 2 PM to 7 PM, windsurfing is out of the question, too, without a wet suit.

What you see instead are campers with small boats, mostly fishing for trout, and occasionally folks in canoes or kayaks paddling and playing around in the water. Rules prohibiting waterskiing and personal watercraft ensure a quiet setting for camping and low-speed boating. The trout fishing is often quite good.

❼ Beardsley Reservoir

Location: Near Strawberry in Stanislaus National Forest; map E4, grid c0.
Directions: From Stockton drive south on Highway 99 to Manteca. Turn east on Highway 120 and drive 56 miles. At the junction of Highways 120 and 108, take Highway 108 northeast and continue to Sonora.

From Sonora drive 29 miles east on Highway 108 (a winding two-laner) to the town of Strawberry. Continue northwest for four more miles to Beardsley Road. Turn left and proceed west to Beardsley Reservoir.

Access: A paved ramp is located on the reservoir's entrance road; watch for the signed turnoff.

Facilities, fees: A picnic area is provided. Campgrounds and supplies are available in Strawberry and along Highway 108. Access to the lake is free.

Water sports, restrictions: Waterskiing, personal watercraft, and windsurfing are permitted. A swimming beach is available at the picnic area.

Contact: Stanislaus National Forest, Summit Ranger District, (209) 965-3434 or fax (209) 965-3372.

About Beardsley Reservoir: Although best known as a good trout fishing lake, Beardsley Reservoir is also the only lake in the district that allows waterskiing. The lake has a paved ramp, nice picnic area, and a fair beach, and all water sports are allowed.

The lake is set in a deep canyon on the Upper Stanislaus River. While the setting is at an elevation of 3,400 feet, it actually feels as if it is much higher in the mountains, like about 6,000 feet. That's no accident.

From the turnoff on Highway 108, you drop nearly 2,000 feet on the eight-mile access road to reach the lake. The road is so long that the Forest Service keeps it gated during icy weather to prevent two-wheel-drive vehicles towing boats from getting stuck so far out there that their drivers are unable to get help.

The water is generally warm enough for swimming by midsummer. Aside from the beach area, the shoreline is steep, rocky in some places and forested in others. Conditions for windsurfing are good in the early summer, but require high expertise due to gusty winds that come shooting up the canyon. You can count on them daily in the late afternoon and early evening.

While there are no developed campgrounds at the lake, there are several Forest Service campgrounds on nearby Highway 108. Many vacationers will set up camp at one of these, then head to Beardsley for day use.

Beardsley can be subject to severe drawdowns, particularly in drought years, making it look something like the Grand Canyon. When the lake is low, you have to drive down on the dry lake bed to hand launch your boat. Believe it or not, that is often preferable to the situation during high water, when the walk up the boat ramp to the parking area is so long that some old-timers call it "Cardiac Hill."

❽ Pinecrest Lake

Location: Near Strawberry in Stanislaus National Forest; map E4, grid d1.

Directions: From Stockton drive south on Highway 99 to Manteca. Turn east on Highway 120 and drive 56 miles. At the junction of Highways 120 and 108, take Highway 108 northeast and continue to Sonora. From Sonora drive 29 miles east on Highway 108 (a winding two-laner) to Pinecrest Lake Road (one mile south of the town of Strawberry). Turn right and continue to the lake.

Access: A unpaved boat ramp is available at Pinecrest Lake Resort.

Facilities, fees: Campgrounds, lodging, picnic area, groceries, gas, and a restaurant are available at the lake. Pinecrest Lake Resort rents out fishing boats, pontoon boats, kayaks, and paddleboats, and has a full-service marina. Access is free. There is no charge for boat launching.

Water sports, restrictions: A 20 mph speed limit is strictly enforced. Windsurfing is permitted; personal watercraft are prohibited. A sandy swimming beach is available next to the picnic area.

Contact: Stanislaus National Forest, Summit Ranger District, (209) 965-3434 or fax (209) 965-3372; Pinecrest Marina, (209) 965-3333.

About Pinecrest Lake: No secrets here. The word is out about Pinecrest Lake, a family-oriented vacation center that is located near the Dodge Ridge Ski Resort. In the summer Pinecrest Lake provides what Dodge Ridge does in the winter: a fun spot with full amenities.

This is the centerpiece of a fully developed family vacation resort, and it gets very heavy use throughout summer. The place is best suited for vacationing families who want to camp, boat, and fish.

The surrounding area is beautiful and heavily forested, with excellent hiking and biking trails. While it is pretty, don't expect the quiet wilderness. The campground usually has plenty of takers.

Pinecrest Lake is set at an elevation of 5,621 feet, covers 300 acres, and has 3.5 miles of shoreline. The water is clear and cold, but by midsummer it is good for swimming on a hot summer day.

Windsurfing can be excellent; lessons and rentals are available.

A bonus is a small but excellent marina that rents all types of boats. Some families rent a pontoon boat so they can enjoy a picnic or barbecue on the water, then use the boat as a swimming platform.

❾ Twin Lakes

Location: Near Bridgeport in Humboldt-Toiyabe National Forest; map E4, grid c7.
Directions: From the north end of Bridgeport on US 395, drive 12 miles southwest on Twin Lakes Road.
Access: Each lake has a paved ramp: on Lower Twin Lake at Twin Lakes Resort, and on Upper Twin Lake at Mono Village Resort. Both are located off Twin Lakes Road.

Facilities, fees: Forest Service campgrounds are provided east of the lakes on Twin Lakes Road. Lodging, restaurants, and groceries are available at the lake. Full-service marinas and fishing boat rentals are available at Twin Lakes and Mono Village Resorts. Access is free. There is a fee for boat launching.

Water sports, restrictions: Waterskiing and personal watercraft are permitted on Upper Twin Lake only. A 5 mph speed limit is enforced on Lower Twin. A beach is available next to the marina at Upper Twin; swimming is available all along the shoreline at Lower Twin. Windsurfing is permitted on both lakes.

Contact: Humboldt-Toiyabe National Forest, Bridgeport Ranger District, (760) 932-7070 or fax (760) 932-1299; Twin Lakes Resort (Lower Twin Lake), (619) 932-7751; Mono Village Resort (Upper Twin Lake), (619) 932-7071.

About Twin Lakes: Surprise, surprise. These are actually two lakes connected by a short stream. Most people think of them as one, but for boating and water sports the prospects are unique at each.

Mono Village Resort is located on Upper Twin, a primary destination for boaters. Waterskiing and other water sports are permitted there. Swimming is especially popular at Upper Twin, where there is a sandy beach at the resort. Upper Twin is also the best spot for windsurfing; you can go as fast, or in some cases as slow, as you deem fit.

Lower Twin, on the other hand, is known as "the fishing lake" for its good catch rates of rainbow trout and a sprinkling of huge brown trout. A 5 mph speed limit here keeps this lake ideal for fishing, especially trolling, and prevents user conflicts between low-speed anglers and any high-speed boaters. Lower Twin also has a fine resort, Twin Lakes Resort.

Remember, these are alpine lakes—set high in the eastern Sierra at an elevation of 7,000 feet—so the water is quite cold, and the bordering landscape to the east is quite stark. These lakes have become very popular in the summer. In addition, an outstanding trailhead (and parking area) just upstream of Upper Twin Lake gives visitors the opportunity to hike into the adjacent Hoover Wilderness.

⑩ Buckeye Creek

Location: East of Bridgeport in Humboldt-Toiyabe National Forest; map E4, grid d8.

Directions: From the town of Bridgeport on US 395, drive seven miles southwest on Twin Lakes Road to Doc & Al's Resort. Turn north on Buckeye Creek Road (dirt) and continue to the creek. A dirt parking area is available about four miles up the road.

Access: There is no boat ramp.

Facilities, fees: Buckeye Campground is located near the creek on Buckeye Creek Road. Supplies can be obtained in Bridgeport. Access is free.

Water sports, restrictions: There are natural hot spring pools at the creek, near the parking area. Swimming is available near the hot springs and at various pools off Buckeye Creek Road.

Contact: Humboldt-Toiyabe National Forest, Bridgeport Ranger District, (760) 932-7070 or fax (760) 932-1299; Doc & Al's Resort, (760) 932-7051. For a detailed map of the area, send $4 to Office of Information, US Forest Service, 1323 Club Drive, Vallejo, CA 94592.

About Buckeye Creek: The star attraction at Buckeye Creek is some little hot springs, and most vacationers don't even realize they exist.

Like nearby Robinson Creek, Buckeye Creek is better known for its brush-free grassy banks, with occasional pools and undercut shoreline, the latter where trout sometimes hide. Because there are few large pools and no sandy banks, this is not much of a destination for swimming, but rather for fishing for small trout. In the course of trout fishing, some fishermen have stumbled upon the hot springs and turned their trip into a far greater success.

The hot springs come down from the canyon walls above the creek, and some people construct rock pools to capture the water on the creekside. During periods of high snowmelt and high flows, the hot springs can be drowned and impossible to find. Most of the summer they can be discovered easily enough, and making new pools is an ongoing effort here.

The hot springs get a fair amount of use, but because they are not publicized, you'll mostly find only locals here. They add a great twist to a vacation in the eastern Sierra.

⑪ Cherry Lake

Location: Northwest of Yosemite National Park in Stanislaus National Forest; map E4, grid e1.

Directions: From the San Francisco Bay Area, drive east on Interstate 580 past Livermore. Continue east on Interstate 205 until it bisects with Interstate 5 and then drive north on Interstate 5 for two miles. Turn east on Highway 120 and proceed to Manteca. Continue east on Highway 120 for approximately 80 miles to Buck Meadows. The road is very narrow and twisty as you head into the mountains. Continue east for four miles to Cherry Valley Road on the left. Turn north and drive 24 miles to the lake.

Access: On Cherry Valley Road take the signed turnoff on the right to reach the unpaved boat ramp. Note: The ramp may be unusable at low water levels.

Facilities, fees: A campground is available about one-quarter mile from the lake. Boat camping is permitted on the lake's east side. Supplies can be obtained in Groveland. Access is free.

Water sports, restrictions: Waterskiing, personal watercraft, and windsurfing are permitted. A rocky beach for swimming is located next to the boat launch. Sandy beaches are available on the lake's east side, and are accessible only by boat.

Contact: Stanislaus National Forest, Groveland Ranger District, (209) 962-7825 or fax (209) 962-7412. For a detailed map of the area, send $4 to Maps, Office of Information, US Forest Service, 1323 Club Drive, Vallejo, CA 94592.

About Cherry Lake: Cherry Lake provides a base of operations for many activities, including camping, boating, swimming, windsurfing, and hiking. The lake is set at an elevation of 4,700 feet, just outside the northwestern border of Yosemite National Park.

All water sports are allowed, yet because it takes so long for most visitors to drive here, you won't find nearly the waterskiing traffic as at other regional lakes, such as Tulloch or Don Pedro in the foothills. It is a great spot for windsurfing, though, with cold, clear water and afternoon winds that are predictable and strong. In the early summer, when winds can blow fiercely, the lake will test the skills of even expert windsurfers.

Most swimmers stick to the 200-yard stretch of rocky beach by the boat ramp, but that is pretty poor pluckings compared to what is available on the lake's far east side. You need a boat to get out there, but the ride is worth it, for you'll have access to a sandy stretch of shore in a far more private setting.

Here's an insider's tip: During periods of campfire restrictions, which is often most of the summer in this national forest, the campground is the only one in the area where campfires are permitted. That makes the idea of camping here extremely compelling.

At the dam at Cherry Lake is a trail that is routed north into the Emigrant Wilderness, or to the east to Lake Eleanor and far-

ther into Yosemite National Park. Between the two wilderness areas, there are literally dozens and dozens of backcountry lakes.

⑫ Virginia Lakes

Location: Near Lee Vining; map E4, grid e9.

Directions: From Bridgeport drive south on US 395 to Virginia Lakes Road. Turn west on Virginia Lakes Road and drive 6.5 miles to Lower Virginia Lake.

Access: An unimproved boat ramp is available at Virginia Lakes Resort on Lower Virginia Lake.

Facilities, fees: A campground is located nearby on Virginia Creek. Lodging, restaurant, and groceries are available at Virginia Lakes Resort, which also offers fishing boat rentals. Rentals for horsepack trips are also available. Supplies can be obtained in Lee Vining. Access is free.

Water sports, restrictions: Gas-powered motors are not permitted on the lake. A 10 mph speed limit is strictly enforced. Swimming and all water-body contact sports are prohibited.

Contact: Virginia Lakes Resort, (760) 647-6484.

About Virginia Lakes: This pair of lakes connected by a channel is the gateway to a beautiful high mountain basin where there are eight small alpine lakes within a two-mile circle. They are set at an elevation of 9,600 feet, between mountain peaks that rise 12,000 feet high.

The lakes are known for providing visitors with quiet solitude and trout fishing. The speed limit allows canoeists to enjoy calm waters. No swimming or water sports are allowed, which keeps away families looking for a vacation site with lots of water sport activities.

Big Virginia gets the heaviest fishing traffic. Guests at Virginia Lakes Lodge usually stick to the lower lake.

A nearby trail is routed just north of Blue Lake, located inside the boundary for the Hoover Wilderness, then leads west to Frog Lake, Summit Lake, and beyond into a remote section of Yosemite National Park. The entire area has great natural beauty that is best seen on foot, allowing you to explore the different lakes as you go.

⑬ Tuolumne River

🏕🐟✕🏊   🔟

Location: East of Yosemite National Park in Stanislaus National Forest; map E4, grid f0.

Directions: From Stockton drive south on Highway 99 to Manteca. Turn east on Highway 120 and drive approximately 70 miles to the small town of Groveland. Continue east on Highway 120 for about eight miles, turn left on Ferretti Road (the turnoff is located about a mile past the turnoff for County Road J20), and drive north two miles. Turn right on Lumsden Road/Forest Service Road 1N01 and continue approximately six miles down the steep road. Access is available along the road and at Lumsden and Lumsden Bridge Campgrounds.

Another access point is located farther north: Continue east on Highway 120 to Forest Service Road 1N07/Cherry Oil Road and turn north. When you reach a fork, bear left and look for signs indicating Cherry Lake. Continue to the bridge at the powerhouse.

Access: There is no ramp. Two standard runs are available:

Upper Tuolumne: The put-in for this run is actually on Cherry Creek. To reach it, drive 14 miles east of Groveland on Highway 120 to Forest Service Road 1N07/Cherry Oil Road and turn north. When you reach a fork, bear left and look for signs indicating Cherry Lake. Continue to the bridge at the powerhouse. Cross it and continue 1.5 miles to an unsigned paved road on the left. Turn left and continue to the put-in, located just downstream of the powerhouse. Take out at Meral Pool.

Note: The Upper Tuolumne is extremely challenging, with several Class V rapids. Do not attempt it at high flows. Even during the river's low flows, this run is for experts only.

Main Tuolumne: From Groveland drive east on Highway 120 for approximately eight miles, turn left on Ferretti Road (the turnoff is located about a mile past the turnoff for County Road J20), and travel one mile north. Turn right on Lumsden Road/Forest Service Road 1N01 and continue approximately six miles down the steep road to Lumsden Campground. Put in at Meral Pool, just downstream from the campground. Take out at Ward's Ferry, which can be reached by taking Deer Flat Road (off Highway 120, two miles west of Groveland) north to Ward's Ferry Road and then north to where the road crosses the river at the upper arm of Don Pedro Reservoir.

Note: At high flows (above 4,000 cubic feet per second) this run should be paddled by experts only.

Facilities, fees: Several campgrounds are available on and near the river, but they offer no piped water. The two most popular for rafters are Lumsden and Lumsden Bridge. Access is free. Rafting permits are required from May 1 through September 30; obtain forms through the Groveland Ranger District in Groveland.

Water sports, restrictions: Several excellent swimming holes are available along Lumsden Road/Forest Service Road 1N01. A good one is just downstream from Lumsden Campground.

Contact: Stanislaus National Forest, Groveland Ranger District, (209) 962-7825 or fax (209) 962-7412 For a detailed map of the area, send $4 to Maps, Office of Information, US Forest Service, 1323 Club Drive, Vallejo, CA 94592. For guided rafting trips contact Ahwahnee Whitewater Expeditions, (800) 359-9790; All-Outdoors Whitewater Rafting, (800) 247-2387; ARTA, (800) 323-2782; ECHO, (800) 652-3246; OARS, Inc, (800) 346-6277; Outdoor Adventures, (800) 323-4234; Sierra Mac River Trips, (800) 457-2580; Whitewater Voyages, (800) 488-7238; or Zephyr River Expeditions, (209) 532-6249.

About the Tuolumne River: Many rafters get baptized by the cool, clear, and pounding rapids of the Tuolumne. It is one of the most popular runs in California, and yes, that baptism usually includes a full dunking. It's a wildly exciting river with Class IV and Class V water, enough to set the hearts of even the most experienced paddlers pounding.

There are two primary runs, and both are for experts only, usually in oar boats. Newcomers jumping into a raft had better make sure an expert is at the oars, or plan on sprouting gills. Both runs offer prime scenery and wilderness-like settings, not that you'll have a moment to notice as you're hitting rapid after rapid, often with scarcely a second in between to catch your breath. At times you even have to time your breathing for when you aren't smothered by water.

The water is clear and cold. Some people wear dry suits or just the bottom or the top of a dry suit or wet suit.

A great bonus is the long season, which can run from March to October. In wet years, however, both runs can be too high to attempt before May. Even when the river's levels are navigable, the runs will be high, turbulent, and dangerous.

Here are some specifics:

Upper Tuolumne: Pro rafters call this the Upper T for Upper Tuolumne. It peaks out at Class V+, just a half step from certain death. Perfect, eh? The run ranges nine miles from Cherry Creek to Meral Pool. Make absolutely sure that only experts are at the oars of a raft, and never, ever run at high flows.

From the put-in the trip starts with more than a mile of Class IV rapids, and just when you are getting accustomed to the thrills, the excitement is tweaked up a full notch. You then quickly run into several Class V drops, including Corkscrew, Jawbone, Mushroom, Catapult, and Miracle Mile. Any of these can popcorn you from the boat if you don't have a good hold, and even then, there are many times when you are so wet, literally submerged in the river, that you will not know when you are in the raft and when you are not.

At about mile seven you'll hit Flat Rock Falls, a Class V–VI drop that is often portaged. At high water you can buy the farm here. Same with Lumsden Falls, which is always portaged. After you get back in the boat, the run winds out with several more Class IV rapids over the course of 1.5 miles en route to the take-out at Meral Pool.

Main Tuolumne: The T, as it is affectionately known, includes one of the most fun rapids in California, Pinball, and one of the most terrorizing, Clavey Falls. It's an 18-mile run, starting at Meral Pool and running downstream to Ward's Ferry, and is rated Class IV+.

From Meral Pool the first five miles feature encounters with several Class IV rapids and drops, including Nemesis, Sunderland's Chute, Hackamack Hole, Ram's Head, and Evangelist. While this may be exciting and enjoyable, the whole time in the back of your mind you will be anticipating the pending confrontation with Clavey Falls (Class V). You know it's coming, you know it's waiting, and finally, you round a bend and there it is. Before you even realize it, you are plunging down through the white water literally like a snowball in hell. This is the one nobody forgets. Some people surrender and portage.

From here the last nine miles are peppered with more Class IV rapids. Featured are Gray's Grindstone, Thread the Needle, Cabin, Hell's Kitchen, and a half mile upstream of the take-out, Pinball, one of the most fun rapids on the run. So you end on an upbeat note, and with the knowledge that you have experienced firsthand one of life's most exhilarating adventures.

⑭ Saddlebag Lake

Location: West of Lee Vining in Inyo National Forest; map E4, grid f9.

Directions: From US 395 just south of the town of Lee Vining, drive west on Highway 120 for about 11 miles to Saddlebag Lake Road. Turn right and drive about three miles to the lake and boat ramp.

Access: An unimproved boat launch is located at Saddlebag Lake Resort.

Facilities, fees: A campground, snack bar, and a grocery store are available. You can rent fishing boats at Saddlebag Lake Resort. Access is free. There is a fee for boat launching.

Water sports, restrictions: A 10 mph speed limit is enforced. The water is too cold for swimming. Windsurfing is possible with a wet suit.

Contact: Inyo National Forest, Mono Lake Visitor Center, (760) 647-3044 or fax (760) 647-3046; Saddlebag Lake Resort, PO Box 303, Lee Vining, CA 93541.

About Saddlebag Lake: If you want to feel as if you are standing on top of the world, just take a trip here. Your vehicle may gasp for breath as it makes the climb, but when you finally arrive, you will be at the highest lake in California accessible by car, Saddlebag Lake, at elevation 10,087 feet.

If you like to camp, boat, and fish, this is an outstanding destination. It also makes good a jump-off point for a wilderness backpacking trip.

Saddlebag Lake is by far the biggest lake in the region, and is set off by stark, pristine granite well above the treeline.

At this elevation don't even think about getting in the water without a wet suit. In the ideal situation you'll be high and dry in a fishing boat or canoe, enjoying the fantastic wilderness views and quiet water.

Most people who come here are interested in hiking and exploring the adjacent wilderness area, not the lake, so much of the traffic in the campground is generated by hikers, not boaters. This means that even when the campground is packed, the lake is often wide open.

The boat ramp is primitive, the air cool, the water always very cold. Because of the high elevation, the recreation season is short. In high snow years the place becomes accessible in late June, and sometimes not until after the Fourth of July. In low snow years access is often possible by Memorial Day weekend, rarely earlier in May. That makes late July and August the prime time, as the nights again become cold in September. The first big snow cuts off access again in the fall, often by Halloween.

⑮ Tenaya Lake

Location: West of Lee Vining in Yosemite National Park; map E4, grid g6.

Directions: From US 395 just south of the town of Lee Vining, turn west on Highway 120 and drive about 11 miles west to the Yosemite National Park entrance. Continue another 15 miles to the lake.

Access: There is no boat ramp. Cartop boats may be hand launched.

Facilities, fees: A picnic area is provided. Campsites are available nearby at Tuolumne Meadows (first come, first served). Supplies can be obtained in Lee Vining and in the park. A park entrance fee is charged.

Water sports, restrictions: Motors are not permitted on the lake. A swimming beach is available on the eastern shore. Windsurfing is permitted.

Contact: Yosemite National Park, Headquarters, (209) 372-0200 or (209) 372-0265.

About Tenaya Lake: There may be no prettier lake on Earth than Tenaya Lake on a warm, windless evening. Set in a natural rock basin in the pristine, high granite country of Yosemite, this is a rare place.

It is set at an elevation of 8,141 feet and covers 150 acres. The atmosphere feels almost sacred, like a mountain temple. The lake was named after Chief Tenaya of the Ahwahneechee tribe, who was Yosemite's last Native American chief and caretaker until a US Army troop moved the entire tribe to a reservation.

Hiking is the most popular activity here. A very beautiful and easy trail loops around the lake's lower end to the far side. Windsurfing, however, is fast becoming a favorite with many visitors, who like to catch the west winds and skim across the surface in a truly spectacular setting. While there can be many people driving along adjacent Highway 120, or even stopping to picnic or hike, you often have the lake to yourself.

One reason is that the fishing is terrible. Trout have not been stocked for many years, and the lake is now fished out. So you'll see very few anglers and never a fishing boat. It is extremely rare to see people paddling around in canoes or kayaks.

Instead, Tenaya Lake attracts those who want to experience one of the most stunningly beautiful settings on the planet.

⓰ Ellery Lake

Location: West of Lee Vining in Inyo National Forest; map E4, grid g9.
Directions: From US 395 just south of the town of Lee Vining, turn west on Highway 120 and drive about nine miles west to the lake.
Access: There is no boat ramp. Cartop boats may be hand launched.
Facilities, fees: A campground is provided on the lake's west side. More camp-grounds are available within Yosemite National Park. Nearby Tioga Pass Resort offers cabins, café, and fishing boat rentals. Supplies can be obtained in Lee Vining. Access to the lake is free.

Water sports, restrictions: A 10 mph speed limit is strictly enforced. The water is too cold for swimming, and the lake too small for windsurfing.

Contact: Inyo National Forest, Mono Lake Visitor Center, (760) 647-3044 or fax (760) 647-3046.

About Ellery Lake: Congress blew the deal when they set the borders for Yosemite National Park and failed to include Tioga and Ellery Lakes within park boundaries. Both are set just two miles outside the Highway 120 entrance on the eastern side of the park.

Ellery Lake offers spectacular deep-blue waters set in rock at 9,800 feet. It looks like Yosemite, feels like Yosemite, but is not Yosemite.

This is a beautiful lake, although often freezing cold, and it is a popular spot for trout fishing and overflow camping. Small motorized boats are allowed, but you almost never see them. Anglers usually fish from the shore and rarely bring cartop boats such as rowboats, canoes, or float tubes.

Use is heavy in the summertime. The lake is easily accessed off Highway 120, and the campgrounds get a lot of people who arrive late at Yosemite only to discover the camps there are full. The irony is that the camps at Ellery Lake are usually just as full.

⓱ Tioga Lake

Location: West of Lee Vining in Inyo National Forest; map E4, grid g9.
Directions: From US 395 at the town of Lee Vining, drive a short distance south and turn west on Highway 120. Continue 10 miles west to the lake.

Access: A small, unimproved boat ramp is available near the campground.

Facilities, fees: A small campground is provided. More campgrounds are available within Yosemite National Park. Nearby Tioga Pass Resort offers cabins, café, and fishing boat rentals. Supplies can be obtained in Lee Vining. Access to the lake is free.

Water sports, restrictions: A 10 mph speed limit is strictly enforced. The water is too cold for swimming, and the lake too small for windsurfing.

Contact: Inyo National Forest, Mono Lake Visitor Center, (760) 647-3044 or fax (760) 647-3046.

About Tioga Lake: Tioga, like nearby Ellery, is a gorgeous spot located just outside the borders of Yosemite National Park and set at an elevation of 9,700 feet.

Conditions here are much like those at neighboring Ellery, with one giant difference: Tioga has a boat ramp. Though small and primitive, the ramp makes the lake accessible for campers with trailered boats.

Most of those who do launch here are fishing for trout, trolling about slowly and enjoying the panoramic views of the many high granite peaks nearby. The campground is often full.

Note that the four major lakes in this region—Tioga, Ellery, Tenaya, and Saddleback—are usually locked up by snow and ice until late May, and in big snow years all the way into July. The 15 hike-to lakes in the vicinity don't usually become accessible until mid-June, with the high mountain spring arriving in July.

---

⑱ Merced River

Location: West of Yosemite National Park in Sierra National Forest; map E4, grid h0.

Directions: From Merced on Highway 99, drive approximately 45 miles northeast on Highway 140 to the historical site of Briceburg. Continue north; the road parallels the river, and direct access is available. Limited access is also available in Yosemite National Park; enter at the El Portal entrance on Highway 140.

Access: There is no boat ramp. The standard put-in is at the Red Bud Launch Site, just across a bridge from Red Bud Picnic Area, located on Highway 140, 29 miles east of Mariposa. At high flows boaters can put in about three miles downstream at Cranberry Gulch in order to avoid the difficult rapids below Red Bud. There are several access spots to take out along the run; the last possible take-out is at Bagby, near McClure Reservoir. To reach it, return to the junction of Highways 140 and 49 in Mariposa and then drive 18 miles north on Highway 49 to a dirt road that heads toward McClure Reservoir. An easy Class I float is also available in Yosemite National Park; enter at El Portal entrance on Highway 140.

Facilities, fees: Indian Flat Campground is located four miles south of El Portal on Highway 140. Other camps are located along the river west of the park entrance near El Portal. Supplies can be obtained in El Portal. Small rafts are rented inside Yosemite National Park. Access is free, except for two spots: Yosemite National Park, where an entrance fee is charged, and at the lowermost take-out north of Bagby, where vehicles using the access road must pay a fee. On the main run, rafting permits are required only for parties with more than 24 people; contact the Bureau of Land Management for information.

Water sports, restrictions: There are several great swimming holes along Highway 140. Look for turnouts and access points off the highway. Some of the most popular and easily accessible holes are near Indian Flat Campground.

Contact: Bureau of Land Management, Folsom Field Office, (916) 985-4474; Sierra National Forest, Minarets-Mariposa Ranger District, (559) 683-4665 or fax (559) 877-

3108; Yosemite National Park, Headquarters, (209) 372-0265. For guided rafting trips contact Ahwahnee Whitewater Expeditions, (800) 359-9790; All-Outdoors Whitewater Rafting, (800) 247-2387; American River Recreation, (916) 622-6802; ARTA, (800) 323-2782; Beyond Limits Adventures, (800) 234-7238; Mariah Wilderness Expeditions, (800) 462-7424; OARS, Inc, (800) 346-6277; Whitewater Voyages, (800) 488-7238; or Zephyr River Expeditions, (209) 532-6249.

About the Merced River: So many vacationers drive right by this stream in their mad scramble to get to Yosemite National Park. It's a beautiful river, offering outstanding rafting and gorgeous scenery, and an opportunity to go swimming and fly-fishing for trout.

There are also several Bureau of Land Management campgrounds available along the Merced that have far fewer people in them then the camps in Yosemite, along with good river access. In the summer it is an ideal river to jump into during the daytime, with many deep holes and rocks perfectly situated for jumping platforms (always check the depth of the hole before jumping in and never dive headfirst into a river, of course).

But the true attraction is rafting. An extraordinarily long stretch of river (29 miles) can be run from the put-in at Red Bud to the take-out at Bagby. The first nine miles and the last 13 miles are rated Class IV+; the seven miles in between those two stretches are rated Class II.

Excellent scenery surrounds the river, and the run has a remote feel, even though much of it is paralleled by the highway. The water is cold and high early in the season, but becomes quite warm by the end of summer. In a year with average rainfall, the season lasts approximately from April to early July, with smaller boats capable of floating it from July to early August. In big snow years the ensuing snowmelt can turn this river into a torrent when the weather gets hot. In any case, always go with an experienced guide.

Within the first half hour after putting in at Red Bud, you will confront some of the river's nastiest rapids. The first 2.5 miles contain some Class IV white water, most notably Chipped Tooth and Nightmare Island. At high flows, in fact, it's often better to avoid these completely and put in farther downstream at Cranberry Gulch.

Five miles downstream of Cranberry Gulch, you come face-to-face with Ned's Gulch, another Class IV rapid. After that you can enjoy the scenery and relaxed Class II water for about seven miles.

Then prepare yourself for a series of more Class IV rapids that will spring you back to full attention. The guides call them Split Rock, Corner Pocket, and Quarter Mile. At mile 23, boaters encounter North Fork Falls, which must be portaged by all. It's a 25-foot vertical, rocky drop.

Afterwards it's easy going from here to the take-out, rated Class II. All in all, this is a beautiful, dramatic, and rewarding rafting trip.

Map of Northern California—Page 28

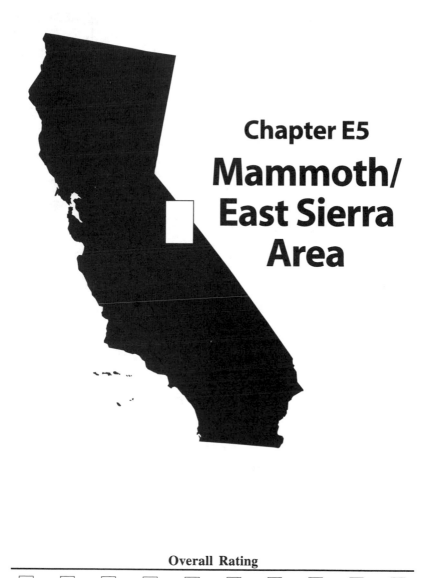

Chapter E5
Mammoth/ East Sierra Area

E5–Mammoth/E Sierra Area Map

One inch equals approximately 10.7 miles.
See page 12 for California state map.

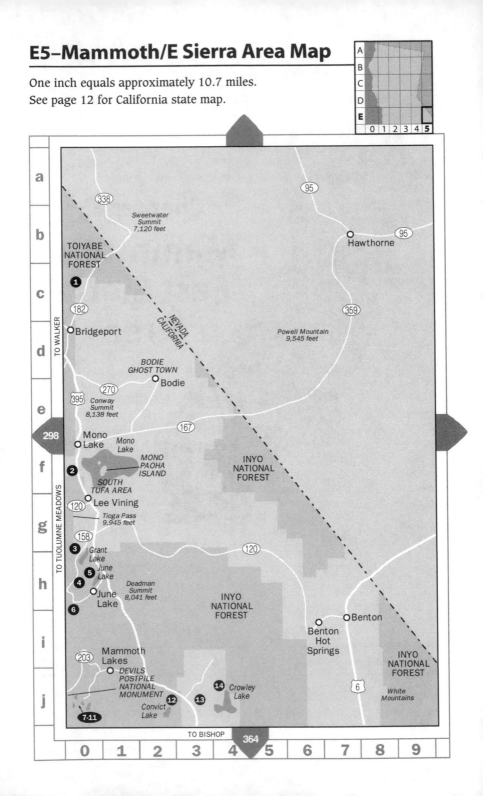

Chapter E5 features:

1 Bridgeport Reservoir

Location: Near Bridgeport; map E5, grid c0.

Directions: From Southern California take US 395 north to Bishop and continue to Bridgeport. At Bridgeport turn east on Highway 182 and continue for one mile to the lake.

From Northern California take Interstate 50 east from Sacramento to Echo Summit (near South Lake Tahoe); then turn south on Highway 89 and drive to its junction with US 395. Turn south on US 395, drive through Bridgeport, turn north on Highway 182, and continue to the lake.

Access: There are three boat ramps:

Bridgeport Public Ramp: From Bridgeport drive 3.5 miles north on Highway 182 to the sign for public access. A paved ramp is available.

Falling Rock Marina: From Bridgeport drive about three miles north on Highway 182 to the marina, which has a paved ramp and docks.

Paradise Shores RV Park: From Bridgeport drive north on Highway 182. The park is just past Falling Rock Marina. A dirt launching area is available.

Facilities, fees: You can camp at Falling Rock Marina and at Paradise Shores RV Park (no tents). Picnic areas are provided along the eastern shore. Falling Rock Marina has a full-service marina and fishing boat rent-

als. Supplies can be obtained in Bridgeport. Access is free.

Water sports, restrictions: Waterskiing, personal watercraft, and windsurfing are permitted. Although there are no designated beaches, swimming is permitted anywhere along the shoreline.

Contact: Falling Rock Marina, (760) 932-7001; Paradise Shores RV Park, (760) 932-7735.

For a free travel packet on the area, phone the Mammoth Lakes Visitor Bureau, (800) 367-6572 or (888) 466-2666.

About Bridgeport Reservoir: On the high desert edge of the Great Basin, just east of the Sierra Nevada, you'll find Bridgeport Reservoir. This is a big lake, covering 4,400 surface acres when full. It is nestled in a valley at an elevation of 6,500 feet and is quite pretty, filled with bright blue water that contrasts with the stark surrounding countryside of the eastern Sierra.

Though winters can be bitter cold here, by summer the water is warm, even laden with algae by August. The algae, along with the fact that the lake is not too deep, keeps most folks from waterskiing or swimming. While there are no restrictions on water sports, it's just not the greatest lake to get plunged into in this region. Water-skiers tend to head instead to Twin Lakes (although the water is cold there, too).

If you don't mind the algae, windsurfing here can be excellent, with brisk afternoon west winds in the summer and a lot of room to really let it rip. A good deal of shoreline is grassy, and as long as water levels are high, the put-ins are clean and not muddy.

Bridgeport Reservoir has its share of large trout, including some truly monster-sized brown trout. So most of the traffic here is from anglers, along with a few US 395 travelers who are curious about what the lake looks like.

That is because Bridgeport Reservoir attracted national attention late in the summer of 1989 when it was completely drained to provide water to some hay farmers in Nevada who wanted to get an extra crop in at the end of the year. In the process they ruined this lake, as well as the East Walker River (which was covered with silt from the lake bottom). But Bridgeport has been dried up before and has always come back as a premier body of water. And so it is again.

❷ Lundy Lake

Location: Near Lee Vining; map E5, grid f0.

Directions: From the town of Lee Vining on US 395, drive north for seven miles north and then turn left (west) on Lundy Lake Road. Continue for five miles to the lake at the road's end.

Access: An unimproved boat ramp is located at the lake's far west corner, near Lundy Lake Resort.

Facilities, fees: A picnic area and primitive campsites are provided near the lake's east side on Mill Creek. Cabins, a small campground, and fishing boat rentals are available at Lundy Lake Resort. Limited groceries and supplies can be obtained at the lake; for full supplies, try in Lee Vining. Access is free.

Water sports, restrictions: A 10 mph speed limit is strictly enforced. The lake is usually too cold for swimming and windsurfing.

Contact: Inyo National Forest, Lee Vining Visitor Center, (760) 647-3044 or fax (760)

647-3046; Lundy Lake Resort, PO Box 550, Lee Vining, CA 93541. No phone is available at the resort, but for information during the off-season, call (626) 309-0415.

For a free travel packet on the area, phone the Mammoth Lakes Visitor Bureau, (800) 367-6572 or (888) 466-2666.

About Lundy Lake: Looking for good fishing, campground, and a jump-off point for hikes into the wilderness? Try Lundy Lake, which is set in a high mountain valley (at elevation 7,800 feet) in the stark eastern Sierra, just a short drive from US 395.

Fantastic scenery surrounds this narrow lake, which is one mile long and one-half mile wide. Much of the shoreline is sprinkled with pine and aspen trees, and the old resort provides a rustic, New England–type feel, especially in the fall when the aspens turn color.

The water at Lundy Lake is clear and very cold, direct from snowmelt, even through the summer. Swimming is not recommended. Neither is windsurfing, not only because of the water temperature, but because there's usually just not enough wind.

That makes it an excellent choice for people with a canoe, rowboat, or small fishing boat. A 10 mph speed limit and typically calm or very light winds are two big boating pluses.

While use at the lake is moderate throughout the year, it's usually not too crowded, even on summer weekends. The resort, however, is a different story, and their cabins are often booked far in advance.

For a great side trip, hike up the trail that starts beyond the west end of Lundy Lake and is routed along upper Mill Creek and into the Hoover Wilderness. That trek alone makes a satisfying day hike. More ambitious hikers with two cars (one for a shuttle) will find an excellent short but steep trip by hiking from Lundy Lake, up over Lundy Pass, and then over to Saddlebag Lake.

Lundy Lake is sometimes overlooked because many travelers become fascinated instead with giant Mono Lake, located just to the east of the highway. The area is akin to a moonscape, the centerpiece of which is this giant saline lake. It is the nesting site for nearly every species of gull in California. If you ever have seen seagulls in the mountains and wondered what they are doing there, Mono Lake provides the answer. As vacationers stare at the lake, though, they don't even see the adjacent turnoff signed Lundy Lake Road.

❸ Grant Lake

Location: Near Lee Vining in Inyo National Forest; map E5, grid h0.

Directions: From Carson City on US 50 or Reno on Interstate 89, drive south on US 395 past Mono Lake. Turn right at the first Highway 158/June Lake Loop turnoff. Drive west on Highway 158 to the lake.

Access: A paved ramp is located at Grant Lake Marina.

Facilities, fees: A campground, picnic area, store, and small marina are provided. Fishing boat and dock rentals are also available. Access is free. There is a fee for boat launching.

Water sports, restrictions: Waterskiing, personal watercraft, and windsurfing are permitted. A sandy watercraft/swimming beach is available near the marina.

Contact: Grant Lake Marina, (760) 648-7964.

For a free travel packet on the area, phone the Mammoth Lakes Visitor Bureau, (800) 367-6572 or (888) 466-2666.

About Grant Lake: The June Lakes Loop is highlighted by a series of quality lakes accessible by car along a loop road (Highway 158) off US 395. These include Grant Lake, Silver Lake, Gull Lake, and June Lake.

Dramatic panoramic sunsets make Grant Lake a special place, the largest of the waters among the June Loop Lakes. Shaped like an hourglass, the lake is set at an elevation of 7,600 feet and covers 1,100 surface acres. Though the surroundings here are by far the most stark of all the lakes in the loop, it is still a very attractive destination for boaters and water sports enthusiasts, with (also by far) the most tolerant boating rules.

Grant Lake is the only lake in the loop where waterskiing and personal watercraft are allowed. Because of that, it tends to attract more of a boater/party crowd, while the others get primarily anglers and campers.

The water can be cold, but it is still good for swimming and waterskiing. Windsurfing conditions are often excellent in late summer, even for experts, as the lake gets a west wind that really sends sailboarders across the lake at a fast clip. There is one large, fully developed campground that usually has some open sites, even on crowded summer weekends.

The lake is subject to drawdowns courtesy of the Los Angeles Department of Water & Power. In years with a light snowfall and a corresponding low snowpack, the water level can get quite low.

❹ Gull Lake

Location: Near Lee Vining in Inyo National Forest; map E5, grid h0.

Directions: From Carson City on US 50 or Reno on Interstate 89, drive south on US 395 past Mono Lake. Turn right at the first Highway 158/June Lake Loop turnoff. Drive west on Highway 158, past June Lake, and then continue another mile to Gull Lake.

Access: A paved boat ramp is located at Gull Lake Boat Landing. Look for the turnoff on Highway 158, past June Lake. Another old, unmaintained boat ramp is available near Gull Lake Campground.

Facilities, fees: A campground and picnic area are provided. Fishing boat rentals and a full-service marina are available at Gull Lake Boat Landing. Groceries can be obtained nearby. Access is free. There is a fee to launch your boat at the marina; the old Forest Service ramp is free, but in poor condition.

Water sports, restrictions: A 10 mph speed limit is strictly enforced. Swimming is permitted, although most of the shoreline is quite steep. The lake is too small for windsurfing.

Contact: Inyo National Forest, Lee Vining Visitor Center, (760) 647-3044 or fax (760) 647-3046; Gull Lake Boat Landing, (619) 648-7539.

For a free travel packet on the area, phone the Mammoth Lakes Visitor Bureau, (800) 367-6572 or (888) 466-2666.

About Gull Lake: Little Gull Lake is the smallest of the June Loop Lakes, covering just 64 acres. Set at an elevation of 7,600 feet below the peaks of the eastern Sierra, it is intimate yet dramatic, tiny yet beautiful.

The lake, which is easily accessible off Highway 158, is excellent for fishing and paddling around in small boats. Swimming is generally not recommended because of the steep shoreline and the cold water. People who want to swim should head instead to the developed swimming beach at nearby June Lake. However, there is a rope swing at Gull Lake that the local kids play on.

If this pretty lake were in the middle of nowhere, it would be treated like a slice of heaven. But with June Lake right down the road providing better fishing, boating, swimming, and camping, this place gets only moderate use throughout the summer.

❺ June Lake

Location: Near Lee Vining in Inyo National Forest; map E5, grid h0.
Directions: From Carson City on US 50 or

Reno on Interstate 89, drive south on US 395 past Mono Lake. Turn right at the first Highway 158/June Lakes Loop Road turnoff. Turn west on Highway 158 and drive three miles to June Lake.

Access: Two paved boat ramps are available: one at June Lake Marina and one at Big Rock Resort, both located off Highway 158.

Facilities, fees: Two campgrounds are provided. A full-service marina, docks, and fishing boat rentals are available at June Lake Marina. Cabins, small marina, and fishing boat rentals are also available at Big Rock Resort. Groceries and other supplies can be obtained nearby. Access is free. There is a fee for boat launching.

Water sports, restrictions: A 10 mph speed limit is strictly enforced. Windsurfing is permitted. A large, developed swimming beach is available.

Contact: Inyo National Forest, Lee Vining Visitor Center, (760) 647-3044 or fax (760) 647-3046; June Lake Marina, (760) 648-7726; Big Rock Resort, (760) 648-7717. For lodging information, phone (760) 648-7794.

For a free travel packet on the area, phone the Mammoth Lakes Visitor Bureau, (800) 367-6572 or (888) 466-2666.

About June Lake: This lake is the centerpiece of a fully developed resort area. It has everything going for it except solitude. Beauty? Try a 160-acre mountain lake set at 7,600 feet below awesome peaks that are often edged with snow. Accommodations? There are campsites near the water, cabins, a good boat ramp, and stores within a mile. If you need something you can get it here.

June Lake is very beautiful and easily accessible off Highway 158. It gets the highest use by far of all the lakes in the June Lakes Loop for many reasons: It has the best fishing, best campground, best swimming, and best windsurfing. That's a lot of bests.

Even when the place is crowded, the 10

mph speed limit ensures at least a modicum of serenity. Most of the boaters you'll see are fishers, and they are up early, getting their fishing done before the predictable afternoon wind comes up. That wind, along with the rules that prohibit waterskiing, makes windsurfing extremely popular here. Sailboarders enjoy clear, open water and brisk afternoon winds almost every day, and there are no water-skiers to get in the way.

This is also the best lake in the loop for swimming, as well as the only one with a developed beach.

Newcomers will need a little attitude adjustment when they arrive and discover two factors: the cold water and the number of other visitors. Windsurfers should wear wet suits, and swimmers should be prepared to turn into ice cubes. And even though it takes a long drive from almost anywhere to reach June Lake, the quality of the place is high enough that a number of people are willing to pay that price. Get the message? Right: always have reservations for lodging.

❻ Silver Lake

Location: Near Lee Vining in Inyo National Forest; map E5, grid i0.

Directions: From Carson City on US 50 or Reno on Interstate 89, drive south on US 395 past Mono Lake. Turn right at the first Highway 158/June Lakes Loop Road turnoff. Drive past June Lake and Gull Lake and continue for another three miles to Silver Lake.

Or from the town of Lee Vining on US 395, drive 11 miles south to June Lake Junction. Turn south on Highway 158/June Lakes Loop Road and drive six miles to the lake.

Access: A paved boat ramp is located at the lake's south end, at Silver Lake Resort.

Facilities, fees: A Forest Service campground is provided. An RV park, cabins, general store, gas, RV supplies, groceries, and a restaurant are available at Silver Lake Resort. There's a small marina where you can rent canoes and fishing boats. Access is free. There is a fee for boat launching.

Water sports, restrictions: A 5 mph speed limit is strictly enforced. Swimming is not recommended due to the rocky shoreline. The lake is too small for windsurfing.

Contact: Inyo National Forest, Lee Vining Visitor Center, (760) 647-3044 or fax (760) 647-3046; Silver Lake Resort, (619) 648-7525.

For a free travel packet on the area, phone the Mammoth Lakes Visitor Bureau, (800) 367-6572 or (888) 466-2666.

About Silver Lake: Small and intimate Silver Lake was named for the way it looks when afternoon winds cause the surface waters to sparkle in refracted silvers—a beautiful sight against a background of several high but stark Sierra peaks. This lake, set at elevation 7,600 feet, covers just 80 acres. Yet all services are provided, including boat rentals, cabins, and a campground; and there is an outstanding trailhead that is routed up the beautiful Rush Creek drainage.

Silver Lake has the most developed resort in the June Lakes Loop, which makes it a tourist magnet in the summer. Most visitors are campers/anglers who stay at the large, open campground just east of the lake at the adjacent RV park or in the resort's cabins. If you prefer fewer people, consider nearby Gull Lake instead, which gets far less use.

A 5 mph speed limit is designed to eliminate user conflict, as well as fast boats. That makes it ideal for fishing.

Even with the speed limit, swimming is not recommended because the shoreline is rocky, the bottom somewhat mucky, the water cold, and by the afternoon, it's often windy.

Unlike Grant Lake, Silver Lake doesn't seem to have problems with water drawdowns. Snowmelt in spring and glacial water in summer flow into the lake, creating a pure setting that is usually full to the brim.

While the lake does not have a wilderness setting, you don't have to go too far to find that, with the Ansel Adams Wilderness only a two-hour hike from a signed trailhead just south of the lake. From here a trail is routed west from Silver Lake along the Rush Creek drainage and up to Agnew Lake, a great day hike that provides access not only to a pristine lake, but wonderful views of the June Lake Basin.

❼ Horseshoe Lake

Location: Near Mammoth Lakes in Inyo National Forest; map E5, grid j0.
Directions: From the town of Bishop on US 395, drive north for 39 miles to Mammoth Junction. Continue straight on Highway 203, driving four miles to the Mammoth Lakes Basin, and follow signs to the lake.
Access: There is no boat ramp. Cartop boats may be hand launched.
Facilities, fees: A picnic area and group campground are available; campground reservations are required. Note: The campground and picnic area may be closed. Phone ahead for status. Supplies can be obtained in Mammoth Lakes and at Lake Mary. Access to the lake is free.
Water sports, restrictions: A 10 mph speed limit is strictly enforced. There is a swimming beach available. Windsurfing is permitted, but the lake is generally considered too small.
Contact: For information and a free travel packet phone Mammoth Lakes Visitor Center, (760) 924-5500 or (888) 466-2666.

For a free travel packet on the area, contact Mammoth Lakes Visitor Bureau, (800) 367-6572 or (888) 466-2666.
About Horseshoe Lake: The Mammoth Lakes Basin features a series of small high mountain lakes that are as pretty as any other drive-to lakes in the world. Little Horseshoe Lake is one of the better examples of the kind of natural beauty common to the eastern Sierra.

The lake, set at elevation 8,900 feet, is one of several found along Lake Mary Road. Of all the destinations at Mammoth, this is the best choice for swimming and cartop boating. A resort, boat rentals, and boat ramp are not available; for those reasons it gets less use than the other lakes—Mary, Mamie, Twin, and George.

You do get a nice swimming beach, though; in fact, this is the only lake in the Mammoth Basin where swimming is allowed. In addition, boaters can hand launch canoes or small boats from the shore. A number of fly fishers float around in inner tubes, officially called float tubes or belly boats, as they try for trout.

What also makes this lake special is the trailhead at the lake's northern side. The trail leads west up to Mammoth Pass (and then connects shortly thereafter with the Pacific Crest Trail), providing incredible sweeping views.

On a different note, in 1995 the campground and picnic area were closed temporarily after volcanic carbon dioxide emissions were detected here. After conducting a study, the Forest Service determined that the levels were safe and reopened the facilities. Guess it's just another unique element of one of the most wondrous areas on the planet.

❽ Twin Lakes

Location: Near Mammoth Lakes in Inyo National Forest; map E5, grid j0.
Directions: From the town of Bishop on US 395, drive north 39 miles to Mammoth Lakes Junction. Turn west on Highway 203/ Minaret Summit Road, drive four miles,

then turn left onto Lake Mary Road, and drive three miles to the lake.

Access: There is no boat ramp. Cartop boats may be hand launched.

Facilities, fees: A campground is available. Cabins and a restaurant are available at Tamarack Lodge. Twin Lakes Store rents rowboats and canoes. Supplies can be obtained nearby. Access is free.

Water sports, restrictions: Motors are not permitted on the lake. Swimming and windsurfing are not allowed.

Contact: Inyo National Forest, Lee Vining Visitor Center, (760) 647-3044 or fax (760) 647-3046; Tamarack Lodge, (760) 934-2442; Mammoth Lakes Visitor Center, (760) 924-5500.

For a free travel packet on the area, phone the Mammoth Lakes Visitor Bureau, (800) 367-6572 or (888) 466-2666.

About Twin Lakes: Don't get these Twin Lakes confused with the Twin Lakes that are located farther north just west of Bridgeport. They are two different animals.

The Twin Lakes near Bridgeport (see chapter E4) are a set of large lakes in a well-developed area. These Twin Lakes, located west of Mammoth, are a pair of small lakes on little Mammoth Creek, high in Inyo National Forest at an elevation of 8,700 feet.

These Twin Lakes are extremely pretty, a paradise for those with a canoe, rowboat, or float tube. That's about all you can do here water-wise, since powerboating and windsurfing are not permitted, and the folks at the lodge discourage swimming (to take a dip, head instead to nearby Horseshoe Lake).

When you first drive here, go to the foot of the lake, where there is a perfect place to park, get out, and enjoy the view of this lake. See the pretty waterfall entering its upper end. Often there are a number of anglers in float tubes bobbing around near the bridge and fishing for trout. Most people enjoy the view from this vantage point, then head on to one of the lakes with more developed boating facilities, such as Lake Mary.

There is a large Forest Service campground, as well as excellent hiking trails in the area. Use is heavy at the campground, and for that reason, stays are limited to seven days. Often there will be people lined up, waiting for another family's weeklong vacation to end so theirs can start. Right: in the summer, when a campsite is vacated here, it is immediately filled.

❾ Lake Mamie

Location: Near Mammoth Lakes in Inyo National Forest; map E5, grid j0.

Directions: From the town of Bishop on US 395, drive north for 39 miles to Mammoth Lakes Junction. Turn west on Highway 203/Minaret Summit Road, drive four miles, turn left onto Lake Mary Road, and drive five miles to the lake.

Access: A boat ramp is available at Wildyrie Lodge.

Facilities, fees: Rental cabins, rowboat rentals, and groceries are available at Wildyrie Lodge. Campgrounds are available at nearby lakes. Access is free. There is a fee for boat launching.

Water sports, restrictions: Motors are not permitted on the lake. Swimming and windsurfing are not allowed.

Contact: Inyo National Forest, Lee Vining Visitor Center, (760) 647-3044 or fax (760) 647-3046; Wildyrie Lodge, (760) 934-2444; Mammoth Lakes Visitor Center, (760) 924-5500.

For a free travel packet on the area, phone the Mammoth Lakes Visitor Bureau, (800) 367-6572 or (888) 466-2666.

About Lake Mamie: What an idyllic site little Lake Mamie makes, this beautiful high mountain lake filled with clear, cold water. For some, when they learn that cabins are available for rent, it's as if they have found their own Golden Pond.

For others it scarcely elicits a pulse, because even though the scenic beauty here is fantastic, the opportunities for boating and water sports are quite scant. No motors are permitted, and the same goes for swimming and windsurfing. That leaves one option for boaters: bring a cartop boat, such as a canoe or rowboat, and paddle about a bit, maybe fishing for trout.

Vacationers who rent cabins here often pick up a rowboat at the small marina and then spend some time oaring about the calm, serene waters. Lake use is lighter than elsewhere in the Mammoth Lakes Basin, primarily because there is no campground directly near the lake and motors are restricted.

⑩ Lake Mary

Location: Near Mammoth Lakes in Inyo National Forest; map E5, grid j0.

Directions: From the town of Bishop on US 395, drive north for 39 miles to Mammoth Lakes Junction. Turn west on Highway 203/Minaret Summit Road, drive four miles, turn left onto Lake Mary Road, and drive three miles to the lake.

Access: There are two paved ramps; one at Pokonobe Resort and one at Lake Mary Marina. Both are located off Lake Mary Road.

Facilities, fees: A Forest Service campground is provided. RV camping is available at Mammoth Mountain RV Park. Cabins and fishing boat rentals are available at Crystal Crag Lodge. A campground, store, and docks are available at Pokonobe Resort, along with pontoon boat, fishing boat, canoe, and paddleboat rentals. Lake Mary Marina has docks and rents out fishing boats, pontoon boats, canoes, and paddleboats. Access is free. There is a fee for boat launching.

Water sports, restrictions: A 10 mph speed limit is strictly enforced. Swimming and windsurfing are not allowed.

Contact: Inyo National Forest, Lee Vining Visitor Center, (760) 647-3044 or fax (760) 647-3046; Crystal Crag Lodge, (760) 934-2436; Pokonobe Resort, (760) 934-2437; Lake Mary Marina, (760) 934-5353; Mammoth Lakes Visitor Center, (760) 924-5500.

For a free travel packet on the area, phone the Mammoth Lakes Visitor Bureau, (800) 367-6572 or (888) 466-2666.

About Lake Mary: It only takes one look to see why this lake is so popular: the natural beauty is astounding. The lake is set high in the mountains at 8,900 feet, just below Crystal Crag, amid some of nature's most perfect artwork.

To campers, boaters, and anglers, Lake Mary is the headquarters for the Mammoth Lakes area. Of the 11 lakes in the immediate vicinity, Lake Mary is the largest and most developed. It provides a resort, boat launch, and boat rentals.

Like the other lakes in the basin (except Horseshoe), no water/body contact sports are permitted, including swimming and windsurfing. However, the rules at Lake Mary do permit motors, and boats with small motors are available at the resorts. Rentals are popular and, along with the number of vacationers who bring their own trailered boats, have made this the most-used lake at Mammoth Lakes. Most of the visitors are here to fish for trout, which include some trophy-size rainbows.

The Forest Service campsites here are available on a first-come, first-served basis. In the summer, visitors should arrive as early as possible to secure a spot. Reservations are necessary to stay at one of the lodges.

Most people staying at Lake Mary will fish a bit, drive around and tour a bit, and maybe hike a bit. For those who get excited about hiking, an excellent trailhead is available on the lake's east side. The trail is routed south along Mammoth Creek to Arrowhead Lake, Skeleton Lake, Barney Lake, and then finally to big Duck Lake. The lat-

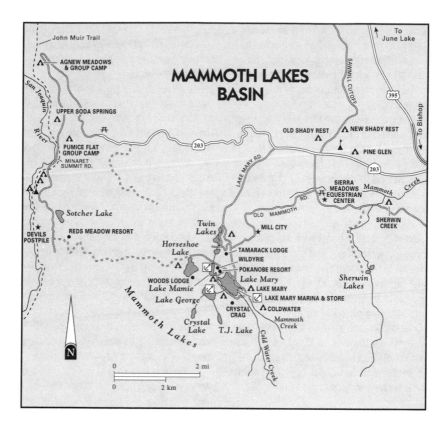

MAMMOTH LAKES BASIN

ter lake is larger than Lake Mary and is set just a mile from the junction with the Pacific Crest Trail.

⑪ Lake George

Location: Near Mammoth Lakes in Inyo National Forest; map E5, grid j0.

Directions: From the town of Bishop on US 395, drive north for 39 miles to Mammoth Junction. Turn west on Highway 203/Minaret Summit Road, drive four miles, turn left onto Lake Mary Road, and drive four miles, past Lake Mary, to Lake George.

Access: A primitive boat launch is available at Woods Lodge.

Facilities, fees: A campground is provided. Cabins, dock, fishing boats, and row-boats are available at Woods Lodge. Access is free. There is a fee for boat launching.

Water sports, restrictions: Motors are limited to six horsepower. Swimming and windsurfing are not allowed.

Contact: Inyo National Forest, Lee Vining Visitor Center, (760) 647-3044 or fax (760) 647-3046; Woods Lodge, (760) 934-2261 (summer) or (760) 934-2342 (winter); Mammoth Lakes Visitor Center, (760) 924-5500.

For a free travel packet on the area, phone the Mammoth Lakes Visitor Bureau, (800) 367-6572 or (888) 466-2666.

About Lake George: An awesome granite mountain provides the backdrop for Lake George, a small, round lake set at the 9,000-foot range. The setting is so beautiful it's spectacular.

For some this is the perfect place to

camp (with lake-view sites) or stay in a cabin. You get outstanding hiking, fair fishing, and decent boating for a high mountain lake. Only small motors (six horsepower or less) are permitted; basically this rule allows trolling for trout in small boats, but nothing else. That's just fine because it keeps this small lake intimate as well as pristine.

Though Lake George is set just west of Lake Mary, it doesn't lure nearly as many people and has a completely different atmosphere—higher, more remote, and closer to wilderness.

Swimming and windsurfing are not permitted here, just boats with small motors that are perfect for going out on the water to fish for rainbow and brook trout. While the campsites are in no way secluded, they do provide prime views of the lake. There are also two excellent short hikes, one to Crystal Lake and another to TJ Lake (separate trails). The trek to TJ Lake takes only about 20 to 25 minutes, and it's about a 45-minute romp to Crystal Lake, a beautiful lake set below giant Crystal Crag.

---

⑫ Convict Lake

Location: North of Bishop in Inyo National Forest; map E5, grid j2.

Directions: From the town of Bishop on US 395, drive 35 miles north to Convict Lake Road on the left. Turn south and travel two miles to the boat ramp.

Access: A paved boat ramp is available at Convict Lake Resort.

Facilities, fees: The Forest Service provides a campground and a picnic area. Boat docks, small marina, and fishing boat, canoe, and rowboat rentals are available at Convict Lake Resort. Groceries can be obtained at the lake. Access is free.

Water sports, restrictions: A 10 mph speed limit is strictly enforced. Swimming and windsurfing are not recommended.

Contact: Mammoth Lakes Visitor Center,

(760) 924-5500; Convict Lake Resort, (800) 992-2260 or (760) 934-1133 (November through March) or (760) 934-3800 (April through October).

For a free travel packet on the area, phone the Mammoth Lakes Visitor Bureau, (800) 367-6572 or (888) 466-2666.

About Convict Lake: People who love untouched, natural beauty can practice their religion at this mountain shrine. The lake is framed by a back wall of wilderness mountain peaks and fronted by a shore that's dotted with giant rocks and a few pines. All this is set at an elevation of 7,583 feet and bordered by the John Muir Wilderness to the west, yet is very easily accessed off US 395 to the east.

We're talking simply spectacular beauty. And even if that weren't enough, consider that the adjacent facilities include a boat ramp, boat rentals, cabin rentals, Forest Service campground, small store, fine restaurant, horse rentals, and a wilderness trailhead.

The lake is known primarily for fishing, particularly for having good catch rates of rainbow trout and rare but huge brown trout. What it's not ideal for is water sports. While swimming is permitted, nobody ever tries it because the water is typically so cold that you'll freeze your little petunia off. Though winds are common here out of the west, it is also extremely rare to see somebody try to windsurf; the gusty winds can really howl, driving everybody off the lake.

Most mornings are extremely calm, so conditions are excellent for canoeing. However, most visitors have small boats that they've either hauled in or rented and use them to fish for trout. The water, which is fed at the upper end by Convict Creek, is extremely clear.

An outstanding trail circles the lake, providing a great day hike. If you walk (or ride horseback) along the southern shoreline, you discover that the trail branches off and heads up the canyon along Convict Creek. This is where you find seclusion and a perfect picnic spot along the creek, as well as picture-perfect views of the lake below on the return trip.

⑬ Hot Creek

Location: Near Mammoth Lakes; map E5, grid j3.

Directions: From the town of Lee Vining, turn south on US 395 and drive about 30 miles to the Hot Creek Hatchery. Turn left on Hot Creek Hatchery Road and look for the sign indicating public access. Continue straight to the dirt parking areas and hike down to the creek.

Access: The creek is not suitable for boating.

Facilities, fees: A picnic area with rest rooms is provided near the fish hatchery. Campgrounds, lodging, and supplies are available in the Mammoth Lakes area. Access is free.

Water sports, restrictions: A developed swimming area is located at the bridge near the hatchery. Hot springs are also available.

Contact: Inyo National Forest, Lee Vining Visitor Center, (760) 647-3044 or fax (760) 647-3046.

For a free travel packet on the area, phone the Mammoth Lakes Visitor Bureau, (800) 367-6572 or fax (888) 466-2666.

About Hot Creek: A classic meandering spring creek, Hot Creek wanders through a meadow in the eastern Sierra on a course like a pretzel. Only two small pieces, totaling just three miles, are accessible. Below the Hot Creek Hatchery are two miles of stream bordered by private land, with access limited to fly fishers who book one of the nine cabins at Hot Creek Ranch. Downstream of that section is another piece of water, just under a mile long, that is accessible to the public.

At the latter stretch are a large parking area and paved trail down to a remarkable

hot spring area. While the ice-cold stream is running past, it is fed by scalding-hot water at the far side of the stream. What results is a remarkable sensation in which the water temperatures are constantly changing as they swirl around you. Your first steps in the stream, for instance, can be shocking because the water is quite cold. But when you get shoulder deep, it is possible to feel very hot water at your chest and shoulders, cold water at your thighs, and warm water at your feet. You can then move a step in any direction and the mix will change completely.

It is advisable to bring some kind of wading shoes, either sandals or old tennis shoes, not only for walking to and from the parking lot, but for wading in the stream.

Hot Creek has become very popular, and that has inspired the Forest Service to develop an area where people can play in the hot springs and have a picnic.

For an excellent hike, try the adjacent trail that fly fishers use to walk up and down the stream.

⑭ Crowley Lake

Location: North of Bishop; map E5, grid j3.

Directions: From the town of Bishop, drive 29 miles north on US 395 to the well-marked lake entrance on the right.

Access: A paved ramp is available at the marina, located at the end of the access road.

Facilities, fees: A small campground is provided. On opening weekend of fishing season and on summer weekends, the campground is expanded to accommodate unlimited visitors. Crowley Lake Fish Camp offers a full-service marina, docks, and fishing boat rentals. Limited supplies are also available. A use fee is charged for all motorized craft; there is an additional fee for boat launching. All boats must be registered at the lake entrance.

Water sports, restrictions: Waterskiing, personal watercraft, and windsurfing are permitted. Swimming is not allowed.

Contact: Crowley Lake Fish Camp, (760) 935-4301.

For a free travel packet on the area, phone the Mammoth Lakes Visitor Bureau, (800) 367-6572 or fax (888) 466-2666.

About Crowley Lake: Don't get your heart set on a pretty sight. In fact, Crowley Lake is kind of like an ugly dog who grows on you. It's a huge lake, with 45 miles of shoreline, at elevation 6,720 feet just east of US 395. Bordering the lake is high desert country that is sparse and dry looking. In addition, the winds out of the west can be nasty, particularly on early summer afternoons.

Like the bulk of the lakes in the eastern Sierra, Crowley is known primarily for its fishing opportunities. But unlike at the others, almost all water sports are permitted here. All types of boating are allowed from Memorial Day to Labor Day. Windsurfing, boogie boarding, waterskiing, and personal watercraft are all doable, and of those sports, windsurfing can really shine. That is because the surface water of this lake warms considerably in the summer and the afternoon winds are often ideal. The most popular jump-off point is at the beach next to the boat launch.

Note: Swimming is prohibited because the lake is a domestic water source.

The opening of trout season at Crowley is often an amazing event, with a flare or fireworks being shot into the dawn sky to commemorate the magic minute when the season is officially under way. Incredible numbers of anglers are drawn to Crowley for the opener and are often rewarded with good catch rates of large trout, both rainbows and browns.

Central California
Recreational Lakes
and Rivers

Overall Rating

| 1 | 2 | 3 | 4 | 5 | 6 | 7 | 8 | 9 | 10 |

Poor .... Fair .... Great

Key to the Symbols

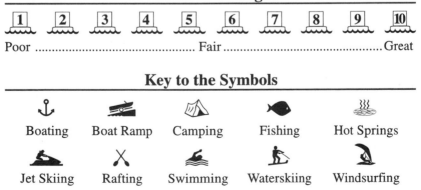

| Boating | Boat Ramp | Camping | Fishing | Hot Springs |

| Jet Skiing | Rafting | Swimming | Waterskiing | Windsurfing |

Central California Overview

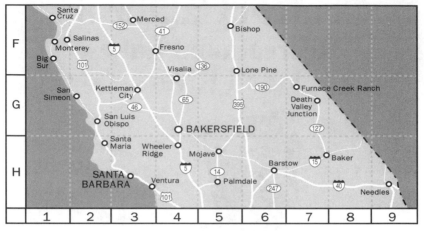

Chapter F1
Monterey/ Big Sur Area

Overall Rating

| 1 | 2 | 3 | 4 | 5 | 6 | 7 | 8 | 9 | 10 |

Poor .... Fair .... Great

F1–Monterey/Big Sur Area Map

One inch equals approximately 10.7 miles.
See page 12 for California state map.

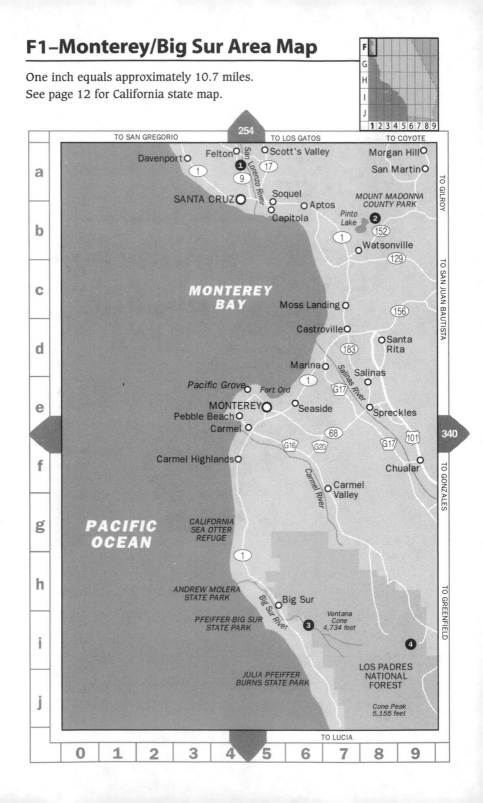

❶ San Lorenzo River

Location: In Santa Cruz; map F1, grid a4.
Directions: The only swimming access is available at Henry Cowell State Park. From Santa Cruz drive three miles north on Highway 17. Take the Mount Herman Road exit, travel west over the freeway, and continue for 3.5 miles to the road's end. Turn right on Graham Hill Road and travel 0.3 mile to the stoplight in Felton. Turn left on Highway 9 and head a short distance south to the park on the left.
Access: There is no boat ramp. Rafting and boating are not recommended.
Facilities, fees: Henry Cowell State Park provides a campground and picnic areas. There is an entrance fee at Henry Cowell State Park.
Water sports, restrictions: A swimming hole is available at the Garden of Eden, which is accessible via Ox Road Trail in the park.
Contact: Henry Cowell State Park, (831) 335-4598 or fax (831) 649-2986.
About the San Lorenzo River: The San Lorenzo starts as a trickle in the Santa Cruz Mountains, then flows westward to the sea near Santa Cruz. Highway 9 parallels much of the route, and for most visitors, driving alongside the river in a car is as close as they get.

As with most short coastal streams, the recreational opportunities here are only fair. The most fun activity is actually not a water sport, but a ride aboard the Roaring Camp Train, a slow-moving steam engine. It runs from Felton to Santa Cruz, much of the route along the San Lorenzo River. This is the best way to see the river and learn about the recreation it offers.

The first thing you may notice is that there are few prospects for swimming and water sports. The only good swimming hole is at the Garden of Eden near Henry Cowell State Park, a beautiful spot set in a picturesque redwood grove. Upstream there are no other spots suitable for swimming; the water is too shallow for anything but wading.

Downstream there is some potential at the seasonal lagoon, located just upstream from the reiver's mouth. In summer the river is closed by a large sandbar, and though flows are reduced to a trickle, it creates a coastal lagoon. This small but pleasant area is ideal for youngsters to paddle around on rafts or float on inner tubes.

The river is narrow, and although shallow most of the year, it is subject to rapid rises during heavy rainstorms. That makes it extremely poor for kayaking. People occasionally attempt to inner tube or kayak here, but they rarely make it far.

Fishing (for steelhead) is permitted only on Wednesdays and weekends from November through February. The fish are very difficult to catch, but anglers do enjoy one special perk: they can ride the train along the river, get dropped off at their chosen spot, and be retrieved later in the day. For information phone the Roaring Camp Train, (408) 335-4484.

❷ Pinto Lake

Location: Near Watsonville; map F1, grid b8.
Directions: From Santa Cruz drive south on Highway 1 to the Highway 152 turnoff. Head east to Green Valley Road, then turn left, and continue north to Pinto Lake.
Access: A paved ramp is available on the lake's south side.

Facilities, fees: A campground, picnic areas, and a snack bar are provided. You can rent rowboats. A day-use fee is charged.

Water sports, restrictions: A 5 mph speed limit is strictly enforced. Windsurfing is allowed; note the speed limit. Swimming and wading are not permitted.

Contact: Pinto Lake County Park, (831) 722-8129.

About Pinto Lake: Learning about Pinto Lake is a major surprise to many people, especially if they have been driving right by on nearby Highway 1 for years with nary a clue as to its existence.

Not only does this pretty spot offer good recreational opportunities, it is one of the few lakes in the greater Bay Area that has a campground. With the state beach campgrounds typically jammed day after day, the campground at Pinto Lake provides an excellent alternative.

The lake is best known as a fishing lake, with trout stocks and a small resident population of crappie. The speed limit is strictly enforced; if park employees see a wake behind your boat, they'll call the cops out to give you a ticket. Gotcha!

Alas, swimming is no longer allowed at Pinto Lake. The rules were changed to ensure the safety of swimmers, who would be threatened by the 20-year accumulation of old fishing line, hooks, and gear; this underwater hazard is a testimonial to the habits of some of the low-life slobs who think littering is their privilege. Oh well, the water is usually laden with algae anyway by mid-summer.

In the spring, windsurfing conditions are often excellent, providing sailboarders can stick to the 5 mph speed limit. This is not a beginner's territory, though; the strong winds can easily blow a windsurfer well out into the lake, leaving the inexperienced to face a long, exhausting paddle back to shore.

Want a great wild card suggestion for your visit to Pinto Lake? Try bird-watching from a canoe or a kayak.

❸ Big Sur River

⛺ 🐟 ✕ 🏊   6

Location: Near Big Sur in Los Padres National Forest; map F1, grid i6.

Directions: From Monterey drive approximately 30 miles south on Highway 1 to Big Sur. Limited access is available off the highway; access is excellent at Pfeiffer–Big Sur State Park.

Access: There is no boat ramp. Rafters and kayakers may put in at Pfeiffer–Big Sur State Park and float about seven miles to the river mouth at Andrew Molera State Park. Alternate take-outs are available at several campgrounds in between on Highway 1.

Facilities, fees: Campgrounds, picnic areas, and supplies are available along Highway 1. A day-use fee is charged for vehicles at Pfeiffer–Big Sur State Park; walk-in access is free. Rafting permits are not required.

Water sports, restrictions: Deep pools for swimming are available at Andrew Molera State Park, Pfeiffer–Big Sur State Park, Fernwood Campground, Big Sur Campground, Riverside Campground, and at a few spots along the highway.

Contact: Pfeiffer–Big Sur State Park and Andrew Molera State Park, (831) 667-2315 or fax (831) 667-2886.

About the Big Sur River: This stream is set amid the southernmost stand of coastal redwoods, a pretty spot known primarily as a summer vacation site and tourist destination. But Big Sur also offers a unique opportunity to take a minor-league float trip through big-league surroundings.

Because this is a short coastal stream, rafting is possible only in spring, after the rainy season has provided sufficient runoff and stream flows. No commercial rafting trips are offered. Instead most folks use inner tubes or kayaks. It is an easy float, with no drops or any sight of white water for seven miles. The standard run spans from

Pfeiffer–Big Sur State Park to Andrew Molera State Park, but many people just float on inner tubes between campgrounds along Highway 1. In the summer inner tubers can get away with short floats, but by then the river is generally too low for kayaks.

The water is clear and cool, and swimming is excellent. Large, deep pools are found at all the campgrounds along the highway. For those who desire a more remote experience, you can hike to the headwaters of the Big Sur River in the Ventana Wilderness, where you'll discover some secret swimming holes.

❹ Abbott Lakes

Location: Near Greenfield in Los Padres National Forest; map F1, grid i9.

Directions: From Salinas drive approximately 25 miles south on US 101 to County Road G17/Arroyo Seco Road. Turn south and continue southwest for 21 miles to the lakes.

From San Luis Obispo drive about 90 miles north on US 101 to the town of Greenfield. Turn left on County Road G16/Elm Avenue and drive six miles west, until the road joins Arroyo Seco Road. Continue 10 miles west on Arroyo Seco Road to the lakes. The road runs right aside the northernmost of the two lakes; a short hike to the south brings you to the smaller lake.

Access: There is no boat ramp. Cartop boats may be hand launched.

Facilities, fees: A campground and a picnic area are provided. Access to the lakes is free.

Water sports, restrictions: Motors are not permitted on the lakes. They are too small for windsurfing. No swimming allowed.

Contact: Los Padres National Forest, Monterey Ranger District, (831) 385-5434 or fax (831) 385-0628.

About Abbott Lakes: These two little reservoirs nestled in the Los Padres foothills are actually more like ponds, and upon first sight you might think this is the kind of place where on a hot summer day with nobody around, you'd like to get buck naked and take a quick dunk.

Wrong! First off, the rules prohibit you from swimming here. Second, you wouldn't want to anyway because these lakes are really a pair of mucky little ponds. The only thing swimming around and feeling any degree of happiness are the pint-size sunfish.

About all you can do is paddle your canoe in a circle and try not to get sunstroke. Huh? Yeah, it gets smokin' hot here because the surrounding canyon traps heat, often making it 10 degrees hotter than down in the valley. You might feel as if you're sitting in a pizza oven, not a boat.

Map of Central California—Page 330

Chapter F2
San Luis Area

Overall Rating

| 1 | 2 | 3 | 4 | 5 | 6 | 7 | 8 | 9 | 10 |

Poor .... Fair .... Great

F2–San Luis Area Map

One inch equals approximately 10.7 miles.
See page 12 for California state map.

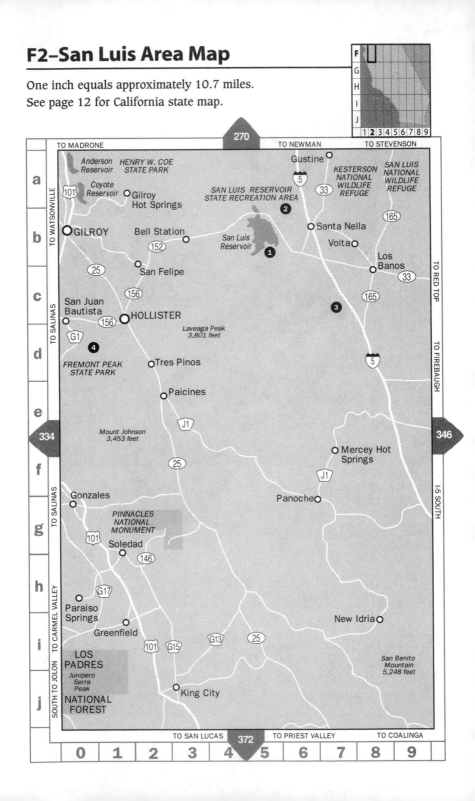

Chapter F2 features:

1 San Luis Reservoir

Location: Near Gilroy in San Luis Reservoir State Recreation Area; map F2, grid b5.

Directions: From the San Francisco Bay Area, drive south on US 101 to Gilroy. Turn east on Highway 152 and continue approximately 23 miles to the reservoir. If approaching from Interstate 5, take the Highway 152 exit. Turn west and drive 10 miles to the park entrance.

Access: Two paved launch ramps are available:

Dinosaur Point: From Highway 152 on reservoir's west side, turn east on Dinosaur Point Road and continue to the boat ramp at the road's end.

Quien Sabe Point: From Highway 152 on the reservoir's east side, take the main park entrance and continue to the boat ramp, located just before Quien Sabe Point.

Facilities, fees: Campgrounds and picnic areas are provided. Supplies can be obtained in Gilroy and Los Baños. A day-use fee is charged; boat launching privileges are included.

Water sports, restrictions: Waterskiing and personal watercrafting are permitted. Boaters must wear life jackets. Windsurfing and swimming are allowed, although there are no developed beaches.

Contact: California State Parks, Four Rivers District, (209) 826-1196 or fax (209) 826-0284.

About San Luis Reservoir: San Luis Reservoir is literally a water hole, and it's one of the biggest water holes imaginable. The primarily stark, man-made reservoir was built on the edge of the San Joaquin Valley for the sole purpose of storing waters on line with the California Aqueduct. When pumped full, usually by spring, it covers 13,800 acres and has 65 miles of shoreline. By fall the water gets drawn way down, and its vast, barren appearance can seem quite weird.

Build a water-storage facility and you get an interesting by-product, opportunities for boating and recreation. In this area though, most boaters head instead to the adjoining O'Neill Forebay, which has full facilities, boat rentals, and a large beach.

That leaves San Luis, which is largely undeveloped, to be used primarily by anglers, water-skiers, and windsurfers.

In the spring and early summer, boaters should use extreme caution on San Luis. That is because the wind comes caterwauling out of the west, pounding the lake as it roars on its course from Monterey Bay to the San Joaquin Valley. Lights and horns have even been installed to alert boaters to get off the lake during dangerous wind warnings.

Most of the year the winds are tolerable enough to present a significant challenge to windsurfers. The stark, vast surroundings and choppy water don't add much ambience to the affair, however.

Regardless, boater use is significant in the summer when the winds are down, and this enormous reservoir provides plenty of space compared to the oft-cramped quarters of O'Neill Forebay. After all, just combine a huge body of cool water and a hot climate, provide a boat, and this is where many people are apt to come.

2 O'Neill Forebay

Location: Near Gilroy in San Luis Reservoir State Recreation Area; map F2, grid b6.

Directions: From the San Francisco Bay Area, drive south on US 101 to Gilroy. Turn east on Highway 152 and continue approximately 25 miles to the forebay entrance on your left. If approaching from Interstate 5, take the Highway 152 exit. Turn west and drive 11 miles to the forebay entrance. Turn north and continue to the beach area.

Access: Two paved launch ramps are available:

Medeiros: From Highway 152 turn north at the sign for the Medeiros picnic area and drive a short distance to the boat ramp.

San Luis Creek: From Highway 152 turn north at the sign for San Luis Creek Beach and continue to the boat ramp.

Facilities, fees: Two campgrounds, picnic areas, rest rooms, and showers are provided. Fishing boats and personal watercraft can be rented at Felton's, (209) 826-7059. A day-use fee is charged; boat launching privileges are included.

Water sports, restrictions: Waterskiing and personal watercrafting are permitted. All boaters must wear life jackets. Windsurfing and swimming are allowed; a large, sandy beach is available on the west side of the forebay.

Contact: California State Parks, Four Rivers District, (209) 826-1196 or fax (209) 826-0284.

About O'Neill Forebay: Sometimes bigger is not better, and that theory is proven at San Luis Reservoir State Recreation Area. O'Neill Forebay is the little brother of the adjacent and giant San Luis Reservoir, but even though it's by far the smaller of the pair, the opportunities for boating and water sports are far more attractive here.

O'Neill Forebay covers 2,000 surface acres with 14 miles of shoreline, providing the recreation for the recreation area. While the main reservoir is used primarily for fishing, O'Neill Forebay caters to swimmers, water-skiers, and personal watercraft. Even anglers, however, will be pleased here, as there are some huge striped bass roaming these waters.

A large developed beach is available for swimmers, complete with outdoor showers for rinsing off. Boaters can dock at the beach to have lunch, go for a swim, then head back out on the water to ski. Windsurfing is decent, but in the spring winds can get just as gusty as at San Luis, driving everybody off the water.

O'Neill Forebay is a very attractive recreation lake, but sometimes it can be too attractive. Weekends and holidays, May through October, can get so congested that some folks simply surrender and head over to San Luis Reservoir in order to avoid the crowds. Windsurfers, who like having some room to zoom, are the most likely to flee.

---

❸ Los Baños Reservoir

Location: Near Los Baños; map F2, grid c7.

Directions: From Interstate 5 turn east on Highway 152 and travel three miles to Volta Road. Turn right, drive one mile south; then turn left on Pioneer Road, and head one mile east. Turn right on Canyon Road and continue south for five miles to the reservoir.

Access: A paved launch ramp is available on the reservoir's northeast side.

Facilities, fees: A campground and picnic areas are provided. A day-use fee is charged; boat launching privileges are included.

Water sports, restrictions: A 5 mph speed limit is strictly enforced. Windsurfing and swimming are permitted.

Contact: California State Parks, Four Rivers District, (209) 826-1196 or fax (209) 826-0284.

About Los Baños Reservoir: Set in a long, narrow valley, this lake covers 410 acres and has 12 miles of shoreline. The surrounding hills are often baked brown by late May, and on the typical summer day, it gets really hot out here.

Like nearby San Luis Reservoir, the wind can howl through this country in the early summer. That is why the number one activity has become windsurfing (the 5 mph speed limit is often exceeded) and sailing. While not exactly paradise, it makes an excellent choice for an overnight stay, a quick respite from the grinding drive, or a couple hours of windsurfing for anybody making the long cruise up or down nearby Interstate 5

Sailboarders soon discover that the winds are less gusty and more predictable than at San Luis Reservoir and O'Neill Forebay. In addition the 5 mph speed limit keeps out personal watercraft and waterskiers, a bonus for windsurfers. Swimmers will find the best spots near the picnic area and campgrounds. Because of the speed limit, use at Los Baños Reservoir is moderate.

❹ San Justo Reservoir

⚓ 🚤 🐟 🛶   5

Location: Near Hollister; map F2, grid d1.
Directions: From US 101 north of Salinas, turn east on Highway 156 and drive seven miles, through San Juan Bautista, to Union Road. Turn south and continue a short distance to the reservoir.
Access: A paved launch ramp is available on the lake's northeast side.
Facilities, fees: Portable toilets, picnic area, and snack bar are provided. Full facilities are available in Hollister. Fees are charged for day use and boat launching.
Water sports, restrictions: Electric motors are permitted on the lake, but gasoline motors are not. Windsurfing is permitted. Swimming is not allowed.
Contact: San Justo Reservoir, (831) 638-3300; San Benito County Parks, 815 Union Road, Hollister, CA 95023.
About San Justo Reservoir: Strong, steady winds that are predictable in the afternoon on most warm days make San Justo Reservoir an excellent spot for windsurfing and sailing.

A rule prohibiting gas motors means that there are no speedboats or personal watercraft rocketing around, another plus for enthusiasts of nonpowered water sports—except for people who want to take a dip, because swimming is not permitted.

San Justo Reservoir covers 200 surface acres. The surrounding landscape is sparse, with no facilities other than covered picnic areas. There are no trees, no grass, and no beach, just dirt and rocks. In addition, the reservoir is subject to closure due to low water levels. Always call ahead for conditions. It is typically open throughout summer, but almost always closes by October 1.

In addition to windsurfing and sailing, fishing is the other primary activity, with prospects for bass and catfish. Paradise it is not, but on hot days out Hollister way, it's still a decent enough spot to plunk a boat or sailboard, cool off, and have some fun.

Map of Central California—Page 330

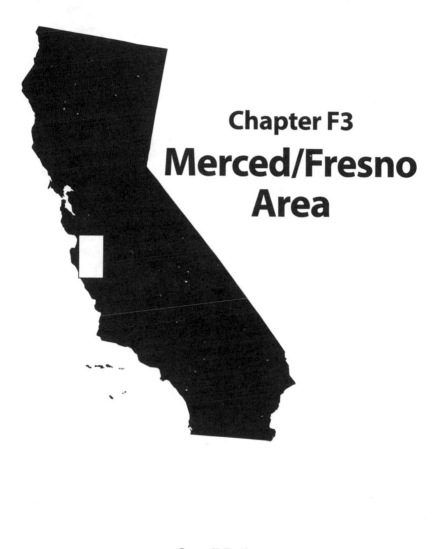

Chapter F3
Merced/Fresno Area

F3–Merced/Fresno Area Map

One inch equals approximately 10.7 miles.
See page 12 for California state map.

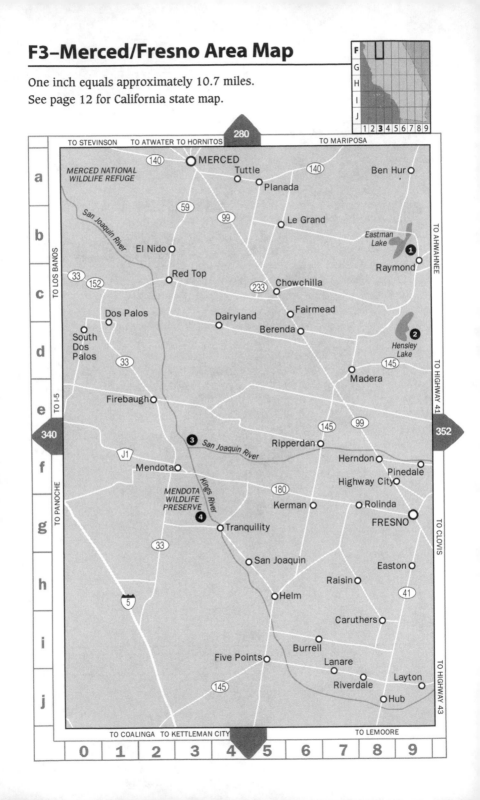

Chapter F3 features:

1 Eastman Lake

Location: Southeast of Merced; map F3, grid b9.

Directions: From Merced drive 15 miles south on Highway 99 to the town of Chowchilla. Take the Robertson Boulevard exit and turn east onto Avenue 26. Continue east for 17 miles, turn north on County Road 29, and drive eight miles to the lake.

Access: Two paved ramps are available, one on lake's east side, and one on the west side.

Facilities, fees: Campgrounds and picnic areas are provided. Supplies can be obtained in Chowchilla. Access to the lake is free. There is a fee for boat launching.

Water sports, restrictions: Waterskiing and personal watercraft are permitted. Windsurfing is also allowed. A large, sandy swimming beach is available on the lake's west side at Chowchilla Recreation Area. Swimming access is available all along the shoreline.

Note: Boating is only permitted during daylight hours. Due to rampant growth of the weed hydrilla, boating is not allowed in the lake's upper end; a keep-out buoy line marks the dividing point.

Contact: US Army Corps of Engineers, Eastman Lake, (559) 689-3255 or (559) 689-3408.

About Eastman Lake: Tucked in the foothills of the San Joaquin Valley at an elevation of 650 feet, Eastman Lake covers 1,800 surface acres. The reservoir was created when the federal government built a dam on the Chowchilla River. On your typical 100-degree summer day, it makes a nice tub to cool off in, ideal in early summer for waterskiing, swimming, or just taking a quick dunk.

All water sports have a place at this lake, including waterskiing and windsurfing, particularly early in the summer, and fishing for bass, which is best in late winter and spring. Swimming is best at the large beach on the west side, but boaters will discover a number of smaller, more private spots all along the shoreline. The lakeshore is edged with brush and oak trees, and the campgrounds and picnic areas are clean and well maintained.

Nothing is perfect, and unfortunately, neither is Eastman Lake. The problem here is weed growth, more specifically, hydrilla, the feared aquatic weed that can spread at such tremendous rates that it will choke off lakes and slow-moving streams. Until 1996 boating was not permitted from May to December at Eastman for fear that the weed might be passed to other lakes after getting chopped up and caught on boat propellers. That danger has largely been alleviated by closing the lake's upper end to boating (now separated by a buoy line), where the weed growth is most rampant. In late summer the blowtorch heat of the San Joaquin Valley can inspire hydrilla to grow like crazy, so if you are concerned, always call ahead for weed conditions before hitting the road.

2 Hensley Lake

Location: North of Fresno; map F3, grid c9.

Directions: From Fresno drive 20 miles north on Highway 99 to Madera. Take the Highway 145 exit and turn east. Travel about six miles, bear left on County Road

400, and drive 10 miles north to the lake.

Access: Two paved launch ramps are available: one on the lake's east side, off County Road 400, and one on the west side, next to Hidden View Campground.

Facilities, fees: Campgrounds and picnic areas are provided. Supplies can be obtained in Madera. Access to the lake is free.

Water sports, restrictions: Waterskiing, personal watercraft, and windsurfing are permitted. Swimming beaches are available on each side of the lake, Buck Ridge on the east side and Hidden View on the west side.

Contact: US Army Corps of Engineers, Hensley Lake, (559) 673-5151 (559) 673-2044.

About Hensley Lake: Set in the foothills of Madera County at 540 feet in elevation, Hensley is one hot place. When full, it covers 1,500 surface acres and has 24 miles of shoreline. As long as water levels are sufficient, it is big enough to be a wonderful water playland.

Popular with water-skiers and personal watercraft in spring and summer, it has prospects for bass fishing as well. Swimming is good, with two beaches to choose from. The best spot is at Buck Ridge on lake's east side, where there are picnic tables and trees for shade.

In the spring, conditions for windsurfing can be decent, but they are inconsistent. One day the winds will be strong and steady, the next day gusty, followed by a day with no wind at all. Yeah, it drives everybody nuts, especially fishermen, who find the bass bite goes up and down like a yo-yo because of the fluctuating barometric pressure that drives winds.

By late spring the lake is at its fullest, the days are warm, and area boaters show in full strength, meaning heavy use through midsummer. That's typically when the water levels start to drop, as the water is shipped out for irrigation purposes to valley farmers. In low rain years the lake level can fall way down and bear little resemblance to its appearance when full.

---

❸ Mendota Pool

Location: Near Mendota; map F3, grid f3.

Directions from Highway 99: From Fresno drive about 32 miles west on Highway 180/White Bridges Road to the town of Mendota. Turn north on Bass Avenue and drive three miles to the entrance to Mendota Park.

Directions from Interstate 5: In Fresno County west of Fresno, take the exit for County Road J1 and head east to Mendota. The road has several 90-degree turns. In Mendota turn north on Bass Avenue and drive three miles to the entrance to Mendota Park.

Access: A paved launch ramp is available.

Facilities, fees: Rest rooms, picnic areas, softball field, and barbecue pits are provided. Supplies can be obtained in Mendota. There is an entrance fee.

Water sports, restrictions: Waterskiing and personal watercraft are permitted from Mendota Pool to the Highway 180/White Bridges Road overpass; you cannot ski south of this point. Windsurfing is not recommended. Swimming is permitted.

Contact: Jack's Resort, (559) 655-2520.

About Mendota Pool: Actually just the northern access point to Fresno Slough, Mendota Pool is the centerpiece of the surrounding county parkland.

This is basically little more than a boat-launching site for water-skiers. There is no beach or developed facilities, and the water can be a bit too mucky for swimming. Water-ski boats may run down to the Highway 180/White Bridges Road overpass, then turn around, and make the run back; be sure not to water-ski past the overpass. For swimming and recreation better prospects are to be found at Jack's Resort at Fresno Slough (see the next listing).

4 Fresno Slough

Location: West of Fresno in Mendota Wildlife Refuge; map F3, grid g3.

Directions: From Fresno turn west on Highway 180/White Bridges Road and drive about 30 miles, through the town of Kerman, to where the road crosses the slough. The wildlife refuge entrance is directly across from Jack's Resort. If approaching from Interstate 5, take the Road J1 exit, drive east to Mendota. Turn south on Highway 180/White Bridges Road, and continue to the slough.

Access: A paved ramp is available at Jack's Resort on Highway 180/White Bridges Road.

Facilities, fees: Limited facilities are provided at Jack's Resort. There are fees for day use and boat launching.

Water sports, restrictions: Waterskiing and personal watercraft are prohibited south of the Highway 180/White Bridges Road overpass. Windsurfing is not recommended. A swimming beach is available at Jack's Resort.

Contact: Mendota Wildlife Refuge, PO Box 37, Mendota, CA 93640; (559) 655-4645; Jack's Resort, (559) 655-2520.

About Fresno Slough: If you're planning a visit, make every effort to get here before dawn so you can see the surrounding marshland wake up with the rising sun. Fresno Slough is truly one of the highlights of the San Joaquin Valley. You get to watch all manner of waterfowl wake up, lift off, and fly past in huge flocks while the morning sun casts an orange hue over everything in sight.

The prime spot for boaters is Jack's Resort, a popular lunch break spot for boaters and swimmers. A swimming beach and day-use facilities are available. The boat launch at Jack's is more popular with anglers than with water-skiers, since no waterskiing is permitted south of the Highway 180/White Bridges Road overpass. For better waterskiing access, launch at Mendota Pool (see the previous listing).

The Fresno Slough is the water source for the surrounding Mendota Wildlife Refuge, as well as a source of tranquillity for anglers who want to fish for catfish amid a wetland vibrant with life.

Chapter F4
Sierra West Area

Overall Rating

Poor .... Fair .... Great

F4–Sierra West Area Map

One inch equals approximately 10.7 miles.
See page 12 for California state map.

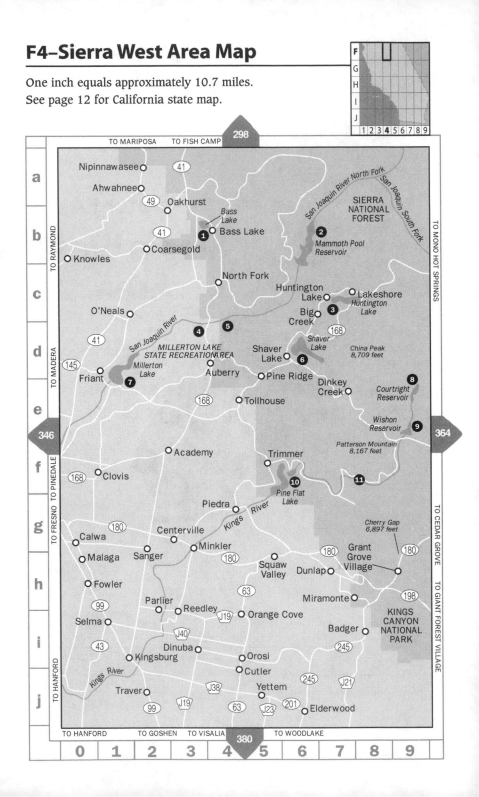

Chapter F4 features:

1 Bass Lake

Location: Northeast of Fresno in Sierra National Forest; map F4, grid b4.

Directions: From Fresno drive about 45 miles north on Highway 41 to County Road 22 in the town of Oakhurst. Then turn right, and drive to the lake. The lake can be accessed farther north as well. Drive 25 miles farther on Highway 41 to Yosemite Forks, turn right on County Road 222, and drive six miles east to the lake.

Access: Two paved boat ramps are available, one on the lake's northeast side, off Road 274 at The Pines Resort, and one on the southwest side, off County Road 222 near Miller's Landing.

Facilities, fees: Several campgrounds, picnic areas, gas, snack bars, full-service marinas, and groceries are available at the lake. Ski boats, personal watercraft, patio boats, fishing boats, and canoes are available at Miller's Landing and The Pines Marina. The Forks Resort rents fishing boats, patio boats, rowboats, and canoes. Access is free. There is a fee for boat launching at the northern boat ramp.

Water sports, restrictions: Personal watercraft and windsurfing are permitted within a specified area. Swimming beaches are available all along the shoreline.

Contact: Sierra National Forest, District Office, Minarets-Mariposa Ranger District, (559) 683-4665 or fax (559) 877-3108; Bass Lake Chamber of Commerce, (559) 642-3676. For boating information contact Miller's Landing, (559) 642-3633; The Pines Marina, (559) 642-3565; or The Forks Resort, (559) 642-3737.

About Bass Lake: The first time I visited Bass Lake, I could have mistaken it for the Hells Angels National Monument. Turned out they make a run here once a year, and despite some apprehension by family campers around the lake, the bikers kept the peace, didn't litter, and won over a lot of doubters before roaring off down Highway 41, one after another, like bullets coming out of a machine gun.

By now you should have figured out that Bass Lake is popular with a diverse mix of people. That makes sense. This is a long, beautiful lake, set in a canyon at 3,400 feet and surrounded by national forestland. It covers nearly 1,200 acres when full, and has five campgrounds, four resorts, and two boat launches.

Waterskiing, personal watercraft, fishing, and swimming are all extremely popular here. On a hot summer day, you can always count on seeing jet boats zooming about, as the roar from their big V8 engines echoes down the lake.

A great plus is that the shoreline is quite sandy nearly all around the lake. So even though there are no designated swimming beaches, you can pull off the road almost anywhere and find a place to swim and sunbathe. In addition, larger beach areas are available near the campgrounds and resorts. Windsurfing prospects are poor because of inconsistent winds and boating traffic.

Bass Lake is hardly a quiet, pristine lake.

In fact, it offers full facilities, including a movie theater. It gets extremely crowded in the summer, especially in late summer, when temperatures are very hot and water levels creep down low enough to expose large expanses of beach. Although a family vacation destination within an hour's drive of the Yosemite National Park southern entrance, the lake also hosts bass fishermen and hotshot water-skiers.

❷ Mammoth Pool Reservoir

Location: Northeast of Fresno in Sierra National Forest; map F4, grid b7.

Directions: From Fresno drive about 25 miles north on Highway 41 to North Fork Road/County Road 200. Turn right and drive 18 miles northeast to the town of North Fork. Turn right on County Road 225/Mammoth Pool Road and travel east and south to Forest Seuse Road 4S01/Minusts Road. Turn left and continue north to the reservoir. The boat ramp is on the lake's north shore. The total distance from North Fork is 42 miles on a narrow, twisty road.

Access: A paved boat ramp is located on the reservoir's north side, next to Mammoth Pool Campground. A gravel launch is available on the south side, next to the picnic areas.

Facilities, fees: Campgrounds, picnic areas, snack bar, and a grocery store are provided. Access to the lake is free.

Water sports, restrictions: The reservoir is closed to all boating from May 1 to June 16. During the rest of the year, waterskiing and personal watercraft are permitted, but a 35 mph speed limit is strictly enforced. Windsurfing is permitted. Swimming is available all along the shoreline.

Contact: Sierra National Forest, District Office, Minarets-Mariposa Ranger District,

(559) 683-4665 or fax (559) 877-3108.

About Mammoth Pool Reservoir: This lake was created by a dam in the San Joaquin River gorge, a steep canyon that drops nearly 3,000 feet, creating a long, narrow lake with steep, high walls. Mammoth Pool always seems to be much higher in elevation than its listed 3,330 feet. That is because of the surrounding high ridges.

One word of caution: If you'll be visiting from late August through November, always call ahead and ask about lake levels. Because the water is used to generate hydroelectric power at the dam, water levels can drop significantly late in the season. The lake covers 1,100 surface acres when full early in the season, but usually drops about 90 feet by the close of summer. This often renders the paved launch ramp useless.

All water sports are permitted at Mammoth Pool Reservoir, and waterskiing and personal watercraft are very popular. There are no designated beaches, but people swim all along the shoreline and the picnic areas and campgrounds. Even though strong winds do kick up most summer days in the late afternoon, it is rare to see people windsurfing at this lake.

❸ Huntington Lake

Location: Northeast of Fresno in Sierra National Forest; map F4, grid c7.

Directions: From Fresno drive 72 miles northeast on Highway 168 (a narrow, winding two laner).

Access: A paved ramp is located on the northeast shore, near Lakeshore Resort, and a primitive launch is located on the northwest shore, at Huntington Lake Resort.

Facilities, fees: Campgrounds, lodging, picnic areas, marina, restaurants, and groceries are available at the lake. Fishing boats, patio boats, and sailboats can be rented at Huntington Lake Marina on the west shore. Access is free.

Water sports, restrictions: Waterskiing, personal watercraft, and windsurfing are permitted. A large, sandy swimming beach is available on the northeast shore at Lakeshore Resort.

Contact: Sierra National Forest, District Office, Minarets-Mariposa Ranger District, (559) 683-4665 or fax (559) 877-3108; Huntington Lake Resort Marina, (559) 893-6750.

About Huntington Lake: Boy Scouts fantasize about spending a week or two here, and now and then they actually get the chance at specially arranged camp outs. The fact that they like it means that you probably will, too.

Huntington Lake is set at an elevation of 7,000 feet in the Sierra Nevada. The four-mile-long, half-mile-wide lake has 14 miles of shoreline, five campgrounds, and five resorts, and is a jump-off point for a backpack trip into the nearby Kaiser Wilderness. Hikers entering the wilderness are required to have a wilderness permit, which can be obtained nearby at a Forest Service office located at the lake's upper end, just off the loop road east of Highway 168.

The is a great mountain lake for almost all boating and water sports. Sailing is particularly popular, and well-known races are held here every year. That means windsurfing is pretty good, too, though there's no place at the lake to rent sailboards.

The lake water comes from snowmelt, so it is cold through the early summer and doesn't begin to get tolerably warm for swimming, about 65 degrees, until mid- to late July. A lot of people swim anyway, and many scouts earn a merit badge by completing a mile-long swim.

Lake use is heavy from May through September and diminishes greatly after Labor Day weekend. By mid-October, when the cold weather moves in for good, all operations shut down for winter.

---

❹ Kerckhoff Reservoir

Location: Northeast of Fresno in Sierra National Forest; map F4, grid d4.

Directions: From Fresno drive north on Highway 99 to Madera. Turn east on Highway 145 and drive 19 miles. Turn right on County Road 206 and drive south to the town of Friant. From Friant drive 19 miles northeast on Millerton and Auberry Roads to the town of Auberry. Turn north on Powerhouse Road and drive about eight miles to the reservoir.

Access: An unimproved boat ramp is located on the north shore.

Facilities, fees: A picnic area and small campground are provided. Supplies can be obtained in Auberry and North Fork. Access is free.

Water sports, restrictions: Motors are not permitted on the lake. Windsurfing and swimming are allowed.

Contact: Sierra National Forest, District Office, Minarets-Mariposa Ranger District, (559) 683-4665 or fax (559) 877-3108; PG&E Building & Land Services, (916) 386-5164 or fax (916) 386-5388.

About Kerckhoff Reservoir: It can seem hotter than the interior of Mount Vesuvius at Kerckhoff Reservoir, which is set in the foothill country east of Fresno. If you camp here, be sure to bring a plastic tarp and some poles so you can rig a makeshift roof to provide some shelter from the sun.

Because the reservoir is remote and small and the use of motors on boats is prohibited, it gets fairly light use, even in summer. Most of the visitors are anglers and folks out paddling canoes and other small boats. Swimming is permitted, and the best spot is the small beach next to the picnic area and campground.

❺ Redinger Lake

Location: Northeast of Fresno in Sierra National Forest; map F4, grid d4.

Directions: From Fresno drive north on Highway 99 to Madera. Turn east on Highway 145 and drive 19 miles. Turn right on County Road 206 and drive south to the town of Friant. From Friant drive 19 miles northeast on Millerton and Auberry Roads to the town of Auberry. Turn north on Powerhouse Road and drive about eight miles to Kerckhoff Reservoir. Turn right on Road 235 and drive six miles to Redinger Lake.

Access: A paved ramp is located on the lake's south end.

Facilities, fees: A primitive campground and a picnic area are provided. Supplies can be obtained in Auberry. Access to the lake is free.

Water sports, restrictions: Waterskiing and personal watercraft are permitted, but a 35 mph speed limit is enforced. Windsurfing and swimming are allowed.

Contact: Sierra National Forest, District Office, Minarets-Mariposa Ranger District, (559) 683-4665 or fax (559) 877-3108

About Redinger Lake: Only about an hour's drive east from Fresno brings you to Redinger Lake, set at elevation 1,400 feet in the hot Sierra foothills. The lake is three miles long and a quarter mile wide, and has a 35 mph speed limit that is tested by every jet boater who launches here.

Since it is so remote and undeveloped, Redinger Lake gets far lighter boating traffic than nearby Shaver and Huntington Lakes. Still, there's a fair number of waterskiers and personal watercraft plying the water throughout summer. After all, with hot weather, cool water, and a good boat ramp, you've got the recipe for fun.

From April through June, you can count on steady breezes out of the west. That makes this lake excellent for windsurfing,

especially after winds force most water-skiers to shut down for the day.

While there are no designated swimming beaches, there are many sandy areas for sunbathing all around the lake's shoreline.

❻ Shaver Lake

Location: Northeast of Fresno in Sierra National Forest; map F4, grid d6.

Directions: From Fresno turn north on Highway 168 and drive 50 miles to Shaver Lake.

Access: A paved boat ramp is located at Sierra Marina, seven miles north of the town of Shaver Lake on Highway 168.

Facilities, fees: Campgrounds, lodging, picnic areas, restaurant, bar, and groceries are available. Sierra Marina has full services and rents out pontoon boats and fishing boats. Fishing boat, pontoon boat, canoe, and kayak rentals are available at Shaver Lake Lodge. Access is free. There is a fee for boat launching.

Water sports, restrictions: Waterskiing, personal watercraft, and windsurfing are permitted. Sandy swimming beaches are available at the day-use areas on Road 1 and Road 2 on the lake's east side.

Contact: Sierra National Forest, Pineridge Ranger District, (559) 855-5360 or fax (559) 855-5375; Sierra Marina, (559) 841-3324; Shaver Lake Lodge, (559) 841-3538.

About Shaver Lake: You have to pass by Shaver Lake if you are heading to Huntington Lake, and a lot of folks can't stand the tease. They stop and check it out. Most like what they see, and considering the longer drive to Huntington, make this their lake of choice.

Though Shaver is not as high in elevation as Huntington (Shaver is set at 5,370 feet, while Huntington is at 7,000 feet), it is very pretty just the same. And as you might expect, by summer this becomes a very busy lake.

Waterskiing is extremely popular. Hey, there are usually tons of water-skiers, and personal watercraft, too, along with the family campers on their annual weeklong vacation. But let me tell you a little secret: there is one boat-in day-use area on the lake's back side for those who want to relax and at least have some semblance of privacy.

A better-known secret is that the best area for swimming and playing in the water is on the lake's east side. Though more difficult to reach, this part of the lake offers sandy beaches rather than the rocky drop-offs so common on the west side. Fishing prospects at Shaver are better on the west side as well, so by making the effort to reach the lake's other side, you will be avoiding a potential user conflict.

Most windsurfers bypass Shaver Lake, which is well sheltered and rarely gets much wind.

❼ Millerton Lake

Location: North of Fresno in Millerton Lake State Recreation Area; map F4, grid e2.
Directions: From Fresno drive north on Highway 41 to the Friant Road exit. Drive north on Friant Road for about 15 miles, then turn right (east) on Millerton Road, and continue to the lake entrance and the day-use areas. To reach the campgrounds continue past the Friant exit on Highway 41 to Highway 145 and turn east. Proceed into the park and follow signs to the campgrounds.
Access: There are three paved boat ramps: two on the south side by the day-use areas, and one at the end of the campground entrance road.
Facilities, fees: Campgrounds, picnic areas, full-service marina, and a snack bar are provided. Fishing boats are rented out at the marina. Supplies can be obtained in Friant. Fees are charged for day use and boat launching.

Water sports, restrictions: Waterskiing, personal watercraft, and windsurfing are permitted. Sandy swimming beaches are available on both sides of the lake.
Contact: Millerton Lake State Recreation Area, (559) 822-2332 or fax (559) 822-2319.
About Millerton Lake: Located at 578 feet elevation in the foothills of the San Joaquin Valley, Millerton gets very hot weather during midsummer. You can count on it. You can also count on this lake being a perennial victim of low water levels by the summer's end due to drawdowns that diminish the area's natural beauty.

Regardless, Millerton gets a lot of traffic because of its proximity to Fresno and Madera. In addition the shape of the lake—a large lake body and a long, narrow inlet, with 43 miles of shoreline in all—helps to separate water-skiers from anglers. Fishermen head upstream, water-skiers downstream.

If you're just coming for the day, head to the lake's south side, which has a huge day-use area. If you'll be camping, head instead to the north side. There's a boat launch directly adjacent to the campgrounds, and if you snare a shoreline site, you can even moor your boat right at the site, a great plus

Waterskiing is popular here, as are sailing and windsurfing. Boat traffic is often heavy. The water-skiers and jet boats dominate the lake on most summer days to about 3 PM. Then a strong, steady wind usually comes up, driving the water-skiers off the lake. Just like that, windsurfers appear, ready to partake of the excellent prospects.

One of the quirks of Millerton Lake is that in the rare times when the lake is full (and quite pretty), the high water covers all the beaches. When the lake levels drop, the beaches become available, just right for swimming and wading, especially for kids who like horsing around in the water. So in the ideal situation, the lake is not quite full, but there's good lakeside access and swimming around most of the shore.

❽ Courtright Reservoir

⚓ 🛥 ⛺ 🐟 🏊   7️⃣

Location: Northeast of Fresno in Sierra National Forest; map F4, grid e9.

Directions: From Fresno drive 63 miles northeast on Highway 168 to the town of Shaver Lake. Turn east on Dinkey Creek Road, drive 12 miles, turn right on McKinley Grove Road, and drive 14 miles east. When the road forks, bear left on Courtright Reservoir Road and drive 10 miles north to the lake.

Access: A paved boat ramp is located on the lake's south side.

Facilities, fees: Campgrounds and picnic areas are provided. Supplies can be obtained in Fresno and the town of Shaver Lake. Access to the lake is free.

Water sports, restrictions: A 15 mph speed limit is strictly enforced. Waterskiing, personal watercraft, and windsurfing are not permitted. Swimming is allowed, but the water is generally too cold.

Contact: Sierra National Forest, Kings River Ranger District, (559) 855-8321 or fax (559) 855-2666; PG&E Building & Land Services, (916) 386-5164 or fax (916) 386-5388.

About Courtright Reservoir: Courtright Reservoir is one great recreation destination. You can camp, boat, and fish, or you can park at the trailhead at Voyager Rock Campground (on the lake's northeast side) and head off into the John Muir Wilderness.

Courtright is set in the high Sierra at an elevation of 8,200 feet. If you plan to stick around, the early summer is the best time to visit. That is when the lake level is the highest by far. It can drop quickly from mid-August on through fall.

The surrounding scenery is very pretty, and this is a good choice for a picnic site, typically very peaceful and quiet. With a 15 mph speed limit, all the fast boats, water-skiers, and personal watercraft head elsewhere. What you get here is the ideal lake for fishing, camping, and low-speed boat use, especially paddling about in a canoe or kayak.

In fact, much of the visitor traffic is not from boaters, but from wilderness backpackers. They use the lake's campground as home base before heading off into the John Muir Wilderness.

And by the way, if you hope to swim while you're at Courtright, plan on joining the Polar Bear Club. Yow! This water is cold!

❾ Wishon Reservoir

⚓ 🛥 ⛺ 🐟 🏊   7️⃣

Location: Northeast of Fresno in Sierra National Forest; map F4, grid e9.

Directions: From Fresno drive 63 miles northeast on Highway 168 to the town of Shaver Lake. Turn east on Dinkey Creek Road, drive 12 miles, turn right on McKinley Grove Road, and drive 14 miles east. When the road forks, bear right and continue for about three miles to the boat ramp on the southeast shore.

Access: A paved ramp is available on the lake's west side.

Facilities, fees: Campgrounds, a picnic area, gas, and limited groceries are available. Fishing boats can be rented at Wishon Village. Access to the lake is free.

Water sports, restrictions: A 15 mph speed limit is strictly enforced. Waterskiing, personal watercraft, and windsurfing are not permitted. Swimming is allowed, but the water is generally too cold.

Contact: Sierra National Forest, Kings River Ranger District, (559) 855-8321 or fax (559) 855-2666; PG&E Building & Land Services, (916) 386-5164 or fax (916) 386-5388.

About Wishon Reservoir: When full,

Wishon is an attractive lake surrounded by national forest land and filled with snowmelt poured from the North Fork Kings River. The hitch is that Wishon Reservoir doesn't ever seem to be full.

This PG&E-managed lake is set at elevation 6,500 feet, and conditions are much the same as at nearby Courtright Reservoir, with a campground and a 15 mph speed limit. However, Wishon is easier to reach and more developed than Courtright.

This is the kind of place where a family might take a short vacation, a pretty spot that promotes a sense of tranquillity. The 15 mph speed limit keeps it that way. Just like that, there are no loud, fast boats and no personal watercraft.

Sometimes, just paddling a canoe at Wishon Reservoir and trailing a fishing line out the back can make for a memorable and relaxing evening.

⑩ Pine Flat Lake

Location: East of Fresno; map F4, grid f6.

Directions: From Fresno turn east on Highway 180 and drive 15.5 miles to the town of Centerville. Turn left on Trimmer Springs Road and proceed eight miles to the lake.

Access: Boat ramps are located on the north shore off Trimmer Springs Road, and on the south shore off Sunnyslope Road.

Facilities, fees: Campgrounds, picnic areas, full-service marinas, snack bars, and groceries are available. Fishing boats, patio boats, houseboats, and personal watercraft can be rented Lakeridge Marina. Patio boats are also available at Trimmer Marina. Access to the lake is free. There is a nominal fee for boat launching when water levels are low.

Water sports, restrictions: Personal watercraft and windsurfing are permitted. There are no sandy swimming beaches, but swimming is available along the shoreline.

Contact: US Army Corps of Engineers, Pine Flat Field Office, (559) 787-2589; Lakeridge Marina, (559) 787-2506; Trimmer Marina, (559) 855-2039.

About Pine Flat Lake: When Pine Flat Lake is full or close to full, it is surprisingly pretty. Set in the foothills east of Fresno at 961 feet in elevation, the lake is 21 miles long with 67 miles of shoreline and 4,270 surface acres—a big lake with seemingly unlimited recreation potential. It fills courtesy of monsoon-level snowstorms in the Sierra and the ensuing melt-off in the spring and summer.

That is when Pine Flat becomes one of the most popular lakes in the entire region. This is a highly developed, commercial destination that includes a resort and numerous private campgrounds and RV parks that offer full facilities, even boat rentals.

Fresno is such a short drive away that boater and camper traffic is extremely heavy from the first warm days of spring on through Labor Day. Reservations are advised for anybody who plans on camping.

Pine Flat features hot summer days and warm water, a combination that often results in large amounts of liquid refreshments being consumed, oil being applied to bodies, and fast boats zooming around. Water-skiing, powerboating, fishing for white bass, and swimming can be quite good here.

Most people who jump in the water to cool off and maybe swim around a bit do so from houseboats and patio boats on the main lake body. The problem is that there aren't many sandy spots on the shoreline. The few good areas are located near the resorts, where you can hike on steep trails that are routed down to little sandy patches.

Because the water is warm even in the spring, this lake is excellent for all water/body contact sports. That includes windsurfing, though the winds are very inconsistent. Call ahead for conditions before heading out here.

One crazy element about Pine Flat is that the conditions are actually best in the fall, when the weather is cooler and much more bearable, yet during that season the lake can be empty.

That is because the lake has a terrible reputation for being extremely low. How low? Would you believe about 80 to 90 percent empty? That was the situation for several years during the recent drought. The lake was always at its lowest in the fall, so boaters just abandoned the place.

---

⑪ Kings River

⛺ 🐟 ✕ 🚣 ⑩

Location: Northeast of Fresno; map F4, grid g5.

Directions: To the Kings River south of Pine Flat Lake, from Fresno turn east on Highway 180 and drive 15.5 miles to Centerville. Turn left (north) on Trimmer Springs Road, which parallels the west side of the river, or continue a few miles east to Minkler and turn left (north) on Piedra Road, which borders the river's east side. Access is available here all the way upstream to the bridge at Piedra and downstream off numerous county roads.

To the Kings River north of Pine Flat Lake, from Fresno turn east on Highway 180 and drive 15.5 miles to Centerville. Turn left (north) on Trimmer Springs Road and drive 26 miles north, past Pine Flat Lake. Continue east on Trimmer Springs Road for seven miles to Garneuske Camp. Access is available off the road and off unimproved roads that parallel both sides of the river.

Access: No boat ramp is available. There are three runs:

Upper Kings: To reach the put-in, drive east of Fresno on Highway 180 to Yucca Point, located about 15 miles east of Grant Grove Village. Park and hike two steep miles down to the river. Do not attempt to put in

farther upstream where the highway crosses the river; the section above Yucca Point should not be run. Take out 10 miles downstream at Garnet Dike Campground.

Note: The Upper Kings is an extremely difficult Class V+ stretch that is rarely run; only experts should attempt it.

Main Kings: From Fresno turn east on Highway 180 and drive 15.5 miles to Centerville. Turn left on Trimmer Springs Road and then proceed 26 miles north, past Pine Flat Lake. Continue east on Trimmer Springs Road for seven miles to the put-in at Garnet Dike Campground. The take-out is 9.5 miles downstream at Kirch Flat Campground, also on Trimmer Springs Road.

Lower Kings: From Fresno drive 15.5 miles east on Highway 180 to the small town of Centerville. Continue a short distance east to Pierce's Canoeing, located where Highway 180 crosses the river. Canoeists may put in here and take out about 15 miles downstream at Cricket Hollow.

Facilities, fees: Several campgrounds are available along Trimmer Springs Road. Supplies can be obtained in Piedra. Canoe rentals are available at Pierce's. Access is free. Rafting permits are not required.

Water sports, restrictions: No swimming access is available on the Upper Kings. A few swimming holes are located on the Main Kings, but swimming is not recommended due to the swift current and cold water. There is a beach at the take-out at Cricket Hollow on the Lower Kings.

Contact: Sequoia National Forest, Hume Lake Ranger District, 35860 East Kings Canyon Road, Dunlap, CA 93621; (559) 338-2251; Pierce's Canoeing, (559) 787-3450. For guided rafting trips contact one of the following outfitters: Kings River Expeditions, (559) 233-4881; Spirit Kings River Whitewater, (559) 332-2227; or Zephyr River Expeditions, (800) 431-3636 or (559) 532-6249.

About the Kings River: The Kings is well known for providing some of the best rafting and kayaking water in California. There are three primary runs, but the one that is ideal for most is the Main Kings, a great Class III run that spans just under 10 miles. The other two are quite different. The Upper Kings is a scintillating stretch of water for daredevil experts only, rated Class V+, with incredible views and death-defying drops. The Lower Kings, on the other hand, is pretty much an easy float that has only fair scenic value. Because the water is so cold, wet suits or dry suits are recommended and are usually required by commercial rafting companies through June.

Here are more precise descriptions of all three runs:

Main Kings: 9.5 miles; Class III. This is a very popular run for commercial outfitters, with daily trips from spring through midsummer. The scenery is excellent; the river winds through a pretty canyon, and there's little auto traffic to disturb the wild river ambience. Highlights include white-water rapids named Banzai (the most difficult rapid on the run), Mule Rock, Fang Tooth, Sidewinder, and Rooster Tail. Kayak races are held here every year. The season runs from April through July.

Upper Kings: 10 miles; Class V+. This stretch of the river is very, very, very difficult (got that?), practically untouched by humankind. Even experts rarely try it. Get-

ting to the put-in requires a long, steep hike, and you must carry in your gear and your boat.

Still with us? The first three miles are Class IV–V, which include several possible portages. After that it's Class V+ all the way, with many portages, huge drops, and terrifying rapids.

The reward is unequaled wilderness scenery, including a spectacular view of Garlic Falls (on the right at mile five), 650 feet high in four dramatic tiers. Nonboaters must hike in five miles to get a glimpse.

In addition, no trails access this river stretch, save for the trail to the put-in. This means that rafters and kayakers must be confident about their skills, because there is no turning back and no chance of being rescued here. The season is short, usually from July 1 to August 1.

Lower Kings: 15 miles; Class I–II. This run is basically advertised as a scenic float, except that it is not all that scenic. But it does make for an easy canoe or inner tube float. Note that Pierce's Canoeing on Highway 180 has the monopoly on canoe rentals because it's the only place around for miles. Numerous roads and highways cross the river along the way. So even though this is technically the same river as the Upper Kings, it is a world apart in character. The season runs from April through July.

Map of Chapter F4—Page 352

Map of Central California—Page 330

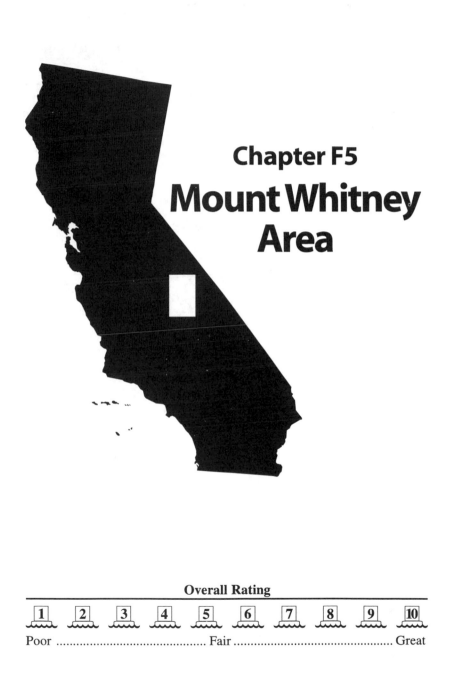

Chapter F5
Mount Whitney Area

Overall Rating

| 1 | 2 | 3 | 4 | 5 | 6 | 7 | 8 | 9 | 10 |

Poor .... Fair .... Great

F5–Mount Whitney Area Map

One inch equals approximately 10.7 miles.
See page 12 for California state map.

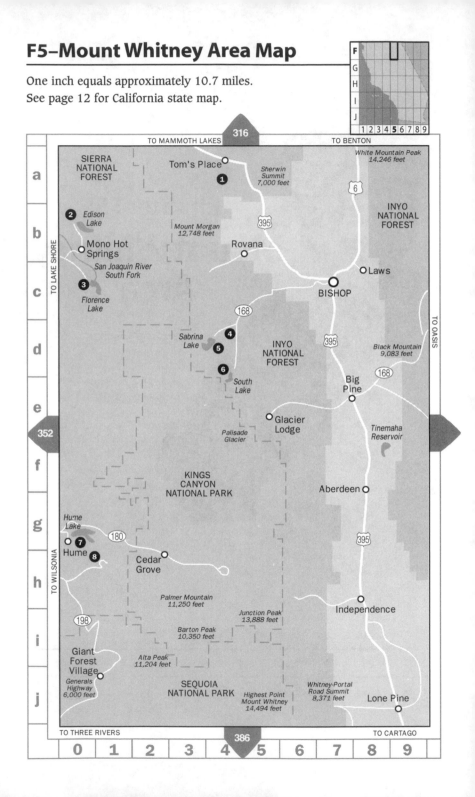

TO MAMMOTH LAKES **316** TO BENTON

SIERRA NATIONAL FOREST

Tom's Place ❶

White Mountain Peak 14,246 feet

Sherwin Summit 7,000 feet

❷ Edison Lake

Mount Morgan 12,748 feet

INYO NATIONAL FOREST

Mono Hot Springs

San Joaquin River South Fork

Rovana

❸ Florence Lake

Laws

BISHOP

Sabrina Lake ❹

❺

INYO NATIONAL FOREST

Black Mountain 9,083 feet

❻ South Lake

Big Pine

Glacier Lodge

Palisade Glacier

Tinemaha Reservoir

KINGS CANYON NATIONAL PARK

Aberdeen

Hume Lake

Hume ❼ ❽

Cedar Grove

Palmer Mountain 11,250 feet

Junction Peak 13,888 feet

Independence

Barton Peak 10,350 feet

Giant Forest Village

Alta Peak 11,204 feet

Generals Highway 6,000 feet

SEQUOIA NATIONAL PARK

Highest Point Mount Whitney 14,494 feet

Whitney-Portal Road Summit 8,371 feet

Lone Pine

TO THREE RIVERS **386** TO CARTAGO

TO LAKE SHORE

TO WILSONIA

352

TO OASIS

0 1 2 3 4 5 6 7 8 9

1 Rock Creek Lake

Location: Northwest of Bishop in Inyo National Forest; map F5, grid a4.

Directions: From the town of Bishop, drive 30 miles north on US 395 to the town of Tom's Place. Turn west on Rock Creek Road and drive eight miles to Rock Creek Lake.

Access: An unimproved launch ramp is available at Rock Creek Lake Resort.

Facilities, fees: Lodging, campground, picnic area, restaurant, and groceries are available at the lake. Fishing boats and rowboats can be rented at Rock Creek Lake Resort. Access is free.

Water sports, restrictions: A 5 mph speed limit is strictly enforced. Windsurfing is permitted; note the speed limit. Swimming is allowed.

Contact: Inyo National Forest, White Mountain Ranger District, (760) 873-2500 or fax (760) 873-2563; Rock Creek Lake Resort, (760) 935-4311; Rock Creek Lodge, (760) 935-4452.

About Rock Creek Lake: This is a small lake that exudes great natural beauty. Located just north of the boundary to the John Muir Wilderness, Rock Creek Lake is nestled in the Little Lakes Valley of the high Sierra at an elevation of 9,682 feet.

This is an excellent destination for a camping/hiking vacation. Some 35 other lakes are located nearby, many of which can be reached in a one-day round-trip hike. The trek out west to Mono Pass is a butt kicker, but you can stop on the way at Ruby Lake, named for its gemlike qualities.

You mainly see small fishing boats on the lake, rarely canoes. A 5 mph speed limit gives boaters a guarantee of quiet water.

At just 63 surface acres, the lake is not big, but its beauty and resident rainbow trout make it popular for shoreline fishing. Unfortunately, years of fishing have made swimming here somewhat hazardous. Along the shore there are quite a few old fishing hooks and lines that have become snagged and broken off on the bottom. This puts anybody wading at risk, especially children. However, not many people will be disappointed, since the water is very cold anyway.

It's so cold that windsurfers are advised to wear wet suits. This sport is best in the fall. The lake is set in a slot in a high mountain canyon, and the wind can whip right on through.

Traffic is heavy in the summer months, with a lot of people using this as a base camp and jump-off point for trips into the nearby John Muir Wilderness.

Special note: An excellent trailhead is available here for wilderness trips into the Little Lakes Valley. You can rent horses for pack trips at the Rock Creek Pack Station, (619) 935-4493.

2 Edison Lake

Location: Northeast of Fresno in Sierra National Forest; map F5, grid b0.

Directions: From Fresno drive 72 miles northeast on Highway 168 (a narrow, winding two-laner) to the town of Huntington Lake. Continue northeast on Kaiser Pass Road for 21 miles to Edison Lake.

Access: A paved boat ramp is located on

the west shore; Kaiser Pass Road leads directly to it.

Facilities, fees: Lodging, campground, picnic area, restaurant, and groceries are available at the lake. Fishing boat and canoe rentals are offered at Vermillion Valley Resort. Access is free.

Water sports, restrictions: A 15 mph speed limit is strictly enforced on the lake. Windsurfing and swimming are permitted.

Contact: Sierra National Forest, Pineridge Ranger District, (559) 855-5360 or fax (559) 855-5375; Vermillion Valley Resort, (559) 855-6558.

About Edison Lake: Here is one of the great family camping destinations in California. Edison Lake offers four lakeside camps, a resort, boat launch, boat rentals, horse rentals, nearby trailhead to the Pacific Crest Trail—and good fishing. A 15 mph speed limit keeps it quiet, and there's a ferry that runs across the lake to the trailhead twice a day.

Edison Lake, which is set at an elevation of 7,650 feet, is fed by Mono Creek, a cold, pure, and pristine trout stream. Camping and fishing are the main activities, with people either renting small fishing boats or bringing their own trailered boats. Because many people start their backpacking trips here, lake use is very high in the summer.

All along the shoreline there are beach areas for swimming, but the water is quite cold. If you're looking for the kind of water that won't chill your bones, nearby Mono Hot Springs offers mineral baths and lodging.

For hikers Edison Lake provides one of the better jump-off points around. The trail along the lake's north side is routed along Mono Creek and then connects to the Pacific Crest Trail (where a bridge crosses the stream). From there, if you don't mind a steep climb, head south up Bear Mountain. It takes about 40 minutes to reach an absolutely wondrous aspen grove that is pretty year-round.

❸ Florence Lake

🪝🚣⛺🐟🏊🚶 🔟

Location: Northeast of Fresno in Sierra National Forest; map F5, grid c0.

Directions: From Fresno drive 72 miles northeast on Highway 168 (a narrow, winding two-laner) to the town of Huntington Lake. Continue northeast on Kaiser Pass Road to Florence Lake Road (two miles south of Mono Hot Springs). Turn south and continue to the lake.

Access: A paved boat ramp is available at Florence Lake Resort on the lake's northwest side.

Facilities, fees: A campground, picnic area, and limited groceries are available at the lake. Fishing boat rentals are provided at Florence Lake Resort. Access is free.

Water sports, restrictions: A 15 mph speed limit is strictly enforced. Windsurfing and swimming are permitted.

Contact: Sierra National Forest, Pineridge Ranger District, (559) 855-5360 or fax (559) 855-5375; Florence Lake Resort, (559) 966-3195.

About Florence Lake: Like nearby Edison Lake to the north, Florence Lake is a great vacation destination with excellent hiking opportunities. Located at an elevation of 7,327 feet, the lake features a beautiful mountain setting (just as pretty as Edison), with the awesome Glacier Divide country providing a backdrop to the east. A 15 mph speed limit maintains a degree of serenity.

Most years the lake becomes ice-free around Memorial Day weekend. The resort is usually open from June through September, sometimes later.

Although Florence is smaller and less developed than its northerly neighbor Edison, conditions are much the same. Fewer people know about this place, however; it does not get the amount of camping traffic that Edison does.

If you like hiking, this is a great place to

start your trip. From the lake inlet a trail is routed up the South Fork San Joaquin River to the Pacific Crest Trail (about five miles in). From there you can continue southeast along the San Joaquin, turning into Evolution Valley, one of the prettiest meadow/woodlands in the entire high Sierra.

❹ North Lake

Location: Southwest of Bishop in Inyo National Forest; map F5, grid d4.

Directions: From US 395 in Bishop, turn west on Highway 168 and drive 17 miles to the North Lake turnoff on the right. Turn west and continue to the lake.

Access: There is no boat ramp. Cartop boats may be hand launched.

Facilities, fees: A campground is provided. Supplies can be obtained in Bishop. Access is free.

Water sports, restrictions: Motors are not permitted on the lake. The lake is too small for windsurfing. Swimming is not recommended.

Contact: Inyo National Forest, White Mountain Ranger Station, (760) 873-2500 or fax (760) 873-2563.

About North Lake: If you prefer a tiny, intimate setting in the high country, then little North Lake might work for you. The lake sits at an elevation of 9,500 feet, and the surface area is just 13 acres, more the size of a high mountain pond.

Some visitors bring cartop boats for improved access, but the lake is too small and too shallow for anything but canoes; boats with motors are not permitted. This is not a good choice for swimming because the water is often mucky and very cold. Hence the place gets light use year-round.

North Lake is best used as a layover spot before heading off on a backpacking expedition. Just west of the lake is a trailhead for a route that follows the North Fork of Bishop Creek up to a remarkable granite basin loaded with similar small mountain lakes. Loch Leven and Plute Lake are just a three-mile hike away; and if you head over the pass into Humphreys Basin, you can venture cross-country to your choice of 25 lakes, many filled with golden trout.

If you don't want to hike, nearby Sabrina Lake and South Lake provide better prospects for boating and water recreation.

❺ Sabrina Lake

Location: Southwest of Bishop in Inyo National Forest; map F5, grid d4.

Directions: From US 395 in Bishop, turn west on Highway 168 and drive 18.5 miles southwest to the lake.

Access: An unimproved boat ramp is located on the lake's north end.

Facilities, fees: A campground is available nearby. Fishing boats are rented out at Sabrina Lake Boat Landing. Supplies can be obtained in Bishop. Access is free.

Water sports, restrictions: A 5 mph speed limit is strictly enforced. Windsurfing and swimming are not recommended.

Contact: Inyo National Forest, White Mountain Ranger Station, (760) 873-2500 or fax (760) 873-2563; Sabrina Lake Boat Landing, (760) 873-7425.

About Sabrina Lake: The largest of the four lakes in the Bishop Creek drainage, Sabrina Lake is also the most popular. It is set at an elevation of 9,130 feet and covers nearly 200 acres, yet it is only a 20-mile ride out of Bishop.

Sound good? It is. Sabrina provides a boat ramp, enforces a 5 mph speed limit to guarantee quiet water, and has good hiking destinations nearby, with two lakes within a 2.5-mile hike from here.

Camping, trout fishing, and low-speed boating are the major attractions. A small concessionaire operation offers boat rentals, but there are no other facilities at the lake. Use is moderate, primarily by anglers.

The water in the lake comes from glacier runoff, so it is freezing cold. Swimming is out of the question for most people, but hey, sometimes you'll see visitors having contests to see who can keep their feet in the water the longest. Some last less than 10 seconds.

If you want solitude, the trail on the lake's southeast side provides an ideal opportunity to strike out on your own. Shortly after leaving the lake's shore, the trail forks; head to the left and you can hike to Lake George; head to the right and you will hit Blue , Donkey, and Baboon Lakes. All are excellent day-hike destinations.

Insider's note: It's pronounced "Sa-*bry*-na," not "Sa-*bree*-na."

⑥ South Lake

⚓ 🚤 ⛺ 🐟   7️⃣

Location: Southwest of Bishop in Inyo National Forest; map F5, grid e4.
Directions: From US 395 in Bishop, turn west on Highway 168 and drive 15 miles southwest to South Lake Road on the left. Turn and drive seven miles south to the lake.
Access: An unimproved boat ramp is located on the lake's north end.
Facilities, fees: Several campgrounds are provided on South Lake Road. Lodging and picnic areas are available at the lake. Fishing boat rentals are available at South Lake Boat Landing. Access is free.
Water sports, restrictions: A 5 mph speed limit is strictly enforced. Windsurfing and swimming are not recommended.
Contact: Inyo National Forest, White Mountain Ranger Station, (760) 873-2500 or fax (760) 873-2563; South Lake Boat Landing, (760) 873-4177.
About South Lake: When a small dam was built on the South Fork of Bishop Creek, South Lake was created. This 166-acre lake is set in the high country at 9,755 feet. There's a good boat ramp, which makes it

popular among owners of trailered aluminum boats. A 5 mph speed limit is in effect, allowing trolling for trout and not much more.

South Lake is the most developed of the three lakes in the area (the others are North and Sabrina), but doesn't offer anything more in the way of water sports. You still get the ice-cold glacial runoff, which prohibits swimming and windsurfing, and the 5 mph speed limit restricts all boating save for fishing. Of course, canoeing and kayaking are always possible.

⑦ Hume Lake

⚓ 🚤 ⛺ 🐟 🌊   6️⃣

Location: East of Fresno in Sequoia National Forest; map F5, grid h0.
Directions: From Fresno turn east on Highway 180 and drive approximately 55 miles on the winding two-laner to the town of Wilsonia in Kings Canyon National Park. Continue east on Highway 180 for six miles to the Hume Lake Road junction. Turn right on Ten Mile Road and drive three miles south to the lake.
Access: A primitive launch ramp is located on the lake's south side.
Facilities, fees: A campground and picnic area are provided. Groceries, gas, and a restaurant are also available. Fishing boats can be rented at Hume Lake Christian Camp. Access is free.
Water sports, restrictions: A 5 mph speed limit is enforced. Gas-powered motors are not permitted. Windsurfing is not allowed. Swimming is available at Sandy Cove Beach on the lake's east side.
Contact: Sequoia National Forest, Hume Lake Ranger District, (559) 338-2251; Hume Lake Christian Camp, (559) 335-2000.
About Hume Lake: This gorgeous lake is set at 5,200 feet in elevation and is bordered by Kings Canyon National Park, Sequoia National Forest, and the Hume Lake Christian Camp (we'll get to that later).

The lake covers 85 acres and is filled with emerald green water. Swimmers will find an excellent spot for jumping in at Sandy Cove Beach, a large day-use area surrounded by huge sequoia trees. This is a very peaceful, pretty place, and the 5 mph speed limit ensures that things stay that way. In addition to swimming, other activities include low-speed boating and paddling, trout fishing, and Bible study.

Right: Hume Lake Christian Camp has jurisdiction over the lake's south side, but they are friendly folks, and will be more than happy to rent you a boat.

---

⑧ Ten Mile Creek

Location: East of Fresno; map F5, grid h1.
Directions: From Fresno turn east on Highway 180 and drive approximately 55 miles on the winding two-laner to the town of Wilsonia in Kings Canyon National Park. Continue east on Highway 180 for six miles to the Hume Lake Road junction. Turn right and continue on about four miles, passing Hume Lake. Access is available directly off Ten Mile Road.
Access: There is no boat ramp.

Facilities, fees: Three campgrounds are available on Ten Mile Road. Limited supplies can be obtained at Hume Lake and the town of Wilsonia. Access is free.
Water sports, restrictions: Several swimming holes are available near pullouts off of Ten Mile Road, near the campgrounds.
Contact: Sequoia National Forest, Hume Lake Ranger District, (559) 338-2251.
About Ten Mile Creek: Vacationers and campers who want to alleviate the intense summer heat by taking a quick dunk have made Ten Mile Creek a popular place.

The trout fishing is lousy here, as the trout are practically nonexistent at times, but swimming can be good. The best fishing areas are found off pullouts on Ten Mile Road, close to Hume Lake. All of these spots are do-it-yourself specials, undeveloped, and difficult to find; keep a close eye out for the little parking pullouts along the road.

Beautiful forest land surrounds the creekside campgrounds, which get quite a bit of traffic. Swimming conditions are poor directly adjacent to the campgrounds. Instead, you need to drive a bit and find those secret little swimming holes. It's like a fortune hunt.

Map of Central California—Page 330

Chapter G2
Morro Bay/ Nacimiento Area

Overall Rating

Poor .... Fair .... Great

G2–Morro Bay/Nacimiento Area Map

One inch equals approximately 10.7 miles.
See page 12 for California state map.

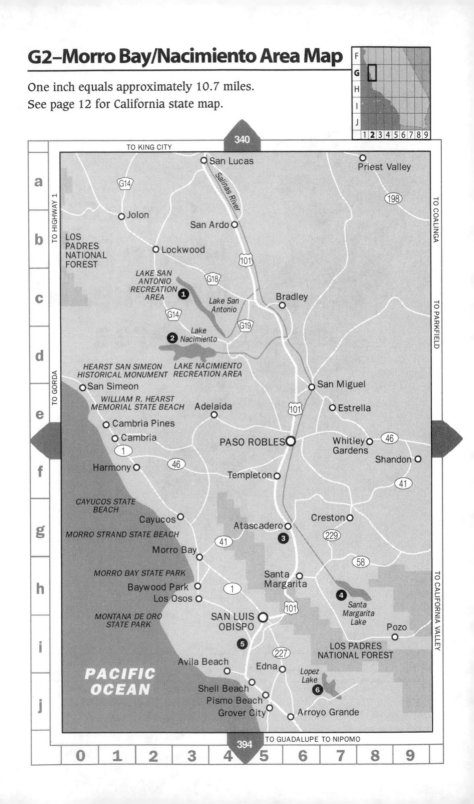

Chapter G2 features:

1 Lake San Antonio

Location North of San Luis Obispo; map G2, grid c3.

Directions: From San Luis Obispo drive approximately 47 miles north on US 101. Turn west on County Road G18/Jolon Road to reach the north shore. To reach the south shore, take the 24th Street exit west. This turns into County Road G19/Nacimiento Road. Turn left on Interlake Road and follow it 3.5 miles to the lake.

Access: Two paved ramps are available. To reach the north shore ramp, turn south off Jolon Road onto New Pleyto Road and continue to the marina at the road's end. To reach the south shore ramp, turn north off Interlake Road onto San Antonio Road and continue to the marina.

Facilities, fees: Campgrounds, picnic areas, a full-service marina, snack bar, restaurant, gas station, laundromat, and groceries are available. Fishing boats, patio boats, ski boats, and personal watercraft can be rented at Lake San Antonio Marina. Fees are charged for day use and lake use (includes boat launching).

Water sports, restrictions: Waterskiing, personal watercraft, and windsurfing are permitted. A sandy swimming beach is available on the south shore between the marina and Harris Creek Day-Use Area.

Contact: Lake San Antonio, (805) 472-2311; Lake San Antonio Marina, (805) 472-2818.

About Lake San Antonio: Have you ever felt like someone or something was watching you? At Lake San Antonio—which has the largest population of bald eagles in central California—that perception is usually accurate.

That's just one of the special things about the San Antonio experience. This is a big lake, long and narrow, covering 5,500 surface acres with 60 miles of shoreline. The setting is at an elevation of 900 feet in the southern Monterey County foothills.

Lake San Antonio, thanks to its large size and warm water, is the most popular waterskiing lake in the region. In the winter, eagle-watching tours are the main attraction, and the chances of seeing both bald and golden eagles by boat are excellent. But no matter when you come, keep an eye out to the skies. The eagles are always watching.

In addition to two boat ramps and several campgrounds, the lake offers full facilities. With all these attractions, it gets significant use and can be extremely crowded on holiday weekends as well as on summer weekends when the weather is good.

Surface temperatures are warm and comfortable, making waterskiing and watercrafting very popular year-round. And providing you can avoid all the fast action, swimming is also excellent. The best spot for swimming is at the sandy beach on the south shore.

Prospects for windsurfing are decent in the spring, but are generally only fair; most sailboarders head to the other side of the hill to Lake Nacimiento (see the next listing), which tends to get steadier winds than at San Antonio.

2 Lake Nacimiento

Location: North of San Luis Obispo; map G2, grid d3.

Directions: From San Luis Obispo drive 25 miles north on US 101 to Paso Robles.

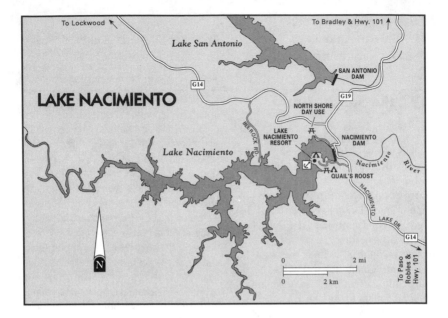

Turn west on County Road G14/Nacimiento Lake Drive and continue west to the dam. Or continue north on US 101 to the turnoff for County Road G19/Nacimiento Road, turn west, and continue to the lake.

Access: A paved boat ramp is located on the southeast shore, next to Lake Nacimiento Resort.

Facilities, fees: A campground, picnic area, lodgings, restaurant, gas, full-service marina, and groceries are available. Fishing boats, pontoon boats, ski boats, personal watercraft, canoes, and kayaks can be rented at the Lake Nacimiento Marina. Fees are charged for day use and lake use (includes boat launching).

Water sports, restrictions: Waterskiing, personal watercraft, and windsurfing are permitted. Swimming is available all along the shoreline (you need a boat to reach the best spots).

Contact: Lake Nacimiento Resort, (805) 238-3256; Lake Nacimiento Marina, (805) 238-1056.

About Lake Nacimiento: A remarkable number of lake arms and coves add to the boundary of Lake Nacimiento, a big lake set in the coastal foothill country. When full, the lake covers more than 5,000 acres and has 165 miles of shoreline.

That combination—a huge surface area with many private coves—provides the ideal conditions for high-speed boating, waterskiing, and personal watercraft, as well as low-speed boating, canoeing, and fishing.

In the main lake body, water-skiers and personal watercraft often dominate the scene. There is even a slalom course on the lake for expert water-skiers. If you have a fast boat, you will feel right at home. But if you don't, well, don't despair.

That is because you can explore the rest of the lake and hunt down a quiet, private spot for fishing or swimming in one of the coves. Fishing is often excellent for white bass and largemouth bass, with high catch rates common in the spring and early summer.

While there is no drive-to swimming beach, with a boat you can access any number of private little beaches in the coves. Swimming is very pleasant here, as the water temperature hovers in the 67- to 72-degree range most of the summer.

Nacimiento is also good for windsurfing in the spring, when coastal winds whip in from the ocean and through the lake canyons en route to the valley. However, the main lake is big enough to get quite choppy and provide a rough riding surface, often making it difficult for novices.

This is a fully developed resort destination that is popular with families. Use is highest in the summer, of course, but holds steady year-round. Its location near US 101 in central California puts it within reach of residents to the south in Santa Barbara as well as those from up north in San Jose—a rarity.

❸ Atascadero Lake

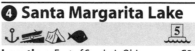

Location: North of San Luis Obispo in Atascadero Memorial Park; map G2, grid g6.
Directions: From San Luis Obispo drive north on US 101 to Atascadero. Turn left on Highway 41 and drive two miles west to the park entrance on the left.
Access: There is no boat ramp. Cartop boats may be hand launched.
Facilities, fees: Rest rooms, a concession stand, and paddleboat rentals are available. Access is free.
Water sports, restrictions: Gas-powered motors are not permitted on the lake. A 5 mph speed limit is strictly enforced. Windsurfing is not allowed. Swimming is limited to a children's swimming pool at the park.
Contact: City of Atascadero Parks & Recreation Department, 6500 Palma Avenue, Room 107, Atascadero, CA 93422; (805) 461-5000 or fax (805) 461-7612.
About Atascadero Lake: This 30-acre lake is the centerpiece of a friendly city park that provides the chance to enjoy a variety of activities.

Unfortunately, those activities do not include most water sports. There are lots of nos: No gas motors, no boat ramp, no waterskiing, no windsurfing, no swimming, no wading.

What that leaves is the opportunity for kids to play, usually pedaling around the lake in a paddleboat. Visitors can hand launch a cartop boat, such as a canoe or a rowboat, and then paddle about, but that's about it. That leaves fishing, and the prospects for that are practically zilch.

Most of the folks you'll see at Atascadero Lake are just out for a lakeside picnic.

❹ Santa Margarita Lake

Location: East of San Luis Obispo; map G2, grid h7.
Directions: From San Luis Obispo drive eight miles north on US 101. Take the Highway 58 exit and drive four miles east, past Santa Margarita, to Pozo Road. Turn right, drive seven miles southeast, turn north on Santa Margarita Lake Road, and continue to the lake.
Access: A paved boat ramp is located on the southwest shore.
Facilities, fees: A campground is set near the lake. Picnic areas, a full-service marina, snack bar, and groceries are available. Fishing and pontoon boats can be rented. There are fees for day use and boat launching.
Water sports, restrictions: The speed limit is 30 mph. Waterskiing, personal watercraft, windsurfing, swimming, and water/body contact are not allowed. Boaters with craft under 10 feet long must sign a safety waiver.
Contact: Santa Margarita Lake Marina, (805) 438-5485.
About Santa Margarita Lake: This lake should have a sign that declares, "Fishing only!" because the rules here do not allow waterskiing or any water contact: no swimming, wading, windsurfing, or anything else, just fishing.

The lake covers nearly 800 acres, most of it long and narrow. It is set at an elevation of 1,300 feet in a dammed-up valley in the foothill country five miles southeast of the town of Santa Margarita.

Anglers from near and far are enamored with the idea of a fishing-only lake, as well as being equally fascinated with the fine bass prospects here. Expect heavy fishing traffic on weekends virtually year-round.

Note the peculiar rule that owners of boats under 10 feet long must sign a safety waiver before they are permitted on the lake. Another rule is that no lawyers are permitted within one mile of the lake. Heh, heh. Just kidding.

⑤ Laguna Lake

Location: Near San Luis Obispo; map G2, grid i5.

Directions: From San Luis Obispo drive two miles south on US 101 to Madonna Road. Turn west and continue to the park entrance.

Access: An unimproved boat ramp is available.

Facilities, fees: Rest rooms, picnic area, and a playground are provided. Access is free.

Water sports, restrictions: Motors are not permitted on the lake. Windsurfing is allowed. No swimming is permitted.

Contact: City of San Luis, Parks & Recreation Department, (805) 781-7300 or fax (805) 781-7292.

About Laguna Lake: Basically a big neighborhood lake, this is the kind of place where locals unwind on the weekends and on summer evenings. Most fish a little, jog a bit, or have a picnic.

What most people don't realize is that Laguna Lake is a great spot for windsurfing. The winds come up nearly every day in the afternoon, and by 4 PM they are usually whipping sailboarders at a fast clip. Conditions

can be ideal because, unlike at larger lakes, the surface here doesn't get choppy when pushed by strong winds. Still, be forewarned that this is no place for a novice windsurfer.

The best thing about Laguna is that windsurfers practically have the lake to themselves. You see, swimming and motorized boats are not allowed.

The lake is far more popular with picnickers and joggers, however. There is even a fitness trail in the park. Big events, including weddings, are often held in the park, which is also the starting point for some running and walking races.

⑥ Lopez Lake

Location: East of San Luis Obispo; map G2, grid j7.

Directions: From San Luis Obispo drive 16 miles south on US 101 to Arroyo Grande. Take Grand Avenue east (which eventually becomes Lopez Drive) and continue 10 miles to the lake.

Access: A paved boat ramp is located at the marina, just past the lake entrance on the left.

Facilities, fees: A campground, full-service marina, gas, laundromat, and groceries are available. Fishing boats and pontoon boats can be rented at Lopez Lake Marina. Fees are charged for day use and boat launching.

Water sports, restrictions: There is a 40 mph speed limit. Waterskiing, personal watercraft, and windsurfing are allowed. A swimming area is available on the lake's east side.

Contact: Lopez Lake Marina, (805) 489-1006; Lopez Lake, Main Office, (805) 489-1122.

About Lopez Lake: They've got it right at Lopez Lake. This lake can be ideal for waterskiing, personal watercraft, windsurfing, and fishing, but not when the participants attempt to practice their sports in the same place. That can result in World War III.

So here they set aside special marked areas devoted exclusively to waterskiing, personal watercraft, and windsurfing. That keeps everybody happy and out of each other's way—a perfect example of the best way to manage a recreational lake.

There are also full facilities for swimming, with a big swimming beach and two giant water slides, along with a nice picnic area. Another bonus is the scenic boat tours, which are touristy, to be sure, and get plenty of takers.

So it will come as no surprise to hear that visitor use is extremely high in the summer. After all, do you know of any lake that provides all this? Nope. Neither do we, and hey, we checked every lake in California.

All these activities and special-use rules work so well because Lopez Lake is a decent-sized lake, 940 acres when full, and it gets excellent summer weather in the foothills southeast of San Luis Obispo.

One word of caution: In the spring, this isn't the place to bring a canoe or, for that matter, any boat that can't handle wind. Why? You guessed it. It gets very windy here in the spring, especially in the afternoon, making it great for windsurfers and sailboaters.

Chapter G4
Bakersfield Foothills Area

Overall Rating

| 1 | 2 | 3 | 4 | 5 | 6 | 7 | 8 | 9 | 10 |

Poor .... Fair .... Great

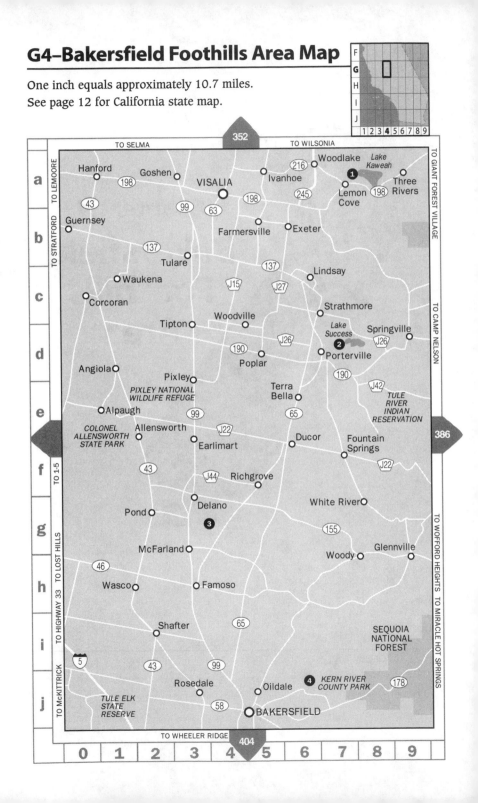

G4–Bakersfield Foothills Area Map

One inch equals approximately 10.7 miles.
See page 12 for California state map.

Chapter G4 features:

① Lake Kaweah

Location: East of Visalia; map G4, grid a8.

Directions: From Visalia drive 20 miles east on Highway 198 to the lake.

Access: Two boat ramps are available on the lake's west end.

Facilities, fees: A campground, picnic areas, full-service marina, and a concession stand are provided at the lake. Fishing boats and patio boats can be rented at the marina. Access is free. There is a fee for boat launching.

Water sports, restrictions: Waterskiing, personal watercraft, and windsurfing are permitted. Swimming is available on the lake's west side near the boat docks, and on the east side at Slick Rock Day-Use Area.

Contact: US Army Corps of Engineers, Lake Kaweah, (559) 597-2301; Kaweah Marina, (559) 597-2526.

About Lake Kaweah: If you visit Kaweah in late March, April, or early May, you discover a big, pretty reservoir set in the foothill country. When full, the lake covers nearly 2,000 acres, with 22 miles of shoreline. You may even think you have found paradise.

But if you visit Kaweah in late summer or fall, you will be greeted by a pit of a water hole and weather so hot you may expect the lake to start boiling at any minute.

Don't blow the deal and show up at the wrong time. Many people do, thinking the late summer heat is the perfect excuse to head to the lake to cool off. Wrong. The annual water drawdown here shrinks the lake and makes it look like a dust bowl.

In the spring, however, this is a boater's heaven. Bass fishing is good in the coves, and there is plenty of room for personal watercraft and water-skiers to steer clear of those who are fishing. Some people even roam around in patio boats and enjoy the warm temperatures and cool water. There are some huge bass in this lake, and they inspire a lot of fishermen.

When the lake is full, prospects for swimming are decent in two spots: the lake's west side near the boat docks, and the east side at Slick Rock Day-Use Area. Over the years the fluctuating water levels have killed any prospects for developed beaches for swimming and wading.

Winds are erratic, coming and going far too unpredictably to make this a reliable destination for windsurfing or sailing. Then comes summer and out goes the water. In late summer and fall, when Kaweah starts to get low, unmarked rocks just beneath the surface can create boating hazards, and boaters should be sure to stay in deep water.

② Lake Success

Location: Near Porterville; map G4, grid d7.

Directions: From Bakersfield on Highway 99, take the Highway 65 turnoff and drive 44 miles north to the junction with Highway 190 south of Porterville. Turn right and drive east on Highway 190 for seven miles to the lake.

Access: Two paved ramps are available: one on the west shore just north of the dam, and one on the east shore adjacent to the campgrounds.

Facilities, fees: A campground, full-service marina, picnic areas, and groceries are available. You can rent fishing boats, patio boats, and houseboats at Success Marina. Access to the lake is free. There is a fee for boat launching.

Water sports, restrictions: Waterskiing, personal watercraft, and windsurfing are permitted. There are no designated swimming beaches, but you can swim at the Tule Day-Use Area, just past the south parking area.

Contact: US Army Corps of Engineers, Lake Success, (559) 784-0215; Success Marina, (559) 781-2078.

About Lake Success: Lake Success is a big lake with a series of major lake arms. When full it covers nearly 2,500 acres and has 30 miles of shoreline, yet is much shallower than most reservoirs. It is set in the bare foothill country at an elevation of 650 feet. Those stark surroundings and the very hot temperatures that set in during the summer can make this lake look like a dream to boaters when they first arrive.

Waterskiing and personal watercraft are very big here, along with trout fishing in the winter and bass fishing in the spring. The water is quite warm by late May, and winds are typically light, so conditions are usually excellent for waterskiing.

The lack of wind, however, makes conditions poor for windsurfing most of the year. The exception is in late March and early April or rarely May, the one period when this area can get some wind. This also happens to be the season when the lake is at its fullest, and the combination means outstanding opportunities for windsurfing.

The biggest problem with Lake Success is that the water levels can fluctuate from day to day, typically with major drawdowns during the summer. That is one reason why there are no beaches, although the day-use area does have a somewhat sloped stretch of shore that is good for swimming.

Lake use is moderate year-round, and there are lots of water-skiers in the summer. That's what you can expect.

➌ Lake Woollomes

Location: Near Delano; map G4, grid g4.

Directions: From Bakersfield drive 25 miles north on Highway 99 to Delano. Turn east on Highway 155, drive one mile, and then turn south on Mast Avenue. Drive one mile, turn east on Woollomes Avenue, and continue to the lake.

Access: An unimproved boat ramp for cartop boats is located next to the picnic areas.

Facilities, fees: Picnic areas, rest rooms, boat docks, and a concession stand are provided. An entrance fee is charged on weekends.

Water sports, restrictions: Motors are not permitted on the lake. All boats are required to have a permit; boaters may purchase one at the park. Windsurfing is not allowed. Swimming is available at a small lagoon area.

Contact: Kern County Parks and Recreation Department, (661) 861-2063.

About Lake Woollomes: It's hard to believe that there is much of anything out in this country. This land is dry, hot, and flat. Little Lake Woollomes provides a respite, set in a small park, the kind that has lawns and even a few picnic spots. Woollomes does cover about 300 acres, and in the barren South Valley, any lake, even this one, is considered something special.

This nice, quiet little spot is used mainly for picnicking, but it does attract a few anglers now and then. No motors are permitted, so people plop in a canoe and paddle around, a popular activity. Use is moderate year-round, mostly families on picnics.

➍ Lake Ming

Location: Near Bakersfield in Kern River County Park; map G4, grid j6.

Directions: From Bakersfield drive 11 miles northeast on Alfred Harrell Highway to Kern River County Park.

Access: A paved ramp is located on the lake's east side.

Facilities, fees: A campground is available approximately one-quarter mile west of the lake. A picnic area, rest rooms, and a concession stand are provided. Access is free.

Water sports, restrictions: Sailing and windsurfing are permitted on the second weekend of every month and on Tuesday and Thursday afternoons. All motorized boating, including waterskiing and personal watercraft, is permitted on the remaining days. All boats are required to have a permit; boaters may purchase one at the park. Swimming is not allowed.

Contact: Kern County Parks and Recreation Department, (661) 861-2063.

About Lake Ming: Squint your eyes just right in February when things have greened up a bit, and Lake Ming can almost look pretty. Almost.

The lake is set near the Kern River at 450 feet in elevation and covers just 107 acres. Instead of scenic beauty, you will find that Lake Ming is mainly a big playground for speed demon boaters and their friends who drink a lot of beer. Jet boat races are even held here, and sailing, windsurfing, and fishing can be restricted to a few days per month. As for swimming, forget it (and we'll get to that).

About 20 days each year, the lake is closed to the public when private boat races and other events are scheduled; always call ahead if you are planning a day trip. To keep water-skiers and race boats out of each other's way, there is a designated lake area for waterskiing.

Sailing and windsurfing are only permitted on the second weekend of every month and on Tuesday and Thursday afternoons, but they are very popular during those times. The only activity more popular on Tuesday and Thursday afternoons is beer drinking, and if you don't believe it, just check out the windsurfers waiting in line for their permits.

All other boating is permitted on the remaining days; be aware that a $40 per year boating permit is required for all craft.

You might ask why no swimming? Well, windsurfers and water-skiers should take note: There is a parasite in the lake that has been known to cause "swimmer's itch." Sounds like fun.

Map of Central California—Page 330

Chapter G5
South Sequoia Area

Overall Rating

| 1 | 2 | 3 | 4 | 5 | 6 | 7 | 8 | 9 | 10 |

Poor .... Fair .... Great

G5–South Sequoia Area Map

One inch equals approximately 10.7 miles.
See page 12 for California state map.

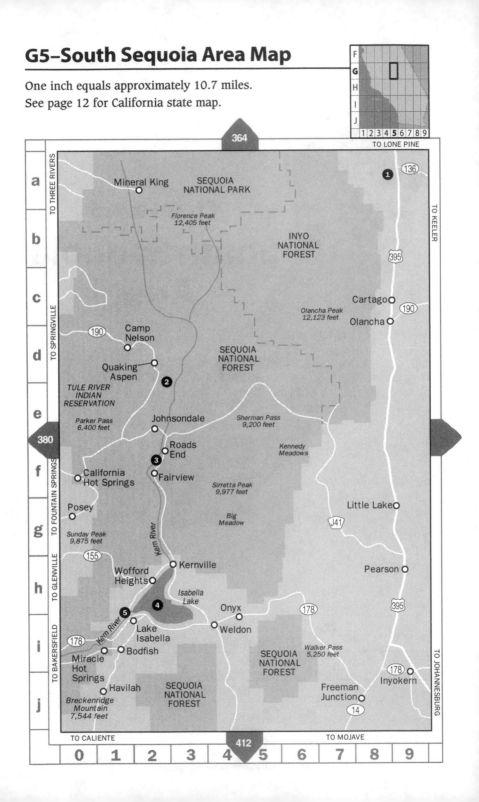

Chapter G5 features:

1 Diaz Lake

Location: South of Lone Pine; map G5, grid a9.

Directions: From the town of Lone Pine on US 395, drive three miles south to the lake.

Access: A paved boat ramp is located on the lake's east side.

Facilities, fees: A campground, picnic area, boat dock, and a golf course are provided. Supplies can be obtained in Lone Pine. Access is free. There is a fee for boat launching.

Water sports, restrictions: Waterskiing, personal watercraft, and windsurfing are permitted. Boats over 22 feet long are prohibited. The speed limit is 35 mph from May through October, and 15 mph from November through April. Swimming is available at the day-use area on the west shore.

Contact: Diaz Lake Campground, (760) 876-5656 or fax (760) 873-5599; Inyo County Parks Department, (760) 878-0272.

About Diaz Lake: Little Diaz Lake is set at 3,650 feet in the Owens Valley, where it gets overshadowed by nearby Mount Whitney and the Sierra range to the west. The lake has three campgrounds along the western shore, making it a decent spot for camper/boaters.

Covering 85 acres, the lake is small enough to provide a degree of intimacy, yet just large enough for waterskiing, and is close enough to Mount Whitney to have a looming sense of grandeur. Those features, along with clear, cool water, make Diaz Lake extremely popular for waterskiing and swimming, and often good for windsurfing.

A 15 mph speed limit during the prime fishing season, November through April, makes this an ideal setting for fishing. By May anglers head north on US 395 to find better prospects in the eastern Sierra, the speed limit is bumped up to 35 mph here, warm weather sets in, and in come the water-skiers. For swimmers there is an excellent beach area.

One sidelight here is hang gliding, which is very popular from May through July on the leeward side of Mount Whitney. On the rare day you might even see hang gliders along the Whitney face as high as 14,000 feet, an extraordinary sight.

2 Forks of the Kern River

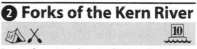

Location: Northeast of Bakersfield in Sequoia National Forest; map G5, grid e3.

Directions: From Bakersfield drive approximately 45 miles east on Highway 178 to the town of Lake Isabella. Turn north on Highway 155 and continue seven miles to Wofford Heights. Look for Burlando Road; turn right and drive four miles to Kernville. Turn north on Sierra Way and drive all the way to the abandoned town of Johnsondale. Look for a sign indicating Lloyds Meadow and turn right. Continue for about 15 miles and bear right when you see the sign that says "Fork of the Kern 4." Drive two miles on the dirt road and park at its end; then hike approximately two miles down to the river. This trail offers the only developed access to this river section.

Access: There is no boat ramp. To reach the put-in see the directions above. Take out 17 miles downstream at the Johnsondale Bridge, located 20 miles north of Kernville.

Facilities, fees: Boat-in campsites are

provided along the river. Access is free. Rafting permits are required from May 15 to September 15; contact the Sequoia National Forest, Cannell Ranger District office, for information.

Water sports, restrictions: Swimming is not recommended. Rafters are advised to wear wet suits.

Contact: Sequoia National Forest, Cannell Meadow Ranger District, (760) 376-3781 or fax (760) 376-3795. For rafting trips contact Chuck Richards Whitewater, (760) 642-9725; Kern River Tours, (760) 379-4616; Outdoor Adventures, (800) 323-4234; or Whitewater Voyages, (800) 488-7238.

About the Forks of the Kern River: You have to be a little crazy to raft the Forks of the Kern, and that's exactly why we like it.

This river stretch is famous for having one heart-pumping rapid after another set in a beautiful wilderness canyon that is extremely difficult to access. The run is rated Class V—and just a notch below a Class VI, which is certain death. Only experts should attempt the run, and even for them it can be a death-defying act.

The run is 17 miles long, most of it amid complete wilderness, all of it on clear, icy water that's fed primarily by Whitney snowmelt from May through July. There are no access roads anywhere, a factor that is of paramount importance. It means that if an accident should occur, a timely rescue would be virtually impossible. It also means that once you start downriver, there is no turning back, because the only way out is down the river to the take-out.

Getting to the put-in requires a two-mile descent into a canyon. That's why most parties hire pack mules to cart in their stuff. Even then it is wise to pack light, as portages are common on this run and you'll end up carrying your gear anyway. Still with us?

If so then note that the run starts in the Golden Trout Wilderness near the confluence with the Little Kern River. This is an absolutely beautiful river canyon, but few rafters have time to admire it because right off the bat you hit Class V water, a river section considered a world-class rafting run for its series of sensational miniature falls.

Highlights include Upper (Class IV+) and Lower (Class V) Freeman Creek Falls, Needlerock Falls (Class IV+), Slalom (Class IV+), Vortex (Class V–VI), Rincon Aisle (Class IV+), Westwall (Class V), and Carson Falls (Class V–VI).

Even the best experts often portage Vortex and Carson Falls. The longest successive piece of white water is Rincon Aisle, which features three consecutive rapids over the course of three-quarters of a mile.

This is considered the most popular expert white-water rafting run in the state, and only one commercial trip per day is allowed.

❸ Upper Kern River

⛺ 🐟 🏐 ✕ 🏊   [10]

Location: Northeast of Bakersfield in Sequoia National Forest; map G5, grid f2.

Directions: From Bakersfield drive approximately 45 miles east on Highway 178 to the town of Lake Isabella. Turn north on Highway 155 and continue seven miles to Wofford Heights. Look for Burlando Road; turn right and drive four miles to Kernville. Turn north on Mountain Road 99. Direct access is available off the road.

Access: There is no boat ramp. To reach the put-in once you are in Kernville, turn north on Sierra Way and drive 20 miles to the Johnsondale Bridge. There are several good take-outs along the way; the final take-out is 18 miles downstream at Riverside Park in Kernville. Note: Sections of the river are unrunnable; be sure to take out above Fairview Dam (mile 2.5) and above Salmon Falls (mile eight).

Facilities, fees: Campgrounds are provided on Highway 178 and Sierra Way, as well as at Isabella Lake. Supplies can be obtained in Bakersfield, Kernville, and Kernvale. Access is free. Rafting permits are required

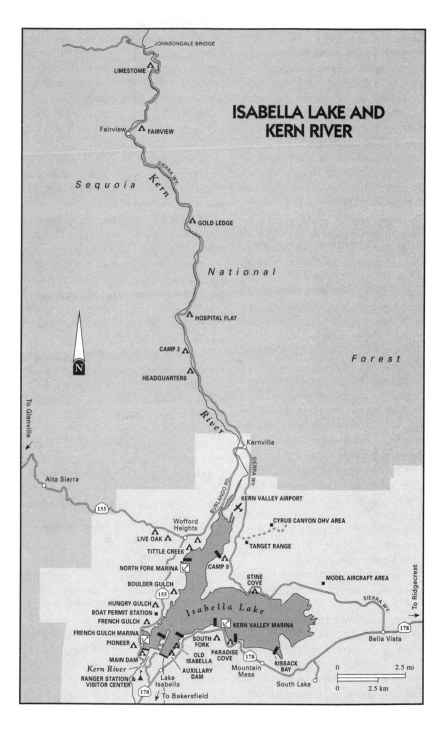

ISABELLA LAKE AND KERN RIVER

JOHNSONDALE BRIDGE

LIMESTOME

Fairview FAIRVIEW

Sequoia Kern SIERRA HWY.

GOLD LEDGE

National

HOSPITAL FLAT

CAMP 3

HEADQUARTERS

Forest

To Glenville

River

Kernville

SIERRA WY.

Alta Sierra

BURLANDO RD.

KERN VALLEY AIRPORT

155

CYRUS CANYON OHV AREA

Wofford Heights

LIVE OAK

TARGET RANGE

TITTLE CREEK

NORTH FORK MARINA   CAMP 9

STINE COVE

MODEL AIRCRAFT AREA

BOULDER GULCH

To Ridgecrest

HUNGRY GULCH

BOAT PERMIT STATION

FRENCH GULCH

FRENCH GULCH MARINA

PIONEER

Isabella Lake

KERN VALLEY MARINA

SIERRA WY.

Bella Vista

178

MAIN DAM

SOUTH FORK

OLD ISABELLA

PARADISE COVE

178

KISSACK BAY

Kern River

RANGER STATION & VISITOR CENTER

AUXILLARY DAM

Lake Isabella

Mountain Mesa

South Lake

178 To Bakersfield

0   2.5 mi

0   2.5 km

Map of Chapter G5—Page 386

from May 15 to September 15; contact the Sequoia National Forest, Cannell Ranger District, for information.

Water sports, restrictions: Swimming is available at several holes along Sierra Way, north of Kernville. The best are near the Forest Service campgrounds.

Contact: Sequoia National Forest, Cannell Meadow Ranger District, (760) 376-3781. For rafting trips contact Chuck Richards Whitewater, (760) 642-9725; Kern River Tours, (760) 379-4616; Outdoor Adventures, (800) 323-4234; or Whitewater Voyages, (800) 488-7238.

About the Upper Kern River: Merle Haggard vowed, "I'll never swim Kern River again," in one of his favorite songs. Why not? Because he lost his "little darlin'" on the Kern when the "swiftness took her life away." And as Haggard sums it up, "It's not deep or wide, but it's a mean piece of water, my friend."

There is some truth to that. The Upper Kern has some of the better stretches of white water for rafting, and it can be dangerous for the inexperienced.

Great white water, beautiful canyon, easy access, and numerous commercial rafting trips have made this run one of the most popular in California. The season typically lasts from April to June, even later in big snow years. The water is always clear and very cold, fresh from snowmelt. The only downer, besides the fate of Merle's little darlin', is that the road parallels most of the river and is within view for nearly the entire run.

The run spans 21 miles, but few people float the entire length. Most rafting companies will break it down into shorter runs because there's a wide range of difficulty over the course of the river. For instance, some stretches are Class III, a good exciting run for beginners, yet others are Class V, where even seasoned professionals can find their hearts pounding like pile drivers. Rafters who will be going in their own boats without guides should note that there are two mandatory take-out points, Fairview Dam and Salmon Falls, which provide natural break points.

Here are the run's highlights, starting at the Johnsondale Bridge put-in:

Miles 0-2.5: This section is rated Class IV and features Limestone (Class IV) and Joe's Diner (IV).

Miles 2.5-6: Rated Class III, with the exception of Bombs Away, a Class V cataract followed by a hydraulic suckhole that'll scare you out of your britches.

Miles 6-8: Rated Class IV+ and featuring Entrance and Satan's Slot, both Class IV+ white water.

Miles 9.5-16.5: Yeah, this is a pulse-pounder, with three Class V rapids and two Class IVs. In sequence, they are Squashed Paddler (Class V), Sock-em-Dog (Class V), The Flume (Class IV+), Fender Bender (Class V), and The Cable (Class IV).

Miles 16.5-19: A great piece of water rated at Class IV. Highlights, as you encounter them heading downriver, are The Wall (Class IV), Tombstone (Class IV), Buzzard's Perch (Class III+), Tequila Chute (Class IV), and Powerhouse (Class III+).

Miles 19-21: The last stretch is a Class III run through private property, highlighted by Big Daddy (Class III-) and Ewing's (Class III-). Do not take out until you reach the town of Kernville, provided you are still in one piece.

---

❹ Isabella Lake

Location: East of Bakersfield; map G5, grid h2.

Directions: From Bakersfield drive approximately 45 miles east on Highway 178 to the lake.

Access: Paved ramps with boat docks are available at the following locations:

1. From the town of Lake Isabella, con-

tinue east on Highway 178 to Sierra Way. Turn north and drive approximately 14 miles to Camp Nine. Note: This ramp may be unusable when water levels are low.

2. From the town of Lake Isabella, turn west on Highway 155, drive a short distance, then turn right at the sign for the boat ramp.

3. From the town of Lake Isabella, turn west on Highway 155 and drive around the lake's west side. The ramp is located between North Fork Marina and Tillie Creek Campground. Note: This ramp may be unusable when water levels are low.

4. From the town of Lake Isabella, continue east on Highway 178 to Old Isabella Road. Turn left and continue to the ramp.

5. From the town of Lake Isabella, continue east on Highway 178 to the sign for South Fork Recreation Area. Turn left and continue to the ramp, located between Paradise Cove and Kern Valley Marina.

Facilities, fees: Several campgrounds and picnic areas are provided. Full-service marinas, restaurants, gas, lodging, and groceries are also available. Rent fishing boats and pontoon boats at Red's Kern Valley Marina, (760) 379-1634. Fishing boats, pontoon boats, ski boats, and personal watercraft can be rented at Dean's North Fork Marina, (760) 376-1812, and at French Gulch Marina, (760) 379-8774. All boaters must purchase an annual permit to boat on the lake; obtain one at any of the three marinas. Permit includes launching privileges.

Water sports, restrictions: Both waterskiing and personal watercraft are permitted. Windsurfing is also allowed; the best spot is on Auxiliary Dam's east side, off Old Isabella Road. Swimming is available all along the shoreline; a popular site is at French Gulch Bridge on the west shore.

Contact: Sequoia National Forest, Greenhorn Ranger District, (760) 379-5646 or fax (760) 379-8597; Kern County Parks, (661) 861-2063.

About Isabella Lake: The largest freshwater lake in Southern California is Isabella, covering 38,400 acres when full. Here you will find what is among the most complete and dynamic array of facilities available anywhere.

The lake, which is set at an elevation of 2,600 feet in the foothills east of Bakersfield, is the centerpiece for a wide variety of activities, namely waterskiing and camping. The majority of visitors are boater/campers who dominate much of the lake, waterskiing on most summer days. There are two major lake arms, each wide and long, and campgrounds are situated along the western shoreline. The weather is hot, the water cool, and with lots of boats and bodies, this is the kind of place where the suntan oil and various liquid refreshments can flow faster than the nearby Kern River.

Windsurfing is extremely popular at Isabella Lake. The best spot is east of Auxiliary Dam, where the winds come up and sail right over the dam; it's quite ideal, usually a steady breeze in the afternoon, not gusty. This area near the dam is also out of target range of the water-ski boats, some of which are navigated and controlled by drivers of questionable sobriety and ability.

The cool, clear Kern River waters feed into the lake and make for excellent swimming conditions. While there are no designated beaches, there are some beachlike areas. The shoreline is mostly hard-packed dirt and sagebrush.

Boater/camper traffic is heavy well into fall. After that, when the cool weather arrives, anglers show up in significant numbers. There is good bird-watching in the area, and of course with the nearby Kern River feeding the lake, there are excellent opportunities for white-water rafting (see listings 2, 3, and 5).

⑤ Lower Kern River

Location: East of Bakersfield; map G5, grid i2.

Directions: From Bakersfield drive approximately 45 miles east on Highway 178 to Lake Isabella. Access to the lower river is available directly off the highway from 10 miles east of Bakersfield all the way to Kernvale.

Access: There is no boat ramp. To reach the put-in drive approximately 45 miles east of Bakersfield on Highway 178 to the town of Lake Isabella. Turn north on Highway 155 and drive just under a mile. Look for the US Army Corps of Engineers sign on your right; directly across the highway is a dirt road. Turn left and drive about one-half mile to a dirt parking area. Put in on the left bank. Take out 18 miles downstream at Democrat Picnic Area (reached by taking a signed dirt road off Highway 178).

Facilities, fees: A primitive camping area is provided at Miracle Hot Springs, located on Kern River Canyon Road off Highway 178. More developed drive-to campgrounds are available at Lake Isabella. Supplies can be obtained in Kernvale. Access is free. Rafting permits are required from May 15 to September 15; contact the Cannell Meadow or Greenhorn Ranger District offices for information.

Water sports, restrictions: Swimming is not recommended.

Contact: Sequoia National Forest, Cannell Meadow Ranger District, (760) 376-3781, or Greenhorn Ranger District, (805) 871-2223. For guided rafting trips contact Chuck Richards Whitewater, (760) 642-9725; Kern River Tours, (760) 379-4616; Outdoor Adventures, (800) 323-4234; or Whitewater Voyages, (800) 488-7238.

About the Lower Kern River: While not as perilous as the Upper Kern, this stretch of river can provide rafters with plenty of thrills and chills. There are a few caveats about safety, however, but we'll get to that in a bit.

This 18-mile-long run is rated Class IV, best for intermediate–advanced rafters. The white-water season is a long one, from Memorial Day weekend to August. One reason is that the Lower Kern is set below Isabella Lake, so water releases from the dam keep this river pumping well through summer. It also means that the water is far warmer than at the stretches of the Kern located upriver of the lake, which are fed by snowmelt.

Access is excellent because the highway parallels the river. And despite the proximity of the road, the steep canyon provides great scenery and has an almost wilderness-like feel.

At first the warm water may seem ideal for swimming, especially when compared to the icy flows of the Upper Kern, but it can be a trip, and swimming is not recommended. This river can be swift and dangerous, particularly when dam releases are increased without warning, and there are numerous holes and brushy sections for swimmers to contend with. People have lost their lives by assuming conditions were kinder.

A challenging intermediate-advanced section is the run's star attraction. Most of the white water is rated Class III+, though a few Class IVs are sprinkled along the route, including White Maiden's Walkway, Dead Man's Curve, Hari-Kari, Horseshoe Falls, and Pinball.

Anybody without a guide should note that there is one Class V–VI rapid called Royal Flush that is nearly always a mandatory portage. Do not attempt to run this piece, and if you are unfamiliar with its location, then you should not be on the river without a guide.

Here's an insider's tip: There are hot springs at the Miracle Hot Springs camping area. Since the old hotel there burned down a few years ago, this area is no longer developed. But if you search, you can still find hot pools.

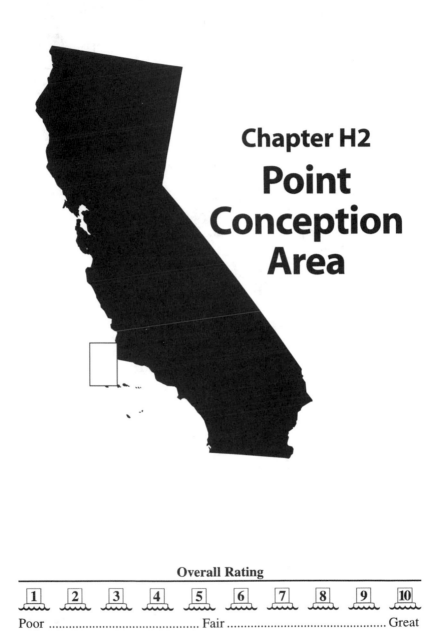

Chapter H2
Point Conception Area

Overall Rating

| 1 | 2 | 3 | 4 | 5 | 6 | 7 | 8 | 9 | 10 |

Poor .... Fair .... Great

H2–Point Conception Area Map

One inch equals approximately 10.7 miles.
See page 12 for California state map.

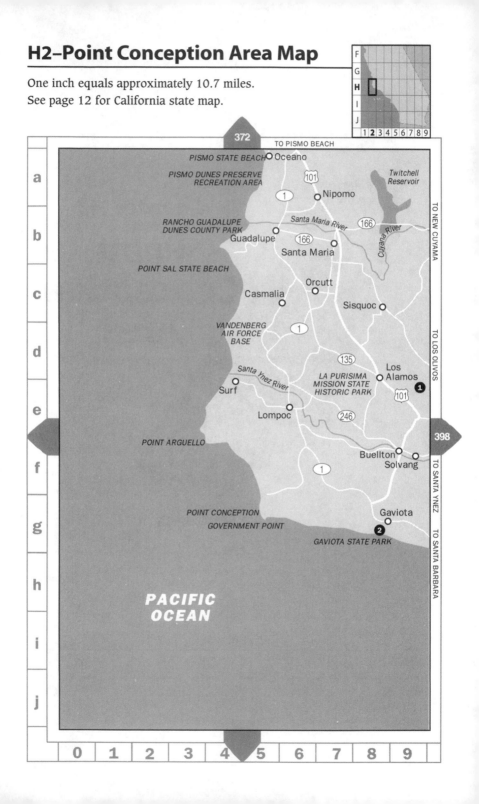

Chapter H2 features:

1 Zaca Lake

Location: South of Santa Maria in Los Padres National Forest; map H2, grid e9.

Directions: From the junction of US 101 and Highway 154 south of Santa Maria, turn east on Highway 154 and drive a short distance. Turn left on a signed dirt road and proceed about 10 miles to the lake entrance.

Access: An unimproved launch ramp is located on the lake's northern side.

Facilities, fees: Primitive campsites, lodging, picnic areas, and a restaurant are provided. Canoes and rowboats can be rented. There are fees for day use and boat launching.

Water sports, restrictions: Motors are not permitted on the lake. Windsurfing and swimming are allowed. The lake is closed to fishing.

Contact: Zaca Lake Resort, (805) 688-5699.

About Zaca Lake: Little Zaca Lake is the perfect retreat for the boater whose ideal vacation wouldn't be complete without a cabin to bed down in.

This small lake, covering just 25 acres, is set at a 2,400-foot elevation in Los Padres National Forest, about 40 miles north of Santa Barbara. Boating is restricted to nonmotorized craft, which keeps the mood nice and quiet here. A full-service lodge rents canoes and rowboats and operates a restaurant.

The few people who have learned about the charms of Zaca Lake have been pretty successful at keeping the place a secret. That hasn't been too difficult because fishing is not permitted, which keeps it out of the loop of most mainstream boaters/campers/anglers.

Swimming is popular, and a buoy line marks a swimming area and rocky beach at the lake's south end. Because of the lake's proximity to the coast, there are steady afternoon winds almost daily, meaning conditions for windsurfing are often excellent. Amazingly, rarely does one see windsurfers taking advantage of it—perhaps they simply haven't heard the word on Zaca.

Side trip options include hiking and horseback riding. Some good trails are routed into the national forestland located north of the lake.

2 Gaviota State Park

Location: North of Santa Barbara; map H2, grid g8.

Directions: From Santa Barbara drive 33 miles north on US 101 to the park entrance.

Access: A boat hoist is available; boaters must provide their own slings. The weight limit is three tons, and the length limit is 22 feet. Driving on the pier is not permitted, so boat owners must have their own transport dolly if they can't tow it by hand.

Facilities, fees: There's a pier and a campground. Supplies can be obtained nearby. Fees are charged for boat hoisting and day use.

Water sports, restrictions: Waterskiing and personal watercraft are permitted; however, water-skiers and personal watercraft must stay within 200 yards of the shoreline. Windsurfing and swimming are not recommended.

Contact: Gaviota State Park, (805) 968-1033.

About Gaviota State Park: If only there were better boating access, this beautiful and spectacular stretch of California coast would have pulled down a perfect 10 rating.

What boaters have to contend with here is a hoist that comes with a hook, and that's all. That means you must supply your own strap, rarely a standard piece of equipment for boaters. But wait, it gets worse. Since driving is not permitted on the pier, boats have to be "walked" on their trailers to the hoist. In other words moving boats in the 17- to 22-foot class requires a transport dolly, and smaller, lighter boats on trailers must be pulled along by hand. These limitations keep most boaters from even considering a visit to this area.

Although there is a pleasant beach for sunbathing and picnicking, conditions are poor to fair for most water sports. The water is too cold for swimming, for instance, and when the wind comes up, it is usually so strong that conditions quickly become hazardous for windsurfers.

So there you have it: a beautiful piece of the central California coast, a state park that gets moderate use year-round, yet far too much hassle to attract many boaters.

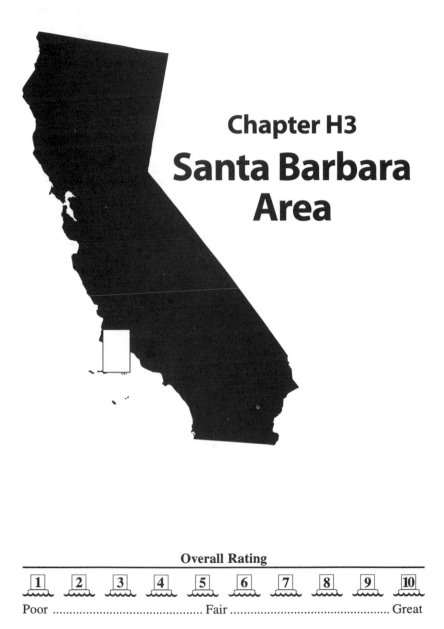

Chapter H3
Santa Barbara Area

Overall Rating

| 1 | 2 | 3 | 4 | 5 | 6 | 7 | 8 | 9 | 10 |

Poor .... Fair .... Great

H3–Santa Barbara Area Map

One inch equals approximately 10.7 miles.
See page 12 for California state map.

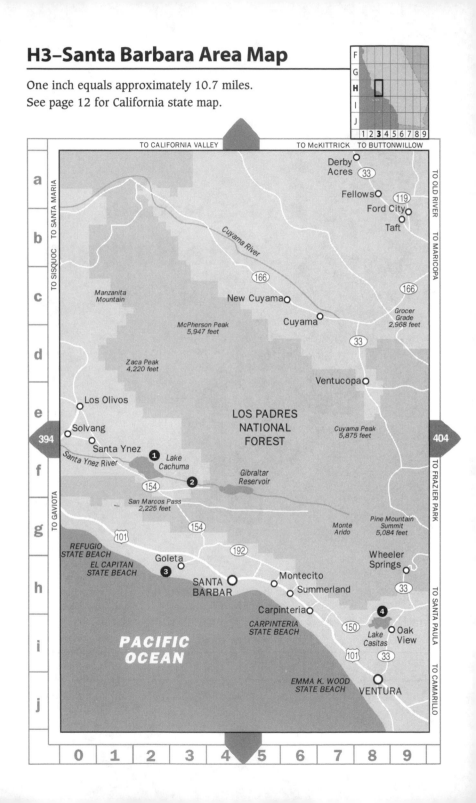

Chapter H3 features:

❶ Lake Cachuma

Location: North of Santa Barbara; map H3, grid f2.

Directions: From Santa Barbara drive about 17 miles north on Highway 154 to the lake on the right.

Access: The unpaved boat ramp is located on the south shore.

Facilities, fees: A campground, picnic areas, full-service marina, rest rooms with showers, snack bar, coin laundry, and groceries are available. Fishing boats and pontoon boats are available for rent. There is a day-use fee.

Water sports, restrictions: Waterskiing and personal watercraft are not permitted. The speed limit is 40 mph in the middle of Lake Cachuma, 5 mph in the coves. Craft under 10 feet long are prohibited. No windsurfing, swimming, or water/body contact is allowed. Swimming pools are available just outside the lake.

Contact: Lake Cachuma, (805) 688-4658 or (805) 688-8780.

About Lake Cachuma: Here's a place that can be transformed from hell to heaven in one fell swoop.

Hell? Because water levels at Cachuma depend solely on rain runoff, it takes only one winter with subpar rains for this lake to become a relative puddle edged by miles of barren, exposed lake bottom. The lake got so low during a recent drought that locals will never forget it.

They will also never forget how the lake filled in a mere 11 days during an onslaught of monsoonlike rains, nor how pretty it suddenly was once again. The high water meant heaven for anglers, and as the bass population boomed (with lots of big fish), Cachuma became one of the best bass lakes in America. Furthermore, boating restrictions have made this lake perfect for fishing.

Very little water recreation is permitted because this is a reservoir used to store drinking water (at least that's the excuse that's provided). No waterskiing, personal watercraft, swimming, or windsurfing is allowed. Canoes and kayaks are prohibited from the lake, as are boats under 10 feet long. That leaves it all to the fishing boats, and with a speed limit of 5 mph in the coves and 40 mph elsewhere, it's just about the perfect setup for high-speed bass boats.

Cachuma is set at an elevation of 780 feet in the foothills east of Santa Ynez. When the lake is full, it is big and beautiful, covering 3,200 acres. But as mentioned, in low rain years the drawdowns are so significant that you'd hardly recognize it.

After fishing, picnicking and camping come in a distant second and third in popularity, respectively. Use is steady year-round, but in summers when the lake is full, the camping traffic skyrockets.

❷ Santa Ynez River

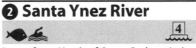

Location: North of Santa Barbara in Los Padres National Forest; map H3, grid g3.

Directions: From US 101 at the north end of Santa Barbara, turn north on Highway 154 and travel 12 miles. Turn right on Paradise Road and drive east to the ranger station. Access is available off Paradise Road. Note: Paradise Road is sometimes closed due to high water. Phone the ranger station before making your trip, (805) 967-3481.

Access: There is no boat ramp. Rafting is not recommended.

Facilities, fees: Several campgrounds are located on the river. Supplies can be obtained in Santa Barbara. Access is free.

Water sports, restrictions: Excellent swimming holes are available at campgrounds and picnic areas along Paradise Road; the best spots are at Fremont Campground, White Rock Picnic Area, Sage Hill Campground, Lower Oso Picnic Area, Falls Picnic Area, and Santa Ynez Campground.

Contact: Los Padres National Forest, Santa Barbara Ranger District, (805) 967-3481 or fax (805) 967-7312. For a detailed map of the area, send $4 to Maps, Office of Information, US Forest Service, 1323 Club Drive, Vallejo, CA 94592.

About the Santa Ynez River: This river is at the mercy of water releases out of Lake Cachuma, and in dry years they can be pretty sparse. The flow is sometimes reduced to a mere trickle in the summer. But when it's right, there are some great swimming holes in this stream—in fact, some of the best in any river in Southern California.

But it seems to be either feast or famine here, with extremely high stream flows in spring that taper off to nothing by late summer. When the water level is reasonably high, swimming is excellent. It gets very hot down here and the river provides the perfect respite, especially at the developed recreation spots along Paradise Road, which come complete with shady sites for picnicking and camping. The best spots typically get heavy use in the summer.

Rafting and boating are not recommended because the river becomes quite brushy in places and can be difficult to navigate.

---

❸ Goleta Beach County Park

🔱🐟⚓🎣🏄🚣   ⟨7⟩

Location: North of Santa Barbara; map H3, grid h2.

Directions: From Santa Barbara drive north on US 101 to Goleta. Turn west on Highway 217 and head toward the University of California at Santa Barbara. Just before the entrance to the university, turn left onto Sandspit Road and continue to the beach.

Access: There is a boat hoist, but boaters must provide their own slings. Note: The hoist is open only on weekends.

Facilities, fees: A pier, picnic areas, restaurant, and bait are available. Access to the beach is free. There is a charge for using the boat hoist.

Water sports, restrictions: Waterskiing and personal watercraft are permitted outside of the swimming area. Windsurfing is allowed. A large beach with a roped-off swimming area is available.

Contact: County Parks Department, (805) 568-2461; Park Ranger, (805) 967-1300.

About Goleta Beach County Park: The real attraction here is the huge beach, a sweeping swath of sandy oceanfront ideal for sunbathing, picnicking, swimming, and beachcombing. Work? What's that? There are summer days when you see so many people lolling about that you wonder, "Hey, doesn't anybody work anymore?"

The water stays warm enough for swimming well into the fall, and you'll see people jumping into the ocean as late as October.

Though there is a boat hoist, most boaters launch at the ramp at the harbor (see the next listing). All that is provided here is a hoist with a hook. Right, you have to supply your own strap, and that's just too much trouble for most folks. If you do launch, you will find that the nearby coast is often quite benign, ideal for boating, with winds soft and predictable most of the year.

It's those calm winds that make windsurfing prospects here less than great, though they're decent for beginners. Only rarely do you see personal watercraft or water-skiers at Goleta Beach, and rules mandate that they stay clear of the swimming area and the pier.

❹ Lake Casitas

⚓ 🚤 ⛺ 🐟   🔲6

Location: North of Ventura; map H3, grid i8.

Directions: From the north end of Ventura on US 101, turn north on Highway 33 and drive 12 miles to Highway 150. Turn left (west) and continue for four miles to the lake.

Or from Santa Barbara turn south on US 101 and drive about 11 miles to Highway 150 on the left. Turn east and continue for 17 miles to the lake.

Access: Two paved boat ramps are located on the lake's north side.

Facilities, fees: Campgrounds, picnic areas, full-service marina, showers, snack bar, and groceries are available. Fishing boats and patio boats can be rented at Lake Casitas Boat Rentals, (805) 649-2043. Fees are charged for day use and boat launching.

Water sports, restrictions: The speed limit is 40 mph except in specially designated areas, where it is 15 mph. Craft under 11 feet long or over 25 feet long are prohibited. Waterskiing and personal watercraft are not allowed. No windsurfing, swimming, or water/body contact is permitted.

Contact: Lake Casitas, (805) 649-2233.

About Lake Casitas: To bass fishermen Lake Casitas is something of a legend, but to other boaters and water users, it is just something.

The legend grew from the fact that there are so many huge bass here, as many in the 10-pound-plus class as you'll find anywhere. Some say that if the next world-record bass isn't landed at Lake Castaic, it will be here. Hopes for that prize often have anglers lining up at the entrance gate before dawn, and even if they don't catch the world record, the prospect of a legendary 10-pounder tends to keeps things exciting just the same. Hey, it could be you!

Casitas is located north of Ventura, at an elevation of 285 feet in the foothill country bordering Los Padres National Forest. The lake has 32 miles of shoreline with a remarkable number of sheltered coves. When full of water, it covers 2,700 acres.

But remember, the regulations prohibit waterskiing, personal watercraft, and all water/body contact sports. That means no swimming and no windsurfing. In addition there are strict rules about what size boat you can use, with no craft under 11 feet or over 25 feet long permitted. These restrictions are very similar to those at Lake Cachuma.

The boating regulations are so stringently enforced that you shouldn't even try to sneak in with a kayak or anything else you have in mind that doesn't meet the standards. Note that the entire shoreline, except for the developed north shore, is closed to the public.

Map of Central California—Page 330

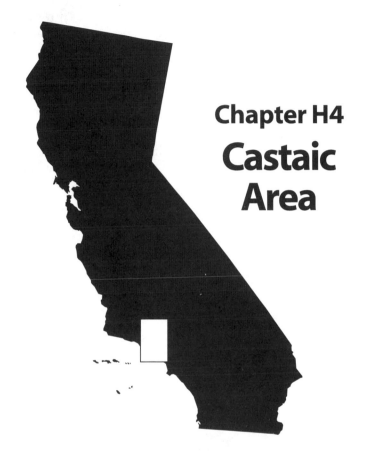

Chapter H4
Castaic Area

Overall Rating

Poor .... Fair .... Great

H4–Castaic Area Map

One inch equals approximately 10.7 miles.
See page 12 for California state map.

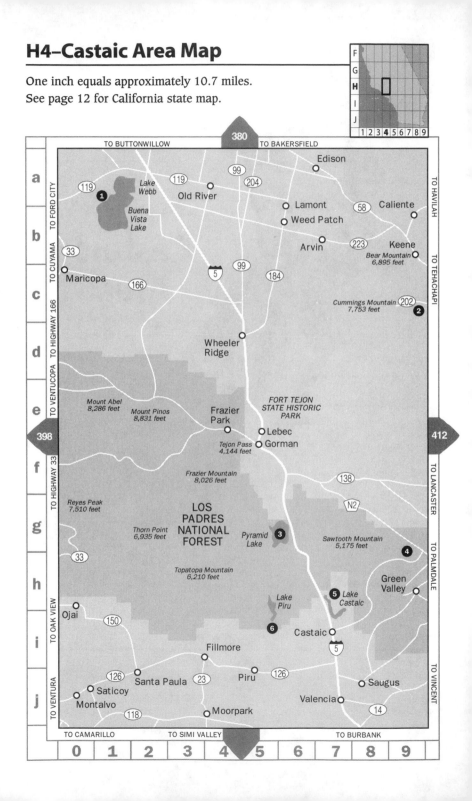

Chapter H4 features:

1 Buena Vista Aquatic Recreation Area

Location: Near Bakersfield; map H4, grid a1.

Directions: From Interstate 5 east of Bakersfield, turn west on Highway 119 and drive two miles. Turn south on Enos Lane and continue to the park entrance.

Access: A paved boat ramp is available on the north side of Lake Webb.

Facilities, fees: A campground, picnic areas, marina, coin laundry, gas, snack bar, and groceries are available. Waterskiing equipment can be rented. Fees are charged for day use and boat launching.

Water sports, restrictions: Waterskiing and windsurfing are allowed at Lake Webb. The speed limit is 45 mph. One area on the lake's north side is off-limits to skiers; only sailboats, windsurfers, and fishing boats are allowed. Powerboating is allowed at Lake Evans, but a speed limit of 5 mph is strictly enforced. Personal watercraft are not allowed at either lake. Swimming is prohibited at both lakes; special swimming lagoons are provided on each lake's north shore.

Contact: Buena Vista Aquatic Recreation Area, (661) 763-1526.

About Buena Vista Aquatic Recreation Area: It may not resemble your idea of paradise, but in the desolate western San Joaquin Valley, any body of water is something of a haven. Buena Vista is actually two connected lakes fed by the West Side Canal: little Lake Evans to the west and larger Lake Webb to the east. To get the most out of your visit, it is critical that you know the differences between the two. Lake Webb, which covers 875 acres, is open to all boat-ing (except personal watercraft), and jet boats towing skiers are a common sight all summer long. On the other hand, Lake Evans is small, only 85 acres, quiet, and has a five mph speed limit.

The Buena Vista Aquatic Recreation Area is primarily a family-oriented park that offers full facilities. It attracts fairly heavy use in the summer; things slow down quite a bit in the fall.

Beaches are provided at Lake Webb for windsurfers and water-skiers, but no swimming is allowed. While all boating is permitted (except for personal watercraft) at Lake Webb, the regulations are strict and enforced quickly here. Try to water-ski in the no-ski area, for instance, and you will be slapped immediately with a hefty ticket and told to leave the lake. Right on.

2 Brite Valley Lake

Location: Near Tehachapi at Brite Valley Recreation Area; map H4, grid c9.

Directions: From Bakersfield turn east on Highway 58 and drive 40 miles toward the town of Tehachapi. Take the Highway 202 exit and drive three miles west to Banducci Road. Turn left and head south to the park.

Access: A primitive boat ramp is located on the lake's south shore.

Facilities, fees: A campground and picnic areas are provided. Groceries can be purchased nearby. A day-use fee is charged.

Water sports, restrictions: Motors are not permitted on the lake. Windsurfing and swimming are not allowed.

Contact: Kern County Parks & Recreation, Brite Valley Recreation Area, (661) 822-3228 or fax (661) 823-8529.

About Brite Valley Lake: Here's a hidden spot that is often overlooked. Little Brite Valley Lake is a speck of a water hole (90 acres) in the northern flanks of the Tehachapi Mountains at an elevation of 4,000 feet. Motors are prohibited, but that makes this a good lake for hand-powered craft such as canoes or rafts.

Fishing prospects are only mediocre. Instead, the lake is best used for picnicking, canoeing, or kayaking. Right; this is the kind of place where you have a picnic, then plunk in a canoe and paddle around a bit, maybe casting a line for small trout without any delusions of grandeur. Use is moderate year-round, primarily picnickers and anglers enjoying the warm temperatures and cool water. A nearby golf course is a popular attraction.

Note: The lake is closed to the public from November through late April.

❸ Pyramid Lake

Location: North of Los Angeles in Angeles National Forest; map H4, grid g6.

Directions: From Los Angeles drive about 60 miles north on Interstate 5. Take the Smokey Bear Road exit (about eight miles south of Gorman) and turn west. Continue to the lake.

Access: A paved launch ramp is located on the lake's north side.

Facilities, fees: A campground, picnic areas, and a concession stand are provided. Fishing boats can be rented at Pyramid

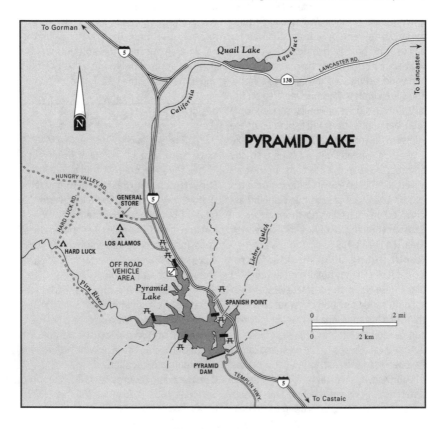

Lake Marina. There is a fee for day use; boat launching is included.

Water sports, restrictions: Waterskiing, personal watercraft, and windsurfing are allowed. Swimming is available at a sandy beach near the marina and at several boat-in sites around the lake.

Contact: Pyramid Lake Marina, (661) 257-2892; or Pyramid Lake Gate House, (661) 257-2790.

About Pyramid Lake: One of the cornerstones of California's Central Valley Project, Pyramid Lake is a major storage facility for water as it is moved from north to south.

Pyramid Lake is set at an elevation of 2,600 feet. Although the lake is surrounded by Angeles National Forest, Interstate 5 is routed right past several lake arms, making it one of the more easily accessible bodies of water in California. It is a favorite destination for powerboaters, especially waterskiers (a 35 mph speed limit is enforced).

The lake covers 1,300 acres and has 20 miles of shoreline. Because it's a showpiece, the water masters tend to keep it fuller than other lakes on line with the California Aqueduct. The primary activities are waterskiing and fishing, though the two are not always compatible. Some anglers feel that the water-skiers are trying to drive them off the lake, and the situation would be greatly improved if the powers that be would set aside special areas for low-speed boating. As it is, you typically see anglers here in the spring and fall; then the water-skiers take over the lake during the summer months.

Several pretty boat-in picnic sites with nice sandy beaches are located along the shoreline. Since most of the shoreline is inaccessible by car, these spots offer that rarity—extreme seclusion. This is one great bonus for boaters.

Windsurfing can be excellent here as well, and the sport seems to be gaining in popularity each year. The best jump-off spot is at the northern launching area, where you can sail off to access any of Pyramid Lake's more private arms.

There is one major drawback: much of the western shore marks the beginning of a large off-road-vehicle area, so on busy weekends the whine of ATVs can be heard in the background.

❹ Elizabeth Lake

Location: West of Lancaster in Angeles National Forest; map H4, grid g9.

Directions: From Los Angeles drive about 40 miles north on Interstate 5 to Castaic. Turn north on Lake Hughes Road and continue to Elizabeth Lake Road. Turn right and drive about three miles east, past Lake Hughes and Munz Lake to Elizabeth Lake.

Access: A primitive boat ramp is located on the lake's northwestern shore.

Facilities, fees: Picnic areas are provided. Access to the lake is free.

Water sports, restrictions: Waterskiing and personal watercraft are not allowed. Motors are restricted to a maximum of 10 horsepower. Windsurfing and swimming are allowed.

Contact: Angeles National Forest, Santa Clara/Mojave Rivers Ranger District, (661) 296-9710 or fax (661) 296-5847.

About Elizabeth Lake: It might be wise to bring in some Mi-Wok medicine men to conduct a rain dance here every winter because Elizabeth Lake is often extremely low. It is a prisoner of rainfall; so is nearby Lake Hughes to the west, which is privately owned.

A pretty lake, Elizabeth is set at 3,300 feet in elevation in the northern outskirts of Angeles National Forest below Portal Ridge. There's a good picnic area and a nice, sandy shoreline. Windsurfing can be excellent, although conditions tend to be inconsistent. Use is light year-round, slightly heavier in summer.

For an exceptional side trip, head over

to the Antelope Valley California Poppy State Reserve, located a few miles to the north. In the spring it can be blanketed wall-to-wall with blooming poppies, about nine square miles of them—a fantastic sight.

Special note: Newcomers should pay special attention to the fact that the lake's eastern half is private. If you try to fish from the shore here or gain access in any way, you will be removed. Should you persist, you will be arrested.

❺ Lake Castaic

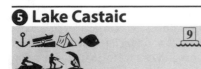

Location: North of Los Angeles; map H4, grid h7.

Directions: From Los Angeles drive about 40 miles north on Interstate 5 to Castaic. Turn north on Lake Hughes Road and continue to the lake entrance.

Access: Paved boat ramps are located on the main lake's east and west arms and on the afterbay's south shore; follow the ramp signs from the lake entrance.

Facilities, fees: A campground is available one-half mile west of the afterbay. Picnic areas are provided at both the lake and the afterbay. Castaic Boat Rentals (on the main lake) rents out fishing boats and personal watercraft. Rowboats and Aquacycles are available for rent at the afterbay. Fees are charged for day use and boat launching.

Water sports, restrictions: The speed limit on the main lake is 35 mph, except at one designated area on the east arm where the speed limit is reduced to 20 mph. Personal watercraft and waterskiing is allowed. No motorized boats are allowed on the afterbay. At both lakes windsurfing is allowed, but swimming is prohibited.

Contact: Lake Castaic, (661) 257-4050; Castaic Boat Rentals, (661) 257-2049; Castaic Afterbay, (661) 295-0849.

About Lake Castaic: Lake Castaic is known the world over as the lake most

likely to produce the next world-record bass. After all, this is where in 1991 Bob Crupi caught, weighed, photographed, and released a 22-pound largemouth bass, just four ounces shy of the world record. Who knows where that fish is swimming around now. Or how big it might be.

But the lake is famous for more than fish. It's a boater's paradise, an outstanding choice for all water sports, with even a specially designated area for personal watercraft.

Castaic is easy to reach, just a short hop from the junction of Interstate 5 and Highway 126. It is set at 1,500 feet in the foothills adjoining Angeles National Forest to the north. Shaped like a giant V, it covers nearly 9,000 acres when full. That's right: it's huge. There is also an adjacent afterbay, which provides additional facilities. Locals call Castaic the upper lake, and the afterbay is referred to as the lower lake or the lagoon.

Of course it is the big brother, the upper lake, that attracts most of the attention. This is where the giant bass roam and where waterskiing is most popular. In general, people who are fishing for bass stick to the coves, while the water-skiers run in a counterclockwise direction from the dam on up the northern lake arm. Note that a buoy line marks the boundary of a restricted area on the far end of the northern lake arm.

If you prefer quiet water, try the nearby afterbay, commonly known as the Castaic Lagoon. It is located just below the Castaic Dam. No motorized boats are permitted here, and even though a few rental watercraft are allowed, for the most part the place is very low-key compared to the main lake. A bonus is that fishing is allowed 24 hours a day at the lagoon.

Windsurfing is quite popular. The best areas are the upper lake's west arm and all over the afterbay. Swimming is prohibited at both Lake Castaic and the Castaic Lagoon. Use is quite heavy into fall.

⑥ Lake Piru

Location: Northwest of Los Angeles; map H4, grid i5.

Directions: From Los Angeles drive about 35 miles north on Interstate 5 to the Highway 126 exit. Turn west and drive 12 miles to the Piru Canyon Road exit. Turn north and drive six miles northeast to the lake entrance. You may also park at the dam or along the road and walk in for free.

Access: A multilane paved launch ramp is located on the lake's western side.

Facilities, fees: A campground, picnic areas, full-service marina, snack bar, and groceries are available. Fishing boats and pontoon boats can be rented at the marina. There is a fee for day use; boat launching privileges are included.

Water sports, restrictions: Motorized boats under 12 feet long are prohibited. Canoes and kayaks over eight feet long are permitted; anything smaller is prohibited. Waterskiing is permitted. Personal watercraft and windsurfers are not allowed. Swimming is allowed only in designated areas; a beach is available on the west shore, past the gatehouse.

Contact: Lake Piru Recreation Area, (805) 521-1500; Lake Piru Marina, (805) 521-1231.

About Lake Piru: Things can get crazy at Piru. Luckily, it's usually a happy crazy, not an insane crazy.

You see, this lake is within a pretty quick drive from the Los Angeles Basin, and it's no secret either, so quite a lot of people come here for boating, waterskiing, fishing, swimming, and sunbathing. The weather is warm, and the water often seems to be the perfect temperature.

But it's not all rosy. Because there are no off-limits areas to water-skiers, in the spring fishers and water-skiers can turn the coves into combat areas. In addition, the wind can really kick up here in the spring and early summer. At times conditions are excellent for sailing, but then the winds can make the lake look something like a washing machine in full spin—enough to scare everybody off the water.

The lake covers 1,200 acres when full and is set at an elevation of 1,055 feet. Most summer mornings are quite beautiful here, with the warm temperatures, pretty scenery, and emerald green water adding to the charm. If you're looking for a good spot for swimming and picnicking, head to the west shore, where there is a large sandy beach.

Most boaters come here in the summer to go waterskiing or sailing. Afternoon winds are predictable on most days, and fishing is popular from fall through spring. Use is quite heavy from May through mid-September, as you might figure. Because the place is so popular, especially with boaters on summer weekends, all boating rules are strictly enforced.

Map of Central California—Page 330

Chapter H5
Tehachapi
Area

Overall Rating

Poor .... Fair .... Great

H5–Tehachapi Area Map

One inch equals approximately 10.7 miles.
See page 12 for California state map.

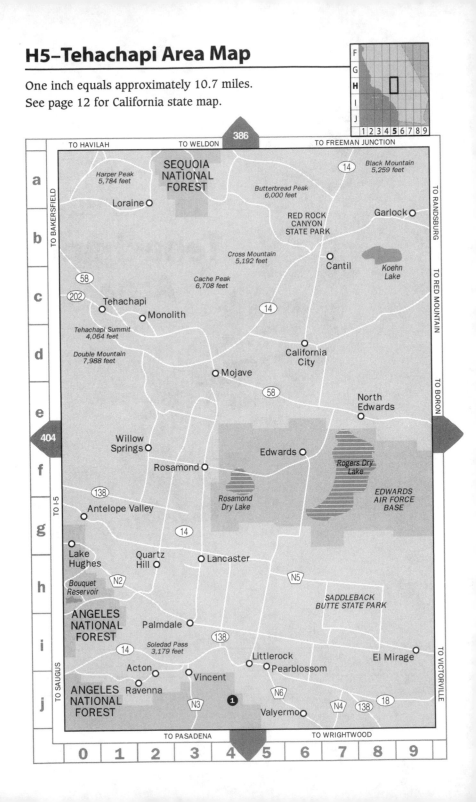

TO HAVILAH TO WELDON 386 TO FREEMAN JUNCTION

a

SEQUOIA NATIONAL FOREST

Harper Peak 5,784 feet

14 Black Mountain 5,259 feet

Loraine

Butterbread Peak 6,000 feet

TO BAKERSFIELD

b

RED ROCK CANYON STATE PARK

Garlock

Cross Mountain 5,192 feet

Cantil

Koehn Lake

TO RANDSBURG

58

Cache Peak 6,708 feet

c

202 Tehachapi

Monolith

14

TO RED MOUNTAIN

Tehachapi Summit 4,064 feet

d

Double Mountain 7,988 feet

Mojave

California City

58

North Edwards

TO BORON

e

404 Willow Springs

Edwards

Rogers Dry Lake

f

Rosamond

EDWARDS AIR FORCE BASE

138

TO I-5

Rosamond Dry Lake

g

Antelope Valley

14

Lake Hughes

Quartz Hill

Lancaster

N5

SADDLEBACK BUTTE STATE PARK

h

Bouquet Reservoir

N2

ANGELES NATIONAL FOREST

Palmdale

i

14 Soledad Pass 3,179 feet

138

Littlerock

Pearblossom

El Mirage

TO VICTORVILLE

TO SAUGUS

Acton

Vincent

j

ANGELES NATIONAL FOREST

Ravenna

N3

1

N6

Valyermo

N4

138

18

TO PASADENA TO WRIGHTWOOD

0 1 2 3 4 5 6 7 8 9

Chapter H5 features:

❶ Little Rock Reservoir

⚓ 🏕 🎣 🏊 [5]

Location: Near Palmdale in Angeles National Forest; map H5, grid j4.

Directions: From Los Angeles drive north on Interstate 5 to the Highway 14/Palmdale exit. Turn east, continue to Palmdale, turn east on Highway 138, and drive through the stoplight at the intersection. Turn right on Cheseboro Road and continue for four miles to the reservoir.

Access: A primitive launching area is located on the lake's northwest shore.

Facilities, fees: A campground, picnic areas, and groceries are available. Little Rock Lake Store rents fishing boats. Access is free.

Water sports, restrictions: A 5 mph speed limit is strictly enforced. Personal watercraft and waterskiing are not allowed. Swimming is permitted.

Contact: Angeles National Forest, Valyermo Ranger Station, Little Rock Gatehouse, (805) 533-2424; Little Rock Lake Store, (805) 533-1923.

About Little Rock Reservoir: In the summer when Little Rock Reservoir is the only cool place around for miles, this is quite a popular spot.

This small lake is set at an elevation of 3,258 feet in Angeles National Forest and covers just 150 acres. It's open year-round, and although fishing is the number one activity most of the time, in the summer camping and swimming attract their fair share of attention.

The 5 mph speed limit keeps things quiet, eliminating most powerboating, personal watercraft, and windsurfing. Note, however, that the wind can really whip through here in the late afternoon.

From late winter to spring to early summer, Little Rock Reservoir is a pretty little mountain lake. But when the water starts to be drained down the Palmdale Ditch and into the California Aqueduct, the lake can be turned into a miniature Grand Canyon. In low water years it might even resemble a moonscape by late fall. When that happens, you might as well see when the next spaceship is departing because you won't find anything in the way of recreation here.

Map of Central California—Page 330

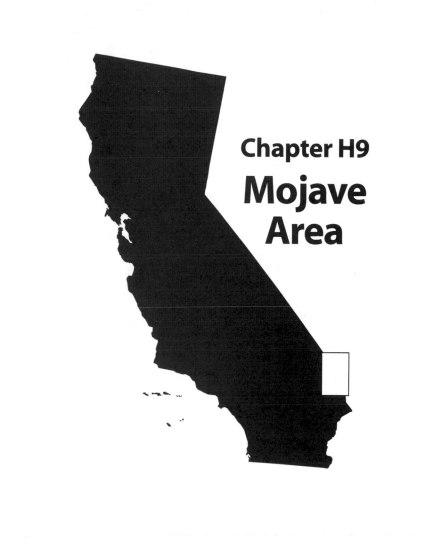

Chapter H9
Mojave
Area

Overall Rating

Poor .... Fair .... Great

H9–Mojave Area Map

One inch equals approximately 10.7 miles.
See page 12 for California state map.

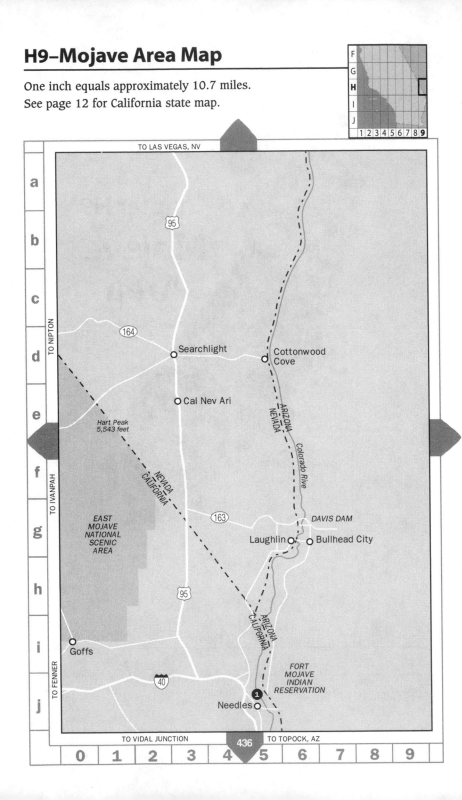

Chapter H9 features:

❶ Colorado River

Location: From the California/Nevada border to Lake Havasu; map H9, grid j5.

Directions: From Southern California, take Interstate 15 north to Interstate 40 at Barstow and drive approximately 150 miles east to Needles.

From Northern California, drive south on US 395 to Highway 58 at Kramer Junction; then drive east, and cross over on Interstate 15 to Interstate 40. Proceed approximately 150 miles east to Needles.

Access: Paved boat-launch ramps are available at the following locations:

Jack Smith Memorial Park: From Interstate 40 eastbound take the Needles Highway/West Broadway exit and turn left. Stay in the left-hand lane; when the road splits, continue straight on Needles Highway (Broadway heads to the right into town). When you reach the four-way stop, proceed straight through; the road turns into River Road. Continue about one mile until the road dead-ends at the park.

Needles Marina: From Interstate 40 eastbound, take the Needles Highway/West Broadway exit and turn left. Stay in the left-hand lane; when the road splits, continue straight on Needles Highway (Broadway heads to the right into town). When you reach the four-way stop, proceed straight through; the road turns into River Road. Look for a sign on the left for Needles Marina; turn left on Marina Drive and proceed into the marina.

Park Moabi Marina: From Interstate 40 eastbound take the Park Moabi Road exit and turn left. Continue until you reach the sign for the boat ramp, turn left again, and continue to the marina.

Canoeists and kayakers may put in at any of the launch ramps listed above. For those who desire a longer trip, a popular put-in is located farther north, at Bullhead City, Arizona. To reach the launching area, take Interstate 40 east to the Needles Highway/West Broadway exit. Take the exit and turn left. Stay in the left-hand lane; when the road splits, continue straight on Needles Highway (Broadway heads to the right into town). When you reach the four-way stop, turn left on Harbor Avenue. The road crosses the California/Arizona border and becomes Highway 95. Continue north for about 25 miles to Bullhead City. Turn left on Riverview Drive and proceed down to the launching area. Boaters may take out downstream at one of several river access sites in Needles or continue all the way to Lake Havasu. Note: The last take-out before Lake Havasu is at the town of Topock, Arizona, where Interstate 40 intersects with the river. If you miss it, you will have to float approximately 17 more miles to the next take-out at Lake Havasu.

Facilities, fees: Lodging, campgrounds, full-service marinas, picnic areas, restaurants, tackle, and groceries are available in the Needles area. Park Moabi Marina rents fishing, ski, and pontoon boats. Jerkwater, (800) 421-7803 or (520) 768-7753, provides canoe rentals and tours. Day-use and/or boat launching fees are charged at the private marinas; access and boat launching at Jack Smith Memorial Park are free.

Water sports, restrictions: No-wake restrictions are enforced around all marina areas. Waterskiing is prohibited in the Topoek Gorge but is allowed everywhere else. Personal watercraft are permitted everywhere. River currents make windsurfing impractical. The only designated swimming beach is located at Park Moabi Marina, but there are numerous undeveloped sandy beaches all along the river.

Contact: Needles Area Chamber of Commerce, (760) 326-2050. For boating information contact Park Moabi Marina, (760) 326-4777; Rainbow Beach Resort, (760) 326-3101; or Needles Marina Park, (760) 326-2197.

About the Colorado River: Bring your suntan lotion and a beach towel. This section of the Colorado River is a big tourist spot where the body oil and beer can flow faster than the river. There are a lot of hot bodies and hot boats, and waterskiing is the dominant activity in the summer. But it's not all craziness; there are also some relatively private beaches and a chance for canoeing and kayaking.

Waterskiing and personal watercraft are, of course, the most popular boating activities. It gets extremely crowded in the summer, when the general tourist traffic is compounded by the speedboat racers who show up every year for various competitions. The roar of the big V8s in the jet boats can be unbelievable.

The only designated swimming beach is at Park Moabi Marina, but as mentioned above, there are several out-of-the-way beaches that offer a little more privacy. Boats are not restricted from these areas, however, so families with small children who are either wading or floating in the water should be on the lookout for boats and personal watercraft, which can come roaring through without notice.

Canoeists and kayakers can paddle anywhere from Bullhead City, Arizona, down to Lake Havasu, but the best bet is the Needles–Castle Rock Run, the most scenic run in these parts. A two-day affair, the Needles–Castle Rock Run is about 26 miles long and flows through the scenic Topoek Gorge, a steep, narrow canyon. Waterskiing is prohibited here. Alas, if only watercraft were also banned, this easy run would have a good chance at attaining canoeing acclaim. If you're interested in this run, an Arizona company called Jerkwater (see "Facilities, fees" above) will provide equipment and shuttle service for very reasonable rates.

Upstream of the Needles put-in, canoeing and kayaking are possible, but the scenery is, well, blah, and canoeists run the risk of being terrorized by water-skiers who sometimes look like kamikazes on a mission.

Southern California
Recreational Lakes
and Rivers

Overall Rating

| 1 | 2 | 3 | 4 | 5 | 6 | 7 | 8 | 9 | 10 |

Poor .... Fair .... Great

Key to the Symbols

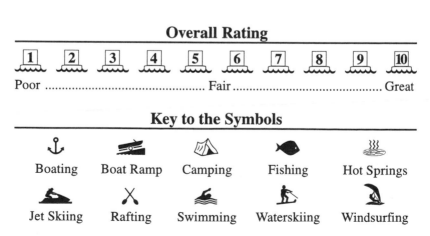

| Boating | Boat Ramp | Camping | Fishing | Hot Springs |
| Jet Skiing | Rafting | Swimming | Waterskiing | Windsurfing |

Southern California Overview

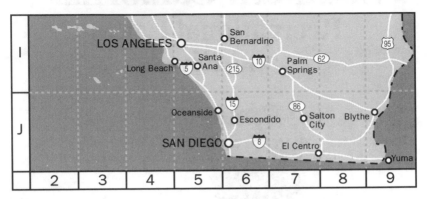

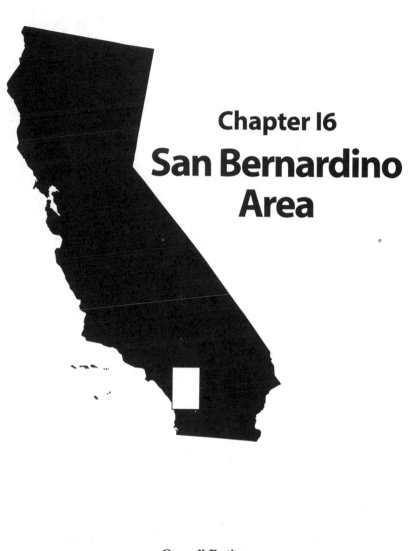

Chapter 16
San Bernardino Area

Overall Rating

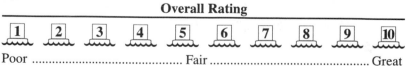

Poor .... Fair .... Great

I6-San Bernardino Area Map

One inch equals approximately 10.7 miles.
See page 12 for California state map.

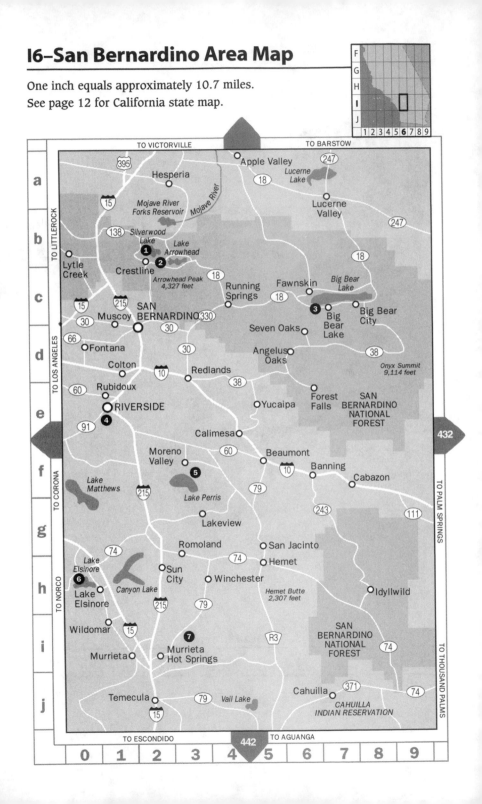

Chapter 16 features:

1 Silverwood Lake

Location: North of San Bernardino in Silverwood Lake State Recreation Area; map 16, grid b2.

Directions: From San Bernardino drive north on Interstates 215 and 15 to the Silverwood Lake exit at Cajon Junction. Turn east on Highway 138 and continue for 12 miles to the lake.

Access: A paved boat ramp is located on the lake's south shore. There is an unimproved ramp for cartop boats on the northwest shore.

Facilities, fees: Campgrounds, a full-service marina, picnic areas, and groceries are available at the lake. Fishing boats and pontoon boats can be rented at the marina. Supplies can be obtained in Cajon Junction and Crestline. Fees are charged for day use and boat launching.

Water sports, restrictions: There is a 35 mph speed limit (5 mph in the major coves). Waterskiing and personal watercraft are permitted. Boats must be off the water by sundown. Windsurfing is permitted in designated areas. A large, sandy swimming beach is available on the lake's southeast side at the Sawpit Recreation Area.

Contact: Silverwood Lake State Recreation Area, Los Lagos District, 14651 Cedar Circle, Hesperia, CA 92345; (909) 940-5600; Silverwood Lake Marina, (760) 389-2299.

About Silverwood Lake: Silverwood Lake is bordered by San Bernardino National Forest to the south and high desert to the north, and its proximity to San Bernardino makes it very popular with boaters, especially on hot summer days. It is set at an elevation of 3,378 feet, and when full to the brim, covers 1,000 acres with 13 miles of shoreline.

The speed limit is 5 mph in all of the major coves, and there are several other boating rules that keep the place relatively sane. The main lake area south of the dam is the hot spot for waterskiing, with a 35 mph speed limit.

Tourists of every kind are attracted to the clear and cool water in the summer. All boating is allowed, as well as waterskiing, personal watercraft, fishing, and windsurfing, though the latter is restricted to designated areas.

The lake facilities are fully developed and include an excellent marina, boat rentals, and a small store. Some people make a great day of it by renting a pontoon boat, having a floating barbecue or picnic, then parking in a cove and using the boat as a swimming platform. In addition to drive-in campsites, there are some hike-in and bike-in campsites—a rare treat. The lake also has excellent trails for hiking and biking.

Because of its location on the edge of the high desert, there are times when the winds can really kick up here, making boating potentially hazardous. Aside from that, Silverwood Lake is a great spot.

2 Lake Gregory

Location: North of San Bernardino in Lake Gregory Regional Park; map 16, grid b2.

Directions: From San Bernardino drive north on Highway 18 to the town of Crestline. Turn east on Highway 138, drive a short distance, turn right on Lake Drive, and continue east to the lake.

Access: Private boats may not be launched here; only boats rented at Lake Gregory may be used.

Facilities, fees: A campground, picnic area, and a snack bar are provided. Rowboats, paddleboats, and water bikes can be rented at the boathouse. Supplies are available in Lake Gregory Village. There is a day-use fee.

Water sports, restrictions: No private boats are permitted, but you may bring your own electric motor to use with a rental boat. Gas-powered motors aren't allowed. Windsurfing is permitted. A large, sandy swimming beach, open from June to September, is available on the northwest shore.

Contact: Lake Gregory, (909) 338-2233 or fax (909) 338-4590.

About Lake Gregory: An adjacent regional park, good swimming (no gas-powered motors permitted on boats), and an opportunity to paddling a canoe or kayak in a family setting make Lake Gregory a winner. It is also one of the relatively few lakes in California where you can buy waterside property. The trip here is a pleasant one, too, on Rim of the World Drive, a winding but pretty road that builds up a bit of anticipation before your arrival.

Little Lake Gregory (120 acres) is set at an elevation of 4,520 feet, just north of San Bernardino on the edge of San Bernardino National Forest. Nearby Silverwood Lake to the northwest and Lake Arrowhead to the east are larger and are good alternate choices.

While no privately owned boats are permitted here, a real downer, boats can be rented at the marina. Beauty, intimacy, and cool waters make this a very popular destination, and it is often packed to capacity on summer weekends.

The setup is family oriented, and rules that forbid motors keep the lake quiet and safe for swimming. There is a large swimming beach that even has a water slide, along with nearby dressing rooms.

❸ Big Bear Lake

Location: Northeast of San Bernardino in San Bernardino National Forest; map I6, grid c6.

Directions: From Interstate 10 at Redlands, drive north on Highway 30 for five miles. Drive north on Highway 330 for 13 miles. At Running Springs turn east on Highway 18 and drive 14 miles to Big Bear Lake.

Access: A boating permit, available at most marinas, must be obtained for all private boats. Boats under eight feet or over 26 feet long are prohibited. Paved boat ramps are provided at the following locations:

Big Bear Marina: From Highway 18 on the lake's south shore, head toward Big Bear Lake Village and look for the big wooden arch that goes across the road. Turn left on Paine Road and continue about two blocks to the marina. Fishing boats, pontoon boats, paddleboats, canoes, and kayaks are available for rent. Personal watercraft are available in the summer. For information phone (909) 866-3218 or fax (909) 866-3846.

Holloway's Marina & RV Park: From Highway 18 on the lake's south shore, head toward Big Bear Lake Village. Drive three miles past the dam and look for the Log Cabin Restaurant. Turn left on Edgemore Street and continue about one-half mile to the marina. Fishing boats, pontoon boats, sailboats, paddleboats, and personal watercraft are available for rent. For information phone (909) 866-5706.

Municipal Water District East Launch: From the dam at the junction of Highways 18 and 38, turn east on Highway 38 and continue approximately nine miles to the sign for the public launch on the

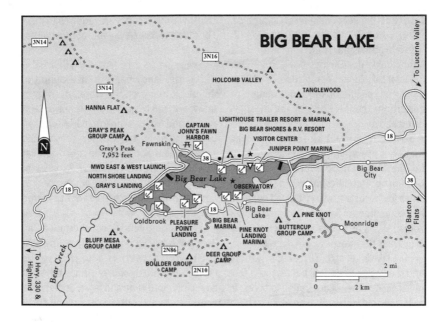

northeast shore. For information phone (909) 866-2917.

Municipal Water District West Launch: From the dam at the junction of Highways 18 and 38, turn east on Highway 38 and continue approximately two miles to the sign for the public launch on the northwest shore. For information phone (909) 866-2917.

Pine Knot Landing: From Highway 18 on the lake's south shore, head toward Big Bear Lake Village. Go past the wooden arch and at the stop sign, turn left on Pine Knot Avenue. Continue to the marina at the road's end. Fishing boats, pontoon boats, speedboats, and canoes are available for rent. For information phone (909) 866-2628.

Pleasure Point Landing: From Highway 18 on the lake's south shore, head toward Big Bear Lake Village. About two miles past the dam, turn left on Cienega Way and continue to Landlock Landing Road. Turn right and proceed into the marina. Parasailing and waterskiing are permitted. For information phone (909) 866-2455.

Facilities, fees: Campgrounds, picnic areas, full-service marinas, restaurants, and groceries are available. Full facilities are provided in Big Bear Lake Village. Boats can be rented at several of the marinas listed above and at any of the following locations: Boulder Bay Marina, (909) 866-7557, fishing boats and canoes; Gray's Landing, (909) 866-2443, fishing boats and pontoon boats. Windsurfer rentals and lessons are offered at North Shore Landing, (909) 878-4386. There are fees for boat launching at all private marinas; the Municipal Water District launches are free.

Water sports, restrictions: Waterskiing is allowed if you bring your own boat, but you may not water-ski with any rental boat unless you hire a driver. Drivers and equipment are available at Pine Knot Marina and Holloway's Marina. Personal watercraft and windsurfing are allowed. Much of the shoreline is sandy and suitable for swimming; developed beaches are available at the Municipal Water District Day-Use Areas on the north shore and at Meadow Park Swim Beach on the south shore.

Map of Chapter 16—Page 422

Contact: Big Bear Chamber of Commerce, (909) 866-4607 or fax (909) 866-5412; info@bigbearchamber.com; Big Bear Municipal Water District, (909) 866-5796; Big Bear Lake Resort Association, (909) 866-6190. For specific boating information or conditions, contact any of the marinas listed above.

About Big Bear Lake: Here is a lake that's got everything: It is big and beautiful. The lake has good trout fishing, quality boating opportunities, many campgrounds, and a few resorts. And it is located near the highest regions of San Bernardino National Forest. Alas, it often has a lot of people, too. Like I said, this place has got everything.

The lake is set at 6,738 feet in elevation, and the Pacific Crest Trail passes just a few miles north of here. Easy trailhead access is available, so if you want to break away from the crowds, you can.

Among the waters in the region, Big Bear is unmatched for beauty, particularly in the spring when the snow is melting. The deep-blue water contrasts strikingly with the surrounding white mountaintops. The lake covers over 3,000 acres, offers 22 miles of shoreline, and has a faithful vacation following, something like the Lake Tahoe of Southern California.

This is a great choice for trout fishing as well as waterskiing, and for the most part skiers and anglers manage to stay out of each other's way. Trout fishing is best during the spring and summer in the morning and the evening, when the water is cool; water-skiers tend to be out in force on warm summer afternoons. Personal watercraft are also very popular in the summer.

If you're renting a boat, note the previously mentioned restrictions on waterskiing; no one and nothing (not even inner tubes) can be pulled behind a rental boat unless a designated driver is hired. In addition, while all types of boating are allowed (as long as your craft is between eight and 26 feet long), all private boats are required to have a permit; these are available at most of the marinas.

Swimming is excellent at Big Bear Lake, with large, sandy beaches all around the shoreline. However, the water, fresh from snowmelt, can be cold until late spring, and in big snow years, even into early summer. During most of the vacation season, the water is clear and cool. The most popular swimming spot is Meadow Park Swim Beach on the south shore, where there is not only a good stretch of beach but a large swimming raft as well.

Windsurfing conditions are erratic at Big Bear, but overall this is a good site. The best advice for windsurfers is to stick to the more open north shore, which tends to have a bit more wind and fewer anglers. The south shore, in contrast, has many small coves that are favorites of people looking for a quiet spot to fish.

❹ Lake Evans

Location: In Riverside at Fairmount Park; map I6, grid e1.

Directions: From Highway 60 at the north end of Riverside, take the Market Street exit. Turn left; the park will be directly on your right.

Access: A primitive launching area is provided. Boats under eight feet or over 15 feet long are prohibited, with the exception of canoes. A free boating permit must be obtained at the park.

Facilities, fees: Rest rooms and picnic areas are provided. Supplies are available in Riverside. Access is free.

Water sports, restrictions: Motorized boats and inflatables are not permitted. No swimming or windsurfing is allowed.

Contact: Riverside County Department of Parks and Recreation, (909) 715-3440 or fax (909) 715-3479.

About Lake Evans: Quit your yelpin'.

Sure Lake Evans is a far cry from Big Bear Lake (see the previous listing), but considering how hot it can be out here, and how few lakes there are in the area, this little lake is one of the few places that can provide a respite from the sweltering summer heat.

Evans is a good spot to bring a small rowboat or canoe, go fishing for a bit, or have a picnic. Rules prohibit most boats and water sports. What you usually see here are fishermen out to catch some small rainbow trout, which are planted when the water is cool enough, plus a few folks just paddling canoes.

The surrounding park is grassy and pleasant, and a golf course and a bowling green are located nearby. Lake use is relatively light.

⑤ Lake Perris

Location: Southeast of Riverside at Lake Perris State Recreation Area; map I6, grid f3.
Directions: From Riverside turn south on Interstate 215 and drive about 11 miles. Take the Ramona Expressway exit and turn east. Continue to Lake Perris Drive, turn left, and continue to the park.
Access: A large, multilane paved launching area is located on the lake's north shore, just east of the marina.
Facilities, fees: Campgrounds, picnic areas, a full-service marina, snack bar, and groceries are available at the lake. Fishing boats, patio boats, personal watercraft, and waterskiing equipment can be rented at the marina. Fees are charged for day use and boat launching.
Water sports, restrictions: The speed limit is 35 mph, except in a few areas where it is reduced to 5 mph. Waterskiing, personal watercraft, and windsurfing are permitted. Ski beaches are available on the lake's north and south shores. A large, sandy swimming beach is available on the north shore, east of the boat ramps.

Contact: Lake Perris State Recreation Area, (909) 940-5603 or fax (909) 943-3986; Lake Perris Marina, (909) 657-2179 or fax (909) 940-4208.

About Lake Perris: The weather out here in the summer and fall can make you feel like you're standing in a fire pit, and that's why waterskiing and swimming are such big hits at Lake Perris.

The lake is set in Moreno Valley, just southwest of the Badlands foothills, at an elevation of 1,500 feet. It has a roundish shape, covering 2,200 acres, with an island that provides a unique boat-in picnic site.

Although known primarily for fishing (many records for spotted bass have been set here), Lake Perris is an extremely popular vacation destination for all types of boating and water recreation in the summer. In addition to fishing, favorite activities are waterskiing, windsurfing, sailing, and swimming.

With large ski beaches on the northeast and southeast shores, the lake can be great for waterskiing and personal watercraft. There is a designated sailing cove on the northwest side, an ideal spot for windsurfing and sailing.

Swimming is also excellent. The best place to swim is at the developed beach at Lake Perris State Recreation Area.

For an out-of-the-ordinary picnic site, steer your boat over to the island, where you can hike up 200 feet to get a unique view of the surrounding country. In addition, there are many trails near the lake that are ideal for mountain biking, horseback riding, and hiking. On the lake's south side, there is even a rock climbing area.

As you might figure, visitor traffic at Perris is extremely high in the summer. Crowds are considerably smaller in the spring and fall, but the attractions are just as compelling then.

❻ Lake Elsinore

Location: South of Riverside at Lake Elsinore; map I6, grid h0.

Directions: From Riverside drive south on Highway 91 to Interstate 15. Turn south and drive about 20 miles on Interstate 15 to the town of Lake Elsinore. Turn west on Highway 74 and drive three miles to the park entrance.

Access: Boat ramps are provided at the following locations:

Cranes Lakeside Park: From Interstate 15 take the Bundy Canyon Road exit and turn left. Go back under the freeway until the road dead-ends. Turn right on Mission Trail and continue to a stop sign. Turn left on Corydon Road, follow it for one mile to its end, and then turn right on Grand Avenue. Continue six miles to the park on the right. Note: If you reach the Ortega Highway, you've gone too far. For information phone (909) 678-2112.

Kay Jordan's Campground: From Interstate 15 take the Central Avenue/Highway 74 exit and turn west on Highway 74. Continue down the hill; the resort is one mile past the stoplight on the left. This ramp is suitable for personal watercraft and small boats only. For information phone (909) 674-2766.

Lake Elsinore West Marina: From Interstate 15 take the Central Avenue/Highway 74 exit and turn west on Highway 74. Drive to Collier Street, turn right, and proceed to Riverside. Turn left and continue four miles to the marina. For information phone (909) 678-1300 or fax (909) 678-6377.

Facilities, fees: Campgrounds, marina, rowboat rentals, picnic areas, snack bar, bait, and groceries are available at the lake. Fishing boats can be rented at Lake Elsinore West Marina, (909) 678-1300. Fishing boats and pontoon boats are rented out at Pro Marina, (909) 678-4028. Personal watercraft can be rented at Playland Park, (909) 678-4663. A day-use fee and boating fee are charged; the boat fee includes a lake permit and launching privileges.

Water sports, restrictions: The speed limit is 35 mph. Waterskiing, personal watercraft, and windsurfing are allowed. Swimming beaches are available at Lake Park Resort, Kay Jordan's Campground, and Cranes Lakeside Park.

Contact: City of Lake Elsinore , (909) 674-3124; Lake Elsinore Chamber of Commerce, (909) 245-8848 or fax (909) 245-9127. For boating information phone any of the resorts listed above.

About Lake Elsinore: Whoosh! Whoosh! What's faster than a speeding bullet? Whoosh! Whoosh! If it's at Lake Elsinore, then the answer is a water-skier being towed by a jet boat. The place is loaded with them. You can't blame them though, not with day after day of barn-burner weather all summer and into the fall, and few anglers to get in their way.

Lake Elsinore is set at 1,239 feet in an area hot enough to make the water here more valuable to boaters than gold. The lake is big enough to accommodate all kinds of boats. It's a winner, and a lot of people take advantage of its offerings.

Most of the developed recreation areas are situated on the northern shore along Highway 74, and that's where the adventure usually starts. Elsinore is extremely popular, and here you will find anglers, water-skiers, personal watercraft, and windsurfers. But get this: If you like to go the daredevil route, there are a few more activities you can participate in, namely hang gliding and parachuting. As you are coursing across the lake, you can often look up and see these adventurers soaring overhead, an incredible sight.

Swimming access is good at Elsinore, but you should stick to the developed beaches at the Lake Elsinore State Recreation Area and the private resorts. These are by far the best spots, with beaches, marked swimming areas, and a fairly gently sloping lake bottom.

There are also several trails for hiking, biking, and horseback riding. In addition, if you drive up the Ortega Highway to Glen Ivy, you will find some hot springs.

One word of caution: In low rain years Elsinore's water level can be subject to extreme and erratic fluctuations, and it is advisable to call ahead for lake conditions before planning a trip. In high rain years the problem isn't nearly as extreme.

❼ Lake Skinner

Location: Near Temecula in Lake Skinner County Park; map I6, grid i3.

Directions: From Interstate 15 at Temecula, take the Rancho California exit and drive nine miles northeast on Rancho California Avenue to Lake Skinner County Park.

Access: Paved launch ramps are available on the lake's northeast and southeast arms. Boats less than 10 feet long and 42 inches wide are prohibited. Sailboats must be a minimum of 12 feet long and have at least 12 inches of freeboard.

Facilities, fees: Campgrounds, picnic area, coin laundry, snack bar, and groceries are available at the lake. Fishing boats and pontoon boats can be rented. There are fees for day use, fishing, and boat launching.

Water sports, restrictions: A 10 mph speed limit is strictly enforced. Waterskiing and personal watercraft are not allowed. No windsurfing, swimming, or other water/body contact is permitted.

Contact: Lake Skinner/Riverside County Park, (909) 926-1541; Lake Skinner Marina, (909) 926-1505.

About Lake Skinner: Don't like waterskiers? Don't like personal watercraft? Don't like fast boats of any kind? Well, you've come to the right place. While Lake Elsinore to the nearby west is dominated by waterskiers, Skinner is dominated by anglers.

Lake Skinner is set within a county park at an elevation of 1,479 feet in sparse foothill country. When full, it covers 1,200 surface acres.

No sports that involve body contact with water are permitted here, and you know what that means. Right: no waterskiing. It also means no other contact sports, including swimming and windsurfing. A large swimming pool is available at the park, however, and considering how hot it can get, taking a dip here can feel like you are being submerged in magic waters.

It's a shame that windsurfing is not permitted, because winds are fairly consistent and it would be a great site for sailboarders. Instead, only folks with small sailboats can take advantage of the wind, and right, it makes a great sailing lake. But the predominant users are anglers who come to fish for trout or striped bass.

Hiking and horseback riding trails are available at the park, and they provide a good option for day trips.

Map of Southern California—Page 420

Chapter 17
Joshua Tree Area

Overall Rating

| 1 | 2 | 3 | 4 | 5 | 6 | 7 | 8 | 9 | 10 |

Poor .... Fair .... Great

17–Joshua Tree Area Map

One inch equals approximately 10.7 miles.
See page 12 for California state map.

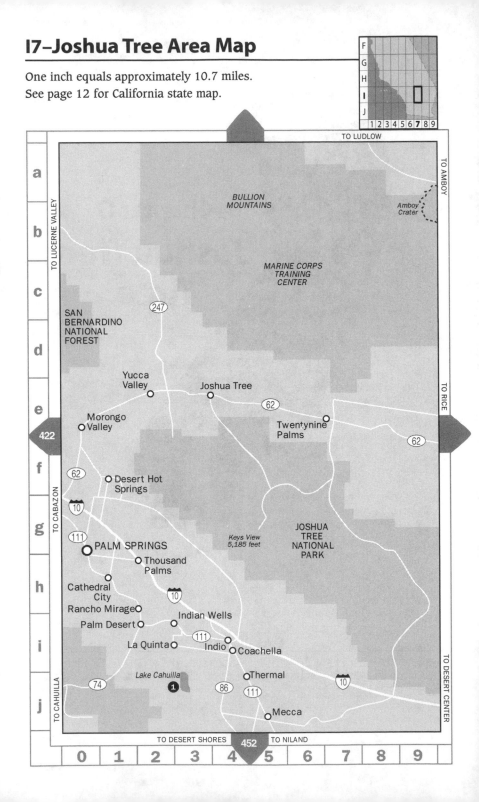

❶ Lake Cahuilla

Location: Near Indio in Lake Cahuilla County Park; map I7, grid j3.

Directions: From the Los Angeles area, drive east on Interstate 10 to the town of Indio. Take the Monroe Street exit and turn right. Keep going on Monroe Street until you reach Avenue 58. Turn right and follow the signs straight to the lake.

Access: A primitive hand-launch ramp is located on the west shore.

Facilities, fees: A campground, picnic areas, and a snack bar are provided. Supplies can be obtained in Indio. A day-use fee is charged.

Water sports, restrictions: Gas-powered motors are not permitted on the lake. A 10 mph speed limit is strictly enforced. Windsurfing is permitted. A 10-acre sandy swimming beach is available on the west shore.

Contact: Lake Cahuilla County Park, (760) 564-4712 or fax (760) 564-2506.

About Lake Cahuilla: What a place. If it weren't for this little patch of water, there would be times when it would be quite appropriate to put up a sign on Interstate 10 that says, "You are now entering hell."

Temperatures are commonly in the 100-degree range, and the desert winds can blow at gale force. In fact, there used to be a little boat ramp at the lake, but it was destroyed by high winds.

Lake Cahuilla covers just 135 acres, but those are the most important acres in the entire region. The park here—complete with large, shady palm trees and a 10-acre beach/water play area—offers a bit of relief from the heat. The lake is excellent for swimming, but at times the water can even be too warm, almost like swimming in a big hot tub. Where else might you actually sweat while you are swimming?

Boating is strictly small-time. Only cartop boats may be used, and the 10 mph speed limit keeps things quiet.

Windsurfing conditions can be good in the late fall, but the wind is too strong in the spring for decent sailboard prospects. Because of the hot summer temperatures, use is highest in the fall and winter months.

If you find yourself out this way during the winter, a good side trip is to Joshua Tree National Park to the northeast. God help you if you are here at any other time.

Map of Southern California—Page 420

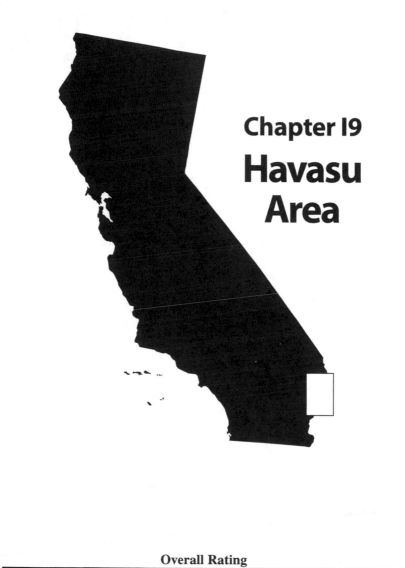

Chapter 19
Havasu Area

Overall Rating

| 1 | 2 | 3 | 4 | 5 | 6 | 7 | 8 | 9 | 10 |

Poor .... Fair .... Great

I9–Havasu Area Map

One inch equals approximately 10.7 miles.
See page 12 for California state map.

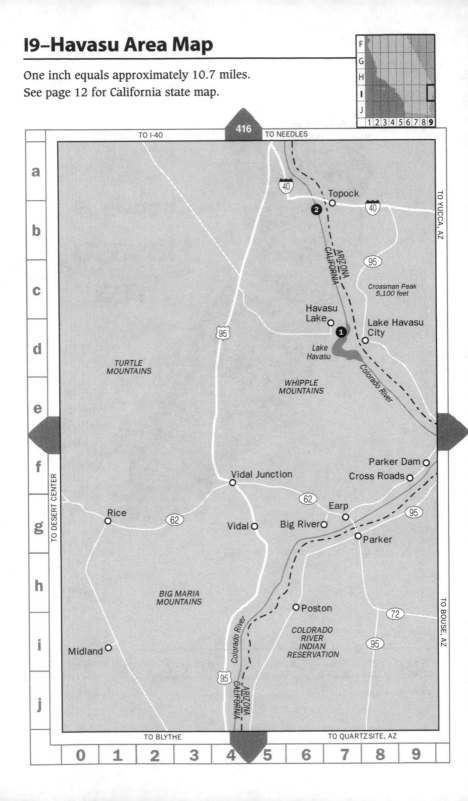

Chapter 19 features:

1 Lake Havasu

Location: From Topock to Parker Dam on the Colorado River; map I9, grid d7.

Directions: From Southern California to Vidal Junction, take Interstate 10 east to Blythe and turn north on US 95. Continue to Vidal Junction at the intersection of US 95 and Highway 62. Or take Highway 62 directly east to Vidal Junction.

From Northern California to Vidal Junction, drive south on US 395 to Interstate 10. Proceed east on Interstate 10 all the way to Blythe, then turn north on US 95, and continue to Vidal Junction at the intersection of US 95 and Highway 62. Or turn north off Interstate 10 onto Highway 62 near Palm Springs and continue northeast to Vidal Junction.

To access the lake's west side, turn north on US 95 and drive about 28 miles to Havasu Lake Road. Turn east and continue to the lake.

To reach the lake's east side, drive east on Highway 62 to Parker, then turn north on Arizona Highway 95 (the Arizona side) or Parker Dam Road (the California side), and drive to Parker Dam. Continue north on Highway 95 to Lake Havasu City.

Access: Paved ramps are available at the following locations:

Black Meadow Landing, California: From Vidal Junction turn east on Highway 62 and drive to Earp. Turn north on Parker Dam Road and continue almost all the way to the dam. Look for a sign for Black Meadow Landing and turn left. For information phone (760) 663-4901 or fax (760) 663-3088.

Cat Tail Cove State Park, Arizona: Drive north on Arizona Highway 95 to mile-

post 168 and turn into the park. For information phone (520) 855-1223 or fax (520) 855-1730.

Crazy Horse Campground, Arizona: From Arizona Highway 95 drive north to Lake Havasu City. Once in town the highway intersects with Swanson Boulevard; turn right. Proceed to Lake Havasu Boulevard, turn left, and then turn left on McCulloch Boulevard. Cross the London Bridge. The resort is approximately one-half mile past the bridge on the right. For information phone (520) 855-4033.

Havasu Landing Resort, California: From Vidal Junction head north on US 95 toward Needles. The resort is halfway between Vidal Junction and Needles; look for a large billboard indicating the turnoff. Personal watercraft are available for rent here. For information phone (760) 858-4593.

Islander RV Resort, Arizona: From Arizona Highway 95 drive north to Lake Havasu City. Once in town the highway intersects with Swanson Boulevard; turn right. Proceed to Lake Havasu Boulevard, turn left, and then turn left on McCulloch Boulevard. Cross the London Bridge and drive approximately two miles (McCulloch Boulevard will turn into Beachcomber Boulevard) to the resort on the left. For information phone (520) 855-5005 or fax (520) 855-1261.

Lake Havasu Marina, Arizona: From Arizona Highway 95 drive north to Lake Havasu City. Once in town the highway intersects with Swanson Boulevard; turn right. Proceed to Lake Havasu Boulevard, turn left, and then turn left on McCulloch Boulevard. Cross the London Bridge and continue to the marina at 1100 McCulloch Boulevard. Fishing boats, pontoon boats, and personal watercraft are available for rent. For information phone (520) 855-2159 or (520) 855-4702.

Sandpoint Marina & RV Park, Arizona: From Arizona Highway 95 northbound, drive approximately 15 miles north of Parker and take the Cat Tail Cove/Sandpoint Marina exit. Turn left and continue into the park entrance. Fishing boats, pontoon boats, and houseboats are available for rent here. For information phone (520) 855-0549 or fax (520) 855-3008.

Facilities, fees: Campgrounds, resorts, full-service marinas, and supplies are available off Arizona Highway 95 in the vicinity of Lake Havasu City. There are 40 shoreline miles of boat-access camping on the lake's Arizona side between the dam and Lake Havasu City. Boats can be rented at many of the marinas listed. Boat rentals are also available at Havasu City Service, (760) 858-4392; Fun Time Boat Rentals, (520) 680-1003; and Arizona Jet Ski Rentals, (520) 453-5558. A fee is charged at most resorts and marinas for day use and/or boat launching.

Water sports, restrictions: Waterskiing, personal watercraft, and windsurfing are permitted. Swimming beaches are available at the following locations: Havasu Landing Resort, Sandpoint Marina, Crazy Horse Campground, and Islander RV Resort. There are numerous undesignated beaches all along the shoreline.

Contact: For general information contact the Lake Havasu City Chamber of Commerce, (520) 855-4115. For boating information phone any of the resorts listed.

About Lake Havasu: Giant Lake Havasu is like a lone sapphire in a vast coal field. Only the mighty Colorado River breaks up a measureless expanse of desert. Havasu was created when the Parker Dam was built across the river, and it is currently one of the most popular boating areas in the southwestern United States.

The lake is 45 miles long, covers 19,300 acres, and is located at the low elevation of 482 feet. Size, hot weather, warm water, and proximity to Las Vegas make this one of the top vacation and waterskiing hot spots in the West. The lake is used year-round, although fewer people use it in the late winter months.

During spring, summer, and fall, it's considered a boating wonderland. Much of the boating activity is located around Pittsburgh Point, the big island across from Lake Havasu City. To get there, you must cross the famous London Bridge, and that alone gives people quite a charge.

Waterskiing and personal watercraft are very popular activities. While competitions are held here yearly, most boaters do their own thing, heading off on this great expanse of water in search of wild fun and frolic. Most find it. Over the course of a year, enough suntan oil is poured at Lake Havasu to fill many small lakes, and enough liquid refreshment is poured to fill the California Aqueduct.

The hot weather and lukewarm surface waters make this lake ideal for swimming. Many boaters search out relatively private beaches, then set up shop to have picnics, swim a little, play a little, and then maybe water-ski or tow somebody around on a Boogie board.

Southern California is well known for being home to a vast amount of people, and Lake Havasu definitely attracts many of them. However, this lake is big enough to handle all of the people who throng here, and big enough for all of them to have the time of their lives.

❷ Colorado River

Location: From Parker Dam south to Palo Verde Dam on the California/Arizona border; map I9, grid a6.

Directions: If coming from Southern California, take Interstate 10 east to Blythe and turn north on US 95. Or take Highway 62 east to Vidal Junction at the intersection of

US 95 and Highway 62 and turn south on US 95. There are numerous access points off US 95 between Blythe and Vidal Junction in the Parker Valley area.

If coming from Northern California, drive south on US 395 to Interstate 10. Proceed east on Interstate 10 all the way to Blythe and then turn north on US 95. Or turn north off Interstate 10 on Highway 62 near Palm Springs and continue northeast to Vidal Junction at the intersection of US 95 and Highway 62. Turn south on US 95. There are numerous access points off US 95 between Blythe and Vidal Junction in the Parker Valley area.

To reach the Parker Dam section of the river, drive about 20 miles east of Vidal Junction on Highway 62 to the town of Parker. From Parker turn north on either Arizona Highway 95 or Parker Dam Road. Numerous access points are available off these roads.

Access: Paved boat ramps are provided at the following locations:

Big Bend Resort, California: From Vidal Junction turn east on Highway 62 and drive to Earp. Turn north on Parker Dam Road and continue 11 miles to the resort. For information phone (760) 663-3755 or fax (760) 663-3068.

La Paz County Park, Arizona: From Vidal Junction turn east on Highway 62 and drive to Parker. Turn north on Arizona Highway 95, drive approximately seven miles, turn left on Golf Course Drive, and continue to the park on the right. For information phone (520) 667-2069 or fax (520) 667-2757.

Parker Public Ramp, Arizona: From Vidal Junction turn east on Highway 62 and drive to Parker. Turn north on Business 95 and drive approximately five miles to the ramp.

Patria Flats Ramp, Arizona: From Vidal Junction turn east on Highway 62 and drive to Parker. Turn north on Business 95 and drive approximately eight miles to the

ramp. For information phone (520) 667-2069 or fax (520) 667-2757.

River Land Resort, California: From Vidal Junction turn east on Highway 62 and drive to Earp. Turn north on Parker Dam Road and continue five miles to the resort. For information phone (760) 663-3733 or fax (760) 663-3203.

Facilities, fees: Campgrounds, resorts, marinas, and supplies are available off Highway 95 near Parker. Boats may be rented at resorts on Lake Havasu (see the previous listing for details). A fee is charged at some resorts for boat launching.

Water sports, restrictions: Waterskiing and personal watercraft are permitted. Windsurfing is not recommended. Swimming is available at La Paz County Park and at several undesignated areas along the riverbanks. Canoeists can put in at any of the boat ramps listed.

Contact: For general information phone the Parker Area Chamber of Commerce, (520) 669-2174 or fax (520) 669-6304, or any of the resorts listed.

Note: The Parker Valley portion of the river is part of the Colorado River Indian Reservation, and the tribe requires that all anglers obtain a permit. Permits are available at the Department of Fish and Game in Parker, (602) 669-9285.

About the Colorado River: Whoa, look at all the water-skiers. On hot summer days the Colorado River is about the only thing liquid around these parts that isn't in a can or bottle. One way or another the natural response is to get in the water, then boat, water-ski, swim, float around on an inner tube, anything—just get on the river. If this sounds like a prime place for water recreation, that's because it is.

The boating season here is a long one, courtesy of that wonderful desert climate. Day after day this place is turned into one of the waterskiing capitals of America. Some days it can seem like a competition to determine who has the loudest boat. No matter where you access the river, you will share in the happy/wild/nutso romance with the water, where hot sun and speedboats make this a water-ski winner.

Families with youngsters who desire a more quiet pace, perhaps a calm spot where they can play in the water or swim, should head to La Paz County Park.

One of the surprising things about this area is that the most difficult time to find a campsite is not during the summer, as at most places, but in the winter. True, even though temperatures can get pretty cold, around 40 degrees at night, the campgrounds fill because of the yearly migration of snowbirds, retired folks with RVs and trailers who leave the snow country (or the rain country in Oregon and Washington) and spend much of their winter here every year.

Chapter J6
San Diego Area

Overall Rating

| 1 | 2 | 3 | 4 | 5 | 6 | 7 | 8 | 9 | 10 |

Poor .... Fair .... Great

J6–San Diego Area Map

One inch equals approximately 10.7 miles.
See page 12 for California state map.

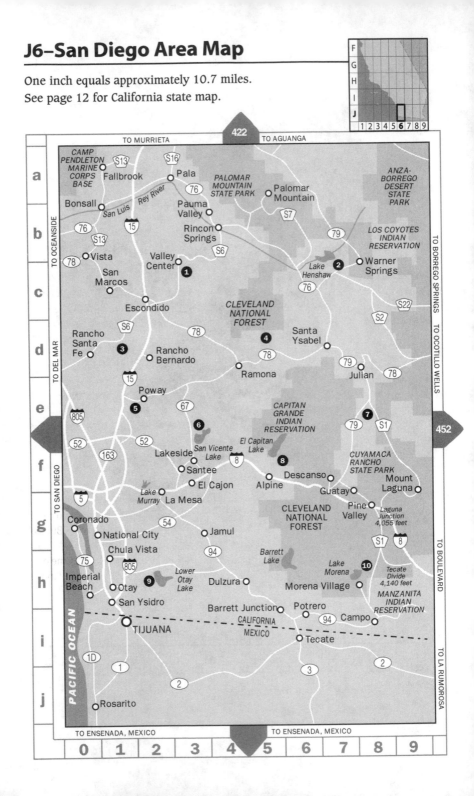

Chapter J6 features:

1 Lake Wohlford

Location: East of Escondido; map J6, grid c3.

Directions: From Escondido on Interstate 15, turn east on County Road S6 and drive five miles to Lake Wohlford Road. Turn right and continue about two miles to the lake.

Access: A paved boat ramp is located on the north shore.

Facilities, fees: A campground, picnic areas, bait, snack bar, and limited supplies are available. Fishing boats can be rented at the lake. Access is free.

Water sports, restrictions: A 5 mph speed limit is strictly enforced. Canoes, inflatables, sailboats, and boats that are under 10 feet or over 18 feet long are prohibited. No water/body contact sports are permitted.

Contact: Lake Wohlford and Oakvale RV Park, (760) 749-2895.

About Lake Wohlford: It's no secret that Lake Wohlford is set up for one thing—fishing—and that all other water sports fall by the wayside.

The lake is set at 1,500 feet in elevation, and that's right, it gets scorching hot out here in the summer. That is why the prime time to visit is in spring and fall, when the campground gets a fair amount of use. Even though fishing is the lone activity possible here, the prospects are only poor to fair for bass, bluegill, and crappie.

The nos really add up: No swimming, no canoeing, and no windsurfing, not to mention the regulations governing boat size. But that's typical; many lakes in the greater San Diego area enforce similar restrictions.

2 Lake Henshaw

Location: East of Escondido; map J6, grid c7.

Directions: From Escondido turn north on Interstate 15 and drive about 15 miles to the Highway 76 exit. Turn east and drive 30 miles to the lake entrance on the left.

Access: A paved boat ramp is located along the access road.

Facilities, fees: A campground, picnic areas, snack bar, groceries, and a restaurant are available. Fishing boats can be rented. Access is free.

Water sports, restrictions: A 10 mph speed limit is strictly enforced. No canoes, inflatables, or craft under 10 feet long are permitted. No water/body contact sports are permitted.

Contact: Lake Henshaw Resort, (760) 782-3501.

About Lake Henshaw: This is a good-sized lake, covering 1,100 acres with 25 miles of shoreline. Henshaw was designed to be used for fishing and not much else. But despite the fact that the lake's record-holding bass weighed 14 pounds, 4 ounces, the bass fishing prospects here are only middling.

Lake Henshaw is set at an elevation of 2,700 feet near Cleveland National Forest. Don't expect to find yourself out in the wilderness, though; you see, the lake is bordered by a permanent-residence mobile home park. However, there are some nice hiking trails through nearby oak tree groves. A large developed campground is also available.

Like many reservoirs Lake Henshaw is sometimes plagued by low water levels. In big rain years, of course, that is never a problem.

❸ Lake Hodges

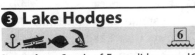

Location: South of Escondido; map J6, grid d1.

Directions: From Interstate 15 at Escondido, turn southwest on County Road S6 (via Rancho Parkway) and continue five miles to the lake's entrance road.

Access: A boat launch is located at the beach at Hidden Cove.

Facilities, fees: A picnic area and a snack bar are provided. Full facilities are available in Escondido to the north or San Diego to the south. Access is free. There is a boat launching fee.

Water sports, restrictions: A 35 mph speed limit is strictly enforced. Windsurfing is allowed. No other water/body contact sports are permitted.

Contact: San Diego Water Utilities, Lake Department, 12375 Moreno Avenue, Lakeside, CA 92040-1135; (760) 668-2050 or fax (760) 443-7681.

About Lake Hodges: How you feel about Lake Hodges depends entirely on your perspective. If you like to catch big bass and you are lucky enough to get a few, you might think that this is the best lake in America. If you are a boater looking for some excitement, you will probably be frustrated by the strict rules prohibiting most water sports, as well as the fact that the high number of anglers can turn this lake into the aquatic version of the San Diego Zoo.

Lake Hodges is set at an elevation of 314 feet in the coastal foothills just west of Interstate 15. The long, narrow, snakelike reservoir is shaped like an inverted V and covers 1,250 acres. For four days out of every week between March and October the lake is shut down; during these closures some anglers will park their trucks and trailered boats in line at the boat ramp, actually pay-

ing college kids to "car-sit" for as long as it takes, in order to grab one of the first spots in line. It gets worse. Once on the water it's every man for himself, with anglers often moving in right on top of each other if they believe there is even the remotest possibility of snaring one of the lake's fish.

People put up with the hassle because Hodges is a fantastic producer of big bass, including the monster-size lake record, 20 pounds, 4 ounces. Typically, all the good spots have been hit by 10 AM.

During the spring, early summer, and fall, there are usually good afternoon winds, and prospects for windsurfing are better than at any lake in the region. What? You say Hodges is the only lake in the region that even allows windsurfing? Yeah? Well, yeah, that's true.

Special note: From March through October the lake is open only on Wednesdays, Saturdays, and Sundays.

❹ Lake Sutherland

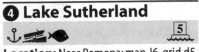

Location: Near Ramona; map J6, grid d5.

Directions: From Interstate 15 at Escondido, turn east on Highway 78 and drive about 30 miles to Sutherland Dam Road (located about eight miles past Ramona). Turn left and drive north to the lake.

Access: A paved boat ramp is located on the west shore.

Facilities, fees: Picnic areas and a snack bar are provided. Supplies can be obtained in Ramona. Rowboat and motorboat rentals are available. A fee is charged for boat launching.

Water sports, restrictions: A 20 mph speed limit is strictly enforced. No water/body contact sports are permitted.

Contact: San Diego Water Utilities, Lake Department, 12375 Moreno Avenue, Lakeside, CA 92040-1135; (760) 668-2050 or fax (760) 443-7681.

About Lake Sutherland: The intense number of anglers that hammer away at Hodges, El Capitan, San Vicente, and Lower Otay don't seem to make it out here. The lake is just distant enough from the San Diego metropolitan area and just small enough (only 560 acres) that many of the go-getters do their go-getting elsewhere.

The lake is set at an elevation of 2,058 feet in the foothills near Cleveland National Forest. It was created from the dammed flows of Santa Ysabel Creek and Bloomdale Creek, and there are 11 miles of shoreline.

Strict rules prohibit all water sports except for low-speed boating and fishing. A bonus is that anglers can rent small fishing boats at the lake.

Special note: From March through October the lake is open only on Fridays and Saturdays.

❺ Lake Miramar

Location: North of San Diego; map J6, grid e2.

Directions: From San Diego turn north on Interstate 15 and drive about 10 miles to Mira Mesa. Take the Mira Mesa Boulevard exit and turn east. Continue to Scripps Lake Drive and turn south; proceed to the lake.

Access: A paved boat ramp is located on the lake's south.

Facilities, fees: A picnic area and a snack bar are provided. Supplies can be obtained in Mira Mesa. Full facilities are available in San Diego. Canoes and paddleboats are available for rent. Access is free. There is a fee for boat launching and fishing.

Water sports, restrictions: A 5 mph speed limit is strictly enforced. No water/body contact sports are permitted.

Contact: San Diego Water Utilities, Lake Department, 12375 Moreno Avenue, Lakeside, CA 92040-1135; (760) 668-2050 or fax (760) 443-7681.

About Lake Miramar: Little Lake Miramar, covering 160 acres with four miles of shoreline, is a pretty spot in the San Diego foothills at an elevation of 700 feet.

It is best known as the place where someone caught a 21-pound, 10-ounce bass that was later discovered to have a lead diving weight in its stomach! This tiny lake is a great one for producing fish stories. In the cool months it is stocked with trout, which seem to work like growing pills for the big bass.

The rental canoes at Miramar are a real treat, and paddling around in one of them for a bit is the only possible activity besides fishing. Miramar is really more of a large pond, with little underwater structure and clear water, and is small enough that anglers can pick over the same spots day after day. That has a way of smartening up the bass. There are days when you can see the fish but not catch them, and believe me, it will drive you crazy. But hey, you can always just give up and paddle about in a canoe instead.

Special note: The lake is open Saturday through Tuesday from November 1 through September 30.

❻ San Vicente Lake

Location: Northeast of San Diego; map J6, grid e4.

Directions: From San Diego turn east on Interstate 8 and drive to El Cajon. Turn north on Highway 67 and drive about 10 miles to Morena Drive. Turn left and continue to the lake.

Access: A paved boat ramp is located on the lake's south side.

Facilities, fees: A picnic area and a snack bar are provided. Supplies can be obtained in Lakeside. Access is free. There is a fee for boat launching.

Water sports, restrictions: A 10 mph speed limit is strictly enforced on Thursdays and Fridays, when fishing boats, canoes, and inflatables are permitted.

Waterskiing is allowed only on Saturdays and Sundays in the summer. From mid-October to mid-May no waterskiing is permitted. Swimming and windsurfing are not allowed.

Contact: San Diego Water Utilities, Lake Department, 12375 Moreno Avenue, Lakeside, CA 92040-1135; (760) 668-2050 or fax (760) 443-7681.

Special note: The lake is open Thursday through Sunday year-round.

About San Vicente Lake: Compared to other lakes in the San Diego area, this one looks different. The shoreline includes some steep, rocky banks, which provide ideal terrain for the aquatic food chain. The underwater habitat fosters the growth of zooplankton and insects, which in turn attract minnows, then trout and bass. That is why the fishing here is often so good.

San Vicente is located in arid foothills at an elevation of 659 feet and comes complete with an island. When full, the lake has 14 miles of shoreline and covers 1,070 acres. Like most lakes in the San Diego area, the rules here are designed primarily to cater to anglers. On weekends, however, San Vicente is a rare breed: one of the few lakes around where waterskiing is allowed.

To prevent conflicts, no waterskiing is permitted on fishing day (Friday), and no fishing is permitted on waterskiing days (Thursday, Saturday, and Sunday). On Friday a 10 mph speed limit is in effect, so people with low-speed boats such as canoes, inflatables, and small fishing boats have a chance to enjoy themselves without high-speed boats zipping around on all sides. Only on extremely rare occasions are exceptions made to this schedule.

What you get here is good fishing in the late winter, spring, and fall, and good waterskiing in the summer. But the highlight, of course, is the bass fishing. More than 500 bass weighing five pounds or more are caught here every year.

❼ Lake Cuyamaca

Location: Northeast of San Diego near Cuyamaca Rancho State Park; map J6, grid e8.

Directions: From Interstate 15 at Escondido, turn east on Highway 78 and drive about 45 miles to the town of Julian. Take Highway 79 south and continue nine miles to the lake.

Access: Two paved boat ramps and one unimproved launch area are located on the lake's west shore, off Highway 79. Boats under 10 feet or over 18 feet long are prohibited. Sailboats, inflatables, and rafts are not permitted on the lake.

Facilities, fees: Campgrounds, picnic areas, restaurant, and a snack bar are provided. Fishing boats, canoes, and paddleboats are available for rent. There is a small access fee for non-anglers. There is a fee for boat launching.

Water sports, restrictions: A 10 mph speed limit is strictly enforced. No water/body contact sports are permitted.

Contact: Lake Cuyamaca, (760) 765-0515.

About Lake Cuyamaca: This lake is just far enough away from the San Diego area to make a trip here something special, and many visitors are rewarded appropriately for their efforts.

Lake Cuyamaca, a small lake covering just 110 acres, is set at 4,620 feet in elevation on the Cuyamaca Mountains' eastern slopes. Surrounding the lake is Cuyamaca Rancho State Park, which offers a network of pretty hiking and horseback riding trails.

First and foremost, Lake Cuyamaca is a fishing lake, and it gets relatively high use by anglers year-round. The rest of the visitors are pretty much hikers and backpackers who come to explore the adjacent park in the summer months.

Fishing prospects are often good. Many trout are stocked by the Department of Fish and Game, and there are sizable resident

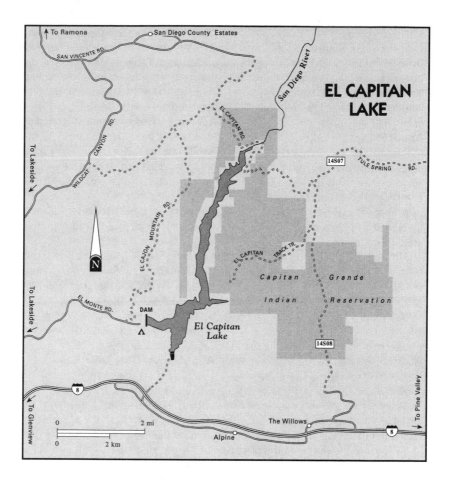

EL CAPITAN LAKE

populations of crappie and bass as well.

A campground is available at the state park. That makes Cuyamaca a good choice for the boater/angler/camper. In addition, fishing boats, canoes, and paddleboats can be rented at the lake, a plus. The lake is just the right size and has a low enough speed limit (10 mph) to make paddling around quite fun for families in the summer.

❽ El Capitan Lake

Location: Northeast of San Diego; map J6, grid f6.

Directions: From San Diego turn east on Interstate 8 and drive 16 miles to Jennings Park Road. Turn north and drive about two miles to the town of Lakeside. Turn right on El Monte Road and continue driving east to the lake.

Access: A paved boat ramp is located on the south shore. Boats under 10 feet or over 20 feet long are prohibited.

Facilities, fees: Picnic areas and a snack bar are provided. Full facilities and supplies are available in the San Diego area. Access is free. There is a fee for boat launching.

Water sports, restrictions: Waterskiing and personal watercraft are permitted on select days; phone San Diego Water Utilities for a current schedule. On all other days a 35 mph speed limit is strictly enforced. Swimming and windsurfing are not allowed.

Contact: San Diego Water Utilities, Lake Department, 12375 Moreno Avenue, Lakeside, CA 92040-1135, (760) 668-2050 or fax (760) 443-7681.

About El Capitan Lake: The bassers call this place "El Cap" and rarely without a touch of reverence. While you may hear stories about the bass at other lakes, El Cap is the one that produces them. The lake is set in a long canyon at an elevation of 750 feet. It is the biggest of the lakes managed by the City of San Diego, covering 1,575 acres when full.

Although this place is primarily set up for fishing, a few quirks have been thrown in. First, this is the only reservoir in the City of San Diego's system where personal watercraft are permitted, though only on certain days; call headquarters for the schedule. Second, the water level fluctuates, which can throw off the fishing, and in rainy years, runoff causes the lake to be somewhat murky in the spring. The latter is actually a boon for anglers because the fish are far less skittish than those at lakes with high water clarity, such as Miramar.

As you might have figured, this place is special and gets a lot of use in the summer months; it attracts a moderately sized crowd the rest of the time. When the lake is opened to the public in February, anglers get delirious, even jittery, at the prospects of casting a line to fish that have had four months of downtime to forget all about hooks and lures.

Special note: Most years, the lake is open only on weekends and Mondays beginning in late February or early March through October.

❾ Lower Otay Lake

Location: Southeast of San Diego; map J6, grid h2.

Directions: From San Diego drive south on Interstate 805 to Chula Vista. Turn east on Telegraph Canyon Road and drive approximately five miles to Otay Lake Road. Turn right, travel two miles east, and then turn south on Wueste Road.

Access: A paved boat ramp is located off Wueste Road on the west shore.

Facilities, fees: Picnic areas and a snack bar are provided. Fishing boats are available for rent. Access is free. There is a fee for boat launching and fishing.

Water sports, restrictions: A 20 mph speed limit is strictly enforced. No water/body contact sports are permitted.

Contact: San Diego Water Utilities, Lake Department, 12375 Moreno Avenue, Lakeside, CA 92040-1135; (760) 668-2050 or fax (760) 443-7681.

Special note: From January through late-September the lake is open on Wednesdays, Saturdays, and Sundays.

About Lower Otay Lake: It could make your brain gears squeak trying to imagine a five-bass limit that weighs in at 53 pounds, 14 ounces. But that is what the scales read when Jack Neu of San Diego weighed the five bass he caught at Otay, the largest single bass limit ever documented on the planet.

I fished with Jack on that record day, and if by now you have figured that Otay is set up mainly for fishing, well, you got that right. A 10 mph speed limit and a prohibition on sports involving water/body contact make this lake ideal for anglers only.

Otay is set at an elevation of 490 feet in the foothills near Chula Vista, just north of the California/Mexico border. When full, the lake covers 1,265 acres with 13 miles of shoreline. There's a variety of aquatic habitats, including submerged trees, tules, underwater holes, and ledges; hey, there's even a metal building down there. What occurs here are long periods of slow to fair fishing results despite intense fishing, followed by short periods of unbelievable snaps with giant bass.

The lake is surrounded by rolling foothills, and if you're interested in a side trip, there are some places where you can hike. But most people are here for one reason: the bass. And the dream of catching a stringer of fish just like the one Jack Neu did.

⑩ Lake Morena

Location: East of San Diego in Lake Morena County Park; map J6, grid h8.

Directions: From San Diego drive approximately 53 miles east on Interstate 8. Take the County Road S1/Buckman Springs Road exit and drive five miles south to Oak Drive. Turn right and follow the signs to the park.

Access: A paved launch ramp is available on the lake's south side.

Facilities, fees: A campground, picnic areas, and a snack bar are provided. More developed facilities are available at Morena Village to the east. Access is free. There is a fee for boat launching.

Water sports, restrictions: A 10 mph speed limit is strictly enforced. No water/body contact sports are permitted.

Contact: Lake Morena San Diego County Park, (619) 565-3600.

About Lake Morena: Yes, Lake Morena is located out in the boondocks, but it's well worth the trip. If you like bass, don't miss it.

The lake is set at an elevation of 3,200 feet just south of Cleveland National Forest and only seven or eight miles from the California/Mexico border. When full, the lake covers 1,500 surface acres. However, water levels can fluctuate wildly, which can have a tremendous impact on the quality of your visit. In low rain years it is advisable to call ahead before planning a trip to the lake.

Because the elevation is much higher than the other lakes in the greater San Diego area, everything gets going a little later, with the best fishing in April, May, and June.

Lake use is limited to fishing only. No other water sports are permitted, and a 10 mph speed limit keeps even the fastest boats at a reasonable pace.

Lakeside camping is a major bonus, and because of it, use is heavy in late spring and summer. In addition, the surrounding national forest offers the chance for lots of other activities, including hiking and horseback riding.

Map of Southern California—Page 420

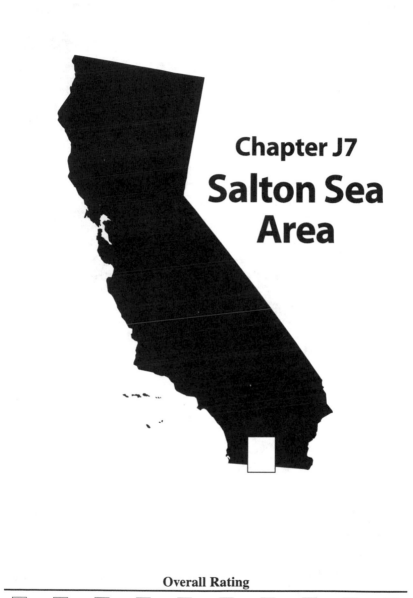

Chapter J7
Salton Sea Area

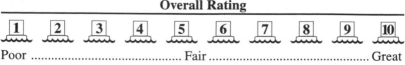

Overall Rating

| 1 | 2 | 3 | 4 | 5 | 6 | 7 | 8 | 9 | 10 |

Poor .... Fair .... Great

J7–Salton Sea Area Map

One inch equals approximately 10.7 miles.
See page 12 for California state map.

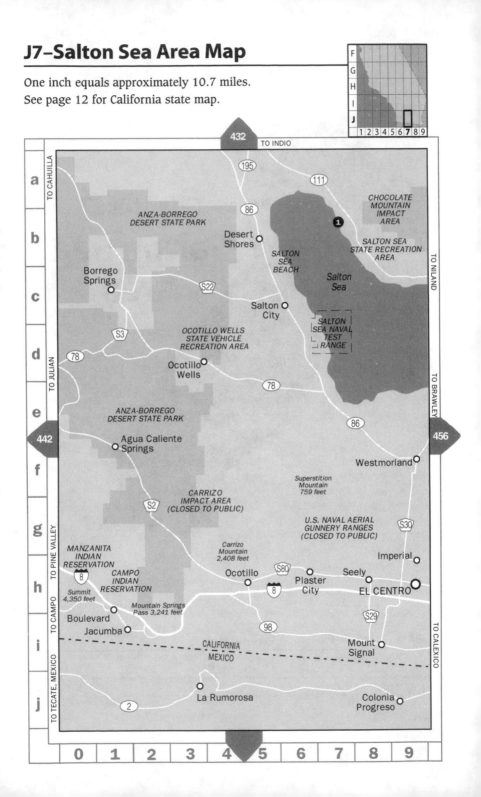

Chapter J7 features:

❶ Salton Sea

Location: East of San Diego; map J7, grid b7.

Directions: From the Los Angeles area, head east on Interstate 10. Drive east past Indio and then turn south on Highway 111. To reach the lake's east shore, continue south on Highway 111 at the Mecca/Niland exit. Follow the freeway to the end. At the stop sign turn right onto Avenue 58. Drive over the railroad tracks in the left lane. Turn left at the light onto Old Highway 111 and drive approximately 13 miles to the lake. To reach the west shore, take the Mecca/Niland exit south to Highway 195. Follow Highway 195 until you reach Highway 86; then turn south and continue to the lake.

Access: Boat ramps are available at the following locations:

Desert Shores Marina (west shore): From the junction of Interstate 10 and Highway 111, turn south on Highway 111 and drive to Highway 86. Turn south and continue to the resort at Desert Shores. For information phone (760) 395-5280.

Red Hill Marina (east shore): From the junction of Interstate 10 and Highway 111, turn south on Highway 111. Drive through Niland to Saint Clair Road, turn right, and drive 3.5 miles to Garse Road. Turn right and drive 1.5 miles to the marina. For information phone (760) 348-2310.

Salton Sea Beach Marina (west shore): From the junction of Interstate 10 and Highway 111, turn south on Highway 111 and drive to the small town of Salton Sea Beach. Turn left on Coachella Street; the resort is located at 288 Coachella. For in-formation phone (760) 395-5212.

Salton Sea State Recreation Area (west shore): From the junction of Interstate 10 and Highway 111, turn south on Highway 111 and continue to the state park entrance on the right. For information phone (760) 393-3052.

West Shores RV Park (west shore): From the junction of Interstate 10 and Highway 111, turn south on Highway 111 and drive to Highway 86. Turn south and continue to Salton City. Turn left on North Marina Drive and continue to the sign for Johnson's Landing. Turn left on Sea Garden and continue to the resort at the road's end. For information phone (760) 394-4755.

Facilities, fees: Campgrounds, full-service marinas, picnic areas, lodging, restaurants, and groceries are available at various locations around the lake. Boats can be rented at Bob's Playa Riviera and Bombay Marina. A fee is charged at most marinas and resorts for day use and/or boat launching.

Water sports, restrictions: Waterskiing, personal watercraft, and windsurfing are permitted. Swimming is available anywhere around the lake; a good spot is Mecca Beach in Salton Sea State Recreation Area.

Contact: For information contact Salton Sea State Recreation Area, (760) 393-3052, the resorts listed, or the Salton Sea West Shore Chamber of Commerce, (760) 394-4112.

About the Salton Sea: Some people pray for love. Some people pray for riches. At the Salton Sea you pray for the wind not to blow in the spring, and for it not to be too hot in the summer and fall.

When you first arrive at the Salton Sea, it appears to be a desolate, godforsaken wasteland. The lake is 35 miles long but has an average depth of just 10 feet. Nothingness surrounds you for miles in all directions. When the wind blows, there's no obstacle to slow it down, and it can howl across the water, whipping up large waves that are dangerous to boaters. To help alert boaters when hazardous winds are in the offing, local authorities have posted a flashing red light on the northeast shore that warns boaters to get off the lake.

Damn, it's hot—terrible at times. This vast water covering 360 square miles is set at 228 feet below sea level. The nearby mountain range is stark and reaches up to 10,000 feet, creating an eerie backdrop.

In addition to the weird setting, scorching temperatures, and occasional frothing winds, this lake is known for being a good place to fish for corvina, a warmish spot for camping in the winter, and an odd place to go swimming.

Since the water is, for the most part, quite shallow, boaters who aren't used to the place should be aware of unmarked underwater obstacles located at the lake's far north and south ends, which can pose navigational hazards. Most of the boaters here are fishermen casting about for corvina, and they rarely have any unusual problems.

Salton Sea is not only visually unique, it is an extremely unusual place to swim. Because of the water's high salinity level, swimmers kind of bob around effortlessly, their buoyancy obviously boosted by all the salt. It is possible to swim pretty much anywhere on the east and west shores, but note that some areas on the west shore tend to be more mud than sand. Yeah, right, very ugly.

Use is moderate at Salton Sea year-round but is lowest in the summer and highest in the winter, when quite a few retirees make the trip in order to take advantage of the temperate off-season climate. Other activities in the area include golfing, bird-watching, and hiking.

When it gets really hot here in the summer, with the mercury hovering in the 110-degree range for days in a row, you may think you are in hell—and you might be right.

Chapter J8
Chocolate Mountain Area

Overall Rating

| 1 | 2 | 3 | 4 | 5 | 6 | 7 | 8 | 9 | 10 |

Poor .... Fair .... Great

J8–Chocolate Mountain Area Map

One inch equals approximately 10.7 miles.
See page 12 for California state map.

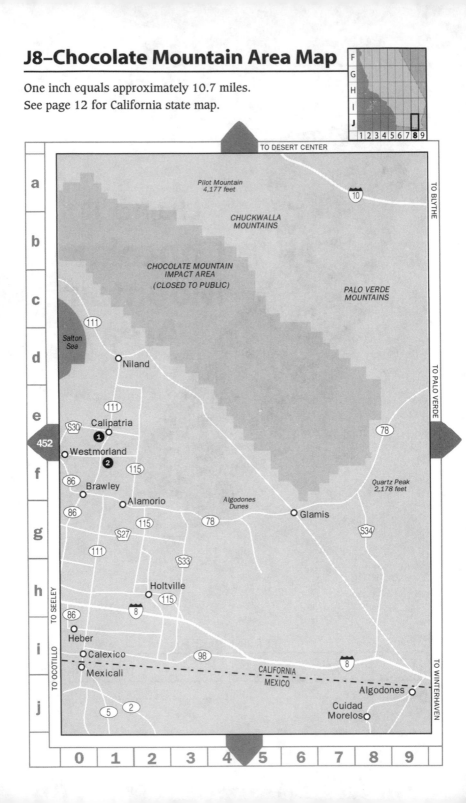

① Ramer Lake

Location: Near Calipatria in the Imperial Wildlife Area; map J8, grid f1.

Directions: From the Los Angeles area, turn east on Interstate 10 and drive to Indio. Then turn south on Highway 111 and drive about 70 miles. As you leave Calipatria, look for the sign for Ramer Lake. Turn left and continue to the lake.

Access: A paved ramp is located on the east shore of the lake.

Facilities, fees: Vault toilets are provided. A campground is available to the south at Weist Lake. Supplies can be obtained in Calipatria and El Centro. Access to the lake is free.

Water sports, restrictions: Motorized boats are not permitted. All water/body contact sports are prohibited.

Contact: California State Fish & Game, Imperial Wildlife Area, (760) 348-2493 or (760) 359-0577.

About Ramer Lake: Almost nobody knows about little Ramer Lake—nobody, that is, except for a few duck hunters. The lake is located in the Imperial Wildlife Area, which provides waterfowl habitat and duck-hunting grounds during the winter. The rest of the year it is largely ignored, save for a handful of folks who fish the lake for bass, catfish, and that world favorite, carp.

Set in the Imperial Valley, Ramer is surrounded by farmland and is overshadowed by the massive Salton Sea to the near north. You must register at the entrance station, then leave a written record of anything you've caught because it is part of the wildlife area. That way they can keep track of the carp. Heh, heh.

There is not much in the area except for this little fishing pond. Wildlife lovers are welcome to toss in a canoe and paddle around, using their binoculars to look for birds. Hiking trails and nature-study sites are available in the wildlife area.

② Weist Lake

Location: South of Calipatria in Weist Lake County Park; map J8, grid f1.

Directions: From the Los Angeles area, turn east on Interstate 10 and drive to Indio. Then turn south on Highway 111 and drive about 75 miles to Rutherford Road (about five miles south of Calipatria). Turn left and continue east to the park.

Access: A paved boat ramp is located on the lake's east side.

Facilities, fees: A campground, picnic areas, and a snack bar are provided. Supplies can be obtained in Calipatria and El Centro. A day-use fee is charged; rates may change from season to season. The entrance fee includes boat-launching privileges.

Water sports, restrictions: Waterskiing, personal watercraft, windsurfing, and swimming are allowed. A beach with a designated swimming area is located on the southeast shore, near the campground.

Contact: Weist Lake County Park, (760) 344-3712.

About Weist Lake: Ask somebody what a Weist Lake is and they will probably go into brainlock. But there really is such a place.

A Weist Lake, it turns out, is a little lake, just 50 acres, set at 110 feet below sea level amid desolate country that is scorching hot most of the year. Because there is not much else around, this place can seem almost like an oasis.

The lake is filled by the Alamo River, and despite its small size it is actually a pretty fair setting for waterskiing. Windsurfing conditions can be excellent, though relatively few windsurfers realize it. After all, most people don't even know there is such a thing as a Weist Lake.

Use is moderate in spring, fall, and winter, and very light in summer when scorching temperatures keep away all but the most desperate vacationers. Arrive then and you'll begin to feel kind of like an iguana. Arrive in the spring and you'll get the chance to have some good times. Enjoy!

Saltwater Appendix

Overall Rating

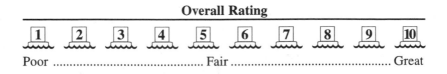

| 1 | 2 | 3 | 4 | 5 | 6 | 7 | 8 | 9 | 10 |

Poor .... Fair .... Great

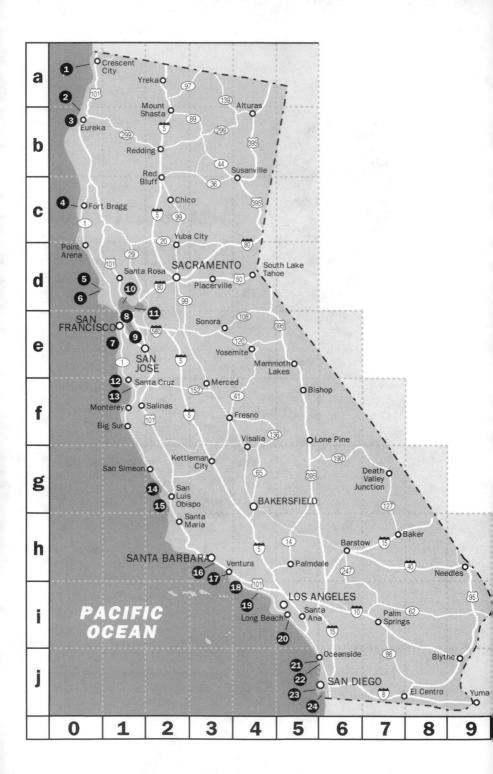

Saltwater Appendix features:

1 Crescent City Harbor

Location: In Crescent City; map AØ, grid e6.

Directions: Just south of Crescent City, drive north on US 101, turn west at Citizen's Dock Road, then continue to the harbor.

Access: Two paved, two-lane boat ramps and a hoist are located within the harbor.

Facilities, fees: A full-service marina is available, including a maintenance area, boat wash, bait and tackle shop, fuel, public rest rooms and showers, restaurants, and a coin laundry. Boat rentals are not available. A privately owned RV park is located adjacent to the harbor. Access is free. There is a charge for using the boat ramps or hoist.

Water sports, restrictions: The speed limit is 25 mph in the harbor and 5 mph near the docking area. All water sports are permitted. Personal watercrafting and windsurfing are popular here. There is a long, sandy beach just south of the harbor. The water is quite cold for swimming, even in the summer.

Contact: Crescent City Harbor District, (707) 464-6174; the Chart Room Marina, (707) 464-5993. For general information

and a free travel packet, contact the Crescent City–Del Norte Chamber of Commerce, 1001 Front Street, Crescent City, CA 95531; (707) 464-3174.

About Crescent City Harbor: In the summer and fall, there's always a stream of vacationing out-of-towners arriving via US 101 to discover this magic place where the redwoods meet the sea. If you approach from the south, your first sight of the harbor is a beautiful view from the roadside lookout. This is a natural crescent-shaped harbor that provides refuge from the terrible spring winds out of the northwest. Full services, including a harbormaster and a restaurant, are within walking distance of the harbor's parking lot.

The harbor gets heavy use, mostly by anglers who enjoy excellent salmon and deep-sea fishing in the summer and fall, as well as a good boat ramp and an adjacent parking area. Whether you have your own boat or plan to take a charter trip, it is critical that you call ahead to check on wind and sea conditions and to obtain a reliable weather forecast. Other popular sports are beachcombing and windsurfing. Just south of the parking area is a long, sandy beach that has excellent pickings during low tides. It is one of the best accessible beach walks in California. As for windsurfing the annual winds out of the north make this harbor a choice spot for experts, even though the water is cold, often ranging from 48 to 55 degrees , and the winds can be particularly fierce. Just about no one swims out here because it's far too cold. Personal watercraft are popular, but it is essential that riders wear wet suits.

On calm, foggy summer days in Crescent City, it can be difficult to fathom the volatile weather that has pounded this harbor. In 1964 the Juneau earthquake precipitated the most famous event in the town's history. In the middle of the night, most of the water was sucked out of the harbor; then a tidal wave buried the town. One guy was asleep at home as his bed floated eight feet high. When he awoke, he poked his head right through the ceiling and thought the roof had collapsed on him. Imagine that.

In the winter, storms can arrive extremely quickly, and hardly a year goes by without a commercial crabber getting trapped in bad weather, often capsized. Wind and rain pound the coast here, and anybody who lives in Del Norte County year-round gazes at the sea with respect and a little fear, as well as an appreciation for its vast beauty.

❷ Trinidad Harbor

Location: In Trinidad; map BØ, grid a4.
Directions: From Eureka drive 22 miles north on US 101 and take the Trinidad exit. As you head west the road becomes Main/Trinity/Edwards and goes all the way down to a parking lot adjacent to the Seascape Restaurant.
Access: A boat hoist and a primitive boat launch are available at Bob's Boat Basin, located on Bay Street in Trinidad.
Facilities, fees: Bob's Boat Basin provides skiff rentals, tackle shop, restaurant, and a gift shop. Party boat charters are also avail-

able at Bob's. Nearby Patrick's Point State Park has a campground, and there are several motels that offer good, low-cost lodging. Access is free. There is a charge for boat launching.
Water sports, restrictions: Windsurfing and personal watercraft are permitted. There are beaches, but swimming is not recommended due to frequent shark sightings.
Contact: For general information and a free travel packet, contact the Trinidad Chamber of Commerce, (707) 677-3448. For boating and fishing information, contact Bob's Boat Basin, (707) 677-3625.
About Trinidad Harbor: So many people miss out on Trinidad. But it only takes one good trip here to keep you coming back for the rest of your life. This is a beautiful chunk of coast, a protected bay sprinkled with rock-tipped islands and prime fishing grounds off the Trinidad Head. Just north is Patrick's Point State Park, one of the prettiest small parks in California, something of a rain forest/jungle with Sitka spruce, heavy fern undergrowth, hiking trails winding through tunnels of vegetation, and spectacular coastal lookouts.

Boaters should heed this word of caution: Hone your navigational skills. These parts often get quite foggy in the summer, and the worst of it comes in July and August, which happen to be when fishing prospects are best. Boaters unfamiliar with the area can find themselves cloaked in the stuff. That is why GPS and Loran navigation devices are so popular with people who use the harbor, as are professional charter boat services. The wind really kicks up in the late winter and spring, and you have to time it right to get on the water. It's worth battling the fog, however, as this is a spectacular place to visit.

Of course if you visit when the harbor is fog-free, all the better. If you come on a calm day in the winter or spring, you might consider crabbing. The area is a prime habitat for Dungeness crab. Just set out a series of traps, spend the day rock fishing, and return to add a few big Dungeness crabs to your bag. What a feast to be had for the wise!

❸ Humboldt Bay

⚓ 🚤 🐟 🚣 🧍 🛶   8

Location: In Eureka; map BØ, grid c2.
Directions: From Eureka drive south on US 101 to Field's Landing, or west on Highway 255.
Access: Five boat ramps are located on the bay:
Eureka Boat Basin: From US 101 in Eureka, turn south on Commercial Street and continue to the paved boat ramp.
Field's Landing: From Eureka drive south on US 101 to the Field's Landing exit. Drive two blocks, then turn right, and continue west to the paved boat ramp at the waterfront.
Samoa Bridge: From US 101 in Eureka, take Highway 255 west. Turn right just before the Samoa Bridge, continue two blocks, and turn left on T Street. Continue to the paved ramp at the bay.
Samoa Peninsula: From US 101 in Eureka, take Highway 255 west. Cross the Samoa Bridge and continue to the peninsula and the two-lane paved boat ramp.
Woodley Island Marina: From US 101 in Eureka, take Highway 255 west and follow the signs to the marina on Woodley Island, which has a paved boat ramp.
Facilities, fees: Full-service marinas are located at Woodley Island and Johnny's Marina, four miles south of Eureka at King Salmon. Camping, lodging, food, and bait and tackle are available in Eureka. Sailboats, powerboats, canoes, and kayaks can be rented from Humboldt State University Center Activities in Arcata. Access is free.
Water sports, restrictions: A 5 mph speed limit is strictly enforced in designated areas. Personal watercraft and waterskiing are permitted but are not recommended due to heavy boating traffic. Windsurfing is allowed. The bay is generally too cold for swimming.
Contact: Humboldt Bay Harbor District, (707) 443-0801; Humboldt State Center Activities, (707) 826-3357. For a free travel packet, contact the Eureka Chamber of Commerce, (800) 356-6381 or (707) 442-3738.
About Humboldt Bay: Here is one of the many vast bodies of water in Northern California that is often overlooked by boaters. It is a narrow bay, 21 miles long, with tidal wetlands bordering the northern flats near Arcata and the southern flats south of Eureka.

My life-pal Michael Furniss taught me what a great place this is for canoeing. On calm days, especially in late summer and fall, plop a canoe or kayak in, paddle for 20 minutes or so, and find yourself in the center of the bay. Surrounded by this huge expanse of water, you feel as if you're a million miles away from the nearest creature. Except, of course, for your bird friends. A wide variety of marine birds and waterfowl can be spotted at the Arcata Marsh at the bay's north end; at the south end the Humboldt National Wildlife Refuge is home to egrets, plovers, and even the occasional otter.

The water is far too cold for most body/water contact sports. Although people occasionally use personal watercraft or go windsurfing here, they are always protected by thick wet suits.

Salmon fishing is very popular in the summer, a primary attraction for powerboaters. Inexperienced boaters should use caution when leaving the harbor, which locals refer to as "venturing out the jaws"—especially if a big swell is coming in from the west. Of course fog is common here, and boaters should be skilled in the use of navigational equipment and charts to ensure a safe journey to the ocean.

❹ Noyo Harbor

Location: In Fort Bragg; map CØ, grid f3.

Directions: From Highway 1 in Fort Bragg, turn east on Highway 20 and drive south to North Harbor Drive (right before the Noyo Bridge) or South Harbor Drive (just after the bridge). Turn west; you can access the river from both sides.

Access: There are two public boat ramps:

Noyo Mooring Basin: From Highway 1 in Fort Bragg, turn east on Highway 20 and cross the Noyo Bridge. Turn left on South Harbor Drive and continue straight to the paved ramp at the harbor.

Noyo Public Ramp: From Highway 1 in Fort Bragg, turn east on Highway 20. Just before the Noyo Bridge, turn onto North Harbor Drive and head toward the marina. Follow the road around the marina until you come to the paved launch ramp.

Facilities, fees: Limited marina services are provided at Noyo Mooring Basin. A full-service marina, dock, coin laundry, and campground are available at Dolphin Isle Marina, which also has a gravel boat ramp for customers only. More campgrounds, lodging, and groceries are available nearby at Fort Bragg. Access is free. There is a charge for boat launching.

Water sports, restrictions: There is a 5 mph speed limit near the harbor. It is not possible to swim here.

Contact: Noyo Harbor District, (707) 964-4719 or fax (707) 964-4710; Dolphin Isle Marina, (707) 964-4113. For general information contact the Fort Bragg–Mendocino Coast Chamber of Commerce, (707) 961-6300 or fax (707) 964-2056.

About Noyo Harbor: Fort Bragg was once a classic fisherman's town, but in recent years it has become more of a summer tourist destination where the ambience of the old harbor seems to be more important than the fishing.

Still, this is an outstanding harbor for boaters. Set where the lower Noyo River enters the Pacific Ocean, the harbor has extensive boat docking, restaurants, and a jetty at its entrance to the ocean. Boat ramps are extremely well sheltered from coastal winds and ocean surge, and the only problem boaters will encounter is their own eagerness; they often surpass the 5 mph speed limit near the harbor in the rush to reach open water.

When the ocean is calm, there is excellent fishing, best from summer through fall, especially for rockfish at nearby Cleone Reef (three miles north of Fort Bragg) and for salmon in July. Another great bonus: unlike at other harbors to the south where you must often take a long boat ride to reach the fish, here the fish swim close to land.

In recent years the harbor scene, with its packed restaurants and parking lots, has detracted from the boating and fishing industries that have been the mainstay of this area for the past century. The tide has definitely turned.

A wild card activity is to plunk in a small boat or a canoe and explore the lower Noyo River. The tidewaters are more like a lagoon than a river, and getting an up-close view from a small boat is far more peaceful than being in a crowded restaurant.

❺ Bodega Bay

Location: North of San Francisco; map DØ, grid h7.

Directions: From US 101 in Petaluma, take the East Washington Boulevard exit, drive west through Petaluma (Washington Boulevard becomes Bodega Avenue), and continue to Highway 1. Turn north on Highway 1 and drive to Bodega Bay.

Access: There are three paved, public ramps:

Doran County Park: The ramp is located on the bay's south end. Enter the park directly off Highway 1.

Porto Bodega: From Highway 1 take East Shore Road along the bay to the ramp.

Westside Ramp: From Highway 1 take West Shore Road out to the ramp at Bodega Head.

Facilities, fees: Campgrounds are located at Doran County Park and Westside Park. Porto Bodega has an RV park. A hoist and marina facilities are provided at Spud Point Marina, and other marina services are available at Mason's Marina and Porto Bodega. There are no boat rentals. Supplies can be obtained in the town of Bodega Bay. There is a fee for boat launching. A day-use fee is charged at the county parks.

Water sports, restrictions: Waterskiing and personal watercraft are permitted 50 yards from the shoreline. Doran Beach is a good spot for swimming. Windsurfing is allowed everywhere.

Contact: Bodega Bay Chamber of Commerce, (707) 875-3422; Spud Point Marina, (707) 875-3535; Mason's Marina, (707) 875-3811; Porto Bodega, (707) 875-2354; Doran and Westside Parks, (707) 875-3540.

About Bodega Bay: Boaters have found that Spud Point Marina and Bodega Bay Harbor offer the best access for ocean fishing anywhere from Monterey to Oregon.

With Bodega Head shielding the harbor from west winds and a beautiful, large concrete boat ramp on the bay's west side, the Bodega Bay setting has always been ideal. And now that Spud Point Marina is fully established, boaters have the advantage of full services, including docking and gas.

During low tide Bodega Bay becomes a fairly narrow channel bordered by miles of exposed mudflats. Therefore it is critical that boaters always stay inside the channel markers. After launching, a short, sheltered ride gets you out to the mouth of the bay, with a jetty protecting you as you enter the ocean. The prime reason people come here is to go salmon fishing; it can be

a real treat because the fish are often close by, a 15-minute ride out to the Whistle Buoy just west of Bodega Head. At other times salmon can be found near Tomales Point to the south or to the north at the mouth of Salmon Creek. Deep-sea fishing from Bodega Bay is often great, though it's a long ride to the prime spot, Cordell Bank.

In Bodega Bay, waterskiing and personal watercraft—sports that are growing surprisingly popular here—are permitted 50 yards from shore. Just make sure you stick to high tides. Windsurfing is also popular.

The shoreline is rocky, not great for swimming, but a hard-core few do swim all along the bay. The only beach is at Doran Park.

Though it is close to the Bay Area, Bodega Bay retains a rural feel. The drive here is a nice one, along a two-laner that is routed through rolling hills and country-style dairy farms.

Of course Bodega Bay will always have legendary status as the place where Alfred Hitchcock filmed his thriller *The Birds*. One time while returning from a salmon trip here, I actually saw a deer swimming straight out of the harbor, heading toward the sea. A Coast Guard crew went out and rescued the deer and placed it on land, whereupon it reentered the water and started swimming out to sea again. That is as strange as it gets here.

❻ Tomales Bay

Location: North of San Francisco; map DØ, grid i8.

Directions: From US 101 in Marin, take the Sir Francis Drake Boulevard exit (toward San Anselmo) and drive west about 20 miles to Olema. Turn right on Highway 1, drive a short distance, then turn left at Bear Valley Road, and drive north for 8.2 miles to Pierce Ranch Road. (Bear Valley Road rejoins with Sir Francis Drake Boulevard). Turn right on Pierce Point Road and drive 1.2 miles to the access road to Tomales Bay State Park on the right.

Access: There are no public ramps. Two private ramps are available: a paved ramp at Golden Hind Inn and Marina, and a sand ramp at Lawson's Landing.

Facilities, fees: A small campground is provided for bicyclists and hikers at Tomales Bay State Park, which also has picnic areas and rest rooms. Fishing boats can be rented at Lawson's Landing. In Marin Seatrek offers kayak rentals and guided trips. A day-use fee is charged at Tomales Bay State Park. There are fees for boat launching.

Water sports, restrictions: Waterskiing and personal watercraft are not permitted in the bay. Swimming, kayaking, and windsurfing are allowed at Shell Beach, Heart's Desire Beach, Pebble Beach, and Indian Beach (all within Tomales Bay State Park), and at Chicken Coop Beach (a free, public beach).

Contact: Tomales Bay State Park, (415) 669-1140; Golden Hind Marina, (415) 669-1389; Lawson's Landing, (707) 878-2443. For kayak rentals or guided trips, contact Seatrek, (415) 488-1000 or fax (415) 332-8790.

About Tomales Bay: Because Tomales Point, Inverness Ridge, and Point Reyes shield Tomales Bay from north winds, this is a perfect place to paddle a kayak or motor around in a small boat.

Tomales Bay is largely undeveloped, bordered on the west by the Point Reyes National Seashore and on the east by Highway 1 and several very small towns—geography that creates quiet, calm conditions and protection from the wind. Long and narrow, the bay is fed by Papermill Creek (also known as Lagunitas Creek) to the south and enters the ocean through a small, shallow reefed mouth.

Sea kayakers of all experience levels will find this makes an excellent destination. Kayaking and swimming are popular, particularly at Shell Beach and Heart's Desire Beach at Tomales Bay State Park. Seatrek, a local kayak company, offers guided kayaking trips and oyster-tasting tours.

Tomales Bay State Park receives heavy visitor use in the summer, especially at the beaches already mentioned. But even when the area is inundated with people, which is quite rare, you can always find instant tranquillity by plunking a small boat into adjoining Tomales Bay and taking a few strokes out into the open water where peace and serenity reign.

Special Note: Although a few people do it, it is unwise to try to "shoot the jaws"— or head out through the mouth of Tomales Bay and into the ocean—in a small boat. It is very shallow near the buoy here, and the water can be choppy and dangerous. Plus this happens to be a breeding ground for great white sharks. One great white actually bit the propeller off a boat in this area. That is warning enough.

---

❼ Half Moon Bay

Location: From Martin's Beach to Devil's Slide; map E1, grid f1.

Directions: From San Francisco drive south on Highway 280 to Daly City and the junction with Highway 1. Turn south on Highway 1, drive through Pacifica, over Devil's Slide, and continue five miles to Princeton. Turn right, drive a quarter mile; then turn left into Pillar Point Harbor.

From the East Bay or the Peninsula, drive west on Highway 92 into Half Moon Bay and the junction with Highway 1. Turn north and drive five miles to Princeton. Turn left, drive a quarter mile, and turn left into Pillar Point Harbor.

Access: A paved boat ramp is located at Pillar Point Harbor at Princeton Street in the town of Half Moon Bay.

Facilities, fees: A full-service marina and a pier are provided. Lodging and supplies can be obtained nearby. Campsites are provided at Half Moon Bay State Beach to the south. Boat rentals are not available in the area; the nearest businesses offering rentals are north at San Francisco Bay. There is a fee for boat launching.

Water sports, restrictions: Waterskiing and personal watercraft are not recommended. It is possible to windsurf in the outer harbor when afternoon winds kick up. Although there are several miles of sandy beach, the water is generally too cold for swimming.

Contact: Pillar Point Harbor, (650) 726-5727 or fax (650) 726-7740; Hilltop Grocery Bait & Tackle, (650) 726-4950.

About Half Moon Bay: One of the great success stories of the California coast is here at Half Moon Bay.

Not long ago the old launch ramp had lines extending to the highway, the parking lot was always jammed, the marina was old and dilapidated, and the party boats were slow and needed a paint job. On top of all that, gillnetters were wiping out the inshore fisheries and commercial fishermen were shooting sea lions. But one by one, all of these problems have been fixed. Gillnetting was banned in water shallower than 240 feet, commercial fishermen stopped shooting anything that moved (after two were arrested), a new launch ramp was completed, a breakwater was added inside the harbor, new boat slips were built, new skippers brought in fast and well-maintained boats, and a new parking lot was added.

Suddenly Half Moon Bay became a quality act. The best features are the new six-lane boat ramp and the inner jetty. Though there can still be considerable lines on summer weekends, launching at the boat ramp is a snap most of the year, particularly on weekdays. With six lanes boaters no longer suffer the old nightmare of getting jammed up when one boater has difficulty getting in or out. The inner jetty solved the old problem of ocean surge, and along with it came an added benefit.

The jetty has made the harbor calm enough for people with small boats, including canoes, to enjoy the pretty setting. The west harbor is somewhat secluded, as well as beautiful, and is home to grebes, cormorants, pelicans, and other marine birds. Most boaters launch from the ramp, then make the trip out of the harbor en route to nearby fishing grounds. The best nearby spot is Deep Reef, 12 miles southwest of the harbor, where rockfish are available year-round and where salmon often school in the spring. The Farallon Islands are located 25 miles to the northwest. Another great ride is on the nearby coast to the north, along Devil's Slide, where you can see just how precipitous the cliff is that holds the little shelf on which Highway 1 is perched.

Just south of the harbor along the south jetty is an area popular with surfers. Though danger looms in those adjoining rocks, the jetty creates waves even when other areas are flat and calm. When the conditions are right, this spot is also a favorite of skilled windsurfers and, to a lesser extent, of personal watercraft users. The latter have sometimes come into conflict with surfers, and most personal watercraft users now stay well south of the surfing area.

Forget about swimming; the water temperature ranges from 48 to 56 degrees most of the year. All surfers and windsurfers wear thick full-body wet suits.

There are 11.5 miles of beaches suitable for beachcombing, picnicking, and sunbathing. Beach walks are excellent along the harbor's west side, just below the Pillar Point Radar Station. From the parking lot here, you can walk on a trail routed on a raised bluff on out to the north jetty, with access to a secluded beach at Pillar Point that often has many sea lions cavorting about nearby.

❽ San Francisco Bay

Location: From the Richmond Bridge to the Oakland Bay Bridge; map E1, grid c4.

Directions: Access is available off roads and highways that connect with Highway 101 to the west and Interstate 80 to the east. See Boat ramp for specific directions.

Access: Paved ramps are available at the following locations:

Berkeley Marina, Berkeley: From Interstate 80 in Berkeley, take the University Avenue exit and turn left toward the bay. At Marina Boulevard turn right and go past the Marriott Hotel to Spinnaker Way. Turn left and continue to a signed turnoff just before the boatyard. For information phone (510) 644-6376.

Clipper Yacht Harbor, Sausalito: From US 101 near Sausalito, take the Sausalito–Marin City exit and bear left, heading under the freeway. Turn right on Bridgeway and proceed a few blocks to Harbor. Turn left and continue to the marina. For information phone (415) 332-3500 or fax (415) 332-0257.

Emeryville Marina, Emeryville: From Interstate 80 south of Berkeley, take the Emeryville-Powell exit. Turn south on Powell and follow it for approximately two miles to the marina at the road's end. For information phone (510) 596-4330.

Richmond Marina Bay Harbor, Richmond: Heading north on Interstate 80, take the Marina Bay Parkway exit and turn west on Marina Bay Parkway. Turn right on Regatta Street, proceed to Marina Way South, turn left, and continue to Hall Street. Turn left on Hall Street and take it back around to Marina Way South. Follow the signs to the marina, located at 1340 Marina Way South. If you're heading south on Interstate 80, take the El Cerrito–San Rafael Bridge exit and proceed to Cutting Boulevard. Turn right and continue to Marina Way South. Turn left and continue to the marina. For information phone (510) 236-1013.

Facilities, fees: Lodging and full facilities are available in San Francisco and in the surrounding cities along the bay. Campsites for tents are provided at Angel Island State Park; RV parks are available in San Francisco. Full-service marinas are available at most of the launch ramps listed. Powerboats can be rented at Captain Case's Boat Rentals in Sausalito, (415) 331-0444. Sailboats can be rented at the following locations: Marina Plaza Harbor, in Sausalito, (415) 332-4723; Cass' Marina, in Sausalito, (415) 332-6789; or Rendezvous Charters, at Pier 40 in San Francisco, (415) 543-7333. Fees may be charged for boat launching and/or parking.

Water sports, restrictions: A 5 mph speed limit is enforced near harbor areas. Waterskiing and personal watercraft are permitted on the main bay. Beaches for swimming and windsurfing are available at South Sailing Basin, on the south side of the Berkeley Marina in Berkeley, at Friendship Park in Richmond, and at Miller-Knox Regional Shoreline in Richmond. Windsurfing is also popular at Larkspur Landing, near the Richmond Bridge, and at the south side of the Golden Gate Bridge, near Crissy Field and the downtown marina.

Contact: For boating tours and general information, phone the San Francisco Convention & Visitor Bureau, (415) 391-2000. For boating information and regulations, contact the US Coast Guard, Bay Area Marine Safety Office, (510) 437-3073. For information on specific areas, phone any of the marinas listed.

About the San Francisco Bay: One of the greatest boating experiences is a ride in the San Francisco Bay among national treasures such as Alcatraz and the Golden Gate Bridge. How can you beat that?

Many people agree that you can't. This is one of the premier places in the world to cruise a sailboat, an activity made extra special by mooring at Ayala Cove on Angel Island for dinner. But anybody with a boat big enough to handle the occasional wind chop and strong enough to power through the sometimes powerful tides can enjoy world-class beauty on the water, surrounded by some of the most famous landmarks in America. Windsurfing can be nothing short of incredible for the highly skilled, and there are also stellar opportunities for sea kayaking and fishing. One thing about boating in the bay, however, is that it can require skill and talent, particularly when you're confronted with strong currents, fog, high winds, and heavy boating traffic.

This is why renting a boat around here is so difficult; for liability reasons, almost no one wants to rent boats to the inexperienced. Only one place on the entire bay, Captain Case's in Sausalito, rents boats with motors. Other rental services have sailboats, but they charge a hefty fee and require proof of experience. However, most will provide a skipper for a price and give you a guided tour.

Newcomers might consider sea kayaking as an alternative. Sea kayaks have flat bottoms, so they don't tip over, and the tandem jobs can make for a great romantic getaway. Sea Trek in Sausalito provides great beginner packages that include a short lesson and the necessary equipment; go that route and you'll soon be paddling away in the quiet waters of lovely Richardson Bay. Sea kayak rentals are also offered by Sea Trek at Angel Island State Park.

Windsurfing is extremely popular on the bay. The best spots are listed under "Water sports," but there are many other undesignated sites where you can windsurf. For experts the top spot is at Crissy Field, where windsurfers can pick up afternoon winds and go shooting across the bay at warp speeds. Some daredevils even windsurf in the wakes of the afternoon ferryboats heading from San Fran-

cisco to Tiburon. The water temperature is cold year-round, making it necessary to wear wet suits. A few notes: Fishing is best in the summer, when striped bass and halibut enter the bay. In December and January boaters should beware of the large number of commercial fishing boats netting for herring. Whenever there is a chance of fog, boaters should have GPS navigation equipment and know how to use it. Excelent boating safety programs directed by the US Coast Guard Auxiliary and the US Power Squadron are conducted at locations around the Bay Area.

❾ South San Francisco Bay

Location: From the Oakland Bay Bridge to Alviso; map E1, grid e4.

Directions: Access is available off roads that intersect with US 101 to the west and Interstate 580 to the east. See "Access" for specific directions.

Access: Paved ramps are available at the following locations:

Ballena Isle Marina, Alameda: From Interstate 880 near Oakland, take the Broadway exit and turn right. Continue to the next stoplight, make another right, and proceed through a tube that runs under the estuary. Stay to the right; when you emerge from the tube, continue on Webster Street to Central. Turn right on Central and continue until you see the high school (look for a big jet on the front lawn). Just past the high school, there is a paved driveway; turn into it and continue down to the marina. The boat ramp is located just past the marina. For information phone (510) 523-5528.

Coyote Point Marina, San Mateo: If you're heading southbound on US 101, take the Poplar exit in San Mateo and continue to the first stoplight. Turn right on

Humboldt and continue to Peninsula. Turn right, continue up and over the highway, bear left, and loop back around under the overpass. You will reach a stop sign on the left; proceed straight through and look for the Coyote Point Park gatehouse. From there follow the signs to the marina. If you're going northbound on US 101, take the Dore exit, make an immediate left on the frontage road, and continue to Peninsula. Turn right, continue to the Coyote Point Park gatehouse, and follow the signs to the marina. For information phone (650) 573-2594.

Grand Street Public Ramp, Alameda: From Interstate 880 near Oakland, take the 23rd Avenue exit and go across the Park Street Bridge. At the first stoplight turn right on Clement and continue until the street dead-ends at Grand. Turn right on Grand and proceed to the boat ramp. For information phone the Alameda Marina, (510) 521-1133 or fax (510) 521-1185.

Oyster Point Marina, South San Francisco: From US 101 in South San Francisco, take the Oyster Point Boulevard exit. Follow Oyster Point Boulevard to Marine Boulevard, turn right, and continue to the sign indicating the public ramp. For information phone (650) 871-7344.

Port of Redwood City: From US 101 in Redwood City, take the Seaport Boulevard–Woodside Road exit and bear east on Seaport Boulevard. Continue toward the water to Chesapeake Street, turn left, and continue to the launching area sign on your right. For information phone (650) 306-4150 or fax (650) 369-7636.

San Leandro Marina: From Highway 17/Nimitz Freeway in San Leandro, take the Marina exit and continue straight down to the marina. Follow the signs to the public launch ramp. For information phone (510) 357-7447.

Facilities, fees: Lodging and full facilities are available at cities along the bay. RV campers are accommodated at Candlestick Park and in Redwood City. Full-service marinas are available at most of the boat ramp listings above. Sailboat lessons and rentals are provided at Spinnaker Sailing in Redwood City, (650) 363-1390. Sailboats can be rented at Club Nautique in Alameda, (510) 865-4700. Windsurfer rentals are available at the Mountain View branch of Spinnaker Sailing, (650) 965-7474. Fees may be charged for boat launching and/or parking.

Water sports, restrictions: A 5 mph speed limit is enforced near harbor areas. Waterskiing and personal watercraft are permitted on the main bay. Sandy beaches are available at Crown Beach in Alameda, Coyote Point Park in San Mateo, and on the west side of Oyster Point Marina in South San Francisco. Windsurfing access is available near the fishing pier at Oyster Point, at Candlestick Point State Recreation Area in San Francisco, and at Crown Beach in Alameda.

Contact: For tours and general information, contact the San Francisco Convention & Visitor Bureau, (415) 391-2000 or fax (415) 362-7323. For boating information and regulations, contact the US Coast Guard, Bay Area Marine Safety Office, (510) 437-3073. For information on specific areas, phone any of the marinas listed above.

About the South San Francisco Bay: For such a huge expanse of water and with so many people living nearby in need of open space, the South Bay should be a boating wonderland. Instead, it gets relatively light use. With the adjacent San Francisco Bay offering so many amazing attractions, many boaters just launch from a South Bay harbor, particularly those near Alameda, then head to the main bay to take advantage of its dramatic surroundings and first-class recreation. Regardless, the South Bay does have its own unique charm. South of the Bay Bridge the waterway borders shipyards on each side, then spans south to Hunter's Point, Candlestick

Point, San Francisco International Airport, the San Mateo Bridge, and the Dumbarton Bridge, with outstanding waterfowl habitat along each shore. As you head south, access becomes quite poor, with former boat ramps at Palo Alto and Alviso now filled in with silt.

At high tide the South Bay appears to be a vast expanse, but this is largely a mirage. It is actually a fairly narrow channel that floods over miles of mudflats at high tide; low tide often leaves the mudflats exposed. Boaters should stick to marked channels and always carry a navigation chart to avoid being marooned on a mud dob. Such strandings happen quite a bit, and there is nothing you can do except wait for a high tide to float you off.

Shore access is poor for water sports. The best spot for windsurfing is at Candlestick Cove, where the infamous winds that make playing baseball here so miserable create a challenging setting for windsurfing. The water is often choppy, pushed by 25-knot afternoon winds, which makes for a bumpy ride.

One little-known recreational option is sea kayaking or canoeing (no rentals available) in the far South Bay near Alviso, at the Environmental Education Center, and the sloughs adjoining Coyote Creek. This area is often remarkably peaceful and calm, providing the few who are in on the secret with the chance to enjoy a great San Francisco Bay adventure in relative solitude.

❿ San Pablo Bay

Location: From the Richmond Bridge to the Carquinez Bridge; map E1, grid a3.
Access: Paved launch ramps are available at the following locations:

Benicia Marina, Benicia: From Interstate 780 in Benicia, take the Fifth Street exit and follow Fifth Street south for approximately one-half mile to the ma-

rina. At the street's end turn right and proceed to the boat ramp. For information phone (707) 745-2628.

Loch Lomond Marina, San Rafael: From US 101 in San Rafael, take the downtown San Rafael exit and turn east on Second Street. After you pass the Montecito Shopping Center, the road becomes South San Pedro Road. Follow it for two miles, turn right on Loch Lomond Drive, and continue to the marina. For information phone (415) 454-7228.

Vallejo Public Ramp, Vallejo: From Interstate 80 in Vallejo, take the Interstate 780 exit and turn south on Curtola Parkway. Continue to the public ramp, located adjacent to Brinkman's Marine. For information phone (707) 642-7521 or (707) 642-6490.

Facilities, fees: Lodging and full facilities are available in San Rafael and Vallejo. A campground is provided at China Camp State Park. The nearest boat rentals are in Sausalito: powerboats can be rented at Captain Case's Boat Rentals, (415) 331-0444. Sailboats can be rented at Marina Plaza Harbor, (415) 332-4723, and Cass' Marina, (415) 332-6789. Fees may be charged for boat launching and/or parking.

Water sports, restrictions: A 5 mph speed limit is enforced near harbor areas. Waterskiing and personal watercraft are not recommended. Swimming and windsurfing access is available at China Camp State Park.

Contact: For boating information and regulations, contact the US Coast Guard, Bay Area Marine Safety Office, (510) 437-3073. For camping and windsurfing information, contact China Camp State Park, (415) 456-0766, or California State Parks, Marin District, (415) 893-1580. For conditions or specific boating information, phone one of the marinas listed above.

About San Pablo Bay: Based on scenic beauty alone, San Pablo Bay appears to be a place of great wonder. When you're out on the water, you see Mount Tamalpais to the southeast, Mount Diablo to the southwest, the Richmond Bridge to the south, and the Carquinez Bridge to the east, while out on the shipping channel a procession of giant tankers and freighters parades by. Marine birds are abundant, from millions of little mud hens and clouds of cormorants to the lesser-seen night heron and the snowy egret.

Recreation on San Pablo Bay is pretty much limited to fishing and to nature watching. Because the bay is set in the migration path of striped bass and sturgeon, fishing is often excellent. On a flat and calm day, most common in late summer and early fall, you may encounter a water-skier, but these days are rare. For the most part you see fishing boats. San Pablo Bay is well known among boaters for its unusual navigational landmarks. While the channel is marked with buoys, northwestern San Pablo Bay features a landmark that looks like an outhouse on stilts, referred to as the "pump house." Just west of the Carquinez Strait is the Mare Island Rock Wall, and on the southern shore is Point Pinole and its adjoining regional parkland. On the shore of San Rafael there's another park, China Camp.

China Camp State Park offers the best territory for windsurfing, at China Camp Village and Bullhead Flats. The latter commonly gets powerful winds and is recommended only for experts. Both launch points have beaches, and China Camp Village is set along a protected cove.

A rare opportunity to see many unusual birds up close is presented in San Rafael at Loch Lomond Harbor at the end of Dock A. This is the site of a small bait shop whose owner, Keith Fraser, has taken to feeding a variety of birds; some will even let him feed them by hand. They include a night heron, blue heron, pelican, snowy egret, and giant egret, along with many other suspects, such as gulls and cormorants. Bring your camera.

⑪ Carquinez Strait/ Suisun Bay

Location: From the Carquinez Bridge to Pittsburg; map E1, grid a6.

Directions: From San Francisco turn east on Interstate 80 and drive approximately 25 miles to Hercules. Turn east on Highway 4, or continue six miles on Interstate 80 to Vallejo, then turn east on Interstate 780. Access is available off roads that intersect Highway 4 and Interstate 780.

Access: Paved ramps are available at the following locations:

Benicia Marina, Benicia: From Interstate 780 in Benicia, take the Fifth Street exit and follow Fifth Street south for approximately one-half mile to the marina. At the street's end turn right and proceed to the boat ramp. For information phone (707) 745-2628.

Harris Yacht Harbor, Bay Point: From Highway 4 west of Antioch, take the Bay Point turnoff and bear left on Willow Pass Road. Go through a few stoplights and turn left on Port Chicago Highway. Continue down the hill to the marina area and turn right toward Harris Harbor. For information phone (925) 458-1606.

Martinez Marina, Martinez: From Interstate 680 in Martinez, take the Marina Vista exit (the northernmost Martinez exit) and turn west on Marina Vista. Stay on Marina Vista until you reach Ferry Street; then turn right, cross the train tracks, and drive into the marina area. Stay on the main road; the launch ramp is at the end. For information phone (925) 313-0942.

McAvoy Yacht Harbor, Bay Point: From Highway 4 west of Antioch, take the Bay Point turnoff and bear left on Willow Pass Road. Go through a few stoplights and turn left on Port Chicago Highway. Continue down the hill to the marina area and proceed straight to McAvoy Harbor. For information phone (925) 458-2568.

Pittsburg Marina, Pittsburg: From Highway 4 west of Antioch, take the Pittsburg Marina exit and head north to Third Street. Turn left on Third Street, drive to Marina Boulevard; then turn right, and follow Marina Boulevard to the launch ramp at the road's end. For information phone (925) 439-4958.

Vallejo Public Ramp, Vallejo: From Interstate 80 in Vallejo, take the Interstate 780 exit and turn south on Curtola Parkway. Continue to the public ramp, located adjacent to Brinkman's Marine. For information phone (707) 642-7521.

Facilities, fees: Lodging and full facilities are available in Vallejo, Benicia, and Martinez. A picnic area is provided at Benicia State Recreation Area. Full-service marinas are available at the boat ramps listed above. There are no boat rental services in the area. Fees are charged for boat launching.

Water sports, restrictions: A sandy beach for swimmers and windsurfers is located at Ninth Street in Benicia.

Contact: For boating information and regulations, contact the US Coast Guard, Bay Area Marine Safety Office, (510) 437-3073. For conditions and specific information, contact Benicia Marina, (707) 745-2628.

About Carquinez Strait/Suisun Bay: This is where a thousand miles of Delta waterways join and pour into the salty environs of the San Francisco Bay. The result is Suisun Bay and the narrow Carquinez Strait, a largely brackish and muddy-colored water that is perfect for fishing and bird-watching, with the bonus of some unusual features.

The most unusual of these is the Mothball Fleet, rows of old navy ships set out to pasture along the north shore, just across the water from Martinez. This is a famous fishing spot for sturgeon, and you might see dozens of boats anchored near the old Mothball Fleet when the fishing is good.

Another unique element is the old army munitions dump, set along the south shore east of Martinez. Note that this area is restricted to boaters and is under surveillance. If you get too close, you will be told to back off, and failing to do that, you will be arrested. The northeast end of Suisun Bay is called Honker Bay and Grizzly Bay, and it abuts the Grizzly Island Wildlife Area. This is an outstanding habitat for nesting ducks, particularly mallards, and boaters may even be treated to a rare sighting of tule elk near the shore. Grizzly Bay is shallow, and most boaters will venture in along a string of markers called the Firing Line.

While the muddy-looking water may not appear too appealing for swimming or windsurfing, diehards do both here. For access there is only one good beach area, at Ninth Street in Benicia, where people often swim and windsurf.

On a rare day you'll see personal watercraft carousing around the Mothball Fleet, but they drive anglers crazy, and there have been several confrontations on the water. Personal watercraft will find a better area upstream in Honker Bay or near Chipps Island.

---

⑫ Santa Cruz Shoreline

Location: At Santa Cruz Wharf; map F1, grid b4.

Directions: From the San Francisco Bay Area, drive south on Highway 1 and take any Santa Cruz or Capitola exit west to reach the shoreline. For specific directions, see "Access."

Access: Boat launching facilities are available at the following locations:

Capitola Wharf: From Highway 1 in

Capitola, take 41st Avenue west to Capitola Road. Turn left and drive down toward the water. When you see the Venetian Hotel, turn on a small signed access road and proceed to the wharf, where you'll find a hoist.

Santa Cruz Harbor: From Highway 1 in Santa Cruz, head west on Soquel Avenue and follow the signs to the harbor. A paved launch ramp is available.

Facilities, fees: Lodging, campgrounds, and supplies are available in Santa Cruz. Santa Cruz Municipal Wharf and Capitola Wharf offer full-service marinas and fishing boat rentals. There is a fee for boat launching.

Water sports, restrictions: Waterskiing and personal watercraft are permitted; craft must stay within 300 yards of the shoreline. Windsurfing is also permitted. Wet suits are recommended. Swimming is possible all along the shoreline; there are sandy beaches staffed with lifeguards.

Contact: Santa Cruz Harbor, (831) 475-6161; Capitola Wharf, (831) 462-2208. For general information about the area, contact the Santa Cruz Area Chamber of Commerce, (831) 423-1111.

About the Santa Cruz Shoreline: Santa Cruz is a beautiful area, set on the northwestern tip of Monterey Bay. Among the many highlights are a rejuvenated boardwalk, pretty beach, and nearby redwood forests. Access is excellent, and the place offers boat rentals, launches, and charters.

In fact, this is the only coastal area in the Bay Area region where boat rentals are available. Skiffs with motors can be rented at Capitola Wharf and Santa Cruz Wharf. This is where the "Stienstra Navy"—my dad, Robert Stienstra, Sr.; my older brother, Bob Stienstra, Jr.; and I—took its first voyages. We rented a boat out of Capitola and rowed out to fish near the kelp beds. Some 30 years later, anybody can do the same.

Many other water sports and activities are possible in the area. The most popular are lying around on the beach, surfing, lying around on the beach, waterskiing, lying around on the beach, whale watching, fishing, and—lying around on the beach. The entire Santa Cruz shoreline is one big, sandy beach, excellent for sunbathing and beachcombing.

Charter boats make whale watching runs in the winter, salmon fishing trips in the spring, and deep-sea trips for rockfish in the summer and fall. Monterey Bay is often far more calm than the ocean north of Pigeon Point, making it ideal for those who are novices at coastal boating.

On the odd day it is even calm enough for waterskiing, though you rarely will see anyone doing this. Riding personal watercraft is a much more common sport, with people launching at the ramp at Santa Cruz Harbor and heading off from there. When the water is rough, inexperienced skiers (and boaters, too, of course) should either play it safe or wait for a calmer day.

Sailing is popular in Santa Cruz, and boaters will often use a motor assist to get farther out to sea, then pick up the coastal winds, and head off into the wild blue yonder.

The water is a little cold for swimming, typically around 55 to 60 degrees , but it's okay for a dunk. Surfers, windsurfers, and anyone else planning to be in the water for extended periods of time should wear a wet suit. This area is extremely popular with surfers despite a few nasty shark bite incidents. Shark attacks are rare, and surfers are most vulnerable in late winter and early spring, when birthing elephant seals at Año Nuevo to the north attract great white sharks who come to the area to feed. The most popular time for surfing is in the summer, of course. This is a college town, so there are lots of young surfer types using the beaches year-round, and a fair amount of tourist traffic keeps the shoreline busy.

While windsurfing is only fair in the vicinity of Santa Cruz, just ahead about 10 miles north on Highway 1 to Davenport, and you'll find one of the prime windsurfing spots in California. A large, beautiful beach is bordered by sheer cliffs to the south. The combination of north winds in the spring, the beach, and the cliffs makes some of the best conditions imaginable for windsurfing and hang gliding, for experts only. Be prepared for a remarkable sight: windsurfing masters clipping along on their sailboards at high speeds, often whipping just beyond the breaker line and, rarely, even plunging right through ocean breakers—while hang gliders hover about like giant pelicans.

⑬ Monterey Bay Shoreline

Location: Along Monterey Bay; map F1, grid b6.

Directions: From the San Francisco Bay Area, drive south on Highway 1 to Monterey. For specific directions, see Boat ramp.

Access: Boat launching facilities are available at the following locations:

Breakwater Cove Marina: From Highway 1 in Monterey, take the Pacific Grove–Del Monte Boulevard exit (don't take the Del Monte exit in Marina, located a few miles north of Monterey). Turn west and drive through a tunnel (the road turns into Lighthouse Boulevard). Immediately after the tunnel turn right on Foam Street and continue to Cannery Row. Turn right and proceed straight, down to the parking area. A paved public launch is available.

Monterey Harbor: From Highway 1 in Monterey, take the Pacific Grove–Del Monte Boulevard exit (don't take the Del Monte exit in Marina, located a few miles north of Monterey). Turn toward the water and follow the signs to Fisherman's Wharf

and Monterey Harbor. Two paved public ramps are available: one at the Monterey Yacht Club, and the other at the Coast Guard station.

Moss Landing Harbor: From Watsonville drive six miles south on Highway 1. Look for the PG&E power stacks; the boat ramp entrance is just north of them, next to the Little Baja store.

Facilities, fees: Campgrounds are available at Sunset State Beach in Watsonville and in the town of Marina. Lodging and supplies can be obtained in Monterey. Full-service marinas are available in Monterey. No motorized boat rentals are available. You can rent kayaks at Monterey Bay Kayaks, (831) 373-5357. There are fees for boat launching at private marinas; public ramps are free. Additional parking fees are often charged.

Water sports, restrictions: Waterskiing and personal watercraft are permitted; craft must stay within 300 yards of the shoreline. Personal watercraft can only be launched at the Coast Guard launch ramp, on the northwest side of Monterey Harbor. Windsurfing is permitted; a popular spot is at Del Monte Beach near Monterey Harbor. Wet suits are recommended. You can swim at several state beaches, including Moss Landing State Beach, Marina State Beach, Monterey State Beach, Asilomar State Beach, and Carmel River State Beach.

Contact: Monterey Harbor, (831) 646-3950; Breakwater Cove Marina, (831) 373-7857; Moss Landing Harbor, (831) 633-2461. For general information contact the Monterey Peninsula Chamber of Commerce, (831) 649-1770, or the Carmel Visitor Bureau, (831) 624-2522.

About the Monterey Bay Shoreline: Monterey Bay is often one of the most stunning places in the world. Even the water has a special quality—more of a deeper blue green than the murky greens to the north off San Francisco. The water tends to be calmer and warmer than at points north, and when it laps at the sandy beaches you might think you were experiencing a calm day in Hawaii.

What you have is the perfect setting for powerboating, sailing, windsurfing, and sea kayaking, all of which are quite popular in Monterey.

For first-timers the best kickoff to your visit is a tour of the Monterey Aquarium, which provides not only great entertainment, but a good orientation to Monterey Bay. You will learn how upwelling in the deep underwater canyon in the bay's center starts the marine food chain, giving rise to a flourishing aquatic environment. After that lesson you will appreciate Monterey Bay even more, regardless of your favorite sport.

Most powerboaters launch to go fishing (for salmon in the spring and rockfish in the summer). Restrictions on commercial fishing, especially the ban on gill nets, have helped fisheries make a major comeback here. If you fish here in March, you might get a bonus, because the launch ramp at Moss Landing is often within close range of the salmon.

Monterey is also a great spot for sailing and windsurfing. Afternoon winds out of the north are common, and the beautiful scenery makes it all the more special. The best spot for windsurfing is right smack in Monterey, near the harbor. Water temperatures are typically 56 to 64 degrees, spring through fall, respectively, and everybody wears wet suits.

For a truly unique and wondrous experience, you should consider sea kayaking. It is possible to paddle around in kelp beds as sea otters actually play hide-and-seek with you. Sea kayaks are built completely differently from ocean kayaks; they're much wider, flatter, and longer, sometimes with enough space for two paddlers. That means they are stable, don't tip over, and can make for an intimate experience without getting too intimate with the water. Severe regulations regarding personal watercraft guar-antee quiet water.

There are also several designated beaches for swimming, sunbathing, and beachcombing, but the water is quite cold. A better choice for swimming is the large pool at the Monterey Sports Center.

Expect lots of tourists, along with heavy fishing traffic. After all, this is one of the most beautiful places on Earth. When you experience it from on the water, it can also be one of the most special.

⑭ Morro Bay

Location: North of San Luis Obispo; map G2, grid h3.

Directions: From San Luis Obispo drive 13 miles north on Highway 1 until you reach Morro Bay. Take the Main Street exit and turn right. Continue up the grade, under the freeway, to Beach Street. Turn right, continue to Embarcadero Street, turn right again, and continue to the facilities at the bay.

Access: Boat launching facilities are available at the following locations:

Morro Bay City Public Launch: From Highway 1 in Morro Bay, take the Main Street exit and turn right. Continue up the grade, under the freeway, to Beach Street. Turn right and continue to Embarcadero; turn on Embarcadero Street and continue to the paved ramp at the street's end.

Morro Bay State Park: From Highway 1 take the Morro Bay State Park exit and drive west to the boat ramp. A primitive hand launch is provided for nonmotorized craft only.

Facilities, fees: Lodging, restaurants, and supplies are available in the town of Morro Bay. A campground is provided at Morro Bay State Park. Canoes and kayaks are available for rent at Morro Bay Marina, (805) 772-8085, and at the Morro Bay State Park Marina, (805) 772-8796. Access to Morro Bay is free.

Water sports, restrictions: A 5 mph speed limit is strictly enforced within the bay. Waterskiing and personal watercraft are not allowed. Windsurfing is permitted. Swimming is possible at a beach near what is called "The Rock" at the bay's north end.

Contact: For general information and a free travel packet, contact the Morro Bay Chamber of Commerce, (805) 772-4467. For boating information contact the Morro Bay Harbormaster's Office, (805) 772-6254; Morro Bay Harbor Patrol, (805) 772-1214; or Morro Bay State Park, (805) 772-7434.

About Morro Bay: The drive to Morro Bay along beautiful Highway 1 can be worth the trip itself. Cruising the great coastal highway, whether you're coming from the north or the south, is one of the most satisfying driving experiences anywhere. But even more compelling attractions await your arrival.

Morro Bay is an excellent vacation destination. This is a good fishing town that offers the opportunities to fish aboard a rental boat or on a charter, or to see migrating whales in the winter—two activities that have become very popular.

In the harbor itself there is a paved boat ramp that is free to the public. The 5 mph speed limit in the harbor is designed to prohibit watercraft, as well as keep boat wakes down, in order to ensure that the surrounding habitat for marine birds is not disturbed.

The area rarely gets much wind in the summer, a great plus. Another bonus is that the fishing grounds are nearby. Halibut can often be caught right in Morro Bay during the summer months, and rockfish are abundant at nearby offshore reefs.

The best spot for swimming is at the beach at Morro Rock. The rest of Morro Bay is poor for swimming and windsurfing, and the water clarity is typically poor.

Morro Bay really gets popping in the summer with the many vacationers who stop by as they cruise the coastal highway.

In the off-season the place takes on a completely different character, often very quiet and with relatively few people.

One safety note is that in periods of heavy ocean swells, which occur rarely in the winter and spring months, boaters heading out of Morro Bay should use extreme caution or even delay their trips. Although extremely rare, just outside the bay those big swells have been known to trap boats, which, if they broach, can flip over. Not a happy time.

On the average day, however, what you'll find at Morro Bay is a little wind, fairly benign seas, and the unusual opportunity to rent a boat and catch fish in the bay after only a short ride.

⓯ San Luis Obispo Bay

Location: South of San Luis Obispo at Port San Luis; map G2, grid j4.

Directions: From San Luis Obispo drive south on US 101 to the San Luis Drive exit. Turn west and continue until you reach Avila Drive. Turn right and continue west to the parking area at the street's end.

Access: A hoist is provided at Port San Luis Harbor; follow the directions above to reach it.

Facilities, fees: A campground with hot mineral pools is located at Avila Beach. Picnic areas, pier, and supplies are available at the harbor. Lodging is available inland at San Luis Obispo. Access is free. There is a fee to use the boat hoist.

Water sports, restrictions: Waterskiing is not recommended. A special area is set aside for personal watercraft. Windsurfing is allowed. Swimming is available all along the shoreline; a good spot is at Avila State Beach.

Contact: For general information and a free travel packet, contact the San Luis Obispo Chamber of Commerce, (805) 781-2777. For boating information contact the

Port San Luis Harbor District, (805) 595-5400; or Port Side Marine Tackleshop, (805) 595-7214.

About San Luis Obispo Bay: The drive to San Luis Obispo is a pretty one, particularly from the south, with the road winding its way along the coast around the Sierra Padre range. As they journey here from LA, big city anglers leave behind the crowds, the traffic, and the stoplights, and instead look forward to the open sea and a great day, free on the earth.

Avila Beach is a popular fishing destination, primarily for charter boat operators, but also for private boaters fishing nearby for calico bass and sand bass. The only major drawback is that boat rentals, once very much in demand, are no longer offered.

Other sports get a fair amount of attention, too. A special area in the harbor is set aside just for watercrafts, and lots of young adults from the nearby university take full advantage of it. Having a separate, marked area for watercrafts is an excellent idea, and is probably the only way to solve water-sport user conflicts.

A wild card here is windsurfing. Conditions can be excellent when winds are high, but you discover that the winds are very inconsistent, and they are down far more often than they are up. Locals have the best prospects, as they are able to respond immediately when they see conditions are good.

Sandy beaches are available all along the shoreline for swimming, wading, sunbathing, and beachcombing. However, don't plan on finding seclusion. During the summer the entire area gets heavy visitor traffic.

⑯ Santa Barbara Shoreline

Location: In Santa Barbara; map H3, grid h5.

Directions: From US 101 southbound take the Castillo exit in Santa Barbara and turn right on Cabrillo Boulevard. Continue to Harbor Way, and turn left. Turn immediately into the parking lot and proceed to the boat ramp. From US 101 northbound take the Cabrillo Way exit and follow Cabrillo to Harbor Way. Proceed as above.

Access: A paved boat ramp is provided at the harbor.

Facilities, fees: A pier, rest rooms, restaurants, and shops are available at the harbor. Full facilities are available in Santa Barbara. Sailboats can be rented at Santa Barbara Sailing Center, (805) 962-2826. They also conduct champagne sunset cruises. There is a fee for parking at the harbor; boat launching is included.

Water sports, restrictions: Waterskiing and personal watercraft are permitted outside of the harbor. Windsurfing is also allowed. Swimming is available at West Beach and Leadbetter Beach, located on either side of the harbor, and all along the shoreline south and north of Santa Barbara.

Contact: Santa Barbara Visitor Center, (805) 965-3021. For boating information contact the Santa Barbara Harbor Department, (805) 564-5520 or the Santa Barbara Sailing Center, 133 Harbor Way, Santa Barbara, CA 93109; (805) 962-2826 or fax (805) 966-7435.

About the Santa Barbara Shoreline: Beautiful beaches? An emerald green sea that's warm to the touch? Waves that often lap at the shore? An excellent boat ramp and harbor with easy access to nearby fishing grounds? Perhaps the best climate anywhere on the California coast?

Right on all counts, and that makes the Santa Barbara coast an extraordinary place: a classic beach area complete with a university and all the extracurricular activities that students bring to the beach.

The first thing you need to know is that the University of California at Santa Barbara is actually located a bit to the north, near

Isla Vista, where the college crowd hangs out. So if you want to join the students, that's the spot. Otherwise, head south of Isla Vista.

Surfing is popular, but conditions are actually only fair at best. What you get most of the time here are surfers floating around on their boards, talking and having a great old time as they await the proverbial "ninth wave" from which surf legends are born. It can be a long wait.

Conditions are better for windsurfing, and the sport is extremely popular at the beaches on either side of the harbor. Winds are not strong; often they're just right, with only a mild chop on the water surface.

That makes the area extremely appealing to watercrafters. In fact, personal watercraft has become such a big thing on weekends that locals have been pushing to restrict watercraft from several spots.

Powerboaters who launch at the harbor discover that boating along this stretch of coastline can be an odyssey through dense kelp forests, oil platform drilling rigs, and the Channel Islands. A variety of offshore trips are offered by different charter boat companies in the area.

⑰ Ventura Shoreline

Location: North of Los Angeles; map H3, grid j8.

Directions: From Los Angeles drive north on US 101 to Ventura. Take the Seaward exit and turn left. Continue to Harbor Boulevard, turn left, and drive 1.5 miles to Schooner Street. Turn right and continue until the street dead-ends at Anchors Way. Turn right and continue a short distance to the harbor on the left.

Access: A paved ramp is located at the harbor.

Facilities, fees: A full-service marina, restaurants, shops, rest rooms, and a pier are provided at the harbor. Full facilities are available in Ventura. There is a fee for parking.

Water sports, restrictions: Waterskiing and personal watercraft are allowed outside of the harbor. Windsurfing and swimming are available at the swimming beach in the harbor. You can also swim at several state beaches along the surrounding shoreline, including Emma Wood State Beach, San Buenaventura State Beach, Peninsula State Beach, and McGrath State Beach.

Contact: Ventura Chamber of Commerce, (805) 648-2875 or fax (805) 648-3535. For boating information phone Ventura Harbor Village, (805) 644-0169.

About the Ventura Shoreline: Any boater who has ever been stuck in highway traffic knows the great value of being on the open ocean, where there are no traffic jams and no stoplights, just boundless water and freedom. That in itself is the greatest value of the Ventura shoreline. Terrible traffic problems are common inland here, but get in a boat, push that throttle forward, and your cares will drop away like waves receding from the beach.

This area is very popular, especially for sunbathing, swimming, and windsurfing. The best spots for these activities are at the beach in the Ventura Harbor, as well as at the nearby state beaches, including Emma Wood State Beach, San Buenaventura State Beach, Peninsula State Beach, and McGrath State Beach.

Outside the harbor, riding personal watercraft is another favorite. Although the water can be a bit choppy, it is actually often just right, with enough of a bump to add some thrills to the ride.

Just about the only downer is that there are no rental boats available, only partyboat charters for fishing. These operators fish the adjacent coastal waters, which are among the most distinctive in Southern California. Directly offshore of Port Hueneme in Oxnard is the Hueneme Canyon, a massive underwater gorge that drops quickly to never-never land. Yet just north of the canyon, right offshore of Ventura, are the Ventura Flats, and just 15 miles west are the tops of an undersea mountain range, including Anacapa Island and Santa Rosa Island.

⑱ Channel Islands Harbor

Location: Offshore of Oxnard; map l3, grid a9.

Directions: From Los Angeles drive north on US 101 to the Victoria Avenue–Channel Islands Harbor exit. Turn left and continue to the harbor.

Access: Follow the directions above to the harbor and look for the sign for the launch ramp on Victoria Avenue. A paved ramp and a hoist are available. Note: If you reach the Coast Guard office, you've gone too far.

Facilities, fees: Full-service marinas are provided at the harbor. Full facilities are available in Ventura and Oxnard. There are fees for parking and using the boat hoist. Island Packers offers round-trip boat transportation to Anacapa Island, Santa Cruz Island, Santa Barbara Island, Santa Rosa Island, and San Miguel Island. Fares range from $50 to $80, depending on the distance of the trip. Kayak rentals are also available.

Water sports, restrictions: A 5 mph speed limit is strictly enforced within the harbor. Personal watercraft are permitted outside the harbor in front of the breakwater. Waterskiing is not recommended. Windsurfing is permitted. A sandy beach with lifeguards is available in the harbor; you can also swim along the coast at Silver Strand Beach and Hollywood Beach.

Contact: Island Packers, (805) 642-7688; Channel Islands Harbor Patrol, (805) 385-8693; US Coast Guard, (805) 985-9823; Ventura Visitor Bureau, (800) 333-2989 or fax (805) 648-2150.

About Channel Islands Harbor: Venturing out to any of the Channel Islands is one of the greatest boating odysseys in North America. Here is a place of remarkable beauty, with perhaps the best sea kayaking anywhere, as well as outstanding camping and hiking. Furthermore it's just far enough away to make the trip feel rare and special.

The Channel Islands include Anacapa Island, Santa Cruz Island, Santa Rosa Island, San Miguel Island, and Santa Barbara Island. The best way to access them is by boarding a charter boat run by Island Packers and making the long but fun trip out to your chosen destination. The boats are often accompanied on the route by porpoises who jump alongside as if they were in an aquatic circus.

The rugged island chain is an extraordinary habitat surrounded by pristine, clear waters, with hardly anyone around for miles and miles—well, at least 20 miles. These offshore retreats are the perfect places to hike, swim, snorkel, and camp. And with remarkable sea caves, there is no better setting for kayaking, even for people who have never tried it.

Kayaking here is a dreamlike experience. The water is warm, typically about 70 degrees in the summer and fall, quite calm, and much clearer than along the inshore waters. You can see deep into the water, and you'll probably spot some bright gold fish; they are garibaldi, a protected species and now the state marine fish. Island Packers provides a guide and equipment. After practicing for 20 minutes, you will have mastered the easy paddle strokes and will get a chance to explore the mazelike cave systems. These caves have been carved out by thousands of years of sea action and add a mysterious dimension to the trip—one that you will never forget.

Here is a synopsis of the trips to each island:

Anacapa Island: Little Anacapa, long and narrow, is known for its awesome caves, cliffs, and sea-lion rookeries near huge kelp beds. After landing you face a 154-step staircase trail that brings you to a perch on an ocean bluff. Trails leading from this point provide vast views of the channel. The inshore waters are an ecological preserve loaded with marine life, and because the water is so clear, this makes a great destination for snorkeling. The boat ride takes only 90 minutes.

Santa Barbara Island: A veritable dot of an island set well to the south of the other four, Santa Barbara is known for having miles of hiking trails, solitude, and opportunities for snorkeling, swimming, and excellent viewing of marine mammals. This is a breeding ground for elephant seals; dolphins, sea lions, and whales are all common to the area. Snorkeling here is so fun it can make you ecstatic as you dive amid playful seals. The only negative is the long boat ride, which takes 3.5 hours from the mainland, too long to allow enough time for much recreation on a one-day adventure.

Santa Cruz Island: The Painted Cave of Santa Cruz makes this a world-class destination for kayakers. This is the largest of the islands, making it perfect for camping and multiday visits. The camp is set in a eucalyptus grove in a valley, and there's a trailhead that hikers can take to reach the ridgeline. One great hike is from Pelican Bay to Prisoner's Harbor, a three-miler routed through the island's interior to a beautiful beach. Visitor have the chance to experience some excellent kayaking through sea caves.

San Miguel Island: The most unusual of the five islands, this one is small, distant (located outside the region covered on map I3), and extremely rugged. Unusual birds and abundant wildlife make San Miguel their home. It receives the fewest visitors because getting here takes five hours by boat. A true island wilderness.

Santa Rosa Island: A stand of rare Torrey pines, a three-mile stretch of sand dunes, tide pools, and Indian archaeological sites lure visitors here from Friday through Sunday (no trips are available during the week). Because the boat ride to Santa Rosa takes longer than the one to Santa Cruz, few will try to complete the adventure in one day.

Meanwhile, a variety of additional recreation possibilities await at Channel Islands Harbor on the mainland.

Silver Strand Beach is the most popular area for surfing, windsurfing is good at Hollywood Beach and in the harbor, and personal watercraft are popular just outside the harbor.

Swimmers can head to Silver Strand Beach and Hollywood Beach. The best area for children is at the small beach in the harbor, where there are no currents; it is roped off and lifeguards are present in the summer.

While this area gets a lot of tourist traffic year-round, most of the private boaters are here to fish. However, it is the renowned islands, not the fish, that hold unparalleled appeal.

⑲ Santa Monica–Redondo Shoreline

Location: From Malibu to San Pedro; map I4, grid c5.

Directions: Access is available all along the coast off roads that intersect Highway 1.

Access: Paved launch ramps are provided at the following locations:

Cabrillo Beach, San Pedro: From Los Angeles drive south on Interstate 110 to San Pedro. The interstate ends at Gaffey Street; turn left and travel to 22nd Street. Continue to Pacific, turn right, proceed to the next stoplight, and turn left. Look for the sign for Cabrillo Marine Aquarium and head into the parking lot.

Marina del Rey Public Launch: From Los Angeles drive south on Highway 1 past Venice to Lincoln Boulevard. Turn right on

Lincoln Boulevard and drive to Fiji Way. Turn right on Fiji Way, which leads to Harbor Village. Look for a sign for the boat ramp.

Portofino Inn and Marina, Redondo Beach: From Highway 1 in Redondo Beach, turn west on Burl Street. Burl Street turns into Portofino Way; continue to the hotel and marina at King Harbor.

Facilities, fees: Lodging, restaurants, and shops are available in towns along the coast. Fishing boats and kayaks can be rented at Portofino Marina in Redondo Beach, (310) 379-8481 (ask for Rocky Point). Sailboats and powerboats are rented at EuroSail Charters in San Pedro, (310) 831-2363. Cruises on Los Angeles Harbor are available by reservation through Spirit Cruises in San Pedro, (310) 831-1073. Fees are usually charged for parking and/or boat launching.

Water sports, restrictions: Waterskiing is generally not recommended due to choppy conditions. Personal watercraft are permitted in most areas; check with city harbormasters for specific regulations. Windsurfing is permitted all along the shoreline; the best spot is at Cabrillo Beach in San Pedro. Swimming is possible at numerous beaches all along the shoreline but is usually prohibited in the harbor areas.

Contact: Santa Monica Chamber of Commerce, (310) 393-9825; Marina del Rey Chamber of Commerce, (310) 821-0555; Marina del Rey Harbormaster, (310) 823-7762; Los Angeles Harbor Department, Cabrillo Beach Park, (310) 548-2645; Redondo Beach Chamber of Commerce, (310) 376-6911; Portofino Marina, (310) 379-8481.

About the Santa Monica–Redondo Shoreline: This is where fiction meshes with reality, where it is difficult to discern where illusion ends and real life begins. If you have ever seen one of those grade B beach babe movies, this is where it was filmed. After spending even a few minutes here, you start wondering if everyone else is pretending they are in one of those movies. The scene comes complete with weight-lifting areas and adjacent parkways where unsuspecting newcomers are in danger of being mowed down by in-line skaters and cyclists.

The beach areas are fully developed, complete with lifeguard towers (yeah, just like the movies). Besides lying around in the sun (doesn't anybody work anymore?), the favorite recreation activities are looking at each other (as far as I could tell) and swimming. As for the latter you can swim at any of the beaches along the coast, but not in the harbors.

Windsurfing is only fair, with the best prospects at Cabrillo Beach in San Pedro. Personal watercraft are allowed most everywhere, but there are often designated areas for the sport; sometimes personal watercraft are permitted only in certain harbor sections, but more often they may only be used outside the harbor.

Most of the boaters here are going fishing. Rockfish provides a consistent fishery on the edges of Redondo and Santa Monica Canyons and at the kelp beds offshore of Zuma Beach north of Malibu. Skiffs are rented out in Redondo Harbor, along with an open-water fishing barge, and bonito can provide a fun fishery. When these barges get filled with people, however, they are sometimes called cattle boats.

This place gets tons of traffic. After all, it sits on the edge of one of the most densely populated areas in America. Not only that, but anybody who has ever dreamed of starring in one of those beach movies can simply show up here and act out their own personal screenplay.

⑳ Los Angeles Shoreline

Location: From San Pedro to San Clemente; map I5, grid f0.

Directions: Public access marinas are available at the following locations:

To Long Beach Harbor trom Los Angeles, drive south on Interstate 405 to the Interstate 710 cutoff. Continue south on Interstate 710 (stay in the left-hand lane) and take Shoreline Drive. Continue on Shoreline Drive to the harbor area at Shoreline Village.

To Newport Harbor from Los Angeles, take Interstate 405 south to Highway 55. Drive south to Newport Beach, where the highway becomes Newport Boulevard. Continue past Highway 1. About one-quarter mile past the bridge, Newport Boulevard becomes Balboa Boulevard. Follow the signs to the harbor.

To Dana Point Harbor from Los Angeles, take Interstate 5 south to the Dana Point–Pacific Coast Highway exit. Turn north on Highway 1 and continue to Dana Point Harbor Drive. Continue past Doheny State Beach to Embarcadero Place, then turn left and continue into the harbor.

Access: Paved boat ramps are available at the following locations:

Davies Launch Ramp, Long Beach: From Los Angeles take Interstate 405 south to Interstate 710. Continue south to the Studebaker off-ramp and turn south. Proceed to Second Street and turn right (if you go left, it's Westminster). Continue to Marina Drive, turn right, and make an immediate left at the sign for Davies. For information phone (562) 594-0951.

Embarcadero Marina, Dana Point: From Los Angeles take Interstate 5 south to the Dana Point–Pacific Coast Highway exit. Turn north on Highway 1 and continue to Dana Point Harbor Drive. Continue past Doheny State Beach to Embarcadero Place, then turn left, and continue into the harbor. Both a multilane launch ramp and a hoist are provided. Note: The launch is open 24 hours a day and is a self-service operation; you need exact change ($7) to enter the gate. For information phone (949) 496-6177.

Marine Stadium Ramp, Long Beach: From Los Angeles take Interstate 405 south to Interstate 710. Continue south to the Studebaker off-ramp and turn south. Proceed to Second Street and turn right (if you go left, it's Westminster). Continue to the sign for Mother's Beach and then follow the signs to Marine Stadium.

Newport Dunes Marina, Newport Beach: From Los Angeles take Interstate 405 south to Highway 55 (the sign says "Beach Cities"). Take Highway 55 west (it eventually becomes Newport Boulevard) until you reach Highway 1. Turn south and continue to Jamboree Street. Turn left, continue to Backbay Drive, turn left, and proceed to the boat launching area. For information phone (949) 729-1100.

Sunset Aquatic Marina, Huntington Beach: From Los Angeles take Interstate 405 south to Long Beach and follow the signs for Seal Beach and the Garden Grove Freeway (stay in the far right-hand lanes). Take the Bolsa Chica off-ramp just before the Garden Grove Freeway and head south on Bolsa Chica for roughly five miles to Edinger Street. Turn right and continue toward the harbor. You will cross a bridge; the road makes a sharp left and heads toward the shipyard. Pass the shipyard and follow the signs to the launch ramp. Note: The launch is open 24 hours a day and is a self-service operation; you need exact change ($7) to enter the gate. For information phone (562) 592-2833 or fax (562) 592-1853.

Facilities, fees: Lodging, campgrounds, piers, restaurants, shops, and groceries are available all along the coast. Sailboat rentals are provided in Long Beach at Marina Sailing, (562) 432-4672. Motorboat rentals are available at Davey's Locker in Newport Beach, (949) 673-1434. Resort Water Sports in Newport Beach rents sailboards, sailboats, fishing boats, canoes, and kayaks. Parking and/or boat launching fees are charged at most marinas and launch ramps.

Water sports, restrictions: Waterskiing is generally not recommended due to choppy conditions. Personal watercraft are usually not allowed within harbor areas, but are permitted on the open water. No personal watercraft are allowed from the Huntington Beach launch ramp; you must tow your craft to open water. Windsurfing is possible all along the coast; two popular spots are at the Newport Beach Harbor and at Mother's Beach at Dana Point Harbor. Swimming is possible at any of the beaches along the shoreline; families with children should stick to the Mother's Beaches in the city harbors, which offer lifeguards and safe swimming conditions for children.

Contact: Long Beach Visitor Bureau, (800) 452-7829; Long Beach Harbormaster, (310) 437-0041; Newport Beach Chamber of Commerce, (949) 729-4400; Newport Beach Harbormaster, (949) 644-3044; Dana Point Chamber of Commerce, (949) 496-1555; Dana Point Harbormaster, (949) 496-1094. For specific boating information phone any of the marinas listed above.

About the Los Angeles Shoreline: The closest thing to freedom in Southern California is time on the open ocean, cruising across the smooth briny green: no traffic jams, no stoplights, no concrete, no angry people, and no problems. You just get the wide-open sea, the friendly hum of a boat engine, and a clean wake as you leave your troubles behind on the mainland.

This stretch of coast is extremely popular with tourists. If you don't have a boat that will take you to the open ocean, don't come here hoping to find peace and quiet, because you will never find it. But there is much to do. This area is fully developed, with huge, sandy beaches, and is just the place for anyone who is looking for the quintessential Southern California beach experience. Every water sport can be practiced here.

With a boat you can access a tremendous variety of habitat settings, most of which are frequented by fishermen. They include inshore kelp beds off Point Vicente, off Royal Palms State Beach, south of Newport, northwest of Laguna Beach, south of Dana Point, between San Clemente and Dana Harbor, and between San Clemente and San Mateo Point, all good spots for catching bass and rockfish. There are also flat-bottomed areas—primarily mud and sand—offshore of Huntington Beach, just off Point Fermin, and in San Pedro Bay, places that attract halibut in the summer. There are both shallow and deepwater reefs; the largest reef area is just beyond the 50-fathom line west of Huntington Beach. Finally, there are tremendous underwater canyons, the most famous being the Newport Submarine Canyon, located southwest of the pier at Newport Beach, and the Santa Monica Canyon, located in the center of Santa Monica Bay.

Along the near shore surfing, swimming, sunbathing, windsurfing, and personal watercraft are all popular. For special regulations see "Water sports/restrictions."

Huntington Beach is a hot spot for surfing. As far as swimming goes, any of the beaches along the shoreline will do; families with children should stick to the Mother's Beaches in the city harbors, which are overseen by lifeguards and have safe water conditions for youngsters.

㉑ Oceanside Shoreline

Location: North of San Diego; map J5, grid b9.

Directions: From Interstate 5 at Oceanside, take the Oceanside-Harbor Drive exit. Turn west and continue to the harbor.

Access: A paved ramp is located at Oceanside Harbor. Take Interstate 5 to the Oceanside–Harbor Drive exit and turn west.

At the dead-end (look for the Jolly Roger sign), turn left and continue to the bottom of the hill, bear left again, on South Harbor Drive. Continue to a stop sign, turn right, and proceed two blocks to the ramp.

Facilities, fees: Campgrounds and lodging are provided in Oceanside. A picnic area and some supplies are available at the harbor. There is a parking fee at the harbor.

Water sports, restrictions: Waterskiing and personal watercraft are permitted outside the harbor. Windsurfing is not recommended. There are several beaches for swimming along the coast.

Contact: Oceanside Chamber of Commerce, (760) 722-1534 or fax (760) 722-8336.

About the Oceanside Shoreline: The quaint Southern California town of Oceanside is the jump-off point for a visit to one of the prettiest coastal stretches in America, with long sandy beaches, a warm sea, and outstanding boating.

The beaches are extraordinary, expansive and clean, with waves that often lap at the land. The water temperature is tepid most of the year and downright warm in El Niño years, perfect for playing in. This is no secret, of course, and tons of people flock here throughout summer to take advantage of the conditions.

There is just one boat ramp, the only ramp for many miles around with direct access to the coast. Most of the boaters here are fishermen who have discovered that it only takes a short ride, two to three miles either northwest or southwest of the harbor, to reach underwater ledges where fishing prospects are good for a variety of rockfish.

For nonboaters there are charter operators who run fishing trips daily. In El Niño years when the water is warm, abundant bait fish populations near the coast can attract many migratory fish, even marlin and tuna, within relatively close range of the shore. There are also trips that head off-

shore to Catalina Island and, occasionally, to San Clemente Island.

Sea kayaks are available for rent here (see "Facilities"), and this is an excellent location for learning the sport. That is because the water is often warm and the seas benign, and you can paddle away in the mild surf or beyond. Doing so can provide a great sensation of freedom, especially when the beaches are very crowded.

Special Note: Boaters venturing out near San Clemente Island should monitor channel 16 on the marine radio for special closures. San Clemente is a Naval gunnery range, and nearby waters are occasionally closed to boating.

㉒ Agua Hedionda Lagoon

Location: Near Carlsbad; map J5, grid c9.

Directions: From Oceanside drive south on Interstate 5 to Tamarack Street. Turn left, travel to Adams Street, then turn right, and follow the road to Chiquapin. Continue to Harrison Street and follow Harrison Street to the lagoon.

Access: A paved ramp is located on the lagoon's north end.

Facilities, fees: Campsites are available at Carlsbad State Beach. A picnic area and a snack bar are provided at the lagoon. You must obtain a permit and show proof of insurance before you may boat here; phone the marina for details. Waterskiing and personal watercraft lessons and rentals are available. There are fees for boat launching and parking.

Water sports, restrictions: The speed limit is 45 mph. Waterskiing, personal watercraft, and windsurfing are permitted, but retricted to a specified area. Swimming is not allowed.

Contact: Snug Harbor Marina, (760) 434-3089.

About Agua Hedionda Lagoon: Wild

times are the order of the day at this saltwater lagoon, where the rules are designed primarily for speed demons. Exclusive? Yes. Crazy? Yes. Popular? You better believe it.

What you've got here is a spot where jet boats will tow water-skiers at up to 50 mph (no kidding). The boats are loud and really let it rip, often shooting engine spray 50 feet into the sky. Every once in a while, somebody will plow into a shoal in a spectacular crash.

Then you have the windsurfers, who damn near fly across the place when the north wind is whipping. This is for experts only, and even they have to come with their attitudes properly adjusted to deal with plenty of fast company.

From November to February the place is only open on weekends and you must make reservations if you want to boat. In addition, boaters must show proof of insurance coverage of at least $300,000 before they are allowed on the water.

When you show up with a boat and someone asks to see your insurance policy, well, that should tell you everything you need to know about Agua Hedionda.

㉓ Mission Bay

Location: Northwest of San Diego; map J5, grid g9.

Directions: From Interstate 5 north of San Diego, take the Sea World Drive exit. Turn west and travel to Mission Bay Drive. Continue west to the bay.

Access: Boat launching facilities are available at the following locations:

Campland on the Bay: From Interstate 5 northbound in San Diego, take the Grand Avenue exit and stay in the left lane. At the first stoplight turn left on Grand Avenue and continue to Olney. Turn left and follow Olney to its end; proceed into the resort. From Interstate 5 southbound take the Balboa–Garnet Avenue exit and proceed to Grand Avenue. Turn right, drive to Olney, and take a left into the resort. Both a ramp and a sling hoist are provided. For information phone (619) 581-4200.

Dana Landing Marina: From Interstate 5 in San Diego, take the Sea World Drive exit and turn west. Continue past the main Sea World entrance to Ingraham Street and turn right. Drive to the first stoplight and turn left on South Shores. Follow the road as it loops around and proceed into the launching area. For information phone (619) 224-2513.

De Anza Harbor Resort: From Interstate 5 in San Diego, take the Claremont Drive exit and turn left. At the first stop sign, turn right on North Mission Bay Drive. Follow it for 1.5 miles and look for the De Anza Harbor sign on the left. Turn right into the resort. For information phone (619) 273-3211.

Facilities, fees: You can camp at Campland on the Bay. Supplies, restaurants, and shops are available on the bay. Boats are rented out at Seaforth Boat Rentals. There may be a fee for boat launching.

Water sports, restrictions: A 5 mph speed limit is strictly enforced on the northern bay, and on the entire bay after sunset. Waterskiing, personal watercraft, windsurfing, and swimming are permitted in designated areas.

Contact: San Diego Coastal Division, (619) 221-8901; Campland on the Bay Marina, (619) 581-4224; Sea World Marina, (619) 226-3915; Seaforth Boat Rentals, (619) 223-1681.

About Mission Bay: Mission Bay is treated like private parkland, even like a big lake, and its preeminent qualities attract unbelievable numbers of visitors. The bay has 27 miles of shoreline, expansive beach frontage within walking distance of shops, and ocean access for boats.

The place provides complete facilities,

and all water sports are allowed, with waterskiing and windsurfing being extremely popular. But with so many people, it sometimes feels as if you have to fight for even a small piece of the action, even down to finding a parking spot.

If you can get past the reality of the crowds, which some people cannot, you'll find it is quite beautiful here, with calm, warm water and often perfect weather, temperate with light coastal breezes.

Boaters have a tremendous advantage since they are able to leave the beach and tourist hordes behind and head off across the bay or if they want, out to the ocean. Most of the boaters who head to the open sea are fishermen, who have many outstanding fishing grounds nearby to choose from. A series of easily accessible kelp forests provide havens for a wide variety of species; one large expanse of kelp is located between Point La Jolla on south past Bird Rock, and another is set to the south, spanning from offshore *Ocean Beach* to Point Loma. In addition, directly west of Mission Bay between kelp and Point Loma kelp there is a flat-bottomed area within easy reach of small boats; you'll find good halibut fishing there in the spring.

Also, several party boat operators run trips from the bay. If this interests you, always get a reservation. These boats often fill up during the summer, and it can be very difficult to get a spot if you show up on the fly.

㉔ San Diego Bay

Location: At San Diego; map J6, grid h0.
Directions: From Interstate 5 in San Diego, take the Hawthorne Street/Airport exit. Turn west on Harbor Drive and continue to the harbor.
Access: Paved boat ramps are available at the following locations:

Chula Vista Public Ramp: From Interstate 5 take the J Street exit and drive to a stop sign. The road becomes Marina Parkway; continue straight and look for the sign for the boat ramp.

Coronado Public Ramp: From Interstate 5 take the Coronado exit, cross the bridge, then turn south on Silver Strand Boulevard, and look for the launching area on the right.

Shelter Cove Public Launch: From Interstate 5 take the Rosecrans exit and head west for approximately four miles to Shelter Island Drive. Turn left and proceed around the traffic circle to the launching area on the left.

Facilities, fees: Full-service marinas, restaurants, lodging, and supplies are available at the bay. Boats can be rented at Seaforth Boat Rentals, (619) 233-9311; Coronado Boat Rentals, (619) 437-1514; Harbor Sailboats, (619) 291-9568. Boat launching is free; there may be a fee to park.

Water sports, restrictions: There are designated areas for waterskiing and personal watercraft. Windsurfing is permitted throughout the bay. An excellent swimming beach is available at Point Loma.

Contact: San Diego Bay Harbor Patrol, (619) 686-6272; San Diego Visitor's Bureau, (619) 232-3101. For information on fishing boats, see the Foghorn Press book *California Fishing*.

About San Diego Bay: This may be a world-class destination for fishing, but boaters, too, find that the remarkable marine beauty, warm water, and benign seas put San Diego Bay and the nearby coastline in a class rarely seen anywhere in the United States.

Unfortunately, it's often very crowded. To deal with the large number of visitors, the people who make the rules have established extremely complex boating regulations that permit all water sports but only in designated areas within the bay. If you are new to the area or are unsure about the regulations, contact the San Diego Bay Harbor Patrol before heading out. Failure to heed any of the rules can result in an immediate citation.

Some people compare San Diego Bay to Mission Bay. But while both are extremely popular, the activities at San Diego Bay are more spread out, so you don't get the suffocating congestion that sometimes occurs at Mission Bay. In San Diego Bay itself, waterskiing and personal watercraft are popular, but again, are permitted only in designated areas. Windsurfing is permitted throughout the bay. Swimmers will discover a fine beach at Point Loma.

The main attraction, however, is fishing, and some of the most famous long-range boats in the world are based here. The *Royal Polaris, Polaris Supreme, Red Rooster,* and *Qualifier* are among some 50 boats that take people out to fish. There are quick trips for albacore, yellowtail, or white sea bass at Coronado and Catalina Islands, and more extensive trips lasting from a week to 10 days that head all the way south of Cabo San Lucas to Clarion Island and other regional hot spots.

When there are multiple hookups, it can become absolute bedlam, with fishers ducking under each other's rods and lines, chasing the fish along the railing, often in different directions. Yes, this is some of the most exciting fishing you can find anywhere in the world.

ABCs
of the
California
Boating Law

Preparation

Education

The Department of Boating and Waterways recommends taking a boating-safety class offered by the U.S. Coast Guard Auxiliary, the U.S. Power Squadrons, or certain chapters of the American Red Cross. For more information on the Coast Guard Auxiliary and Power Squadron classes, call:

Toll-Free:

U.S. Coast Guard Auxiliary:	**(800) 869-SAIL(7245)**
U.S. Power Squadrons:	**(800) SEA-SKIL (732-7545)**
U.S. Coast Guard Customer Infoline:	**(800) 368-5647**

In addition, the Department of Boating and Waterways offers a free home-study guide called the *California Boating Safety Course*.

Weather

Before you begin a cruise, check the local weather and sea conditions. Detailed information can be obtained by tuning to local radio stations or the National Weather Radio broadcasts on frequencies of 162.400, 162.475, and 162.550 MHz in areas where available, or by consulting local newspapers.

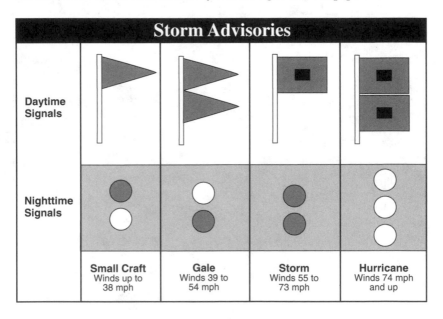

Storm Advisories

	Small Craft Winds up to 38 mph	Gale Winds 39 to 54 mph	Storm Winds 55 to 73 mph	Hurricane Winds 74 mph and up
Daytime Signals				
Nighttime Signals				

Note: In some areas, the display of storm-advisory flags has been discontinued. Boaters should always check current weather conditions before getting under way.

At selected locations in and near boating areas, storm advisories are displayed by flag hoists or lights. Coast Guard stations and many marinas no longer display storm-advisory flags. Remaining display points are located at some park ranger stations, marinas, or municipal piers. A boater should become familiar with the display stations in the area and the meanings of the signals.

EPIRB or VHF Marine Radio Licensing Information

For information on getting a license for a VHF marine radio or Emergency Position Indicating Radio Beacon (EPIRB), contact the U.S. Federal Communications Commission (FCC) at (800) 418-3676 for forms, or (717) 337-1311 for assistance.

Fueling

Most fires happen after fueling. To prevent fires, follow these rules:
- Don't smoke or strike matches.
- Shut off motors. Turn off electric equipment.
- Close all windows, doors, and openings.
- Take portable tanks out of the boat and fill them on the dock.
- Keep the filling nozzle in contact with the tank.
- Wipe up any spilled gas. Discard the cloth in a safe manner.
- Ventilate for at least five minutes. Sniff to make sure there is no gasoline odor anywhere in the boat.
- Periodically check the system for fuel leaks.
- Visually check for leaks or fuel in the bilges.

Boat Capacity

Single-hull motorboats less than 20 feet in length manufactured after 1972 must display capacity and safe-horsepower information. The maximum weight in persons, gear, and motors is offered as a guide to boaters, and should not be exceeded. It is not a violation of federal or California state law to exceed recommended maximums. However, other states may cite an operator who exceeds capacity and horsepower limitations. Some insurance companies will not insure craft exceeding horsepower maximums, and some boat manufacturers will void any applicable warranties for the same reason.

Loading

It's the operator's responsibility to ensure that supplies are carefully loaded and passengers are properly seated. Remember:
- Spread weight evenly.
- Fasten gear to prevent shifting.
- Keep passengers seated.
- Don't overload.

Checklist and Float Plan

CHECKLIST

Before embarking on a cruise:

1. File a float plan (see below)

2. Give consideration to basic safety items, including the following:

- ☐ Vessel in good condition
- ☐ Vessel properly loaded
- ☐ Ample supply of fuel
- ☐ Check weather reports
- ☐ Compass and charts
- ☐ Good anchoring equipment
- ☐ Bailing device
- ☐ Spare parts
- ☐ First-aid kit

- ☐ Flashlight
- ☐ Tools
- ☐ Extra starting battery
- ☐ Personal flotation devices (Coast Guard-approved)
- ☐ Fire extinguishers (Coast Guard-approved)
- ☐ Visual distress signals
- ☐ Oars or paddles
- ☐ VHF marine radio

3. Cancel your "Float Plan" when you return

FLOAT PLAN

Operator _____
          Name and address of operator   Phone number

A search for an overdue boat has a much greater chance of success if the Coast Guard or other rescue agencies have certain facts. For your own safety, complete this form before leaving on a cruise and leave it with a reliable person who will notify authorities if necessary.

If overdue, contact _____
                  Name and phone number of rescue agency near point of departure

Vessel _____
          Name   CF number   Length

_____
   Power, inboard–outboard   Rig, if sail   Hull color

_____
      Type/style   Range   Speed

Persons _____   **Radio** _____
          Number of persons aboard   Frequencies

Departure _____
              Place   Date/time departed

_____
  Parked car license number   Parked trailer license number   Where parked

Destination _____
              Place   Stops en route   Date/time returned

Important: Don't forget to cancel your float plan when you return.

Aids to Navigation

The waters of the United States are marked for safe navigation by the lateral system of buoyage. This system employs a simple arrangement of colors, shapes, numbers, and light characteristics to show the side on which a buoy should be passed when proceeding in a given direction. The characteristics are determined by the position of the buoy with respect to the navigable channels as the channels are entered from seaward.

The expression "red right returning" has long been used by seafarers as a reminder that red buoys are kept to the starboard (right) side when proceeding from the open sea into port (upstream). Likewise, green buoys are kept to the port (left) side (see page 505). Conversely, when proceeding toward the sea or leaving port, red buoys are kept to the port side and green buoys to the starboard side. Green buoys are always odd-numbered and red buoys are even-numbered. Red and white vertically striped buoys mark the center of the channel.

Uniform State-Waterway Marking System

Most waterways used by boaters are located entirely within the boundaries of the state. The California Uniform State-Waterway Marking System has been devised for these waters. Examples of such aids are found on page 504.

The waterway marking system employs buoys and signs with distinctive, standard shapes to show regulatory or advisory information. These markers are white with black letters and orange borders. They signify speed zones, restricted areas, danger areas, and general information.

Aids to navigation on state waters use red and green buoys to mark channel limits. Red and green buoys are generally used in pairs. The boat should pass between the red buoy and its accompanying green buoy.

Mooring to Buoys

Tying up to or hanging onto any navigation buoy (except a mooring buoy) or beacon is prohibited.

Aids to Navigation

In recent years certain aids to navigation located on coastal and inland waters have been modified. These changes apply to aids used in both the lateral and state-waterway marking systems. (See the charts that follow.)

- Port-hand buoys are painted green, with green fixed or flashing lights.
- Starboard-hand buoys are painted red, with red fixed or flashing lights.
- Safe-water buoys, also called midchannel or fairway buoys, and approach buoys are painted with red and white vertical stripes and have flashing lights.
- Preferred-channel buoys, or junction buoys, are painted with red and green horizontal bands and have flashing lights.
- Special marks (traffic separation, anchorage areas, dredging, fishnet areas, etc.) are painted yellow. If lighted, the light may be fixed or flashing.

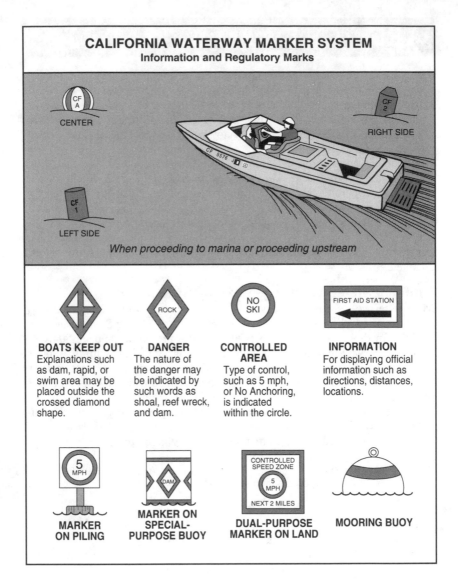

CALIFORNIA WATERWAY MARKER SYSTEM
Information and Regulatory Marks

CF A — CENTER

CF 2 — RIGHT SIDE

CF 1 — LEFT SIDE

When proceeding to marina or proceeding upstream

BOATS KEEP OUT
Explanations such as dam, rapid, or swim area may be placed outside the crossed diamond shape.

DANGER
The nature of the danger may be indicated by such words as shoal, reef wreck, and dam.

CONTROLLED AREA
Type of control, such as 5 mph, or No Anchoring, is indicated within the circle.

INFORMATION
For displaying official information such as directions, distances, locations.

MARKER ON PILING

MARKER ON SPECIAL-PURPOSE BUOY

DUAL-PURPOSE MARKER ON LAND

MOORING BUOY

FEDERAL-CHANNEL MARKING SYSTEM
Lateral System as Seen Entering from Seaward

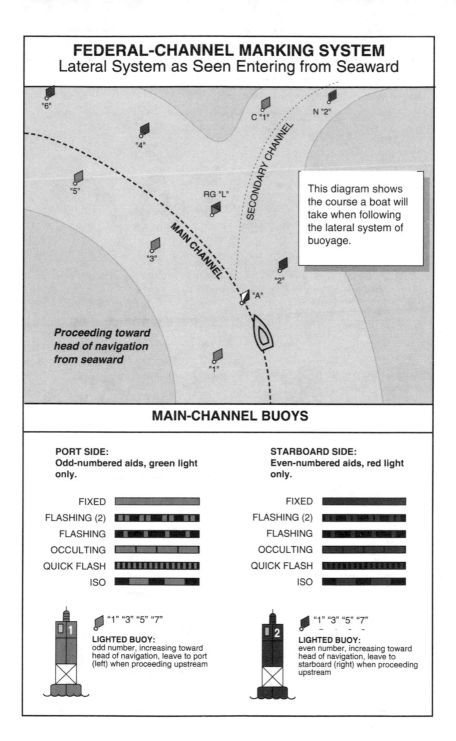

This diagram shows the course a boat will take when following the lateral system of buoyage.

"6"

C "1"

N "2"

"4"

"5"

RG "L"

SECONDARY CHANNEL

"3"

MAIN CHANNEL

"2"

"A"

Proceeding toward head of navigation from seaward

"1"

MAIN-CHANNEL BUOYS

PORT SIDE:
Odd-numbered aids, green light only.

FIXED	
FLASHING (2)	
FLASHING	
OCCULTING	
QUICK FLASH	
ISO	

"1" "3" "5" "7"

LIGHTED BUOY:
odd number, increasing toward head of navigation, leave to port (left) when proceeding upstream

STARBOARD SIDE:
Even-numbered aids, red light only.

FIXED	
FLASHING (2)	
FLASHING	
OCCULTING	
QUICK FLASH	
ISO	

"1" "3" "5" "7"

LIGHTED BUOY:
even number, increasing toward head of navigation, leave to starboard (right) when proceeding upstream

SAFE-WATER BUOY— MARKS MIDCHANNEL:
No numbers, may be lettered, white light only

MORSE CODE (A)

"A"

UNLIGHTED

LIGHTED AND/OR SOUND:
marks midchannel, pass on either side; not numbered, may be lettered; letter has no lateral significance—used for identification and location purposes

SPHERICAL

MR

PREFERRED-CHANNEL BUOY: No numbers, may be lettered

Topmost band denotes preferred channel. Letter has no lateral significance—used for identification and location purposes.

COMPOSITE GROUP FLASHING (2 + 1)

STARBOARD

LIGHTED BUOY "L"

UNLIGHTED CAN "L"

PORT

LIGHTED BUOY "L"

UNLIGHTED NUN "L"

DAYMARK

DAYMARK

SECONDARY-CHANNEL BUOYS
Starts New Numbering System

PORT

C 1

UNLIGHTED CAN BUOY: odd number, leave to port

DAYMARK

STARBOARD

N 2

UNLIGHTED NUN BUOY: even number, leave to starboard

DAYMARK

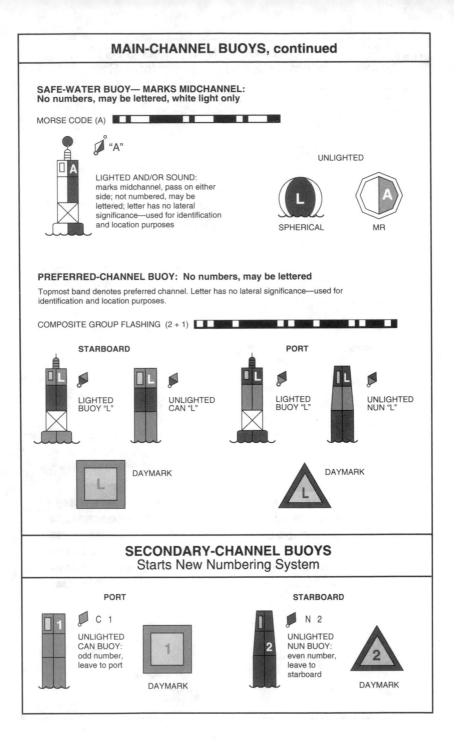

Inland Rules of the Road

Navigation Rules

The inland navigational rules, commonly called the "rules of the road," govern the operation of boats and specify the light and sound signals on inland waters in order to prevent collisions.

Existing law requires that a complete copy of the new inland navigational rules must be kept onboard all boats with a length of 39 feet, 4 inches (12 meters) or more, operating on inland waters. A copy of the *Navigation Rules International—Inland* booklet, which is published by the Coast Guard, may be ordered from: Superintendent of Documents, U.S. Government Printing Office, Attn: Customer Service, Washington, DC 20402.

There is a charge for this booklet. Please call (202) 783-3238 for availability and price.

Responsibility

Nothing in the rules of the road exonerates the operator of a vessel from the consequences of neglecting to comply with the inland rules of the road or from neglecting any precaution that may be required by the ordinary practice of boaters or by the special circumstances of the case.

In construing and complying with the inland rules of the road, due regard shall be given to all the dangers of navigation and collision, and to any special circumstances—including the limitations of the vessels involved—that may make a departure from the rules of the road necessary to avoid immediate danger.

Navigation Signals

The law prescribes signals for vessels in sight of each other, to indicate the intended course of a vessel when necessary for safe navigation.

- **One short blast (one second)** will show an intention to direct the course of the vessel to the operator's own starboard (right).
- **Two short blasts** will show an intention to direct the course of the vessel to the operator's own port (left).
- **Three short blasts** will indicate that the vessel's engines are going astern (in reverse).
- **Five or more short and rapid blasts** of the horn or whistle is a danger signal used when the other vessel's intentions are not understood or when the other vessel's indicated course is dangerous.
- **One prolonged blast (four to six seconds)** will indicate situations of restricted visibility or maneuverability (see "Fog Signals," page 510).

Motorboats should not use cross signals, that is, answer one blast with two blasts or two blasts with one blast.

Meeting or Crossing Situations

When motorboats are in sight of one another, and meeting or crossing at a distance within half a mile of each other, each vessel shall indicate its intended maneuver with the following signals: one short blast—*I intend to leave you on my port side;* two short blasts—*I intend to leave you on my starboard side;* or three short blasts—*I am operating astern propulsion.* Upon hearing the one- or two-blast signal, the other vessel shall, if in agreement, sound the same signal and take steps to effect a safe passing. If the proposed maneuver is unsafe, the danger signal (five or more short and rapid blasts) should be sounded and each vessel should take appropriate action until a safe-passing agreement is made.

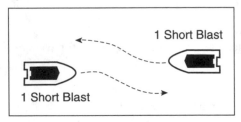

1 Short Blast

1 Short Blast

When meeting head-on, or nearly so, either vessel shall signal its intention with one short blast, which the other vessel shall answer promptly. Both vessels should alter their course to starboard (right) so that each will pass to the port (left) side of the other.

As the two vessels cross, the vessel that has the other on the starboard (right) side shall keep out of the way. The give-way vessel (the vessel directed to keep out of the way) shall take early and substantial action to keep well

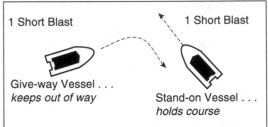

1 Short Blast

1 Short Blast

Give-way Vessel . . .
keeps out of way

Stand-on Vessel . . .
holds course

clear of the other vessel (the stand-on vessel). This latter vessel should hold course and speed. However it may, as the stand-on vessel, take action to avoid collision by maneuvering as soon as it becomes apparent that the vessel required to keep out of the way is not taking appropriate action.

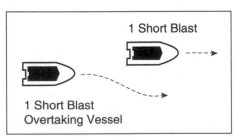

1 Short Blast

1 Short Blast
Overtaking Vessel

Overtaking Situations

If two motorboats are running in the same direction and the vessel astern desires to pass, it shall give one short blast to indicate a desire to pass on the overtaken vessel's starboard. The vessel ahead shall answer with one blast if the course is safe.

If the vessel astern desires to pass to port of the overtaken vessel, it shall give two short blasts. The vessel ahead shall answer with two short blasts if the course is safe. If it is unsafe to pass, the vessel being overtaken should answer with the danger signal (five or more short and rapid blasts).

A vessel approaching and overtaking another vessel from the stern shall keep out of the way of the overtaken vessel. The overtaken vessel shall hold its course and speed.

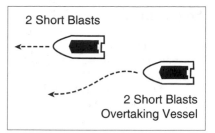

Other Situations

- A boat nearing a channel bend where vessels approaching from the other direction cannot be seen shall signal with a prolonged blast (four to six seconds), which shall be answered with the same signal by any approaching boat within hearing. Should such a signal be answered by a boat on the farther side of the bend, then the usual signals for meeting and passing shall be given upon sighting. If the signal goes unanswered, the channel may be considered clear.
- Boats shall keep to the starboard side of narrow channels whenever safe and practicable.
- Motorboats leaving a dock or berth shall sound one prolonged blast.
- Motorboats shall keep out of the way of sailing vessels where courses involve the risk of collision.
- In narrow channels, do not hamper the safe passage of vessels such as deep-draft liners and freighters, which can navigate only inside such channels.

Rules for Sailing Vessels

When two sailing vessels are approaching one another, so as to involve risk of collision, one of them shall keep out of the way of the other as follows:

- When each sailing vessel has the wind on a different side, the vessel that has the wind on the port side shall keep out of the way of the other vessel.
- When both sailing vessels have the wind on the same side, the vessel that is to windward shall keep out of the way of the vessel that is to leeward.
- If a vessel with the wind on the port side encounters a vessel to windward and cannot determine with certainty whether the other vessel has the wind on the port or on the starboard side, it shall keep out of the way of the other.

The windward side shall be deemed to be the side opposite to that on which the mainsail is carried or, in the case of a square-rigged vessel, the side opposite to that on which the largest fore-and-aft sail is carried. The international rules for sailing are the same as the above.

Fog Signals

The law also prescribes signals to identify vessels navigating in or near areas of restricted visibility.

Upon hearing a fog signal apparently forward of the beam, the operator should reduce speed to the minimum velocity at which the boat can be kept on course, unless it has been determined by radar or other means that the risk of collision does not exist. If necessary, the operator should use reverse propulsion. In any event, navigate with extreme caution until the threat of danger is over.

Motorboats:

- Making way through the water, sound (at intervals of not more than two minutes) one prolonged blast.
- Under way but stopped and making no way through the water, sound (at intervals of not more than two minutes) two prolonged blasts in succession with an interval of about two seconds between them.

Sailboats or Vessels Not Under Command, Restricted in Ability to Maneuver, Towing or Pushing Another Vessel, or Engaged in Fishing with Nets or Trawling:

- Sound, at intervals of not more than two minutes, one prolonged blast followed by two short blasts.

Boats at Anchor:

- Ring, at intervals of not more than one minute, a bell rapidly for about five seconds. In addition, one short blast followed by one prolonged and one short blast may be sounded to give a warning of position and of the possibility of collision to an approaching vessel.
- Boats less than 39 feet, 4 inches (12 meters) in length may, instead of the above, make an efficient sound signal at intervals of not more than two minutes.
- Boats less than 65 feet, 7 inches (20 meters) in length are not required to sound signals when anchored in a federally designated anchorage area.

Operational Law

Peace Officers

Every peace officer of the state, city, county, harbor district, or other political subdivision of the state is empowered to enforce California boating law. Such officers have the authority to stop and board any vessel subject to the state boating law.

Peace officers are also authorized to order the operator of an unsafe vessel to shore. A vessel can be ordered to the nearest safe moorage if an unsafe condition cannot be corrected on the spot and if, in the judgment of the officer, the continued operation of the vessel would be especially hazardous.

Any vessel approaching, overtaking, being approached, or being overtaken by a moving law-enforcement vessel operating with a siren or an illuminated blue light, or any vessel approaching a stationary law enforcement vessel displaying an illuminated blue light, shall immediately slow to a speed sufficient to maintain steerage only; shall alter its course, within its ability, so as not to inhibit or interfere with the operation of the law-enforcement vessel; and shall proceed, unless otherwise directed by the operator of the law-enforcement vessel, at the reduced speed until beyond the area of operation of the law-enforcement vessel.

Trailering

It is against the law to tow a trailered vessel containing a passenger, except when engaged in launching or retrieving a vessel.

Stolen Vessels

If a numbered vessel is stolen, the owner or legal owner should notify the local law-enforcement agency as soon as possible. The owner shall also notify the local law-enforcement agency if the vessel originally reported stolen is recovered.

County and City Laws

In addition to state law, many counties, cities, and districts have special laws or ordinances that restrict activities in certain areas, prohibit certain acts at certain times, or establish additional requirements. These ordinances may regulate speed, set aside certain areas or hours for special purposes, and prohibit acts that would be contrary to public interest. Boaters must comply with these local rules as well as with the state laws. Check with your local waterway operator for special laws or ordinances in your area.

Age Restrictions

No person under 16 years of age may operate a motorboat of more than 15 horsepower, except for a sailboat that does not exceed 30 feet in length or a dinghy used directly between a moored boat and the shore, or between two moored boats. The law allows persons 12 to 15 years of age to operate motorboats of more than 15 horsepower or sailboats over 30 beet if supervised on board by a person at least 18 years of age. A violation of these provisions is an infraction.

Speed

Speed is limited by law for certain conditions and areas. The maximum speed for motorboats within 100 feet of a bather (but not a water-skier) and within 200 feet of a bathing beach, swimming float, diving platform, lifeline, passenger landing being used, or landing where boats are tied up, is 5 mph.

A safe speed should be maintained at all times so that: (a) action can be taken to avoid a collision, and (b) the boat can stop within a distance appropriate to the prevailing circumstances and conditions.

In restricted visibility, motorboats should have the engines ready for immediate maneuvering. An operator should be prepared to stop the vessel within the space of half the distance of forward visibility.

Reckless or Negligent Boat Operation

No person shall operate any vessel or manipulate any water skis, aquaplane, or similar device in a reckless or negligent manner so as to endanger the life, limb, or property of any person. Examples of such operation include, but are not limited to:

1. Riding on the bow, gunwale, or transom of a vessel under way, or propelled by machinery, when such a position is not protected by a railing or other reasonable deterrents to falling overboard; or riding in a position or manner that is obviously dangerous. These provisions shall not apply to a vessel's crew in the act of anchoring, mooring, or making fast to a dock or another vessel, or in the necessary management of a sail.
2. Maneuvering towed skiers, or devices, so as to pass the towline over another vessel or its skier.
3. Navigating a vessel, skis, or other devices between a towing vessel and its tow or tows.
4. Operating under the influence of intoxicants or narcotics.

Other actions, such as speeding in confined or restricted areas, "buzzing" or "wetting down" others, or skiing at prohibited times or in restricted areas can also be construed as reckless or negligent operation.

"Hit and run"

Any person involved in a boating accident resulting in injury, death, or disappearance, who is convicted of leaving the scene without furnishing appropriate information to others involved or to any peace officer at the scene and/or rendering any reasonable assistance to any injured person, is liable for a fine of up to $10,000, imprisonment for up to one year, or both.

Intoxicated Boat Operation

Alcohol is a factor in 39 percent of all fatal motorboat accidents in California. Please do not drink and operate a boat! State law specifies that:

1. No person shall operate any vessel, water skis, or similar device while under the influence of intoxicating liquor or drugs or when addicted to any drug.

2. No person 21 years of age or older shall operate any vessel, water skis, or similar device who has .08 percent or more, by weight, of alcohol in their blood. A level of at least .05 percent, but less than .08 percent, may be used with other evidence in determining whether the person was under the influence of alcohol. No person under 21 years of age may operate a vessel, waterskis, or similar device who has a 0.1% or more, by weight, of alcohol in their blood.

3. A person who has been arrested for operating a mechanically propelled vessel while "under the influence" may be requested to submit to a chemical test to determine blood alcohol content. Refusal may result in increased penalties upon conviction. A person convicted of intoxicated boat operation could receive up to a $1,000 fine and six months in jail.

4. If you are convicted of operating a vessel while intoxicated, the Department of Motor Vehicles may suspend or revoke your vehicle driver's license. Depending upon the number and type of vehicle and/or vessel violations accumulated, this suspension or revocation could be for up to five years and could also result in fines of up to $1,000.

Court-Ordered Boating Education

A person convicted of a moving violation such as reckless or negligent operation, speeding, or operating a vessel under the influence of drugs or alcohol *may* be ordered by the court upon a first conviction, and *must* be ordered by the court upon a subsequent conviction within seven years of a previous conviction, to complete and pass a boating-safety course.

Any person convicted of operating a motorboat under the influence of alcohol must be ordered by the court to take a boating safety course approved by the Department of Boating and Waterways.

Personal Watercraft Operation

"Personal watercraft" means a vessel less than 12 feet in length, propelled by machinery, that is designed to be operated by a person sitting, standing, or kneeling on the vessel rather than in the conventional manner of sitting or standing inside the vessel.

Personal watercraft (PWC) are subject to the same laws governing the operation of motorboats of the same size. For proper display of registration numbers and stickers, see the "Registration" section. For more information, see the Department of Boating and Waterways publication, *Safe Boating Hints for Personal Watercraft.*

Lanyard/Self-Circling Device—The law requires a person operating a personal watercraft equipped with a lanyard cutoff switch to attach the lanyard to his or her person. Operating a personal watercraft equipped with a self-circling device is prohibited if the self-circling device has been altered.

Nighttime Operation Prohibited—The law prohibits the operation of a personal watercraft at any time bertween the hours from one-half hour after sunset to one-half hour before sunrise.

Operator Age—It is an infraction for a person under 16 years of age to operate a motorboat of more than 15 horesepower, including personal watercraft. Any person who permits a person under the age of 16 to do so is guilty of an infraction. A person 12 to 15 may operate a motorboat of more than 15 if supervised by a person on board who is at least 18 years of age.

Reasonable and Prudent Operation—California law holds that no person shall operate any craft in a reckless or negligent manner so as to endanger the life, limb, or property of any person. Some examples are:

- Navigating a vessel, skis, or other devices between a towing vessel and its tow or tows.
- Operating under the influence of intoxicants or narcotics.
- Jumping or attempting to jump the wake of another vessel within 100 feet of the other vessel constitutes unsafe operation.

Other actions which constitute unsafe operation are operating a PWC toward any person or vessel in the water and turning sharply so as to spray the person or vessel; and operating at a rate of speed and proximity to another vessel so that either operator is required to swerve at the last minute to avoid collision. Operating a PWC toward any person or vessel in the water and turning sharply so as to spray the person or vessel; and operating at a rate of speed and proximity to another vessel so that either operator is required to swerve at the last minute to avoid collision. Operating a PWC at night (between the hours from one-half hour after sunset to one-half hour before sunrise) is illegal, even if the PWC is equipped with the proper nagivational lights.

Waterskiing

When using a boat to tow a person on water skis or an aquaplane, there must be in the boat, in addition to the operator, one other person who can observe the person being towed. The observer must be at least 12 years of age.

The towing of water-skiers from sunset to sunrise is prohibited by state law. Local laws may also restrict waterskiing at certain times during the day and in certain areas.

Water skis and aquaplanes must not be operated in a manner that endangers the safety of persons or property. Passing the towline over another vessel or skier is prohibited. Towing a skier or navigating between a vessel and its tow is prohibited. Towing a skier does not give the operator of the vessel any special privileges. The rules of the road must be observed.

Water-skiers being towed are considered to be persons on board, in terms of personal flotation device requirements. For more information on waterskiing, send for the free pamphlet titled "Safety Hints for Waterskiing," from the Department of Boating and Waterways, 2000 Evergreen Street, Suite 100, Sacramento, CA 95815-3896.

Water-ski Flag

It is mandatory for the operator of a vessel involved in towing a water-skier to display, or cause to be displayed, a red or orange water-ski flag, to indicate:

- a downed water-skier;
- a water-skier in the water preparing to ski;
- a ski line extended from the vessel;
- or a waterski in the water in the vicinity of the vessel.

The flag must be no less than 12 inches on each side and square or rectangular in shape. The display of the water-ski flag does not in itself restrict the use of the water, but when operating in the area, boaters should exercise caution.

Diving

▬▬ Superhighway	• Point of Interest	▬ Boat Ramp
▬▬ Primary Road	• Accommodation	⚑ Ranger Station
▬▬ Secondary Road	• Other Location	⚘ Picnic Area
······ Trail	○ City	⚑ State Park
⟳ U.S. Interstate	○ Town	⚘ Waterfall
▢ U.S. Highway	✗ Airfield/Airstrip	⚑ Golf Course
◯ State Highway	∧ Campground	
▢ County or Forest Road	⛴ Marina	

Required for use by vessels engaged in diving operations and restricted in their ability to maneuver.

When the size of a vessel engaged in daytime-hour diving operations makes it impracticable to exhibit the daytime shapes required of a vessel with restricted ability to maneuver, the display of a rigid replica of the international blue-and-white code flag (Alpha) is required. The flag must measure not less than three feet, three inches (one meter) in height and must be visible all around the horizon.

For boats tending free-swimming divers where the diving does not interfere with the maneuverability of the boat, the Alpha Flag is not required and they may display the Divers-Down Flag (see below).

Divers-Down Flag

Recognized for use by persons engaged in diving.

State law recognizes that a red flag with a white diagonal stripe—commonly called the divers-down flag—indicates a person engaged in diving in the immediate area. Displaying the divers-down flag is not required by law and does not in itself restrict the use of the water. When operating in an area where this flag is displayed, boaters should exercise caution.

Radio Procedures—Marine and Emergency Distress

Speak Slowly and Clearly—Call:

A. If you are in distress (i.e., threatened by grave and imminent danger) or are observing a vessel in distress, transmit the International Distress Call on Channel 16: "MAYDAY, MAYDAY, MAYDAY, THIS IS (state vessel's name and assigned call letters, repeated three times)."

If Aboard a Vessel in Trouble—State:

1. WHO you are (your vessel's call letters and name);
2. WHERE you are (your vessel's position in latitude/longitude or true bearing and distance in nautical miles from a widely known geographical point);
3. WHAT is wrong;
4. kind of assistance desired;
5. number of persons aboard and the condition of any injured;
6. present seaworthiness of your vessel;
7. description of your vessel—length, type, cabin, masts, power, color of hull, superstructure, and trim;
8. and your listening frequency and schedule.

If Observing Another Vessel in Distress—Give:

1. your position and, if possible, the bearing and distance of the vessel in difficulty;
2. nature of distress;
3. description of the vessel in distress (see item 7 above);
4. your intentions, course, and speed;
5. and your radio call sign, name of your vessel, listening frequency, and schedule.

Note: The international sign for an aircraft that wants to direct a surface craft to a vessel in distress is: circling the surface craft, opening and closing the throttle or changing propeller pitch (which is noticeable by a change in sound) while crossing ahead of the surface craft, and proceeding in the direction of the vessel in distress. If you receive such a signal, you should follow the aircraft. If you cannot do so, try to inform the aircraft by any available means. If your assistance is no longer needed, the aircraft will cross your wake, opening and closing the throttle, or changing the propeller pitch. If you are radio equipped, you should attempt to communicate with the aircraft on Channel 16 when the aircraft makes the above signals or makes any obvious attempt to attract your attention. In the event you cannot communicate by radio, be alert for a message block dropped from the aircraft.

B. If you need INFORMATION OR ASSISTANCE FROM THE COAST GUARD (other than in a distress), call the COAST GUARD on Channel 16 (The Distress and Calling Frequency). In this situation, you will normally be shifted to a common working frequency (21, 22, or 23), which allows the DISTRESS frequency to remain open.

Radio Checks

Do not use Channel 16 to call the Coast Guard merely for a radio check. Such use is prohibited by the Federal Communications Commission.

Notify the Coast Guard immediately after the emergency terminates.

Accident Reporting

Boat operators involved in an accident must provide their name, address, and vessel registration number to other involved parties; provide assistance to any injured persons; and, in the case of a death or disappearance, report the accident without delay to law-enforcement officials.

Boat operators or owners must also make a written report of a boating accident to the Department of Boating and Waterways when:

- a person dies, disappears, or is injured and requires medical treatment beyond first aid;
- and total damage to all vessels involved and other property is more than $500, or there is complete loss of a vessel.

This report must be made within 48 hours of the accident in cases involving a disappearance, death that occurs within 24 hours of the accident, or injury that requires medical treatment beyond first aid. In all other incidents where a written accident report is required, the report must be made within 10 days of the accident.

An accident report form is contained in this booklet and may be used for such reports. Forms are available through most sheriffs' and harbormasters' offices and many police departments. They may also be obtained by writing to the Department of Boating and Waterways, 2000 Evergreen Street, Suite 100, Sacramento, CA 95815-3896. Failure to comply with the above requirements is punishable by a fine of up to $1,000, imprisonment up to six months, or both.

Required Equipment

Recreational vessels are required to carry specified safety equipment which may vary according to type of propulsion, type of construction, area and time of use, and number of people aboard. Unless otherwise noted, all Coast Guard-approved, required equipment must be kept in good, serviceable condition, be readily accessible, and be of the proper type and/or size.

Recreational vessels may carry extra equipment that is not Coast Guard approved, provided that the minimum requirements for approved equipment are satisfied. For equipment purposes, sailboats, canoes, rowboats, and inflatable rafts equipped with motors are considered to be "motorboats." Requirements vary considerably for commercial vessels and vessels engaged in racing.

Sailboats and Manually Propelled Vessels

Personal Flotation Devices: Requirements for *federally navigable waterways*–Vessels less than 16 feet in length and all canoes and kayaks, regardless of length, must carry one Type I, II, III, or V Coast Guard-approved personal flotation device for each person on board. They must be readily accessible and of a suitable size for the intended wearer. For state requirements, see "Personal Flotation Devices (PFDs)" on page 521.

Vessels 16 feet and over, except canoes and kayaks, must have one Type I, II, III, or V Coast Guard-approved wearable device for each person aboard, plus at least one Type IV throwable device. The throwable device must be immediately available. Wearable devices must be of a suitable size for the intended wearer.

Navigation Lights: All vessels are required to display navigation lights between sunset and sunrise and during times of restricted visibility. In inland and international waters, sailing vessels under sail alone shall exhibit the navigation lights described on page 529. The tricolored lantern and the all-round green and red lights should *never* be used together.

A sailing vessel of less than 23 feet (7 meters) in length or a vessel under oars shall, if practicable, exhibit those lights prescribed or have ready at hand an electric torch or lighted lantern showing a white light which shall be exhibited in sufficient time to prevent a collision.

Sound Signaling Devices: A vessel of less than 39 feet, 4 inches (12 meters) is not required to carry a whistle or bell, but must be able to provide some other means of making an efficient sound signal.

Visual Distress Signals (Coastal Waters Only): Boats less than 16 feet, manually propelled craft of any size; sailboats under 26 feet and of completely open construction and not equipped with propulsion machinery; and boats competing in an organized marine parade, regatta, race, or similar event are required to carry aboard devices that are suitable for night use (see Table C, page 530) between sunset and sunrise.

Motorboats Less Than 16 Feet in Length

Personal Flotation Device: One Type I, II, III, or V Coast Guard-approved personal flotation device must be carried for each person on board. They must be readily accessible and of a suitable size for the intended wearer.

Fire Extinguisher: One Type B-I Coast Guard-approved fire extinguisher must be carried when no fixed fire-extinguishing system is installed in machinery spaces. Extinguishers are not required for outboard motorboats less than 26 feet in length and of open construction. No portable extinguishers are required if an approved, fixed fire-extinguishing system is installed in machinery spaces.

Backfire Flame Arrester: A Coast Guard-approved backfire flame arrester is required for inboard gasoline motors that are not exposed to the atmosphere above the level of the gunwale.

Muffling System: An effective muffling system is required for the exhaust of each engine. Unmodified outboards usually meet legal requirements (see page 524).

Ventilation System: For details, see page 526.

Sound Signaling Devices: A vessel of less than 39 feet, 4 inches (12 meters) must be able to make an efficient sound signal but is not required to carry a whistle or a bell.

Visual Distress Signals (Coastal Waters Only): Boats less than 16 feet of completely open construction and not equipped with propulsion machinery, and boats competing in an organized marine parade, regatta, race, or similar event are only required to carry aboard devices that are suitable for night use (see Table C, page 530) between sunset and sunrise.

Navigation Lights: Navigation lights must be kept in serviceable condition and displayed between sunset and sunrise and at times of restricted visibility. For motorboats operating during these times, see page 529.

Motorboats 16 Feet to Less Than 26 Feet
Personal Flotation Devices: One Type I, II, III, or V Coast Guard-approved, wearable personal flotation device must be carried for each person aboard. They must be readily accessible and of a suitable size for the intended wearer. In addition, the vessel must carry an approved, immediately available Type IV throwable device.

Fire Extinguisher: One Type B-I Coast Guard-approved fire extinguisher must be carried when no fixed fire-extinguishing system is installed in machinery spaces. Extinguishers are not required for outboard motorboats less than 26 feet in length and of open construction. No portable extinguishers are required if an approved, fixed fire-extinguishing system is installed in machinery spaces.

Backfire Flame Arrester: A Coast Guard-approved backfire flame arrester is required for inboard gasoline motors that are not exposed to the atmosphere above the level of the gunwale.

Muffling System: An effective muffling system is required for the exhaust of each engine. Unmodified outboards usually meet legal requirements (see page 524).

Ventilation System: For details, see page 526.

Sound Signaling Devices: A vessel of less than 39 feet, 4 inches (12 meters) must be able to make an efficient sound signal but is not required to carry a whistle or a bell.

Visual Distress Signals (Coastal Waters Only): All boats 16 feet or more in length must carry devices aboard at all times. Boaters must carry *either* (a) devices suitable for day use and devices suitable for night use, *or* (b) devices suitable for both day and night use (see Table C, page 530).

Navigation Lights: Navigation lights must be kept in serviceable condition and be displayed between sunset and sunrise and at times of restricted visibility. For motorboats operating during these times, see page 529.

Motorboats 26 Feet to Less Than 40 Feet

Personal Flotation Devices: One Type I, II, III, or V Coast Guard-approved, wearable personal flotation device must be carried for each person aboard. They must be readily accessible and of a suitable size for the intended wearer. In addition, the vessel must carry an approved, immediately available Type IV throwable device.

Fire Extinguisher: Two Type B-I or one Type B-II Coast Guard-approved fire extinguisher must be carried when no fixed fire-extinguishing system is installed in machinery spaces. With a fixed system in the machinery space, one Type B-I fire extinguisher must be carried.

Backfire Flame Arrester: A Coast Guard-approved backfire flame arrester is required for inboard gasoline motors that are not exposed to the atmosphere above the level of the gunwale.

Muffling System: A muffling system is required for the exhaust of each engine. Unmodified outboards usually meet legal requirements (see page 524).

Ventilation System: For details, see page 526.

Sound Signaling Devices: A vessel of less than 39 feet, 4 inches (12 meters) must be able to make an efficient sound signal but is not required to carry a whistle or a bell. See page XX for vessels over 12 meters.

Visual Distress Signals (Coastal Waters Only): All boats 16 feet or more in length must carry devices aboard at all times. Boaters must carry *either* (a) devices suitable for day use and devices suitable for night use, *or* (b) devices suitable for both day and night use (see Table C, page 530).

Navigation Lights: Navigation lights must be kept in serviceable condition and be displayed between sunset and sunrise and at times of restricted visibility. For motorboats operating during these times, see page 529.

Motorboats 40 Feet to 65 Feet in Length

Personal Flotation Devices: One Type I, II, III, or V Coast Guard-approved, wearable personal flotation device must be carried for each person aboard. They must be readily accessible and of a suitable size for the intended wearer. In addition, the vessel must carry an approved, immediately available Type IV throwable device.

Fire Extinguisher: Three Type B-I, or one Type B-I and one Type B-II Coast

Guard-approved fire extinguishers must be carried when there is no fixed fire-extinguishing system installed in machinery spaces. With a fixed system in the machinery space, two Type B-I extinguishers or one Type B-II extinguisher must be carried.

Backfire Flame Arrester: A Coast Guard-approved backfire flame arrester is required for inboard gasoline motors that are not exposed to the atmosphere above the level of the gunwale.

Muffling System: An effective muffling system is required for the exhaust of each engine. Unmodified outboards usually meet legal requirements (see page 524).

Ventilation System: For details, see page 526.

Sound Signaling Devices: A vessel 39 feet, 4 inches (12 meters) or more in length is required to carry a whistle and a bell.

Visual Distress Signals (Coastal Waters Only): All boats 16 feet or more in length must carry devices aboard at all times. Boaters must carry *either* (a) devices suitable for day use and devices suitable for night, *or* (b) devices suitable for both day and night use (see Table C, page 530).

Navigation Lights: Navigation lights must be kept in serviceable condition and displayed between sunset and sunrise and at times of restricted visibility. For motorboats operating during these times, see page 529.

Personal Flotation Devices (PFDs)

The minimum requirements are as follows:

- Except canoes and kayaks, all boats 16 feet or more in length: One wearable life jacket (Type I, II, III, or V) for each person on board and one throwable (Type IV) in each boat.
- Canoes and kayaks of any length and all other boats less than 16 feet in length: One Type I, II, III, or V PFD for each person on board.

Under state law, it is an infraction, punishable by a fine of up to $250, to operate a vessel that is 26 feet or less in length unless every child six years of age or younger on board is wearing a Type I, II or III Coast Guard approved personal flotation device (life jacket). The law does not apply to the following:

- The operator of a sailboat on which every child under seven is restrained by a harness tethered to the sailboat.
- The operator of a vessel on which every child under seven is in an enclosed cabin.

Inflatable PFDs—The US Coast Guard approved inflatable PFDs in 1996. Only certain brands are US Coast Guard approved, so check the label. While activation upon impact is not a required feature, inflatables must be equipped, at a minimum, with both manual (pull) and oral inflation systems. They are only approved for adults, and must be wearable, not throwable-type PFDs. Inflatables are not recommended for nonswimmers and are not intended for use while water-skiing or on personal watercraft.

Personal Flotation Devices (PFDs)

Offshore Life Jacket
(Type I PFD)

Best in open, rough, or remote water where rescue may be slow. Type Is float you best, turn most unconscious wearers face up in the water, and are highly visible.

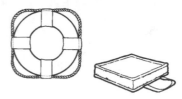

Throwable Device
(Type IV PFD)

Use in calm inland water with heavy boat traffic where help is always nearby. Type IVs do not help unconscious persons, and are not designed for nonswimmers or children. Type IVs are not suitable for many hours in rough water.

Nearshore Buoyant Vest
(Type II PFD)

Good in calm, inland water or where there is a good chance of fast rescue. Less bulk. Type IIs will turn many, but not all, unconscious wearers face up in the water, but are not suitable for long hours in rough water.

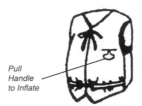

Pull Handle to Inflate

Hybrid Device
(Type V PFD)

High flotation when inflated. Good for continuous wear. However, this PFD may not adequately float some wearers unless it is partially inflated. Type Vs must be worn and require care of the inflation chamber.

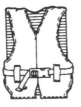

Flotation Aid (Type III PFD)

Good in calm, inland water or where there is a good chance of fast rescue. Generally the most comfortable PFD, Type IIIs are not good for use in rough water and the wearer may have to tilt her or his head back to avoid a face-down position in the water.

In addition to the above requirements, all boats, powered or nonpowered, must carry at least one wearable Coast Guard-approved personal flotation device for every person aboard. PFDs bearing Coast Guard approval are identified by Types I, II, III, IV, or V. Coast Guard approval is shown by a stencil marking or tag on the PFD. This tag or marking shows the name and address of the manufacturer and the Coast Guard approval number. It also shows the amount of flotation in the device and the PFD Type (I, II, III, IV, V). Failure to have a sufficient number of approved devices aboard constitutes a violation of state and federal law.

California boating law requires that all Type I, II, and III PFDs must be readily accessible, and all Type IV (throwable) PFDs must be immediately available. All PFDs must be kept in serviceable condition. If the PFD is badly torn, damaged, rotted, punctured, or otherwise unserviceable, it no longer meets legal requirements and should be replaced.

Persons towed on skis or other contrivances are considered "persons on board." If the skier is not wearing an approved device, one device must be in the boat. Except for some Type V PFDs, and the requirements for children under seven, California boating law does not require that persons wear life jackets while under way. However, it is highly recommended that all persons, especially nonswimmers, wear life jackets. All wearable life jackets must be of suitable size.

Nonapproved devices such as ski belts may only be carried aboard as excess equipment. Buoyant cushions should never be worn on the back when in use. For further details concerning the types and designs of PFDs, send for the free pamphlet titled "Safe Boating Hints for Personal Flotation Devices" from the Department of Boating and Waterways.

Fire Extinguishers

Motorboats are required to carry readily accessible fire extinguishers accepted for marine use by the Coast Guard. The size and number of extinguishers accepted for use on motorboats depend on the size of the boat and whether or not there is a fixed extinguishing system installed aboard the boat. Fire extinguishers are not required for outboard pleasure boats less than 26 feet in length, not carrying passengers for hire, without permanently installed fuel tanks, and which do not have spaces in which explosive or flammable gases or vapors can collect. (See Table A for specific requirements.) The minimum size approved for use aboard pleasure boats is the B-I extinguisher.

All extinguishers must be readily accessible (preferably not stowed next to common fire sources) and must be kept in serviceable condition.

Carbon Dioxide
Extinguisher

Halon
Extinguisher

Dry Chemical
Extinguisher

TABLE A—FIRE EXTINGUISHER REQUIREMENTS

Boat Length	Without Fixed Extinguishing System in Machinery Space	With Fixed Extinguishing System in Machinery Space
Less than 26 ft.	1 B-I	None
26 ft. to under 40 ft.	2 B-I or 1 B-II	1 B-I
40 ft. to 65 ft.	3 B-I or 1 B-I and 1 B-II	2 B-I or 1 B-II

TABLE B—FIRE EXTINGUISHER CHARACTERISTICS

UL-listed extinguishers of the type and weight shown below may be selected to meet the type and size requirements for the corresponding Coast Guard classification (see Table A). For example, if a Coast Guard Type B, Size II extinguisher is required, a 10 lb. dry-chemical extinguisher would be one of the equivalents. The following specifies only the minimum net-agent weight. A larger extinguisher would be acceptable.

Coast Guard Classes	UL-Listed Equivalent	Dry-Chemical lb.	Carbon-Dioxide lb.	Halon 1211 / 1301 lb.
B-I	5-B:C	2	4	2.5
B-II	10-B:C	10	15	10

REMEMBER, the number required by law is only the minimum. Extra extinguishers provide additional safety.

An extinguisher is suitable for marine use when it bears either:

- a label that includes Coast Guard approval numbers, "Marine Type USCG," or both markings;

- or a label that states the extinguisher is listed with Underwriters Laboratories (UL) and is suitable for marine use. It must be of the type and size described in Table B. UL-listed extinguishers must bear a UL rating of 5-B:C or higher. (All recently manufactured UL marine-type extinguishers will bear both the UL and Coast Guard label markings.)

All carbon tetrachloride extinguishers and others of the toxic vaporizing-liquid type, such as chlorobromomethane, are not approved and are not accepted as required fire extinguishers on any motorboats.

For further details concerning the types and designs of approved fire extinguishers, send for the free pamphlet titled "Safe Boating Hints for Fire Extinguishers" from the Department of Boating and Waterways.

Muffling Systems

Any motorboat operated on the inland waters of this state must be muffled or otherwise prevented from exceeding the following noise levels when recorded at a distance of 50 feet:

- 82 dB (A) for engines manufactured on or after January 1, 1978;
- 84 dB (A) for engines manufactured on or after January 1, 1976 and before January 1, 1978;
- or 86 dB (A) for engines manufactured before January 1, 1976.

Authorities generally agree that unbaffled exhaust pipes (stacks) and most types of water-injected pipe do not meet any of the noise-level requirements listed above.

Recommended Additional Equipment

Items E = essential D = desirable	Less than 16 ft.			16 ft. to under 26 ft.			26 ft. to under 40 ft.			40 ft. to 65 ft.		
	Open Waters	Semi-protected	Protected	Open Waters	Semi-protected	Protected	Open Waters	Semi-protected	Protected	Open Waters	Semi-protected	Protected
Anchor, cable (line, chain, etc.)	E	E	E	E	E	E	E	E	E	E	E	E
Bailing device (pump, etc.)	E	E	E	E	E	E	E	E	E	E	E	E
Boat hook	—	—	—	D	D	D	E	E	E	E	E	E
Bucket (fire fighting/ bailing)	E	E	E	E	E	E	E	E	E	E	E	E
Compass	E	E	D	E	E	D	E	E	E	E	E	E
Distress signals*	E	E	E	E	E	E	E	E	E	E	E	E
Emergency drinking water	E	D	—	E	D	—	E	D	—	E	D	—
Fenders	D	D	D	D	D	D	D	D	D	D	D	D
First-aid kit and manual (10- to 20-unit)	E	E	E	E	E	E	E	E	E	E	E	E
Flashlight	E	E	E	E	E	E	E	E	E	E	E	E
Heaving Line	—	—	—	—	—	—	D	D	D	D	D	D
Light list	D	D	—	E	E	D	E	E	E	E	E	E
Local chart(s)	E	D	—	E	E	E	E	E	E	E	E	E
Mirror (for signaling)	D	D	—	D	D	—	D	D	—	D	D	—
Mooring lines	E	E	E	E	E	E	E	E	E	E	E	E
Motor oil and grease (extra supply)	—	—	—	D	D	D	D	D	D	D	D	D
Oars, spare	E	E	E	E	E	E	—	—	—	—	—	—
Radio direction finder	—	—	—	D	—	—	D	—	—	D	—	—
Radio, telephone	D	—	—	D	D	—	D	D	—	D	D	—
Ring buoy(s) (additional)	D	D	D	D	D	D	D	D	D	D	D	D
Shear pins (if used)	E	E	D	E	E	D	—	—	—	—	—	—
Depth-sounding device (lead line, etc.)	D	D	—	D	D	D	E	E	E	E	E	E
Spare batteries	D	D	D	D	D	D	D	D	D	D	D	D
Spare parts	E	D	—	E	E	D	E	E	D	E	E	D
Tables, current	—	—	—	—	—	—	—	D	D	—	E	E
Tables, tide	—	—	D	—	—	D	—	D	D	—	E	E
Tools	E	D	—	E	E	D	E	E	D	E	E	D

* Distress signal devices are required on coastal waters on certain sized boats or during certain times.

Ventilation Systems

All motorboats or motor vessels (except open boats) made after 1940 and using gasoline as a fuel must have at least two ventilator ducts fitted with cowls, or their equivalent, for the efficient removal of explosive or flammable gases from the bilges of every engine and fuel-tank compartment. If engine and fuel-tank compartments are closed and separated, two such ventilation systems are required.

There must be at least one exhaust duct installed to extend from the open atmosphere to the lower portion of the bilge, and at least one intake duct installed to extend to a point at least midway to the bilge or at least below the level of the carburetor air intake. The cowls must be located and trimmed for maximum effectiveness to prevent displaced fumes from being recirculated in the vessel.

Boats built after July 31, 1980, with a gasoline engine for electrical generation, mechanical power, or propulsion must be equipped with an operable ventilation system. A compartment containing a permanently installed gasoline engine must either be open to the atmosphere or ventilated by an exhaust blower system. The intake duct for an exhaust blower must be in the lower one-third of the compartment and above the normal level of accumulated bilge water. A combination of more than one exhaust blower may be used to meet specified requirements.

Boats equipped with outboard motors or inboard motors, not enclosed and of "open" construction, are exempt from ventilation requirements.

Backfire Flame-Control Devices

Backfire flame-control devices are designed to prevent open flame from leaving the carburetion system in the event of a backfire.

Vessels equipped with gasoline engines, except outboard motors, must have a backfire flame-control device installed on the engine. These can be either:

- a Coast Guard-approved backfire flame arrester, suitably secured to the air intake with flame-tight connection;
- a backfire flame arrester marked "SAEJ-1928" or "UL 1111," and suitably secured to the air intake with a flame-tight connection;
- an approved engine air-and-fuel induction system that provides adequate protection from propagation of backfire flame to the atmosphere, equivalent to that provided by an acceptable backfire flame arrester; or
- a flame-tight metallic carburetor air-intake attachment, located or positioned so backfire flames would be dispersed to the atmosphere outside the vessel. This latter device must be acceptable to the Coast Guard and be such that the flames will not endanger the vessel, persons on board, or nearby vessels and structures.

Marine-Sanitation Devices

Federal law forbids the dumping of sewage (treated or untreated), or any waste derived from sewage, into the lakes, reservoirs, or freshwater impoundments of this state.

Federal regulations and equipment standards established jointly by the Federal Environmental Protection Agency and the Coast Guard govern the use of marine-sanitation devices (MSDs). For a pamphlet on the federal MSD regulations, including a list of coastal harbors whose waters have been declared "no-discharge" areas, write to the Department of Boating and Waterways.

State law provides that it is a misdemeanor to disconnect, bypass, or operate an MSD so as to discharge sewage into the waters of this state, unless expressly authorized or permitted by law. In no-discharge areas: (a) no person shall disconnect, bypass, or operate an MSD so as to potentially discharge sewage, and (b) no person shall occupy or operate a vessel in which an MSD is installed unless the MSD is properly secured. A first violation is an infraction and any subsequent violation is a misdemeanor. State and local peace officers may enforce state laws relating to MSDs and may inspect vessels if there is reasonable cause to suspect noncompliance with those laws.

Oily Waste Discharge Placard

Federal law requires all boats 26 feet or longer to display an Oily Waste Discharge Placard in the engine compartment or near the fuel tank. For more information, call the U.S. Coast Guard's toll-free boating safety information line at (800) 368-5647.

Marine-Pollution Placard

Federal law now requires all boats 26 feet or more in length, when operating in waters under federal jurisdiction, to display an informational placard on the subject of the federal marine-pollution prevention laws. Under the Marine Pollution (MARPOL) International Convention to Prevent Pollution From Ships, the discharge of the following into the navigable waters of the U.S. is prohibited:

- plastic, paper, rags, glass, metal, crockery, dunnage (lining or packing materials that float), or food in U.S. lakes, rivers, bays, sounds, and up to three miles from shore;
- any plastic, or any of the above items if not ground to less than an inch in size, between 3 and 12 miles from shore;
- plastic or dunnage 12 to 25 miles from shore;
- and plastic outside 25 miles from shore.

The required placard details the above prohibitions. The placard must be displayed in a prominent location where the crew and passengers can read it, must be at least nine inches wide by four inches high, and must be made of durable material bearing letters at least 0.8 of an inch high. The placards can be purchased at marine-supply dealers or a free placard can be obtained by writing to the Department of Boating and Waterways, 2000 Evergreen Street, Suite 100, Sacramento, CA 95815-3896, or by calling (916) 445-2616.

Additionally, all U.S. vessels 40 feet or more in length and equipped with a galley and berthing must carry a Waste-Management Plan if the vessel operates beyond three miles from shore. The Waste-Management Plan must be in writing; designate the person who is in charge of carrying out the plan; and describe procedures for collecting, processing, storing, and properly disposing of garbage in keeping with the prohibitions described above.

Marine Pollution (MARPOL) Regulations

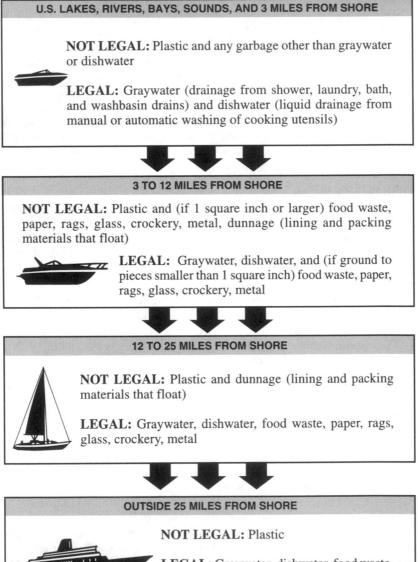

U.S. LAKES, RIVERS, BAYS, SOUNDS, AND 3 MILES FROM SHORE

NOT LEGAL: Plastic and any garbage other than graywater or dishwater

LEGAL: Graywater (drainage from shower, laundry, bath, and washbasin drains) and dishwater (liquid drainage from manual or automatic washing of cooking utensils)

3 TO 12 MILES FROM SHORE

NOT LEGAL: Plastic and (if 1 square inch or larger) food waste, paper, rags, glass, crockery, metal, dunnage (lining and packing materials that float)

LEGAL: Graywater, dishwater, and (if ground to pieces smaller than 1 square inch) food waste, paper, rags, glass, crockery, metal

12 TO 25 MILES FROM SHORE

NOT LEGAL: Plastic and dunnage (lining and packing materials that float)

LEGAL: Graywater, dishwater, food waste, paper, rags, glass, crockery, metal

OUTSIDE 25 MILES FROM SHORE

NOT LEGAL: Plastic

LEGAL: Graywater, dishwater, food waste, crockery, metal, dunnage (lining and packing materials that float)

Running Lights—Inland and International

Operating a boat at night without lights is not only dangerous, it is against the law. Running lights make it possible for boat operators to properly interpret and react to the movements of other boats in darkness. *If a boat is used exclusively in the daylight hours, and not during periods of restricted visibility, running lights are not required.*

All vessels must show required running lights between sunset and sunrise and during periods of restricted visibility. Light requirements vary, based on vessel length and propulsion type. In most cases requirements for a particular vessel are the same under both inland and international rules.

Power-Driven Vessels: A recreational powerboat under way is required to display a masthead light forward, red and green sidelights, and a sternlight. A recreational powerboat under 39 feet, 4 inches (12 meters) may instead display a 360° all-round sternlight and combination red and green sidelights.

Sailing Vessels and Vessels Under Oar: A sailing vessel operating solely under power of sail must exhibit sidelights and a sternlight. A sailing vessel of less than 23 feet (7 meters) in length must, if practicable, exhibit sidelights and a sternlight, or a lighted lantern showing a white light that must be exhibited in sufficient time to prevent a collision. *A sailing vessel operating under machinery power only or under power and sails is considered a power-driven vessel and must display the proper lights for a powerboat.*

A vessel under oars may: (a) display those lights prescribed for sailing vessels, or (b) have ready at hand an electric torch or lighted lantern showing a white light that must be exhibited in sufficient time to prevent a collision.

Boaters operating at night should be aware that there are other possible combinations of lights; the ones presented above are the most common.

Anchor Lights

An anchor light is an all-round white light exhibited where it can best be seen and is visible for two miles.

Power-driven vessels and sailing vessels at anchor must display anchor lights. Exceptions are: (a) vessels less than 23 feet (7 meters) in length are not required to display anchor lights unless anchored in or near a narrow channel, fairway, anchorage, or where other vessels normally navigate, and (b) vessels less than 65 feet, 7 inches (20 meters) in inland waters, when at anchor in a special anchorage area designated by the Secretary of Transportation, are not required to exhibit an anchor light.

Visual Distress-Signaling Devices

Vessels operating on coastal waters must carry the required number of approved visual distress-signaling devices selected from Table C.

Coastal waters include: (a) territorial seas and (b) those waters directly connected to the territorial seas (bays, sounds, harbors, rivers, inlets, etc.) where any entrance exceeds two nautical miles between opposite shorelines, to the first point where the largest distance between shorelines narrows to two miles. The carriage requirements for vessels operating on coastal waters are:

1. All boats 16 feet or more in length must carry devices aboard at all times.

Boaters must carry *either:* (a) devices suitable for day use and devices suitable for night use, *or* (b) devices suitable for both day and night use.

2. Boats less than 16 feet; manually propelled craft of any size; sailboats under 26 feet, of completely open construction, and not equipped with propulsion machinery; and boats competing in any organized marine parade, regatta, race, or similar event are only required between sunset and sunrise to carry aboard devices that are suitable for night use.

All visual distress-signaling devices must be Coast Guard approved, readily accessible, and in serviceable condition. Devices carried aboard beyond the date stamped on each device will not meet legal minimum requirements.

TABLE C—VISUAL DISTRESS REQUIREMENTS

Boaters may select a group or any combination, as long as it meets the specific requirement for their boat.

Number on device	Device description	Accepted use for	Number required
160.021	Hand red flare, distress signals	Day and night[1]	3
160.022	Floating orange-smoke distress signals	Day only	3
160.024	Pistol-projected, parachute red flare distress signals	Day and night[2]	3
160.036	Handheld rocket-propelled parachute red	Day and night	3
160.037	Handheld orange-smoke distress signals	Day only	3
160.057	Floating orange-smoke distress signals	Day only	3
160.066	Distress signal for boats, red aerial pyrotechnic flare	Day and night[3]	3
160.072	Distress signal for boats, orange flag	Day only	1
160.013	Electric distress light for boat	Night only	1

[1] These signals must have a date of manufacture of October 1, 1980, or later to be acceptable.

[2] These signals require use in combination with a suitable launching device approved under 46 CFR 160.028.

[3] These devices may be either self-contained or pistol-launched, and either meteor- or parachute-assisted type. Some of these signals may require use in combination with a suitable launching device approved under 46 CFR 160.028.

Recognized Distress Signals

Other signals that indicate distress and need of assistance include white light flashing (inland waters only), radio-telephone alarm, foghorn continues sounding, mayday by radio, and smoke. On coastal waters, boaters must carry Coast Guard-approved visual distress-signaling devices (see Table C, page 530).

Registration

California law requires current registration of most vessels. This includes moored vessels, whether or not they are used. All vessels must be registered and numbered except:

1. boats propelled manually;
2. boats eight feet or less in length propelled solely by sail;
3. certain vessels owned by public agencies;

4. vessels documented by the Coast Guard;

5. foreign vessels;

6. ship's lifeboats used solely for lifesaving purposes;

7. vessels having valid registration in the state of principal use and not remaining in California over 90 consecutive days;

8. and sailboards.

How to Register

An application to register a vessel may be made at any office of the Department of Motor Vehicles (DMV). Upon receipt of the required information and fees, the DMV will issue a Certificate of Number, a Certificate of Ownership, and a set of registration stickers. The boat registration number is the number (beginning with CF) shown on the certificates.

Upon registration, your vessel may be subject to a Use Tax based on the purchase price if it is acquired out-of-state or from a private party. For additional information regarding the Use Tax, contact your local Board of Equalization or DMV office.

The Certificate of Ownership is your evidence of title to the vessel and therefore should be kept in a safe place. Certificates issued will also contain the boat's identifying number (known as the hull identification number), which is the number permanently marked on the transom by the manufacturer or builder, or the number assigned by the DMV and marked on the transom by the owner. The reverse side of the Certificate of Ownership is an application for transfer of ownership.

The Certificate of Number, or temporary Certificate of Number, must be available for inspection on the vessel whenever it is used on the water. Proper display of the current registration stickers on the vessel, next to the CF number, is required to permit law-enforcement officers to determine, without boarding, that the vessel is currently registered.

Although the DMV is responsible for the collection of annual vessel registration fees, boat owners may still be subject to local county taxes. Boats are subject to personal property taxes assessed by the assessor in the county where the boat is principally located. Failure to pay personal property taxes assessed on a boat may result in the nonrenewal of the boat's registration. Questions concerning taxes on boats should be directed to the assessor of that particular county.

Registration Fees

Original Registration (including stickers)	$ 9.00
Penalty, Late Original Registration	$ 4.00
Renewal of Registration (two-year)	$ 10.00
Renewal of Registration (annual)	$ 5.00
Penalty, Late Renewal	$ 2.00
Nonresident Original Registration	$ 37.00
Penalty, Late NR Original Registration	$ 18.00
Boat-Trailer Registration	$ 30.00 + VLF*
Transfer of Ownership, Single	$ 15.00
for Each Additional Transfer	$ 15.00

Penalty, Late Transfer	$ 7.00
Duplicate Certificate of Number	$ 15.00
Duplicate Certificate of Ownership	$ 15.00
Duplicate Set of Stickers	$ 15.00
Repossession	$ 15.00
Historical Vessel Plaque	$ 20.00

* The VLF, or Vehicle License Fee, is part of the annual fee due upon initial registration and registration renewal. The formula for VLF assessment is established by the legislature and is based upon the vehicle's purchase price. An 11-year depreciation schedule is used to calculate the VLF.

Display of Numbers and Stickers

Numbers and stickers issued at the time of registration must be placed on each side of the forward half of the vessel, usually on the bow, in the manner indicated below. If placement of a number on a flared bow would result in difficult reading, the number should be placed on some other part of the forward half of the vessel where it can be easily read.

For personal watercraft, the numbers and stickers must also be affixed on each side of the vessel's forward half on a nonremovable portion of the hull.

On inflatable boats or vessels configured so that a number will not properly adhere or cannot be clearly seen, the number should be painted on or attached to a backing plate along with the registration sticker. The number must be visible from each side of the vessel. No other numbers, letters, or devices may be placed in the vicinity of the state-assigned number, except for the U.S. Recreational-Vessel Fee decal.

To separate the numerals from the letters, spaces the width of the letter "C" or hyphens may be used between the prefix and the number, and between the number and the suffix. Letters and numerals must be at least three inches high, of block character, and of a color that will form a good contrast with the color of the hull or the backing plate. In determining height and contrast, any border, trim, outlining, or shading around the number shall not be considered.

Notification Requirements

The owner is required to notify the DMV in writing whenever any of the following takes place:

1. The vessel has been destroyed or abandoned. This notice must be given within 15 days and be accompanied by the Certificate of Number and the Certificate of Ownership.
2. The owner's mailing address has changed. This notice must be given within 15 days.
3. The vessel is sold. This notice must be provided within five calendar days and must include the date of sale, a description of the vessel, and the name and address of the new owner.

Registration forms may be obtained from any local DMV office, or authorized registration agent, or by writing:

> Department of Motor Vehicles
> Registration Processing Units
> P.O. Box 942869
> Sacramento, CA 94269-0001

Proposed Changes in the California Boating Law

At press time a bill before the California legislature would require among other provisions:

1. Children under the age of 12 wear a life jacket when aboard an underway vessel that is 26 feet long or less, with exceptions.

2. Personal watercraft users and water skiers to wear life jackets.

3. The Department of Boating and Waterways to develop a model educational course in safe boating principles and regulations.

4. The Department's Director to appoint a Boating Advisory Committee from among the boating community to advise the Director in the development of the model educational course.

5. The Department to administer a written test of knowledge and understanding of the curriculum and authorize the Department to issue lifetime certificates to those who pass the examination. A class A certificate would be issued for residents of the state and a Class B certificate for short-term visitors and boat renters.

6. Operators of vessels powered by a motor of greater than 15 horesepower to pass an examination developed by the Department, and possess a valid certificate by a scheduled date between September 1, 2002, and June 1, 2005.

California Recreational Lakes and Rivers Reference Map

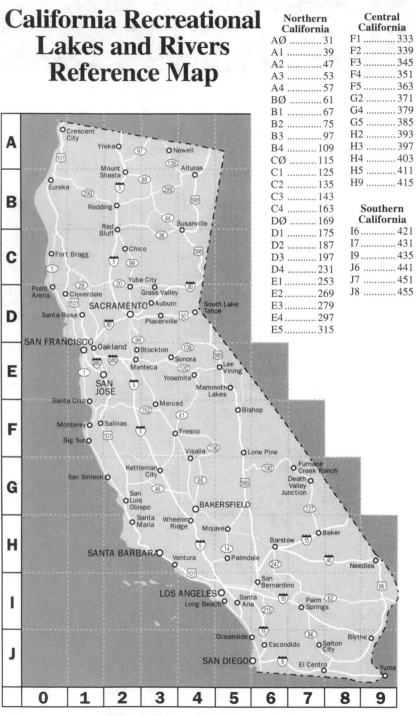

Index

Index

Index

Index

Index

Acknowledgments

We visited hundreds of lakes, streams, and coastal ports in the state, and hundreds of people provided additional information. Many thanks to Diane Strachan and numerous other river guides who provided their personal know-how about white-water rafting in California and to the U.S. Forest Service and lake managers for their personal reports. A special thanks to the Department of Boating and Waterways for allowing us to reprint the "ABCs of the California Boating Law."

ABOUT THE AUTHOR

Tom Stienstra has made it his life's work to explore the West—hiking, camping, fishing, and boating—searching for the best of the great outdoors and writing about it.

He is the outdoors writer for the *San Francisco Examiner,* which distributes his column on the New York Times News Service, and an associate editor for *Western Outdoor News.* In the 1990s, he was twice named National Outdoor Writer of the Year (newspaper division) by the Outdoor Writers Association of America, and three times named California Outdoor Writer of the Year.

Tom Stienstra's best-selling outdoor guidebooks with Foghorn Press include:

Easy Camping in Northern California • California Hiking
Tom Stienstra's Outdoor Getaway Guide
California Fishing • Pacific Northwest Camping
California Recreational Lakes and Rivers
Sunshine Jobs: Career Opportunities Working Outdoors
California Wildlife: The Complete Guide

FOGHORN ⋈ OUTDOORS

Founded in 1985, Foghorn Press has quickly become one of the country's premier publishers of outdoor recreation guidebooks. Foghorn Press books are available throughout the United States in bookstores and some outdoor retailers.

101 Great Hikes of the San Francisco Bay Area, 1st ed.	1-57354-068-4	$15.95
Alaska Fishing, 2nd ed.	0-935701-51-6	$20.95
America's Wilderness, 1st ed.	0-935701-47-8	$19.95
Arizona and New Mexico Camping, 3rd ed.	1-57354-044-7	$18.95
Atlanta Dog Lover's Companion, 1st ed.	1-57354-008-0	$17.95
Baja Camping, 3rd ed.	1-57354-069-2	$14.95
Bay Area Dog Lover's Companion, 3rd ed.	1-57354-039-0	$17.95
Boston Dog Lover's Companion, 2nd ed.	1-57354-074-9	$17.95
California Beaches, 2nd ed.	1-57354-060-9	$19.95
California Camping, 11th ed.	1-57354-053-6	$20.95
California Dog Lover's Companion, 3rd ed.	1-57354-046-3	$20.95
California Fishing, 5th ed.	1-57354-052-8	$20.95
California Golf, 9th ed.	1-57354-091-9	$24.95
California Hiking, 4th ed.	1-57354-056-0	$20.95
California Recreational Lakes and Rivers, 2nd ed.	1-57354-065-x	$19.95
California Waterfalls, 2nd ed.	1-57354-070-6	$17.95
California Wildlife: The Complete Guide, 1st ed.	1-57354-087-0	$16.95
Camper's Companion, 3rd ed.	1-57354-000-5	$15.95
Colorado Camping, 2nd ed.	1-57354-085-4	$18.95
Day-Hiking California's National Parks, 1st ed.	1-57354-055-2	$18.95
Easy Biking in Northern California, 2nd ed.	1-57354-061-7	$12.95
Easy Camping in Northern California, 2nd ed.	1-57354-064-1	$12.95
Easy Camping in Southern California, 1st ed.	1-57354-004-8	$12.95
Easy Hiking in Northern California, 2nd ed.	1-57354-062-5	$12.95
Easy Hiking in Southern California, 1st ed.	1-57354-006-4	$12.95
Florida Beaches, 1st ed.	1-57354-054-4	$19.95
Florida Camping, 1st ed.	1-57354-018-8	$20.95
Florida Dog Lover's Companion, 2nd ed.	1-57354-042-0	$20.95
Montana, Wyoming and Idaho Camping, 1st ed.	1-57354-086-2	$18.95
New England Camping, 2nd ed.	1-57354-058-7	$19.95
New England Hiking, 2nd ed.	1-57354-057-9	$18.95
Outdoor Getaway Guide: Southern CA, 1st ed.	1-57354-011-0	$14.95
Pacific Northwest Camping, 7th ed.	1-57354-080-3	$19.95
Pacific Northwest Hiking, 3rd ed.	1-57354-059-5	$20.95
Seattle Dog Lover's Companion, 1st ed.	1-57354-002-1	$17.95
Tahoe, 2nd ed.	1-57354-024-2	$20.95
Texas Dog Lover's Companion, 1st ed.	1-57354-045-5	$20.95
Texas Handbook, 4th ed.	1-56691-112-5	$18.95
Tom Stienstra's Outdoor Getaway Guide: No. CA, 3rd ed.	1-57354-038-2	$18.95
Utah and Nevada Camping, 1st ed.	1-57354-012-9	$18.95
Utah Hiking, 1st ed.	1-57354-043-9	$15.95
Washington Boating and Water Sports, 1st ed.	1-57354-071-4	$19.95
Washington Fishing, 3rd ed.	1-57354-084-6	$18.95
Washington, DC-Baltimore Dog Lover's Companion, 1st ed.	1-57354-041-2	$17.95

For more information, call 1-800-FOGHORN
email: travel@moon.com
or write to: Avalon Travel Publishing, Foghorn Outdoors
5855 Beaudry St., Emeryville, CA 94608